LIBRARY OF THE HISTORY OF IDEAS

VOLUME II

Philosophy, Religion and Science in
the Seventeenth and Eighteenth Centuries

LIBRARY OF THE HISTORY OF IDEAS

ISSN 1050–1053

Series Editor: JOHN W. YOLTON

PREVIOUS VOLUMES

I   The History of Ideas: Canon and Variations, *ed. Donald R. Kelley*

PHILOSOPHY, RELIGION AND SCIENCE

IN THE
SEVENTEENTH AND EIGHTEENTH CENTURIES

Edited by
JOHN W. YOLTON

UNIVERSITY OF ROCHESTER PRESS

This collection first published 1990

University of Rochester Press
200 Administration Building, University of Rochester
Rochester, New York 14627, USA
and at PO Box 9, Woodbridge, Suffolk IP12 3DF, UK

ISBN   1 878822 01 2

A CIP catalogue record for this book is available from the British Library

This publication is printed on acid-free paper

Printed in the United States of America

TABLE OF CONTENTS

PART FIVE: LARGER ISSUES

ACKNOWLEDGEMENTS

The articles in this volume first appeared in the *Journal of the History of Ideas* as indicated below, by volume, year and pages, in order.

Barnouw, Jeffrey, "The Separation of Reason and Faith in Bacon and Hobbs, and Leibniz's *Theodicy*", 42 (1981) 607–28.

Batz, W. G., "The Historical Anthropology of John Locke", 35 (1974) 663–70.

Biddle, J. C., "Locke's Critique of Innate Principles and Toland's Deism", 37 (1976) 411–22.

Cantor, G. N., "Berkeley, Reid, and the Mathematization of Mid-Eighteenth-Century Optics", 38 (1977) 429–48.

Farr, James, "The Way of Hypothesis: Locke on Method", 48 (1987) 51–72.

Force, James E., "Hume and Johnson on Prophecy and Miracles: Historical Context", 43 (1982) 463–75.

Force, James E., "Hume and the Relation of Science to Religion Among Certain Members of the Royal Society", 45 (1984) 517–36.

Guerlac, Henry, "Can There be Colors in the Dark? Physical Color Theory Before Newton", 47 (1986) 3–20.

Guerlac, Henry, "Theological Voluntarism and Biological Analogies in Newton's Physical Thought", 44 (1983) 219–29.

Heiman, P. M., "Voluntarism and Immanence: Conceptions of Nature in Eighteenth-Century Thought", 39 (1978) 271–83.

Jacob, Margaret C., "Millenarianism and Science in the Late Seventeenth Century", 37 (1976) 335–41.

Jolley, Nicholas, "Leibniz on Locke and Socinianism", 39 (1978) 233–50.

Laudan, L., "The Nature and Sources of Locke's Views on Hypotheses", 28 (1967) 211–23.

Moravia, Sergio, "From *Homme Machine* to *Homme Sensible*: Changing Eighteenth-Century Models of Man's Image", 39 (1978) 45–60.

Mossner, Ernest Campbell, "The Religion of David Hume", 39 (1978) 653–63.

Osler, Margaret J., "Locke and the Changing Ideal of Scientific Knowledge", 31 (1970) 3–16.

Perl, Margula R., "Physics and Metaphysics in Newton, Leibniz and Clarke", 30 (1969) 507–26.

Rigotti, Francesca, "Biology and Society in the Age of Enlightenment", 47 (1986) 215–33.

Roe, Shirley, A., "Voltaire vs. Needham: Atheism, Materialism and the Generation of Life", 46 (1985) 65–87.

Rogers, G. A. J., "Boyle, Locke, and Reason", 27 (1966) 205–16.

Rogers, G. A. J., "Locke, Newton, and the Cambridge Platonists on Innate Ideas", 40 (1979) 191–206.

Rogers, G. A. J., "Locke's Essay and Newton's Principia", 39 (1978) 217–32.

Schankula, H. A. S., "Locke, Descartes, and the Science of Nature", 41 (1980) 459–77.

Siebert, Donald T., Jr., "Johnson and Hume on Miracles", 36 (1975) 543–47.

Stewart, Larry, "Samuel Clarke, Newtonianism and the Factions of Post-Revolutionary England", 42 (1981) 53–72.

Tennant, R. C., "The Anglican Response to Locke's Theory of Personal Identity", 43 (1982) 73–90.

Thrane, Gary, "Berkeley's 'Proper Object of Vision' ", 38 (1977) 243–60.

Wallace, Dewey D., "Socinianism, Justification by Faith, and the Sources of John Locke's *The Reasonableness of Christianity*", 45 (1984) 49–66.

Wilson, Catherine, "Visual Surface and Visual Symbol: The Microscope and the Occult in Early Modern Science", 49 (1988) 85–108.

Wright, John P., "Hysteria and Mechanical Man", 41 (1980) 233–47.

Yolton, John W., "As in a Looking-Glass: Perceptual Acquaintance in Eighteenth-Century Britain", 40 (1979) 207–34.

Yost, R. M., "Locke's Rejection of Hypotheses about Submicroscopic Events", 12 (1951) 111–30.

Chapter I

INTRODUCTION

By John W. Yolton

Philosophy has had a varied role in the history of thought. Sometimes considered the Queen of the Sciences, at other times the handmaiden of theology, in different periods identified with logic and rhetoric. To offer a rough generalization, more often than not, what we recognize as philosophy has been closely linked with other areas and fields. Only infrequently has it been a stand-alone discipline, as it was for a while in the English-speaking world between the two world wars. Today in that same world, and especially in North America, philosophy has once again joined hands with other disciplines, e.g., computer science, cognitive psychology, and linguistics.

When we think of philosophy, we usually think of it as an academic discipline. Sometimes, members of philosophy departments hold cross-appointments in other disciplines, but philosophers in our country have been notorious for their isolation within their own technical jargon. The very existence of academic disciplines, with the inevitable proliferation of specialist journals, has encouraged sharp demarcations, protection of turf, and often, some disdain of general education and interdisciplinary programs. When it comes to studying and writing about the history of one's discipline, philosophy has again frequently shunned its past or else casually consulted some historical figure to see what, if anything, in that person's writings might bear upon contemporary interests.

The definition or identification of any field or discipline has not always been consistent over time. Histories of philosophy do not always discuss the same figures, although there is general agreement over the canonical members. Sometimes the official canon is influenced by judgments of quality, at other times omission from the list of philosophers can be a result of a writer's corpus including 'non-philosophical' material, e.g., theological or medical writings. Introductory courses in philosophy tend to concentrate on contemporary issues or, when some historical perspective is allowed, to particular features of a writer's work. Hume's history of England is usually excluded or not even mentioned in such courses. Locke's writings on religion or money are placed outside the canon of philosophy.

These concentrations and attitudes are not always exemplified in our courses or views of the history of our discipline. There is a healthier attitude prevailing in many places. I raise these pedagogical and historiographical concerns as a way of reminding ourselves of some basic differences between twentieth *and* seventeenth and eighteenth century activities. In those two centuries, it was difficult to isolate philosophical from scientific, theological, and even medical issues. Even the writers admitted to philosophy's canon in those centuries wrote on a wide range of topics, issues and questions. Philosophical, scientific and religious interests were intertwined. The papers in this collection illustrate this fact. The issues and problems around which they are grouped reflect most of the dominant themes and ideas involving philosophy, science and religion in those two centuries: concern with problems of perception, especially vision; the philosophers' challenges to religious beliefs and church doctrine by new concepts and approaches; Locke's special close relations to the science of his time; and the relations between biological developments and what Hume called the 'science of man', the formation of a concept of human nature. The final section of this collection addresses some of the larger questions about the relation between the three areas in the title.

I

There are several ways in which we can illustrate the interdisciplinary nature of the issues and problems presented in this volume. One is to remind ourselves of the contents of that remarkable early eighteenth century document, *A Collection of Papers Which Passed Between the Late Learned Mr. Leibnitz and Dr. Clarke in the Years 1715 and 1717, Relating to the Principles of Natural Philosophy and Religion* (1717). Leibniz had written on mathematics and logic, physics and metaphysics, theology. His pre-established harmony theory on the relation between mind and body was from 1695 a strong rival to Malebranche's occasionalism. Both systems were widely discussed in tracts and journals in the eighteenth century. Leibniz had been involved in controversy with various writers in Europe and, most prominently, with Newtonians in England. Samuel Clarke was a prominent divine, friend of Newton (who was, himself, we should remember, a close student of the Bible and alchemy), whose Boyle lectures in 1705 quickly became a popular text for those with an interest in *A Demonstration of the Being and Attributes of God*, the title of Clarke's lectures.

The exchange between the polymath Leibniz and the English divine Clarke was initiated by Leibniz, as Clarke explains in the Dedication to the Princess of Wales in the *Collection*, because of his "Suspicions that the Foundations of *Natural Religion* were in danger of being hurt by Sir ISAAC Newton's Philosophy" (p.v). By some orthodox divines, natural religion, with its deist versions, was seen as a threat. Clarke considered the order and relations within the universe as the best evidence of God and his attributes. That was what he understood by 'natural religion'. "Christianity presupposes", he said, "the Truth of Natural Religion" (p.ij). The scientific study of nature, Clarke believed, supported, not subverted revealed religion. The theme of the Boyle lectures was based on this same conviction. When William Wollaston published his *The Religion of Nature Delineated* (1722), he gave expression to this same confidence in the compatibility of natural philosophy and Christianity. Clarke even believed that explicit moral obligations (e.g., acting in agreement with justice, equity, goodness and truth) could be derived from considerations of the natural relations of things.

If natural religion was so strongly endorsed by such a respected figure as Samuel Clarke, with its roots in Newton's natural philosophy, what in it did Leibniz find as marks of its decay? He directed his charge against natural religion in England. If we are to judge from the subsequent discussions in that *Collection*, the marks of decay were certain metaphysical concepts and doctrines in Newton's *Principia* and *Opticks*, concepts such as space and time, God's presence in the world, the nature of mind-body relations. Leibniz assumes that natural religion must rest upon proper ontological principles. It was not only such austere concepts as those I have just mentioned which sparked his reactions. The second and third sentences in his First Paper identify more urgent concerns: "Many will have Human *Souls* to be material: Others make *God himself* a corporeal Being. Mr. *Locke*, and his Followers, are *uncertain* at least, whether the *Soul* be not *Material*, and naturally perishable."

Locke's suggestion about thinking matter had become implicated in and used by other publications within England. William Carroll, a Spinoza-hater who had accused Locke with being a Spinozist (in his *Spinoza Revived*, 1705), published in the same year a similar charge against Clarke (in his *Remarks upon Mr. Clarke's Sermons*). Carroll had linked Locke's sceptical claims about not knowing the essence of substance with his suggestion of the possibility of thought being a property of matter. Clarke gave Carroll some brief attention in volume 2 of his Boyle lectures, *A Discourse concerning the Unchangeable Obligations of Natural Religion and the Truth and Certainty of the Christian Revelation* (1706). In the Preface to that work, Clarke pointed out that Carroll reviled Locke and charged Clarke's Boyle lectures with being Locke-Spinoza in slightly new garb. Carroll was not one of the century's best or most rational pamphleteers. His attempts to show that the whole of Locke's *Essay* was written to defend Spinoza's one substance ontology sink to the level of name-calling and a feverish search for hidden meanings. Nevertheless, Carroll reflects worries that many others in Britain and France had about Locke's suggestion in *Essay* 4.3.6, the possibility of God adding thought as a property to matter. Leibniz's comment to Clarke about this aspect of Locke's work constitutes one of the more rational reactions, but this issue was not the focus of Leibniz's exchange with Clarke.

Just why Leibniz throws in that remark at the beginning of what turns out to be a comprehensive attack on Newton's concepts of space and God's relations with the world is not entirely clear. It may reflect the fact that Leibniz had recently completed his critique of Locke's *Essay* with his *Nouveaux essais* (written around 1705–06). As Nicholas Jolley has argued, that work was a detailed reaction to what Leibniz took to be the "pervasively materialist tendency" of Locke's *Essay*. (See Jolley's *Leibniz and Locke: A Study of the New Essays on Human Understanding*, 1984). Clarke did not allow Leibniz's opening remark about materialism, or the implied association of Newton with Locke's suggestion, to go unchallenged. Clarke did seem to agree with Leibniz about Locke: "Mr. Locke *doubted* whether the *Soul* was *immaterial*" (Clarke's First Paper, §2); but he turns the charge against Leibniz, claiming that Newton's mathematical principles are the best defense against "the false Philosophy of the *Materialists*" (§1). In characterizing his pre-established harmony theory, Leibniz had used the analogy for the soul-body relation of two synchronous clocks which keep the same time but never interact. Using that analogy against Newton, but applying it to the world as a machine, Leibniz said that according to Newton, "God Almighty wants to *wind up* his Watch from Time to Time" (Leibniz's First Paper, §4). Leibniz had even described the soul as an immaterial automaton, trying to explain his notion of the internal unfolding of the states of the soul. Frequent comparisons were made in tracts and pamphlets between the mind's relations to the body and God's relation to the world. As others had done earlier, Clarke seized on the clock analogy with respect to the unfolding of the world: "The Notion of the World's being a great *Machine*, going on *without the Interposition of God*, as a Clock continues to go without the assistance of a Clockmaker; is the Notion of *Materialism* and *Fate*. . ."(§4). Thereby, one of the main issues between Leibniz and Clarke (and Newton) was joined.

The charge of materialism against Locke was thus used by Clarke as a way of raising a range of questions found in many writings of the seventeenth and eighteenth centuries, questions to which Leibniz responded at length in his subsequent papers. These questions covered ones about perception ('how can physical objects be known if the mind or soul is immaterial?'), the interaction between mind and body ('can causation work between different kinds of substances?'), the location of the soul ('where in the body does it reside or exercise its function?'), freedom versus necessity in human action. There are many sub-heads and issues falling under these questions in the exchange between Leibniz and Clarke. To work through that collection of papers is to become immersed in most of the topics in those centuries. A number of these topics appear in the papers in this volume of the Library of the History of Ideas.

II

Another way to appreciate the diverse and interdisciplinary nature of philosophy, science and religion in these centuries is to consider the range of topics covered by Locke in his various publications. Locke was not atypical in the catholicity of his interests. He studied medicine at Oxford; lectured there on the laws of nature (moral laws of rights, duties and obligations); wrote topical tracts on money while secretary to the Earl of Shaftesbury; advised friends on medical problems, prescribing cures and regimens; wrote out a system of education for his friends Mr. and Mrs. Edward Clarke; organized his thoughts on government and political structure at a time of social unrest; kept up an extensive correspondence with theologians and philosophers in Holland, France and England; published a series of pleas for toleration, but not for Catholics or atheists; developed his own minimalist principles for religious belief and for the reasonableness of Christianity; conducted an extensive defense of his metaphysical and epistemological doctrines with an important bishop (Edward Stillingfleet, Bishop of Worcester); turned his attention late in life to biblical exegesis; and of course completed over a span of some fifteen or twenty years his major work on knowledge, belief and opinion.

After the appearance of his *Essay concerning Human Understanding* in 1690, Locke was quickly attacked by theologians and defenders of Christian dogma. Most of the doctrines considered by these people as central to Christianity Locke openly rejected, questioned, or silently ignored. The vigorous attacks on innate principles, principles held almost sacred by traditionalists, were bad enough: no innate ideas of God, no common moral rules 'written on the hearts' of infants. Worse was to come in later books of the *Essay*. When Locke exposed the absence of any sound knowledge of the essential attributes of material or immaterial substances (body or soul), he was seen as questioning or, Bishop Stillingfleet charged, rejecting the doctrine of the Trinity and even allowing for the possibility of only one substance (material) with the dual properties of thought and extension. These dangerous and evil implications of Locke's account of knowledge were seen as reinforcing Socinianism, deism, and materialism. Locke must have known that his exposure of the belief in innate ideas and principles would rouse the ire of traditional advocates of religion. Indeed, his examples and the language of innateness used in his polemic are all taken from contemporary sermons and tracts. Commentators have been strangely reluctant to recognize the context for and the targets of Locke's Book I. In responding to the prevalent appeals to and assumption of innate, 'congenite' knowledge of moral principles found in many seventeenth-century publications, Locke reveals the topicality of his interests. He usually wrote with an eye to some pressing concerns of his contemporaries. Whether he was writing on religious toleration, the jurisdiction of the magistrate over religious practices, reason and faith, clipped coins, or the nature and limits of knowledge, Locke always had his eye on live issues current at that time.

The local rootedness of Locke's concerns is nowhere more evident than in his reflections on knowledge in his *Essay*. Those concerns were probably initially related to religious and moral questions, but his analysis soon encompassed scientific matters as well. A not-too active member of the Royal Society, friend and correspondent of such scientists as Boyle, Newton, Molyneux and Sydenham, Locke's interest in science is the background to much of his *Essay*. He accepted the corpuscular account of matter as the most probable general hypothesis, substituting it for the vague metaphysical doctrine of substance. Chary of the use of hypotheses before ample experience and observation have yielded descriptive accounts of phenomena (what he called the 'plain, historical method'), he insisted upon the importance of careful observation and description in science. He still seemed to believe that there are necessary connections in the physical world, necessary connections between observed properties or events and the inner structure of matter (see his excessive discussion of what a knowledge of that inner structure would yield, an *a priori* science), he was firmly convinced that man lacks the tools for such penetration and necessary knowledge. Whether there are real classes, generic kinds, in nature (he vacillates a bit on this question), *we* can only classify objects on the basis of observed qualities, in terms of our interests and needs.

For Locke, the descriptive account of our cognitive states, processes and faculties does not raise questions about an underlying psychic structure. In his insistence that there can be no unconscious cognitive states, no ideas without an awareness of them, Locke could proceed with his analysis of idea-acquisition and belief-formation without any caveat about our knowledge of these processes and faculties being limited to observation and experience. Our knowledge in this area *does* come from careful introspection and perhaps observation of learning in children, but not in contrast with another sort of access which lies beyond our abilities. There is no indication in the text of the *Essay* that Locke ever entertained the notion of an unconscious or subconscious structure behind the cognitive life available to us in experience. He did, of course, recognize, as most people did, that physiological events within the body *are* related to awareness and cognition, but he says explicitly that he will not consider that physical basis of the mind. The *Essay* is a work of psychology and epistemology, not a work of physiology.

Locke was fully acquainted with the work of physiologists and anatomists. He studied with Willis at Oxford and he had read other physical treatises on the human body. It was difficult for anyone to deny the central role for the functioning of the body played by physical and physiological events in nerves and muscles. That same physiology was held necessary for perception, but powerful metaphysical reasons drove many to deny that the connection between sense awareness and physical or physiological processes is causal. Malebranche's occasionalism and Leibniz's pre-established harmony systems were denials of the third system for mind-body relation, the system of causal influence. Nevertheless, changes in the concept of man and of human nature were under way. Increased knowledge and understanding of the mechanism of the body, of its biological structure, made inroads into those doctrines which tried to keep body and mind separate. The feared danger of mechanizing the mind as well as the body prolonged the separation, but the growth of biological knowledge, together with the change from the concept of corpuscular, inactive matter to the concept of a dynamic force-matter, led to basic changes in the human sciences, in the understanding of the cognitive and affective nature of man. The essays in part IV of this volume illuminate these exciting changes.

III

The spread of scientific knowledge forced some writers to adhere even more strongly and blindly to their metaphysical and theological doctrines. Religious movements such as Socinianism or deism were more easily seen as in harmony with some of the newer developments in science and philosophy. To speak more precisely, the newer developments in science (force concept of matter) and philosophy (stress on experience and observation) were considered by traditionalists as support for heterodoxy in religion. In the end, orthodoxy lost, at least for a time. The Enlightenment, especially in France, built upon the changes in science and philosophy, forcing new alliances, producing new concepts of man and nature which, if not absorbed by religion, did mark the disappearance of much of the older metaphysical baggage. The challenge to faith in favor of reason, the rejection of miracles were skirmishes in the larger dialectic between old and new. The interplay between science, philosophy and religion in these two centuries provides us with a fascinating set of documents in intellectual history and the history of ideas.

PART ONE

OPTICS AND THEORIES OF VISION

Chapter II

BERKELEY, REID, AND THE MATHEMATIZATION OF MID-EIGHTEENTH-CENTURY OPTICS

By G. N. Cantor*

I. The "mathematization of nature" has been identified by Koyré and other historians of science as the principal conceptual development during the "scientific revolution" of the seventeenth century. The qualitative science of Aristotle was replaced by quantitative relationships involving space, motion, and, for Descartes, matter. Many leading natural philosophers of the period considered nature to be written in mathematical characters, and the program they advocated for scientific research involved the analysis of natural phenomena into mathematical, or, more specifically, into geometrical terms.

This program for research proved highly successful, particularly in astronomy, mechanics, and optics.[1] Only the last of these sciences, optics, will be discussed in this paper. During this period both catoptrics and dioptrics were placed on a firm mathematical basis. Furthermore, the eye which was considered to function like a machine appeared a suitable candidate for scientific analysis. But the finest and final achievement of the program was Newton's success in showing that "the Science of Colours . . . [is] as truly mathematical as any other part of Opticks."[2]

Although the program to mathematize optics was highly successful, it rested on a number of unexamined assumptions. One of these assumptions, and the only one to concern us here, was that all optical phenomena could legitimately be described in mathematical terms. Newton, for example, did not analyze this assumption. Thus in defining refrangibility he merely offered two disconnected alternatives, one describing the bending of a physical ray, the other representing the bent ray by a geometrical line.[3] For Newton and his contemporaries it was

* A shortened version of this paper was read at the summer meeting of the British Society for the History of Science, Canterbury, July 1975. For valuable criticisms during the preparation of this paper the author is indebted to John Christie and Jonathan Hodge.

[1] A. Koyré, "The Significance of the Newtonian Synthesis," *Newtonian Studies* (Chicago, 1968), 3-24; V. Ronchi, *The Nature of Light: An Historical Survey*, trans. V. Barocas (London, 1970). See also primary sources; e.g., Galileo Galilei, *Dialogue Concerning the Two Chief World Systems*, trans. S. Drake (Los Angeles, 1967), 103-04; E. Halley, "An Instance of the Excellence of the Modern Algebra," *Philosophical Transactions*, 17(1693), 960-69.

[2] I. Newton, *Opticks* (New York, 1952; based on 4th London, edition 1730), 244. [3] *Ibid.*, 2.

1

unquestionable that nature could be interpreted in mathematical terms. It will be helpful in the following discussion to specify this belief in the essential mathematization of nature as the geometrical model or analogy.[4]

In one specific area the validity of this assumption was particularly open to question. The correct method for explaining the phenomena of perception, particularly the apparent magnitudes and distances of objects, had long been disputed. The perception of distance was problematical since any point on a straight line extending from the eye would project the same point image on the retina. Hence, it was argued, distance was not immediately perceptible. Instead, two basic geometrical models were employed to ascertain distance. One model concentrated on the degree of divergency with which rays, emanating from a distant point, entered the eye. Divergency was considered to be a measure of distance since the divergency tended towards zero as the distance between object and observer increased. The height of the object could then be calculated from the triangle having its base in the object and its apex in the eye. The other basic model involved binocular vision in which the distance of a point from the observer could be ascertained from the geometry of the triangle having its base in the line joining the two eyes and its apex in the object. Using constructions like these the geometrical model seemed able to explain perception of distance and magnitude. Indeed, the explanation of these phenomena by geometrical means prompted Huygens to declare that there "is nothing in which God has more clearly employed the art of geometry."[5]

Irrespective of whether geometrical methods could be used to ascertain distance and magnitude, the problem of how we actually judge distance and magnitude raised some awkward epistemological questions. Descartes acted as spokesman for the theory of visual perception prevalent in the seventeenth century. He had likened the process of visual perception to the way in which a blind man holding two intersecting sticks, one in each hand, could discover the distance of an object. In Descartes' theory the mind employed "as it were . . . [a form of] natural geometry" involving "a simple judgment characterized . . . by intricate reasoning similar to that done by geometers."[6] Thus according to Descartes, the mind utilized a rational procedure like that used in geometry. Hence the geometrical analogy could specify the relation between visual

---

[4] M. Hesse, *Models and Analogies in Science* (Notre Dame, 1966); M. Black, *Models and Metaphors* (Ithaca, 1962); C. M. Turbayne, *The Myth of Metaphor* (New Haven, 1962).

[5] C. Huygens, *Cosmotheoros* (1698), cited on the title page of Robert Smith, *A Compleat System of Opticks in Four Books* (Cambridge, 1738).

[6] R. Descartes, *Dioptrique* (1637), sixth discourse. Neo-Cartesian theories of vision were not uncommon in the eighteenth century: e.g., C. N. Le Cat, *A Physical Essay on the Senses* (London, 1750), 190-91, esp. Plate ix, Fig. 3.

perception and geometry in Descartes' system. According to this analogy, similitude exists between the manner in which distance is perceived by the mind and the geometrical method for calculating distance given the bearings of an object from two points of known separation. Starting with this model a natural philosopher could pursue some of its implications in mathematical detail. However, the analogy might also be adopted as a specification of the natural order and not merely used in metaphorical vein; in other words, it might be seen to imply the proposition that we really employ an innate geometry in the process of perception. Thus the realist interpretation implied a non-empiricist psychology which attributed to the mind an innate ability to perform complex mathematical manipulations on visual sensations.

Despite the success of geometrical optics, certain problems of perception caused some embarrassment. These were not, however, generally considered as dangerous anomalies or as refutations of the geometrical method by most of its proponents. One such anomaly was clearly delineated by Isaac Barrow in his *Eighteen Lectures* (1669). Barrow, having developed at length applications of the geometrical model, ended his final lecture by pointing out "a certain untoward difficulty which seems directly opposite to the doctrine I have been hitherto inculcating."[7] The anomaly occurred when an object was placed at a distance greater than the focal length from either a convex lens or a concave mirror, and its image viewed from a point between the lens or mirror and the image point. With the eye close to the lens or mirror the image appeared near the object point, but on moving the eye back towards the image point the image appeared to approach closer to the eye and to become more confused. Barrow considered that this appearance was inexplicable in terms of the divergency of the rays, which instead of diverging converged on the eye. This anomaly, known as the Barrovian problem, was discussed by many late seventeenth and eighteenth century natural philosophers.[8]

A second problem which did not clearly fall within the scope of geometrical optics was why the moon's diameter appeared three or four times larger when near the horizon than in the zenith. Numerous explanations had been proposed for this phenomenon, many of which attributed to it the status of an optical illusion.[9] Furthermore, there were several difficulties concerning vision which seemed to border on the

[7] I. Barrow, *Lectiones XVIII, Cantabrigiae in Scholis publicis habitae; in quibus Opticorum Phaenomenon genuinae rationes investigantur, ac exponuntur* (London, 1669), 152-53.

[8] E.g., William Molyneux, *Dioptrica Nova. A Treatise of Dioptricks, in two Parts* (London, 1692), 118.

[9] For the history of the horizontal moon illusion, see E. Reimann, "Die scheinbare Vergrösserung der Sonne und des Mondes am Horizont," *Zeitschrift für Psychologie und Physiologie der Sinnesorgane*, **30**(1902), 1-38, 161-95.

philosophy of mind. One of these problems was why objects appeared single when the images painted on the two retinas were slightly different. A further problem of this type was why objects appeared upright when the retinal image was inverted. Thus, even in the seventeenth century slight anomalies existed, but these were usually considered peripheral to the main program of research in geometrical optics.

In 1709, only five years after the first edition of Newton's *Opticks*, the on-going and highly successful program in geometrical optics was devastatingly criticized by George Berkeley in his *Essay Towards a New Theory of Vision*.[10] Berkeley challenged this program by showing, first, that the phenomena of visual perception could not be explained in geometrical terms and, secondly, that the assumed mathematizability of nature was untenable.

In the *Theory of Vision* Berkeley offered a sensationalist critique of the geometrical model. He tried to explain all aspects of visual perception in terms of the immediate objects of sense. In vision, four phenomenal qualities were involved; we have direct perception of (1) shape, (2) color, (3) the degree of faintness or clearness of that shape, and (4) the degree of confusion or distinctness. These four parameters were the only immediate visual inputs to the mind. To these must be added the information obtained through the sense of touch. According to Berkeley, no necessary connection existed between the ideas of sight and touch; however, he claimed that we learn from experience to correlate these independent sets of ideas. Employing these and only these immediate objects of sense Berkeley showed how other aspects of visual perception were attained. Thus the idea of distance, which was not known from immediate sensory data, had to be judged by the mind on the basis of our past experience. According to Berkeley, experience has taught us to associate distance, which we know directly only from the sense of touch, with some of the immediate objects of vision such as the degree of confusion of a perceived image.

With this sensationalist epistemology Berkeley criticized those theories of perception which employed lines and angles in space, since these lines and angles were not immediate objects of visual perception. As a further objection aimed at the realist interpretation of the geometrical analogy he pointed out that those untutored in the "hypotheses framed

[10] G. Berkeley, *An Essay Towards a New Theory of Vision* (Dublin, 1709), hereafter *Theory of Vision*. Two editions appeared in 1709, and two or three others in 1732 as an appendix to *Alciphron*. Modern editions include *George Berkeley: Works on Vision*, ed. C. M. Turbayne (Indianapolis, 1963) and *George Berkeley, Philosophical Works, including the Works on Vision*, ed. M. R. Ayers (London, 1975). For further analyses of Berkeley's argument: D. M. Armstrong, *Berkeley's Theory of Vision: A Critical Examination of Bishop Berkeley's Essay Towards a New Theory of Vision* (Melbourne, 1961); R. J. Brook, *Berkeley's Philosophy of Science* (The Hague, 1973).

by the mathematicians" were nevertheless perfectly able to judge distances. "In vain shall all the mathematicians in the world tell me," wrote Berkeley, the sensationalist, "that I perceive certain lines and angles which introduce into my mind the various ideas of distance so long as I myself am conscious of no such thing."[11]

Berkeley was not arguing that geometry had no place in optics; to the contrary, he utilized ray diagrams in the *Theory of Vision* and claimed a specific but limited role for geometrical methods.[12] He considered that the lines and angles of geometry formed a synthetic language in the tangible realm and could thus signify tangible extension. Thus the geometrical language was applicable to physical optics, for example, in representing a ray. However, it could not signify how we see an object since visual extension was not necessarily connected with tangible extension. Hence Berkeley contended that the calculation of apparent magnitudes by using ray diagrams was neither an accurate nor an appropriate representation of visual perception since the mind formed judgments which depend on experiential factors and did not merely compute the necessary relationships implicit in the "optic triangle." Thus according to Berkeley the eye might act like a *camera obscura* but the mind does not receive the image passively. Instead the mind, actively operating on the signs, effectively interpreted the visual language in accordance with past experience.

In rejecting the geometrical analogy for vision Berkeley proposed a rival, the model of a visual language.[13] He likened the process of visual perception to the way in which the mind infers a thing signified by a word; the inference being founded on custom and not on necessary connection. "I think we may fairly conclude," wrote Berkeley, "that the proper objects of vision constitute a universal language of the Author of nature." This language, like a written or spoken language, could be learnt only by experience. Berkeley's principal contribution to the theory of vision was to show how the radical elements in Lockean empiricism could be extended to account for visual perception.

Berkeley also elaborated on the language metaphor to show how it could be used to solve specific optical problems. In discussing the Barrovian problem[14] Berkeley claimed that experience has taught us that the more confused an object appears, the closer it is to the eye. Hence, when the eye was close to the lens or speculum and the image appeared distinct, the image was assumed to stand at some distance from the eye. However, in moving the eye away from the lens or mir-

---

[11] *Theory of Vision*, sects. 2-15.

[12] *Ibid.*, sects. 78, 149-60.

[13] *Ibid.*, sect. 147. This concept is discussed in detail by Turbayne, *op. cit.*, notes 4 and 10 above.

[14] *Theory of Vision*, sects. 29-40.

ror the image became progressively more confused, and this confusion was interpreted by the mind as a sign that the image was approaching close to the eye. Even for Berkeley this phenomenon was an illusion since the mind wrongly interpreted the sign. He likened the process to reading a language which employed English words as signs but where the words signified ideas with which they were not normally connected.

In his explanation of the horizontal moon illusion[15] Berkeley employed the correlation between faintness and distance. He claimed that the sun and moon appeared fainter and thus more distant in the horizon than in the zenith. The mind therefore compensated for the increased distance in the former case by augmenting the body's apparent size. In discussing both the Barrovian problem and the horizontal moon illusion Berkeley went beyond his sensationalist program when he explained the physical basis of the phenomena. He attributed the appearance of confusion in the Barrovian problem to the rays not being focused on the retina owing to their degree of convergency when entering the eye. Similarly, the physical explanation of the moon appearing fainter near the horizon was that more light was lost in passing through a greater thickness of atmosphere.

The relationship between the sight and touch was extensively discussed in the *Theory of Vision*.[16] Berkeley denied that "visible ideas" and "tangible ideas" were necessarily connected, and claimed instead that they were independent and incommensurable; however, by experience the mind came to associate them. One implication of this theory was that a disembodied spirit having sight but not touch could not judge distance. More mundanely, Berkeley proposed a solution to the problem of retinal inversion. He claimed that since the mind does not perceive the inverted retinal image its existence must not be assumed in accounting for perception. Instead, he argued, we define the directions up and down in the visual field by correlating these with our tactile experience.

Following Locke most eighteenth-century philosophers emphasized the importance of empiricism, yet the conventionally-accepted form of empiricism incorporated many *a priori* beliefs about the structure of the universe. Locke's theory of matter, for example, assumed the existence of minute particles endowed with primary qualities,[17] while the prevalent theory of vision incorporated "a form of natural geometry."

[15] *Ibid.*, sects. 67-78.

[16] *Ibid.*, sects. 79-160.

[17] J. Locke, *An Essay concerning Human Understanding* (London, 1690), Bk.II, Ch. VIII; G. Berkeley, *A Treatise concerning the Principles of Human Knowledge* (Dublin, 1710). Berkeley also attacked Newton's philosophy of mathematics in *The Analyst, or a Discourse addressed to an Infidel Mathematician* (London, 1734).

Berkeley's criticisms of the latter marked a significant extension of the philosophy of empiricism. Furthermore, Berkeley's sensationalism challenged some of the fundamental assumptions of the scientific world view. In particular, Berkeley denied the validity of applying the geometrical method to problems of visual perception, and offered in its place the analogy with a visual language. This challenge did not pass unnoticed by eighteenth-century writers. Their response to the geometrical model, to Berkeley's criticism of it, and to the language metaphor will be examined in the next section.

II. Berkeley's theory of visual perception entered into the discourse among British writers in 1738.[18] Few, if any, adopted the theory in its totality; rather, like Lévi-Strauss's "bricoleur,"[19] eighteenth-century writers of diverse interests selectively utilized specific parts of the book which were relevant to their own problem situations. This selective borrowing was facilitated by the large range of topics discussed in the *Theory of Vision* and by the intimate inter-relationship of natural with mental philosophy in eighteenth-century thought. Furthermore, although Berkeley came to be labelled as an immaterialist, his writings on vision can be read without reference to the immaterialist thesis and this interpretation was adopted by many of the eighteenth-century writers discussed below.[20] For example, Thomas Reid considered that Berkeley's *Theory of Vision* "taken by itself, and without relation to the main branch of his system, contains very important discoveries, and marks of great genius."[21]

Berkeley's explanation of specific phenomena, the Barrovian problem and the horizontal moon illusion in particular, were often employed in an *ad hoc* manner even by writers who did not doubt the efficacy of the geometrical method. Thus Richard Helsham, a close friend of Berkeley's who held the chair of Physic and Natural Philosophy at Trinity College Dublin, employed Berkeley's "natural and satisfactory" solution to the Barrovian problem in his *A Course of Lectures in Natural Philosophy* (1739).[22] Of greater significance to the present paper were

[18] There were few references to the *Theory of Vision* between 1709 and 1738. An anonymous criticism appeared in the *Daily Post-Boy* (9 Sept. 1732) to which Berkeley replied in his *The Theory of Vision, or Visual Language, shewing the immediate presence and providence of a Deity, Vindicated and Explained* (London, 1733).

[19] C. Lévi-Strauss, *The Savage Mind* (London, 1966).

[20] This interpretation is also adopted by Brook, *op. cit.* Other commentators have sought the seeds of Berkeley's immaterialism in the *Theory of Vision*.

[21] T. Reid, *Essays on the Intellectual Powers of Man* (Cambridge, Mass., 1969), 169; hereafter *Essays*.

[22] R. Helsham, *A Course of Lectures in Natural Philosophy* (London, 1739), 331-33.

7

the many eighteenth-century writers[23] who emphasized the role of
experience in visual perception, a topic which was first explored in
detail by Berkeley. Explanations based on experiential associations,
but often omitting the physical details of Berkeley's arguments, were
frequently offered for the perception of distance, magnitude, erect and
single vision. Furthermore, Berkeley's emphasis on the role of experience received impressive confirmation in William Cheselden's experiments.[24] Cheselden reported the Molyneux problem of a man born
blind who, on gaining his sight in an operation, could not initially distinguish by sight a cube from a sphere. After sustaining an injury,
another of Cheselden's patients who saw everything double took a few
months to "learn to see objects singly again."

Many writers accepted that in vision the mind employed an asso-
ciative principle which they often expressed in terms of Berkeley's language analogy. In some of these instances the analogy was simply acknowledged as appropriate but not further discussed while in others
this model was subsumed within a wider philosophical framework. The
example of David Hartley, whose ontological and epistemological views
differed considerably from Berkeley's, effectively illustrates one aspect
of Berkeley's influence. In his *Observations on Man* (1748)[25] Hartley
agreed with Berkeley that the sense of touch had primacy over the
sense of sight, and he proceeded to argue that "we judge tangible qualities chiefly by sight; which therefore may be considered, agreeable to
Bishop Berkeley's remark, as a philosophical language for the ideas of
feeling; being, for the most part, an adequate representative of them, and
a language common to all mankind, and in which they all agree or very
nearly, after a moderate degree of experience." In the context of Hartley's book, however, the language model became merely an example
of a more general principle, the association of ideas.

Probably the only writer who totally and uncritically accepted
Berkeley's thesis was Voltaire. A whole chapter of his popular book
The Elements of Sir Isaac Newton's Philosophy (1738)[26] was devoted

[23] Among them were Cheselden, Hartley, Helsham, Reid, Adam Smith, Robert
Smith, and Voltaire, all of whom are cited in this paper.

[24] W. Cheselden, *The Anatomy of the Human Body* (10th ed., London, 1773),
295-304. The theories of perception adopted by Locke, Molyneux, Berkeley,
and Cheselden are discussed in N. Pastore, *Selective History of Theories of Visual
Perception: 1650-1950* (Toronto, 1971).

[25] D. Hartley, *Observations on Man, his Frame, his Duty, and his Expectations* (6th ed., London, 1834), 87, 120-28.

[26] F. M. A. de Voltaire, *The Elements of Sir Isaac Newton's Philosophy* (London, 1738), 57-71. Berkeley is mentioned by name on 63-64. This work,
originally published in French in the same year is included here owing to its
popularity in Britain and to Voltaire's extreme enthusiasm for Berkeley's *Theory
of Vision*. In France, particularly in the 1740s and 1750s, a major controversy
raged over the relationship between mathematics and physics: T. L. Hankins,
Jean d'Alembert: Science and the Enlightenment (Oxford, 1970), 74-117.

to problems of visual perception. He cited the example of seeing a man to be of the same apparent height whether he was at four or at eight paces distance. This appearance, Voltaire claimed, offered decisive refutation of the geometrical method since it predicted that the heights should be approximately in the ratio of two to one. He even repeated Berkeley's argument that the lines and angles of geometry were not immediately perceptible and that they were not related to our judgments of distance and magnitude. In true Berkeleyan language he proclaimed that we see size and distance in the same way "as we imagine the Passions of Men, by the Colours which those Passions paint on their Faces. . . . This is the Language which Nature speaks to every Eye; but a Language to be learnt only by Experience."[27] It is incongruous to read this one chapter of pure Berkeleyan sensationalism in the middle of a famous work on "Newtonian" philosophy. Newton's name was not mentioned in this chapter, and Voltaire did not consistently employ a sensationalist philosophy of science in other sections of this book.

Voltaire's response to Berkeley was exceptional. At the opposite end of the spectrum were those writers on physical optics who unflinchingly adhered to the geometrical method. A typical technical work on geometrical optics was Benjamin Martin's *A New and Compendious System of Optics* (1740). According to Martin the "Principles and Theorems of Optics are of a peculiar Nature, wonderful in their harmonious Origin, and *express a whole Science in a Line.*"[28] Unconcerned with the attendant philosophical problems, Martin showed how catoptrical and dioptrical problems could be solved by ray diagrams "as large as the Life." In these full black lines denoted "the Rays of the Sun's Light, as they are seen to go [sic] to and from the Mirrour in a darkened Chamber; and the *dotted lines* denote[d] only the Course or Tendency of the reflected Rays."[29] Martin's very language betrayed his belief in the geometricization of nature. Throughout the majority of the book he proceeded on the assumption that ray diagrams accurately represented physical reality. However, in discussing optical instruments he admitted that we do not see the true size and distance of objects.[30] He attributed this to the influence of certain habits of mind which interfered with our sensory data and thus prevented us from perceiving true spatial relationships. Hence, without querying the universality of applied geometry, Martin explained apparent anomalies by interference on the part of the mind.

Significantly many of the natural philosophers working in the geometrical tradition neither acknowledged Berkeley's criticisms nor de-

[27] Voltaire, *op. cit.,* 66.
[28] B. Martin, *A New and Compendious System of Optics* (London, 1740), ix. My emphases.
[29] *Ibid.,* 32.
[30] *Ibid.,* 151-52.

fended their own approach. Instead they pursued their research un-
deterred, possibly on the assumption that their program should be
judged by its success.[31] One outstanding objective was to show that
apparent anomalies could be explained mathematically. Samuel Dunn
writing in the *Philosophical Transactions* for 1762 confronted one such
problem.[32] He chastised those opticians who, having failed to explain
the horizontal moon phenomenon by geometrical principles falsely
claimed it to be a mere optical illusion. Dunn preferred his own physical solution to the problem which ignored the crucial distinction between the measured and perceived diameters of the moon. Instead,
:ollowing a simple experiment in which an object under water appeared
magnified, Dunn proposed the general principle that "certain accidents
making the rays more divergent than they otherwise would be, at their
entrance into the eye, seem to me to be the cause of" the horizontal
moon and similar appearances. The "accidents" to which Dunn referred
were allegedly produced either by the atmospheres of planets or by
the distribution of ether in the solar system, and he even conjectured
that the ether distribution could be discovered by studying the refraction of light in celestial regions. Despite the speculative nature of his
argument, Dunn was clearly trying to defend the universality of the
geometrical program against those who countenanced untidy optical
illusions.

Probably the only writer on physical optics who seriously responded
to the philosophical implications of Berkeley's theory was Joseph Harris
whose *Treatise on Optics* was published posthumously in 1775. In this
work Harris emphasized the role played by experience in the perception of distance and magnitude. Branding immaterialism as contrary
to religion and scientific truth he asserted that external objects exist at
some distance from us in the direction of the incident rays.[33] In accepting that no necessary connection existed between an object and the
visual idea formed of it, Harris clearly felt the need to legitimate the
role of the geometrical method in the light of Berkeley's criticisms. The
"optic angle," he asserted, need not be measured either with an instrument or by the angle of intersection of two imaginary lines. Instead,

[31] E.g., the mathematician William Emerson asserted that "vision is not made
at random, but is performed by certain uniform and steady laws"; W. Emerson,
The Elements of Optics. In Four Books (London, 1768), iv. In the appended
treatise on perspective (iv) Emerson, like most other writers on this subject,
claimed that the truth of a painting is guaranteed if the rules of perspective
are followed.

[32] S. Dunn, "An Attempt to Assign the cause, why the Sun and Moon appear
to the naked Eye, larger when they are near the Horizon," *Philosophical Transactions,* 52(1762), 462-73.

[33] J. Harris, *Treatise of Optics: containing Elements of the Science; in Two
Books* (London, 1775), 101-03.

it was itself a measure of the inclination of our eyes which, from experience, we know to be correlated with distance. The inclination of the optical axes was thus "always analogous to the *optic angle,* so we may express them by that angle." By thus asserting the synthetic nature of geometry Harris effectively reconciled Berkeley's critcisms with the geometrical model. Furthermore, Harris defended the efficacy of the geometrical method by arguing that the "lines and angles in optics, are not only useful in communicating our ideas to one another, but they are also not without their foundation in nature." The "foundation in nature" in this case referring to the analogy between the "optic angle" and the inclination of the optical axes.[34] In other words, Harris merely postulated an analogical relationship between physical reality and its geometrical representation. Although Harris did not refute Berkeley's criticisms, nevertheless, he argued quite convincingly for the suitability of the geometrical analogy in a specific problem area.

Another realist was William Porterfield, the Scottish physician, whose response to Berkeley was very different from Harris's. His *Treatise on the Eye* (1759) included a scholium which was clearly aimed at undermining the Berkeleyan position. In part this read: "the Judgments we form of the Situation and Distance of visual Objects, depend not on Custom and Experience, but on an original, connate and immutable Law to which our Minds have been subjected from the Time they were first united with our Bodies."[35] Porterfield distinguished between perception and judgment: perceptions he defined as modifications of the mind produced by vibrations in the sensorium, while judgments were the conclusions which the mind drew from these perceptions. Thus Porterfield considered that we do not merely perceive a red blob, we also form the judgment that the color belongs to the real external object which we observe. While distinguishing between these two acts he adopted Berkeley's view that since no necessary connection existed between perceptions and judgments, some other type of relationship must exist. Porterfield therefore enumerated two possibilities; either the connection depended on experience, or it was a law of our constitution. Since visual judgments must precede experience, for otherwise a young child would be precluded from making its first judgment, visual judgments must therefore be founded on a natural and immutable law and were not the result of experience. In rejecting the role of experience Porterfield not only attributed an innate and rather arbitrary faculty to the mind, but also provided a realist account of perception. The mind, he was forced to acknowledge, had literally to "trace back the Perceptions it has by Sight, from the *Sensorium* to the *Retina,* and from

[34] *Ibid.,* 153-54.
[35] W. Porterfield, *A Treatise on the Eye, the Manner and Phaenomena of Vision* (Edinburgh, 1759), II, 299.

thence *along those perpendicular Lines to the Object itself.*"[36] He thus attributed to the mind the extraordinary faculty of tracing geometrical lines in external space. In this statement, which appears to be a response to Berkeley, Porterfield not only adopted the geometrical analogy but also accepted it as an expression of literal truth and articulated one of its non-empirical assumptions. Also, in reacting against Berkeley's theory and its idealist connotations, Porterfield propounded a crude and over-stated form of common-sense philosophy.

In the eighteenth century there was extensive discussion of whether visual perception depended solely on experience or on an innate mental law. While Porterfield adopted the latter position, Adam Smith, the author of the *Wealth of Nations,* queried the extreme empiricist view of mind implicit in the language model. Smith considered Berkeley's *Theory of Vision* "one of the finest examples of philosophical analysis," and he drew on it extensively in his discussion of the visual sense.[37] However, he disagreed with Berkeley on the question of whether the visual language, like a written language, was founded purely on convention. Smith argued on teleological and necessitarian grounds that the language of nature, unlike that of man, contained some intrinsic order which made any particular visual sign most appropriate for representing one particular tangible object. This argument also called into question the very foundations of sensationalism, since if there was some intrinsic coherence in nature, then man might be endowed with an innate visual sense to help him comprehend the language of vision. In support of this thesis Smith cited the example of chickens which appear to understand the language of vision as soon as they are born. Also, children and blind people when first given the sense of light learn the visual language very quickly, which further confirmed Smith's view that some preferential connection existed between visible signs and the objects they signified. In the language of nature Smith concluded, "the analogies are more perfect; the etymologies, the declensions, and conjugations, if one may say so, are more regular those those of any human language. The rules are fewer, and those rules admit of no exceptions."[38]

The above responses to Berkeley's *Theory of Vision* may for simplicity be divided into two classes. Martin, Dunn, Harris and Porterfield subscribed to versions of the geometrical model, while Voltaire, Adam Smith and Hartley adopted the language metaphor. Of those

[36] *Ibid.,* 301. Emphasis added in latter part of quotation.
[37] A. Smith, "Of the Sense of Seeing," *Essays* (London, 1872), 450-68. Although not first published until 1795, five years after Smith's death, this essay was probably written about the mid-century. It is significant that this essay bears some marked similarities with Reid's philosophy.
[38] *Ibid.,* 461.

named only Harris attempted to answer Berkeley's criticisms of the geometrical model by trying to support it on scientific and philosophical grounds. Two further writers need to be discussed. They attempted the more exacting task of reconciling geometrical optics with Berkeley's theory of visual perception. In the first case, that of Robert Smith, the reconciliation was aimed at explaining optical phenomena, but his synthesis was unsatisfactory since he sinned against the fundamental doctrines of physical optics. By contrast, the other attempt was made by Thomas Reid, the common-sense philosopher, who was concerned with the science of mind.

Robert Smith, Plumian professor of Astronomy and Experimental Philosophy at Cambridge and a friend of Berkeley, wrote the most famous eighteenth-century work on Newtonian optics. However, his *Compleat System of Opticks* (1738) represents an unhappy amalgam of Berkeleyan and geometrical methods. Smith, in adopting a corpuscular theory of light, claimed that the motion of these corpuscles (or the rays of light) could be represented adequately by physical lines, but not by idealized mathematical lines.[39] Although Robert Smith followed Berkeley in rejecting the language of abstract mathematics, he championed the general pragmatic program of numbering, weighing, and measuring as the only method of obtaining truth in science. He pointed out that those qualities, color in particular, which had once been considered non-mathematizable were now expressed in mathematical terms. Therefore, he concluded, Berkeley had been over-cautious about applying mathematics to physical problems.[40]

In discussing perception Robert Smith followed Berkeley in rejecting geometrical methods in the judgment of distance and magnitude. He repeated many of Berkeley's arguments, including the ability of those unskilled in geometry to judge distance. However, Smith refuted Berkeley's specific explanations of the Barrovian problem and of the horizontal moon illusion with simple experiments and observations. For example, Berkeley's theory predicted that at the time of a lunar eclipse the moon being fainter should appear larger; but, as Smith pointed out, this prediction was not confirmed.[41]

Despite rejecting Berkeley's explanations of these two specific phenomena Robert Smith adopted and elaborated Berkeley's metaphor of a visual language: "the manner, wherein external objects are signified to us, by the sensation of light and colours, is the same with that

---

[39] Robert Smith, *op. cit.* (see n.5), 2. William Molyneux had likewise stressed the difference between physical lines and points and the lines and points of abstract mathematics. Molyneux, *op. cit.*, dedication to the reader and 9-10.

[40] R. Smith, *Remarks* appended to his *A Compleat System of Opticks in Four Books* (Cambridge, 1738), 56.

[41] R. Smith, *op. cit.* (see n.5), 49-51; *Remarks, op. cit.*, 31-42, 55-56.

of language and signs of human appointment: which do not suggest
the things signified by any likeness or identity of nature, but only by an
habitual connection that constant experience has made us observe between them."[42] Smith also considered that when we are unable to recall
a similar experience, the signification of the signs "like the words of an
unknown language . . . is entirely unknown."[43] In other instances, however, he asserted that we relate our sensations to similar past experiences.
James Jurin, in the appendix to Smith's book, discussed the association
of ideas and argued, following Berkeley, that "the ideas of sight constitute a visual language, because they as readily suggest to us the corresponding ideas of touch, as the terms of a language excite the ideas answering to them."[44] Smith proceeded to show how this associationist
psychology could explain the apparent sizes and distances of visual objects. For example, the horizontal moon illusion was explained in terms
of the vaulted appearance of the sky. He claimed that past experience
of cloud movements had taught us that the sky is much closer to us in
the zenith than in the horizon. Hence when the moon is seen near the
horizon it is assumed to be at a very great distance and the mind therefore augments its apparent diameter by a factor of three or four.[45]

Smith considered that when we observe objects through lens systems
or in mirrors our judgments "are indisputably derived from our experience in vision with the naked eye." Furthermore, the judgment of distance depended "principally or solely" on the object's apparent magnitude; in other words, the distance or angle it subtends in the visual field.
The mind, he contended, worked on the assumption that the linear real
magnitude of the image was the same as that of the object itself. The
image was therefore assumed to stand at such a distance that had the
object been viewed with the naked eye, the same visual angle would
have been subtended. This was Smith's novel though unsatisfactory
solution to the perennial problem of distance perception.[46] Clearly,
his principle was developed from Berkeley's empiricist theory, but in
applying this principle to specific cases Smith faltered over the accepted
principles of geometrical optics. For example, in his analysis of a flat
horizontal object placed under water he located the image parallel to
the object and of an equal linear magnitude but closer to the surface by
a factor of one quarter. This construction, however, was incommensurable with the sine law of refraction which implied a foreshortening of
the object as the angle of incidence increased. This example effectively
illustrates Smith's failure to demarcate the roles of associationist psychology and synthetic geometry. By overstating the former, he ignored
important features of geometrical optics.

[42] R. Smith, *op. cit.* (see n.5), 46.   [43] *Ibid.,* 50.
[44] R. Smith, *Remarks, op. cit.,* 27-29.   [45] R. Smith, *op. cit.* (see n.5), 63-64.
[46] *Ibid.,* 35, 51-58; *Remarks, op. cit.,* 42-55.

Benjamin Robins, one of Berkeley's foremost antagonists in the *Analyst* controversy[47] and a skilled applied mathematician who was suspicious of philosophical subtleties, was quick to chastise Smith. Many instances existed, Robins pointed out, where Smith's principle was untenable; for example, when the real size of an object was not previously known. Again, when an object was viewed through a powerful microscope Smith's principle implied that the image would have to stand at an impossibly small distance from the eye. Furthermore, Robins claimed that an observer could easily falsify Smith's principle by simultaneously viewing a candle and its image in a convex mirror and by comparing the distances and apparent magnitudes.[48] Although Smith's discussion of visual perception was unsatisfactory, it represented an impressive attempt to bring Berkeley's theory into the service of optics.

The final mid-eighteenth-century writer under discussion is Thomas Reid, the doyen of the Scottish school of common-sense philosophy. His extensive and constructive analysis of Berkeley's *Theory of Vision* appeared in his *An Inquiry into the Human Mind* (1764) and, more briefly, in his *Essays on the Intellectual Powers of Man* (1785). Although Reid was a realist and rejected Berkeley's idealism, the relationship between the two authors is subtle and complex. Reid derived many important ideas from Berkeley's *Theory of Vision* and incorporated them into a realist framework. For example, Berkeley had distinguished between the tangible magnitude of an object and its apparent visible magnitude. The latter quantity was an idea in the Lockean sense and existed only in the mind, and it was also logically unconnected with the idea of tangible magnitude. However, in adopting this distinction Reid denied that either magnitude was an idea *per se*. Instead, he asserted that we have measurable sensations of both visible and tangible magnitude, and that a necessary relationship existed between the two.[49]

Reid also used Berkeley's language metaphor extensively. Firstly, it expressed the relationship between sensation and perception: sensation being the sign which, in the act of perception, the mind instinctively interpreted as indicating the real existence of some external

[47] B. Robins, *A Discourse concerning the Nature and Certainty of Sir Isaac Newton's Methods of Fluxions, and of the prime and ultimate Ratios* (London, 1735).

[48] B. Robins, *Remarks on Mr. Euler's Treatise of Motion, Dr. Smith's Compleat System of Opticks, and Dr. Jurin's Essay upon Distinct and Indistinct Vision* (London, 1739), 36-41.

[49] T. Reid, *An Inquiry into the Human Mind, on the Principles of Common Sense* (Cupar, 1823), 111; hereafter *Inquiry;* also *Essays,* 169-70, 224. For Reid on visual perception: L. Turco, *Dal Sistema al Senso Comune* (Bologna, 1974), ch. V.

object. Secondly, Reid considered that the mind frequently employs original perceptions to signify our acquired perceptions. As in the synthetic languages devised by man, we instantly infer from these signs the objects signified, this mental act depending solely on custom but not on reasoning. For example, in vision only color, figure, and visible place are original perceptions, but by experience we learn to infer from these signs other perceptions: thus a faint color might be used to infer distance. Reid praised the "just and important observation of the Bishop of Cloyne, that the visible appearance of objects is a kind of language used by nature, to inform us of their distance, magnitude and figure."[50] As an example of the use of the visual language metaphor Reid cited the appearances seen through a telescope or microscope which had not been explained on geometrical principles. They must, he stated, "be resolved into habits of perception, which are acquired by custom. . . . The Bishop of Cloyne first furnished the world with the proper key for opening up these mysterious appearances."[51]

At this point in the argument Reid departed from Berkeley. As a realist he needed to establish that the judgments connected with vision were not purely in the mind but were truly founded in nature. Thus he claimed that while we may instinctively infer the existence of an object from its sign, the sign bore a necessary and exact relationship to the object it signified. Furthermore, he argued that those empirically acquired perceptions were also sanctioned by the structure of the real world: in particular that visible magnitude and distance were necessarily connected with the body's real tangible magnitude and distance. In establishing these claims he utilized geometrical reasoning.

Reid followed Berkeley in rejecting Euclidean geometry as appropriate for representing vision, not because judgments were based on experience as Berkeley had contended, but because a different form of geometry could accurately represent the relationship between an object and its associated sign. He therefore devised a form of geometry commensurable with vision. In this "geometry of visibles" objects in three dimensions were represented as projections on the two dimensional spherical field of the eye.[52] Reid's new geometry provided a set of rules of perspective which formally related the real linear extension of an object to its visual extension, measured either by an angle or by a line on the surface of the visual sphere. These rules showed, for example,

[50] Inquiry, 97, 89-100, 119-20, 202-28. Reid considered that Berkeley and Robert Smith "attribute too much to custom; Dr. Porterfield, too little." Ibid., 189.
[51] Ibid., 228.
[52] Ibid., 121-32. Norman Daniels has discussed in detail Reid's "geometry of visibles" in terms of his realist response to Berkeley's idealism; N. Daniels, Thomas Reid's Inquiry: The Geometry of Visibles and the Case for Realism (New York, 1974). For Reid's philosophy of mathematics and its Scottish context: R. Olson, Scottish Philosophy and British Physics, 1740-1880 (Princeton, 1975).

how the visible magnitude decreased with distance, and why a circle viewed obliquely was seen as an ellipse. By means of his geometry Reid established the necessary connection in nature between any object and its associated visual sign.

Reid's "geometry of visibles" provided the means by which the "visible figure, magnitude, and position, may, by *mathematical reasoning,* be deduced from the real."[53] He claimed that with these rules even a blind mathematician could have good understanding of vision, and could predict the visible magnitude of an object given its tangible magnitude and distance from the eye. The principle role of the "geometry of visibles" in Reid's argument was to refute Berkeley's "capital mistake"; that no resemblance existed between visible extension and the extension perceived by touch.[54] Instead, with the aid of a geometry commensurable with vision, he demonstrated that in nature visible extension is "a necessary consequence" of the tangible.[55]

Reid shared with Adam Smith and some of the other writers discussed above a profound sympathy for voluntarist and theological arguments. For Reid the eye's structure indicated the creator's "consummate wisdom and perfect skill in optics."[56] The human senses were fashioned by God to enable man to carry out his functions with safety, the eyes being particularly useful. Thus it was essential to Reid's metaphysical beliefs that the sensations of sight and touch were intimately connected and provided reliable and non-contradictory information about the external world. While the uniformity of nature guaranteed our sign reading under normal conditions, Reid allowed that "we sometimes mistake the meaning of the signs, either through ignorance of the laws of nature, or through ignorance of the circumstances which attend those signs."[57]

In replying to Berkeley, Reid divided the phenomenon of vision into two parts corresponding to physical optics and to the "psychology" of vision. In the physical universe the laws of nature guaranteed the exact correspondence between objects and their signs. Natural philosophers had discovered these laws and had expressed them abstractly in mathematical form as the rules of perspective or the "geometry of visibles." For Reid this form of mathematization posed no insuperable philosophical problems.[58] In the mind, as opposed to external space, these signs which formed the language of vision were read and sometimes misinterpreted. This process did not depend on geometry or on reasoning but on instinct or custom. By dividing the problem of vision into two parts,

[53] *Inquiry,* 111. My emphasis. [54] *Ibid.,* 140.
[55] *Essays,* 286; *Inquiry,* 139-40, 233.
[56] *Ibid.,* 88; A. Smith, *op. cit.,* 457. [57] *Inquiry,* 231.
[58] R. Olson, "Scottish Philosophy and Mathematics: 1750-1830," JHI **32** (1971), 29-44.

corresponding to Cartesian dualism, Reid assigned complementary roles to geometry and to the language metaphor. In response to the *Theory of Vision* he proposed a compromise between Berkeley's theory and that of the mathematicians.

III. Berkeley introduced into the discourse among eighteenth-century natural philosophers a lucid and damaging criticism of geometrical optics. In the ensuing debate fundamental beliefs were at stake about the structure of the world, and the assumption was challenged that in visual perception the mind operated like a computer in a universe constructed by God on geometrical principles. Berkeley questioned the scope of geometrical and mechanistic science and also an underlying ideology which had become very powerful during the preceding century. In place of the geometrical model Berkeley proposed the metaphor of a visual language. In a world created and supervised by God the linguist, and not God the geometrician, the mind had to create its own conception of the world by means of association founded on experience. By destroying the symmetry between mind and matter Berkeley offered a philosophy of mind which could provide a new paradigm for science on an empiricist basis. However, Berkeley's programme violated the prevalent eighteenth-century belief that a science of mind could be constructed analogous to the physicist's paradigm for science.

In historical terms the *Theory of Vision* relates not only to the role of geometry in science, but also to the rise of physical optics as distinct from theories of vision. Historians[59] have stressed the importance of Kepler, Descartes, and other early modern writers who achieved this disjunction which was essential for the development of physical optics on mathematical principles. One significant aspect of Berkeley's theory is that it blurred this distinction and instead offered a unified account of physical optics and the psychological aspects of vision. The mid-eighteenth-century writers discussed above adopted different approaches towards this definitional problem. Opticians like Martin and mathematicians like Robins accepted the modern physicist's definition of optics, while Adam Smith was concerned with vision as a mental process. It was Reid in his reply to Berkeley who reaffirmed the distinction between physical optics and the psychology of vision.

Central to the debate was the problem of the viability of different definitions of science. Berkeley's *Theory of Vision* bore several of the hall-marks of contemporary philosophy of science. For example, his attack on mathematical hypotheses is reminiscent of some of Newton's methodological pronouncements,[60] while furthermore he supported a

[59] E.g., Ronchi, *op. cit.*

[60] *Theory of Vision*, sect. 14. Cf., for example, the General Scholium added to the 2nd ed. (1713) of Newton's *Principia*.

popular cause by attacking the Cartesian theory with empirical arguments. Several of the mid-eighteenth-century writers discussed above found much in Berkeley that was truly scientific in the sense that he propounded general phenomenal laws. Robert Smith even tried to legitimate the associationist theory for judging distance by linking it with the methodological precepts stated in the 31st query to Newton's *Opticks*.[61] However, Berkeley's idealism, his sensationalism and his attack on geometrical methods were not compatible with contemporary views about the philosophy and practice of science. On these issues Reid attempted to defend science, as he understood it, from Berkeley's criticisms. For Reid, physical science aimed at the discovery of nature's laws by means of an admixture of empiricism and a set of *a priori* common sense assumptions, including the asserted realism of the external world and the assumption that it could be represented in geometrical terms.

Another significant facet of Berkeley's impact on eighteenth-century philosophy concerned the debate over whether the mind was a *tabula rasa* at birth. With Berkeley's sensationalism the physical world seemed in danger of dissolving into mere ideas. Many of the writers discussed above, but particularly Porterfield, Reid, and Harris, felt the need to support Cartesian dualism on both physical and theological grounds. But the common sense philosophers did not disentangle Berkeley's ontology from his epistemology, and in combating his idealism they had to postulate a simple correspondence between things and perceptions. They considered that even if the mind was a *tabula rasa* at birth it had to be endowed with some basic principles. In emphasizing sensory experience Berkeley did not really face up to this problem. Later, however, Porterfield and Reid insisted on the existence of certain innate mental laws. Adam Smith wavered on this point, finding it difficult to decide whether some fundamental laws preceded all experience, although he considered that man was born with certain basic instincts.

Berkeley discredited the concept of an innate geometry by showing its incompatibility with the prevailing philosophy of empiricism. In turn, Reid, reacting against Berkeley's idealism, argued that geometry was applicable to physical optics, but he simultaneously adopted a more conventional form of empiricism. Yet Reid's version of empiricism also countenanced a form of innate faculty psychology, since he postulated a number of basic laws of mind. One of these effectively illustrates Reid's compromise between Berkeley's empiricism and Porterfield's nativism: "every point of the object is seen in the direction of a right line passing from the picture of that point on the *retina* through the centre of the eye."[62] The geometricization of nature, mind excepted, was reaffirmed on common sense principles.

[61] R. Smith, *Remarks, op. cit.*, 39; Newton, *op. cit.*, 404-05.
[62] *Inquiry*, 145.

19

Following Reid's tame interpretation of the *Theory of Vision,* a reaction set in against Berkeley for nearly a century.[63] Thus James Hutton, writing at the end of the eighteenth century, judged Berkeley's view of science as too constricting to permit progress.[64] In a sense history, at least in the short term, favored Reid's view that philosophy should be subordinated to common sense.[65] The man of common sense triumphed over the sensationalist philosopher.

University of Leeds.

[63] A number of mid-nineteenth-century writers reexamined the *Theory of Vision:* T. K. Abbott, *Sight and Touch; an attempt to disprove the received (or Berkeleyan) Theory of Vision* (London, 1864); S. Bailey, *A Review of Berkeley's Theory of Vision, designed to show the unsoundness of that celebrated Speculation* (London, 1842); J. S. Mill, *Dissertations and Discussions Political, Philosophical and Historical* (London, 1867), 2, 84-119.

[64] J. Hutton, *An Investigation of the Principles of Knowledge, and of the Progress of Reason, from Sense to Science and Philosophy* (Edinburgh, 1794), I, 371. Berkeley's philosophy is extensively discussed in this volume.

[65] *Inquiry,* 11. Reid even considered that it "is genius, and not want of it, that adulterates philosophy"; *ibid.,* 7.

Chapter III

BERKELEY'S "PROPER OBJECT OF VISION"

By Gary Thrane

1. In this paper I give an exegesis of Berkeley's doctrine of the "proper object of vision." This conception is, of course, a central part of his theory of vision. The principal exegetical difficulty here surrounds the relation of the proper object of vision to the pattern of light on the retina. There are three relatively well-known positions on this issue. In the nineteenth century it was usually held that (1) Berkeley's proper object of vision was the pattern of light on the retina and (2) that this was a reasonable thesis. A second, more recent position, is that Berkeley indeed thought (1) that we see the pattern of light on the retina but (2) that this is absurd (D. M. Armstrong). And, finally, it has been held (Colin Turbayne) that, (1) since it is absurd to hold that we see the pattern on the retina, (2) Berkeley could not have meant that the proper object of vision is the retinal pattern. I shall urge that Berkeley does indeed hold that the proper object of vision is the pattern of light on the retina. In part, my case rests on showing that this is not an absurd thesis. Further, I will show how Berkeley's characterization of the proper object of vision follows from the thesis that the proper object *is* the retinal pattern.

2. Berkeley's *New Theory of Vision* (1709) has had a curious history. The first of Berkeley's precocious philosophical works, the *New Theory of Vision* grew in influence. While the *New Theory of Vision* did well, most learned men regarded the rest of Berkeley's writings as somewhat mad, of interest mainly to philosophers and lovers of paradox. So well, however, did the *New Theory of Vision* do, that Charles Saunders Peirce, in 1868, matter-of-factly writes,

There can be no doubt that before the publication of Berkeley's book on vision, it had generally been believed that the third dimension of space was immediately intuited, although, at present, nearly all admit that it is known by inference.[1]

Indeed, throughout the nineteenth century, Berkeley's theory was regarded as the standard or "received" account of vision. The influence of Berkeley's theory was pervasive as well as profound. Even the art critics were under its spell. Perhaps best known is the famous remark of

---

[1]Charles Saunders Peirce, "Questions Concerning Certain Faculties," *Charles S. Peirce: Selected Writings,* ed. Philip P. Wiener (New York, 1966), 21; cf. *Journal of Speculative Philosophy* (1868), 103–114.

Bernard Berenson: "The painter can accomplish his task only by giving tactile values to retinal impressions."[2]

Ironically, in the twentieth century, Berkeley's *New Theory of Vision* has fallen into disrepute, while his other writings have been rehabilitated. In modern treatments of perception, Berkeley's *New Theory of Vision* is either attacked or, more usually and worse yet, ignored. Not all philosophers, of course, are so oblivious. Nelson Goodman, for example, in his short review of Armstrong's book on Berkeley's theory, begins his remarks with the warm reflection that, "Berkeley's great small *Essay,* after long neglect, is beginning to receive some of the attention it deserves."[3] Berkeley thought enough of the *New Theory of Vision* to append it to the first edition of the much later *Alciphron* (1732). And an anonymous critique of the appended *Essay* provoked Berkeley's last systematic philosophical work, the *Theory of Vision Vindicated.* Apparently, Berkeley was never shaken in his belief that his theory of vision was correct in all its essentials.

3. The *New Theory of Vision* constitutes a thoroughgoing attempt to characterize the nature of one phenomenal field. Berkeley lays out the objective and plan of the work in the opening section.

My design is to shew the manner wherein we perceive by sight the distance, magnitude, and situation of objects. Also to consider the difference there is betwixt the ideas of sight and touch, and whether there be any idea common to both senses.[4]

Of these, the two most important contentions of the *New Theory of Vision* are: (1) the visual field is, strictly speaking, bidimensional; it has no depth; (2) heterogeneity: there are no perceptions common to the visual and tactile fields.

With regard to the limited thesis of visual immaterialism, the most important contention in the *New Theory* is that distance (from the eye) is not immediately seen. Indeed, Armstrong contends that "almost every conclusion that Berkeley comes to in the *New Theory of Vision* follows *simply* from the view that all that is immediately seen is a two-dimensional arrangement of light and colours."[5] Unfortunately, as we shall see, Berkeley does not explicitly argue in any detail why we should believe a view so contrary to what most of us regard as common experience. But in the *Principles of Human Knowledge* he does explain

[2]Cited by E. Gombrich, *Art and Illusion* (Princeton, 1961), 16; cf. Richard Wollheim, *Art and Its Objects* (New York, 1971), 45.

[3]Nelson Goodman, "Review of Armstrong's *Berkeley's Theory of Vision,"* *Problems and Projects* (New York, 1972), 80.

[4]Berkeley, *An Essay Towards a New Theory of Vision* (1709), *The Works of George Berkeley,* eds. A. A. Luce and T. E. Jessop, 9 vols. (Edinburgh & New York, 1948), I, 171, sect. 1; hereafter *Works.*

[5]D. M. Armstrong, *Berkeley's Theory of Vision* (London, 1960), 8.

why he conceives it to be important to the immaterialist case that we accept this doctrine.

For, that we should in truth *see* external space, and bodies actually existing in it, some nearer, others farther off, seems to carry with it some opposition to what hath been said of their existing nowhere without the mind. The consideration of this difficulty it was that gave birth to my *Essay towards a New Theory of Vision,* which was published not long since.[6]

The logic behind this is simple. Berkeley is not concerned with how the (unextended) mind can "contain" a three-dimensional array of ideas. Indeed, in the *Three Dialogues between Hylas and Philonous,* he explicitly notes this.

Philonous: But, allowing that distance was truly and immediately perceived by the mind, yet it would not thence follow it existed out of the mind. For, whatever is immediately perceived is an idea: and can any idea exist out of the mind?[7]

Also, Berkeley is not, after all, much concerned with explaining how the mind can "contain" a two-dimensional array of ideas. A three-dimensional visual field is not in the end incompatible with phenomenalism. Russell's sensibilia are, for example, in three-dimensional perspectives.[8]

What then is the "opposition" to immaterialism in the notion that we see three dimensions? Actually, the answer here relates to his doctrine of the utter heterogeneity of the objects of touch and sight. This doctrine *is* central to Berkeley's immaterialism. If what we see is a two-dimensional array, it is apparent that we do not see (immediately) the same things that we touch. For we touch things that have the property of being solids; consequently, to establish that what we see (immediately) are two-dimensional objects is to establish the immaterialism of sight. Since sight is commonly deemed the best access we have to the world, to establish the immaterialism of sight is to go a long way toward establishing the general doctrine of immaterialism. It should be emphasized that the principle of heterogeneity follows from the view that the visual field is, strictly speaking, bidimensional. I shall confine my attention to what now can be seen to be the fundamental principle of the *New Theory of Vision:* the proper object of vision, strictly speaking, has no depth.

4. Let us turn then to the arguments that Berkeley advances in support of his contention that the visual field is, strictly speaking, bidimensional. Berkeley does not argue at any length in *A New Theory of Vision* that distance, or as he sometimes quaintly calls it, "outness," cannot be immediately seen. Polemically, such argumentation was unnecessary.

[6] *Works,* II, 58, sect. 43.   [7] *Ibid.,* 202.
[8] Bertrand Russell, *Our Knowledge of the External World* (New York, 1960), 72–80.

For, it was a commonplace among contemporaneous opticians that distance could not be immediately seen. The standard account and a succinct statement of its rationale are given by Berkeley in section 2, of *A New Theory of Vision*,

It is, I think, agreed by all that distance, of itself and immediately, cannot be seen. For, distance being a line directed endwise to the eye, it projects only one point in the fund of the eye, which point remains invariably the same, whether the distance be longer or shorter.[9]

For the sake of brevity, I shall call this "the physiological argument."

In the *Three Dialogues*,[10] the argument just cited undergoes a subtle transformation.

Philonous: . . . Is not distance a line turned endwise to the eye?
Hylas: It is.
Philonous: And can a line so situated be perceived by sight?
Hylas: It cannot.

Notice that there is here no mention whatever of what occurs on the retina. I shall call this "the phenomenological argument."

More interesting yet is the form the argument takes in the still later *Alciphron* (1732).

Euphranor: Tell me, Alciphron, is not distance a line turned endwise to the eye?
Alciphron: Doubtless.
Euphranor: And can a line, in that situation, project more than one single point on the bottom of the eye?
Alciphron: It cannot.
Euphranor: Therefore the appearance of a long and of a short distance is of the same magnitude, or rather of no magnitude at all—being in all cases one single point.
Alciphron: It seems so.[11]

What is interesting about this version is that it combines the physiological and phenomenological arguments. The gap in the argument occurs at Euphranor's "therefore". But this gap can be bridged as I shall argue below. It should be remembered, too, that *Alciphron* is a rather late work and bears the weight of considered thought.[12] I shall call this interesting version of the argument "the physio-phenomenological argument."

Although these arguments may seem compelling, the conclusion is

[9] *Works*, I, 171, sect. 2.   [10] *Ibid.*, II, 202.
[11] *Ibid.*, III, 150.

[12] It should be noted, however, that Berkeley does not raise any form of the distance argument in the *Theory of Vision Vindicated*. Of course, there he is much more concerned to defend and explain the heterogeneity thesis against the anonymous critic. Moreover, Berkeley's technique in the *Theory of Vision Vindicated* is "synthetic" (cf. sect. 38), proceeding deductively *from his conclusion* not inductively from his evidence.

most implausible. It takes a considerable effort of imagination even to pretend that the visual field is bidimensional. It is in fact quite impossible to do this in any adequate way if the objects in view are anything like near to hand.

Naturally Berkeley is quite aware of this. He gives us many eloquent complaints against the intransigence of habit and ordinary speech. In *A New Theory of Vision,* Berkeley reluctantly notes:

We are nevertheless exceedingly prone to imagine those things which are perceived only by the mediation of others to be themselves the immediate objects of sight; or, at least, to have in their own nature a fitness to be suggested by them, before ever they had been experienced to coexist with them. From which prejudice every one, perhaps, will not find it easy to emancipate himself, by any the clearest convictions of reason.[13]

Unraveling the colors that we see from the habitual interpretation that we put on them proves to be impossible (at least for me). Artists sometimes claim to be able to do this. But such a claim is clearly hard to assess. The implausibility just noted is not, however, incompatible with Berkeley's view of the nature of natural philosophy.

The work of science and speculation is to unravel our prejudices and mistakes, untwisting the closest connexions, distinguishing things that are different, instead of confused and perplexed, giving us distinct views, gradually correcting our judgment, and reducing it to a philosophical exactness.[14]

5. Most discussions of Berkeley and Berkeleyan theses have turned on the putative distinction between "immediately see" and "mediately see." Although this seems a natural place to begin an analysis, such a distinction is, as is well-known, fraught with controversy. Instead, then, I shall concentrate on Berkeley's positive characterization of the proper object of vision.

To begin, then, Berkeley tells us, "The real objects of sight we see, and what we see we know."[15] This is not very helpful. Or, again, we see "visible ideas,"[16] or "the proper objects of sight." Many have noticed such tautologous "explications," but not everyone has paid close attention to Berkeley's more enlightening accounts.

One of the best phenomenological descriptions occurs in *The Theory of Vision Vindicated.*

The proper, immediate object of vision is light, in all its modes and variations, various colours in kind, in degree, in quantity; some lively, others faint; more of some and less of others; various in their order and situation.[17]

[13]*Works,* I, 195, sect. 66.
[14]Berkeley, *The Theory of Vision or Visual Language Showing the Immediate Presence and Providence of a Deity Vindicated and Explained* (London, 1733), *Works,* I, 263, sect. 35.
[15]*Ibid.,* 258, sect. 20.   [16]*Ibid.,* 256, sect. 10.   [17]*Ibid.,* 266, sect. 44.

Again, in the early *New Theory of Vision,*

... it is to be observed that what we immediately and properly see are only
lights and colours in sundry situations and shades and degrees of faintness and
clearness, confusion and distinctness.[18]

We see, then, colors alone immediately. What properties do these colors
have? They assume shapes (although they may be indistinct or
"confused"). It is clear also that these colored shapes that are arranged
in an order are, in Berkeley's words, "various in their order and situation." But Berkeley is adamant that these colored shapes are at no
distance. In the *New Theory of Vision,* Berkeley writes, "they may,
indeed, grow greater or smaller, more confused, or more clear, or more
faint. But they do not, cannot approach, (or even seem to approach) or
recede from us."[19] In his notebooks, Berkeley wrote these entries:

1   No extension but surface perceivable by sight.[20]
   3
      X,
1   W^t I see is onely variety of colours & light. w^t I feel
   3   is hard or soft, hot or cold, rough or smooth &c. w^t resemblance
      X,   have these thoughts with those?[21]

One question that deserves clearing up is suggested by the first of
the above-quoted journal entries. Berkeley there speaks of perceiving
only *surfaces.* But such a way of speaking is confusing. Surfaces are surfaces of solids. In his published work Berkeley makes quite clear that
the visual field is not a surface. He also rejects the notion that the visual
field is a *plane.* For, a plane is a bidimensional space with, as we might
say, a zero curvature *in a third dimension.* Speaking of a purely visual
intelligence, Berkeley writes,

And perhaps upon a nice inquiry it will be found he cannot even have an idea of
plain figures any more than he can of solids; since some idea of distance is
necessary to form the idea of a geometrical plain, as will appear to whoever
shall reflect a little on it.[22] [And again][23] ... plains are no more the immediate
object of sight than solids. What we strictly see are not solids, nor yet plains
variously colored: they are only diversity of colours.

The visual field, if the argument from the bidimensionality of the retina
is any indication, is bidimensional, but neither is it a surface nor a plane.
This sounds paradoxical, but there is no contradiction. This point is convincingly made by Armstrong.

The paradox vanishes if we assume that what is immediately seen is a two-di-

[18]*Ibid.,* 202, sect. 77.   [19]*Ibid.,* 197, sect. 50.
[20]Berkeley, *Philosophical Commentaries, Works,* I, 11, #35.   [21]*Ibid.,* 29, #226.
[22]Berkeley, *New Theory of Vision, Works,* I, 234, sect. 155.   [23]*Ibid.,* 235, sect. 158.

mensional manifold, for since the two-dimensional manifold is not a *surface,* it is quite capable of independent existence.[24]

Thus, quite apart from the data of the other senses (notably touch), Berkeley would hold that the visual field consists of colored shapes situated next to one another; but, I take it, the third-dimensional shape of the visual field as a whole is *indeterminate.* It is a bidimensional space with no determinate third-dimensional shape.

Berkeley is not always very helpful on this point. In the *Theory of Vision Vindicated,* Berkeley illustrates his contention that there is no natural relation between apparent magnitude and real (i.e., tangible) magnitude, by imagining that there is a diaphanous plane erected before the eye.[25] In so far as this suggests that we see planes, the illustration is poorly taken. Another illustration that may also confuse is that of the picture plane. This last is used to emphasize the disparity of the worlds of sight and touch.[26] Indeed, the nineteenth-century critic and aesthetician, John Ruskin, appears to have read Berkeley to be saying that we see flat pictures.

The perception of solid Form is entirely a matter of experience. We see nothing but flat colours; and it is only by a series of experiments that we find out that a stain of black or grey indicates the dark side of a solid substance. . . .[27]

Yet another erroneous interpretation is offered by Luce in his notes on the *Philosophical Commentaries.* Referring to entry #97, Luce writes, "the visual sphere must be the total field of vision from a point, which seems spherical, but which Berkeley holds, has a zero radius, i.e., the objects in it are seen at no distance."[28] In the entry in question Berkeley notes,

+Two demonstrations that blind made to see would not take all things he saw
Xto be without his mind or not in a point, yᵉ one from microscope eyes, the
other from not perceiving distance i.e. radius of the visual sphere.[29]

There is, to use an eighteenth-century turn of phrase, a certain repugnancy in the notion of a sphere of zero radius. The status to accord this entry is not too unclear. First, the marginal plus sign, as Luce notes in another connection, "may be an obelus, marking entries not needing attention."[30] Luce's remark may well be a correct description of

[24]Armstrong, *Berkeley's Theory of Vision, op. cit.,* 14.

[25]Berkeley, *Works,* I, 270, sect. 55. Berkeley's "diaphanous plane" is antedated at least by Leonardo da Vinci's similar conception of a window. I have developed a like idea, "the occlusion screen," in my paper, "The Proper Object of Vision," *Studies in History and Philosophy of Science,* 6 (1975), 13–14.

[26]Berkeley, *New Theory of Vision, Works,* I, 2i4, sect. 108.

[27]Cited by Gombrich, *Art and Illusion,* 296.   [28]Luce, *Works,* I, 111.

[29]Berkeley, *Philosophical Commentaries, Works,* I, 17, #97.

[30]Luce, "Introduction," *Works,* I, 4.

Berkeley's embryonic thought on the matter. Yet, it is hard to believe
that Berkeley could long rest content with so abstract a notion as a
sphere of zero radius. Its use would serve no purpose. And, in fact, so
far as I can determine, the notion appears nowhere in Berkeley's
published works.

Most decisively of all, however, there is an advantage in holding that
the shape of the visual field is indeterminate. It would be hard to see how
the "diversity of colors" could "suggest" objects at different distances if
the visual field had its own intrinsic, clearly determinate shape. Since
the visual field is of indeterminate shape, it may, like a piece of India
rubber, be "pushed" and "stretched," according to various cues, to a
pimply topography.

The literal description of the proper object of vision is then this: The
proper object of vision is a bidimensional array of light "in all its modes
and variations" (a "diversity of colors"). But this bidimensional array
has no intrinsic shape; it is not, for example, a plane. Nor is it at any determinate distance "from the mind," neither "near" nor "far."

6. These last considerations suggest a possible explication of
"mediately see." For we say something is mediate, meaning thereby
that it stands between, or is (spatially) intervening. It might be tempting
to suppose that it is this spatial sense of "mediate" that Berkeley has in
mind. The visual field would thus be a two dimensional array that stands
between us and the tangible objects arranged at distances from us.

But this is quite clearly *not* what Berkeley means by "mediate." The
trouble, in a sentence that only a philosopher could write, surrounds the
word "between." The visual field can only be between the mind and the
tangible objects in three dimensional space if the field is itself in the
three dimensional space. But Berkeley is quite clear about this. The visual field is, strictly speaking, spatially unrelated to the tangible field.

Or rather, to speak truly, the proper objects of sight are at no distance, neither
near nor far from any tangible thing . . . if they are one tangible and the other
visible, the distance between them doth neither consist of points perceivable by
sight nor by touch, *i.e.* it is utterly inconceivable.[31]

The only "link" between the tangible and visual fields is contingent (and
therefore learned) association. This point is elaborately made by
Berkeley in his discussion of situation. Indeed, Berkeley holds that *all* of
the spatial attributions we normally make of the elements of the visual
field are "metaphorical."

It is true that terms denoting tangible extension, figure, location, motion, and
the like, are also applied to denote the quantity, relation, and order of the
proper visible objects or ideas of sight. But this proceeds only from experience
and analogy. There is a *higher* and *lower* in the notes of music. Men speak in a

[31]Berkeley, *New Theory of Vision, Works,* I, 216, sect. 112.

high or low key, and this, it is plain, is no more than metaphor or analogy. So likewise, to express the order of visible ideas, the words *situation, high* and *low, up* and *down,* are made use of, and their sense, when so applied is analogical.[32]

Thus, the bidimensional space of the visual field is, according to Berkeley, completely separate from (real) tactile space. It is worth listing these "geometrical" features. What is immediately seen is a (1) bidimensional array of "light and colors," (2) indeterminate in its third-dimensional shape, (3) such that its elements cannot be treated of by (plane) geometry, (4) not oriented in three-dimensional space, (5) with no intrinsic metric (size) relation between its elements and ordinary three-dimensional objects. Thus, while we still have no fully satisfactory account of what *"immediate* seeing" is, we do now, I hope, have a very clear account of what is immediately seen. Berkeley's proper object of vision is a very strange brute, indeed. It is this latter fact, I think, that has led exegeticists largely to ignore it. It is now appropriate to question, however, whether Berkeley's conception here is a sober theoretical posit or an unusually grotesque chimera.

7. The reader will recall that in section 4 above, I cited three versions of Berkeley's argument that we do not immediately see depth. The first of these I called the physiological argument. None of the arguments are as explicit as one might wish, but of the three the physiological argument is the most truncated. The argument, it will be recalled, may be stated in a single sentence: we cannot (immediately) see distance because distance is a line directed end-wise to the eye and as such invariably projects but one point on the retina.

The foregoing argument, concerning what is projected on the retina, is not usually admired. Ritchie refers to it as "ill-fated."[33] And it is widely thought that the argument is, as Armstrong asserts, "valid only if we assume that the immediate object of sight *is* the fund of the eye. But this is obviously false."[34] Berkeley does indeed seem to commit himself to the idea that we see the pattern of light projected on the retina. In the *New Theory of Vision* he roundly declares,

There is at this day no one ignorant that the pictures of external objects are painted on the retina or fund of the eye; that we see nothing which is not so painted; and that, according as the picture is more distinct or confused, so also is the perception we have of the object.[35]

[32]Berkeley, *Theory of Vision Vindicated, Works,* I, 267, sect. 46.

[33]Arthur Ritchie, *George Berkeley:A Reappraisal* (London, 1960), 1.

[34]Armstrong, *Berkeley's Theory of Vision,* 9.

[35]Berkeley, *Works,* I, 206, sect. 88. Turbayne suggests in his "Berkeley and Molyneux on Retinal Images," *JHI,* **16** (1955), that Berkeley does not really hold this hypothesis. Rather, he suggests, Berkeley is merely assuming a "vulgar error" for the sake of argument. But, if this is so, it is hard to see why retinal inversion is a problem for Berkeley. And, Berkeley set great store by his solution of this "knot." Further, there is Berkeley's language itself in the passage cited above: he scarcely seems to be saying

Berkeley then goes on to discuss his solution of the "mighty difficulty"—retinal inversion—that arises on this hypothesis.

Two things, however, should be noted. First, saying that we see the
pattern of light on the retina is not necessarily equivalent to saying we
see the retina (of this, more below, section 9). Second, there are
passages in Berkeley's notebooks (1708) which suggest that Berkeley
was quite aware of a possible fallacy here. In one of these preparatory
notebooks there is the reminder:

1x2Mem: To discuss copiously how & why we do not see the pictures.[36]

In the face of such contradictory indications and in view of the im-
poverished character of the argument, it is hard to know how to
continue the exegesis. Armstrong and Warnock,[37] who have both written on Berkeley's distance thesis, dismiss the physiological argument
and proceed to develop alternative arguments. Such a course is tempting. However, it seems to me that it is the part of charity to assume that
the physiological argument of the *New Theory of Vision* may be but an
abbreviated form of the physiophenomenological argument in *Alciphron.* Accordingly, having noted the weakness of the pure physiological
argument, let us turn to the other forms of the argument.

8. Since the physiological argument is not widely admired, those
who are favorably disposed to Berkeley's contention here tend to
construe the physiological argument as a version of the phenomenological argument. Merleau-Ponty's embarrassment over the physiological argument and his preference for the phenomenological argument
are apparent in the following:

If one retorted that after the criticism of the "constancy hypothesis" we cannot
judge what we see by what is pictured on our retinas, Berkeley would probably
reply that, whatever may be true of the retinal image, depth cannot be seen because it is not spread out before our eyes, but appears to them only in
foreshortened form. . . . Berkeley's argument, made quite explicit, runs
roughly like this. What I call depth is in reality a juxtaposition of points, making
it comparable to breadth. I am simply badly placed to see it. I should see it if I
were in the position of a spectator looking on from the side, who can take in at a
glance the series of objects spread out in front of me, whereas from me they
conceal each other—or see the distance from my body to the first object,
whereas for me this distance is compressed into a point.[38]

Warnock, too, explicitly analyzes the physical argument as a variant of
the phenomenological argument.

"Let us assume for the sake of argument,. . . ." For more, see section 10, below, and
Furlong, "Berkeley and the 'Knot' . . .," *Australasian Journal of Philosophy,* **41** (1963),
311–16.
[36]Berkeley, *Philosophical Commentaries, Works,* **I,** 33, #268.
[37]*Op. cit.,* note 23, above.
[38]Merleau-Ponty, *Phenomenology of Perception* (London, 1962), 255.

But the point which, in this rather odd way, Berkeley is seeking to make is a different one. . . . The gap between myself and any object at which I look is a gap which, we might say, I can only look at from one end; and of course from the end it does not *look* like a gap—not like the gap between the two trees. It is to this that Berkeley wishes to point.[39]

It is interesting to note that both authors speak as if they are unaware of the explicit phenomenological argument in the *Three Dialogues*.

Armstrong is also guilty of this exegetical oversight. In his book on Berkeley's *New Theory of Vision,* Armstrong is very keen on demonstrating that Berkeley really was deluded into thinking that we see the "fund of the eye." Armstrong discusses only what I have called the physiological argument. Since this is the only argument in the *New Theory of Vision,* there is some justice in his narrow inquiry. Yet, Armstrong does freely use the *Theory of Vision Vindicated,* and refers on occasion to the *Principles of Human Knowledge* and the *Three Dialogues between Hylas and Philonous.* Armstrong himself develops a version of the phenomenological argument which, he says, "does seem to tell a little in Berkeley's favor."[40] Surprisingly, however, he presents this as an argument Berkeley *should* have used. Since a purely phenomenological argument does occur in the *Three Dialogues,* it would seem that Armstrong has read only the *New Theory of Vision* with care. He makes no mention of the most explicit argument in *Alciphron.* One can take one of two attitudes here: first, one could hold that the physiological argument in *A New Theory of Vision* is the full and explicit argument; or, second, one could hold that the physiological argument is but a condensed version of the still none-too-explicit argument in *Alciphron.* My attitude is the second. That is, I hold that each of these arguments is but a version of the *same* argument. The fullest version of the argument is that in *Alciphron.* Indeed, the physio-phenomenological argument in *Alciphron* is Berkeley's explicit combination of the other two versions.

In any case, whether one notes Berkeley's own phenomenological argument or "charitably" invents one for Berkeley, still any *purely* phenomenological argument is subject to serious objections. Each of the above-mentioned commentators is aware of the limitations of this sort of argument, for depth is a phenomenological given of the visual field. True, the gap between me and distant objects is not "spread out" before my eyes. Yet, I do see objects as distant from me. The argument that I do not see the gap spread out before me only raises questions about the mechanism of depth-perception. What one ought to conclude from phenomenological inspection is simply that one does not see depth by viewing the gap between oneself and distant objects, instead of concluding that one does not see depth. Those that resist a purely phenom-

[39]Warnock, *Berkeley,* 27. Warnock then cites the *physiological* argument from section 2 of *The New Theory of Vision.*

[40]Armstrong, *Berkeley's Theory of Vision,* 15.

enological argument here most likely do so (correctly in my view) on precisely these grounds.

This is a feature which will plague any purely phenomenological argument. As long as we merely inspect our visual field, we will find solids ordered in a three-dimensional array. What may become puzzling, *just* from phenomenological inspection, is how this is possible. The discussion of the gap is but one variant of a consideration that makes this possible puzzlement vivid. More generally, I may wonder how I can see something as *there* even though I am here. But, again, what seems transparent is that we shall not be tempted to doubt the three-dimensional nature of the visual field; rather, we shall be, at worst, puzzled as to how it is possible. If, on the other hand, one chooses the method of phenomenological reduction, one runs up against the following difficulty: however many properties are "reduced away," no amount of plausible phenomenological reduction will rob the objects of vision of their three-dimensionality. Three-dimensionality is not consciously inferred, estimated, nor even "suggested" to the mind. All of these processes are far too cognitive to adequately characterize the vivid and immediate solidity of the objects we see about us. Writing of the traditions he calls "Empiricism" and "Intellectualism," Merleau-Ponty points to this flaw (if I understand him rightly): "the two philosophies take for granted the result of a constitutive process the stages of which we must, in fact, trace back."[41] Of course, it is just this "tracing back" of the supposed constitutive steps in the perception of depth that cannot be done on a cognitive level. It is a brute psychological fact that the visual world of solids in a three dimensional array is conceptually primary. It is there that any conceptual tracing back will *end,* at least if that tracing back is based on phenomenological reduction.

9. It may well seem now that Berkeley's case is hopeless. The phenomenological argument seems to be profoundly inadequate. And the physiological argument seems to rest on the patently false assumption that we see the retina. Let us look, then, at the physio-phenomenological argument in *Alciphron.* The argument in *Alciphron* represents the most explicit version of the argument. The reader will recall that Euphranor points out that the line which constitutes distance from the eye projects "one single point on the bottom of the eye"; "therefore," he concludes, "the appearance of a long and of a short distance is of the same magnitude, or rather of no magnitude at all—being in all cases one single point."[42] Euphranor's "therefore" clearly turns on the principle that we could not see the line out from the eye as anything but a point since that is all that there is, as it were, a record of on the retina.

Now there are clear correlations between the (phenomenal) visual

[41]Merleau-Ponty, *The Phenomenology of Perception,* 255.
[42]Berkeley, *Alciphron, or the Minute Philosopher* (London, 1732), *Works,* III, 150.

field and occurrences on the retina. When I remove my glasses, for example, my visual field is blurred (or "confused" in Berkeley's language). This is because without corrective lenses the "little pictures" are themselves confused. Objects high and low in my visual field are low and high in the (inverted) "little picture." Faint things in my visual field are the result of faint projections on the retina. Apparent (phenomenal) magnitudes are correlated rather closely with the magnitude of the projections. Phenomenal colors, too, are correlated rather closely at least with the colors projected on the retina.

But ought we to say that we *see* the pattern of light projected on the retina? Is the pattern of light projected on the retina the "proper object of vision"? It seems to me that close reading of Berkeley reveals that the answer is inescapably "Yes". Berkeley's argument, reformulated, goes like this: strictly speaking, all that *could* be immediately seen are those features of the optical stimulus to which the photo-sensitive surface (the retina) is sensitive. The retina is sensitive to a bidimensional array of colors and to the intensity and hue of those colors, but the retina is sensitive to nothing else.[43]

The puzzle, then, to which Berkeley's theory addresses itself is roughly this: seeing, even at its most cautious, is far richer and more informative than the retinal irradiation pattern; but the retinal pattern of light contains the entirety of the information "intromitted" by the eye. It would seem that all that is physically possible to see, without "processing," is this pattern of light—yet we always see more than this.

One standard objection should be dealt with at once. As has been already noted, Armstrong claims that the physiological argument is "valid only if we assume that the immediate object of sight is the fund of the eye."[44] Why does Armstrong think that such a view is entailed by Berkeley's theory? Consider the following argument which Armstrong develops in this connection:

. . .suppose it were true that the fund of the eye was the object immediately seen. Would we not need *another* eye to see the fund of the eye? After all, seeing requires eyes. But then, by parity of reasoning, all that would be immediately seen would be the fund of this second eye, which would have to be observed by a third eye, and so on indefinitely.[45]

This argument seems very plausible at first. Yet it rests on two false premises. First, there is the assumption that seeing the two-dimensional

[43]It is this insensitivity of the retina that accounts for the indeterminacy and "free-floating" character of the proper object of vision.

[44]Armstrong, *Berkeley's Theory of Vison*, 9.

[45]*Loc. cit.* Armstrong may have gotten the argument from J. J. Gibson whom he cites in another connection. Gibson, who is also opposed to the Berkeleyan position, writes: "If the retinal image were really a picture there would have to be another eye behind the eye with which to see it." *Perception of the Visual World* (Boston, 1950), 54.

pattern of light on retina is equivalent to seeing the retina, and second, that all seeing requires eyes. As will be seen shortly, the first of these aberrant premises follows from the second.

First, what is the cognitive status of "All seeing requires eyes"? It is clearly not analytic. If it is a fact, it is most assuredly just an empirical fact. The world might have been such that eyes were never requisite for seeing. Thus, despite the *prima facie* triviality of Armstrong's principle, we must consider whether or not it is empirically correct.

Is it true that all seeing requires eyes? It is clear that, if my interpretation of Berkeley is correct, one of the following is true: either we look at our retinas with another eye or it is not the case that all seeing requires eyes.[46] It must be conceded that the first of these propositions is oddly tempting. It is all too easy to think of the eyes as windows from which a "little man" peers; or, noting the existence of the retina, to think of the retina as a screen at which the "little man" looks. Armstrong is of the opinion that Berkeley is still subtly influenced by this picture.

> ...what is formed on the retina is a two dimensional simulacrum of the object seen. . . . This physiological accident has profoundly confused both philosophers and scientists. Normally it has operated to reinforce the idea that perception was a matter of seeing *pictures* of the external world; Berkeley does not believe this, but he is still deceived by the *two-dimensional* nature of the simulacrum. And, . . . accepting this argument as he does here, lands him in a great deal of trouble when he comes to discuss the 'knot' caused by the fact that the retinal image is inverted.[47]

Since Berkeley renounces the idea that we see the retina either he is confused on this point or he would reject Armstrong's principle, "All seeing requires eyes."

If Berkeley's views are to be saved from Armstrong's interpretation (which involves the allegation of incoherency), it must be argued that it is false that all seeing requires eyes. This may seem a *reductio ad absurdum,* but it is not. What is the function of the lens mechanism? By means of it a focused image is projected on the retina. So far as we know the only biological solution to the problem of discriminating sight involves the formation of images by crystalline lenses. Once the image is formed, however, what else is requisite to seeing? A sensitive retina and a working optic nerve. Consequently, although the entire mechanism of the eye is requisite to see distant objects, seeing the pattern of light on the retina does not require another eye. The retina, or "fund of the eye," just *is* the photosensitive surface.

---

[46]It follows from this disjunct that not all seeing requires looking—at least if all looking requires (directing the) eyes.

[47]Armstrong, *Berkeley's Theory of Vision,* 10. The physiological argument is Armstrong's reference.

Actually, Armstrong's principle may be meant as "All seeing requires looking at something with the eyes." This would be more in keeping with the "little-man" model. This principle is so incompatible with Berkeley's position that it is virtually a denial that we can see the pattern of light on the retina. Hence, this assumption of Armstrong's "refutation" is very close to begging the question. Obviously, too, on my account, the corollary that we must see the fund of the eye goes by the boards. We see the pattern of light projected on the retina but not the retina itself.

It is interesting to speculate that seeing may have been unconsciously assimilated to touch. When I feel this page, I also feel the telltale pressure in my fingers. Whenever we feel an object, we feel the part of our body that is in contact with the object felt. Not so, seeing. We do not feel where the light impinges on the retina: we just see light. Seeing is not proprioceptive. It is only an externally discoverable fact that seeing is connected with the eyes. This is obviously closely related to Berkeley's contention that there is no sensed (seen or felt) connection between the visual and tactile fields. It is this fact, too, of course, that solves the "knot" of retinal inversion. That we just see a bidimensional field of light (and not its shape or setting) is sufficient to explain why we do not see upside down.

As further confirmation of the above interpretation consider the following remark that Berkeley makes with regard to the problem of retinal inversion:

Farther what greatly contributes to make us mistake in this matter is that when we think of the pictures in the fund of the eye, we imagine ourselves looking on the fund of another's eye, or another looking on the fund of our own eye, and beholding the pictures painted thereon.[48]

Berkeley, thus, appears to understand the matter very well: we do not see the pattern of light on the fund of the eye by looking at the fund of the eye (with, of course, *another* eye).

Interpretive confusion about what Berkeley means is not entirely the fault of his readers. His own discussion of this issue suffers from an uncharacteristic turgidity.

Pictures, therefore, may be understood in a twofold sense, or as two kinds quite dissimilar and heterogeneous, the one consisting of light, shade, and colours; the other not properly pictures, but images projected on the retina. Accordingly, for distinction, I shall call those *pictures,* and these *images.* The former are visible, and the peculiar objects of sight. The latter are so far otherwise, that a man blind from his birth may perfectly imagine, understand, and comprehend them.[49]

[48]Berkeley, *New Theory of Vision, Works,* I, 217, sect. 116.
[49]Berkeley, *Theory of Vision Vindicated, Works,* I, 268, sect. 50.

It is easy, then, to see how one might well become confused.

Berkeley's way of drawing the distinction is thus infelicitous. Berkeley's immediate object of vision is most emphatically *not* a picture; it consists *merely,* as he goes on to say, of "light, shade and colours." The retinal irradiation pattern as immediately seen is just a three-dimensionally indeterminate bidimensional array of colors that is "free-floating" and metric-free. As seen in an ophthalmoscope, the "image" (as Berkeley would call it) is indeed tiny, upside down and curved. But the "image" in the ophthalmoscope and the "picture" caused by the irritation of the photosensitive surface of the body are quite different. This is all that Berkeley needs to say to obviate the kind of objections that Armstrong and others have raised.

10. A more apologetic tack has been taken by one of Berkeley's best known contemporary commentators. Because he accepts Armstrong's argument that we cannot see retinal events, he urges that Berkeley never maintained such a thesis. In an article devoted to this subject, Colin Turbayne concludes,

> To say that pictures on the retina are the proper objects of sight is to commit "the psychologist's fallacy", a fallacy to which the writers of optics were prone, and which Berkeley was particularly anxious to avoid. It involves the supposition that we may be directly aware of things which we can only *know about.* Of what occurs on our retinas we can never be directly aware. It is therefore most unlikely that Berkeley, who never once categorically stated that pictures on the retina are the proper or immediate objects of sight meant that they are.[50]

Several things need to be said about Turbayne's argument. First, some argument is indeed necessary. For, as we have seen, Berkeley's own writings are somewhat confusing on this score. Indeed, I agree with Turbayne that we are stuck with arguing, as he does, about what Berkeley *must* have meant.[51] Turbayne and I would also agree that Berkeley was far too clever to have thought that we see by *looking* at retinal patterns (with another eye). Any view (such as Armstrong's) which imputes such naiveté to Berkeley is therefore *prima facie* implausible.

What, then, of Turbayne's contention that it is absurd to speak of being directly aware of retinal events? I certainly see no fallacy in supposing that we see the light that (as it happens) is projected on the retina. True, we do not know by seeing that this is what happens. The physiologist must tell us about the structure of the eye. But, do we not see a light when the oculist shines one in our eye? Do we not fail to see when the lights are out? When we (as it happens) project little pictures on the retinas of our eyes with a stereopticon, do we not see scenes?

---

[50]"Berkeley and Molyneux on Retinal Images," *loc. cit.,* 351.

[51]In his article (*op. cit.,* note 35, above) on this subject Furlong notes, "what are we to say on this issue? I think it is no easy matter to decide" (311).

What, in the end, is the retina sensitive to if not light? Such, I would suggest are Berkeley's questions. And the obvious answer to them is indeed the answer he gives, "light in all its modes and variations."

Turbayne's argument is thus curiously unsound. The trouble is not the "psychologist's fallacy," but rather the "philosopher's fallacy." Crudely put, this fallacy is the view that what we do not know about cannot happen or exist. Perhaps, it is not a fallacy so much as a rather extreme form of idealism. Nonetheless, it is some such view that must be behind Turbayne's argument. It is true that knowledge of retinas, lenses, etc. is rather recondite; but it is also true that these are requisite for seeing. We do not know *by seeing the retina* that we see light impinging there. But it scarcely follows from this that we therefore do not see the light that (as it happens) does impinge on the retina. Berkeley is after all offering a *theory* of vision in which he discusses these recondite facts in great detail. Why would he do this, if he thought it was a fallacy to do so? Turbayne's argument is, thus, rather close to Armstrong's which involves the erroneous assumption that seeing the retinal pattern is equivalent to seeing the retina.

Two personal examples may make this more vivid. The lenses of this author's eyes do not give focused images on the retinas of his eyes;[52] things look blurred (out of focus) without glasses. I know things look blurred without my glasses for this reason because my oculist tells me this—not by seeing my retinas. Nonetheless, the oculist's reason is (as it happens) the reason. Like most people, I also, when staring at the sky, see several small specks. These are "vitreous floaters," bits of lens debris floating in the aqueous humor of my eyes (no longer a "clear-eyed youth"). Once again, the expert, the ophthalmologist explains just what it is I am seeing: I do not take my eyes out to examine them. But, note again, it scarcely follows that I am not seeing "vitreous floaters." I am in fact (as it turns out) seeing debris floating *in* my eyes. Turbayne would have to maintain that I do not *really* see this debris because it had to be explained to me what I was seeing.

Finally, it has been suggested by some apologists that Berkeley changed his mind about vision during the course of his philosophical career. He was indeed deluded, they say, in a *New Theory of Vision* (1709), into thinking that one sees one's retinal patterns. But, they go on, he certainly had given up this view by the time he published *The Theory of Vision Vindicated and Explained* (1733).

How does the *TVV* [*Theory of Vison Vindicated*] solution compare with that in the *TV* [*A New Theory of Vision*]? With both solutions we begin with two apparently conflicting things and end by abolishing one of them. In the *TV* Berkeley abolished the erect appearance and retained the retinal picture, deny-

---

[52]This is Euphranor's "therefore."

ing that this is inverted. In the *TVV* he leaves the erect appearance, but denies the retinal picture.[53]

Despite textual difficulties, such a view has little merit. First, such a theory is contradicted by the very title of the later essay. Second, the fullest argument that we do not see distance (because of what happens on the retina) is to be found in *Alciphron,* and *Alciphron* (1732) is nearly contemporaneous with *The Theory of Vision Vindicated* (1733). Third, the absence of any distance-argument in *The Theory of Vision Vindicated* results from Berkeley's announced method in that work. He there proceeds deductively from his conclusions not (as he does elsewhere) inductively from his evidence. These considerations are, I think, sufficient to lay to rest the notion that Berkeley had a last-minute change of heart.

In any case, once it is recognized that Berkeley's thesis in *A New Theory of Vision* is not absurd, the need for such apologetics evaporates. Notice what seems to me decisive on this issue: that Berkeley took the proper object of vision to be the retinal pattern (as directly sensed—not looked at with "another eye") explains why the proper object of vision has the rather odd features he attributes to it. The proper object of vision is free-floating *because* we do not see (or otherwise sense) its setting. It is bidimensional but lacks any determinate three-dimensional shape *because* (again) we see the pattern but not the setting. A view such as Turbayne's cannot give an account of why Berkeley's proper object of vision has these peculiar features. This alone, it seems to me, should settle the matter.

Illinois Institute of Technology.

[53]Furlong, "Berkeley and the 'Knot' . . .," 314.

Chapter IV

AS IN A LOOKING-GLASS: PERCEPTUAL ACQUAINTANCE IN EIGHTEENTH-CENTURY BRITAIN

By John W. Yolton

Anyone working within the history of thought appreciates the importance of small phrases, even single words, for illuminating the context of arguments and claims. The presence in a particular author of some phrase taken from a prior tradition does not, of course, necessarily mean that the author has accepted that earlier doctrine or theory, certainly not without modifications. But such words and phrases do serve as signals to us of reverberations of some doctrine which it behooves us to track down. We can decide later to what extent the prior history of that doctrine does help us understand its eighteenth-century use.

There are three such phrases which play a role in studying theories of perception in the eighteenth century. When Hume says, "'tis universally allow'd by philosophers, and is besides pretty obvious of itself, that nothing is ever really present with the mind but its perceptions,"[1] we may think of Malebranche's remark: "Je croi que tout le monde tombe d'accord, que nous n'appercevons point les objets qui sont hors de nous par eux-mêmes."[2] When Hume links the notion of what is "present with the mind" to the further claim that "the very being, which is intimately present to the mind, is the real body or material existence,"[3] we may think we hear an echo of Descartes' notion of the objective reality of ideas. Hume's struggles with the single and double existence views may be seen as an eighteenth-century British version of Cartesianism, the notion that ideas have a dual reality, as modes of mind and as bearers of the reality of objects.

That Hume's discussion does reflect this Cartesian doctrine is, I think, clear, but not quite in the way in which Arnauld and Malebranche (who were much closer in time to Descartes) reflected Descartes' formulation. Much other discussion and transformation of the doctrine had occurred before Hume wrote his analysis. Philosophical theories hardly ever stand still. They are absorbed but modified almost as soon as the next writer turns his attention to the problems which the theory was to solve. But the occurrence of that phrase in Hume, "present with the mind," is a

---

[1] David Hume, *A Treatise of Human Nature* (London, 1739). Quotations are from the Selby-Bigge edition; here, 67.

[2] Malebranche, *De la recherche de la vérité* (Paris, 1674). Citations are from the edition of Geneviève Rodis-Lewis, in the *Oeuvres Complètes* (Paris, 1972). The reference here is to I, 413: Book III, Part II, Ch. I.   [3] *Treatise*, 206.

significant indication of one of the ingredients in his thought about perception and our knowledge of external objects. The fact that that phrase
runs throughout the *Treatise* (it occurs in the *Enquiry* also), and is invoked almost as a litany, suggests that it may have been frequently used
by the writers Hume was reading. In fact, that phrase had an interesting
history from the Cartesians through the eighteenth century.[4] When
William Porterfield says that "Our Mind can never perceive any thing but
its own proper Modifications and the various States and Conditions of
the *Sensorium* to which it is present,"[5] he is just repeating a claim which
he himself had made earlier and one which is found in many other writers
prior to Hume's *Treatise*. In many writers, this notion of what is present
to the mi   was linked with a dictum about the location of things, both
for existence and for knowledge. For example, Porterfield writes in 1737:
"nothing can Act, or be Acted upon where it is not; and therefore our
Mind can never perceive any thing but its own proper Modifications, and
the various States and Conditions of the Sensorium to which it is
present."[6]

Optical theories and the language of optics also played a role in leading some writers to the conclusion that perceptions are what is present to
the mind. There are many optical examples in Hume. One curious phrase,
probably taken from a tradition in optics, is Hume's remark in his section on space and time: "But my senses convey to me only the impressions of colour'd points, dispos'd in a certain manner."[7] While Hume
talks of physical and mathematical points (he rejects the latter for perception) in the rest of this section, he makes no attempt to explain this
remark about the senses and "coloured points." We can recall Berkeley's
discussion of perceptual minima, of seeing visible points.[8] Berkeley also
mentions that Isaac Barrow cited Tacquet's language of visible points.[9]

---

[4] I have made a start at tracing the history in "On Being Present to the Mind:
A Sketch for the History of an Idea," *Dialogue,* 14(1975), 373-88. For a brief
discussion of one very recent use of this notion, see my "Pragmatism Revisited:
An Examination of Professor Rescher's Conceptual Idealism," *Idealistic Studies*
(1976), 218-38.

[5] *A Treatise on the Eye* (London, 1759), II, 356-57.

[6] "An Essay Concerning the Motions of our Eyes," in *Medical Essays*
(Edinburgh, 1737), III, 220. Porterfield cited Newton in support of this principle.
Clarke, in his exchange with Leibniz, had given an explicit formulation of it:
"*How* the Soul of a Seeing Man, sees the Images to which it is *present,* we know
not: But we are sure it cannot perceive what it is *not present* to; because nothing
can Act, or be Acted upon, where it Is not." *A Collection of Papers Which
passed between the late Learned Mr. Leibniz and Dr. Clarke* (London, 1717),
83-84.   [7] *Treatise,* 34.

[8] *New Theory of Vision* (Dublin, 1709). Citations are to the *Works of
George Berkeley,* ed. by A. A. Luce, I. Here, it is Sect. 82, 204-05.

[9] *Ibid.,* 181, Sect. 30.

These references remind us that much of the discussion of vision in optical treatises talks in terms of the geometry of vision, of rays of light and of points on the retina. Newton's Axiom VI in his *Opticks* speaks of rays flowing from points of the object. Axiom VII says that the rays from all the points of the object meet again after converging by reflection or refraction. They "make a Picture of the Object upon any white Body, on which they fall."[10] Thus, in the eye, light is conveyed "in so many Points in the bottom of the Eye, and there to paint the Picture of the Object upon that skin." These pictures, "propagated by Motion along the Fibres of the Optick Nerves into the Brain, are the cause of Vision."[11]

The suspicion that optical theories (not just Berkeley's) play some role in Hume's reference to "coloured points" is further supported by the recognition that earlier writers (in particular, Maurolico and Kepler) on geometric optics used the same language. In his account of these early writers, Vasco Ronchi describes the way in which it was said that an extended object reflects rays on to the retina, there producing a "system of points," from which is derived "a luminous and coloured figure."[12] The problem for Kepler was, how we locate this figure or image (Ronchi uses Hobbes' term "phantasm") where the object is. Ronchi's fascinating account of optical theory sketches some of the ways in which the apparent world, built from the details supplied by the sense organs, can supply us with information about the object world. What we see is the apparent world, Hobbes' phantasms (perhaps we might suggest, Hume's perceptions). Sometimes, under precise conditions, we locate the phantasm or perception where the object is. What is present to us are our perceptions, our phantasms, but we normally take these to be the objects. "En effet, 'voir la table' signifie créer un *phantasme,* identique à la table matérielle, et le localiser exactment où celle-ci se trouve, de façon à pouvoir y poser les objets et lui trouver, en la touchant, des dimensions et la position que la vue lui donne."[13] Ronchi remarks that seeing is for Kepler the result of a physical agent (rays of light), a physiological process (formation of retinal image, impulses along optic nerve), and a psychic or psychological representation (the apparent world). "Le *monde apparent,* celui que l'on voit, avec ses figures, sa luminosité et ses couleurs, est donc un produit psychique, une création de l'observateur, un ensemble de *phantasmes,* c'est-à-dire de figures qui n'ont pas de corps, mais seulement un aspect."[14] A collection of phantasms, a psychic entity of light and colors:

---

[10] *Opticks,* 1704. (Dover Reprint, New York, 1952), 15.   [11] *Ibid.*

[12] See Ronchi's Preface to Paul-Marie Maurin's French translation of Hobbes's *De Homine* (Paris, 1974), 15-16. I am indebted to Professor Jeffrey Barnouw for calling this work to my attention.

[13] Vasco Ronchi, *L'Optique; Science de la Vision* (Paris, 1966), 49. This is the French translation of his *L'Ottica, scienza della visione* (Bologna, 1955).

[14] *Ibid.,* 37.

for Ronchi, this feature of Kepler's theory is most important for understanding perception.

In developing the notion that what we see is the apparent world, Ronchi makes effective use of the photographic picture. The action of the rays of light on the film or plate is well known. When this film is developed and then projected onto a screen, what is on the screen is the image of the building we photographed, having many details similar to those of the building. No one, Ronchi remarks, would think of saying the image on the screen *is* the building. "Pourquoi, au contraire, quand il s'agit de la vision, dit-on que l'image vue *est* l'objet?"[15] He goes on to draw out many analogies between the eye and the film and between the eye as a lens and the camera lens. He also cites a fact about vision which is relevant to our study: when we look up into the sky, we see a dome, a sort of screen for the objects we see there: clouds, sun, moon, stars. These objects are in fact at varying distances from us and from each other. Nevertheless, we see all of them on the same surface, they appear to be on a common plane. From these facts about vision and about the distances of the objects seen in the sky, Ronchi concludes that "les figures vues sur la voûte céleste ne sont pas les corps célestes, comme ils ne sont pas les nuages réels, ni les étoiles filantes. Ce sont seulement des *phantasmes* que la psyché de l'observateur crée et localise où elle peut et comme elle peut. Comme elle n'a aucun moyen de sentir des distances aussi grandes, même si elles sont aussi variables, elle les localise tous à la distance maximale possible, c'est-à-dire à cette distance au-delà de laquelle elle n'a plus aucune information."[16]

Ronchi's book is useful for fixing in our minds how, from facts about vision, we might be led to formulate a problem of perception in the way in which Hume did, in terms of a double (phantasm and real object) or a single (real object only) existence. Am I suggesting that Hume, like Berkeley, had a theory of vision, even that the problem of perception for him was a problem in optics? Such a suggestion would be too strong, although there are a number of passages in the *Treatise* which show that Hume knew the basic facts about vision, just as there are even more passages where he cites and uses the physiology of animal spirits. But Hume was not writing an "optics." Besides the optical theories of Berkeley, Newton, and several other eighteenth-century writers (all of whom I suspect Hume knew), there were *philosophical* theories of perception. These were theories about perceptual acquaintance, rather than about vision. These perceptual theories still employed optical language and they made use of optical examples, e.g., objects seen in mirrors, the eye compared to a lens, the understanding compared to a *camera obscura*. In

[15] *Ibid.*, 41.
[16] *Ibid.*, 45.

varying degrees, these optical examples controlled the analysis of perceptual acquaintance. It was only when the optical model was replaced by a cognitive one that writers were able to point the way around skepticism with regard to external objects. When perception is considered in visual and optical terms, the question is one of relating or matching the image seen with the object. Either the image seen is taken to be the very thing itself or, in some unexplained manner, we are said to see both image and object: "As in a *Looking-glass,* in which he that looks does indeed immediately behold the *Species* in the Glass, but does also at the same time actually behold *Peter* or *Paul* whose Image it is."[17] The alternative was to follow Arnauld's lead in distinguishing *spatial* from *cognitive* presence, to indicate a recognition of the psychic or psychological element in perception, of what one writer in England called the "Apprehension of the Thing seen or heard."[18] Ditton carefully distinguished between the physical and physiological aspects of perception and what he nicely characterized as "that Acquaintance which I have with an Object, in what I call an Act of Perception." It is with the analyses of perceptual acquaintance and of the act of perception that this paper is concerned.[19]

1. Perceptual Optics—Comparing the eye to a *camera obscura* was a standard practice in writings on optics. Robert Hooke remarks that Della Porta, Kepler, and Galileo, among others, used this way of explaining the workings of the eye. Hooke refers to Descartes' use of this model:

He explains then . . . the Organ of Vision the Eye, by the Similitude of it to a dark Room, into which no other Light is admitted but what enters by one round Hole, in which a convenient Convex refracting *Lens* is placed so, as to collect all the Rays from Objects without, and to unite them in their distinct and proper places upon a Wall or Sheet of Paper at a convenient Distance within; whereby the Picture of all those Objects that are without the Room, is made as it were and placed upon the Wall or Sheet within: This Sheet says he in the

---

[17] John Norris, *An Essay Towards the Theory of the Ideal or Intelligible World* (London, 1701), I, 166. Norris is here giving a commentary on Christopher Scheibler's discussion of the question, "Whether Created things are the Object of the Divine Understanding of their own Beings, or only as they are Eminently, Ideally or Vertually contain'd in God?" (165). Norris himself insisted that "I do not feel any thing that is out of my self, but I feel my very self otherwise Modified, and Existing after Another manner than I did before" (199).

[18] The phrase is Humphrey Ditton's, *A Discourse Concerning the Resurrection of Jesus Christ* (London, 1712), 497. Arnauld's distinction is found in his *Des vraies et des fausses idées* (Paris, 1683) in his *Oeuvres complètes,* XXXVIII, 216. He uses the language of *présence locale* and *présence objective,* the latter being rendered as "known": objects are objectively present to the mind when they are known by the mind.

[19] This paper is part of a larger study in which I examine theories of perception from Descartes to Reid. The role and nature of *ideas* in these theories are also traced.

Eye, is the *Tunica Retina,* on which the Picture of all Objects without the Eye are as it were painted and described.[20]

In these same lectures, Hooke describes a "Perspective Box, in which all the appearances that are made in the Eye are in some manner represented." This box contained a hole "large enough to put one's Face into it," as well as the necessary hole with a lens for letting in light. With such a box, one could look in and "see the Species or Pictures of outward Objects upon the bottom."[21] For Hooke the eyes were not only our special access to the world, they were a "Microcosm, or a little World," a duplicate of the outer world. The eye, he says, has "a distinct Point within it self, for every distinct Point without it self in the Universe; and when a Hemisphere of the Heavens is open to its view, it has a Hemisphere within it self, wherein there are as many Respective Points for Reception of the Radiations, as there are differing Points for emission of Radiations."[22] Since Hooke accepted a plenum, the eye informs us in an instant of what is happening in the world.[23] In another passage, he compares the action of the eye, in collecting rays, to a lens for collecting light from the sun to burn: "Now the Action of the Eye being much the same upon the Rays of Light, from any Luminous Object with this of the Burning Glass; it follows that the Eye does by its Power bring all visible Objects into the bottom of it, and make an Impression on the *retina,* the same as if the very Action of the Object were immediately there."[24] The substance of the Retina "is affected or moved by the very same Action, as if it touched the Object." These impressions are then communicated to the brain. The eye in fact "becomes as it were a Hand, by which the Brain feels, and touches the Objects, by creating a Motion in the *Retina,* the same, and at the same Instant, with the Motion of the lucid Object it self."[25]

With his notion of the eyes providing the brain with hands to touch objects, Hooke's optics give us something close to direct realism. At least, we have a "perfect Picture, or Representation of all outward Objects" preserved point by point on the retina. Hooke was unable, however, to explain our awareness of these little images. We find in his further account a material or corporeal notion of ideas. Memory, he says, is an organ in the brain. It is "a Repository of Ideas formed partly by the

[20] "Lectures on Light" (London, 1680), in *The Posthumous Works of Robert Hooke* (London, 1705), 98.

[21] *Ibid.,* 127-28.   [22] *Ibid.,* 121.

[23] The notion of the instantaneous propagation of light was a common doctrine, held by Aristotle, Galen, al-Kindi, Avicenna, Averroes, as well as Grosseteste, Witelo, Kepler, and Descartes. See A. I. Sabra, *Theories of Light from Descartes to Newton* (London, 1967), 46-47. In these lectures, Hooke shows a strong influence from Descartes.

[24] Hooke, *op. cit.,* 123.   [25] *Ibid.,* 124.

Senses, but chiefly by the Soul it self."[26] Impressions from the senses—those impressions being actual motions—are carried to the memory where they become powers "sufficient to effect such Formations of Ideas as the Soul does guide and direct them in." The soul's action is necessary for the formation of ideas. This action is attention: "the Soul in the Action of Attention does really form some material Part of the Repository into such a Shape, and gives it some such a Motion as is from the Senses conveyed thither." He seems to mean this talk quite literally, although he proceeds to help us understand it by making "a mechanical and sensible Figure and Picture thereof."[27] His talk then becomes that of *supposing,* of supposing that ideas have a size and bulk, occupy a place. The soul is incorporeal, but it is "every where as it were actually present, in every point of the Sphere of its Radiation, though yet it may be supposed to be more immediately and forcefully present in the Centre of its Being."[28] He does not understand how the incorporeal soul can act on corporeal ideas, but he even drops a hint that the sphere of influence of the soul may extend "out of the Body, and that to some considerable Distance."[29]

Locke also did not profess to understand the transition from brain impression to awareness. As he said to Malebranche, "Impressions made on the retina by rays of light, I think I understand; and motions from thence continued to the brain may be conceived, and that these produce ideas in our mind, I am persuaded, but in a manner to me incompre-

---

[26] *Ibid.,* 140.   [27] *Ibid.,* 141-42.   [28] *Ibid.,* 146.

[29] Other writers were stressing the importance of physiology in awareness, some (such as Anthony Collins) even moved towards the theory of Joseph Priestley, at the end of the century, that thought is a property of the brain. But it is not easy to find explicit identifications of ideas with brain states. Hume appears to be serious when, in the section on the immateriality of the soul he speaks of some ideas being extended. Hume may be following Hooke. (For a discussion of this passage in Hume, see Robert F. Anderson, 'The Location, Extension, Shape, and Size of Hume's Perceptions," in *Hume, A Re-evaluation,* ed. by Donald W. Livingston and James T. King [New York, 1976], 153-71.) David Hartley might be thought to have come close to making ideas into brain states, but he always maintained that sensations and ideas are "of a mental Nature," while vibrations of nerve fibres are corporeal. *Observations on Man* (London, 1749), 34. Even though he does sometimes speak of ideas leaving traces, more permanent traces than sensations do, he does not explicitly locate those traces in the brain. Descartes did identify ideas or images with brain impressions, in some of his early writings. Also, Voltaire says an idea is "une image, qui se peint dans mon cerveau" (entry, "Idée", in his *Dictionnaire*). Charles Bonnet, who was known in Britain, stressed the close links between ideas and brain impressions but he never drew an identity. See, e.g., his *Essai Analytique sur les Facultés de l'Ame* (Copenhagen, 1760). Bonnet was often compared with Hartley.

hensible."[30] Locke's ideas were not brain impressions. That Locke was well acquainted with the physiology of perception, especially with optical accounts of the eye, is indicated by his detailing the facts about the eye to Malebranche. He was writing to show how an optical species theory—in distinction from the peripatetic species theory against which Malebranche wrote—explains vision. He spoke of the "visible appearances of bodies, being brought into the eye by the rays of light"; of how the bottom of the eye is far from being a point; of the way in which the rays of light "cause their distinct sensations, by striking on distinct parts of the retina"; of how the "figures they paint there must be of some considerable bigness, since it takes up on the retina an area whose diameter is at least thirty seconds of a circle, whereof the circumference is in the retina, and the centre somewhere in the crystaline"; and of how "few eyes can perceive an object less than thirty minutes of a circle, whereof the eye is the centre."[31] Thus, when Locke compared the understanding of man to a *camera obscura,* he did so in full knowledge of this model for the eye. In using that model for the understanding, was he unduly influenced by the optical details? When he talks of ideas *resembling* primary qualities, of ideas *conforming* to things, of ideas not objects being present to the mind, was Locke transferring Hooke's microcosm notion to the understanding? Was there some temptation to think of our awareness being like the face at the Perspective Box scanning the images on the wall of the box?[32]

Other writers used visual images when talking about perception. Henry Lee, in his careful critique of Locke (*Anti-Scepticism,* 1702), says that the proper sense of "idea" is "a visible Representation or Resemblance of the Object, and, in some measure at least, *like* that thing of which it is the *Idea.* Thus a man's Face in the Glass is properly the *Idea* of that Face" (2). John Witty (*The First Principles of Modern Deism Confuted,* London, 1707) speaks of our eyes as natural glasses. Arthur Collier (*Clavis Universalis,* London, 1713) makes heavy appeal to the looking-glass: in such a glass, "I see sun, moon, and stars, even a whole expanded world" (26). But Collier observes that even those who maintain an external world admit that the objects or images in the looking-glass are not the same as the external objects. Collier goes on to apply the parallel to all perception: the images seen in normal vision do not

[30] *Examination of the Opinions of P. Malebranche, Works* (London, 1823), IX, Sect. 10, 217.

[31] *Ibid.,* Sect. 9.

[32] In his recent discussion of Locke and the representative theory, J. L. Mackie makes use of a device very much like Hooke's Perspective Box. "What if someone ever since birth had had a large box attached in front of his eyes, on the inside of which, for him to see, fairly faithful pictures of outside, surrounding things were somehow produced?" (*Problems From Locke* [Oxford, 1976], 44).

differ from those seen in the looking-glass.[33] Vision has always been taken
as the model for perception and understanding, but the Perspective Box
model can raise problems about our knowledge of the external world.
Hooke was not bothered by any of those worries, for which philosophers
are noted, about our knowledge of the external world. That world for
him was all but present to the mind in vision.

   A. Hobbes.—Vasco Ronchi in his preface to Paul-Marie Maurin's
translation of Hobbes's *De Homine*, points out how this work sits firmly
in the tradition of explanation of the location of visual images.[34] Maurin
remarks that in this work Hobbes considers the rays of light from objects
as "un code qui, analysé instant par instant par l'observateur, donne à
ce dernier la possibilité de recréer instant par instant un univers de
phantasmes qui constitue une bonne imitation de l'univers réel."[35] In
chapter II of this treatise, Hobbes speaks of a distinct and figured vision
occurring when light (*lumen*) or color forms a figure of which the parts
originate from the parts of the object and stand in a one-to-one correspondence to those parts of the object. Light thus figured is called *an
image*. By an institution of nature, all animate beings judge that that
vision is the vision *of* the object. People have not always understood that
the sun and stars, for example, are larger than they appear to be. That
writers on vision have so far been unable to explain why objects appear
now larger, now smaller, now farther away, now closer, does not surprise
Hobbes, because no one so far, he says, has had the idea of considering
light (*lux*) and color, not as emanations from the object but as phenomena of our inner world.[36] Later chapters of this treatise identify the apparent place of the object as the place of the image in direct vision (59).
Maurin reads Hobbes as saying all that we are aware of are our images,
our phantasms. (55-56, n. 12) He interprets such a view as idealism, and

----

[33] Arnauld identifies as one of three reasons for philosophers accepting ideas
as real beings (as Malebranche did) that, having seen sensible objects reflected in
mirrors and in water, they come to believe that they never see bodies themselves,
but only their images (*op. cit.*, 190).

[34] *Traité de l'homme*, Traduction et commentaire par Paul-Marie Maurin.
Préface par Vasco Ronchi (Paris, 1974).   [35] *Ibid.*, 29; also 51n.2.

[36] The editor points out that the two different Latin words, *lumen* and *lux*
distinguish light as a physical phenomenon from light as a visual appearance.
Ronchi stresses the importance of this distinction in the history of vision, a
distinction which he laments has not always been followed. See Chapter IV in his
book. Cf. Locke's *Essay*, 3.4.10, where he distinguishes the *cause* of light from
the *idea* of light "as it is such a particular perception in us." What to us may
sound strange in this same passage of the *Essay*—the talk of tennis balls bouncing,
as a way of conceiving of light—is another indication of Locke's knowledge of
optics. For, as Sabra has pointed out, Descartes and earlier writers attempted
to explain refraction and reflection in terms of impact. They used examples of
balls thrown against different surfaces and rebounding from them.

he is puzzled as to how such an idealism can be superimposed upon Hobbes's materialism. Whether we can so quickly take the distinction between *lumen* and *lux*, between physical events and psychological awareness, as idealism, is open to some doubt. It was just this question which is played out by subsequent writers in Britain, especially by Berkeley and Hume. But it is important to appreciate that Hobbes has not changed his views in this late treatise. He never did deny appearances.[37] Just what their status was may not always be clear, but his use of "thought" or "conception" in earlier writings, as well as of "idea," reinforces the fact that he was not saying *all* is matter and motion.

For example, the *Elements of Philosophy* speaks of the effects and appearance of things to sense as "faculties or powers of bodies, which make us distinguish them from one another."[38] Later in this work, Hobbes says that "The first beginnings, therefore, of knowledge are the phantasms of sense and imagination; and that there be such phantasms we know well enough by nature" (66). Sometimes, he uses the term "idea" in close conjunction with—sometimes even as a synonym for—"phantasm." "A man that looks upon the sun, has a certain shining idea of the magnitude of about a foot over, and this he calls the sun, though he knows the sun to be truly a great deal bigger; and, in like manner, the phantasm of the same thing appears sometimes round . . . and sometimes square [i.e., a tower at different distances]."[39] The question then is, "whether that phantasm be matter, or some body natural, or only some accident of body"? As a way of answering this question, he assumes that the whole world, save man, was annihilated. Man would still have the ideas of the world, of bodies, etc.: "that is the memory and imagination of magnitude, motions, sounds, colours, etc.," as well as their order. He then says: "All which things, though they be nothing but ideas and phantasms, happening internally to him that imagineth; yet they will appear as if they were external, and not at all depending upon any power of the mind." Even when the world does still exist, we work only with our phantasms. "For when we calculate the magnitude and motions of heaven or earth, we do not ascend into heaven that we may divide it into parts, or measure the motions thereof, but we do it sitting in our closets

---

[37] See my "Locke and the Seventeenth-Century Logic of Ideas," *JHI*, 16 (Oct., 1955), Section 2, 435-39.

[38] *The English Works of Thomas Hobbes*, ed. by W. Molesworth, I, 5 (Pt. 3, Ch. I). All references to Hobbes will be to this edition, volume and page indicated in the text.

[39] Other passages where "idea" occurs with "phantasm" are: "As a body leaves a phantasm of its magnitude in the mind, so also a moved body leaves a phantasm of its motion, namely, an idea of that body passing out of one space into another by continual succession" (94). "Now, by space I understand, here as formerly, an idea or phantasm of a body" (108).

or in the dark."[40] Hobbes then proceeds to consider the species of external things, "not as really existing, but appearing to exist, or [appearing] to have a being without us." It is the way the world appears that he analyzes, since that is all that we *can* analyze.

Later, in Part IV on "Physics, or the Phenomena of Nature," in the chapter on "Sense and Animal Motion," "perception" is linked with "ideas." "In the first place, therefore, the causes of our perception, that is, the causes of those ideas and phantasms which are perpetually generated within us whilst we make use of our senses, are to be enquired into . . ." (389). The act of sense differs from sense "no otherwise . . . than *fieri,* that is, being a doing, differs from *factum esse,* that is, being done" (392). Sense is also said to be "the judgment we make of objects by their phantasms; namely, by comparing and distinguishing those phantasms" (393). In some passages, Hobbes writes "thought or phantasm" (398). *Leviathan* speaks of the thoughts of man, characterizing them as "a *representation* or *appearance,* of some quality, or other accident of a body without us" (*Works,* III, 1). Mental discourse is a "train of thought" (11). The word "conception" is also used. Hobbes's *Human Nature; Or, The Fundamental Elements of Policy* even speaks of "certain *images* or conceptions of the things without us" (*Works,* IV, 2). The having of images is "that we call our *conception, imagination, idea, notice* or *knowledge* of them" (3). The faculty by which we have such knowledge is the cognitive power. He goes on in the same work to speak of conceptions "proceeding from the action of the thing itself." By sight, "we have a conception or image composed of *colour* and *figure.*" He cites seeing the sun and other visible objects reflected in water and glasses. These experiences show us that color and images generally "may be there where the thing seen is not" (4-5). The image seen by reflection in a glass "is *not* any thing *in* or *behind* the glass." The image and color are "but an apparition to us" of the motion of object and nerves. Thus again, two senses of light are distinguished: motion in and from the object and the appearance or image.

---

[40] Malebranche used this point about the mind not ascending into the heavens to draw his conclusion that what is present to the mind are ideas, not things. "Nous voyons le Soleil, les Etoiles, et une infinité d'objets hors de nous; et il n'est pas vraisemblable que l'ame sorte du corps, et qu'elle aille, pour ainsi dire, se promener dans les cieux pour y contempler tous ces objets. Elle ne les voit donc point par eux-mêmes . . ." (*Recherche,* I, 413-14). Lord Monboddo, late in the eighteenth century, was convinced that the mind does transport itself to a place where the body is not, for the objects are not present with the mind: "Now as we cannot suppose that the objects come to the mind, it is I think of necessity that the mind should go to the objects; for, some way or other, they must be present together" [William Knight: *Lord Monboddo and Some of His Contemporaries* (1900), 231]. The same argument is found in Monboddo's *Antient Metaphysics,* vol. II (Edinburgh, 1782).

We should perhaps be cautious in crediting too strong a psychological content to these various words used by Hobbes. What seems certain,
however, is that he did employ different terms, all of which were his attempt to distinguish the way the world appears to us from the world
itself. *Leviathan* made this point firmly: "And though at some certain
distance, the real and very object seems invested with the fancy it begets
in us; yet still the object is one thing, the image or fancy is another" (2-
3). Similarly, in *Seven Philosophical Problems,* one of the speakers, B,
cites as examples of fancy both "the appearance of your face in a looking-
glass" and an after image, "a spot before the eye that hath stared upon
the sun or fire" (*Works,* VII, 27). The other speaker then asks why that
which "appears before your eyes" when you look towards the sun or
moon is also not fancy? B replies, "So it is. Though the sun itself be a real
body, yet that bright circle of about a foot diameter cannot be the sun,
unless there be two suns . . ." (27-28).

The question Hume raised later, of a single or double existence,
Hobbes clearly answered as "double." Moreover, it seems to have been
the visual image which Hobbes took as his standard, although such terms
as "thought" and "conception" indicate his generalizing of the double
existence view. It was optics which provided Hobbes, certainly in his last
work, *De Homine,* with some convincing evidence for his distinction between image and object. We have found that optical examples play a role
in some of his earlier writings as well.

B. Berkeley.—The most striking case of a perception theory being
based upon vision is that of Berkeley. His *An Essay Towards a New
Theory of Vision* (1709) addressed itself to the way in which we determine the distance of objects. He opens that work with a quick summary
of different theories advanced earlier to explain how we determine the
apparent places of objects (Sects. 4-8). Instead of judging distance by the
"bigness of the angle made by the meeting of the two optic axes" (Sect.
12), as the geometrical opticians claimed, Berkeley argues that distance
perception is based upon (1) the sensations we feel in our eyes when we
widen or lessen the interval between the pupils (Sect. 16) and (2) the
degree of confusion in our vision of the object (Sect. 21).[41] Both these
ways of determining or judging distance (or the location of objects) are

[41] Malebranche notes the role of the sensation felt in the eyes when we try
to focus on objects very near to us. "En effet lorsqu'on force sa vûe pour voir de
fort près un petit objet, on sent l'effort des muscles qui compriment les yeux, et
qui fait même de la peine à ceux-là principalement qui n'ont point pris l'habitude
de regarder de près de petits objets" (*Eclaircissement* XVII, Sect. 32, in *Oeuvres
Complètes,* III, 333). For a recent discussion of Berkeley, in the context of
geometrical theories of optics, see G. Thrane, "Berkeley's 'Proper Object of
Vision,' " *JHI,* 38(1977), 243-60; also G. N. Cantor's "Berkeley, Reid, and the
Mathematization of Mid-Eighteenth Century Optics," *JHI,* 38(1977), 429-48.

a function of the coexistence of these experiences: coexistence of the sensations with the discovery of the place of objects, coexistence of degrees of confusion with varying distances of objects (Sect. 25). He attempts to explain a problem raised by Dr. Barrow about the *locus objecti* and the *locus apparens,* citing Molyneux's use of these two phrases, and appeals to the second of the ways of judging distance, the degrees of confusion in vision. But, as he proceeds, his account of these two places becomes more radical. The *locus objecti* is always *near to* the perceiver (present with the mind) and the *objecta* constantly change. To speak more accurately on this last point, the *objecta* become a series of *apparentia.*

We can witness this double change by examining Berkeley's remarks about the man born blind who later gains his sight. For such a person, "The objects intromitted by sight would seem to him (as in truth they are) no other than a new set of thoughts or sensations, each whereof is as near to him as the perceptions of pain or pleasure, or the most inward passions of his soul" (Sect. 41). In Section 43, he asks rhetorically, "whether the visible extension of any object doth not appear as near to him as the colour of that object?" Since "those who have had any thoughts of that matter" agree that colors are not "without the mind," and since Berkeley here argues that extension, figure, and motion are inseparable from color, the suggestion is that what is seen does not exist outside the mind at any distance. Section 44 then argues that "the immediate objects of sight are not so much as the idea or resemblance of things, placed at a distance." I understand this phrase "not so much as" to be the same as "not." Here is the example Berkeley gives to support his conclusion:

Suppose, for example, that looking at the moon I should say it were fifty or sixty semi-diameters of the earth distant from me. Let us see what moon this is spoken of: It is plain it cannot be the visible moon, or anything like the visible moon, or that which I see, which is only a round, luminous plain of about thirty visible points in diameter. For in case I am carried from the place where I stand directly towards the moon, it is manifest the object varies, still as I go on; and by the time that I am advanced fifty or sixty semi-diameters of the earth, I shall be so far from being near a small, round, luminous flat that I shall perceive nothing like it; this object having long since disappeared, and if I would recover it, it must be by going back to the earth from whence I set out (187).

Berkeley uses other examples to make the same point: a distant tree, a tower, a man. What leads me to think I am seeing a distant object is that I have found that my seeing has usually been accompanied or followed by touching, after a certain movement of my body. But Berkeley claims even further that I do not touch what I see. Both seeing and touching reveal sensations *near to me;* they reveal both *sensations* and sensations *near to me.* Thus, "in truth and strictness of speech, I neither see distance

it self, nor anything that I take to be at a distance" (Sect. 45, p. 188).
Nor do I even see the ideas *of* things at a distance. I have only my ideas,
my perceptions, my phantasms. Hooke's microcosm duplicate world turns
out to *be* my world. We seem to have a single existence, my perceptions.
That dictum about no cognition at a distance, that what is known must
be present to the mind, is at work here: "the things we see being in
truth at no distance from us" (Sect. 52, p. 190), all visible objects "are
only in the mind" (Sect. 77, p. 202).

Berkeley's explication, in his *Principles* and *Dialogues,* of this notion
of objects existing in the mind was summarized by his dictum, *esse est
percipi.* This principle was meant to identify two features of his general
account: that there is no aspect of objects which is insensible (his negative claim against the materialists) and that objects as known are *in* the
mind. This second feature is consistent with those various traditions from
Aristotle to the Schoolmen and to Descartes which said that the object is
present to the mind. Berkeley was fond of pointing out that the materialist's object, the insensible, corpuscular particles of matter, cannot be present to the mind. Nor does the corpuscular account of perception explain
how ideas or perceptions arise. He agreed with many other writers that
corporeal objects cannot cause awareness. If those physical objects which
we take to exist in external space distant from us can neither cause ideas
in us nor be present to our mind, what *is* present there? Berkeley's
answer is "visible objects" and "ideas," where these two terms mean and
designate the same thing. He was quite clear about his analysis of "present to" and "exist in": it means "perceived," "known," or "comprehended" (i.e., "understood"). Early in the *Principles,* where he is explaining
what he means by "mind," "spirit," "soul," or "my self," he says these
words denote "a thing entirely distinct from them [his ideas], wherein they
exist, or, which is the same thing, whereby they are perceived."[42] In the
third of his *Three Dialogues,* Philonous says, "I know what I mean,
when I affirm that there is a spiritual substance or support of ideas, that
is, that a spirit knows and perceives ideas" (234). To reinforce to Hylas
that "exist in" has no literal sense, Philonous tells him that "when I speak
of objects as existing in the mind or imprinted on the senses; I would not
be understood in the gross literal sense, as when bodies are said to exist
in a place, or a seal to make an impression upon wax. My meaning is only
that the mind comprehends or perceives them; and that it is affected from
without, or by some being distinct from itself" (250). More importantly
still, Berkeley's ideas are not modes of mind: they exist in the mind
"not by way of mode or property, but as a thing perceived in that which

[42] Berkeley, *Principles,* in *Works,* II, 42, Principle 2. References to the
Dialogues are also to this same volume.

perceives it" (237). For the corresponding passage in the *Principles,* see Sect. 49 (61).

All these passages explicating the meaning of "exist in" indicate that Berkeley has to this extent escaped the control of the optical model for perception. For "exist in" turns out to have the same *cognitive* meaning as it did for Arnauld and Locke.[43] Berkeley gives the same analysis of "exist in" for "ideas in God's mind." For example, in denying that he is following Malebranche, Philonous says that he does not say "I see things by perceiving that which represents them in the intelligible substance of God. This I do not understand; but I say, the things by me perceived are known by the understanding, and produced by the will, of an infinite spirit" (215). It is the *"Omnipresent eternal Mind,* which knows and comprehends all things" (231), the "real tree existing without" our minds "is truly known and comprehended by (that is, *exists in*) the infinite mind of God" (235). To reinforce that the "that is" phrase is meant to explicate by offering a synonym, Philonous a bit later in the same Dialogue says: "All objects are eternally known by God, or which is the same thing, have an eternal existence in his mind" (252).[44]

In his recent study of Berkeley, I. C. Tipton recognizes this close linking of "exist in" with "perceived by."[45] He even allows that Luce's stressing of this linkage (Luce reads "in the mind" as an abbreviation for "in direct cognitive relation to the mind") is "in a way right" (93). Tipton's reluctance to accept this as Berkeley's full meaning is not clear. What he says is that "if it is true that Berkeley regards existence in the mind as amounting to perception by the mind it is also true that he thinks of perception by the mind as coming down to the existence of an idea in the mind" (93-94). My trouble with this remark is that while Berkeley's translation of "exist in" by "perceived or known by" does give us an intelligible explication, I do not see what we are told by the second part of Tipton's remark, that "perception by the mind" means "existence in the mind." The troublesome phrase is "exist in," not "perceived by." We need to know, especially in the light of the history of the appeals to "present to the mind," just what Berkeley means by "exists in the mind." The passages I have cited seem to tell us unequivocally what that phrase means. It means "to be perceived by." And *what* is perceived by the mind is *not* a mode of mind.

[43] Cf. Arnauld: "Je dis qu'un objet est présent à notre esprit, quand notre esprit l'apperçoit et le connoit" (*op. cit.,* 198). This definition appears in Locke's *Essay* in 1.2.5: "For if these words *(to be in the understanding)* have any propriety, they signify to be understood."

[44] The comparing of God's knowledge of objects with our knowledge of them, via God's presence to all things and the presence of the images of things to our mind, was a frequent occurrence. Clarke and Newton on this point were typical of many writers in the century. See Clarke's exchange with Leibniz.

[45] I. C. Tipton, *Berkeley, The Philosophy of Immaterialism* (1974), 87.

It is this last notion which leads Tipton to hang back from accepting Berkeley's explication of "exists in"; for Tipton is sure that, not being a mode, ideas for Berkeley must be things, entities. Berkeley, Tipton says, "does want us to think of the appearance as itself a thing" (187), he "really does hold that each sense datum is an entity" (185). Tipton has some good comments earlier about how reifying sensations or appearances leads away from direct to representative realism.[46] Ideas for Malebranche were *real beings,* even though there was no clear category in his metaphysics for characterizing these beings. They were substance-like, if not substances.[47] Berkeley's ideas are clearly not these sorts of spiritual things. Nor can we say that his ideas are the appearances *of* objects, for there are no other objects on his account. Tipton says "they are themselves the basic things in the sensible world" (191). As Hume was later to say of the ordinary view, "the very image which is present to the senses, is with us the real body" (*Treatise,* 205). Berkeley's way of expressing this view is succinctly put at the end of his *Dialogues:* the vulgar opinion is that *"those things they immediately perceive are the real things"* (262). His own position combined this vulgar view with the view of the philosophers: "that *the things immediately perceived, are ideas which exist only in the mind."*

In trying to wed these two opinions, Berkeley never wavered from the claim that with the definition of "existence" as "percipi" and "percipere," "the horse is in the stable, the Books are in the study as before."[48] Putting an objection to himself—"Well say you according to this new Doctrine all is but meer Idea, there is nothing wch is not an ens rationis"— he replies: "I answer things are as real and exist in rerum natura as much as ever. The distinction betwixt entia Realia and entia rationis may be made as properly now as ever."[49] Similar passages can be found in the *Principles* and the *Dialogues.*[50] Nor did he ever follow Malebranche in making ideas into special entities. A careful inventory of the many passages on ideas in his writings, together with the statement of those two opinions which he has combined, yields the following summary of Berkeley's account of our knowledge of objects:

[46] See, e.g., 23-24, 35, 66.

[47] In his *Examination of Malebranche,* Locke discusses this aspect of ideas. An eighteenth-century defender of Malebranche against Locke's attack, P. Gerdil Barnabite *(Défense du sentiment du P. Malebranche sur la nature, et l'origine des Idées contre l'Examen de M. Locke,* 1748) denies that Malebranche's ideas are substances, although he characterizes them as spiritual things (61). There were, in eighteenth-century Britain, two main concepts of ideas: ideas as entities and ideas as the same as perceptions. The latter was the view of Arnauld against Malebranche.

[48] *Philosophical Commentaries,* 429, in *Works,* vol. I.   [49] *Ibid.,* 535.

[50] For example, *Principles,* 34, 35; *Dialogues,* 229-30, 244.

1. Ideas are perceptions, sensations, or thoughts.
2. Perceptions or ideas *are* the things themselves.
3. What is known or perceived is present to (near to) the mind.
4. To exist in the mind means to be perceived or known by the mind.
5. To be perceived by the mind is the way things are in the mind.
6. Perceptions or ideas do not (can not?) exist apart from mind.
7. Things do not (can not?) exist apart from mind.

Other writers had accepted (1), (3), (4), and (5). What is distinctive of Berkeley's analysis is (2) and (7). It was easier for people to accept (3), identifying what is present to the mind as our perceptions, while insisting (as Porterfield did) that there is a world of objects independent of our perceptions, to which we ascribe our perceptions, on which we locate our images. It was apparently even easier to accept a veil of perception doctrine, as Henry Grove urged, taking ideas or perceptions as a screen between perceivers and the world.[51] Skepticism seemed to many easier, more intelligible than Berkeley's propositions (2) and (7).

II. Hume on Single and Double Existence.—When Hume began reading in preparation for writing a treatise on the human understanding, there was a number of traditions in philosophy which had been widely explored. There was that tradition which invoked the dictum that what is known must be present to the mind. There were a number of optical treatises addressing the question of where and how the visual image is located on or near the object. A number of philosophers, such as Hobbes and Berkeley, had adapted the knowledge of the structure and workings of the eye to cognitive theories about perceptual acquaintance. There was also a dual concept of ideas, where ideas became separately existing ob-

---

[51] Grove *(An Essay Towards a Demonstration of the Soul's Immateriality)* (London, 1718), suggested that ideas are like a "thin Varnish spread over the Face of Nature, which do not hinder us from passing a Judgment of it; because they express outward Objects, much as the Varnish takes the Form of the Work upon which it is laid" (11-12). Grove, in his Preface, writes against Collier, but he agrees with Collier that we see nothing but ideas. What he objected to in Collier's *Clavis Universalis* was the claim that there is no external world, even that it is impossible. Grove was confident that, were there no external world, God would have made our ideas "appear to be at home in the Mind," rather than, as they do, "having the appearance of something External" (16, 19). He constructs an interesting model to illustrate what it would be like did our ideas have no suggestions of externality: the Perspective Box turned perceiver. "Suppose then a hollow Globe endued with Perception, and painted on the Inside with Birds, Beasts and Fishes, and to have the Knowledge of all that is delineated within it; the whole Delineation being within the Globe, and the Perception the Globe hath of it but one Act, is it not certain that the Appearance which this Representation would most naturally make to the Globe must be of something comprehended within itself? And the same it would probably be with the Mind, if there were not some external World, to signify and represent which of our Ideas, by the Rules of Divine Perspective, appear External" (16-17).

jects; or they were used either interchangeably or in close connection
with perceptions. Almost all writers talked in terms of ideas or perceptions, not objects, being present to the mind.

Confronted with the difficulties in the attempts to accept perceptions
as what is present to the mind and yet hold fast to a realism of objects,
Berkeley with one deft stroke cut a path out to a resolution: he said ideas
are the very things themselves. Both Berkeley and Hume took seriously
this notion that our ideas or perceptions are the objects. Berkeley did not
flinch in the face of the one difficulty with his account: that objects become dependent upon mind, albeit ultimately God's mind. But no matter
how hard he tried, Berkeley could not convince his readers (or us) that
mind-dependency is part of our ordinary belief about the world of objects. Hume saw that, if sense could be made of this ordinary view, we
would have to find an explanation for how we come to consider perceptions, which are discontinuous and mind-dependent, to be objects, which
we believe to be continuous and mind-independent. Hume meets that
problem by saying (a) perceptions are not necessarily related to other
perceptions, each can exist apart, and (b) we feign their continued
existence when not perceived. Thus, Hume accepts the *esse est percipi*
dictum for perceptions but suggests that we (or our imagination) waive
that dictum when we take our perceptions for the objects themselves.
Hume was not entirely satisfied with his account of the way of viewing
perceptions, and his view of the ordinary, vulgar opinion. But in Hume's
discussion of that opinion, and of the philosophical view of perceptions
and objects, we find the most systematic analysis in the century of both
points of view.

Berkeley provided his contemporaries with a clear statement of the
two points of view, the single and double existence view. In Principle
56, he says that:

men knowing they perceived several ideas, whereof they themselves were not
the authors, as not being excited from within, nor depending on the operation
of their wills, this made them maintain, those ideas or objects of perception
had an existence independent of, and without the mind, without ever dreaming
that a contradiction was involved in those words. But philosophers having
plainly seen, that the immediate objects of perception do not exist without the
mind, they in some degree corrected the mistake of the vulgar, but at the
same time run into another which seems no less absurd, to wit, that there are
certain objects really existing without the mind, or having a subsistence distinct from being perceived, of which our ideas are only images or resemblances,
imprinted by those objects on the mind (64-65).

That Hume accepts the identification of objects and perceptions is suggested by his reminder (in I.IV.II of the *Treatise*) that he has shown
earlier that "the notion of external existence, when taken for something
specifically different from our perceptions" is absurd (188). The nature

or kind of identification between perceptions and objects is revealed in Hume's phrase, "specifically different." To fail of *specific* difference does not rule out *numerical* difference. In the earlier passage (I.II.VI), he considered the idea of existence: is this an idea distinct and different from the idea of any particular thing? If so, there would need to be an impression just of existence, not of any particular existing thing (66). Such an idea would be an instance of those abstract ideas against which Berkeley wrote. The alternative is that the idea of existence is the same as the idea of whatever we conceive to be existent. "Whatever we conceive, we conceive to be existent," or, "Any idea we please to form is the idea of a being" (67). The reverse is equally true: "the idea of a being is any idea we please to form." To oppose what Hume says here would be to show that the idea of *entity,* of thing, can be derived from some impression of entity, just of entity. There are no such impressions. Another way of putting Hume's point is to show how two objects differ just in that one exists, the other does not. "But no object can be presented resembling some object with respect to its existence, and different from others in the same particular" (67).

When Hume applies this reasoning to the idea of *external* existence, we see how the application of the principle about what is present to the mind yields his conclusion of no specific difference between perceptions and external existence: "We may observe that 'tis universally allow'd by philosophers, and is besides pretty obvious of itself, that nothing is ever really present with the mind but its perceptions or impressions and ideas, and that external objects become known to us only by those perceptions they occasion" (67). To be able to conceive of something specifically different from ideas and impressions, something other than ideas and impressions (i.e., objects) would have to be present to the mind, from which we could then derive an idea. We never "can conceive any kind of existence, but those perceptions, which have appear'd in that narrow compass" of our mind (67-68).

It was because of this strong belief about what we cannot conceive with respect to existence that Hume so firmly rejected Malebranche's double existence view, in which ideas *are* essentially different from objects. On Malebranche's view, ideas become another kind of object. This philosophy, Hume says (I.IV.V), holds that "no external object can make itself known to the mind immediately, and without the interposition of an image or perception" (*Treatise,* 242). Perceptions are properties of mind, either of finite minds or of an infinite mind. Mind was a substance, immaterial, simple and indivisible. Hume achieves the rejection of this view by comparing it with the materialist account found in Spinoza. The materialist talks of a system of objects. The immaterialist (whom Hume is satirizing in this section) talks of the system of thoughts and ideas. The materialist tells us that all the objects I observe—the sun, moon, stars, earth, seas, plants, men, ships, houses—are not really objects (that is, are not really substances), but are only modes or modifications of a substance in which all these modes inhere, a substance which is simple, uncompounded, and indivisible. The other system, the system of thoughts, is, Hume says, a "system of beings, *viz.* the universe of thought, or my impressions and ideas." Impressions and ideas become real beings. When Hume examines this system of beings, what does he find? "There I observe another sun, moon, and stars; an earth, and seas, cover'd and inhabited by plants and animals; towns, houses, mountains, rivers; and in short, every thing I can discover or conceive in the first system" (242).

While Hume does not name Malebranche, it seems clear that it is Malebranche who is being attacked in this passage. Malebranche accepted the dictum that the mind cannot know what is distant from it, that it can know only what is intimately united to the mind. In cognizing distant objects, then, we must see those objects where they are not located. What we see are other objects, other stars, moon, houses which are intimately united to our mind.[52] There are, Malebranche said, "deux sortes d'être," those which our mind sees immediately, and others which the mind knows only by means of the first sort of beings.[53] There were not many writers in Britain who took this extreme double existence view. Hooke, as we have seen, suggests something like a double existence view, without appealing to immaterial substance. Henry Grove and William Porterfield may also be taken as accepting such a view. Isaac Watts cited Malebranche's doctrine of intelligible sun, moon, and stars, and he had his own version of seeing things in the mind of God.[54] The extreme version depicted by Hume reveals the inherent logic of the approach:

[52] "Il est donc nécessaire, que nôtre ame voye les maisons et les étoiles où elles ne sont pas, puisqu'elle ne sort point du corps où elle est et qu'elle ne laisse pas de les voir hors de lui. Or comme les étoiles qui sont immédiatement unies à l'ame, lesquelles sont les seules que l'ame puisse voir, ne sont pas dans les Cieux, il s'ensuit que tous les hommes qui voyent les étoiles dans les Cieux, et qui jugent ensuite volontairement qu'elles y sont," make a false judgment (*Recherche,* I, 156).

[53] There is a similar remark in Berkeley's *New Theory of Vision,* but he makes it about the ideas of sight and touch: "there are two sorts of objects apprehended by the eye, the one primarily and immediately, the other secondarily and by intervention of the former" (Sect. 50, 189). Hume was not alone in finding Malebranche's doctrine a duplication of the world of ordinary objects. In his *Examination of Malebranche,* Locke questioned the same point, charging Malebranche with skepticism of real objects. See also Arnauld, *op. cit.,* 227-28: Malebranche transports us into an unknown country where we no longer see men, bodies, sun, stars but only intelligible objects.

[54] I. Watts, *Philosophical Essays* (London, 1733).

thoughts, ideas, perceptions become modifications of one simple, un-compounded, and indivisible substance: an exact parallel, Hume wants us to note, with Spinoza's account of modes and one substance. Spinoza's account is treated with "detestation and scorn, and the second with applause and veneration" (243). Both accounts are, Hume insists, equally unintelligible.

For Hume the route to intelligibility clearly lies through his principle of no specific difference between perceptions and objects, as well as through his acceptance of that feature of the ordinary view which said that what is present with the mind are its own perceptions (*Treatise*, 197). There are various formulations given of this latter feature. The generality of mankind perceive, Hume says, only one being, and "can never assent to the opinion of a double existence and representation. Those very sensations . . . are with them the true objects, nor can they readily conceive that this pen or paper, which is immediately perceiv'd, represents another, which is different from, but resembling it" (202). What is required is an explication of what "any common man means by a hat, or shoe, or stone, or any other impression, convey'd to him by his senses." The general principle is repeated: "all the unthinking and unphilosophical part of mankind (that is, all of us, at one time or other) . . . suppose their perceptions to be their only objects and never think of a double existence internal and external, representing and represented" (205). He adds, "the very image which is present to the senses, is with us the real body"; and again (206), he repeats this account: "'Tis certain, that almost all mankind, and even philosophers themselves, for the greatest part of their lives, take their perceptions to be their only objects, and suppose that the very being, which is intimately present to the mind, is the real body or material existence."

It is that ordinary view which is clearly more acceptable to Hume; but making that view intelligible depends upon finding a sense of "present to" which will enable us (in the language of Norris's example) to behold both the image and the object, and will thus explain our acquaintance with objects in the act of perception. Hume faces this question directly: "After what manner we conceive an object to become present to the mind, without some new creation of a perception or image"? (207). This phrase, "without some new creation of a perception or image," is, I think, most important. Is it asking "how can an object be present to the mind without a perception," a direct realism by-passing perceptions; or, is it indicating (what I will be suggesting) that, to be present to the mind, something more than sense perceptions are required? Hume goes on to ask the question, "what we mean by this *seeing*, and *feeling*, and *perceiving*." The reference of "this" can only be, the presence of an object to the mind without a perception or image. To answer this question, Hume says first that what we call a mind is just "a heap or collection of different perceptions, united together by certain relations."[55] Since every perception is distinguishable, it can be separated from this collection and hence be considered as existing independently. He then uses this account of the mind to answer the question about how an object can be present to the mind without a perception, that is, without the addition of a new perception over and above the object. His answer gives, I take it, an analysis of *present to the mind.* "External objects are seen, and felt, and become present to the mind; that is, they acquire such a relation to a connected heap of perceptions, as to influence them very considerably in augmenting their number by present reflexions and passions, and in storing the memory with ideas" (207). Hume might be taken to be saying the same perception can be thought of as separating itself from the heap (and hence becoming an independent object) and rejoining the heap. It would not be a *new* perception added to the *heap,* but an old one returned. But Hume seems to me very carefully *not* to say that the object being present to the mind *is* an old perception rejoining the heap. He talks of the external object influencing the heap by augmenting the number of perceptions through reflexions and passions. It is as if his account here is that objects can be present to the mind in the effects they bring about, not effects in the form of new sense perceptions but effects in stimulating reflection on the contents of the mind. It is present reflections and passions which augment the number of perceptions in the heap.

An example of present reflections and passions occasioned by objects being present to the mind is given in *Treatise,* II.II.VIII. There he says that there is a "general maxim, that no object is presented to the senses, nor image form'd in the fancy, but what is accompany'd with some emotion or movement of spirits proportion'd to it" (373). He is there discussing such emotions as the admiration of large objects, lesser emotions coming with smaller objects. The degree of emotion which "commonly attends every magnitude of an object" influences our perception of the object: "when the emotion encreases, we naturally imagine that the object has likewise encreas'd" (374). The transfer of the judgment of magnitude due to the accompanying emotion is just an instance of a general trait of applying "the judgments and conclusions of the understanding to the senses" (374-75). This general trait is disclosed by what Hume calls "the metaphysical part of optics." The factual part of optics tells us that the retinal image does not vary.

---

[55] It is interesting, as indicating the general context from which Hume's discussion arose, to note those *Philosophical Commentaries* entries where Berkeley says the mind or the understanding is a congeries of perceptions (entries 580, 587, and 614).

When an object augments or diminishes to the eye or imagination from a comparison with others, the image and idea of the object are still the same, and are equally extended in the *retina,* and in the brain or organ of perception. The eyes refract the rays of light, and the optic nerves convey the images to the brain in the very same manner, whether a great or small object has preceded; nor does even the imagination alter the dimensions of its object on account of a comparison with others. The question then is, how from the same impression and the same idea we can form such different judgments concerning the same object, and at one time admire its bulk, and at another despise its littleness. This variation in our judgments must certainly proceed from a variation in some perception; but as the variation lies not in the immediate impression or idea of the object, it must lie in some other impression, that accompanies it[56] (373).

It is the impression of reflection to which Hume refers.

It is important to note in these later passages that Hume is relating the *sensing* of objects (retinal image, brain impression) to the *conceiving* or *judging* of objects: "Every part, then, of extension, and every unite of number has a separate emotion attending it, when conceiv'd by the mind" (373). For an object to be present to the mind, it is not enough that an impression is made on the retina and conveyed to the brain. What is necessary in addition is that a judgment be made, a judgment which is then transferred (or as Porterfield said, traced back to) the senses. Nor do we usually "judge of objects from their intrinsic value, but form our notions of them from a comparison with other objects" and from the emotion which "secretly attends every idea" (375). There are other places in the *Treatise* where Hume makes use of optics in order to show the difference between what is sensed and what is perceived or judged. He accepts Berkeley's claim in *New Theory of Vision* that "our sight informs us not of distance or outness (so to speak) immediately and without a certain reasoning and experience" (191). Earlier, Hume drew the same conclusion from the fact that "all bodies which discover themselves to the eye, appear as if painted on a plain surface, and that their different degrees of remoteness from ourselves are discover'd more by reason than by the senses" (56).[57] There are other optical passages where Hume shows that the phenomena, the appearances, do not justify some judgment: for example, that the idea of extension without visible or tangible objects standing between other objects (i.e., the idea of a vacuum) cannot be given from any of the usual distance cues. "The angles, which the rays of light flowing from them, form with each other; the motion that is requir'd in the eye, in its passage from the one to the other; and the different

---

[56] This passage was called to my attention by reading Anderson's interesting article, *op. cit.*

[57] Cf. Vasco Ronchi's discussion of the "voûte céleste." (*Supra,* n. 16).

parts of the organs, which are affected by them; these produce the only perceptions, from which we can judge of the distance. But as these perceptions are each of them simple and indivisible, they can never give us the idea of extension" (58). He offers the example of looking at two luminous objects against a dark background, or the blue sky seen between the fingers, as possible cases where the idea of empty space might be derived (56-58). He gives a careful analysis of these visual examples, and of some similar tangible ones, to show that the sensations experienced are the same whether visible objects are interposed between other objects (showing the distance between them, a filled distance) or not. In this way, Hume explains how "an invisible and intangible distance is converted into a visible and tangible one, without any change on the distant objects" (59). Similarly, working from the information found in most optical treatises, about rays of light being reflected or refracted from points on the surfaces of objects and being collected in points on the retina, Hume argues that since "my senses convey to me only the impressions of colour'd points, dispos'd in a certain manner" (34), our idea of extension "is nothing but a copy of these colour'd points, and of the manner of their appearance." He uses this account of our idea of extension to argue against infinite divisibility of matter and against mathematical points. As with his analysis of our idea of time, so with space and extension, Hume wants to show what is and is not conceivable, given the sensations and appearances we have. Color and tangibility are not only necessary for *sensation,* they are necessary for our *conceiving* of space and time. "Upon the removal of the idea of these sensible qualities, they [the parts that make up our impressions of extension] are utterly annihilated to the thought or imagination" (38-39).

The same careful discussion of appearances, of our perceptions, is made in the section "Scepticism with regard to the Senses." There, working from the ordinary belief that we see objects, that our perceptions are the objects, Hume wants to discover what it is about these perceptions which leads us to take them to be the objects, where objects are believed to be continuous and independent. What, then, is the presence of objects to mind, what is it to see objects? Hume's answer is that an object is present to the mind, is seen or felt, when the perceptions which we take to be those objects themselves are augmented by reflections and passions. The sorts of reflections necessary for externality are those involving continuity and independence. How, out of resemblance of perceptions can we or do we conceive of continued existence when not present to us? How is it that given specific sensations and perceptions of knocks, footsteps, etc., we reach the idea of unseen doors, intervals of space and time filled with unperceived objects? The phenomena of perceptions are, by themselves, insufficient for giving us the idea of externality, of independent objects being present to the mind. When Hume shows how, out of the constancy and coherence of our sense perceptions, we come to the idea of external objects. he is showing what it must mean, on the vulgar view, for an object to become present to the mind "without some new creation of a perception or image." Just having more perceptions would not make *objects* present to the mind, would not enable the mind to conceive of objects, to be perceptually acquainted with them; for perceptions by themselves are not objects, they lack the two important characteristics of objects, continuity and independence.

In this account of objects being present to us, given that in fact only perceptions are immediately present to the mind, Hume thinks he has described "the natural propensity of the imagination," given the appearances of our perceptions.[58] But reason and a few simple experiments tell us that "the doctrine of the independent existence of our sensible perceptions is" in fact false, "contrary to the plainest experience." When philosophers reflect on phenomena such as double vision, they draw a distinction between "perceptions and objects, of which the former are suppos'd to be interrupted, and perishing, and different at every different return; the latter to be uninterrupted, and to preserve a continu'd existence and identity" (211). Such a distinction is, however, only a temporary "palliative remedy," it does not cure the disease. The concept of an object not only distinct but different from our perceptions is not intelligible. It is a desperate move made in the face of the phenomenological fact that perceptions are mind-dependent and are fleeting though similar. Hume thinks that this move would never be made, were we not first convinced "that our perceptions are our only objects"; so the philosophical view of a double existence is an attempt to patch up the difficulties in the vulgar, single existence view. But the notion of objects different in kind, specifically different, from perceptions is incoherent. Thus, the palliative

---

[58] In his account of how the imagination carries the mind beyond what is given to the senses, Hume exemplifies what Eric Rothstein has identified as an eighteenth-century response: creating in the imagination aspects of scenes, parts of figures not presented in poetry or painting. See his " 'Ideal Presence' and the 'Non Finito' in Eighteenth-Century Aesthetics," in *Eighteenth-Century Studies,* 9(1976), 307-32. Illusory realism, or what Lord Kames called "ideal presence," was practiced by artists and poets: the spectator was expected to fill out what was only hinted or suggested. Rothstein quotes a remark by Jean Starobinski (*The Invention of Liberty,* Geneva, 1964) that the eighteenth-century observer's pleasure "lay in completing mentally, in a complicity of the imagination, the work that the artist had abandoned" (308). Using the art historian's notion of *non finito* — "a work which the artist *intended* to leave unfinished, like a torso or sketch" — Rothstein's discussion suggests to me some fascinating parallels to this notion in Hume. It is as if nature has presented us with an unfinished sensory sketch, which we are expected to complete. From what *is* present to us, we find that we naturally fill out, extend, and complete those perceptions.

remedy reduces to an arbitrary invention of "a new set of perceptions" to which the attributes of objects are ascribed (218). The remedy turns out to double our perceptions, unlike the double existence view of those immaterialists whom Hume satirized which doubles objects, by turning perceptions into objects.[59]

Hume was looking for a conceptual resolution of the tensions between the ordinary and the philosophical views, a way of conceiving externality which would avoid Berkeley's conclusion that perceptions *are* the *objects.* Such a conceptual resolution was prevented by Hume's acceptance of the Berkeleian principle about our being unable to conceive anything specifically different from our perceptions. Hume returns to this point on several occasions in the *Treatise.* A passage in the section on the immateriality of the soul, where he is discussing *that* double existence view, is especially interesting, for it strongly supports the conclusion that Hume does accept the existence of objects as well as perceptions. Repeating his claim that we cannot conceive of an "object or external existence" specifically different from our perceptions, Hume says: "Whatever difference we may suppose betwixt them, 'tis still incomprehensible to us; and we are oblig'd either to conceive an external object merely as a relation without a relative, or to make it the very same with a perception or impression." That odd suggestion of conceiving "an external object merely as a relation without a relative," I take to mean that this alternative would be the concept of an object *related* to our perceptions (it occasions them) but we are unable to fill in any other content for that *relatum.* Such an alternative is not very acceptable, but the other, Berkeleian route of making the object "the very same with a perception" is both unsatisfactory and false. The next paragraph in that passage even suggests that we may *suppose,* even if we cannot *conceive,* a specific difference between object and perception. It is because such a supposal is possible that "any conclusion we form concerning the connexion and repugnance of im-

---

[59] The *Enquiry* discussion of the single and double existence views is much less detailed but is essentially the same. Men are said to be carried by instinct to trust their senses and to suppose an external universe, "which depends not on our perception." Men also always suppose "the very images, presented by the senses, to be the external object, and never entertain any suspicion, that the one are nothing but representations of the other" (152). He cites as an example "this very table." But "the slightest philosophy . . . teaches us, that nothing can ever be present to the mind but an image or perception, and that the senses are only the inlets, through which these images are conveyed, without being able to produce any immediate intercourse between the mind and the object." Reason leads us to say this house, this tree, "are nothing but perceptions in the mind, and fleeting copies or representations of other existences." This "pretended philosophical system" cannot, however, be justified, since "the mind has never anything present to it but the perceptions, and cannot possibly reach any experience of their connexion with objects" (153).

pressions, will not be known certainly to be applicable to objects" (241). The supposal of a specific difference rules out moving from impression or perception to objects, since the conclusion we draw may be based upon just those ways in which objects differ from impressions: "'Tis still possible, that the object may differ from it in that particular" (242). We can, however, go the other way: "whatever conclusion of this kind [of a connection or repugnance] we form concerning objects, will most certainly be applicable to impressions." Whatever reasoning or conclusion we reach about the object must be based upon our conception of the object; and that *conception* is, as we have seen, limited by not being able to go as far as our *supposal*. The "quality of the object, upon which the argument is founded, must at least be conceiv'd by the mind" (242). Even more interesting is Hume's remark in this passage about his I.IV.II. attempts to show how, from the coherence of our perceptions, we come to ascribe continuity and independence to those perceptions. Hume calls this attempt "an irregular kind of reasoning from experience." Thus, he allows that it may not be true that "all the discoverable relations of impressions are common to objects."

A certain amount of caution is in order, in what we take to be Hume's own serious views in this section on the immateriality of the soul, since he is so obviously satirizing, even parodying, the immaterialist's claims.[60] Has he drawn the supposal-conception distinction only to be able to apply (as he does, 243-44) the repugnancies of the materialist to the immaterialist account? He does not use this distinction in any other place, so far as I can discover. Moreover, the whole of Part IV of the *Treatise* has a dialectical quality to it. On each of the topics discussed in that part, Hume takes two extremes, shows the difficulties in each, suggests good reasons for our accepting both, but ends by saying neither is quite satisfactory. Usually this opposition is presented as between reason and sense, or between philosophy and common sense, or between reflection and unreflection. The structure of this part seems to be such that, while Hume invokes some of his basic principles, and while he seems somewhat more partial to common sense than to reason, he does not entirely accept either side of the dialectical oppositions.

Nevertheless, there seems sufficient warrant from the *Treatise* to say that the view of external existence Hume himself accepted was neither Berkeley's single existence theory that perceptions *are* the object, nor the duplicate world double existence theory he ascribes to the immaterialists.

---

[60] There is much obvious good fun in this section. At a time when all serious writers are arguing the possibilities of thinking matter (Locke's suggestion had unleashed a storm of reactions), when most people are defending immaterialism against the atheism of *materialism*, Hume devotes a section of his *Treatise* to arguing the thesis that *immaterialism* is an atheism! (I.IV.V.)

The double existence view, which emerges when the philosopher tries to deal with the problems of the vulgar view that what we *see* are independent objects, seems closer to the view Hume is trying to articulate. For *this* double existence view ends by making objects numerically different but specifically similar to perceptions. But that philosophical account is still not quite what Hume accepts, for it is a view of the world limited by what is conceivable for us. Nothing Hume wrote in the *Treatise* ever supports saying he took the limits of human understanding as an account of the nature of the world. He simply did not think we could penetrate to the secret springs and powers of nature; but that nature works in ways unavailable to us was a conviction he shared with most of his other contemporaries. He took seriously the injunction of Locke and most members of the Royal Society, to pay close attention to the observable features of the world. The frequent use he makes of visual and tactual phenomena, in his account of space and time and of external objects, reveals both an acquaintance with optical writings and a concern to discover what we can and cannot say on the basis of the way the world appears to us. He was reluctant to say external objects *cause* perceptions (for reasons found in his phenomenological analysis of causal phenomena), but he was able to say they *occasion* our perceptions. It is through that occasioning of sense perceptions that external objects become present to the mind, not sensorily present, but present to cognition. That passage in the *Treatise* which I have suggested reveals Hume's analysis of "present to the mind" for objects, through the thoughts and passions aroused by the sense perceptions occasioned by objects, is also found in a brief *Enquiry* passage. Excessive skepticism, Hume there says, is subverted by "the presence of the real objects, which actuate our passions and sentiments" (159). Real, external objects become present to the mind, not through the sense perceptions they occasion (though that is a necessary condition) but through the thoughts and feelings which accompany their perceptions.[61]

Rutgers College, Rutgers University.

[61] I am indebted to John Wright for helping me clarify my ideas on Hume. Discussions we have had on Hume, and on other aspects of my general study, have saved me from misreadings of Hume. The interpretation of Hume which I have given in this paper probably still disagrees from his own reading.

Chapter V

CAN THERE BE COLORS IN THE DARK?

PHYSICAL COLOR THEORY BEFORE NEWTON

Isaac Newton's first scientific paper, setting forth his epoch-making theory of light and colors, appeared in the *Philosophical Transactions* of the Royal Society of London in February 1672.[1] Newton was barely thirty years old, a young don at Trinity College, Cambridge, where he was destined to remain immured for the next quarter century. Yet several years before submitting his classic paper he had been investigating the problem of colors using what one scholar has called his "instrument of choice," the triangular glass prism. Indeed, not long after his appointment, in the autumn of 1669, as Mr. Lucas's Professor of Mathematics, he devoted his first university lectures to these optical discoveries.[2] Only a sampling of the experiments described in these lectures, or recorded in his earlier notebooks, was drawn upon for his first published paper.

A central thrust of this "New Theory of Light and Colors"[3] was to show that color is derived from light which is not a simple entity but appeared to Newton as composed of, or could be analyzed into, different "colorific" rays. These rays, however one might envisage them, differ in refrangibility, i.e., in the degree to which they are bent in passing from a thin transparent medium like air into a denser medium like water or glass. Having established this fact, Newton then set forth in thirteen numbered propositions his "doctrine" of the origin of colors. As the rays differ in "refrangibility" (a word that Newton here introduced into the English scientific vocabulary), so they differ in their disposition to exhibit this or that color. The relation or "analogy," as he calls it, between colors and the degree of refrangibility he described as "very precise and strict." Colors, Newton clearly recognized, have no extra-mental existence, but are internal sensations of our sensory apparatus evoked by the light from luminous or illuminated bodies.

[1] *Philosophical Transactions of the Royal Society*, No. 80, February 19, 1671/72, 3075-3087. Facsimile repr. in I. Bernard Cohen et al., *Isaac Newton's Papers & Letters on Natural Philosophy* (Cambridge, Mass., 1958; 2nd ed. 1978), 47-59.

[2] The Latin Manuscript (ULC MS. Add. 4002) was published in facsimile by the Cambridge University Library, as *The Unpublished First Version of Isaac Newton's Cambridge Lectures on Optics 1670-1672* (1973). Recently it has been included, with annotations and an English trans., in Alan E. Shapiro, ed., *The Optical Papers of Isaac Newton*, Vol. I (Cambridge, 1984) 46-279.

[3] Newton's communication was a letter to Henry Oldenburg, Secretary of the Royal Society, who in effect gave it a title by describing it as a "New Theory about Light and Colors." The last word used what is now American spelling.

In his "New Theory" the propositions setting forth Newton's doctrine of color are followed by a curious paragraph that could well puzzle a modern reader. Here Newton wrote: "These things being so, it can no longer be disputed, whether there be colours in the dark, nor whether they be the qualities of the objects we see." The second clause is easily interpreted, for the word "qualities" was a technical term of peripatetic philosophy, a subject Newton had endured as a Cambridge undergraduate and from which, like his more enlightened contemporaries, he was seeking to free himself.[4] Indeed, he was soon to avoid the word "qualities" altogether because of its Aristotelian overtones, favoring instead the word "properties" in replying to the critics of his first paper; more than thirty years later he used it in the opening sentence of his long-delayed *Opticks* (1704).

But what are we to make of the first clause where he asks whether there can be colors in the dark? This has the ring of some earlier philosophical disagreement, and further inquiry will show this to have been the case. Compared to the copious literature on the history of optics, surprisingly little attention has been paid to physical theories of color before Newton and to the role of light in its production. This, presumably, is because color was not considered part of optics, which, from classical antiquity to Newton's day was—like theoretical astronomy, mechanics, and geodesy—considered a branch of the "mixed," or as we would say, "applied," mathematics. Color theory was left to the painters and to the speculative vagaries of philosophers. Newton, with his discovery of the strict relation between color and the degree of refrangibility of solar rays, was the first to show that numbers could be assigned to colors, in a word that color could be quantified and treated with a rigor justifying its inclusion as a part of optics. Indeed, Newton was fully aware of his temerity, for when he delivered the first of his Lucasian lectures early in 1669/70, he felt obliged to explain to his auditors why he planned to discuss in mathematical lectures the nature of colors, "which is considered to have no relation to mathematics."

An introduction to a forthcoming edition of Newton's *Opticks* clearly calls for some background on traditional geometrical optics, and it was not long before I discovered how rich is the rapidly growing literature on the subject, yet how little, and that limited in scope, has been written about the *physical* theories of light and color before Newton.[5] And with good reason. This I shall try in some degree to remedy.

[4] For this passage see E. A. Burtt, *The Metaphysical Foundations of Modern Science* (New York, 1925), 232-233. Burtt concentrated on the second clause, which I believe he misinterpreted, and ignored the first.

[5] For Antiquity see Arthur Erich Haas, "Antike Lichttheorien," in *Archiv für Geschichte der Philosophie,* 20 (1907), 345-386, and the article by David E. Hahm, "Early Hellenistic Theories of Vision and the Perception of Color," in Peter Machamer and Robert Turnbull, ed. *Studies in Perception* (Columbus, Ohio, 1978), 60-95. Useful back-

I. Ideas held by the earliest Greek philosophers concerning light and colors can be traced only in a fragmentary and conjectural way before the extended treatments by Plato and Aristotle. The first theory of vision, which left traces well into the early eighteenth century, has been called the "extromission" or "visual ray" theory. It assumed that we see external objects by virtue of a fire-like emanation from the eye. An early supporter of this theory was the Pythagorean, Alcmeon of Croton (5th century B.C.), who gave as evidence the flashes of light and color seen when the eye is struck.[6] For Empedocles, who held this theory, we have good evidence, since Aristotle quotes ten lines from the former's poem *On Nature,* in which the theory is clearly invoked.[7]

Plato in the *Timaeus* elaborated this doctrine, describing a particulate fire-matter emitted from the eye as an even stream of a substance akin to the light of everyday life.[8] When daylight, a kind of gentle fire, meets this outstreaming substance, like encounters like, and the two coalesce to form the visual ray. Colors, for Plato, are particulate flames given off from every sort of body. These color-particles differ in size. If equal to the components of the visual effluence, they are imperceptible, and the color is called the "transparent" or the "diaphanous," a term that Aristotle was soon to adapt for his own purposes. Larger particles from these bodies contract the compound, yielding the sensation of black, while smaller particles dilate it, producing white. Here would seem to be the origin of Aristotle's doctrine to be described below.

In his *De Sensu,* Aristotle rejects any extromission theory[9] and in so doing makes some interesting and (in some cases, alas, perdurant) assertions. Each of the five senses has its appropriate object; that of our sense of sight is color; color is what we see,[10] just as flavor is the object of our sense of taste. Color is not an effluence from the seeing eye or from the objects we perceive but an incorporeal "form" or "quality"

---

ground for color theory in the Middle Ages is in William A. Wallace, O.P., *The Scientific Methodology of Theodoric of Freiberg* (Fribourg, Switzerland, 1959), esp. 132-248, to be cited henceforth as Wallace (1959). For the seventeenth-century, A. I. Sabra's *Theories of Light from Descartes to Newton* (London, 1967) is valuable, but color is treated only in passages devoted to Descartes and Robert Hooke.

[6] The theory has sometimes been credited to other early Pythagoreans.

[7] Aristotle's *De Sensu,* 437b-438a. For English versions see William A. Hammond, *Aristotle's Psychology* (London, 1902), and G.T.R. Ross, ed., Aristotle, *De Sensu and De Memoria* (Cambridge, England, 1906), the translation I have used. For references to light and color in Aristotle's works see H. Bonitz, *Index Aristotelicus* (Berlin, 1870).

[8] *Dialogues of Plato,* trans. Benjamin Jowett, 2 vols. (New York, 1937), II, 26.

[9] Aristotle is not consistent throughout his works. In the *De Caelo* (II, viii, 290a) he writes: "The planets are near, so that our vision reaches them with its powers unimpaired; but in reaching to the fixed stars it is extended too far, and the distance causes it to waver." Similar views are invoked in the *Meteorologica,* III, iv, 373b, 374b.

[10] Modern psychologists agree that what we see is color.

inhering in colored bodies. Light, in some mysterious way, makes colors visible.

But what is light? Light—if you will bear with me, or rather with Aristotle—is not a material entity but the *activity* of a fire-like substance, similar to the aether that pervades the outermost sphere of the heavens. When light enters the transparent medium, the *diaphanous,* the result is color. In the bodies of our daily experience color "is the limit of the transparent medium in a definitely bounded body." This is a definition unlikely to illuminate the modern reader, and I give it only to suggest the veil that Aristotle cast over conceptions of the role of light for nearly two millennia.

There are, nevertheless, some comprehensible, if incorrect, things to put down about Aristotle on color. There are two "fundamental" or "primary" colors, black and white, and all the other chromatic colors we commonly distinguish are derived from these primaries. Note that black and white are *opposite* qualities, just as among flavors sweet and bitter are opposite.

Here, we might mention in passing, are two examples of Aristotle's practice of explaining physical phenomena, and much else, in terms of a polarity of antithetical qualities or powers.[11] This basic approach he sets forth in the *Physics,* citing his Pre-Socratic predecessors who spoke of the wet and the dry, the hot and the cold, and (with Democritus) the full (the atoms) and the empty (the void).[12]

How many colors did Aristotle distinguish? The answer would be seven: white, yellow, red, violet, green, blue, and black. But we should not be deluded into thinking that Aristotle ranked colors in a chromatic sequence like that of a prismatic or diffraction spectrum. His listing does, however, seem to represent a rough scale of brightness or luminosity: from white and yellow at one end to the "dark" colors blue and black at the other.[13] It is evident that Aristotle had in mind the colors of familiar opaque objects, or colored liquids, what the schoolmen were later to call "true" or "genuine" colors, distinguishing them from the ephemeral colors displayed by the rainbow, by the spray of a fountain or waterfall, by prismatic crystals or glass with bevelled edges: the so-called "apparent," "emphatical," "false," or "phantastical" colors. Until the seventeenth century this dichotomy proved a real obstacle to attempts at understanding the physical origin of color and its relation to light.

[11] Harold Cherniss, *Aristotle's Criticism of Pre-Socratic Philosophy* (Baltimore, 1935), 12.

[12] Aristotle, *The Physics,* trans. Wicksteed and Cornford (Loeb Classical Library, I, v. 188a, 19-26). Farther on (188b) we read: "And since the intermediates are compounded in various degrees out of the opposite couple (colors, for instance, out of white and black) it follows that all things that come into existence in the course of nature are either opposites themselves or are compounded of opposites."

[13] Hammond, *Aristotle's Psychology,* 160, n.1.

The only "emphatical" colors mentioned by Aristotle are those of the rainbow which, in his *Meteorologica,* he was the first to study in some detail. He reports (incorrectly) that only three colors—red, green, and blue—are readily distinguished, although yellow can sometimes be seen, but he did note the secondary bow in which the same three colors are in reverse order.

In the corpus of Aristotle's writings, to which the Latin West fell heir, are included several works which, although they possess some marked Aristotelian features, cannot, scholars generally agree, be attributed to the master himself. One of these, the *De Coloribus,* deserves, because of its later influence, more than passing attention. That this treatise on colors is not by Aristotle himself was clear to J. G. Schneider, who in 1818 included excerpts from it in his edition of the works of Theophrastus of Eresus, adding the cautionary subheading: *Vulgo Aristoteli Adscripta.* The careful analysis of Prantl (1849) left little doubt that Aristotle could not have been the author.[14] Recent scholarship has somewhat gingerly attributed it to Theophrastus of Eresus or to one of his devoted pupils.[15]

De Coloribus is a strange agglomeration, containing some astute observations, dubious inferences drawn from meteorological color phenomena, and remarks about the color changes in maturing plants, fruit, the hair of animals, and the plumage of birds.[16] There are major departures from Aristotle's opinions, as when, for example, the author asserts that the "primary" colors are the colors of the four traditional elements: Earth, Air, and Water are white, whereas Fire, like sunlight, is yellow. All other colors are derived from the simple ones by mixing.

It is in treating light, a subject central to our discussion, that *De Coloribus* markedly departs from Aristotle's doctrines. For Aristotle, light is immaterial and without color, whereas our Peripatetic author considers it a material substance that can mix with other substances, force its way through air because of its greater "density," and is reflected from solid surfaces. In *De Coloribus* light has the color of fire, which is the only element visible without the help of any other agency, and it makes all other substances visible. Black or darkness (*schotos*) is not a color but only the privation of light; bodies appear black through the paucity or absence of reflected light. Yet bodies derive their chromatic colors from the "primary" colors when their particles mix with each other or with light.

---

[14] Carl von Prantl, *Aristoteles über die Farben, erläutert durch ein Uebersicht der Farbenlehre der Altern* (Munich, 1849).

[15] H.B. Gottschalk, "The De Coloribus and its Author," *Hermes,* 92 (1964), 59-85. Gottshalk gives an admirable analysis of this treatise and translations of salient passages.

[16] For the Greek text and complete trans. of the *De Coloribus* see "Aristotle on Colours," in Aristotle, *Minor Works,* ed. W.S. Hett (Loeb Classical Library), 4-45. Hahm (1978), 83-84, points to the number of places where *De Coloribus* shows an affinity with Epicurean theory.

For the first time we perceive a suspicion that light must do more than make colors visible: it plays a mysterious part in modifying them, for we read (798b): things appear differently when they are seen in shadow or in sunlight, in a strong or weak light, and according to the angle at which they are seen. In this connection the author of the *De Coloribus* anticipates an observation we shall encounter with the Epicureans, that light striking a bird's plumage from different angles changes its color:

Birds' feathers too when held to the light at a certain angle appear violet; if still less light falls upon them, they turn a dark greyish brown; but if much light is mixed with their natural black color they turn crimson, and this becomes the color of fire if it is vivid and glittering.[17]

II. In later Antiquity, Euclid and Ptolemy both revert to the older doctrine of extromission. In Euclid's *Optics,* which treated the geometry of the light ray, it made no difference whether the rays come *from* the eye or from the observed object. Color or the role of light did not concern him. But as an exception to my generalization that classical optics did not treat color, there is an *Optics* attributed, but not with certainty, to Ptolemy (Claudius Ptolemaeus), the great mathematical astronomer who flourished about 150 A.D. In this *Optics* color is the subject of a lost Book I. Something of its contents has been reconstructed from allusions to it in the surviving Books of the work.[18] Ptolemy follows Aristotle in many details of his theory of color. Colors are actually *in* the objects we see; they are inherent "qualities" of the things around us, actually *there.* And Ptolemy accepted and reinforced with his prestige the Aristotelian doctrine that there are two "primary" or "principal" colors, white and black, from which the others are derived by mixing. Ptolemy, however, differed from Aristotle's dominant doctrine by conceiving sight as resulting from visual rays emanating from the eye. More trivially, we learn from Olympiodorus in his commentary on the *Meteorologica* of Aristotle that Ptolemy claimed that seven colors, not just three, could be discerned in the rainbow.

There is little need to encapsulate the history of ancient atomism from Democritus to Lucretius, except to point out that for such thinkers, although the atoms themselves are colorless, their arrangement and physical interconnections, which make up the visible bodies, yield us our sensations of color. Yet as Aristotle wrote, colors for Democritus did not have real independent existence. Then how do we perceive colors? If we may adopt the terminology of Newton's friend, the philosopher John Locke, the classical atomists clearly made a distinction between the "primary qualities" (like shape and texture) and "secondary qualities"

[17] Gottschalk, 64. For a stiffer rendering see Aristotle, *Minor Works,* 11.
[18] Albert Lejeune, *Euclide et Ptolémée* (Louvain, 1948). A critical edition of Ptolemy's *Optics* was later published by Lejeune (Louvain, 1956).

like odor, color or taste. These were said to be the result of convention (*nomos*), apparently meaning "mind-dependent" or "in thought," or (as we would say) *subjective*.

This was a major clarification and eventually exerted a profound effect on speculations about color with the revival of Epicurean atomism in the Renaissance and later. But it still left open the question of what physical processes originate and affect our sense organs. One step lay in the abandonment of the "visual ray" theory of vision and the acceptance of an *intromission* theory. Indeed, one form of this was the atomists's well-known theory of visible emanations *from* objects, the *eidola* or *simulacra,* images that travel to the observing eye, conveying the object's shape, motion, and also its color or colors. The *eidola* were conceived as thin films that peel off objects but are constantly replaced; on reaching the eye the *eidola* retain the relative disposition (*rhythmos*), the interconnections of the atoms, and the colors at the surface of bodies.

If we ask what part light plays in all this, the fragments of Democritus tell us nothing, although from Aristotle we learn that Democritus attributed the whiteness of a body to the smoothness of its surface and black to its roughness or (to use a favored seventeenth-century term) its "asperity." There may be here a suggestion that white and black result when light is reflected diversely or absorbed from differently structured surfaces, which indeed was to be the theory of Pierre Gassendi and Robert Boyle. I know of no passage from the early atomists discussing how the intermediate or chromatic colors arise.

The only extended exposition of a theory of colors, relating it to the theory of the *eidola,* is to be found in the famous letter of Epicurus to his friend Herodotus (not, of course, the famous historian). It is a passage primarily concerned both with Aristotle's theory and that of Empedocles and Plato:

For external things would not stamp on us their own nature of colour and form through the medium of the air which is between them and us, or by means of rays of light or currents of any sort going from us to them, so well as by the entrance into our eyes or minds ... of certain films coming from the things themselves, these films or outlines being of the same colour or shape as the external things themselves.[19]

Though light is mentioned in passing (as an emanation from the eye), Epicurus is here primarily concerned to refute earlier theories. There is, however, something more interesting, although cryptic, in a surviving fragment from Epicurus's treatise *Against Theophrastus.* This signalized a problem destined to engage the curiosity of later writers. Here Epicurus makes clear that light in some way is involved in the origin of colors:

[19] Diogenes Laertius, *Lives of Eminent Philosophers,* trans. R. D. Hicks, 2 vols (London, 1925 and later reprints), II, 579, in The Loeb Classical Library. Another English version is in Whitney J. Oates, *Stoic and Epicurean Philosophers* (New York, 1940), 6.

"I do not know," the fragment says, "how one should say that things in the dark have colour."[20]

In Lucretius, the Roman popularizer in splendid verse of the Epicurean philosophy, there occurs a striking observation specifically linking our perception of different colors to the role of light rays. In a prose translation it reads:

... since colours cannot exist without light and the first beginnings of things [*primordia rerum,* i.e. the atoms] do not come into the light, you may be sure that they are clothed with no colour. For what colour can there be in total darkness?

And Lucretius continued with an observation that the colors of the feathers of birds change when light is reflected to the observer from different angles:

After this fashion the down which encircles and crowns the nape and throat of doves shows itself in the sun; at one time it is ruddy with the hue of bright pyropus; at another it appears by a certain way of looking at it to blend with coral-red green emeralds. The tail of a peacock when it is saturated with abundant light, changes in like fashion its colours as it turns about. And since *these colours are begotten by a certain strike of light, sure enough you must believe they cannot be produced without it.*[21]

This passage, although few classical scholars seem to have noted its portent, was later to be familiar to seventeenth-century investigators of the mysterious problem of color.

III. In the early Middle Ages in the West (where I do not propose to linger) the only available texts on the subject of the physics of color and vision were portions of Plato's *Timaeus* rendered into Latin in the 4th century A.D. by Chalcidius and some passages in St. Augustine. Aristotle's views on colors were not appreciated until the full corpus of his works, including the *De Anima* and the *De Sensu,* were translated, along with the classical commentators, in the 12th and 13th centuries, and when Thomas Aquinas produced, along with much else, a commentary on the *De Sensu.* It was much later that the writings of the Epicurean atomists gained currency.

At roughly the same time as the Greek writings were translated the optical studies by Arab scientists became available in Latin versions. For mathematical and experimental optics the single most important author was Ibn Al-Haytham, known in the West as Alhazen. His *Optics,* given its Latin titles of *Perspectiva* or *De Aspectibus,* was for the later Middle

---

[20] Epicurus, "Fragment against Theophrastus," in Oates, 45. For the notion that colors result from the mixing of light with air see Epicurus, "Letter to Pythocles," in Oates, 25.

[21] Oates, 106. Pyropus, or pyrope, is a deep red species of garnet. The emphasis in the last sentence is mine.

Ages the most influential stimulus for the mathematical and experimental study of light and vision. Alhazen was frequently cited by later optical writers, among them Roger Bacon. But on color Alhazen had little to offer beyond the prescient statement that the form of color "is always intermingled with the form of light,"[22] quoted by Roger Bacon, who derived from Alhazen and Avicenna the view that nothing is seen without light and that color does not have a real existence in darkness.[23] On this question scholars were divided. Averroës led the opponents of Avicenna and insisted that colors *do* exist in the dark. Albertus Magnus, invoking the distinction between material and formal causes which Aristotle had made, chose a middle path and urged that the material differences in bodies, which underlie their different colors, are present not only in light but in darkness; yet to supply the "form" of colors, that is, to actualize them, light is essential. Albert concludes therefore that colors can exist in the dark, but only potentially. A similar position was taken by Thomas Aquinas, who adhered to Aristotle's definition of color and reasoned "that since bodies have no actual surfaces in their interior (only potential ones), they are not colored on the inside except potentially." Yet light, as Thomas put it, is in a certain sense the "substance of color" (*substantia coloris*).

Dietrich of Freiburg (d. *ca.* 1310), one of the notable figures in the history of medieval optics, is perhaps best remembered for his study of the rainbow, his *De Iride.*[24] His small treatise on colors, the *De Coloribus,* was written as an explanatory appendix to the *De Iride.*[25] Aristotle was his principal authority, but he drew significantly from Alhazen, whom he cites as *auctor perspectiva,* to the effect that color does not affect vision without light, nor does light affect vision without color. His definition of light is essentially Aristotelian: it is a real quality or form of the diaphanous. Dietrich's *De Coloribus,* an introduction to the problem of color, opens by taking up the question "that has been greatly agitated among his predecessors and contemporaries: which is, whether colours can exist in the dark." Dietrich's debt to Aristotle and, closer at hand, to Albertus Magnus, is quite apparent, although veiled in his cumbrous terminology. For Dietrich, as Father Wallace puts it, "one can truly say that colors do not exist in darkness, in the sense that they have not been brought to actuality from their accidental potency, and yet one can maintain that they do exist in darkness in the sense that they are already

[22] Wallace (1959), 138 and n. 1. See note 5 above.
[23] *The Opus Majus of Roger Bacon,* trans. Robert Belle Burke, 2 vols. (Philadelphia, 1928), II, 473. But see note 27 below.
[24] For Dietrich (or Theodoric) of Freiberg see Wallace (1959) and the same author's account in the *Dictionary of Scientific Biography,* ed. Charles Coulston Gillispie Vol. IV (1971), 92-94, with bibliography.
[25] Dietrich's opuscule *De Coloribus* is analyzed, with appropriate background, in Wallace (1959), 163-173. The Latin text is in Appendix III, 364-376.

outside their essential potency, and need only an accidental mover [the light] to be actualized."[26]

If we turn to classical atomism, the only sources for the medieval scholar were the critical references to Democritus in Aristotle. Yet, in the 5th century, fragments of the ancient natural philosophy of atomism appeared in the treatise on the Seven Liberal Arts by Martianus Capella, a work very popular in the Middle Ages. In the listing of the philosophers assembled for the marriage of Mercury and Philology, the central and symbolic episode, there is a facetious reference to Democritus, described as "surrounded by atoms," and to Epicurus, about whom the Middle Ages remained largely ignorant until the translation into Latin, early in the 15th century, of the *Lives of the Eminent Philosophers* by Diogenes Laertius and its first printing in 1475.

As a popularizer of Epicurus's physical philosophy Lucretius was unknown to the Middle Ages, or so it has been generally believed. Yet he was often quoted (perhaps following Macrobius, a later Roman writer) as a poetic influence upon Virgil. Indeed Macrobius gives some forty citations where Lucretius is seen as anticipating, and probably influencing, Virgil's prosody. In Seneca, whose *Naturales Questiones* was familiar to the Latin Middle Ages, there is a passage that might ultimately derive from Lucretius on color. Seneca quotes from a poem, which he attributed to his patron, the Emperor Nero, in which the neck of a dove is said to "glisten" when the bird moves about. Seneca follows this with the remark that the *neck* of a peacock (no mention of the spectacular tail) also "gleams" when it moves. Of course these could have been everyday observations, but Lucretius might have been the source. There is no reference as in Lucretius, however, to changing colors.

A full acquaintance with the Lucretian poem is generally thought to have awaited the discovery by Poggio Bracciolini, about 1417, of a manuscript of the *De Rerum natura*. A corollary is that the lines referring to color which I have cited above from the great poem could not have been known before Poggio's discovery. Or so I believed on first noting their significance. But not long ago evidence, ready at hand, suggested that this was not the case. Roger Bacon's *Opus Majus,* written before 1267 (the year he sent a copy to the Pope), has some sentences strongly suggesting that the lines quoted above from Lucretius were known to him. Here, as in Lucretius, the intimate role of light in the production of the different chromatic colors is clearly suggested. Roger writes:

that in accordance with the diversity of the fall of the same light on the same object the aspect is changed, and the color appears different to the vision, as in

---

[26] Wallace (1959), 166. Elsewhere Wallace writes: "The existence of colors in darkness and at the interior of bodies were much discussed questions because they touched upon the mysterious and very intimate relation which apparently existed between light and color" (*ibid.,* 152).

the case of the dove's neck when it turns the neck in different positions to the light, and so too in the case of the peacock's tail.[27]

Roger goes on to remark that without light nothing is seen. No great discovery, to be sure, in view of the gradual approach by his scholastic predecessors to the true solution. But even more clearly than Lucretius he is telling us that light is somehow directly involved in the production of colors.

Needless to say, Aristotle's old theory of color, subject to various minor modifications, remained dominant during the sixteenth century, despite growing anti-Aristotelianism and the emerging popularity of corpuscular theories. René Descartes, a *chef de file* of the burgeoning anti-Aristotelian movement, was quite familiar with classical atomism, for the notion of a void is several times attacked in his correspondence. Yet as his theories of matter testify, he was, in a broad sense, a corpuscularian.

On the subject of light and color, as on other matters, Descartes was a revolutionary figure. He rejected both what he had learned from his conservative teachers at the school of La Flèche and from the atomists. He urged his readers to reject "those little flying images, called intentional species, which so torment the imagination of Philosophers," as well as the *simulacra* of the atomists. For them he substituted a view of light fitted to his mechanically conceived universe. The light (*lumen*) that originates in luminous or light-emitting bodies is simply a rapid circular motion which passes to us as an impulse through the globules of his "second element," reaching us from the sun or the stars "in an instant." This light (*lux*) is not a material entity but a "tendency to motion" passed along by the closely-packed globules. We can visualize these as a compact chain of tiny spheres connecting us, along our line of sight, with the source of light.

Descartes's contributions to optics are contained in two treatises appended to his famous *Discours de la méthode* (1637). The *Dioptrique* dealt with geometrical optics and the design of telescopic lenses and had little or nothing to say about color. But in the *Météores,* where Descartes works out the geometry of the sun's rays in producing a rainbow, he is obliged to confront the problem of the nature of light and color.[28] Here, as in other scattered texts, we find him an important precursor of, and doubtless to some degree an influence upon, Isaac Newton. In the first place, he appears as the earliest modern figure to recognize that light is

---

[27] Roger Bacon, *Opus Majus,* trans. Burke, II, 450. See also 557. Alhazen may have been an influence, for under a passage headed "Color varies according to the quality of light," we read that the feathers of a peacock and a silk cloth, where green is mixed with dark red, change color when seen at different times of day, according to the difference in the light striking them. See the Latin in Friedrich Risner, ed. *Opticae Thesaurus,* (Basel, 1572), 2-3.

[28] Both reprinted in *Oeuvres de Descartes,* eds. Adam and Tannery, VI, 1-228, 231-366.

not merely an auxiliary agent making colors visible to us but *the true source of color.* He is the first as well to insist that color is color and to attack the scholastic philosophers for their sharp distinction between "true" colors and those that are merely "apparent," "false," or "emphatical," like the colors of the rainbow.

In the *Météores,* accompanying his classic analysis of the rainbow's formation, Descartes reports two experiments to illustrate what happens in a raindrop. The first, whether or not he was aware of it, had been performed long before by Dietrich of Freiberg. Passing a beam of the sun's light through a transparent sphere of glass filled with water that acted as an isolated and magnified raindrop, Descartes, like Dietrich, was able to show that the beam suffered two refractions and one reflection in passing into and out of a raindrop. This, of course, did not explain how the colors originate.

Aware that "emphatical" colors like those of a rainbow could be produced by a triangular glass prism, Descartes was the first, so far as I can discover, to undertake *and publish* a serious prismatic experiment. If a beam of the sun's light after passing through a prism is admitted through a narrow aperture, it forms a colored image on a vertical paper, with the red appearing at one extremity of the image and blue or violet at the other. But this is true only if the aperture is small enough; if it was too wide, all Descartes obtained was a white image. Influenced by the still prevailing Aristotelian idea that colors are produced by a mixture of black and white (or light and shadow), he noted that quite different colors were seen at the extremities of the image, where the beam of light grazed the region of shadow. To explain this effect he had recourse to a mechanical model. For him, we recall, light is only an impulse or tendency to motion transmitted by the subtle second matter which itself has no translation motion. Colors, he imagined, could be produced by giving the subtle matter a rotation. The spin producing red is swifter than the spin yielding blue or violet. Intermediate rates of spin give the intermediate colors. Descartes was aware that refraction was somehow a cause of what the scholastics had called the "emphatical" colors, but he applied his theory also to explain the "true" colors of objects, where shadows and refraction were not involved. In their stead the size, shape, situation, and motion "of the parts of bodies we call colored can interact in diverse ways to increase or decrease the rotation of the subtle matter."[29]

IV. Three seventeenth-century scholars are specially important to us as forerunners of Newton and influences upon his thought about light and color: Pierre Gassendi (1592-1655), Gassendi's English disciple Walter Charleton, and Robert Boyle (1627-1691). Gassendi has not received his due from philosophers or historians of science, especially from de-

---

[29] *Oeuvres de Descartes,* VI, 335.

votees of Descartes, whose chief antagonist he was.[30] Gassendi was born in a small village a few miles from Digne, a dreary, sulphurous watering place in the Alps of upper Provence. He had his advanced education at the University of Aix-en-Provence and taught philosophy there with a wide-ranging curiosity and an independence of mind uncommon in the universities of his day. He became a canon and later (in 1634) Provost of the church at Digne.

As firmly anti-Aristotelianism as Descartes, Gassendi took a quite different route, becoming the first influential philosopher of atomism in the modern world. His early interest in Epicurus, with his hope of rehabilitating that Greek thinker's reputation (for Epicurus had been widely proscribed as a hedonistic materialist), was only an aspect of his anti-Aristotelian strategy. The first publication to reveal his conversion to atomism was a small tract published in 1642 on the apparent size of the sun when viewed near the horizon or near the zenith. In this early work, as Robert Boyle was to remark, "The most Learned *Gassendus*" has some passages towards "reviving the Atomical philosophy."[31] Gassendi's first Epicurean work, his *Observations on the Tenth Book of Diogenes Laertius,* published in 1649, treats the life, character, and ethical views of Epicurus, revealing in its title his chief literary source.

Gassendi's atomistic theories are fully set forth in his major work, the *Syntagma philosophicum,* which treats logic, physics (in the seventeenth-century meaning of the word), and ethics. It was published posthumously in the first two volumes of his collected works brought out by friends in 1658. His atomic theory adheres closely to the classical model, and I need not trouble you with it, except to note that he rejects, doubtless in the interest of piety, the notorious "swerve" (*clinamen*) with which Epicurus endowed his atoms.

His physical theory of color, on the other hand, is central to our story, since it indirectly influenced the young Isaac Newton through the works of Walter Charleton and Robert Boyle. Abandoning Aristotle, Gassendi conceived light as a material efflux streaming out of luminous bodies like the sun and the fixed stars, or from an earthly fire, and either propagated directly to us or reflected from other bodies. He rejects the *eidola,* those images that are propagated from luminous or illuminated bodies. For Gassendi they are nothing but light itself; for him light consists of a stream of very fine corpuscles transmitted to us with an incomprehensible speed (*pernicitate ineffabili*) to move our organ of vision. These

[30] As, for example, Alexandre Koyré's picture of Gassendi as "pas un grand savant" in *Actes du Congrès du Tricentenaire de Pierre Gassendi* (Digne, 1957), 175-190. The leading studies on Gassendi are by Bernard Rochot, *Les travaux de Gassendi sur Epicure et sur l'atomisme* (Paris, 1944) and his article in the *Dictionary of Scientific Biography,* V, 1972, with more up-to-date bibliography.

[31] Robert Boyle, *Experiments and Considerations Touching Colours* (London, 1664), 94-95.

fine corpuscles are tiny spheres which, unlike the second element of Descartes, have a translational motion through the void or through air.

Like Descartes, his illustrious opponent, whose support he was willing to invoke on this score, Gassendi firmly rejects the scholastic habit of distinguishing between "true" and "false" or "fantastical" colors. Color is color. And more bluntly than Descartes he states that the essence of color is from the light itself. Light as it originates (*in sua fonte*), undisturbed and unmodified, gives the sensation of white. Black is simply the absence of white light. What of the chromatic colors? To support his view that they are modifications of white light Gassendi cites at length the lines from the *De Rerum natura* already echoed, as we saw, in Roger Bacon, where Lucretius remarks upon the changing color of a dove's neck and of a peacock's tail as the position of the bird or the observer changes.

Gassendi could not accept, as did so many of his contemporaries, the Aristotelian view that the various colors arise from different mixtures of black and white or light and shade. The only result of such mixtures would merely be varying degrees of grey. But since in fact other colors exist, they must be accounted for. Here Gassendi is understandably vague. He invokes different reflections and refractions which affect the different greys and alter the motions or directions (*tenores*) of the rays, thereby confusing the sensorium and producing in us different color sensations.

We must now turn to the person who first brought Gassendi's speculations to England, the physician Walter Charleton. Shortly after taking his medical degree he received, at the onset of the civil war, the short-lived appointment of physician-in-ordinary to Charles I. After the King's execution Charleton turned his talents, such as they were, to writing on medical and other subjects. In the early 1650s, probably under the influence of Thomas Hobbes, he was attracted to the rival exponents of a "New Philosophy," Descartes and Gassendi. In 1654 appeared Charleton's major work, an attempt to present the views of Gassendi and his atomic theories to the English public. Entitled *Physiologia Epicuro-Gassendo-Charletoniana,* with the subtitle "A Fabrick of Science Natural, upon the Hypothesis of Atoms," the subject is further described on the title-page as "Founded" by Epicurus, "Repaired" by Petrus Gassendus, and "Augmented" by Walter Charleton.[32] The book is a hard read: the English is so dreadfully Latinized that it is almost difficult to tell, at some points, in which language he believed himself to be thinking.

Charleton introduces his section dealing with light and color with an account of early theories, remarking that most of the "sects" seem "as remote from each other, as the Zenith from the Nadir," so he had no need to justify his "Adherence to that more verisimilous Doctrine of

[32] Reprinted in facsimile, with an Introduction by Robert H. Kargon, as *The Sources of Science,* No. 31 (Johnson Reprint Corporation, New York and London, 1966).

Democritus and *Epicurus*,"[33] where the atoms are without color and bodies differ in color owing to their surface textures and their influence upon, or modification of, the rays of light. Those rays, Charleston clearly states, are streams of minute particles either emitted directly from their source or "fountain" or reflected from the surfaces of bodies where they are influenced by the excrescences and cavities found there.

At considerable length Charleton argues, as had Gassendi, against the "*Distinction of Colours* into *Real* or *Inhaerent,* and *False* or only *Apparent,* so much celebrated by the Schools" (*ibid.,* 187, Art. 4). The former are the colors of different opaque bodies; the latter are evanescent colors "such as those in the Rainbow, Parheliaes, Paraselens, the trains of Peacocks, necks of Doves, Mallards, &c." (188, Art. 4). To this category belong the colors produced "by *Prisms* or *Triangular Glasses,* vulgarly called *Fools Paradises,*" which sometimes appear less real than others reputed to be only apparent (188, Art. 5). All these must nevertheless be considered real, "being equally produced by Light and Shadow gradually intermixt."

Charleton sums up his discussion by affirming that the difference between evanescent and "durable" colors is that the former derive from light *refracted* by transparent bodies, while the latter are *reflected* from opaque ones whose surface particles "are of this or that Figure, Ordination, and Disposition." Colors, in any case, are not "inhaering" qualities of bodies (189, Art. 1).

At greater length than might seem necessary Charleton discusses that "so Paradoxical assertion" (those are his words) of Epicurus that there are no colors in the dark. Unaware of the complex nature of light, yet believing that in some fashion white light is "modified" to produce "intermediate" colors (i.e., the chromatic colors between the extremes of white and black), he sets forth his position in words that display, in their Latinate English, his inescapable debt to Aristotle. Since all colors vanish in the absence, "the Amotion or defection of Light," he continues, "we are to observe that it is one thing to be *Actually* Colorate, and another to be only *Potentially,* or to have a *Disposition* to exhibit this or that particular Colour, upon the access of the Producent, Light."

Although we agree that bodies are without color in the dark, yet they retain a capacity "whereby each one, upon the access and sollicitation of Light, may appear clad in this or that particular Colour, respective to the determinate ordination and Position of its superficial particles" (186, Art. 1).

Our disciple of Gassendi does not hesitate to advance his own theory of color. In speaking about what, after Newton's introduction of the word into our language, we call the prismatic *spectrum,* he struggles, not too successfully, to explain the production of color as the result of different

---

[33] Charleton, *Physiologia,* p. 184, Art. 6.

proportions of light mingled with shadow. He ends by confessing that the foundation of his theory of color is "not layed in the rock of absolute Demonstration . . . but in the softer mould of meer *Conjecture*" (196, Art. 10). He adopts, of course, the corpuscular theory of light that Gassendi had put forward but does not pretend to know what are the proper figures and essential qualities of the insensible particles of light, with what kind of motion they are radiated from a luminous source, what are the "determinate" positions and shapes of the reflecting and refracting particles at the surface of opaque or diaphanous bodies "which modifie the Light into this or that species of Colour," or "what are the precise proportions of shadows, interwoven with Light, which disguise it into this or that colour" (197, Art. 10).

Let me justify the space given to Charleton, a figure of far lesser worth than Descartes, Gassendi, and Robert Boyle, with whom I shall conclude. It is through Charleton and Boyle rather than from Gassendi's own writings that Newton was led to a corpuscular theory of light and an atomic theory of matter and—most important of all—the realization that light is the "producent," as Charleton put it, of all color. I do not doubt that it was from Walter Charleton that Newton learned of that "so paradoxical assertion" of Epicurus which was echoed in his first paper: that there are no colors in the dark.

The Honourable Robert Boyle, scion of a notable Anglo-Irish family, was one of the founding Fellows of the Royal Society of London and from the beginning a member of its Council. The year of the Society's foundation (1662) saw the appearance of the second edition of Boyle's *Spring of the Air,* to which was added an appendix with the experiments and table we summarize as "Boyle's Law," relating the pressure and volume of air (at constant temperature) and demonstrating quantitatively the elasticity or "spring" of the air. Two years later Boyle brought out a book that was soon to exert a profound influence upon the young Newton, the *Experiments and Considerations Touching Colours* (1664).

Boyle's book on color is something of a miscellany, a collection of his observations on the many different ways that colors can be observed. His chemical interest is very much in evidence, and there is a section on painter's pigments. Theoretical conjectures are widely scattered. He draws upon Gassendi in a number of places, notably for the corpuscular theory of matter and the corpuscular theory of light. The immediate cause of colors is "the modifi'd Light it self, as it affects the Sensory." Colors are not to be thought of as *inherent* in the object, although light can be influenced by the surface texture of objects and so appear colored when reflected to our eyes.

In Isaac Newton's earliest notebooks we find records of his reading of Boyle on colors, and these records, or at least some of them, are echoed in his classic paper of February 1672 and in the *Opticks* itself. Certain of Boyle's observations Newton adduced in support of his own radical theory of the composite nature of white solar light, for example, the peculiar property of gold leaf (Boyle called it "foliated gold" such as apothecaries used to gild pills), or an infusion of that rare and exotic wood *lignum nephriticum* (nephritic wood), which had the curious characteristic of appearing a different color by reflected and by transmitted light. Boyle suggested that transmitted light was "so Temper'd with Shadow, and Modify'd, that the Eye discern'd no more a Golden Colour, but a Greenish Blew."[34] For Newton, on the other hand, these substances are "apt to reflect one sort of light," i.e., one sort of colorific ray, "and transmit another," as he reported in his paper of February 1672.

Perhaps the most important influence of Boyle on Newton was where the former, in one place, described a prism as "the usefullest Instrument Men have yet imploy'd about the Contemplation of Colours." Again he describes it as "the Instrument upon whose effects we may the most Commodiously speculate the Nature of Emphatical Colours (and perhaps that of others too)." Fully as significant is that he urges his reader to use his prism in a darkened room "not (as is usual) in an ordinary Inlightn'd Room."[35]

V. We may now summarize the state of knowledge of the relation of light to color when Newton came upon the scene. The more emancipated thinkers no longer believed that colors have an independent external existence or that they are inherent "qualities" or "forms" that light merely makes visible. The artificial distinction between "real" and "emphatical" colors has been abandoned. Light is increasingly thought to be material or the activity of a material substrate, as in the theories of Descartes and later of Robert Hooke, whose "wave" or pulse theory of light was set forth in his *Micrographia* (1665). Both recognized, as Newton too made clear in his *Opticks,* that color, in any case, was not an objective reality but a subjective response of our visual equipment. Light was increasingly understood to be the chief causative agent of our sensation of color. Aristotle's venerable explanation that the chromatic colors derived from a varied mixture of the two "fundamental" colors, black and white, was still very much alive, expressed most often as the mixture of light and shadow. The colors seen on the surface of bodies, or produced by refraction, result from an alteration or *modification* of the pure, homogeneous light of the sun, generally when the light is mixed with shadow. It will be one of Newton's chief objectives in his *Opticks* to show by various experiments that this hypothesis is untenable.

That light is the principal agent in the production of our color sensation was implied by the ancient atomists, as recorded in the fragment of Epicurus *Against Theophrastus* and in Lucretius's great poem when

[34] Boyle, *Experiments,* 198-99.
[35] *Ibid.,* 191.

writing of the color changes in the neck of a dove or the tail of a peacock. As we saw, this Lucretian passage left its imprint on Roger Bacon and was quoted by Pierre Gassendi and Walter Charleton. Robert Hooke, the first to publish careful observations on the rings of color observed in thin films and plated bodies—"Newton's rings" we call them—saw a similarity between these rings and "the Colours in Peacocks, or other Feathers," but recognized that these color phenomena could better be studied in the plates of "Muscovy glass" (mica), where he had observed them, since "this laminated body is more simple and regular . . . and more manageable, to be divided or joyned, then [sic] the parts of a Peacocks feather."[36]

Newton went further than mentioning a mere similarity between the colored rings observed in thin films and the spectacle of a peacock's tail. He would seem to have carried out experiments on the colored rings independently of Hooke and with an ingenuity and degree of precision that justifies our naming the rings after him. In one of his early notebooks Newton recorded that, in observing the colors produced by a thin film of air between two glasses, he found that the colored rings appeared greater the more obliquely he observed them. Later, when taking notes on Hooke's *Micrographia,* he recalled his earlier observation, adding the comment: "The more oblique position of ye eye to ye glasse makes ye coloured circles dilate."[37] Long after, Newton devoted the greater part of Book Two of the *Opticks* to the ring phenomenon in thin films or plates, and his early observation on the effect of the angle of vision was elaborated into Observations 7 and 19 of the first Part of that Book. In order to demonstrate that the explanation he put forward had wider applications and could apply to "the parts of all natural Bodies being like so many Fragments of a Plate," Newton gave an example, now familiar to my readers:

The finely colour'd Feathers of some Birds, and particularly those of Peacocks Tails, do in the very same part of the Feather appear of several Colours in several Positions of the Eye, after the same manner that thin Plates were found to do in the 7th and 19th Observations, and therefore their Colours arise from the thinness of the transparent parts of the Feathers; that is, from the slenderness of the very fine Hairs, or *Capillamenta,* which grow out of the sides of the grosser lateral Branches or Fibres of those Feathers.[38]

Cornell University.

---

[36] Hooke *Micrographia,* 49.

[37] Newton's notes "Out of Mr. Hook's Micrographia" were published in Appendix IV of Geoffrey Keynes, *A Bibliography of Dr. Robert Hooke* (Oxford, 1960). See esp. 100, item 48 for Newton's comment, given also in A. Rupert Hall and Marie Boas Hall, *Unpublished Papers of Isaac Newton* (Cambridge, 1962), 403.

[38] *Opticks,* ed. 2, 1717/18, Book II, Part III, 226, where in this edition the bracketed words first appear in English. The Latin *Optice* (1706) had made the change: *et proinde Plumarum istarum Colores,* etc.

Chapter VI

VISUAL SURFACE AND VISUAL SYMBOL: THE MICROSCOPE AND THE OCCULT IN EARLY MODERN SCIENCE.

By Catherine Wilson

Like Vesalius's book of skeletons and muscle-men, Robert Hooke's collection of microscopical observations, the *Micrographia* of 1665, exercises a fascination which cannot be well accounted for by reference to its role in any direct or orderly line of scientific development. Indeed Hooke himself was to complain in 1691 that the microscope had almost gone out of service as a scientific instrument and had fallen into the hands of amateurs. Outside of Leeuwenhoek, he says, "I hear of none that make any other Use of that Instrument, but for Diversion and Pastime, and that by reason it is become a portable Instrument, and easy to be carried in one's pocket." [1] Leeuwenhoek himself communicated no observations to the Royal Society, otherwise the major recipient of his letters between 1682 and 1691,[2] and Hooke's own "Discourse concerning Telescopes and Microscopes" devotes approximately nine pages to the use and importance of the telescope as against two for the microscope. "Most of those who formerly promoted these inquiries," he explains not too helpfully, "are gone off the stage"; his own contemporaries are of the opinion that no more is left to be done, or that nothing can be done which will "bring ready Money." [3]

Reading the *Micrographia* is indeed diversion and pastime: the fine, geometrical rows of fish-scales, the tropical forest, and lunar flowers—in fact the ordinary blue mold that grows on oranges—and Hooke's *pièce de resistance*, the startling cancroid body-louse, reproduced on its own outsized fold-out, are as visually interesting to us as they must have been

Earlier versions of this paper were read at the University of Konstanz and the University of Cambridge in May 1985 and in Hannover in 1986. The author gratefully acknowledges the support of the Alexander von Humboldt-Stiftung in 1984-86 and the National Endowment for the Humanities in 1983. For valuable stimulation and criticism I am indebted to Alexander Rüger and Robert S. Westman; for access to unpublished work, Brian Vickers; for helpful comments, Vickers and Brian P. Copenhaver, the referees for this journal.

[1] *Dr. Hook's Discourse concerning Telescopes and Microscopes; with a short Account of their Inventors*, in R. Hooke, *Philosophical Experiments and Observations*, ed. W. Derham (London, 1967), 257. On amateur interest in the microscope, see M. H. Nicolson, "The Microscope and the English Imagination," in *Science and Imagination* (Ithaca, 1956), 155-234.

[2] A. van Leeuwenhoek, *The Collected Letters*, ed., illust. and annot. by a committee of Dutch scientists (Amsterdam, 1939-). Bilingual Dutch-English edition, now complete through 1696.

[3] Hooke, *Discourse*, 261 ff.

to the first generation of readers. The aesthetic pleasure it offers is only slightly enhanced by the knowledge that *Micrographia* is a landmark in the development of a scientific iconography.[4] Does this fact, one might wonder, provide a clue to the microscope's decline?

Gaston Bachelard, who was uniquely sensitive to the intrusion of the non-cognitive into the domain of positive science, took this position, claiming that the microscope functioned as an actual impediment to knowledge. "Its decisive valorization," he argues, "lay in the discovery of the hidden under the manifest, the rich under the poor, the extraordinary under the ordinary.... In truth," he continues, "it was only a case of spinning out the old dreams with the new images which the microscope delivered. That people sustained such excitement over these images for so long and in such literary form is the best proof that they dreamed with them." [5] What is certainly true is that, shortly after its introduction, the microscope became a vehicle of hopes which it could not conceivably fulfill and that therein lay some of the potential for disappointment which Hooke was later to record.

This failure to connect in an immediately fruitful way with theoretical interests is partly to be explained by the purely technical limitations of the instrument. They were of such a serious nature that the leading expert on its history has stated flatly that the microscope ceased to be a plaything only in the second half of the nineteenth century.[6] In a recent study of Leeuwenhoek's attempts to understand generation, another writer notes that his observations "offered a particularly flagrant example of a simple image exploited by preconceptions," a fact inevitable in light of the "impenetrable smallness that cast an unyielding veil over nature's ultimate modus operandi." [7] But the low resolutive power of Hooke's own compound microscopes, the intrinsic limitations of Leeuwenhoek's simple lenses, and the difficulties in specimen preparation and illumination which plagued early microscopy go only part way to explain its relatively sudden fall from grace. Nor can the actual results achieved—represented primarily by the reports prepared by Leeuwenhoek, de Graaf, Malpighi,

---

[4] The comparison between Hooke's volume and the earlier work of Pierre Borel, *De vero telescopii inventores ... accessit etiam Centuria observationes microscoparum* (2 vols.; The Hague, 1655), with its small, crude illustrations, is especially striking.

[5] G. Bachelard, *La Formation de l'esprit scientifique* (4th ed.; Paris, 1965), 160.

[6] While noting that "it was largely the amateur interest that forced the pace of development" in the later period, G. L'E. Turner argues that lack of improvements in the acuity of Hooke's microscopes before 1830, together with the absence of photographic techniques which could provide an objective, neutral means of communication between researchers, condemned it to a marginal status. "Microscopical Communication," *Journal of Microscopy*, 100 (1974), 5. B. Bracegirdle emphasizes the idiosyncrasy of early preparation, mounting and viewing techniques, and the air of secrecy surrounding them: *A History of Microtechnique* (London, 1978), 9ff.

[7] E. G. Ruestow, "Images and Ideas: Leeuwenhoek's Perception of the Spermatozoa," *Journal of the History of Biology*, 16 (1983) 185-224, 223f.

Swammerdam, and Nehemiah Grew—explain the vigorous philosophical interest which attended the use of the microscope. This interest took a variety of forms ranging from a passionate endorsement of microscopical research to curiosity mixed with skepticism to a determined repudiation. We shall consider these reactions later; my intention is first to establish the epistemological background to the introduction of the microscope, an undatable and not entirely locatable event but presumed by Hooke to have occurred first in Italy in 1625,[8] spreading from there to Holland where the Dutch became the acknowledged masters of lens manufacture and microscopical observation.

I. It has recently been argued by Keith Hutchinson that the success of the corpuscular philosophy is to be explained by the promise it offered of incorporating the so-called "occult qualities," those revealed by their effects rather than by sensory observation, within a uniform and comprehensive framework of explanation.[9] The verbal, disputatious, inconclusive character of scholastic philosophy which its seventeenth-century opponents attacked in the harshest of terms was, on this interpretation, less the effect of an ascetic other-worldliness, a contempt for the world of natural things and their powers, than a sensible restriction to topics and questions that could be handled within the limited framework provided by Aristotelian physics. This physics, with its manifest qualities (hot, cold, wet, dry, color, shape, etc.) and its notorious range of "virtues" (dormitive, fossilizing, purgative, etc.) introduced by later writers, notably Galen and his followers, could only "explain" natural and physiological changes in a manner which came to be regarded as tautological or uninformative. The corpuscular philosophy, however, did not accept the principle that effects whose causes could not be seen fell outside the boundaries of human knowledge. And indeed the "corpuscularians," particularly those of the first post-Cartesian generation in England, were particularly concerned to give "mechanical" explanations both for such "occult" (though from our present point of view non-magical) effects as magnetism, gravity, and the action of drugs as well as such "occult" (and from our point of view, magical) non-effects as the cure of wounds at a distance,[10] telepathy, and so on.

As illuminating as Hutchinson's account is, it bypasses two important

---

[8] Hooke credits the Florentine "Academy of the Lynx" with sponsorship of the first set of systematic observations: *Discourse*, 268. More precise information is given by G. L'E. Turner, "Animadversions on the Originals of the Microscope," in J. D. North and J. J. Roche (eds.), *The Light of Nature: Essays Presented to A. C. Crombie* (Dordrecht, 1985), 193-207.

[9] Keith Hutchinson, "What Happened to Occult Qualities in the Scientific Revolution?" *Isis*, 73 (1982), 233-53.

[10] Walter Charleton and Kenneth Digby are the chief examples; see Hutchinson, *ibid.* 244f.

problems. The first is the relation of the so-called "occult" philosophy to the emerging "mechanical" philosophy. Though the scholastics might have been, as Bacon charged, insufficiently attentive to the world,[11] the anti-scholastic current represented primarily by Paracelsus, Agrippa, and van Helmont had been concerned directly with the "occult" both in the sense of the hidden and in the sense of the magical.[12] It is useful in this context to remember that the reforming treatises of Bacon and later of Boyle present the alchemical philosopher of the Paracelsian tradition as an opponent both more dangerous and more interesting than the school-philosopher.[13] The mechanico-corpuscular philosophy, I should now like to argue as an extension of Hutchinson's thesis, gave a sense to the notion of the interpretation of nature *by non-occult means*, and this constituted its primary advantage over a philosophy which could not interpret nature at all. Here the microscope had a role to play.

Second, a point easily overlooked in concentrating on the reception of corpuscularian theory in the first half of the seventeenth century rather than in the second half, a theoretical commitment to mechanico-corpuscular explanations failed significantly to mesh with the ideals of experimentation and observation simultaneously favored by writers like Descartes, Boyle, and Newton. The simplicity, the generality, and the much-praised intelligibility of the doctrine that all qualitative change depends on alterations in the movement and arrangement of invisible corpuscles were offset by a grave disadvantage, namely, that the micromodels invoked to explain such occult phenomena as magnetism or drug-

[11] The schoolmen, Bacon says, "their wits being shut up in the cells of a few authors (chiefly Aristotle their dictator) as their persons were shut up in the cells of monasteries and colleges ... did out of no great quantity of matter and infinite agitation of wit spin out unto us those laborious webs of learning which are extent in their books...." *Advancement of Learning*, ed. A. Johnson (Oxford, 1974), 27-28. R. Millen has recently argued that certain Aristotelians, notably Pomponazzi and Fracastoro, did perceive the challenge presented by the occult; they achieved no real solution to the problem, however, and Pomponazzi shows a tendency to veer off in the direction of the "hermetic adeptus." "Occult qualities in the scientific revolution," in *Religion, Science, and Worldview: Essays in honor of Richard S. Westfall*, ed. M. J. Osler, P. L. Farber (Cambridge, 1985), esp. 190 ff.

[12] Again traditional classification can create confusion. Fernel, who actually popularized the notion of occult qualities in his *De abditis rerum causis*, printed in 1648, and often thereafter, "still follows Aristotle and Galen extensively." L. Thorndike, *History of Magic and Experimental Science* (8 vols.; New York, 1941), VI, 557. The three "occult" authors named are, by contrast, whatever their dependence on elemental theories, distinguished by their anti-Aristotelian rhetoric. See, P. Zambelli, "Magical and Radical Reformation in Agrippa of Nettesheim," *Journal of the Warburg and Courtauld Institutes*, 39 (1976), 69-103, 77.

[13] Bacon, *Novum Organum*, in *Works*, ed. J. Spedding, R. L. Ellis, D. D. Heath (London, 1860), VI, 65. Boyle, *Skeptical Chemist* (London, 1661), in T. Birch (ed.), *Works* (6 vols.; London, 1772), I, 458-586.

action seemed destined to remain forever hypothetical.[14] What Hooke calls "the real, the mechanical, the experimental Philosophy" dealt, in other words, with fictions. Descartes floundered awkwardly and unsuccessfully with this problem in the closing sections of his *Principles of Philosophy*.[15] It remained serious enough to convince the influential Locke, despite his belief that the corpuscular theory was probably true, that it could not be the basis of a science. For Locke, ordinary sensory "experience," i.e., observation, trial-and-error, is the only route to knowledge of nature.[16] Consideration of the role of the microscope helps to explain why the revival of atomism in the mid-seventeenth century was nevertheless successful even when the Boyle-Descartes version allowed no more practical control over nature and offered no more predictive power than had the original Democritean version or the Lucretian version which had been revived earlier in the Renaissance.

As technically-limited and amateur-infested as it was, the microscope thus had a conceptual role to play which has been ignored in discussions of the epistemological foundations of modern science. This is not to say that the microscope drove out the occult, a claim it would be quite impossible to substantiate historically. Interest in Paracelsian doctrine appeared to wane after a surge in the 1640s and 1650s, while the microscope's hour had not yet come. Only in the rare instance, moreover, is it possible to locate a text in which the use of the microscope is depicted as a rival to occult methods.[17] These facts should not, however, affect the argument of the paper. My claim is that the microscope was an instrument of enablement which permitted its devotees to maintain and extend a Baconian theory of the interpretation of nature. This theory was itself anti-occultist in its insistence on the replacement of the direct "reading" of nature by a dispassionate form of visual inspection coupled with processing by the Baconian inductive "machine." Had the entrance of the lens into modern science been delayed, it is difficult in turn to imagine that philosophers of the late seventeenth century would have addressed themselves so energetically to the problems generated by this shift: the problems of visual perception, of the nature and existence of physical minima, and above all of the theological significance of natural forms. The remainder of the essay is directed to making plausible these claims.

II. The "Interpretation of Nature" is a term employed by Bacon in the context of his persistent attempts to renegotiate the relationship

[14] Cf. R. E. Schofield, "Atomism from Newton to Dalton," *American Journal of Physics*, 49 (1981) 211.

[15] Descartes, *Oeuvres complets*, ed. J. Adam and P. Tannery, (Paris, 1974), IX (2), 321ff.

[16] See below, n. 82ff.

[17] But see below, 14, 19.

between the investigator and the natural world.[18] Bacon works towards this goal quite conspicuously in the *Novum Organum* by a process of triangulation, setting the philosophy of the schools at the end of one axis and the practices and theories of the "empirics" at the other. His chief criticism of the former is the endlessness and unfruitfulness of its results. "Like boys," he says, "it can talk, but it cannot generate." [19] This combination of excess and insufficiency was, he argued, a direct consequence of its withdrawal from the world of things. "For the mind of man, if it work upon matter, which is the contemplation of the creatures of God, worketh according to the stuff and is limited thereby; but if it work upon itself, as the spider worketh its web, then it is endless. . . ."[20] By contrast the alchemist, the physician, and even the astrologer, did leave their cloisters to take on the world. Here again however, his criticism is that they do not submit themselves to limitation from the "stuff."

This second point is the key to Bacon's sweeping attack on the interpretation of nature as practiced by astrologers, soothsayers, and Paracelsian chemists. His argument here turns on the notion of "Anticipation": it is the spontaneous tendency of the mind to shape the world according to its own pre-existing prejudices and desires which determine the content of the false sciences. This "tincture of the will and affections," Bacon thought, in particular the longings for fame, wealth, love, and immortality, imposes on the world an imaginary system of signs or correspondences which the mind then pretends to discover. The false sciences are in this sense like poetry, which "doth raise and direct the mind by submitting the shows of things to the desires of the mind," by contrast with reason, which "doth buckle and bow the mind unto the nature of things."[21]

Bacon's supposition is thus that the false sciences have sought to interpret nature—a praiseworthy aim in itself—but have done so by positing correspondences which do not in fact obtain. A clear example of this is the projection of powers supposed relevant to human destiny onto particular stars and planets. However, his critique is not directed simply at astrology, considered as the assignation of occult powers of influence to the heavenly bodies, but at a range of techniques making use of a certain type of intellectual address to the world. He is attacking not only a set of theories about the natural powers of natural objects (indeed he ascribes to many natural objects powers of a highly "occult"

---

[18] These attempts must be considered independently from the persistence or recrudescence of earlier ideas in his physical theories: cf. G. Rees, "Francis Bacon's Semi-Paracelsian Cosmology," *Ambix*, 22 (1975) 81-105.

[19] *Preface* to the *Great Instauration, Works*, IV, 14.

[20] *Advancement of Learning*, 28.

[21] *Ibid.*, 81, cf. Brian Vickers's attempt to characterize such forms of reasoning in "Analogy vs. Identity: the rejection of occult symbolism 1580-1680," in Vickers (ed.), *Occult and Scientific Mentalities in the Renaissance* (Cambridge, 1984), 95-163.

and magical nature) but an epistemology based on a false estimation of the possibilities of interpretation.[22]

If Bacon was correct, the old Book of Nature was not readable in so many ways as had been thought. "All Herbs, Flowers, Trees, and other things which proceed out of the earth," according to Oswald Croll, the neo-Paracelsian, "are Books and Magic Signs, communicated to us by the immense mercy of God, which Signs are our Medicine."[23] This picture of universal legibility is precisely the one which Bacon rejects. Astrological medicine, divination, the deciphering of plant "signatures"—all of these procedures which fall under the general heading of the occult—have in common the fact that they seek to extract information about what cannot directly be seen (future fortune and misfortune, the outcome of a disease, the hidden virtues of an herb) from the visible patterning of natural objects. The heavens, as Paracelsus claims, demand a certain type of decoding. "Just as a man reads a book on paper, so the physician is compelled to spell out the stars of the firmament in order to know his conclusions. . . . It is like a letter which has been sent to us from a hundred miles off, and in which the writer's mind speaks to us. . . ."[24]

This "semiotic" conception of nature helps to explain the much-remarked "obscurity" of Paracelsian writing, its gestural quality, the curious curtailment of the didactic intention. These correspond precisely to the stress of the role of personal involvement with the objects of nature—stars, herbs, the "signs" turned up by the arts of geomancy, chiromancy, of divination by the flight of birds and the swarming of bees, the changes of color and texture in the chemist's glass. For Paracelsus, it is nature herself, the wisest of teachers, who provides the text; the role of the writer is only to give hints which may help others to read for themselves. To write or to depict in a way which is transparently instructional is to usurp her role; the true sciences cannot be written down without becoming dead letter.[25] The things we need to know are disguised; that is one way in which God displays his power. Yet they are not wholly impenetrable mysteries; they require simply a careful, sensitive, spiritually informed reading of the book of nature, which will determine the rela-

---

[22] Bacon's own philosophical writings are, to be sure, powerfully enhanced by the parables, metaphors, and other literary devices whose use in scientific contexts he thoroughly condemns. On Bacon's imagery see Vickers, *Francis Bacon and Renaissance Prose* (Cambridge, 1968), esp. Ch. 6.

[23] O. Croll, *Preface to the Reader*, "Of Signatures," in *Bazilica Chymica* (London, 1670). On Croll, see M. Foucault, *The Order of Things* (New York, 1973), Ch. 2; O. Hannaway, *The Chemists and the Word* (Baltimore, 1975).

[24] Paracelsus, *Saemtliche Werke*, ed. K. Sudhoff (Munich, 1922-25), XI, 176, tr. N. Guterman, in Paracelsus, *Selected Writings*, ed. J. Jacobi (London, 1951), 159.

[25] See O. Temkin, "The Elusiveness of Paracelsus," *Bulletin of the History of Medicine*, 26 (1952), 241ff.

tionship between external "differentiation" and internal virtue. It is "signatures" which provide a point of cognitive access.

"Experience" in Paracelsian epistemology refers thus not merely to simple sensory familiarity, but to the cognitive identification with the object of knowledge achieved through insight; the learning of the physician is described as a faint "echo," an "overhearing" of the *scientia* which teaches scammony how to purge or pear trees how to grow pears. Nature is instructed by God: she "shines as a light from the Holy Ghost," Paracelsus says, "and learns from Him and thus this light reaches man as in a dream."[26]

It is clear why Paracelsus claims that knowledge of the occult—the hidden powers of nature—must be sought in ways that are occult,[27] that is, in ways which cannot be directly taught. Both Agrippa and van Helmont stress with him that the discursive, sequential thought of school-philosophy is incapable of reaching to the inner essences of things. "Every kind of true science or intellectual knowledge," Helmont states, "is not to be demonstrated." Discourse and "reason" only serve to imprint opinions already established; they cannot lead to "things not had." These can only be acquired by "invention or gift."[28] Agrippa describes the acquisition of knowledge in *De occulta philosophia* as "non successione, non tempore, sed subitaneo momente quod cupit assequitur"—the mind grasping in an instant what it seeks[29]—and Helmont speaks of the understanding which "partakes of an unlimited light, is perfected without weariness and labour."[30]

The ideal to be achieved is quite explicitly the knowledge ascribed to the angels by the Christian theologians.[31] Our understanding, St. Thomas comments, by combining or distinguishing concepts, by reasoning from premises to conclusions, is due to the "dimness of the intellectual light in our souls."[32] The angel by contrast is a "pure and brilliant mirror" who sees "manifold things in a simple way; and change in an unchanging way."[33] Thus, setting aside for the moment the differences in epistemology

---

[26] "*De Fundamento scientarum sapientaeque*," in Jacobi (ed.), *Selected Writings*, 255 (*Saemtliche Werke*, I, 13, 325). See W. Pagel, *Paracelsus* (Basel, 1982), 50

[27] *Ibid.*

[28] J. B. van Helmont, *Oriatrike or Physik Refin'd.*, J[ohn] C[handler] (London, 1619), 26.

[29] Agrippa, *De occulta philosophia*, Bk. III, Ch. 53.

[30] *Oriatrike*, 26.

[31] "The soul," says Agrippa, freed of disturbing influences, "needs neither memory nor instruction, but by her understanding ... emulates the angels" (Agrippa, *De occulta philosophia, loc. cit.*).

[32] St. Thomas Aquinas, "How an Angel's Mind Functions," in *Summa Theologica*, XIV, 149. He cites in turn (151) St. Augustine and pseudo-Dionysus, who describes the angels as gathering their knowledge not from "scattered discourses," but by immediate intuition; their intelligence is "alight with the penetrating simplicity of divine concepts."

[33] *Ibid.*, 155.

between these representatives of the occult, we can detect a common theme: the scholastic restriction of human knowledge, as against angelic knowledge, to what can be achieved through logic, the "combining and distinguishing of concepts," is unnecessary and illegitimate. How, in turn, non-discursive knowledge is to be won—whether through Paracelsian "overhearing," through Croll's reading of divine visual language, Helmont's inspired trance states, or Agrippa's and Ficino's explorations of micro-macrocosmic relations with the help of analogy, intuition, and the relics of an enlightened antiquity—varies with the author.

III. The seventeenth century is alleged to be the period in which the occult sciences just discussed were, if not eliminated from the corpus of human wisdom, at any rate segregated from more honored forms of scientific inquiry. Yet this alleged progress was hardly steady or uniform. As Charles Webster has shown, the England of the 1640s and 1650s experienced a dramatic revival of Paracelsianism, evidently because its prophetic, visionary, and anti-authoritarian messages answered to a political state of civil war and violent conflict among radical sects.[34] Elizabeth Eisenstein has suggested in turn that the spread of printing resulted in a flood of occult literature, many earlier works being translated into English for the first time and finding a receptive audience.[35] A work which documents the mid-century interest in the occult as part of the drive for educational reform is John Webster's attack on the Universities, the *Academiarum Examen* of 1654. For this outspoken writer, as for Robert Fludd before him, the semiotic approach was to serve as an instrument of enlightenment against the oppression of the Schools.

In this strenuous attack on the Universities, Webster, a puritan divine, argues that the scholastic curriculum has stifled knowledge, demands the elimination of the "rotten and ruinous fabrick of Aristotle and Ptolemy" and calls for the introduction of the works of, among others, Bacon, Fludd, Croll, Gassendi, Kepler, and Descartes, into university teaching.[36] Special criticism is directed by Webster at the study of "grammar," by which he appears to mean not only the structure of actual languages, but formal modes of reasoning, argument construction, and so on. In its place he recommends that "probable, pleasant, and useful ... Hieroglyphic, Emblematic, Symbolic and Cryptographical Learning."[37] After

---

[34] C. Webster, *From Paracelsus to Newton* (Cambridge, 1982). See also A. S. Debus, *The English Paracelsians*, (London, 1965).

[35] E. Eisenstein, *The Printing Press as an Agent of Change* (Cambridge, 1979), II, 471ff.

[36] *Academiarum Examen* (London, 1654), reprinted in A. G. Debus, *Science and Education in Seventeenth-Century England* (London, 1970), 78 *et passim*.

[37] *Ibid.*, 24. The notion that learning should be pleasant suggests the influence of Comenius, for whom the world is as a "garden" or a "theater" for the delight of youth "who have been so much vexed" by their schoolmasters, but Comenius stresses direct

the manner of Fludd, who had published his own attack on the Academies in 1617, Webster contrasts the "dead paper idolls of creaturely-invented letters" with the "legible characters that are only written and impressed by the finger of the Almighty." The Schools, he complains, are ignorant of the science of "physiognomy," which alone "doth explicate the internal nature and qualities of natural bodies ..." and so teach us "all the salutary and morbidifick lineaments."[38] Living things are "not as mute statues but as living and speaking pictures, not as dead letters, but as Preaching Symbols."[39] He goes on to contrast the "vulgar anatomy and dissection of the dead bodies of men" of Harvey with the "vive and Mystick Anatomy" which alone can penetrate to the causes and cures of disease.[40]

Seth Ward and John Wilkins, speaking for the University, spare no adjectives in their reply, attacking what they call "that canting Discourse about the language of Nature." Webster's admiration for "the Rosicrucians," for Robert Fludd and Jakob Böhme, they maintain, "may sufficiently convince what kind of credulous, fanatick reformer he is likely to prove." Webster's desire to decode the true language of nature, his interest in Hieroglyphs and cryptography, is vigorously attacked. Codes, they suggest, are human inventions made for an explicit purpose: one cannot achieve insight into the secrets of nature by studying Hieroglyphs.[41] Webster, they charge, is incapable of telling the difference between mathematical symbols, the notations of Vieta, Oughtred, and Heridon, and charms and magic signs.[42] He even confuses the fantastic idea of the recovery of the original "Adamic" language, which expressed the true natures of things, with the noble and fully achievable proposal of Wilkins to invent a universal scientific characteristic.[43] Finally, Webster's indiscriminate references to all self-professed reformers show that he has understood none of them. "There are not two waies in the whole World more opposite," Wilkins and Ward state, "than those of the L. Verulam and D. Fludd"; one is a philosophy based on "experiment,"

---

contact with objects; the world is not to be seen "obscurely, perplexedly, and intricately, as if it were a complicated riddle." *The Great Didactic* (1658) (London, 1777), 230.

[38] *Academiarum Examen*, 74.

[39] *Ibid.*, 28. Fludd himself distinguishes between the Egyptian hieroglyphs "whose letters, images and characters are artificial, superficial, like shadows of real things, and the products of human invention," and the things of nature, the "celestial hieroglyphs," which are "not superficial, imaginary, or dead but on the contrary, substantial, real and living." *Tractatus Apologeticus* (London, 1617), 45.

[40] *Ibid.*, 74.

[41] *Vindiciae Academiarum*, in Debus, *Science and Education*, 18.

[42] *Ibid.*, 19. This debate is reminiscent in many ways of the earlier Fludd-Kepler controversy on the role of geometry and geometrical symbolism in the description of the cosmos. See R. S. Westman, "Nature, Art, and Psyche," in Vickers (ed.), *Occult and Scientific Mentalities*, 177-229.

[43] *Ibid.* 25.

the other upon "Mystical Ideal Reasons."[44] We have already seen a sample of Bacon's anti-magical rhetoric: it is now time to examine this confidently asserted distinction.

We need to remark from the outset that the Baconian ideal of scientific knowledge embraced a number of competing models. Both pure, undistorted, direct reception and the elaborated, indirect, tortured "vexing" of nature furnish Bacon with metaphors for the acquisition of knowledge. And both conceptions of the acquisition of knowledge might be contrasted with the winning of knowledge through "occult" methods, through reception distorted by subjective desires. For although the full process of a Baconian Induction can only appear baroque and fantastic to the modern reader, it is essential to remember the radical nature of what it proposed: a route to the occult proceeding by way of the "combining and distinguishing of concepts." The process is one which Bacon describes as the mental equivalent of the physical manipulation of the chemist; as mental equivalent, however, it can dispense with certain of the psychological elements of chemical theory.

Thus the Baconian "waie of experiment" furnishes the "mental alchemy" required to effect "a separation and solution of bodies not indeed by fire, but by the mind," which will in turn "bring to light the true textures and configurations of bodies; on which all the occult, and, as they are called, specific properties and virtues in things depend."[45] The work demands a regime and a discipline; the investigator's exchanges with his subject matter are not—as Webster, for one, hoped—accelerated and intensified, made easy, pleasant, or psychologically meaningful. The vexing out of the Form of Heat, which occupies twenty-eight pages of the *Novum Organum*, generalizes, weakens, and abstracts his bond with this fascinating property of the sun, feathers, fires, damp lime, and living bodies. Only then is he capable of recognizing the relatively dull and colorless but, as Bacon recognizes, productive truth that "heat is a motion, expansive, restrained and acting in its strife upon the smaller particles of bodies."[46]

Yet this same Baconian investigator can at times be a pure and brilliant mirror, an angel and not a torturer. All that is required is that he free himself from the domination of idols of the understanding, whether the linguistic idols of the schools, the idols of the theater represented by the men with theories, or the distorting power of the emotions. "All depends," Bacon says, "on keeping the eye steadily fixed upon the facts of nature and receiving their images simply as they are."[47] Elsewhere he speaks of himself as "dwelling purely and constantly among the facts of

---

[44] *Ibid.*, 46.
[45] Bacon, *Works*, IV, 125.
[46] *Ibid.*, 154.
[47] *Ibid.*, 32f.

nature,"[48] withdrawing his intellect from them "no further than may suffice to let the images and rays of natural objects meet in a point."[49] It is true that Bacon considered mere sense-perception—even instrument assisted sense-perception—inadequate for obtaining the profounder sort of knowledge of nature. This demands, he says, the mediating role of experiment, "wherein the sense decides touching the experiment only, and the experiment touching the point in nature and the thing itself."[50] But there is no mistaking the call for what Svetlana Alpers calls "attentive looking."[51] The greatest hindrance and aberration to the human understanding, Bacon claimed, writing before the development of the microscope, was constituted by the "dullness, incompetency, and deceptions of the senses."[52]

Once the microscope became available, the rhetoric essential for justifying its introduction as an instrument of scientific reform was thus, largely thanks to Bacon, in place and ready for application. The introductory prefaces of both Hooke and Henry Power demonstrate that both have grasped the lessons of the *Novum Organum*. Knowledge of the occult is indeed power—for as Bacon had said, "whosoever is acquainted with the Forms, embraces the unity of nature in substances the most unlike—and is able therefore to detect and bring to light things never yet done."[53] But to achieve knowledge of them, one must correctly diagnose the sources of error and distortion and correct and master them. The use of "artificial helps and instruments," by which Bacon understood primarily artificial methods, is now interpreted by Hooke and Power as referring quite literally to optical devices.

So Hooke begins his *Preface* to the *Micrographia* with a diagnosis of the deficiences of our mental powers, devoting special attention to the inadequacies of our sense-organs relative to those of other creatures. The *"disproportion of the Object to the Organ,"* the vastness of nature and the smallness of its parts, our errors of perception together with the defects of memory threaten to render all of our succeeding works in vain and uncertain.[54] "Not having a full sensation of the Object," he says, "we must be very lame and imperfect in our conceptions about it, and in all the propositions which we build upon it; hence we often take the *shadow* of things for the *substance*, small *appearances* for good *similitudes, similitudes* for *definitions."*[55] What we take to be "definitions" are

[48] *Ibid.,* 19.
[49] *Ibid.*
[50] *Ibid.,* 58.
[51] Alpers, *The Art of Describing* (Chicago, 1985), Ch. 3.
[52] Bacon, *Works,* IV, 58.
[53] *Ibid.,* 120.
[54] *Micrographia: or some Physiological Descriptions of Minute Bodies made by Magnifying Glasses with Observation and Inquiries thereupon* (1665) (Edinburgh, 1894), vi.
[55] *Ibid.,* vif.

"rather expressions of our own misguided apprehensions then [sic] of the true nature of the things themselves."[56] The *"forces of our own minds,"* he says, "conspire to betray us."[57] The first steps to establishing a true philosophy are, then, a *"watchfulness over the failings and an enlargement of the dominions of the senses."*[58] To this end we require first "a *scrupulous* choice and a *strict examination* of the reality, constancy, and certainty of the Particulars; second, a supplying of the infirmities of the sense-organs with instruments," the adding of *"artificial Organs* to the *natural."*[59] By this means we come to discover "the subtlety of composition of Bodies, the structure of their parts, the various texture of their matter, the instruments and manner of their inward motions . . . from which," he continues,

there may arise many admirable advantages towards the increase of the *Operative,* and the *Mechanick* Knowledge, to which this Age seems so much inclined, because we may perhaps be enabled to discover all the secret workings of Nature, almost in the same manner as we do those that are the productions of Art, and are manag'd by Wheels, and Engines and Springs. . . .[60]

Hooke's rhetoric is ostensibly directed against the "Philosophy of *discourse* and *disputation,"* devised by the "luxury of subtil Brains" belonging to the Aristotelians. He does not consider it appropriate or necessary to argue, as had Bacon, against the methods employed by Paracelsians. But his push toward "Operative Knowledge" and his claim that the microscope gives access to "all the secret workings of Nature"— workings in which the school philosophy was frankly uninterested or which it considered dangerous or inappropriate to investigate—establish this link. Hooke's vision of the microscope as an instrument which binds knowledge to power and so permits a control of the forces of nature is Bacon's old dream.[61]

So the microscope figures as the central fixture in what Hooke refers to as "the universal cure of the mind," and the same image of the microscope as the instrument of conceptual salvation figures in the writing of Hooke's colleague, Henry Power, who maintains that without the assistance of the microscope "our best philosophers will prove but empty conjecturalists, and their profoundest speculations herein, but glos'd out-

[56] *Ibid.,* vii.
[57] *Ibid.*
[58] *Ibid.,* viii.
[59] *Ibid.*
[60] *Ibid.,* ix.
[61] On knowledge and power in Bacon see esp. P. Rossi, *Francis Bacon: from Magic to Science,* tr. S. Rabinovitch (London, 1968), Ch. 1.

side fallacies, like our Stage scenes or perspectives that show things inward when they are but superficial. . . ."[62]

Power presumably means to indicate that the mechanical philosophy itself constitutes mere empty conjecture unless it can be given substance by "Dioptrical assistance"; the "Modern Engine," as he calls the microscope, will enable us to see "what the illustrious wits of the Atomical and Corpuscularian Philosophers durst but imagine."[63] The evocations are again directly Baconian. With our "Artificial eyes" we may eventually hope to observe the magnetical effluviums, particles of air and ether, the motion of fluid bodies, and "those infinite, insensible Corpuscles which daily produce those prodigious (though common) effects amongst us."[64] As the telescope, Power suggests, freed men from futile speculation about the heavenly bodies on the basis of analogy,[65] so the microscope by bringing the invisible within reach of the senses—and so of experimental manipulation—will free men from the mythologies they have constructed to explain the unseen.

In addition to a clarification of the mysteries of action-at-a-distance, for example, magnetism and gravity, and the seemingly spontaneous changes within substances, the microscope suggested, first provisionally, then, after Leeuwenhoek, definitively, the possibility of understanding reproduction and growth as a sub-class of these spontaneous internal changes.[66]

What had been for the Renaissance chemist an *explanans* thus achieved the status of a potential *explanandum*.[67] Hooke, along with others, might continue to believe that inanimate bodies such as stones grew in the farmer's fields, but he abandoned fully the occult use of the metaphors of generation and reproduction as fundamental categories for the interpretation of nature. Even before Leeuwenhoek's observations of spermatozoa, however, such a use for the lens is proposed by Wilkins and Ward, attacking John Webster's proposal to discover the "signatures of the invisible Archeus"—perhaps a reference to Fludd's teaching that seeds contain or are *"scripturae et characteres invisibles."* "The schematisms of nature in matters of sensible bulk," Ward indicates, "have been observed amongst us and collections made of them in our inquiries,

---

[62] H. Power, *Experimental Philosophy* (London, 1664), Preface. (Power is known for his poem in praise of the microscope, which is transcribed by T. Cowles in *Isis*, 21 [1934], 70ff.) Bacon had described "all the received systems" as "so many stage-plays, representing worlds by their own creation after an unreal and scenic fashion" (*Works*, IV, 55).

[63] Power, *Experimental Philosophy*, Preface.

[64] *Ibid.*

[65] *Ibid.*

[66] See esp. Ruestow, "Images and Ideas" (n. 7 above).

[67] This is not to say that Leeuwenhoek's research supported mechanical epigenesis; the hope of philosophers like Leibniz was that the microscope would favor a (no less-mechanical but vastly more plausible) preformationism.

and ... when the microscope be brought to the highest, whence it is apace arriving, we shall be able to give the seminall figures of things which regulate them in their production and growth."[68]

For Hooke and Power the microscope was critical for what both (though Power denies that Adam's vision was actually sharper than that of modern man)[69] present as the reestablishment of a conceptual empire, the restitution of what Bacon called "that commerce between the mind of man and the nature of things," corrupted by time. For it permitted a glimpse into what Bacon described as a "new visible World"—and so a world utterly unspoiled by theory, by "dreams of Opinions," by the "work of the Brain and Fancy." The microscopical world was unknown to Aristotle, uninvaded by scholastics, and unguessed at by the philosophers of the occult. It lay waiting to be discovered, as simple and uncorrupted as the other New World, and served in the same manner as a focus for utopian plans, projects, and hopes. By the addition of "artificial Instruments and methods," Hooke reports, "there may be, in some manner, a reparation made for the mischiefs, and imperfection, mankind has drawn upon itself, by negligence, and intemperance, and a willful and superstitious deserting the Prescripts and Rules of Nature, whereby every man, both from a derived corruption, innate and born within him, and from his breeding and converse with men, is very subject to slip into all sorts of errors."[70] In this revealing passage, in which the microscope is proposed as a means of release from an original sin, the return to nature's "Prescripts and Rules" is opposed to the corrupted commerce which is all that human history has achieved. It is of little actual importance for our purposes whether Hooke sincerely believed the use of artificial optical instruments was a gesture of moral purity. He may simply be adhering to convention in an age which often preferred to represent genuine novelties as non-innovative. What is interesting is that such rhetoric is brought into play when the justification of new techniques and procedures for the interpretation of nature is in question.

Hooke's own claim that the reformation of philosophy was less dependent on "strength of Imagination and exactness of Method" or "depth of Contemplation" than on "a sincere Hand and a faithful Eye, to examine, and to record, the things themselves as they appear"[71] and the tacit presumption of the *Micrographia* itself that the depiction and verbal description of the visually differentiating qualities of things constitutes itself a desirable form of knowledge, show how the Baconian rejection of theory might assume extreme forms. Svetlana Alpers is right to suggest

[68] Wilkins and Ward, *Vindiciae Academiarum*, 35.

[69] Power, *Experimental Philosophy*, Preface.

[70] Hooke, *Micrographia*, Preface, 5. Cf. Bacon on reparation through science, *Works*, IV, 247.

[71] Hooke, *Micrographia*, Preface, 9.

a parallel between the interest of the Dutch painters of the seventeenth century in reproducing exactly, often with the help of the lens, the surface textures of cloth, mirrors, glasses, insects, fur, and feathers, and the interest of the first generation of microscopists in studying and reproducing the appearances of everyday objects and substances—dust, hair, cloth, household pests, and so on. As Dutch art tends to extinguish the moral lesson in painting, to efface the significance of the unique historical event by contrast with what happens everyday, presenting instead ordinary things in all their likelihood, so too the microscope leads to a kind of displacement, attention to visual surface substituting for attention to the symbolic meaningfulness of the object.[72]

Both Hooke and Power believed, however, that the microscope would lead to a full understanding of the processes of nature; the mere possession of images clearly did not fulfill the Baconian ambition of the possession of Forms, with its promise of power over nature. Hooke himself is suspicious of an iconography which, by merely revealing outward form and beauty, fills the mind with misleading ideas. Such illustrations belong elsewhere; the trouble with the ancients, he says, with Aristotle and Pliny, was that, although they described natural things, we find "a needless insisting upon the outward Shape and Figure, or Beauty or else of some Magical and superstitious effects Producible by us" aimed at creating pleasure, divertisement, admiration, and wonder "but not such a knowledge of Bodies as might tend to practice."[73] But Hooke's problem—the problem of early microscopy in general—was to answer the objection that this look at the inner workings of things was in fact only a new form of looking at their surfaces, no more capable of binding knowledge and power into one than the older, naive, unassisted form of sense-perception.

Thus Hooke attempts by way of compensation to transform microscopical observation into something else: into geometry or grammar. In his *Preface* he suggests, for example, that the microscope will result in an "alphabet" for the expression of complex forms: "As in geometry we begin with bodies of the most simple nature," he writes, "so we need begin with *letters* before we try to write *sentences* or draw pictures." Beginning with "Fluidity, Orbiculation, Fixation, and Angularization, or Crystalization," we may proceed all the way to "Germination . . . Vegetation, Plant Animation, Animation, Sensation and finally . . . Imagination." From the forms of crystals we may move to those of mushrooms, thence to plants in general and so on, "these several inquiries having no

---

[72] Alpers, *Art of Describing, ibid.* The comparison is not farfetched. Berkeley, in the course of criticizing the "minute philosopher" draws the contrast between the Italian and the Dutch manners of painting to develop a point. *Alciphron*, in *Works*, ed. A. A. Luce and T. E. Jessop (London, 1950), III, 49.

[73] *A General Scheme of Idea of the Present State of Natural Philosophy and How Its Defects May be Remedied*, in *Posthumous Works of Robert Hooke* (London, 1705), 4.

less dependence on one another than any select number of propositions in Mathematical Elements may be made to have."[74]

Micrographia begins, in fact, in the best Euclidean spirit, with the observation of the point of a household needle.[75] No more rapid subversion of a program conceived *a priori* is imaginable, for under the microscope this simplest of things appears blunt, pitted, and scarred. Equally disturbing to one engaged in the search for the alphabet of forms was the simple variability of the image, the problem of knowing exactly what was being seen and how to describe it. Thus Hooke writes:

it is exceedingly difficult in some Objects to distinguish between a *prominency* and a *depression*, between a *shadow* and a *black stain*, or a *reflection* and a *whiteness in the color*. Besides, the transparency of most Objects renders them yet much more difficult than if they were *opacous*. The Eyes of a Fly in one kind of light appears almost like a Lattice, drill'd through with abundance of small holes. . . . In the Sunshine they look like a Surface cover'd with golden Nails, in another posture, like a Surface cover'd with Pyramids; in another with Cones. . . .[76]

So it might seem that a program of "attentive looking" could only begin and end with attentive looking.

IV. It is not surprising, given these difficulties, to find the microscope represented in late seventeenth-century literature as a useless instrument, and microscopy as a trivial, time-wasting, or intrinsically comical pursuit. Three separate sources of criticism are identifiable: first, a satirically-minded popular culture; second, the medical establishment; third, epistemologically-concerned philosophers.

Sir Nicholas Gimcrack, the hero of Thomas Shadwell's play *The Virtuoso* of 1676, is a product of the first source. Gimcrack, who has "spent two thousand pounds in microscopes to find out the Nature of eels in vinegar, mites in a cheese, and the blue of plums," and "broken his brains about the nature of maggots. . ."[77] is given one of Hooke's own speeches from the *Micrographia* which sustains the comedy. While the absorption of the learned in their subject is always potentially comic (because of all that they do not see), the microscope and its subjects had none of the redeeming features of the telescope; and squinting at mites, dust, and decaying cheese is a different matter from contemplating the moon, stars, and planets—objects which are "high" rather than "low," powerful, and mysterious rather, than small, dirty, and troublesome. It was perhaps for this reason that Swammerdam suffered from such fundamental doubt about the value of his work. The conflict between his

---

[74] *Micrographia*, 127.
[75] *Ibid.*, 1.
[76] *Ibid.*, 23.
[77] Shadwell, *The Virtuoso*, ed. M. H. Nicolson and D. S. Rodes (Lincoln, 1966), 22.

love of insects and of microscopical work and the disapproval of his
father, together with his own scruples about the sin of "curiositas,"
eventually led to a collapse in which he sold his collections for an absurd
price and underwent conversion to a radical religious order.[78] And the
same suspicion of triviality or worse destroyed Malpighi's relations with
the surrounding medical community.

Malpighi, whose microscopical studies were carried out under the
auspices of the Royal Society but who lived in a country in which a
traditional medical faculty enjoyed high prestige, experienced sharp opposition. His house was set on fire, and in 1689 his chief rival issued a
tract which Malpighi, in his reply, described as an attempt by a member
of the "empirical sect" to "damn anatomical exercises carried out with
the microscope *ad minima* on man, animals, and plants, [which] censures
and ridicules them as useless and as abortuses of the mind's unlawful
desires."[79] This tract, which Malpighi had reprinted and sent to Boyle
with a reply, is worth a closer look: Sbaraglia, a medical professor at
Bologna, points out in his critique of his opponent that microscopical
anatomy does not contribute to a knowledge of the function of organs,
but only furnishes greater detail. Examination of the lining of the lungs
tells us nothing about the process or use of respiration, just as the visual
study of the brain leaves epilepsy, catalepsy, and dizziness as problematic
as before. Nor is micro-anatomy of any use for pharmacy; the hidden
virtues of plants cannot be discovered by observation alone. "The schools
do not profit from the virtue of the seed of the white poppy because the
eye armed with its microscope has seen that its surface is provided with
many square, pentagonal, and hexagonal figures."[80] As broken bones are
set by the surgeon and heal without our understanding how this takes
place, medicine does not require and cannot obtain theoretical knowledge.
It is specific remedies, gathered from experience, which are needed.

In his reply Malpighi appeals to the Cartesian conception of the body
as a machine composed of invisible sub-machines. Subtle anatomy teaches
us the "cords, filaments, beams, levers, tissues, fluids . . . cisterns, canals,
filters, and sieves of the body," and enables us to form models of them
by means of which the causes of bodily changes can be demonstrated *a*

[78] On Swammerdam's troubles, see H. Boerhaave, *Life of Swammerdam*, in *Book of
Nature*, tr. T. Flloyd (London, 1758). The Augustinian injunction against "curiositas"
was not infrequently directed against the use of the lens. Francis Quarles, for example,
uses optical conceits to stress the value of self-examination as against the examination
of nature (*Emblems* [1635], no. 35). On theological encouragement and discouragement
of natural history, see C. Glacken, *Traces on the Rhodian Shore* (Berkeley, 1973), passim.

[79] G. Sbaraglia, *De recentiorum medicorum studio dissertatio . . .* in H. B. Adelman,
Marcello Malpighi and the Evolution of Embryology, (Ithaca, 1966), I, 556. On the
empiricist/dogmatist controversy in the history of medicine see C. Daremberg, *Histoire
des sciences médicales*, (Paris, 1870), II, 170ff.

[80] *Ibid.*, 563.

priori. Here he cites the *camera obscura* as a model for the visual system and models which demonstrate the nature of blood pressure, the actions of the joints and the workings of the thorax. Interestingly, he goes on to raise the counter-charge of occultism, arguing that it is useless to spend time investigating "the archeus, the sympathies, the archeal diseases, universal medicine, and other strange fantasies which hide the weakness of a totally abstract philosophizing."[81] The specific secret remedies which Sbaraglia wants can only be got from "empirics," who in turn can only get them from "signatures"—a worthless procedure.

Malpighi's conception of scientific activity as involving a succession of movements upwards and downwards between observation and idealized hypothetical models is deeper and more plausible than Power's dream of observing corpuscular interactions directly or Hooke's ambition to construct an alphabet of forms. Moreover, it puts the traditional contrast between rationalist and empiricist trends in seventeenth-century science in a doubtful light. Here, techniques of close observation are bound together with a preexisting commitment to Cartesianism. This suggests that in the late seventeenth century "Empiricism" stood for the claim not that all true knowledge is acquired through sensory experience but that all true knowledge is acquired *through ordinary unassisted sensory experience.* Both the value of artificial enhancement of the senses and the corresponding proposal of hypotheses are rejected as a package.

In this way we can grasp the connection between Locke's anti-rationalism and his anti-microscopical bias. In Book II of the *Essay Concerning Human Understanding*, Locke argues that ". . . if by the help of . . . microscopical eyes (if I may so call them), a man could penetrate further than ordinary into the secret composition and radical texture of bodies, he would not make any great advantage by the change, if such an acute sight would not serve to conduct him to the market and the exchange." It is all very well to peer into the interior of a clock to inspect the minute particles of its spring, but not if the acuteness of the owner makes him unable to tell the time.[82] Locke goes on to consider the case of "spirits" which could adapt their organs of sight so as to see "the figure and motion of the minute particles in the blood and other juices of animals," concluding that this would "perhaps, be of no advantage." For "God has no doubt, made us so as is best for us in our present condition."[83] When in Book IV he discusses the limits of our knowledge of "Substances," it is painfully clear that the subject of the chapter is a struggle between Locke's allegiance to Boyle, representing an hypothetical, corpuscular, but also "experimental" science, and his allegiance to

---

[81] *Ibid.*, 575.
[82] Locke, *Essay Concerning Human Understanding*, ed. A. C. Fraser (Edinburgh, 1894), II, 100.
[83] *Ibid.*

his old teacher Sydenham, representing a sincere and sympathetic, but traditionally "empiricist," anti-theoretical approach to medicine.[84] Though a number of writers have seen in Locke's crusade against Aristotelian "essences" the origins of a distinctively modern conception of natural science aiming at the regular correlation of phenomena,[85] it is important to recognize that there is a reactionary aspect to it as well. Writing in the prime period of disillusionment with the microscope, Locke continually measures microscopical science against angelic science and finds it wanting.[86] His response, unlike Malpighi's, is to retreat to the surface.

Real enthusiasm for the instrument by contrast is demonstrated by Leibniz, who favors, "inquiry into analogies. More and more of them," he says, "are going to be yielded by plants, insects, and the comparative anatomy of animals, especially as the microscope continues to be used more than it has been."[87] The result will be, he claims, a confirmation of his theory of monads, of the existence of *petites perceptions* (and *petites inclinations*). "It will be found," he states, "that all these views are in complete conformity with the analogies among things which come to our notice and that I am merely going on beyond observations, not restricting them to certain portions of matter or to certain kinds of action; and that the only difference is that between large and small, between sensible and insensible."[88] The value of the microscope for Leibniz was thus that it appeared to provide direct confirmation for certain of his metaphysical doctrines by demonstrating the possibility of an endless sequence of life-forms and so their irreducibility to mere machines. Had the microscope actually revealed atoms as Power had hoped, Leibniz could hardly have become such an enthusiastic supporter.[89]

Unlike Leibniz, Berkeley regarded the microscope and the mechanico-

[84] See esp. F. Duchesneau, *L'Empirisme de Locke* (The Hague, 1973), 6, for a favorable assessment of Sydenham's role in determining Locke's epistemology, and K. Dewhurst, *John Locke: Physician and Philosopher* (London, 1963). Sydenham, according to Dewhurst, "set aside all vain philosophical hypotheses in studying the manifest phenomena of disease ... [and] believed that the remote causes of disease were not only outside the scope of the physician's art, but beyond the range of human understanding" (35). Particularly objectionable to Locke was perhaps Boyle's suggestion that the microscope might enable us to understand how shape and figure produce the sensation of color, in *Experiments and Considerations touching Colours* (*Works*, I, 680). On the primary-secondary quality problem, cf. *Essay*, II, 200.

[85] M. J. Osler, "Locke and the Changing Ideal of Scientific Knowledge," *JHI*, 31 (1970), 3-16. See also I. Hacking, *The Emergence of Probability* (Cambridge, 1975), 182f.

[86] Locke, *Essay*, II, 223.

[87] Leibniz, *New Essays*, tr. J. Bennett and P. Remnant (Cambridge, 1981), 474.

[88] *Ibid*. Cf. Letter to Foucher in *Philosophische Schiften*, ed. C. J. Gerhardt (Berlin, 1875-1890), I, 335.

[89] On Leibniz and the microscope see M. Serres, *Leibniz et ses modèles mathématiques*, (Paris, 1968), I, 354ff, and G. L. Linguiti, *Leibniz et la scopertà del mondo microscopica della vita*, (Lucca, 1984).

corpuscular philosophy as mutually reinforcing. In both the *Dialogues* and the *New Theory of Vision* he argues that the microscope cannot be supposed to provide a better, sharper, truer picture of the world than ordinary unassisted vision. But what does the microscope threaten for Berkeley? Indeed we might have expected to find him consistently appealing to the instrument for arguments against, for example, corpuscularian theories of visions.[90] Instead, he takes literally Hooke's claim that the microscope reveals a new visible world: we do not see the same object more clearly with the lens, he says, but another object.[91] Thus the microscope gives us no information about our own world and its objects. At the same time Berkeley attempts to rehabilitate the old idea that visible things are signs of an invisible presence. Natural objects are an "optic language": the world shows us the "production and reproduction of so many signs, combined, dissolved, transposed, diversified, and adapted to such an endless variety of purposes."[92]

Berkeley's attack on physical minima and on the instrument intended to reveal them shows how the tension between the conception of nature as permeated by a divine significance and the glimpse offered by the microscope might assume philosophical expression. Assimilation was another possibility. The microscope was the great weapon of the physico-theologists who sought to demonstrate the existence of a *deus artifex* from the wonders of the tiny insect-machine.[93] Sir Thomas Browne invites us to "collect our Divinitie" in the contemplation of bees, ants, and spiders, in whose "narrow Engines there is more curious Mathematicks" than in the frame of larger animals.[94] But for Browne, who is still fascinated by signatures, by the science of "physiognomy" and by the lines and figures in the hand, the morphology of plants and the significance of the ubiquitous *quincunx*, which he invites us to consider "artificially, naturally and mysteriously,"[95] the notion of subvisible fine structure underwrites a conception of macrocosmic-microcosmic relations. "In the seed of a Plant to the eyes of God, and to the understanding of man, there exist, though in an invisible way, the perfect leaves, flowers, and fruits thereof: (for things that are in *posse* to the sense are actually existent to the understanding.)" At the resurrection, our "glorified senses . . .

[90] On Berkeley's erratic use of microscopical examples see B. Silver, "The Conflicting Microscope Worlds of Berkeley's *Three Dialogues*," *JHI*, 37 (1970), 343-49.

[91] Berkeley, *Three Dialogues* (1710), in *Works*, II, 245; *An Essay Towards a New Theory of Vision* (1709), in *Works*, I, 205.

[92] *Alciphron*, in *Works*, III, 159f.

[93] D. Hume, in *Dialogues Concerning Natural Religion*, ed. H. D. Aiken (New York, 1948), 83.

[94] Sir Thomas Browne, *Religio Medici* (1654) in *Selected Writing*, ed. G. Keynes (Chicago, 1968), 20.

[95] *The Garden of Cyrus, or, The Quincunical, lozenge, or net-work plantations of the ancients artificially, naturally, mystically considered*, in *Selected Writings*, 157-210.

shall as really behold and contemplate the world in its Epitome or contracted essence, as now they doe at large and in its dilated substance." [96]

But suppose that such fine structures were visible not only to God and to glorified sense but also to the ordinary eye, armed with its microscope? There is a wide gulf between the occult idea that nature is instructed and imprinted by God—that, in Croll's words, "Every Creature in this ample Machine of the World, in which the invisible Creator exhibits himself to us to be seen, heard, tasted, smelt, and handled is nothing else but the shadow of God"—and the physico-theological idea that nature is a premise in an argument. Those who still employed the old language, who spoke as Hooke does of the "signatures" of seeds of thyme, were partly attempting to express an altered understanding of the interpretation of nature, partly harkening back to a form of interpretation which the microscope was helping to render obsolete. So many marvelous structures, such intricate design, such undreamt of riches in ordinary pond-water. Who could believe that they were intended for our eyes and not happened on accidentally? Their being happened upon entailed a displacement of human vision and human interests from their old center as decisive as the displacement indicated by the new astronomy.

V. In closing I should like to return to Bachelard's assessment of the microscope. It was his view that the microscope constituted an actual impediment to knowledge in the seventeenth and eighteenth centuries because it revealed things which were beautiful but which could not lead to the acquisition of any new theoretical information, or which suggested to observers theories of the wrong sort—for example, the theory that the world was a *plenum* filled with an infinity of tiny animals—and made a quantitative handling of phenomena seem impossible or unimportant.

We have seen that there are indeed several senses in which people dreamed with the new images presented by the microscope. They dreamed in the sense that they could experience them only in a passive way, unable to put what they saw to further use. They dreamed as well in assigning them a central place in fanciful, premature, or conceptually unsound explanatory programs. They dreamed, finally, in spinning around the instrument a fine web of theological and moral significance, supposing it capable of mitigating the effects of sin or restoring a pure and uncorrupted commerce with the physical world. When researchers of the seventeenth century wanted to defend the theoretical relevance of the microscope by contrast with the purely recreational interest it aroused, they tended to point to the same example: the direct verification of the circulation of the blood in animals with diaphanous blood-vessels, such

[96] *Ibid.*, 58.

as fish and frogs.[97] It would be a long time before anyone could see with this instrument anything which might help to make him, in the sense of Bacon and Descartes, a master and possessor of nature.

Nevertheless the microscope gave a sense to the notion of the interpretation of nature which neither the corpuscular philosophy of Descartes and Boyle nor the mathematical philosophy of Galileo and Newton was able to supply. The all around "excellency" of the mechanical hypothesis notwithstanding, these philosophies created a certain degree of intellectual bewilderment, a bewilderment not confined to the scientifically uneducated, simply on account of their abstract, hypothetical, probabilistic character. Though it was true, Pascal argued, to say that all is made by figure and motion it was "useless, uncertain, and painful."[98] There was no hope of "composing the machine." What the microscope did in revealing layer after layer of articulated structure was to restore the solidity and accessibility to the understanding of an otherwise atomized and mathematicized world. Even for those who were to a greater or lesser degree skeptical about the actual powers of the microscope, what Hume was later to call "hidden mechanism and secret structure of parts" were nevertheless irrevocably proposed as possible objects of experience.

A substantive criticism leveled by the occult philosophers Paracelsus, Croll, and van Helmont against the teaching of the schools and the medicine of the academies was that it was "external." According to Paracelsus, despite all the exertions of Aristotle and his followers there remained in the kernel of nature only "dust and a withered flower."[99] The Aristotelian intellect, according to Helmont, "beholdeth things only on the outside."[100] Neither naive sense perception nor disputation and argument could supply, for these philosophers, a knowledge of nature "in her Root and thingliness." The predictive and interpretive powers which differentiate the sciences from other forms of learning were thus associated, up to the middle of the seventeenth century, with a set of interpretive procedures which were in turn allied with supra-rational techniques. Thus were the hidden causes, meaning, and probable prognosis of otherwise mysterious events to be uncovered. We require, Croll says, "a much higher ingenuity and more subtile Inquisition, than can be obtained by the sight of eyes only."[101] When the state of scientific illumination is achieved, says Helmont, "the things themselves seem to

---

[97] *Malpighi*, I, 580. Cf. C. Huygens, "De Telescopiis et Microscopiis" in *Oeuvres*, (The Hague, 1944), XII, 2, 522, 842.

[98] Pascal, *Pensées*, ed. F. Kaplan (Paris, 1982), 149. (This is not to say that Pascal would have regarded the microscope as more than an outlet for *curiositas*.)

[99] W. Pagel, *Paracelsus*, 52.

[100] *Oriatrike*, 26.

[101] *Bazilica Chymica*, Preface.

talk to us without words, and the understanding pierceth them being shut up no otherwise than if they were dissected and laid open."[102]

These criticisms of the philosophy of the schools were echoed— though not always deliberately—by Bacon and Hooke, who urged the advancement of the understanding beyond "superficies" and "outward forms" to the secret and "occult" workings of things, under which Hooke himself included sympathies and antipathies, influences, influxes, and the works of fantasy and imagination.[103] That the microscope in its early years of development could explain none of these effects, that many of them did not, as it turned out, exist to be explained, does not alter the fact that the instrument gave a sense to the idea of a non-occult interpretation of nature, so binding knowledge to power in a way which the irredeemably fictional mechanical models, as well as the search for linguistic essences, had been unable to accomplish.

University of Oregon.

[102] *Oriatrike*, 26.
[103] Hooke, *A General Scheme*, 43.

PART TWO

PHILOSOPHERS AND RELIGION

Chapter VII

THE RELIGION OF DAVID HUME

By Ernest Campbell Mossner*

The above title may well provoke two antithetical responses. One, it is sheer nonsense to associate Hume with religion of any variety. Or, two, we knew all along Hume was a believer, perhaps even a good Christian, masking his religion behind implicit atheism to gain attention and notoriety. This latter response may be called the Boswellian caper: in a dream some eight years after the death of the philosopher the biographer finally resolved—to his own satisfaction—the longstanding paradox of the virtuous infidel.[1] Both of these hypothetical responses are false. The first, because Hume did not dissociate himself entirely from religion but only from the supernatural element with its connotation of worship. The second, because Hume, in the strict conventional sense of the terms, was neither a believer nor an unbeliever, that is to say, neither a theist nor an atheist. In short, he was a skeptic. His skepticism was well-tempered for he insists that "A true sceptic will be diffident of his philosophical doubts, as well as of his philosophical conviction. . . ." As Philo, his spokesman in the posthumous *Dialogues concerning Natural Religion,* exults, ". . . it is that very Suspence or Ballance, which is the Triumph of Scepticism."[2]

In a recent essay, "Hume and the Legacy of the *Dialogues,*" I presented a new reading of that work chiefly by means of the rhetorical device of irony.[3] (Irony may be taken as "a figure of speech wherein the real meaning

---

*Legend.

Phil. Wks. = *Philosophical Works of David Hume,* edd. T. H. Green and T. H. Grose (London, 1874-75), 4 vols. Reprinted 1964, Scientia Verlag, Aalen.

S-B, T. = *A Treatise of Human Nature by David Hume* (Oxford, 1888 and numerous reprints), ed. L.A. Selby-Bigge.

S-B, E.I and II = *Enquiries concerning the Human Understanding and concerning the Principles of Morals by David Hume,* ed. L.A. Selby-Bigge, 2nd ed. (Oxford, 1902 and numerous reprints).

HL = *Letters of David Hume,* ed. J. Y. T. Greig (Oxford, 1932; reprinted 1969), 2 vols.

NHL = *New Letters of David Hume,* edd. Raymond Klibansky and E. C. Mossner (Oxford, 1954; reprinted 1969).

Life = E. C. Mossner, *Life of David Hume* (London, Edinburgh, and Austin, 1954; reprinted Oxford, 1970), 2nd ed. scheduled 1978.

[1] *Life,* 605-6. Based on *Private Papers of James Boswell from Malahide Castle,* edd. G. Scott and F. A. Pottle (N.Y., 1928-34), XII, 34; XIII, 23.

[2] *Phil. Wks.,* I, 552; S-B,T., 273; *Phil. Wks.,* II, 385; *DNR,* ed., N. K. Smith, 2nd ed. (Edinburgh, 1947), 136; *DNR,* ed. J. V. Price (Oxford, 1976), 152, the definitive text used here.

[3] Originally delivered at the Hume Bicentenary Conference at Edinburgh University in 1976; published in *David Hume: Bicentenary Papers,* ed. George Morice (Edinburgh, 1977), 1-22.

is concealed or contradicted by the words used.") First, there is no rational means *a priori* or *a posteriori* to prove either the being of a God or the non-being of a God; and religious faith is unphilosophical. Moreover, the only concept of a God permitted by the argument from design, the one argument that Hume deems worthy of serious consideration, excludes the moral attributes of a God and, therefore, any remote resemblance to the personal God of Christianity. What is more, reliance on the beneficence of nature, which had characterized Hume's thinking throughout the greater part of his life, is lost in the final period with the apprehension that nature is amoral (Hume's epithet is "indifferent"). So man is left entirely on his own bereft of a personal God and also of a benign nature.[4] Both natural and revealed religions stand impugned.

The second thrust of the argument is that "mitigated" (or "modest" or "moderate") skepticism, Hume's fundamental philosophical position, permits positive thinking and contemplates what I am ironically calling the *religion of man.* My present purpose is to render more explicit this naturalistic and positive *religion of man,* which to my mind constitutes the personal religion of David Hume. Before doing so, however, the predominantly negative slant of his religious thinking needs to be reviewed once again—this time in a somewhat novel way. These two speculations will be detailed as far as possible in Hume's own words.

Part I: *Crusade against the Supernatural*

Hume's war upon the supernatural in religion, both natural and revealed, is plainly visible throughout his career as philosopher. Aside from the presumed late reinterpretation of nature from benign to indifferent, Hume's attitudes toward religion remain essentially unchanged. The assault is incremental, starting intermittently with the Treatise and climaxing pervasively with the *Dialogues.* The *Treatise of Human Nature* (1739–40) and the two ancillary pamphlets, the *Abstract of a Treatise* (1740) in which he explicates causation, "the chief Argument" of the *Treatise,* and the *Letter from a Gentleman* (1745) in which he defends the *Treatise* against charges of atheism, set the tone. Running throughout these works are repeated assertions presented without argument or proof that God exists: God is the Prime Mover and the First Cause and the Author of our being and the Omnipotent

---

[4] *Phil. Wks.,* II, 446-53; DNR (Smith), 205-12; DNR (Price), 234-42. My essay, n.3 above, 21, 24, 34-8. N. Kemp Smith in *The Philosophy of David Hume* (London, 1941), 564, argues that "coming in the dramatic setting of the *Dialogues,* this view of Nature [i.e., "a blind nature"] may not, however, be taken as Hume's own. No other passage in any of his writings is on these lines." I venture to take issue with Kemp Smith on two counts: (1) The "blind nature" paragraph stands, not by itself dramatically, but as the conclusion of an eight-page presentation of the evils in nature. It was added presumably in the last year of Hume's life; (2) there is at least one other passage in Hume's writings that is "on these lines." See NHR (1757) in *Phil. Wks.,* IV, 324 n.1; NHR (Colver), 44 n.v.: "The blind unguided powers of nature, if they could produce men, might produce such beings as *Jupiter* and *Neptune. . . .*"

Mind discernible in the order of the universe. Taken by themselves and without prior knowledge of the later works (the first *Enquiry*, "The Natural History of Religion," and notably the *Dialogues*), these three pieces would prompt perhaps no more than a suspicion, if even that, of a sustained irony in Hume's every statement on religion. With knowledge of the later works together with the revelation that "Of Miracles," which is a thinly disguised attack on the very foundations of Christianity, was originally in one form or another a part of the *Treatise,* the pattern of irony becomes unmistakable— at least to those capable of recognizing irony.

"Of Miracles" was composed at La Flèche as an argument against Christian miracles. It was deleted from the *Treatise* at London—"I am at present castrating my Work, that is, cutting off its noble Parts, that is, endeavouring it shall give as little Offence as possible"—out of consideration for Bishop Butler whom Hume was unsuccessfully attempting to meet and to invite to read the manuscript. It was then kept from publication on the insistence of close friends. Finally, still against their advice, Hume included it in the *Philosophical Essays concerning Human Understanding* (1748), later the first *Enquiry,* fully aware that publication would inevitably brand him with "the character of an infidel."[5]

Readers commonly have not found the *Treatise* ironical; thus it is novel to be told that all statements on religion in the *Treatise* and the two pamphlets are ironical. (Had "Of Miracles" been retained in the *Treatise,* Hume's irony, as well as his skepticism, would have been sufficiently plain from the very beginning.) Here are a few examples which in view of our hindsight are properly to be taken as ironical. From the *Treatise:* (1) "A man, whose memory presents him with a lively image of the *Red-Sea, and the Desert, and Jerusalem, and Galilee,* can never doubt of any miraculous events, which are related either by *Moses or the Evangelists.*"[6] —(2) "The order of the universe proves an omnipotent mind; that is, a mind whose will is *constantly attended* with the obedience of every creature and being. Nothing more is requisite to give a foundation to all the articles of religion, nor is it necessary we shou'd form a distinct idea of the force and energy of the supreme Being."[7] (3) "If *nature* be oppos'd to miracles, not only the distinction betwixt vice and virtue is natural, but also every event, which has ever happen'd in the world, *excepting those miracles, on which our religion is founded.*"[8] Or this one from the *Abstract:* "It would have been necessary, therefore, for *Adam* (if he was not inspired) to have had *experience* of the effect, which followed upon the impulse of these two balls" in the famous billiard-ball illustration of causation.[9] Or this one from the *Letter:* "Wherever I see Order, I infer from Experience that *there,* there hath been Design and Contrivance. And the same Principle which leads me into this Inference, when I contemplate a Building, regular and beautiful in its whole Frame and Structure; the same Principle obliges me to infer an infinitely perfect Architect, from the infinite

[5] NHL, 3; HL, I, 361, 106.   [6] *Phil. Wks.,* I, 410; S-B, T., 110.
[7]*Phil. Wks.,* I,456, n.1; S-B, T., 633 n.1.   [8] *Phil. Wks.,* II, 249; S-B, T., 474.
[9] David Hume, *An Abstract of a Treatise of Human Nature,* edd. J. M. Keynes and P. Sraffa (Cambridge, 1938), 14.

Art and Contrivance which is display'd in the whole Fabrick of the Universe."[10] Two of these citations, the second from the *Treatise* and the one from the *Letter* are prime examples of irony "wherein the real meaning is contradicted by the words used," being direct negatives of Hume's multi-faceted refutations of this very argument in the first *Enquiry,* Section XI (which he was composing at about that time) and, above all, in the somewhat later *Dialogues.*

The *Essays Moral and Political* (1740–48), which are, in general, sim-plified versions and illustrations of major theses of the *Treatise,* continues the campaign against the supernatural in religion, what Hume terms the "religious hypothesis," as found in the predominant "popular" religion of Christianity. For instance, take this passage from "Of Parties in General" (1741): "And the same principles of priestly government continuing, after Christianity became the established religion, they have engendered a spirit of persecution, which has ever since been the poison of human society, and the source of the most inveterate factions in every government."[11] Or consider the following suggestive passage from "The Sceptic" (1742): ". . . an abstract, invisible object, like that which *natural* religion alone presents to us cannot long actu-ate the mind, or be of any moment in life. To render the passion of continu-ance, we must find some method of affecting the senses and imagination, and must embrace some *historical,* as well as *philosophical* account of the divinity. Popular superstitions and observances are even found to be of use in this particular."[12] There are a number of such passages in "Of Superstition and Enthusiasm" (1741), "The Stoic" (1742), "Of National Characters" (1748), as well as in several other essays.

With the advent in 1748 of *Philosophical Essays concerning Human Understanding,* the first *Enquiry,* the assault on Christianity becomes more detailed, somewhat more outspoken, and yet on occasion more skillfully disguised in irony. I refer, it goes without saying, to Section X "Of Miracles" and Section XI "Of a Particular Providence and of a future State," originally titled "Of the Practical Consequences of Natural Religion." It is to be noted in passing that although the original title is more accurately descriptive of the contents, the second title is more provocative to the orthodox—which no doubt is the intention. There is no need to review here the well-known argu-ment of the essay on miracles except to remind ourselves of the conclusion: "So that, upon the whole, we may conclude, that the *Christian Religion* not only was at first attended with miracles, but even at this day cannot be believed by any reasonable person without one. Mere reason is insufficient to convince us of its veracity: And whoever is moved by *Faith* to assent to it, is conscious of a continued miracle in his own person, which subverts all the principles of his understanding and gives him a determination to believe what is most contrary to custom and experience."[13]

The most remarkable feature in the turbulent history of the first *Enquiry* —or so it seems to me—is that although Section X has been refuted scores

---

[10] David Hume, *A Letter from a Gentleman,* edd. E. C. Mossner and J. V. Price (Edinburgh, 1967). 25-6.

[11] *Phil. Wks.,* III, 132.   [12] Ibid., III, 220.

[13] *Ibid.,* IV, 108; S-B, E., I, 131.

of times, Section XI, notwithstanding its provocative title, has been largely passed by until more recent times, and this despite the fact that, judging from the extraordinary precautions that he took, Hume seems to have regarded it as the more controversial and consequently the more perilous to himself. For "Of a particular Providence and of a future State" is presented ironically through a double dissimulation. Not only is it a dialogue in the midst of essays, but also a dialogue with an inversion of speakers: First, is a "friend who loves sceptical paradoxes"—and who could fit the bill better than Hume himself?—who assumes the role of "Epicurus" delivering a harangue to the Athenian people; and second, is "I" who represents the Athenian people and who may be identified as that distinguished theologian and master of the analogy argument, Bishop Butler (who reappears later as Cleanthes in the *Dialogues*). Nor may we ignore Hume's own caveat: "In every dialogue, no more than one person can be supposed to represent the Author."[14] So if in Section X Hume is attacking the miraculous foundations of Christianity, in Section XI he is undertaking the even more hazardous enterprise, the refutation of the then most widely accepted argument for the being of a God, the argument from design.

Here is how "Epicurus" presents his case: "When we infer any particular cause from an effect, we must proportion the one to the other, and can never be allowed to ascribe to the cause any qualities, but what are exactly sufficient to produce the effect. . . . We can never be allowed to mount up from the Universe, the effect, to Jupiter, the cause; and then descend downwards, to infer any new effect from that cause. . . ." So he is bound to conclude: "All the philosophy, therefore, in the world, and all the religion, which is nothing but a species of philosophy, will never be able to carry us beyond the usual course of experience, or give us measures of conduct and behaviour different from those which are furnished by reflections on common life. No new fact can ever be inferred from the religious hypothesis; no event foreseen or foretold; no reward or punishment expected or dreaded, beyond what is already known by practice and observation."[15] In brief, the "religious hypothesis" is empty.

The uncompromisingly secular morality of the *Enquiry concerning the Principles of Morals* (1751), the second *Enquiry*, scorns "Celibacy, fasting, penance, mortification, self-denial, humility, silence, solitude, and the whole train of monkish virtues" on the grounds that "they serve to no manner of purpose . . ." in society but rather "stupify the understanding and harden the heart, obscure the fancy and sour the temper."[16]

Even the *Political Discourses* (1752) provides opportunity for strokes against religion and the clergy, such as: "The heights of popularity and

[14] HL, I, 173. It is perhaps not altogether unreasonable to assume that Section XI, at least some elements of it, was originally a part of the pre-castrated *Treatise*. These two Sections are clearly designed to be taken together. Hume's statement is ambiguous: whether "it's noble parts" refers to one argument or two or more is unresolved. Antony Flew in *Hume's Philosophy of Belief* [A Study of his First *Inquiry*], (London, 1961), 6, takes a similar position.

[15] *Phil. Wks.*, IV, 112-3, 120-1; S-B, E., I, 136, 146.

[16] *Phil. Wks.*, IV, 246-7; S-B, E., II, 270.

patriotism are still the beaten road to power and tyranny; flattery to treachery; standing armies to arbitrary government; and the glory of God to the temporal interest of the clergy."[17] "The Idea of a perfect Commonwealth," the nearest to a utopia that a non-utopian-minded philosopher ever proposed, presents a curious dilemma. "The Church is my Aversion"[18] Hume had confided to a close friend in 1747, yet five years later in his "perfect Commonwealth" he postulates a church with "Presbyterian government." The "assembly or synod," however, he hastens to make clear, could be overruled by the magistrates whenever they pleased. "Without the dependence of the clergy on the civil magistrates . . . it is in vain to think that any free government will ever have security or stability."[19] The dilemma is more fully resolved by the following statement on religion which Hume repeats with slight variations on several occasions: "The proper Office of Religion is to reform Men's Lives, to purify their Hearts, to inforce all moral Duties, & to secure Obedience to the Laws & civil Magistrate."[20] This pragmatic and secular conception of the function of religion in the commonwealth satisfies Hume's moral specifications and dismisses the supernatural.

In "The Natural History of Religion," the first of *Four Dissertations* (1757), Hume examines the origins of religion in human nature. Admittedly an "entertaining exercise in armchair anthropology from secondary sources," this study is yet a searching and fundamentally sound formulation of the origins of religion in the fears and hopes of mankind. Hume's concluding indictment is outspoken, his pen is barbed: "What a noble privilege is it of human reason to attain the knowledge of the supreme being; and, from the visible works of nature, be enabled to infer so sublime a principle as its supreme Creator? But turn the reverse of the medal. Survey most nations and most ages. Examine the religious principles, which have, in fact prevailed in the world. You will scarcely be persuaded, that they are other than sick men's dreams: Or perhaps will regard them more as the playsome whimsies of monkeys in human shape, than the serious, positive dogmatical asseverations of a being, who dignifies himself with the name of rational."[21]

The *Dialogues concerning Natural Religion* (1779), Hume's crowning achievement in religious philosophy, need not detain us long; the bald conclusions as already stated will suffice for present purposes. The critical question remains only to be asked and answered: *After the philosophical exorcism of the supernatural from religion, natural and revealed, what remains?* The answer is brief and simple: *The religion of man.* Put more explicitly it reads: *Man, intrepid and "enlightened" man, stands starkly alone to fend for himself and for the society in which he lives in an indifferent nature.* The full significance of *religion of man* will be delineated in due course.

---

[17] "Of Public Credit in *Phil. Wks.*, III, 372-3.   [18] NHL, 26.

[19] *Phil. Wks.*, III, 485-6, 490.

[20] David Hume, *History of England*, II (1756), 449; *Life*, 306; DNR in *Phil. Wks.*, II, 460; DNR (Smith), 220; DNR (Price), 251-52.

[21] D. G. C. MacNabb, "Hume, David" in *The Encyclopedia of Philosophy* (N.Y., 1967), IV, 89. *Phil. Wks.*, IV, 362; *NHR*, ed. A. W. Colver (Oxford, 1976) 94, the definitive text used here.

To close this brief survey of Hume's lifelong crusade against the supernatural element in religion, we may say that throughout his career he has seized every opportunity with discretion, particularly by means of irony, to nullify the "religious hypothesis," to discredit superstitious and enthusiastic religious beliefs and practices, and to cast doubts on the integrity of the clergy. Hume's assault on the supernatural in religion is more philosophically oriented than, say, Voltaire's bravura *Ecrasez l'infâme*. Yet, as with Voltaire, there is ample reason to conclude that to Hume Christianity has throughout its history brought more harm than good to mankind. His droll deathbed confession to his physician that "he had been very busily employed in making his countrymen wiser and particularly in delivering them from the Christian superstition, but that he had not yet compleated that great work"[22] is no more than the sober truth.

Part II: *Religion of Man*

The *Treatise of Human Nature*, Hume informs us in the Introduction, is designed as a "compleat system of the sciences" based on the "science of man." He might well have added—though he did not—that "Man is the measure of all things." This principle appears in the pre-Socratic sophist, Protagoras. Taken in the sense of "individual man," the man-measure principle is profoundly skeptical as implying that objective truth is unobtainable. Taken in the sense of "mankind," however, the man-measure principle is entirely compatible with Hume's instrumental "mitigated" skepticism as well as his projected "science of man." The understanding, passions, morals, politics (history as well as theory), and criticism (including aesthetics) compromise Hume's comprehensive study of human nature. Moreover, "Even *Mathematics, Natural Philosophy,* and *Natural Religion,* are in some measure dependent on the science of Man; since they lie under the cognizance of men, and are judged of by their powers and faculties." So from the beginning Hume was resolved to keep "a strict philosophic eye"[23] on the science of man. Also noteworthy is the fact that natural religion, the philosophical rationale of revealed religion, is akin to the "science of man" and, therefore, actively to be addressed.

In the Humean view all men are divided into two unequal parts. At the top of the scale, the few, the very few. Down below, the many, the multitude. Those in the lower range are variously called the "generality of men," the "common people," the "ignorant and the thoughtless," the "mere ignorant," the "peasants," and by far most frequently the "vulgar." I shall lump them all together as the "vulgar." Those in the upper range are variously called "the party of human-kind," the "men of genius," the "learned world," the "judicious and knowing," the "learned and wise," the "men of letters," the "philosophers," the "enlightened," and the "heroes in philosophy." This last, the "heroes in philosophy," natural and moral, are so very few, as we

---

[22] *Life*, 601.

[23] Protagoras is presented more or less extensively by Plato, Aristotle, and Sextus Empiricus. Hume mentions Protagoras in the second paragraph of the crucial Section XI of the first *Enquiry. Phil. Wks.,* II, 196; S-B, T., 417.

shall see, that I shall generalize all those others at the top of the scale simply as the "enlightened" who compose, as it were, a natural intellectual elite.

The fullest contrast that Hume makes of the dichotomy between the "vulgar" and the "enlightened," brief as it is, occurs in "The Natural History of Religion": "The vulgar, that is, indeed, all mankind, a few excepted, being ignorant and uninstructed. . . ."[24] He has little more to say about the "vulgar" beyond this indication of their number and their utter helplessness to behave rationally in the sphere of religion, where they constantly fluctuate between polytheism and a nonphilosophical variety of theism. But there is a passage in Book II of the *Treatise* that sheds some further light on the "vulgar." "The skin, pores, muscles, and nerves of a day-labourer are different from those of a man of quality: So are his sentiments, actions, and manners." And this is because "the different stations of life influence the whole fabric, external and internal. . . ."[25] A day-labourer, it would appear, stands at the very bottom of the "vulgar." Yet Hume would be the last, we may be sure, to equate the "man of quality" with the enlightened": "It is wonderful to observe," he comments elsewhere, "what airs of superiority fools and knaves, with large possessions, give themselves above men of the greatest merit in poverty."[26]

The "enlightened" receive considerable, although not systematic, review from Hume because only in them lies whatever hope there is for the continued improvement of mankind. Hume's view of human nature, like that of most thinkers of his day, is universalistic rather than individualistic. "It is universally acknowledged," he observes in the first *Enquiry*, "that there is a great uniformity among the actions of men, in all nations and ages, and that human nature remains still the same, in its principles and operations. . . . Mankind are so much the same, in all times and places, that history informs us of nothing new or strange in this particular. Its chief use is only to discover the constant and universal principles of human nature. . . ."[27]

Acutely conscious of the vast preponderance of the "vulgar," Hume, who is by nature optimistic—"I was ever more disposed to see the favourable than unfavourable side of things"[28]—in an essay (1741) felicitously named "Of the Dignity or Meanness of Human Nature," paints a memorable portrait of "enlightened" and intrepid man. In him ". . . we see a creature, whose thoughts are not limited by any narrow bounds, either of place or time; who carries his researches into the most distant regions of this globe, and beyond this globe, to the planets and heavenly bodies; looks backward to consider the first origin at least, the history of human race; casts his eye forward to see the influence of his actions upon posterity, and the judg-

[24] *Phil. Wks.*, IV, 334; *NHR* (Colver), 57.

[25] *Phil. Wks.*, II, 183; S-B, T., 402.

[26] "Of Impudence and Modesty" in *Phil. Wks.*, IV, 381.

[27] *Ibid.*, IV, 68; S-B, E. I, 63. S. K. Wertz in "Hume, History, and Human Nature," this *Journal*, 36 (1975), argues most competently "that Hume's view of human nature and its use in historical inquiry is more diversified and complex than the commonplace conceptions have made it out to be." As Wertz's argument is only tangential to mine, however, this is not the place to discuss it.

[28] "My Own Life" in *Phil. Wks.*, III, 4; *Life*, 613.

ments which will be formed of his character a thousand years hence; a creature, who traces causes and effects to a great length and intricacy; extracts general principles from particular appearances; improves upon his discoveries; corrects his mistakes; and makes his very errors profitable."[29]

This "enlightened" man who exemplifies the dignity of human nature and who is capable of enriching mankind by means of the experimental method of reasoning may, in fact, be, or become, a "hero in philosophy." "Among the ancients," Hume remarks in the second *Enquiry*, "the heroes in philosophy, as well as those in war and patriotism, have a grandeur and force of sentiment, which astonishes our narrow souls, and is rashly rejected as extravagant and supernatural." Yet in the present enlightened age, he continues, the ancients "would have had equal reason to consider as romantic and incredible, the degree of humanity, clemency, order, tranquillity, and other social virtues, to which in the administration of government we have attained in modern times, had any one been then able to have made a fair representation of them. Such is the compensation, which nature, or rather education, has made in the distribution of excellencies and virtues, in those different ages."[30] The Age of Enlightenment as viewed by Hume transcends the ancient age in regard to humanity, that is, the improvement of the human condition.

This view is somewhat enlarged in the posthumous essay "Of the Immortality of the Soul" (1777): "According to human sentiments, sense, courage, good manners, industry, prudence, genius, &c. are essential parts of personal merits. Shall we therefore erect an elysium for poets and heroes, like that of the ancient mythology? Why confine all rewards to one species of virtue?"[31] One looks in vain to find in *Essays and Treatises* further development of the role of education rather than of nature in distinguishing between the human values of the ancients and of the moderns.

In a poignant passage in the Conclusion of Book I of the *Treatise*, Hume lays bare his motivations for presenting to his fellow "enlightened" his philosophy of human nature: "I cannot forbear having a curiosity to be acquainted with the principles of moral good and evil, the nature and foundation of government, and the cause of those several passions and inclinations, which actuate and govern me. I am uneasy to think I approve of one object, and disapprove of another; call one thing beautiful and another deform'd; decide concerning truth and falsehood, reason and folly, without knowing upon what principles I proceed. I am concern'd for the condition of the learned world, which lies under such a deplorable ignorance in all these particulars. *I feel an ambition to arise in me of contributing to the instruction of mankind, and of acquiring a name by my inventions and discoveries.* These sentiments spring up naturally in my present disposition; and shou'd I endeavour to banish them by attaching myself to any other business or diversion, I *feel* I shou'd be a loser in point of pleasure; and this is the origin of my philosophy."[32] Some twelve years later in the second *Enquiry*, Hume is more explicit and more highly personalized on the same theme: "Give me my choice, and I would rather, for my own happiness and self-enjoyment, have

---

[29] *Phil. Wks.*, III, 152.
[31] *Phil. Wks.*, IV, 402.

[30] *Ibid.*, IV, 236; S-B, E., II, 236.
[32] *Ibid.*, I, 550; S-B, T., 270-1. (My italics.)

a friendly, humane heart, than possess all the other virtues of Demosthenes and Philip united: But *I would rather pass with the world for one endowed with extensive genius and intrepid courage, and thence expect stronger instances of general applause and admiration.*"[33]

It is instructive, as well as pleasant, to be able to recognize in these two intellectual self-portraits that Hume is viewing himself as a "hero in philosophy," but one who has not as yet received full public recognition. He is entirely confident, however, that the rewards of his "extensive genius and intrepid courage," will come in time, the "general applause and admiration."

These basic thoughts and yearnings are confirmed by two sections of Book II of the *Treatise*, "Of the Love of Fame" and "Of Curiosity, or the Love of Truth," and by "Of Greatness of Mind" of Book III. The same sentiment expressed in more universal terms was added to the second *Enquiry* during the last weeks of Hume's life. "Upon the whole, then, it seems undeniable *that* nothing can bestow more merit on any human creature than the sentiment of benevolence in an eminent degree; and *that* a *part,* at least, of its merit arises from its tendency to promote the interest of our species, and bestow happiness on human society."[34] Benevolence in the individual, that is to say, fosters humanity and knowledge in society.

Hume holds the *religion of man,* a religion that is freed from the worship of the supernatural, as well as from reliance on the benignity of nature, in the highest esteem: recognition of worth, of service beneficial to mankind, and of the augumentation of knowledge. What he eschews is worship of even the most exalted station of man, the "heroes in philosophy." (So far as I can determine, Hume was the first, in "The Natural History of Religion" (1757) to employ the term "hero-worship.")[35] Worship with its inherent supernaturalistic overtones was abhorrent to him. In this light consider the following significant statement: "Were we to distinguish the Ranks of Men by their Genius and Capacity more than by their Virtue and Usefulness to the Public, great Philosophers wou'd certainly challenge the first Rank, and must be plac'd at the Top of human Kind. So rare is this Character, that, perhaps, there has not, as yet, been above two in the World, who can lay a just Claim to it. At least *Galileo* and *Newton* seem to me so far to excel all the rest, that I cannot admit any other into the same Class with them."[36] "Honor" and "praise,"[37] "general applause and admiration," doubtless but not hero-worship. These same attributes of "honor" and "admiration" appear in the *History of England,* where Hume characterizes Napier, "the famous inventor of the logarithms, the person to whom the title of a GREAT MAN is more justly due, than to any other whom his country [Scotland] ever produced."[38]

The subtle distinction that Hume is drawing here between men of "Virtue and Usefulness to the Public" and men of Genius and Capacity,"

---

[33] *Phil. Wks.,* IV, 282; S-B, E., II, 315-6. (My italics.)

[34] HL, II, 331-2, n.5; *Phil. Wks.,* IV, 179; S-B, E., II, 181.

[35] The earliest reference in the *OED* is 1774.

[36] "Of the Middle Station of Life" (1742) in *Phil. Wks.,* IV, 379.

[37] The words are Hume's: *Phil. Wks.,* IV, 286; S-B., E., II, 321.

[38] *History of England* (ed. of London, 1792), VII, 44.

more specifically, between the "enlightened" who contribute to humanity and the "heroes in philosophy" who contribute to knowledge, is exemplified, on the one hand, by great statesmen and on the other, by great philosophers. Basic knowledge acquired by astronomers and physicists and moral philosophers, for instance, might also eventually prove useful "to the Public."

(It is not difficult to imagine the scorn with which Hume would have viewed the "religion of Humanity" with its worship of man as proposed in the nineteenth century by Auguste Comte: to parallel in a man-made naturalistic religion the ritual structure of a revealed supernaturalistic religion, with his great friend Adam Smith ensconced in the calendar of positivist saints. One wonders why Comte was unable to find a saintly niche for David Hume, who in his own day had earned from some admirers the title of "Saint David of Scotland.")

In a moment of truth on the occasion of his triumphal and unprecedented reception in Paris, October 1763, is it not altogether likely that Hume indulged himself with the long-husbanded conviction that he would ultimately, by virtue of his "extensive genius and intrepid courage," receive the "honor" and "praise," the "general applause and admiration," due a "hero in philosophy"—conceivably the third such hero after Galileo and Newton? ". . . They consider me," he somewhat shamefacedly confides to a friend, "as one of the greatest geniuses in the world."[39]

Yet Hume always stops short of the hero-worship implicit in the famous chorus of Sophocles' *Antigone*: Numberless are the world's wonders, but none / More wonderful than man." Or of Shakespeare's man, "the beauty of the world! the paragon of animals!" Hume was content rather to echo his favorite poet of the Enlightenment, Pope: "The proper Study of Mankind is Man" and, most significantly, *"Man and for ever?"*[40]

"The vulgar, that is, indeed, all mankind, a few excepted, being ignorant and uninstructed . . . ," lack the capacity to work their own fate and stand in dire need of leadership. It is the function of the intellectual elite, the "enilghtened" and the "heroes in philosophy," to provide that leadership. This function constitutes the *religion of man:* "enlightened" and "heroic" men providing humanity and knowledge for mankind without recourse to the supernatural or to a benign nature. Hume's "enlightened" man and his "hero in philosophy" are the noblest men of all. To them all "honor" and "praise," "general applause and admiration," for they are mankind's last best hope. In a universalist sense, Hume's "enlightened" and "heroic" men *are* the measure of all things. In them germinate and fructify humanity and knowledge. "Be a philosopher," cautions Hume; "but, amidst all your philosophy, be still a man."[41] *Man and for ever!* Such is the religion of David Hume.

University of Texas at Austin.

---

[39] HL, I, 410.

[40] This second quotation from Pope (*Satires*, 6, 252) appears in the final paragraph of "Idea of a perfect Commonwealth" in *Phil. Wks.*, III, 493. Pope's line reads: "Man? and for ever? Wretch! what wouldst thou have?"

[41] First *Enquiry* in *Phil. Wks.*, IV, 6; S-B, E., I, 9.

Chapter VIII

JOHNSON AND HUME ON MIRACLES

By Donald T. Siebert, Jr.

Ernest Mossner has presented Johnson and Hume as the two towering but contrasting intellectual figures of Great Britain in the mid and later eighteenth century—one the great defender of the Christian faith and the other its most successful adversary. Although Mossner has admitted that there are many similarities between the two men and suggested, as well, that Johnson was at heart a skeptic who feared that Hume was right (and hated him for it), the drift of Mossner's analysis is to picture Johnson as an implacable, even impassioned enemy of Hume's thought: not even the meddlesome and foolhardy Boswell, the implication goes, dared to mix Johnson with Hume, as he did Johnson with Wilkes.[1] And Boswell, it must be admitted, surely depicted Johnson as no friend of Hume: one might contend that Boswell needed to view his spiritual mentor as strictly uncompromising when dealing with those sticky problems that held such a malign fascination for Boswell. By focusing on Johnson's treatment of Hume's well-known essay "Of Miracles" (Section X of *An Enquiry concerning Human Understanding*), I wish to argue that regardless of his antagonism to Hume, Johnson by no means blindly rejected Hume's reasoning.

Charles E. Noyes has noticed that in Boswell's *Life,* Johnson shows a familiarity with Hume's argument against the possibility of miracles.[2] As Noyes points out, Johnson is clearly employing some of Hume's methodology when he demonstrates for Boswell that it is plausible, for instance, to disbelieve the British taking of Canada from the French.[3] Such an event violates the normal course of human experience (since the French are more numerous, they can be expected to win—not, of course, a very convincing example of a cause-and-effect whose contravention would be miraculous), and it has been reported by those whose interests would lead them to falsify the results of the war—the British soldiers and ministry. Noyes offers this episode in the Mitre Tavern as Johnson's *reductio ad absurdum* rebuttal of Hume's argument against miracles, but there is in fact no reason to view it that way. A follower of Mossner (and Boswell), Noyes accepts *a priori* Johnson's total rejection of Hume: "This work [Hume's essay "Of Miracles"] almost cried out for an

---

[1] Ernest C. Mossner, *The Forgotten Hume* (New York, 1943), 189–209.

[2] "Samuel Johnson: Student of Hume," *University of Mississippi Studies in English,* 3 (1962), 91–94. Mr. Noyes nicely sums up Hume's argument: "The core of Hume's argument against the validity of miracles is that the evidence against each of them is necessarily greater than the evidence for them—and we cannot, in reason, accept the lesser probability as true. It is more probable, Hume maintains, that those attesting to the miracle should be lying, or should be themselves deceived, than that the miracle should have come about" (93).

[3] *The Life of Samuel Johnson, LL.D., with a Journal of a Tour to the Hebrides with Samuel Johnson,* ed. G. B. Hill, revised and enlarged by L. F. Powell (Oxford, 1934–50), I, 428; hereafter *Life.*

answer from the man who later was to handle Soame Jenyns' 'Enquiry into the Nature and Origin of Evil' so roughly."[4] Need one suggest that it makes little sense to conclude that the way Johnson felt about Jenyns he would also have felt about Hume? The turgid Jenyns and the incisive Hume are hardly in the same class.[5] Moreover, Johnson's final remark that "the weight of common testimony" silences such doubts is not in conflict with Hume's essay. Also referring to historical events such as great battles, Hume had granted that "some human testimony has the utmost force and authority in some cases," as "when it relates the battles of Philippi or Pharsalia."[6] The point is that no one disputed the event of these battles, as indeed the French had not denied the existence of Wolfe or the outcome of the battle of Quebec. However, if rival factions had claimed the victory, whether of Philippi or Quebec, then there would have been difficulty in knowing whom to believe. And when in doubt, one might well have been justified in believing the lesser miracle, on Humean grounds.

It is not my intention to spin out an epistemological web. Rather, I am interested in showing that Johnson must have found much of Hume's inquiry stimulating and useful—a kind of thinking to be reckoned with, certainly not rejected out of hand. It is possible, for example, to read through Hume's essay "Of Miracles" and discover much that Johnson would hardly have questioned. He would have applauded Hume's animadversions against the human love of the wondrous: "With what greediness are the miraculous accounts of travelers received, their descriptions of sea and land monsters, their relations of wonderful adventures, strange men and uncouth manners?" (125). One thinks of the *Preface to Lobo's Voyage,* of *Idler* No. 49 on Will Marvel, or indeed of *A Journey to the Western Islands of Scotland,* a book which illustrates a Johnson at work applying many of Hume's principles of reasoned skepticism. Take the examination of the second sight: Johnson by no means comes away spreading wild tales about visionary miracles. In spite of wishing to believe, he finds in the end that the evidence is insufficient.[7] If human experience is the bedrock of Humean thinking, then *A Journey* shows Johnson sifting through empirical evidence in a manner which Hume could have found only commendable.

Two facts relating to Hume obsessed Boswell: (1) Hume's undermining of the miraculous foundation of the Christian religion; (2) Hume's easiness at the imminence of death. In his conversations with Johnson, Boswell would sometimes introduce those subjects to plumb his friend's reactions. Johnson's talk reveals an awareness of the serious issues raised by Hume's position, and he treats Boswell's doubts by both earnest reasoning and a playful twitting of

[4]Noyes, 92–93.

[5]Johnson's objection to Jenyns is in large measure that Jenyns misused the powers of language, either covering up his ignorance with specious language or dressing up commonplaces in pompous phrasing.

[6]The Library of Liberal Arts edition of *An Inquiry Concerning Human Understanding,* ed. C. W. Hendel (New York, 1955), 134.

[7]*The Yale Edition of the Works of Samuel Johnson,* ed. Mary Lascelles (New Haven, 1971), IX, 110.

Hume. At two different times Boswell confronts Johnson with Hume's argument against miracles. Although he is inclined to dismiss Hume with the cavalier remark that "every thing which Hume has advanced against Christianity had passed through my mind long before he wrote" (*Life*, I, 444), Johnson nonetheless feels compelled to deal seriously with Hume's questioning: "Why, Sir, the great difficulty of proving miracles should make us very cautious in believing them." Johnson's defense of the credibility of the Christian miracles is not a satisfactory reply to Hume, but Johnson does place his arguments in a Humean context:

The miracles which prove it are attested by men who had no interest in deceiving us; but who, on the contrary, were told that they should suffer persecution, and did actually lay down their lives in confirmation of the truth of the facts which they asserted. Indeed, for some centuries the heathens did not pretend to deny the miracles; but said they were performed by the aid of evil spirits. This is a circumstance of great weight (*Life*, I, 445).

Or at other times, Johnson emphasizes that great and learned men like Grotius and Newton—and not always the ignorant and superstitious—have weighed the evidence and been convinced (*Life*, I, 454–55). Nowhere does Johnson simply brush away Hume's arguments without conceding, either implicitly or directly, that they pose problems. In the following passage, he pays them the tribute of considering them as obstacles to be sidestepped:

Talking of Dr. Johnson's unwillingness to believe extraordinary things, I ventured to say, "Sir, you come near Hume's argument against miracles, 'That it is more probable witnesses should lie, or be mistaken, than that they should happen.' " JOHNSON. "Why, Sir, Hume, taking the proposition simply, is right. But the Christian revelation is not proved by the miracles alone, but as connected with prophecies, and with the doctrine in confirmation of which the miracles were wrought" (*Life*, III, 188).

It is worth noting here that "Hume . . . is right," at least "taking the proposition simply."

Johnson's attitude toward ghosts, though the object of some ridicule, was hardly antipodes away from Hume's. Surely Johnson allowed for the possibility of their existence, scarcely a concession Hume would tolerate, but Johnson would admit that " 'a man who thinks he has seen an apparition, can only be convinced himself; his authority will not convince another, and his conviction, if rational, must be founded on being told something which cannot be known but by supernatural means' " (*Life*, IV, 94; cf. I, 405). Hume could not cavil too much at this kind of statement. Imagining the possibility of Hume face to face with a genuine (and fitting) miracle, Johnson suggests, no doubt with a wry grin, that it would take something on the order of this sort of miracle to convert the stubborn Hume: "Here then was a man, who had been at no pains to inquire into the truth of religion, and had continually turned his mind the other way. It was not to be expected that the prospect of death would alter his way of thinking, unless God should send an angel to set him right" (*Life*, III, 153). Johnson's evidence for suggesting that Hume had not inquired into religion was only hearsay (*Life*, III, 153). Johnson was not being fair, of course; he was being satirical—never an impartial mode. Still, it is interesting that his attempt to ridicule Hume should playfully involve some of Hume's own assumptions.

The differences between Johnson and Hume may then be seen as stemming from one man's willingness and determination to believe, and a resistance to belief by the other. Johnson's attempts to combat the corrosive skepticism of Hume were largely ineffectual, yet on the two occasions when Johnson comments on Hume's vaunted indifference to dying, a stance that for Boswell seemed to strike a fatal blow at the consolation of religion, Johnson does prove himself a worthy opponent of the serene and imperturbable Scot. We might observe as well that by ridiculing Hume, Johnson was attacking the ultimate goal of pagan philosophy, the goal of *ataraxia,* discussed, for example, in Thomas Stanley's *History of Philosophy* in the section on Epicurus. Johnson applies Hume's own arguments in the essay "Of Miracles" with the rigor of Hume's most faithful disciple to discount the story Boswell told:

I said he told me he was quite easy at the thought of annihilation. "He lied," said Dr. Johnson. "He had a vanity in being thought easy. It is more probable that he lied than that so very improbable a thing should be as a man not afraid of death; of going into an unknown state and not being uneasy at leaving all that he knew. And you are to consider that upon his own principle of annihilation he had no motive not to lie."[8]

I told him that David Hume said he was no more uneasy to think he should *not be* after this life than that he *had not been* before he began to exist. JOHNSON. "Sir, if a man really thinks so his perceptions are disturbed, he is mad; if he does not think so, he lies. Hume knows he lies. He may tell you he holds his finger in the flame of a candle without feeling pain; would you believe him?"[9]

We notice in both passages Johnson insisting that not to be afraid of death runs counter to common experience. He asks us to judge which is more probable, that Hume really was unafraid or that there are other explanations, such as Hume's derangement or his lying to flatter his vanity and to promote his own philosophy. (Hume himself had warned that no kind of marvelous story was more to be suspected than that which tended to make its narrator a prophet and so establish a religion.) Johnson likens the story to something absurdly contrary to ordinary experience, as if Hume might say he had held his finger in a flame and experienced no pain: could one believe that? Once again, Johnson is not being entirely fair, for history can supply many examples of men who were not afraid to die and even a few who were wonderfully insensitive to physical stimuli. But Johnson is talking for victory; he is attempting to discredit Hume, and discrediting an infidel justifies many strategies for Johnson, including even foul play, if it works. In a discussion that began with a mention of Hume's "Of Miracles," Johnson observed: " 'When a

---

[8] *Boswell In Extremes, 1776–1778,* from *The Yale Editions of The Private Papers of James Boswell,* ed. C. McC. Weis and F. A. Pottle (New York, 1970), 155; cf. *Life,* III, 153.

[9] *Boswell in Search of a Wife, 1766–1769,* from *The Yale Editions of The Private Papers of James Boswell,* ed. F. Brady and F. A. Pottle (New York, 1956), 332; cf. *Life,* II, 106.

man voluntarily engages in an important controversy, he is to do all he can to lessen his antagonist, because authority from personal respect has much weight with most people, and often more than reasoning. . . .' [Dr. William] ADAMS. 'You would not jostle a chimney-sweeper.' JOHNSON. 'Yes, Sir, if it were necessary to jostle him *down*' " (*Life,* II, 443). Thus by Hume's own method Johnson has satirically intimated that one can regard Hume's claim only with a skepticism as deep and as justified as Hume had displayed toward the evidence for Christianity: a man's not fearing death would have to be viewed simply as a miracle. With delightful ironic wit, if not with perfect logic, Johnson has turned the tables by portraying Hume himself as the self-interested exploiter of the miraculous. In this particular instance, at least, Johnson had found a use for Hume's argument.

University of South Carolina.

Chapter IX

HUME AND JOHNSON ON PROPHECY AND MIRACLES: HISTORICAL CONTEXT

By James E. Force

In a discussion in this journal, Donald T. Siebert attempts to revise our picture of the relationship between Dr. Samuel Johnson and David Hume. Siebert questions Mossner's contention that Johnson is an implacable enemy of Hume's thought by showing how often Johnson utilizes Humean philosophy. Siebert states that "By focusing on Johnson's treatment of Hume's well-known essay 'Of Miracles' . . . , I wish to argue that regardless of his antagonism to Hume, Johnson by no means blindly rejected Hume's reasoning."[1] Siebert specifies that he wishes to show "that Johnson must have found much of Hume's inquiry stimulating and useful—a kind of thinking to be reckoned with, certainly not rejected out of hand."[2]

To show that "nowhere does Johnson simply brush away Hume's arguments," Siebert especially emphasizes Boswell's report that Hume's argument is right. Siebert quotes Boswell's account:

Talking of Dr. Johnson's unwillingness to believe extraordinary things, I ventured to say, "Sir, you come near Hume's argument against miracles, 'That it is more probable witnesses should lie, or be mistaken, than that they should happen.'" JOHNSON. "Why, Sir, Hume, taking the proposition simply, is right. But the Christian revelation is not proved by the miracles alone, but as connected with prophecies, and with the doctrine in confirmation of which the miracles were wrought" (*Life*, III, 188).[3]

Siebert is right in his assumption that the hard-headed Johnson often sounds remarkably like Hume when, for example, he refuses to believe the miraculous reports of the vulgar and of travelers.[4] Both men detest "enthusiasm." However, Siebert is mistaken in his assertion that Johnson never rejects Humean reasoning "blindly" or "out of hand." In the lengthy citation above from Boswell's biography where Johnson proclaims Hume's argument against the possibility of believing in a miraculous event on the basis of historical testimony, there is ample evidence against Siebert that Johnson is in fact blindly ignoring the essential element of Hume's essay. Indeed, Johnson's statement that "the Christian revelation is not proved by the miracles alone, but as connected with prophecies" indicates that quite possibly Johnson had not even read Hume's essay and only knew of its line of argument in the most general terms, probably via Boswell. If Johnson

---

[1] Donald T. Siebert, Jr., "Johnson and Hume on Miracles," *Journal of the History of Ideas*, **36** (July-Sept. 1975), 543.   [2] *Ibid*., 544.   [3] *Ibid*.   [4] *Ibid*.

had read Hume's essay "Of Miracles" he would have noticed (given his explicitly stated reliance on prophecy as the chief apologetic argument for Christianity) the concluding paragraph of Hume's discussion "Of Miracles":

What we have said of miracles may be applied, without any variation, to prophecies; and indeed, all prophecies are real miracles, and as such only, can be admitted as proofs of any revelation. If it did not exceed the capacity of human nature to foretell future events, it would be absurd to employ any prophecy as an argument for a divine mission or authority from heaven.[5]

To see how crucial this paragraph is, I will trace the development of the argument from prophecy in the first half of the eighteenth century. Once this historical context is presented, I will show how Hume endeavors to link the argument from prophecy with the argument from miracles only to be able to destroy both. Thus, Hume's attack on prophecies is not accomplished *en passant* but is integral to Hume's skeptical criticism of establishment theism.

I. *The Argument from Prophecy: The Citadel of Orthodoxy*

The argument from prophecy depends on the definition of prophecy prevalent in the first half of the eighteenth century. Johnson's famous dictionary (1755) defines the noun "prophecy" as "a declaration of something to come; prediction" and defines the verb "to prophesy" as "to predict; to foretell; to prognosticate."[6] A prophecy is a prediction and to prophesy is to predict.

In the argument from prophecy, prophetic predictions connect the Old Testament with the figure of Jesus, the anticipated messiah, and thus gives the argument a distinctly historical complexion. With the passage of time, the prediction can be either confirmed, refuted, or reinterpreted.

The argument from prophecy has a long history in Christian philosophizing; it begins with Justin Martyr who is cited, by the deist Anthony Collins, as believing that "predictions fulfilled are the strongest demonstration of the truth."[7] Nearer to Hume's time, Ralph Cudworth makes much of fulfilled prophetic predictions as a test of truth regarding Jesus' messiahship. Unlike the reports of miracles,

---

[5] David Hume, *Enquiries Concerning Human Understanding and Concerning the Principles of Morals*, reprinted from the posthumous edition of 1777 and edited by L.A. Selby-Bigge; Third Edition, with text revised and noted by P.H. Nidditch (Oxford, 1975), 130-31.

[6] Samuel Johnson, *A Dictionary of English Language: in which the Words are deduced from their originals, and illustrated in their different significations by examples from the Lost writers* (London, 1755), s.v. "prophecy" and "prophesy."

[7] Anthony Collins, *The Scheme of Literal Prophecy* (London, 1727), 343.

predictions which are fulfilled with the passage of time cannot "possibly be imputed by Atheists, as other things, to mean *Fear* and *Fancy*, nor yet to the *Fiction of Politicians*."[8] For Cudworth as for Justin Martyr, Christianity is the true religion and its deniers false because the Bible "contained in it so many unquestionable Predictions of Events to follow a long time after . . . ."[9] which in fact did follow.

The argument from prophecy, as shaped just prior to the opening of the eighteenth century by John Locke, guarantees the reasonableness of Christianity because of the way Jesus fulfills the Old Testament prophecies of a miracle-worker. Miracles and prophecies here stand in a mutually supporting synthesis, the latter predicting the former and the former confirming the latter. For Locke, the miracles of Jesus are only significant becaue they were prophesied.[10]

The other major intellect dominating the intellectual gateway to the eighteenth century, Isaac Newton, also regards prophecy as the foundation of Christianity. In such prophecies as the seventy weeks of Daniel, which Newton, the Biblical chronologist,[11] understands as a sure proof that Jesus is the messiah because He fulfills the prediction, Newton finds a guarantee of the reasonableness of Christianity.[12]

---

[8] Ralph Cudworth, *The True Intellectual System of the Universe wherein All the Reason and Philosophy of Atheism is Confuted, and its Impossibility Demonstrated* (London, 1678), 714.   [9]*Ibid.*, 713.

[10] John Locke, *The Reasonableness of Christianity as Delivered in the Scriptures* (London, 1695), 55. See also Edward Stillingfleet, *Origines Sacrae, or a Rational Account of Christian Faith, as the Truth and Divine Authority of the Scriptures, and the matters therein contained* (London, 1662), 262, and George Stanhope, *The Truth and Excellence of the Christian Religion Asserted Against Jews, Infidels, and Hereticks, in sixteen sermons Preached at the Lecture Founded by the Honourable Robert Boyle, Esq; For the Years 1701, 1702* (London, 1702), 26. The eight sermons for 1701 are separately titled *The Christian Interpretation of Prophecies Vindicated*.

[11] Newton, as Manuel has shown, regards himself as an historian, as well as a scientist. He considers the prophecies of Daniel and the Book of Revelations which refer to events already fulfilled in history, i.e., the historical prophecies which include those predicting the messiah, as useful sources for historians, if properly interpreted. The problem, of course, is that the greater part of these works is written in language which does not refer immediately to the historical world although Newton, following Joseph Mede, is convinced that the Book of Daniel and the Book of Revelations is nothing less than the panorama of history "from the beginning of the Captivity of Israel, until the Mystery of God should be finished." See Joseph Mede, *The Apostasy of Latter Times*, in *The Works of Joseph Mede*, ed. J. Worthington (London, 1672), 654. Newton fully accepts this view of the sweep and range of these prophecies and works out a lengthy method which is basically a table of conversion. In his unique hermeneutic method, Newton assumes that an event mentioned figuratively in a historical prophecy in Daniel as occurring in the "world natural" refers to an historical event in the "world politic." See Isaac Newton, *Observations Upon the Prophecies of Daniel and the Apocalypse of St. John* (London, 1733), 16.

[12] Newton, *Observations Upon the Prophecies*, 252.

As a youth Newton conjectures about the actual date of the fulfillment of Christ's second coming by incautiously choosing the year
1680.[13] Later he becomes more reticent about interpreting the exact
date of the fulfillment of apocalyptic prophecies.[14]

Unlike Locke (who appropriates miracles into his version of the
argument from prophecy as one of the prophetic predictions fulfilled
by Jesus), Newton relies almost exclusively on other predictions fulfilled by Jesus and ignores miracles as a rational argument for the truth
of Christianity. Newton rarely discusses miracles and when he does
he indicates that they are not really disturbances or violations in
nature's laws but are simply unusual events which excite wonder in
the mind of the vulgar. Newton says, "For miracles are not so called
because they are the works of God, but because they happen seldom
and for that reason excite wonder."[15] As the debate concerning
prophecies develops, this tendency to ignore miracles and concentrate on grounding Christian apologetics solely in the argument from
prophecy continues until, under pressure from such deists as Anthony
Collins, miracles are once again pressed into service as a completely
independent rational argument.

By 1713 Anthony Collins had become a leader of the "new sect"
of freethinkers whose members regularly convened at the Grecian
Coffee House in the Strand near Temple Bar.[16] In his first major
rationalistic assault on traditional religion in his *A Discourse on Freethinking* (1713), Collins argues that freethinking is based on the foundational rights of a man freely and rationally to ascertain and weigh
the evidence for his beliefs and to stick to what his reason reveals to
him even when such beliefs are contrary to religious authority.[17] Applying his freethinking to the Bible Collins notes the vast number of
widely differing textual interpretations regarding, for example, the
canon of Scripture, the Trinity, the eternity of Hell's torments, and
the text of Scripture itself. Variant readings on these and other points
necessitate free-thought and the supremacy of reason over religion.
For Collins reason inevitably leads rational men to the abandonment
of revealed religion.

The great classicist, Master of Trinity College, Cambridge, and
former Boyle Lecturer, Richard Bentley, replies to Collins' book by
claiming, first, that the most genuine freethinkers and rationalists
such as the Newtonians and the members of the Royal Society utilize

---

[13] Frank E. Manuel, *The Religion of Isaac Newton* (Oxford, 1974), 99-100. Manuel
cites evidence discovered in Newton's manuscripts in Jerusalem.

[14] Newton, *Observations Upon the Prophecies*, 252.

[15] Newton, *Theological Manuscripts*, ed. H. McLachlan (Liverpool, 1950), 17.

[16] J. H. Monk, *The Life of Richard Bentley* (London, 1830), 268.

[17] A. Collins, *A Discourse on Freethinking* (2nd ed., London, 1713), 171-76.

the canon of scientific reason to support religion. The scientists who have cast so much light on the workings of nature have all been "hearty professors and practisers of religion, and among them several priests."[18] Second, Bentley, a genuine expert in textual exegesis (which Collins was clearly not) shows that merely because there are many differing interpretations of a particular passages does not render the text utterly unreliable and open to doubt. The critical apparatus of sound scholarship still serves to elicit both the true text and a sound exegesis but, as Bentley shows in detail, these are jobs for real experts and not for amateurs such as Collins.

Bentley triumphs. He shows clearly that Collins does not show any real contradictions in Holy Writ and that Collins lacks the scholarship to pursue such historical criticism. But in applying the critical tools of the classical philologist to a defense of scripture, the Bible is reduced to the level of any other historical document. As Leslie Stephen points out, such a defense is as damaging as the assault itself.[19] Thoroughly routed by Bentley and by the savage burlesque of Jonathan Swift and the counter-attacks of others,[20] Collins departs for Holland. He reappears on the scene in 1724 with a frontal assault on the argument from prophecy in a work which the strident apologist, William Warburton, declared one of the most plausible arguments against Christianity ever written[21]: A Discourse Concerning the Grounds and Reasons of the Christian Religion.

It is an indication of the importance of prophecy as a proof of Christianity in the first half of the eighteenth century that Collins chooses to attack Christianity by attacking the proofs from prophecy and the claims of interpreters of prophecy. He ignores miracles as inconclusive proofs that Jesus is the messiah even if they did happen. Like his mentor Locke, Collins firmly believes that the importance of miracles in demonstrating the central tenet of Christianity, i.e., that Jesus is the expected messiah, is that they were predicted in prophecy:

Those miracles were prophesy'd of in the Old Testament, like other Matters of the Gospel; and therefore they are no otherwise to be consider'd as Proofs

---

[18] Bentley writes the following work under the pseudonym of Phileleutherus Lipsiensis. Remarks upon a Late Discourse (6th ed., London, 1725), I, 24.

[19] Leslie Stephen, History of English Thought in the Eighteenth Century, 2 vols. (New York, 1962), I, 172.

[20] See Swift, Mr. Collins' Discourse of Freethinking, put into plain English, by way of abstract, for the use of the Poor (London, 1713). Other replies in the storm of protest to Collins' work come from divines such as William Whiston, Benjamin Hoadly, Daniel Williams, Benjamin Ibbot (who directs his Boyle Lectures of 1713 and 1714 against Collins), the Whig Richard Steele, and the philosopher and future Bishop of Cloyne, George Berkeley.

[21] Leslie Stephen, History of English Thought, I, 179.

of those Points, than as fulfilling the Sayings in the Old Testament, other Gospel-matters and Events or (as a Boylean Lecturer well expresses it) as comprehended in, and exactly consonant to the Prophesies concerning the Messias. In that Sense they are good Proofs, and in that Sense only. For, as I have before observed, if Jesus is not the Person prophesy'd of as Messias in the Old Testament, his Miracles will not prove him to be so, nor prove his divine Mission.[22]

Collins perceives that the core of Christianity is that Jesus is the messiah, but also that the only "proof" which can establish this core tenet is the argument from prophecy. If this argument is valid, "Christianity is invincibly establish'd on its true Foundation."[23] If, on the other hand, the argument is invalid, "then is Christianity false."[24] The good deist Collins attempts to show that the argument from prophecy is invalid by casting doubt on any exegetical attempt by Biblical scholars to connect the Old and New Testaments. Relying on the Biblical scholarship of Richard Simon, Collins attacks the *literal* version of the argument, which holds that Jesus directly and literally fulfills Old Testament prophecies, maintaining that the very text of the Bible is so corrupt that a reconstruction of the original text is simply not possible.[25]

Collins' immediate opponent in this assault on the argument from prophecy is his old antagonist, William Whiston.[26] In 1722 Whiston published his long projected response to the deist criticism of the "Ancient Knots and difficulties" involved in the *literal* argument from prophecy entitled *An Essay Towards Restoring the True Text of the Old for Testament And for Vindicating the Citations made thence in the New Testament.* Whiston treats the deist attack on the literal connection between New Testament references to Old Testament prophecies as a problem engendered by corruptions and mistakes in our copies of the Old Testament. Whiston's method of correcting the text is to use the most ancient and uncorrupt versions to correct the text, which is more or less the way Biblical scholars proceed today.

---

[22] Anthony Collins, *A Discourse Concerning the Grounds and Reasons of the Christian Religion* (London, 1737), 33. The "Boylean Lecturer" cited in this text by Collins is George Stanhope, *The Truth and Excellence of the Christian Religion Asserted Against Jews, Infidels, and Hereticks...* (London, 1702), Sermon 8, p. 19.

[23] Collins, *Discourse Concerning the Grounds and Reasons of the Christian Religion*, 24.   [24] *Ibid.*, 28.

[25] *Ibid.*, 193.

[26] Collins, the leader of a group of freethinkers who met regularly at the Grecian Coffee House in the Strand near Temple Bar, mentions that Whiston "frequents the most publick Coffee-Houses, where most are prone to show him respect, and none dare show him any Disrespect; the Clergy either flying before him, or making a feeble Opposition to him." *Ibid.*, 244. From Whiston's *Memoirs* (London, 1753), 158, we know that "he and Collins often dined at Lady Caverly's house in Soho Square, and to have frequent, but friendly debates, about the truth of the bible and the Christian religion."

In one innovative recommendation Whiston proposes a "Great Search" for the most ancient Hebrew copies "in all Parts of the World," anticipating the discovery of the complete text of *Isaiah* from the second century B.C.[27]

For Collins, however, reconstructing the true text of the Bible is impossible in principle because all prophetic texts are mere fables. Besides, Collins argues "that a *Bible restored*, according to Mr. W.'s *Theory*, will be a mere WHISTONIAN BIBLE, a BIBLE confounding and not containing the *True Text* of the Old Testament."[28]

Collins also flays the argument from prophecy in its *allegorical* form which holds that Jesus fulfills Old Testament prophecy "typically" or allegorically, not literally. The butt of this part of his polemic is the "learned Surenhusius," a Dutch writer who claimed to have rediscovered the ancient Jewish method of deriving a prophecy's "hidden," typical meaning. Surenhusius' rules of interpreting prophetic language include such cryptographic embellishments as "changing the order of words, adding words, and retrenching words, which is a method often used by St. Paul."[29] Collins' point is clear: according to Surenhusius' absurd method, prophecies are made meaningless when they are rearranged to suit the requirements of the particular interpreter.

Collins' all out attack on both forms of the argument from prophecy indicates that he (as well as Locke, Newton, and Whiston) assumes Christianity to be founded mainly on that argument. The avalanche of protests shows how sensitive religious writers were to this line of attack. By Collins' own count there had appeared by 1727 thirty-two intensely hostile replies which sought to defend the argument from prophecy.[30]

One of the most interesting replies to Collins, especially in the light of Hume's "Of Miracles," is Whiston's own counter-counter-attack in which he explicitly attempts to apply the constructive criticisms of the Royal Society to the interpretation of prophecy. Whiston argues that feigned hypotheses have no place in scriptural interpretation in which the experimental method should reign supreme as it does in the physical sciences. For Whiston, as well as for some of his philosophic contemporaries, prophecies are predictions which may be verified to a degree of probability ("moral certainty") by examining the testi-

---

[27] Whiston, *An Essay Towards Restoring the True Text of the Old Testament And for Vindicating the Citations made thence in the New Testament* (London, 1722), 333. Whiston does make some glaring errors, most notably in his incorrect dating of the so-called *Apostolic Constitutions*. But his general method is sound and also corresponds on many particular points with modern textual scholarship.

[28] Collins, *Discourse* (London, 1724), 196.

[29] *Ibid.*, 60.

[30] Collins, *Scheme of Literal Prophecy Considered* (London, 1727), Preface.

mony of the most ancient historical testimony. Such a procedure is analogous to a scientific experiment because ultimately these testimonies are based on the sense experience, memory, and documents of the reporters. The following text shows how Whiston clearly believes that he is extending the experimental philosophy of the Royal Society, the College of Physicians, and the law courts into the realms of natural and revealed religion.

Nor do I find that Mankind are usually influenc'd to change their Opinions by any Thing so much, as by Matters of Fact and Experiment; either appealing to their own Senses now; or by the faithful Histories of such Facts and Experiments that appealed to the Senses of former Ages. And if once the Learned come to be as wise in Religious Matters, as they are now generally become in those that are Philosophical and Medical, and Judicial; if they will imitate the Royal Society, the College of Physicians, or the Judges in Courts of Justice; (which last I take to be the most satisfactory Determiners of Right and Wrong, the most impartial and successful *Judges of Controversy* now in the World:) If they will lay no other Preliminaries down but our natural Notions, or the concurrent Sentiments of sober Persons in all Ages and Countries; which we justly call the Law or *Religion of Nature*. . . . And if they will then proceed in their Enquiries about Reveal'd Religion, by real Evidence and Ancient Records, I verily believe, and that upon much examination and Experience of my own, that the Variety of Opinions about those Matters now in the World, will gradually diminish; the Objections against the Bible will greatly wear off; and genuine Christianity, without either *Priestcraft* or *Laycraft*, will more and more take Place among Mankind.[31]

Whiston utilizes the constructive critical methodology proposed by John Wilkins (and, with minor changes in terminology, by Tillotson, Chillingworth, Boyle, Glanville, Locke, and Newton) to argue that the evidence that Old Testament prophecies are literally fulfilled by Jesus yields not absolutely certain knowledge but only morally certain knowledge.[32]

Of the thirty-two adverse replies to Collins' *Discourse,* the most common approach (exemplified by Whiston's own response above), is to defend the argument from prophecy. Collins ignores miracles and most of his respondents do, too, in the mad scramble of 1725 to salvage the argument from prophecy. However a second, minority mode of defense shifts the ground of debate by denying Collins' explicitly proclaimed premise that fulfilled prophecy is the only "reasonable" foundation and attempts to vindicate religion on the

---

[31] William Whiston, *A Supplement to the Literal Accomplishment of Scripture Prophecies Containing Observations on Dr. Clarke's and Bishop Chandler's late Discourses on the Prophecies of the Old Testament* (London, 1725), 5-6. This text is one of the most direct statements of the relationship between religion and science among the Newtonians on this subject. See James E. Force, "Linking History and Rationale Science in the Enlightenment: William Whiston's *Astronomical Principles of Religion, Natural and Reveal'd* (1717)" in the facsimile edition of that work forthcoming from the Georg Olms Verlag in Hildesheim, West Germany.
[32] Whiston, *A Supplement*, 8.

basis of the reported miracles of Jesus. The few thinkers who fall in this category tend to consider the argument from prophecy as a sort of ravelin, a mere outwork, and, conceding its conquest, fall back to what they consider the main line of defense of the Christian religion against the deists, the argument from miracles.

The argument from miracles, considered as separate and independent of that of prophecy, does not, of course, originate in these responses to Collins' attack on the argument from prophecy. If anything, they only breathe new life into an argument which dates back to the early Christian centuries.[33] In the fifty years preceding the writing of Hume's essay there is a steady stream of apologists, from Grotius through Stillingfleet and Charles Leslie, who argue that the miracles which Jesus performed are sufficient to prove the truth of revealed scripture.[34] Nevertheless, the argument from prophecy continued for two decades to be the most important single rational argument for the truth of the Christian revelation. Even Bishop Sherlock, whose famous work, *The Trial of the Witnesses* is one of best defenses of the credibility of such miracles as the Resurrection,[35] accepts

[33] R. M. Grant, *Miracle and Natural Law in the Graeco-Roman and Early Christian Thought* (Amsterdam, 1952).

[34] Hugo Grotius, *The Truth of the Christian Religion*, trans. Simon Patrick (London, 1680), 21. Interestingly enough, even Grotius ultimately understands miracles to confirm Jesus as the Messiah because he performs them as predicted in prophecy. *Ibid.*, 58: Bishop Stillingfleet emphasizes that miracles are the best rational evidence which tends to confirm the truth of a Divine testimony but he also discusses "The Tryal of Prophetical Predictions and Miracles." See his *Origines Sacrae: Or a Rational Account of the Christian Faith, as to the Truth and Divine Authority of the Scriptures, and the Matters Therein contain'd* (London, 1662), 177-78, 184; Charles Leslie, *A Short and Easie Method with the Deists* (London, 1698), 4. Another very important statement of the argument from miracles is one which is independent of and contemporary with the Collins-Whiston controversy over prophecies. This is John Conybeare's sermon, *The Nature, Possibility and Certainty of Miracles Set Forth: and the Truth of the Christian Religion Prov'd from Thence: A Sermon Preach'd before the University of Oxford, at St. Mary's, on Sunday, December 24th 1721* (London, 1722). See also John Green, *Letters to the Author of the Discourse of the Grounds and Reasons of the Christian Religion* (London, 1726) and Theophilus Lobb, *A Brief Defense of the Christian Religion* (London, 1726).

[35] Sherlock's book is written in answer to six essays by Thomas Woolston. In the last line of *The Scheme of Literal Prophecy Considered* (London, 1727), Anthony Collins promises soon to publish "a discourse upon the miracles recorded in the Old and New Testaments" (439). Woolston attempts to carry out this deist enterprise in a work entitled *Six Discourses on Miracles* (London, 1727-1729). Sherlock then answers Woolston by attempting to demonstrate the credibility of the Apostles, who are charged (in a mock trial at one of the Inns of Court) with giving false evidence. Sherlock argues in legal style that their testimony is believable because many men forsake their old beliefs and embrace Christianity because the Apostles are willing to face death rather than renounce their testimony and because there is no *a priori* assumption against miracles. See Thomas Sherlock, *The Trial of the Witnesses*, in *Works* (London, 1830), V, 170 and 182. Like Whiston, Bishop Sherlock puts great stock in the common sense methodology of the law courts.

prophecy as the most fundamental argument for revealed religion. Whether or not Jesus is the Messiah still "must be try'd by the Words of Prophesy."[36]

By the middle of the eighteenth century, the argument from prophecy was still the dominant argument for the truth of revealed religion. Its formulation grew largely out of a controversy between the Newtonian, William Whiston, and the deist, Anthony Collins. Such is the historical context of Johnson's remark that while Hume's argument in "On Miracles" may be telling against (the possibility of believing) miracles, ". . . the Christian revelation is not proved by the miracles alone, but as connected with prophecies, and with the doctrine in confirmation of which the miracles were wrought."[37]

II. *Hume's Quarrel with the Argument from Prophecy*

It is difficult to believe that Hume could have been unaware of this controversy. Perhaps the real mystery is that his essay is not entitled "Of Prophecy." "Of Miracles" appeared in the *Enquiry* of 1748 (it was excised from the *Treatise* published in 1739). It begins with a section designed to show what the proper method of reasoning is in deciding whether to believe a miracle happened. As in the inference from effect to cause, so too in this case, "A wise man proportions his belief to the evidence."[38] The evidence for miracles derives from human testimony and our own experience and is regarded "as a *proof* or a *probability* according to the conjunction between any particular kind of report and any of argument has been found to be constant or variable."[39]

In the first section, Hume concentrates on the conflict between each individual's experience of the operation of natural law and a miracle. Although Hume considers the idea of necessity in causation indemonstrable, he does recognize a regularity of succession in practical human experience because of a generally observed constant

[36] Thomas Sherlock, *The Use and Intent of Prophecy* (London, 1732), 49.

[37] In the phrase ". . . and with the doctrine in confirmation of which the miracles were wrought," Johnson reiterates one of the basic anti-Catholic principles standard since it was first stated by the Bishop of Norwich, Joseph Hall, in the seventeenth century: "Miracles must be judged by the doctrine which they confirme; not the doctrine by the miracles." *The Oxford English Dictionary*, s.v. "Miracles." For the good Anglican Bishop, "Biblical" miracles are true while "Catholic" miracles are false. This polemical point is reiterated in 1752 by John Douglas, later Bishop of Salisbury, in his answer to Hume's essay, *The Criterion: or, Miracles Examined.* Hume's interest in miracles probably begins with the miracles reportedly performed at the tomb of the Abbé Pâris. Mossner conjectures that while on the scene in Paris (Hume stayed in France from 1734 to 1737) Hume's interest in the "problem" of miracles was stirred. See Ernest Campbell Mossner, *The Life of David Hume* (London and Edinburgh, 1954), 95.

[38] David Hume, "Of Miracles," 110.   [39] *Ibid.*, 111.

conjunction of successive events in experience. Laws of nature, for Hume, are established because of universally firm and unalterable human experience of such a succession of events. A miracle, however, is by definition "the violation of laws of nature."[40] Because a miracle is a violation of that for which we have a "firm and unalterable"[41] experience, the evidence for a miraculous event must be of a degree of strength which is impossible to obtain. The more miraculous an event appears to be, the more contrary to our daily experience of the operation of the laws of nature and, consequently, the less believable it is.

Hume acknowledges the possibility of apparent exceptions to natural law but argues, with the example of the native Indian's ignorance of the freezing of water in Northern climates, that such exceptions are due to limited experience. They are not really violations of the law of nature but result from a lack of experience, in this case a lack of experience of the ineluctable regularity with which water freezes below a certain temperature.

To believe in a miracle requires evidence that is impossible to obtain because it runs counter to our unalterable experience to the contrary. And when one considers how susceptible to deception and error are the historical testimonies of such prodigies, the "plain consequence" is the "general maxim":

That no testimony is sufficient to establish a miracle, unless the testimony be of such a kind, that its falsehood would be more miraculous than the fact which it endeavours to establish; and even in that case there is a mutual destruction of arguments, and the superior only gives us an assurance suitable to that degree of force, which remains, after deducting the inferior. When anyone tells me, that he saw a dead man restored to life, I immediately consider with myself, whether it be more probable, that this person should either deceive or be deceived, or that the fact, which he relates, should really have happened. I weigh the one miracle against the other; and according to the superiority, which I discover, I pronounce my decision, and always reject the greater miracle.[42]

The second section of this essay examines the sorts of testimony upon which the credibility of miracles is founded to see if there are any which satisfies the criterion that their falsehood would be a greater miracle than the miracles which it purports to establish in the first place. Hume finds no examples where falsehood of such testimony would be more miraculous than the event it is used to confirm. Hume first indicts the credibility of enthusiasts who rush to affirm the mirac-

---

[40] *Ibid.*, 114.   [41] *Ibid.*

[42] *Ibid.*, 115-16. Hume here neatly uses the same standards recommended in Whiston's mitigated skeptical methodology for the establishment of the plausibility of "Reveal'd Religion, by real Evidence and Ancient Records" to establish their implausibility. See Note 31.

ulous tales of travellers.[43] Johnson echoes this point in places indicated by Siebert, but the agreement is more one of similar temperaments than a sign that Johnson "must have found much of Hume's inquiry stimulating and useful—a kind of thinking to be reckoned with, certainly not rejected out of hand."[44]

Human fascination with miraculous tales is not the only factor which reduces their credibility. According to Hume, there are three others. First, no miracle has ever been testified to by a sufficient number of hard-headed, enlightened Scotsmen, i.e., "men of such unquestioned good-sense, education, and learning, as to secure us against all delusion in themselves."[45] Second, it is only the ignorant and barbaric who believe in miracles and this "forms a strong presumption against them"—to the rational man it is obvious that enlightenment banishes superstition and hence such reports "grow thinner as we advance nearer the enlightened ages."[46] Finally, no testimony for a particular miracle is entirely univocal; there is always counter-testimony.[47]

Johnson tacitly accedes to these points when he states that "taking the proposition [of the possibility of believing in miracles] Hume is right." Nevertheless, Johnson insists that though Hume is right about miracles, the truth of the Christian religion rests on the argument from prophecy. With this opinion, Johnson joins the ranks of most other apologists in the first half of the eighteenth century.

Believing as he did in the primacy of prophecy, it seems highly probable that, if he had been aware of Hume's argument in detail, Johnson would have addressed himself to Hume's final paragraph. There Hume argues that the canons of credibility which subvert belief in miracles likewise subvert belief in prophecy. Prophecy, properly considered, is miraculous because by his own exertions no prophet could foreknow future events.[48] If prophecy is properly understood,

---

[43] Ibid., 129-30.

[44] Siebert, "Johnson and Hume on Miracles," 544. Siebert cites two examples of Johnson's refusal to credit wild tales about miracles which show Johnson "sifting through empirical evidence in a manner which Hume could have found only commendable."

[45] Hume, "Of Miracles," 218.   [46] Ibid., 131-32.   [47] Ibid., 134.

[48] Hume clearly has to interpret prophecy as beyond human power in order to define them as a sub-class of miracles. They thus require proof in their character as miracles, which is impossible both on the grounds of Pt. II which shows why testimony about the occurrence of miracles is too implausible to be believed and on the grounds of Pt. I as contrary to the laws of nature. But it might be asked why a prophetic prediction which comes true *necessarily* violates a law of nature. There is a sense of prophecy which holds that its fulfillment is just a concurrence between the prophet's prediction and the often quite natural events which come to pass as predicted. But neither Hume nor his opponents use "prophecy" in this sense. For them, prophecies are supernatural, miraculous communications between man and God utterly beyond human power. They are thus violations of natural law and require proof in their character as a miracle.

as Locke understood it, for example, then it is a miraculous violation of natural law as established in the course of human experience and, consequently, prophecy is too implausible to be believed. With a single super-Deistic stroke, Hume does away with Biblical criticism. The "true text" really does not matter. As long as the Bible contains miracle stories founded on human testimony and as long as it contains stories of fulfilled prophetic predictions, which it presumably always will, no matter how the text is revised by textual critics, it will be in principle unbelievable. Miracles *and* fulfilled prophecies are violations of the laws of nature and there is nothing which can constitute adequate evidence for such a violation. The ironic tone of Hume's remark at the beginning of the essay that he hopes his one argument will "be an everlasting check to *all* kinds of superstitious delusion"[49] becomes clear.

Johnson avers that "taking the proposition simply" he finds Hume is right in his argument. However, when he also adds "the Christian revelation is not proved by the miracles alone, but as connected with prophecies," Johnson, for whatever reason, blindly rejects Hume's reasoning. In falling back from the argument from miracles to the argument from prophecy, Johnson brushes aside the fact that Hume's essay is explicitly directed against both.[50]

University of Kentucky.

---

[49] Hume, "Of Miracles," 110. Emphasis added. For a recent catalog of specimens of Hume's irony in his assaults on our rational abilities to know if God exists, or what he is like, as well as for an account of Hume's own personal "religion of man" see Ernest Campbell Mossner, "The Religion of David Hume," *Journal of the History of Ideas*, **39**, no. 4 (Oct.-Dec., 1978), 653-63.

[50] Very few interpreters of Hume have seen this point. One of the best critics of Hume's argument, C. S. Peirce, sees the importance for Hume's argument of defining "laws of nature" in such a way as to emphasize their prophetic or predictive nature and presents a cogent criticism of Hume's use of the calculus of probabilities in proportioning his belief or non-belief in historical testimony regarding miracles as the result of our expectations. But even the astute Peirce dismisses Hume's ironic concluding paragraph asserting that its only purpose is to "fling a gratuitous insult to Christians, in order to give *éclat* to the chapter and to provoke angry replies." See Philip P. Wiener, "The Peirce-Langley Correspondence and Peirce's Manuscript on Hume and the Laws of Nature," *Proceedings of the American Philosophical Society*, **91**, no. 2 (1947), esp. 214-28.

Chapter X

LOCKE'S CRITIQUE OF INNATE PRINCIPLES AND TOLAND'S DEISM

By John C. Biddle

F. M. Powicke once related the complaint of an Oxford tutor who was having great difficulty getting his pupils to read Locke intelligently. As the tutor stated his problem, "It is not only that they don't see why Locke should refer to the Scriptures; they don't know what the Scriptures are." Although the scholarly study of Locke has long been almost as neglectful of his religious thought as this tutor's pupils, some attention has recently been given to the influence of his religious concerns on his political and philosophical writings.[1] It is the purpose of this paper to contribute to that discussion by the exploration of the religious intentions that informed the writing of *An Essay Concerning Human Understanding* and the relation of that *Essay* to *The Reasonableness of Christianity*.

I. Reason and Religion in the Essay

For nearly a century it has been known that the occasion that led Locke to the subject of the *Essay* was a conversation among five or six of his friends in the winter of 1670–71 about "the principles of morality and revealed religion."[2] As he later informed his readers, that conversation had led him to believe that "*it was necessary to examine our own Abilities, and see, what Objects our Understandings were, or were not fitted to deal with.*"[3] By shifting the conversation to the subject of human understanding, Locke did not intend to avoid the topic of morality and revealed religion, but sought to lay a foundation for discussing it properly.[4] In addition to his desire to contribute to the advancement of philosophy and science, he intended the *Essay* to fulfill this initial concern of laying a basis in the extent and limits of human understand-

[1] See esp. Hans Aarsleff, "The state of nature and the nature of man in Locke," and Richard Ashcraft, "Faith and knowledge in Locke's philosophy," *John Locke: Problems and Perspectives,* ed. John W. Yolton (Cambridge, 1969); and John W. Yolton, *John Locke and the Way of Ideas* (Oxford, 1956); among older works specifically on Locke's religious thought: S. G. Hefelbower, *The Relation of John Locke to English Deism* (Chicago, 1918), and Herbert McLachlan, *The Religious Opinions of Milton, Locke, and Newton* (Manchester, 1941).

[2] H. R. Fox Bourne, *The Life of John Locke,* 2 vols. (New York, 1876), I, 248–49.

[3] *John Locke: An Essay Concerning Human Understanding,* ed. Peter H. Nidditch (Oxford, 1975), The Epistle to the Reader, 7; hereafter *Essay.* References are normally given to book (capital Roman numerals), chapter (lower case Roman numerals), and section (Arabic numerals), except for references to "The Epistle to the Reader" (as here), where page numbers are cited.   [4] *Essay,* I, i, 7.

ing for morality and revealed religion. It was to these ends that Locke pictured himself as *"an Under-Labourer in clearing Ground a little, and removing some of the Rubbish, that lies in the way to Knowledge."*[5]

Locke sought in the *Essay* to pave a via media between those who suspected that man could not attain a certain knowledge of the truth and those who would "require Demonstration, and demand Certainty, where Probability only is to be had."[6] Against the skeptics, he based his confidence in the sufficiency of human understanding on a passage of Scripture (II Peter 1:3), that (as the Authorized Version had translated it) God had given men "all things that pertain unto life and godliness." With considerable exegetical license Locke interpreted this to mean that God had given men "Whatsoever is necessary for the Conveniences of Life, and Information of Vertue; and has put within the reach of their Discovery the comfortable Provision for this Life and the Way that leads to a better." Although man's knowledge is far from universal or perfect, he asserted, "it yet secures their great Concernments, that they have Light enough to lead them to the Knowledge of their Maker, and the sight of their own Duties."[7] Such an understanding of God and morality leading to eternal life was, for Locke, the "chief end of all our Thoughts" and *"the proper Science, and Business of Mankind in general."*[8]

On the other hand, he sought to refute those who would extend man's inquiries beyond the capacities of human understanding. Such efforts to know more than the limits of understanding allowed and to claim certain knowledge where only probability could be attained, led in Locke's view only to disputes, wranglings, increased doubts, and in turn

---

[5] *Essay,* The Epistle to the Reader, 10.   [6] *Essay,* I, i, 5; cf. I, i, 2, 6.

[7] *Essay,* I, i, 5; cf. *Essay,* II, xxiii, 12, IV, xx, 3, and the journal entry for Feb. 8, 1677, in *An Early Draft of Locke's Essay,* ed. R. I. Aaron and Jocelyn Gibb (Oxford, 1936), 84–90.

[8] *Essay,* II, vii, 6, IV, xii, 11. Cf. "Our Business here is not to know all things, but those which concern our Conduct," *Essay,* I, i, 6; ". . . here comes in another and that the main concernment of mankinde and that is to know what those actions are that he is to doe what those are he is to avoid what the law is he is to live by here and shall be jugd by hereafter, and in this part too he is not left soe in the darke but that he is furnishd with principles of knowledg and facultys able to discover light enough to guid him, his understanding seldome failes him in this part unless where his will would have it soe," journal entry of Feb. 8, 1677, *An Early Draft,* 88. For the preeminence of morality and religion in Locke's thought, see the journal entry of March to May 1677, in Lord King, *The Life and Letters of John Locke* (London, 1884), 97, 107: "Heaven being our great business and interest, the knowledge which may direct us thither is certainly so too," and "That which seems to me to be suited to the end of man, and lie level to his understanding, is the improvement of natural experiments for the conveniences of this life, and the way of ordering himself so as to attain happiness in the other—i.e. moral philosophy, which, in my sense, comprehends religion too, or a man's whole duty." Cf. "Of the Conduct of the Understanding," par. 22, *The Works of John Locke Esq.,* 3 vols. (London, 1714), III, 407; hereafter *Works.*

to "perfect Scepticism."[9] What "gave the first *Rise* to this Essay concerning the Understanding," then, was the concern "to search out the *Bounds* between Opinion and Knowledge," and to examine the means by which man ought to regulate his assent in matters of probability and thereby govern his actions.[10] With such a purpose in mind he attacked the theory of innate principles, not only because it granted more to human understanding than could rightly be claimed, but also because it seemed to Locke to threaten morality and revealed religion.

From his earliest remarks on innate principles, Locke asserted that what men conclude to be "inscribed in our hearts by God and by nature" are actually opinions instilled in one's youth and confirmed by daily practice and the general consent and approval of associates.[11] This analysis of the origin of so-called innate principles was restated in the first draft of the *Essay* with special application to "matters of religion."[12] In the second draft Locke went into greater detail, asserting that "doctrines that have been derived from no better original than the superstition of a nurse, or the authority of an old woman, may, by length of time, and the consent of neighbours, grow up to the dignity of a principle in religion or morality." Such opinions, he there suggested, become the "received opinions" of a country or party and are given a stamp of sanctity as standards established by God. As he warned and was later to experience, dissent from such supposedly innate principles brings upon one the labels of "whimsical, sceptical, or atheist."[13]

Locke frequently repeated this description of the origin of so-called innate or natural principles, usually in regard to religion.[14] He was not opposed *per se* to education, custom, or fashion as sources of legitimate laws in society; on the contrary he cited these as an inevitable and useful type of law.[15] For several reasons, however, he was adamantly opposed to the procedure by which such laws of opinion, reputation, or fashion were given the status of divine law through the claim that they were implanted in men's minds by God. First, the claim of innate principles seemed to be a demand for implicit faith in the judgment of those who

[9] *Essay,* I, i, 7; cf. journal entry of March to May 1677, in Lord King, 107; journal entry of Sept. 1, 1676, in *John Locke: Essays on the Law of Nature,* ed. W. von Leyden (Oxford, 1954), 281.

[10] *Essay,* I, i, 7, 3, 6. In an early draft of the *Essay,* Locke stated his purpose as "to enquire into the original, certainty, and extent of human knowledge, together with the grounds and degrees of opinion, belief, persuasion, or assent." See *An Essay Concerning the Understanding, Knowledge, Opinion, and Assent,* ed. Benjamin Rand (Cambridge, Mass., 1931), 16. The term "Opinion" in the title was substituted by Locke for "Belief."

[11] *Essays on the Law of Nature,* 142–43.   [12] *An Early Draft,* 63.

[13] *An Essay Concerning the Understanding,* 38–41.

[14] Lord King, 101–02; *Essay,* I, iii, 8, 22–26; IV, xx, 9–10; *The Reasonableness of Christianity* (London, 1695), 277–78. Quotations from the *Reasonableness* are corrected in accord with Locke's personal, annotated copy, now in the Harvard College Library.

[15] *Essay,* II, xxviii, 6–13; cf. Lord King, 292–93.

designated them. Such a demand contravened what Locke took to be man's fundamental right, his duty to God, and the necessity of his nature—that he understand the truth for himself. "I can no more know anything by another man's understanding," he maintained, "than I can see by another man's eyes."[16] Secondly, Locke saw a multitude of nefarious consequences in this denial of individual understanding and demand for implicit faith by the proposers of innate principles. All the examples he gave of such consequences are related to morality and religion. "An Hobbist," he asserted, "with his principle of self-preservation, whereof himself is to be judge, will not easily admit a great many plain duties of morality." In a similar fashion, he claimed that the Roman Catholic demand for implicit faith in the principle of infallibility led to the misinterpretation of Scripture and the rejection of reason. The same assertion was made of the principle of a "light within," presumably referring to the Quakers or the like, whom he generally called "Enthusiasts."[17] He feared that one who claimed such a principle as an internal light would be led to the idolatry of taking "monsters lodged in his own mind for the images of the deity, and the workmanship of his hands."[18]

Locke's concern, however, was not limited to the errors in morality and religion to which innate principles led individuals. He was always a political thinker, and saw the political power of the theory of innate ideas. The proponents of such innate principles seemed to Locke to presume "themselves alone to be masters of right reason" and to claim infallibility for their judgments.[19] This demand for "blind Credulity," he explicitly charged, allowed men of skill and office to govern societies more easily by "the Authority to be the Dictator of Principles, and Teacher of unquestionable Truths; and to make a Man swallow that for an innate Principle, which may serve to his purpose, who teacheth them."[20] Examples of such imposition of innate principles to control the minds and actions of men were again drawn from the realm of religion: the Roman Catholic principles of implicit faith and papal infallibility, and the Enthusiast's principle of immediate inspiration.[21] Thus, Locke saw in this doctrine of innate ideas the political potential for some men or parties (perhaps especially Hobbesians, Catholics, and Enthusiasts) to impose their moral and religious opinions on others as carrying divine sanction. While he clearly believed the theory to be false on other

[16] Lord King, 101, 105–06; cf. 94, 103; *Essay,* I, iv, 24, IV, xx, 8.
[17] Lord King, 103; cf. *Essay,* I, iv, 12, IV, xx, 10.
[18] *An Essay Concerning the Understanding,* 40–42; cf. *Essay,* I, iii, 25–26, iv, 15, IV, xii, 4.   [19] *Ibid.,* 36–37; cf. *Essay,* I, iii, 20.
[20] *Essay,* I, iv, 24; cf. *An Essay Concerning the Understanding,* 51.
[21] *Essay,* IV, xx, 9, 10; also *Essay,* II, xxxiii, IV, xix, *"Of the Association of Ideas"* and *"Of Enthusiasm,"* which were apparently first drafted while Locke was writing the *Reasonableness* (letters to Molyneux, March 26 and April 26, 1695, *Works,* III, 533–35).

grounds as well, Locke's concern for liberty and religious toleration seems to have contributed to his rejection of innate principles.

Having dismissed the notion of innate ideas, Locke sought to lay a correct epistemological foundation for morality and religion that would allow and promote religious toleration. But by denying innate knowledge he did not eliminate the possibility of man's knowing natural law. He affirmed in the *Essay* both natural law and natural religion as means of maintaining man's independent judgment in matters of morality and religion, against the possible imposition by others of fallible interpretations of the Bible.[22] Yet he also believed that Christianity rested principally on its revelation, and sought a means of establishing the legitimacy of such revelation.[23] In contrast to the Hobbesian principle of civil authority, the Catholic claims of tradition and an infallible interpreter, and the Enthusiasts' notion of an inner light, Locke advocated the role of "reason" in certifying and interpreting revelation. While his analysis of "reason" and its relation to revelation is by no means thorough, clear, or consistent, certain features merit attention in this context.

Locke maintained that any claim to revelation must be subjected to the test of reason before it is accepted and believed.[24] This does not mean, however, that he thought reason could attain absolute certainty in determining whether a claimed revelation was actually of divine origin. Reason's task of establishing the validity of a revelation was one of judging a probability.[25] Since he laid down no special criteria for judg-

---

[22] *Essay,* I, iii, 6, 8, 13; II, xxiii, 12, xxviii, 7, 8; IV, x, 7, and Locke's letter to James Tyrrell, Aug. 4, 1690, in Lord King, 198–201; cf. his *Essays on the Law of Nature,* and the unfinished chapter intended for the *Essay,* "Of Ethic in General," in Lord King, 308–13. On natural religion, *Essay,* III, ix, 23.

[23] *Essay,* IV, vii, 11, "But I think that no body will therefore say, that the *Christian* Religion is built on these *Maxims,* or that the Knowledge we have of it, is derived from these *Principles.* 'Tis from Revelation we have received it, and without Revelation these *Maxims* had never been able to help us to it." [24] *Essay,* IV, xvi, 14, xviii, 5, 6, 10, xix, 14.

[25] While Locke never made this process explicit, the following factors seem to indicate that it was his position. He took up the matter of revelation in chapter xvi of book IV, which treats the degrees of assent given to the kinds of probabilities outlined in chapter xv. The discussion of probabilities in chapter xv was, in turn, an elucidation of man's faculty of judgment, distinguished from the faculty of knowledge in chapter xiv. He introduced the matter of revelation (IV, xvi, 14) by contrasting it to other sorts of probability. For revelation, he asserted, is assented to upon the "bare Testimony" of God, who "cannot deceive, nor be deceived." Such assent, or "Faith," as Locke called it, "carries with it Assurance beyond Doubt, Evidence beyond Exception," which "as absolutely determines our Minds, and as perfectly excludes all wavering as our Knowledge itself." However, Locke proceeded to assert that such "Assent can be rationally no higher than the Evidence of its being a Revelation" (i.e., truly a revelation from God), "and that this is the meaning of the Expressions it is delivered in." "If the Evidence of its being a Revelation, or that this its true Sense be only on probable Proofs," he added, "our Assent can reach no higher than an Assurance or Diffidence, arising from the more, or less apparent Probability of the Proofs." That Locke conceived of reason's confirmation of revelation as a judgment of probability is con-

ing a revelation, it might be assumed that one must apply the general principles he designated for judging any matter of probability—conformity to one's knowledge, observation and experience, and the validity of testimonies to the claim.[26] Thus, the degree of assent given to any revelation can be no higher than the probability of its being a divine revelation. Locke nowhere stated precisely how reason could judge something to be divine, nor did he ever offer a systematic case for the probability that the Christian Scriptures were a divine revelation. However, he assumed that such a judgment was possible and believed that the Scriptures were, indeed, of divine origin.[27]

It is one of the peculiarities of Locke's thought that he apparently believed that faith, one's assent to a revelation, could carry an assurance or confidence beyond all doubt and wavering, even though the divine authority of the revelation was only a matter of probability.[28] Locke's confidence in the truth of the biblical revelation rested not only on the high probability of its divine origin, which he thought reason could provide from external evidence. His assurance also rested upon reason's ability to confirm certain aspects of the content of Scripture, for he maintained that reason could and must judge the content or parts of a revelation as well as the whole.[29] In this procedure reason could confirm

---

firmed by the following statement in *Essay*, IV, xviii, 10: "There can be no evidence, that any traditional Revelation is of divine Original, in the Words we receive it, and in the Sense we understand it, so clear, and so certain, as that of the Principles of Reason." "Principles of reason" in this context seems to mean certain knowledge of intuition or demonstration (cf. IV, xviii, 4).

[26] *Essay*, IV, xv, 4. Locke cited six tests of the testimony of others: "1. The Number. 2. The Integrity. 3. The Skill of the Witnesses. 4. The Design of the Author, where it is a Testimony out of a Book cited. 5. The Consistency of the Parts, and Circumstances of the Relation. 6. Contrary Testimonies." Cf. Locke's arguments for the divine origin of the Christian revelation in the *Reasonableness*, 154-57, 173-78, 261-64, 278-82, 291-98; most of the arguments fall into these six categories; also his discussion of miracles in *Essay*, IV, xvi, 13, xix, 15; in the *Reasonableness*, 278-82; and in "A Discourse of Miracles," *Works*, III, 451-55. The discussion of testimonies in *Essay*, IV, xvi, 10 may have been specifically in opposition to the theological use of tradition.

[27] *A Letter to the Right Reverend Edward Lord Bishop of Worcester, Works*, I, 387, "The Holy Scripture is to me, and always will be, the constant Guide of my Assent; and I shall always hearken to it, as containing infallible Truth, relating to Things of the highest Concernment." Cf. *Mr. Locke's Reply to the Right Reverend the Lord Bishop of Worcester's Answer to his Second Letter* (hereafter BW3), *Works*, I, 502. On Locke's possible recognition of the problem of determining what is a divine act: "A Discourse of Miracles," *Works*, III, 451-55.

[28] In addition to *Essay*, IV, xvi, 14, discussed in note 25 above, see BW3, *Works*, I, 482: "But tho bare Belief always includes some degrees of Uncertainty, yet it does not therefore necessarily include any degree of wavering; the evidently strong probability may as steddily determine the Man to assent to the Truth, or make him take the Proposition for true, and act accordingly, as Knowledg makes him see or be certain that it is true." This Locke specifically applied to belief in "Truths reveal'd in the Scripture."

[29] *Essay*, IV, xviii, 5, 6, 10, xix, 14. See also *Reasonableness*, 281, "Since they [the writers of the Scriptures] delivered no Precepts but such, as though Reason of itself had

only those aspects of revelation in which natural knowledge could be had, and it could refute and reject only propositions that were contrary to man's natural knowledge.[30] Locke seems to have believed that reason could confirm some of Scripture and could falsify none of it; thus reason's judgment of Scripture's content corroborated its conclusion from external evidence.

Although the right and necessity that reason judge the content as well as the authenticity of revelation appears to be the height of religious rationalism, such an interpretation would grossly belie Locke's intention. His whole analysis of human understanding was designed to show how little proper knowledge man has and how ineffectual that knowledge is in most matters of morality and religion.[31] These aspects of man's principal concern are based not on intuitive or rational knowledge, but on the judgment of probability. In such matters which transcend reason's capacity for certainty, Locke affirmed that assent is to be given to a clear or evident revelation.[32] Thus, he sought in the *Essay* to establish traditional revelation as the primary guide in that proper science and business of mankind, morality and religion.

II. *Deism and Locke's Reasonable Christianity*

While Locke's concern in the *Essay* to lay a foundation for Christian revelation has been inadequately understood, there has been no lack of recognition that John Toland, a principal exponent of Deism, grounded his attack on revealed religion in an interpretation of the *Essay*. A popular reconstruction of the publication of Toland's *Christianity Not Mysterious* in 1696 has been that it incorporated the epistemological principles of the *Essay* to carry to their logical conclusion the rationalistic interpretation of religion, which Locke had set forth in *The*

---

not clearly made out, Yet it could not but assent to when thus discovered; And think itself indebted for the Discovery."

[30] This aspect of Locke's thought depends on the distinction between things *"According to Reason,"* *"Above Reason,"* and *"Contrary to Reason"* laid down in *Essay*, IV, xvii, 23. The significance of this distinction to the relation of reason and faith is drawn out in *Essay*, IV, xviii, 4–10. See below for a fuller discussion of this issue in regard to Toland's appropriation of Locke's thought.

[31] While most of book IV of the *Essay* is directed to this end, see especially xiv and xviii, 1. Perhaps the best illustration of this point is the following passage: ". . . in the greatest part of our Concernment, he [God] has afforded us only the twilight, as I may so say, of *Probability*, suitable, I presume, to that State of Mediocrity and Probationership, he has been pleased to place us in here" (*Essay*, IV, xiv, 2); Richard Ashcraft, 195–202. Locke's theory that ethics were demonstrable might be an exception to this claim, but what he meant by demonstrating ethics is by no means clear.

[32] *Essay*, IV, xviii, 7–9, ". . . in such probable Propositions, I say, an evident *Revelation* ought to determine our Assent even against Probability. For where the Principles of Reason have not evidenced a Proposition to be certainly true or false, there clear Revelation, as another Principle of Truth, and Ground of Assent, may determine; and so it may be Matter of *Faith*, and be also above *Reason*."

Reasonableness of Christianity in 1695.[33] A correct view of the circumstances and the substance of these publications, however, significantly
alters this interpretation.

Locke had met Toland in August 1693, when Toland came to England in search of employment. What assistance Locke gave to the
itinerant scholar is not known, but he may have introduced him to John
Freke, who probably helped support Toland's study at Oxford.[34] It was
rumored in the coffee houses of London by May 1694, that Toland was
at work on a book showing that Christianity contained no mysteries.[35]
At the end of March 1695, Freke sent to Locke a letter from Toland and
on April 8 Locke returned "Mr. T's Papers" to Freke. In his next correspondence Freke acknowledged the return of the papers and asked
Locke for his opinion of "his Tract (I mean as much as you have seen of
it)."[36] It is possible, therefore, that what Locke received early in the
spring of 1695 was a portion of Toland's manuscript of *Christianity Not
Mysterious*.

Through the winter and spring of 1695 Locke had been confined to
the Mashams' manor house of Oates, poring over his New Testaments
and writing his reflections on what was necessary for a man to believe in
order to become a Christian. It was into this context, the writing of *The
Reasonableness of Christianity*, that Toland's papers entered. But were
those papers a part of *Christianity Not Mysterious*, and did they
influence Locke's final composition of the *Reasonableness?*

The *Reasonableness* elicited strong criticism, especially from a
Cambridge divine, John Edwards.[37] Locke twice defended his book
against Edwards' attacks, and in the *Second Vindication*, published in
mid-March 1697, he explained the origins and intentions of his book.
The first occasion he mentioned as having set him to work on the
Reasonableness was a controversy over justification among the

[33] Kuno Fischer, *Geschichte der neuern Philosophie*, 10 vols. in 11 (Heidelberg,
1897–1904), X, 514; Roland Stromberg, *Religious Liberalism in Eighteenth-Century
England* (Oxford, 1954), 98; and G. R. Cragg, *From Puritanism to the Age of Reason*
(Cambridge, 1950), 141, *The Church and the Age of Reason 1648–1789* (Har-
mondsworth, Middlesex, 1960), 77–78, and *Reason and Authority in the Eighteenth
Century* (Cambridge, 1964), 66, 73.

[34] Benjamin Furly's letter to Locke, Aug. 19, 1693, MS Locke c.9 f.108 (such
references are to the Lovelace Collection of Locke manuscripts in the Bodleian Library,
Oxford), and Toland's letter of Jan. 1694, to an anonymous patron, in which a Mr. Freke
is mentioned, in Toland's *Miscellaneous Works*, 2 vols. (London, 1747), II, 292–94. In
Feb. 1697, Locke loaned Toland £5 through John Freke (MSS Locke b.1 f.188 and c.1
p.321); for Freke's contributions see MS Locke c.8 f.227.

[35] See the anonymous letter to Toland in *Miscellaneous Works*, II, 308–14. This important fact was first called to my attention by Dr. M. C. Jacob, to whom I am deeply
indebted.

[36] Freke's letters to Locke, March 29 and April 9, 1695, in MS Locke c.8 ff. 193–94.

[37] John Edwards, *Some Thoughts Concerning the Causes and Occasions of Atheism*
(London, 1695), *Socinianism Unmask'd* (London, 1696), *A Brief Vindication of the Fun-
damental Articles of the Christian Faith* (London, 1697), and *The Socinian Creed*
(London, 1697).

dissenters. He proceeded to note, however, that he was led to share the conclusions of his study with the world, because they answered the objections that Deists made against Christianity. Without naming the Deists in question, he described the positions of those he sought to refute. Two objections against Christianity concerned him:

... either that there was no need of Revelation at all, or that the Revelation of our Saviour required the Belief of such Articles for Salvation, which the settled Notions and their way of reasoning in some, and want of Understanding in others, made impossible to them.[38]

Locke's claim to have written the *Reasonableness* in opposition to the Deists may have been merely a subterfuge, for common opinion would probably have held that a book against so great an evil as Deism could not be all bad. However, this statement of the Deists' two objections against Christianity fits precisely the sort of Deism that Locke may have encountered in 1695. The first objection, "that there was no need of Revelation at all," was a view expressed by Uriel Acosta, whose writing Locke had on his book shelf.[39] In a journal note dated "95" and headed "Deisme," Locke designated Acosta "the father and patriarch of the Deists."[40] The second objection against Christianity seems in part to fit John Toland.

In *Christianity Not Mysterious* Toland did borrow, but subtly changed, the epistemology and views on the relation of reason and revelation that Locke had set forth in the *Essay*. He asserted, as Locke had, that knowledge is of two sorts—intuitive and rational or demonstrative—and that knowledge lies in the comparison of ideas. He also maintained that reason alone could and must determine whether something was a divine revelation.[41] But Toland proceeded to assert a relationship between reason and the content of revelation that was slightly, but significantly, different from Locke's views. Locke had maintained that one must accept in faith any proposition delivered in a clear or evident revelation, if that matter is not contradicted by certain

[38] Locke, *A Second Vindication of the Reasonableness of Christianity, &c.* (London, 1697), sigs. a^v – a2^r.

[39] Acosta's manuscript, "Exemplar Humanae Vitae," was found by Philip Limborch among the papers of his great uncle, Simon Episcopius, and was printed together with Limborch's refutation in his *De Veritate Religionis Christianae* (Gouda, 1687), 341–64. See John Harrison and Peter Laslett, *The Library of John Locke* (Oxford, 1971), entry 1755, p. 175, which indicates that Locke owned two copies.

[40] MS Locke d. 10, p. 33. Since the entry does not specify the month of 1695, it cannot be conclusively proved that Locke encountered Acosta's work before Aug. 1695, when the *Reasonableness* was published.

[41] John Toland, *Christianity Not Mysterious* (London, 1696), 6–20, 30–31. The substantive and verbal similarities between the views set forth at the beginning of Toland's book and those of the *Essay* leave no room to doubt his dependence on Locke. Veiled reference to Locke as "an excellent modern Philosopher" is made on 83 and 87. Toland's adaptation of the *Essay* to his religious program led to the debate between Locke and Edward Stillingfleet, Bishop of Worcester, as noted below.

knowledge. Toland, however, held that the entire content of revelation must be judged by its conformity to man's "natural" or "common Notions." He refused to accept anything that could not be confirmed by one's "clear Perceptions."[42] Thus, according to Toland, one could not receive as revelation any proposition that was "above reason." Defining a mystery as such notions claimed to be above reason, Toland concluded:

... *either the Apostles could not write more intelligibly of the reputed Mysteries, or they would not.* If they would not, then 'tis no longer our Fault if we neither understand nor believe them: And if they could not write more clearly themselves, they were so much less to expect Credit from others.[43]

While Toland pretended that Christianity did not require the belief of anything that is mysterious, i.e., above the common notions of reason, such a statement could easily be interpreted as challenging the acceptance of the Scriptures as revelation. Therefore, Locke's claim that he wrote against Deists who asserted that "the Revelation of our Savior required the Belief of such Articles for Salvation, which the settled Notions and their way of reasoning ... made impossible to them," could well have been directed at Toland.[44]

While the major thesis of the *Reasonableness* concerned the content and nature of justifying faith, Locke devoted a long and significant section of the book to the refutation of the charges which he later explicitly associated with the Deists. Against the claim (made by Acosta) that there was no need for revelation at all, he cited five reasons why a saviour was required: for the revelation of true knowledge of God, knowledge of man's duty, knowledge of the correct forms of worship, knowledge of an afterlife, and the promise of assistance.[45] Within his discussion of these needs for revelation, Locke sought to qualify too great a confidence in reason and natural knowledge, perhaps as espoused by Toland. He did not deny that reason could know the existence of God or man's duties through nature and natural law; this he had affirmed in the *Essay*. But he asserted as historical fact that mankind had not clearly discerned the true nature of God and all of man's obligations before Jesus revealed them. The ancient philosophers' knowledge of these matters was ineffectual in promoting true religion

---

[42] *Ibid.,* 20, 30, 41, 65, 80, 133.   [43] *Ibid.,* 142.

[44] Locke claimed, however, that this same sort of Deist also maintained that the lack of understanding in others necessitated a rejection of revelation. Toland did not explicitly argue that, since the common, uneducated masses could not understand the Christian revelation, they could not be required to accept it. This does not preclude the possibility, however, that Locke could have drawn this inference from Toland's emphasis on the need for full understanding and demonstration of all articles of faith. The final pages of Toland's book assert in answer to an anonymous objection that "the poor and illiterate" (words Locke had used in the *Reasonableness*) could indeed understand the "uncorrupted Doctrines of *Christianity.*" It is possible that Toland was responding to Locke's argument.   [45] *Reasonableness,* 254–90.

and morality, for their teachings could be understood only by the educated and carried no weight of authority.[46] Against the claim (made by Toland) that natural reason could now know and confirm all the truths of revelation, Locke adapted an argument previously used against the theory of innate principles:

A great many things we have been bred up in the belief of from our Cradles, (and are Notions grown Familiar, and as it were Natural to us, under the Gospel,) we take for unquestionable obvious Truths, and easily demonstrable; without considering how long we might have been in doubt or ignorance of them, had Revelation been silent.[47]

Thus, Locke may have seen in the absolute claims of reason (perhaps Toland's particular variety and application of reason) the same sort of threat to religion and morality posed by the theory of innate principles—the claim of the power to prescribe and impose on others one's fallible judgments and opinions.

If Locke's intention in the *Essay* and the *Reasonableness* was to lend support to revealed religion, however, this was not apparent to many contemporaries. His most prestigious critic was Edward Stillingfleet, Bishop of Worcester, who accused Locke of laying the philosophical foundation for Toland's attack on Christianity.[48] Locke responded to Stillingfleet in three increasingly lengthy letters, disassociating himself from Toland and defending his *Essay*. In the course of the debate he clarified to some degree his conception of the relation between faith and knowledge.

As in the *Essay*, Locke limited "knowledge" to certainty derived from the perception of agreement or disagreement of ideas. "What reaches to Knowledg," he wrote, "I think may be call'd Certainty; and what comes short of Certainty, I think cannot be call'd Knowledg."[49] Faith, on the other hand, was for Locke a matter of probability, not certainty. He admitted the possibility of certainty upon the testimony of God, but only where one could *know* that the testimony was truly from God. He also allowed that some doctrines (e.g., the existence of God) could be demonstrated and thereby certainly known, but maintained that most Christians held such doctrines and all others upon "mere faith," without demonstration.[50] Such faith included "some degrees of Uncertainty" for it was founded only on a "strong probability," yet it was sufficient to determine man's assent to the revealed truths of the Scripture and to direct him to proper conduct.[51] The assurance of faith,

[46] *Ibid.,* 256–82. [47] *Ibid.,* 277–78; cf. references cited in notes 11–14 above.
[48] For the bibliographic details on Locke's controversy with Stillingfleet: H. O. Christophersen, *A Bibliographic Introduction to the Study of John Locke* (Oslo, 1930), 35–42. Stillingfleet did not acknowledge the rumors that Locke had written the anonymous *Reasonableness of Christianity.*
[49] *Mr. Locke's Reply to the Right Reverend the Lord Bishop of Worcester's Answer to his Letter* (hereafter BW2), *Works,* I, 410. [50] BW3, *Works,* I, 469–78. [51] *Ibid.,* 482.

Locke asserted, had "nothing to do with the *Certainty of Knowledg.*"

Faith stands by it self, and upon Grounds of its own; nor can be remov'd from them, and plac'd on those of Knowledg. Their Grounds are so far from being the same, or having any thing common, that when it is brought to *Certainty, Faith is destroy'd;* 'tis Knowledg then, and Faith no longer.[52]

Given this radical separation of faith and knowledge, Locke sought to turn the charge of contributing to Deism back onto Stillingfleet. He accused the bishop of arguing that "Divine Revelation abates of its *Credibility* in all those Articles it proposes, proportionably as human Reason fails to support the Testimony of God." The attempt to support revelation by arguments of natural reason seemed to Locke to be both impossible and impious. He considered such doctrines as the nature of the Trinity and the afterlife to be above man's reason, and viewed all desires for their rational demonstration as a subversion of faith in revelation. The same danger lurked in the Anglican apologist as in the Deists: "to resolve all Revelation perfectly and purely into natural Reason, to bound its *Credibility* by that, and leave no room for Faith in other things, than what can be accounted for by natural Reason without Revelation."[53]

Thus, although Toland and later Deists drew heavily upon his philosophy, Locke seems not to have been an intentional party to their emphasis on reason and natural religion. Rather, as an opponent of the Deists and a defender of revelation, he sought a simple, moral Christianity based on faith. As he wrote in the *Reasonableness:*

The greatest part of mankind want leisure or capacity for Demonstration; nor can they carry a train of Proofs; which in that way they must always depend upon for Conviction, and cannot be required to assent to till they see the Demonstration. . . . And you may as soon hope to have all the Day-Labourers and Tradesmen, the Spinsters and Dairy Maids perfect Mathematicians, as to have them perfect in *Ethicks* this way. Hearing plain Commands, is the sure and only course to bring them to Obedience and Practice. The greatest part cannot know, and therefore they must believe.[54]

True Christianity for Locke, was the plain and intelligible doctrine that Jesus was the Messiah—delivered to the poor, ignorant, and illiterate with the clear, authoritative, divine revelation of man's moral duty. The reasonableness of Christianity lay not so much in its conformity to reason as in its simplicity, intelligibility, and effectiveness.

Yale University.

[52] BW2, *Works,* I, 410. Locke refused to speak of the "certainty" of faith, as Stillingfleet demanded, because the Bible nowhere did so. In his support he cited Hebrews 10:22 (the "full assurance of faith") and William Chillingworth, *The Religion of Protestants* (Chap. VI, pars. 2 and 3), which in turn cited Richard Hooker (BW3, *Works,* I, 470–71).   [53] BW3, *Works,* I, 564, 568.   [54] *Reasonableness,* 279.

Chapter XI

SOCINIANISM, JUSTIFICATION BY FAITH, AND THE SOURCES OF JOHN LOCKE'S *THE REASONABLENESS OF CHRISTIANITY*

BY DEWEY D. WALLACE, JR.[1]

The writings of the English Philosopher John Locke deal extensively with religion. He advocated religious freedom,[2] his *Essay Concerning Human Understanding* (1689/1690) had as one of its aims an inquiry into epistemology that would place true religion on a surer foundation,[3] his treatise on *The Reasonableness of Christianity* (1695) expounded his theological opinions, his posthumously published paraphrases of some of the Pauline epistles indicate the effort he put into biblical studies,[4] and it has even been claimed of his political thought that it was grounded in the Puritanism with which he was familiar from his education at Oxford during the Interregnum.[5]

Locke's religious views have been interpreted as revolutionary ever since the publication of his major works. Some of his first opponents accused him of Socinianism, and this claim has been made repeatedly down to the present, not least by modern Unitarians.[6] It has also been asserted that Locke, either intentionally or inadvertently, was a founder

[1] I would like to thank the following persons who consented to read and comment on a preliminary draft of this essay: Roderick S. French and Harry E. Yeide, Jr., my colleagues at The George Washington University; Roger Miles (Folger Shakespeare Library); and John W. Yolton, Dean and Professor of Philosophy, Rutgers University.

[2] See J. T. Moore, "Locke on Assent and Toleration," *Journal of Religion,* **58** (January 1978), 330-36.

[3] This point is persuasively argued by John C. Biddle, "Locke's Critique of Innate Principles and Toland's Deism," *Journal of the History of Ideas,* **39** (July-September 1976), 411-17. Cf. also John W. Yolton, *John Locke and the Way of Ideas* (London, 1956), 117.

[4] *A Paraphrase and Notes on the Epistles of St. Paul to the Galatians, Corinthians, Romans, Ephesians* was published between 1705 and 1707, and constitutes the eighth volume of *The Works of John Locke,* 10 vols. (London, 1823).

[5] Winthrop Hudson, "John Locke—Preparing the Way for the Revolution," *Journal of Presbyterian History,* **42** (March 1964), 19-38.

[6] His most vociferous opponent, John Edwards, repeatedly called Locke a Socinian. Socinianism was a sixteenth-century radical Christian movement which denied the dogma of the Trinity as well as many other elements of traditional orthodoxy. Later Unitarians saw the Socinians as their ancestors. The German philosopher Leibniz also thought Locke a Socinian, but on philosophical grounds, see Nicholas Jolley, "Leibniz on Locke and Socinianism," *Journal of the History of Ideas,* **39** (April-June, 1978), 223-50. A modern biographer thinks that the general tone of Locke's religion "was plainly Unitarian or Socinian," Maurice Cranston, *John Locke: A Biography* (London, 1957), p. 390. The most thorough case for Locke's Unitarianism has been made by a British Unitarian, Herbert McLachlan, *The Religious Opinions of Milton, Locke, and Newton* (Manchester, England, 1941), 69-114. This provides a more careful description of what constituted Unitarianism in Locke's time than appears in much of the literature about Locke, but in my opinion still fails to prove its case for Locke's Unitarianism.

or abettor of Deism.[7] Yet other interpreters of Locke have placed him in the midst of that emerging Anglican liberalism known as Latitudinarianism, or pointed to ideas he shared with the more liberal Dissenters.[8]

Several recent students of Locke have regarded his religious views as more conventionally Christian that had most earlier commentators, and have also noted the centrality of Christian apologetics to his whole philosophical enterprise. A recent article by Samuel C. Pearson, Jr. claims that an "urge to harmonize the potentially conflicting claims of reason and faith was characteristic of Locke throughout his career," that "Locke was deeply committed to the Christian faith which he understood in moral and experiential more than in dogmatic terms but which he believed rested on historic revelation," and that "In the *Essay* no less than in the *Reasonableness* Locke's concern is that of a latitudinarian Anglican firmly committed to the Christian faith."[9] Another recent investigator of Locke, John C. Biddle, maintains that Locke "sought in the *Essay* to establish traditional revelation as the primary guide in that proper science and business of mankind, morality and religion."[10] A third interpeter, Richard

---

[7] This goes back to the claim that John Toland's *Christianity Not Mysterious*, a deistic book published in 1696, was based on Lockean principles. A tract published in London in 1698, F.B., *A Free But Modest Censure of the Late Controversial Writings and Debates of the Lord Bishop of Worcester and Mr. Locke*, declared that "Sceptics and Deists" were Locke's "humble admirers" (10). Edwards also claimed that Locke's views led to Deism; see John Edwards, *The Socinian Creed* (London, 1697), 125. The question was extensively discussed by S. G. Hefelbower, *The Relation of John Locke to English Deism* (Chicago, 1918), who concluded that Locke and the Deists shared a great deal and were treading a common path toward "progress" and "enlightenment." A more recent author, Roland N. Stromberg, *Religious Liberalism in Eighteenth-Century England* (London, 1954), 17, 19, thinks that "Locke's philosophy led logically to scepticism" and that "Locke's *Reasonableness of Christianity* was a signal for the deists." Gerald R. Cragg, on the other hand, says that "It is possible to exaggerate the degree to which the Deists as a whole were the disciples of Locke," *From Puritanism to the Age of Reason* (Cambridge, England, 1950), 141. For an excellent discussion of the matter see Biddle, 417-22, who stresses Locke's differences from the Deists. New light is cast on the relationship of Toland to Locke in Margaret C. Jacob, *The Newtonians and the English Revolution, 1689-1720* (Ithaca, N.Y. 1976), 211-16. The consensus is that Locke disavowed Deism and unlike the Deists believed in revelation; part of his purpose in *The Reasonableness of Christianity* was to refute Deism.

[8] Cragg, 126, and Hefelbower, 51-52, 66, note Locke's affinities with Latitudinarianism; Mclachlan, 75, calls attention to Locke's indebtedness to William Chillingworth. One point which might be supposed to distinguish Locke from the Latitudinarians would be the importance of Platonism in the thought of the latter, which they had imbibed from the Cambridge Platonists. But Locke was on friendly terms with some of the Cambridge group, and recent studies have minimized their differences from Locke, e.g., J. A. Passmore, *Ralph Cudworth: An Interpretation* (Cambridge, England, 1951), p. 245, or Aharon Lichtenstein, *Henry More: The Rational Theology of a Cambridge Platonist* (Cambridge, Mass., 1962), 25.

[9] Samuel C. Pearson, Jr., "The Religion of John Locke and the Character of His Thought," *Journal of Religion*, **58** (July 1978), 244, 248, 256.

[10] Biddle, 417.

Ashcraft, thinks that "Locke's primary commitment was to certain principles of the Christian faith, and that it is within that context the *Essay* should be read in order to gain an appreciation of Locke's viewpoint." Ashcraft feels that where Locke attacks "certain precepts of traditional religion" it is only because he thought they provided a weak basis for the defence of Christianity and that "Once the old foundation of innate ideas is replaced by a 'surer' one, the superstructure of Christianity will stand mightier than ever." Ashcraft considers *The Reasonableness of Christianity* to be the completion of the task begun in the *Essay*: "It is nothing less than a total misconception to regard the *Reasonableness* as a denigration of Christianity and a defence of philosophy. Rather, the precepts of faith are necessary precisely because of the failure of philosophy."[11]

My aims are to further the analysis of Locke's religious views by focusing on his treatise *The Reasonableness of Christianity* as it dealt with the subject of justification, to uncover the sources in Anglican and Baxterian Latitudinarianism for Locke's exposition of justification in that treatise, and then to return to the question of Locke's supposed Socinianism as that term was given meaning in the discussions of justification contemporary with Locke. The centrality for Locke's treatise of a particular view of justification has been overlooked in both the eighteenth century and our own time because *The Reasonableness of Christianity* has been interpreted chiefly as a book about reason and revelation or as an attempt to reduce Christianity to a few essentials. Furthermore, the problem of Locke's sources in *The Reasonableness of Christianity* has been complicated by his insistence that he was following Scripture alone.[12] And the question of his Socinianism has been obscured by a narrowing of the meaning of Socinianism to Antitrinitarianism, whereas Locke himself consistently disavowed the implication that his writings were Antitrinitarian. I shall present evidence to show that a particular view of justification was a central theme of *The Reasonableness of Christianity*, that Locke's ideas on this matter were derived from the Anglican Latitudinarians and the liberal Dissenters who followed Richard Baxter, and that Locke held a view of the atonement of Christ which was in the later seventeenth century widely excoriated as "Socinian," even though Locke shared it with many Latitudinarian churchmen.

Justification and *The Reasonableness of Christianity*

Almost at the very end of *The Reasonableness of Christianity* Locke commented that "justification" was "the subject of this present treatise."[13]

[11] Richard Ashcraft, "Faith and Knowledge in Locke's Philosophy," in John W. Yolton, editor, *John Locke: Problems and Perspectives* (Cambridge, England, 1969), 194, 198, 202, 218-19.
[12] *The Works of John Locke*, VII, 3.   [13] *Ibid.*, 158.

Although students of Locke have noticed that he had something to say about justification,[14] his remark that it was the "subject" of his treatise has not been adequately appreciated as a clue for understanding Locke's religious ideas. Later, in the preface to his *Second Vindication of the Reasonableness of Christianity*, Locke explained how he came to write about justification: earlier in the same year in which he published *The Reasonableness of Christianity* (1695), he said, "the controversy that made so much noise and heat amongst some of the dissenters, coming one day accidentally into my mind, drew me, by degrees, into a stricter and more thorough inquiry into the question about justification. The scripture was direct and plain, that it was faith that justified: The next question then was, what faith that was that justified; what it was which, if a man believed, it should be imputed to him for righteousness."[15]

The controversy Locke referred to concerned Antinomianism and had driven a wedge between moderate and strict Calvinists among the Dissenters. Antinomianism was a term applied, often with the exaggerated implication of lawlessness, to those extreme proponents of divine grace who denied that good works were important as preparation for faith or necessary as sanctifying evidence of justification. In fact, the debate went all the way back to the 1640s and 1650s, when the more moderately Calvinistic Puritans usually called "Presbyterians," typified by Richard Baxter, began to fear the sectarian and Antinomian leanings of the more strictly Calvinistic Congregationalists and Particular Baptists. After the Restoration the issue continued to flare up, not only between the two factions of dissenting Calvinists (as when in 1672 strict Calvinist Congregationalists took exception to Baxter's views on justification) but also between Conformist and Dissenter, as in the exchange between the Anglican Edward Fowler and the Baptist John Bunyan.[16] The charge of Antinomianism had come to be something of a scare tactic, similar to modern charges of "anarchism," and was a favorite of Anglicans attacking Dissent, which explains why the more moderate Dissenters were eager to show themselves innocent of it.

The phase of the controversy to which Locke was referring had begun in 1690 with the republication of *Christ Alone Exalted*, by the notorious Antinomian Tobias Crisp. Attacked as a dangerous book by the Baxterian Presbyterian Daniel Williams, Crisp's book (Tobias Crisp was long since dead) was defended by his son Samuel Crisp, Isaac Chauncey, Richard Davis, and Stephen Lobb. Supporting Williams were two moderate Calvinists long associated with Richard Baxter, John Howe and William

[14] E. g., Cragg, 126-27; Richard I. Aaron, *John Locke* (1937; third edition, Oxford: Clarendon Press, 1971), 296-97; Biddle, 418-19; Pearson, 252.

[15] *The Works of John Locke*, VII, 186-87.

[16] Dewey D. Wallace, Jr., *Puritans and Predestination: Grace in English Protestant Theology, 1525-1695* (Chapel Hill, North Carolina, 1982), 113-20, 136-39, 164-66, 180-82.

Bates. The controversy had come to a head in the latter part of 1694 and the spring of 1695 with a spate of pamphlets produced by both sides, the withdrawal of the Presbyterians from the joint Pinner's Hall lectureship, and their setting up of a separate lecture at Salter's Hall. Polemical tracts continued to be exchanged for the rest of the decade.[17]

In confuting the Antinomian view that justification preceded actual believing and the strict Calvinist view that free grace was compromised if works were in any way joined to faith in justification, the Presbyterian moderates led by Daniel Williams stressed the conditional character of the covenant of grace and described justifying faith in such a way as to involve repentance and the promise of a new life. In the scope that they gave to human freedom and the caution with which they spoke of predestination, these Presbyterians were coming closer to the Arminian position.[18]

The Reasonableness of Christianity was thus Locke's effort to write about justification as he had been awakened to that subject by the Dissenter's debates as well as to inquire into the nature of revealed knowledge wich followed logically upon his investigation of the character of natural reason in his *Essay Concerning Human Understanding*. It began the discussion of justification with a consideration of the "justice" or righteousness which Adam lost by his fall: he forfeited bliss and immortality by his disobedience and involved all his posterity in this ruin, although beyond the loss of immortality no person will be punished except for his own misdeeds.[19] But according to Locke, Christ will restore persons to immortality if they through their own righteousness will "win a title to" it. Thus "if any of the posterity of Adam were just, they shall not lose the reward of it, eternal life and bliss, by being his mortal issue: Christ will bring them all to life again."[20] However, all having sinned, none can be justified by means of the law of God, it being unthinkable that any unrighteous person should come to "paradise." Thus God interposed with a new order of things, "the law of faith," by which, where fulfillment of God's moral law was lacking, "faith is allowed to supply the defect of full obedience," so that "believers are admitted to life and immortality, as if they were righteous." By the law of faith Locke does not intend a

[17] J. Hay Colligan, "The Antinomian Controversy," *Congregational Historical Society Transactions*, vol. 6 (October 1915), 389-96; Olive M. Griffiths, *Religion and Learning: A Study in English Presbyterian Thought from the Bartholomew Ejections (1662) to the Foundation of the Unitarian Movement* (Cambridge, England 1935), 95-105. Not all high Calvinists were Antinomians, but it would be fair to say that they feared Antinomianism less than they did Arminianism, whereas the moderate Calvinists or Presbyterians were horrified by Antinomianism while more tolerant of Arminian tendencies.

[18] *Ibid.*, 103-04; Roger Thomas, *Daniel Williams: Presbyterian Bishop*, Sixteenth Lecture, Friends of Dr. Williams' Library (London, Dr. Williams's Trust, 1964), 6, 11, 23. Daniel Williams, *Gospel-Truth Stated and Vindicated* (third edition, London, 1698), sig. A6^r, 4, 62, 93, 114, 126, 137, 216.

[19] *The Works of John Locke*, VII, 5-8.   [20] *Ibid.*, 9.

new way of serving God but the same moral law, which may, however, under the new covenant be only partially fulfilled, the defect in its ful-fillment being compensated for by the faith of the believer. Justification by faith is that God considers as just those who are not fully so, "by counting their faith for righteousness, i.e., for a complete performance of the law."[21] The faith which God so accepts is to believe that Jesus is the Messiah. There follows biblical evidence which takes up a considerable portion of the whole treatise, marshalled in order to prove that Jesus and the apostles summoned men only to believe this simple and clear proposition, that Jesus was the Messiah sent by God.[22] In response to the inevitable criticism that this was to require only such an historical faith as even devils might have, Locke adds some other elements to his interpretation of justifying faith: such faith is an offer of divine grace made only to human beings, not to devils, and more crucially, such faith involves repentance. "Repentance is as absolute a condition of the cov-enant of grace as faith," and this repentance includes both sorrow for past sins and "a turning from them into a new and contrary life." Thus, "These two, faith and repentance, i.e., believing Jesus to be the Messiah, and a good life, are the indispensable conditions of the new covenant, to be performed by all those who would obtain eternal life."[23] It is this faith, including repentance and an effort toward a new life, "for which God of his free grace justifies sinful man," forgiving sins and conferring immortality, thereby accepting such faith in place of the defect of obe-dience to the moral law. It would be irrational and unjust and also "encourage iniquity" if God "should justify those who had no regard to justice at all." "Only those who have believed Jesus to be the Messiah, and have taken him to be their King, with a sincere endeavour after righteousness, in obeying his law, shall have their past sins not imputed to them; and shall have that faith taken instead of obedience, where frailty and weakness made them transgress. . . ."[24] Locke then listed numerous biblical passages to prove that Christ and the apostles included repentance along with belief in the Messiah in their preaching, so that none would be condemned for unbelief alone, but also for their misdeeds.[25]

Much in Locke's discussion of justification echoes what had been said about that topic by the moderate Dissenters in their confutation of An-tinomianism, but other elements in his argument even more explicitly touch on the issues of the Antinomian controversy. Locke maintained that Christ explicitly declared what misdeeds would lead to condemnation so that his followers would not be deceived "by mistaking the doctrine of faith, grace, free-grace, and the pardon and forgiveness of sins, and salvation by him" for a doctrine of license.[26] The indwelling of the Holy

---

[21] *Ibid.*, 10-11, 14-15.   [22] *Ibid.*, 16-20, 34, 97, 102   [23] *Ibid.*, 102-105.
[24] *Ibid.*, 110-112.   [25] *Ibid.*, 129.   [26] *Ibid.*, 126.

Spirit in the believer, by which through grace the sanctification of the believer was thought by the strict Calvinists to be effected,[27] was entirely omitted by Locke, who instead spoke of the Holy Spirit as an "assistance" given to the believer in the doing of good. Where the Puritan theologians in particular had discoursed endlessly on the ways in which the Holy Spirit worked in the believer, Locke simply commented that "Twill be idle for us, who know not how our own spirits move and act us, to ask in what manner the Spirit of God shall work upon us."[28] And insofar as the strict Calvinist understanding of grace, faith, and justification was strongly dependent upon the epistles of Paul, Locke argued that the epistolary literature of the New Testament consisted of occasional writings addressed to the problems of those already converted to Christianity and therefore did not lay down the minimal requirements of Christianity or the fundamentals of belief.[29] In this way he excluded from the discussion an enormous number of relevant texts.

Locke wrote two vindications of *The Reasonableness of Christianity*, mostly in response to the strictures upon it of the Anglican Calvinist John Edwards.[30] Especially in the much longer second vindication, Locke bogged down in quibbling with his opponent over what seem subsidiary issues, such as the nature of the epistolary literature of the New Testament (Edwards claimed that Locke said the epistles were "waste paper" and that one need not read the New Testament beyond the *Acts of the Apostles!*)[31] or whether essential Christian belief can be reduced to a single article (which Locke denied he had done). But the vindications do return to the question of justification as well as advance upon *The Reasonableness of Christianity* with a more thorough treatment of the atonement. Little about justification which differs from what he had said in the earlier book appears in the two vindications, however, beyond his attempt in the *Second Vindication* to distinguish more carefully between the types of faith. There he noted that while faith first means "a bare assent to any proposition," there is also an "evangelical faith," which is "an active principle of life, a faith working by love and obedience."[32]

[27] This was in particular a major theme of the high Calvinists of the Restoration age, see Wallace, *op. cit.* (n. 16 above), 154-57, 185.

[28] *The Works of John Locke*, VII, 151.

[29] *Ibid.*, 152-56; his later paraphrases and notes on the Pauline epistles were among other things an attempt to minimize the extent to which those epistles were amenable to the Calvinist interpretation of justification (see for example, *The Works of John Locke*, VIII, 19, 28, 250-251, 391) which would account for his labors on these texts, especially as he had been challenged over the epistles by John Edwards.

[30] *A Vindication of the Reasonableness of Christianity . . . From Mr. Edward's Reflections* (London, 1695); *A Second Vindication of the Reasonableness of Christianity* (London, 1697). Both are reprinted in vol. 7 of *The Works of John Locke*.

[31] John Edwards, *The Socinian Creed: Or a Brief Account of the Professed Tenents and Doctrines of the Foreign and English Socinians* (London, 1697), 127; *The Works of John Locke*, VII, 127.

[32] *Ibid.*, 285-86.

A number of distinct emphases and themes emerge as characteristic of Locke's treatment of the doctrine of justification. First, in the Lockean view, faith justifies as it is accepted by God in place of a full righteousness, a position strikingly different from the Reformation Protestant view that it is Christ's righteousness imputed by God to the believer which justifies, faith being the instrument by which advantage is taken of this "alien" righteousness. Next in the Lockean view, such faith is first of all the mind's assent to the truth of revealed testimony; thus faith is reduced to the acceptance of propositions as true rather than being, as it was in Reformation theology, a trusting acceptance of the sufficiency of Christ's righteousness. But Locke and those who agreed with him feared the Antinomian possibilities of any view of faith which joined the more affective elements to the intellectual. However, if faith is intellectual rather than a trusting union with Christ with morally renovative consequences, then the third element of the Lockean view of faith is necessary, the coupling of obediece to faith for justification, and one is justified for a faith which includes not only the sincere resolution to do good works but also actual obedience to the moral law even if not perfect obedience. To strict Calvinists such an outlook seemed plain justification by works and was sometimes assaulted as a surrender to the Roman Catholic view of the matter. That charge was wide of the mark, however, for the Tridentine theology of justification was a subtle blend of divine grace infused through sacramental means and human cooperation with that grace in the production of faith and works that gave less scope than Locke gave to justification by works. Fourthly, grace comes into the Lockean view of justification, not as in classical Reformation theology by the imputation of Christ's righteousness to the believer nor as in Tridentine Catholic theology by sacramental infusion, but simply by the appointment of a new covenant which provides a "law of faith," different from the natural law of works which required full obedience, by which one might be justified. This covenant however is conditional, its condition being the actual faith and obedience of those who accepted its terms. The prominence of covenantal thinking in Puritan and Calvinist thought has long been a commonplace, but their view of the covenant always included the explanation that it was God's grace which enabled his elect to fulfill the terms of the covenant. Variations of that kind of covenant theology appeared even among the Antinomians.[33] The emergence and prominence of a truly conditional covenant theology among later seventeenth-century Anglicans, however, has been given less attention than it deserves. Grace also enters into the picture in a fifth element of the Lockean view of justification, that God gives the grace of his Holy Spirit as an assistance to the believer. There are two final points in the Lockean view of justification that may be singled out: the morality of the Christian dispensation is not a new and different morality based on the spiritual gifts of the indwelling Holy Spirit (as all Calvinists believed) but the same

[33] E.g., see Richard A. Muller, "The Spirit and the Covenant: John Gill's Critique of the *Pactum Salutis*," *Foundations*, **24** (Jan-March, 1981), 4-14.

eternal moral law given new clarity and incentives; and, as the character of Locke's whole treatise testifies, he regarded his interpretation as consonant with reason, unlike more mystical and enthusiastic versions of faith and justification.

Elements of the view of justification, which Locke later expounded, first appeared in English Protestant theology during the era of civil war and Interregnum in the strictures of Richard Baxter against the Antinomians and in the increasingly anti-Calvinist thought of some Anglican theologians. Richard Baxter was a Puritan spokesman who greatly feared the sectarianism unleashed by the unsettledness of the 1640s.[34] In explaining justification in 1649 Baxter argued that obedience and works as well as faith were conditions of justification and that the Gospel commands the same morality as did the law of nature. In his discussion of the covenant he stressed its conditional character and he spoke of the faith of the believer as that which was imputed as righteousness.[35] In a later discourse on *The Reasons of the Christian Religion*, Baxter made much of the congruence of Christianity and reason, and repeated his view of justification in the context of that congruence. He also stated there what Locke was later to assert, that "Christianity was best known in its principles" as those were "delivered by Christ the Author of it."[36]

Laudian Arminians had developed an anti-Calvinist Anglican theology in the generation before the civil wars, and the years of Puritan rule only abetted that kind of theology among the ousted supporters of episcopacy. C.F. Allison has called attention to a turning toward what he calls moralism in their understanding of justification among such Interregnum Anglican spokesmen as Henry Hammond, Jeremy Taylor, George Bull and Herbert Thorndike. He also thinks that their views were very much akin to those of Richard Baxter, and a departure from earlier "classical" Anglicanism, which remained loyal to the Reformation perspective on justification.[37] these same Anglican "moralists" attacked many other aspects of Calvinist theology.[38]

According to Allison, Jeremy Taylor's position was "that our faith and sincere endeavours before justification are accepted as the required righteousness on account of Christ."[39] Locke's opponent John Edwards thought Locke must have derived his view of justification from Taylor.[40]

---

[34] See Geoffrey F. Nuttall, *Richard Baxter* (London, 1965), esp. 35-39.

[35] Richard Baxter, *Aphorisms of Justification* (London, 1649), 96, 107-108, 125-126, 154, 289-290, 292-293, 310, 317; In later writings, such as *Confession of His Faith* (London, 1655), Baxter expressed himself more carefully on these matters, but his basic convictions about faith and the covenant remained the same, see C. F. Allison, *The Rise of Moralism: The Proclamation of the Gospel From Hooker to Baxter* (London: S.P.C.K., 1966), 154-164, esp. 156, "Baxter's original views on justification were never substantially altered."

[36] Richard Baxter, *The Reasons of the Christian Religion* (London, 1667), esp. 221-22, 255; 146.

[37] Allison, see esp. 192-96.   [38] Wallace, 120-29.   [39] Allison, 70.

[40] John Edwards, *Some Thoughts Concerning the Several Causes and Occasions of Atheism, Especially in the Present Age* (London, 1695), 104-05.

The same view of faith itself as imputed appeared in Herbert Thorndike.[41]
For Henry Hammond and George Bull justifying faith included repen-
tance and either the vow to live a good life (Hammond) or good works
themselves (Bull).[42] Allison also thinks that Taylor, Hammond, and
Thorndike held the same view about a conditional covenant as did
Baxter.[43] Hammond not only prefigured Locke's understanding of jus-
tification but also published a book entitled *Of the Reasonableness of
Christian Religion*.[44]

This same interpretation of justification shared by Baxter and the
Interregnum Anglican anti-Calvinists reappeared, in more explicit and
developed form, among the Latitudinarian Anglicans of the Restoration
era. These divines inherited not only the anti-Calvinism and Arminianism
of the preceding Anglican generation but also the more liberal outlook
of the earlier William Chillingworth and of the Cambridge Platonists.
Among prominent Latitudinarians writing about justification were Simon
Patrick, Isaac Barrow, Edward Fowler, William Sherlock, Samuel Parker,
Joseph Glanvill, and John Tillotson. All except Sherlock, Glanvill and
Barrow became bishops of the Church of England, and Tillotson was
Archbishop of Canterbury toward the end of Locke's life. Richard Baxter
too continued to express his ideas about justification throughout the
Restoration period, and by the end of the century this had led to a group
of liberal Calvinist Presbyterians that included Daniel Williams and John
Howe.

Simon Patrick was made Bishop of Chichester after the Glorious
Revolution of 1688-89, but at the opening of the Restoration he was a
young enthusiast for more liberal if not more tolerant views in the Church
of England, as his *A Brief Account of the New Sect of Latitude-Men*
testifies. In that short tract he revealed himself to be an Arminian as
well as a supporter of Platonism rather than scholastic Aristotelianism,
and also to be one who thought that justification entitled "conditions."[45]
In his *Friendly Debate Between a Conformist and a Nonconformist*, published in 1669, Patrick described justifying faith as "An effectual persuasion that God hath sent Jesus into the world. . .[and]. . .that ye
believe on him whom he hath sent." But this faith also included becoming
Christ's disciple in a "sincere profession of his Religion, and living according to it," that is, faith included good works, which Patrick explicitly
said were necessary for justification. God's grace is in giving the gospel
and in accepting repentance and obedience and pardoning failures "when

---

[41] Herbert Thorndike, *The Theological Works*, vol. 3, in two parts (Oxford, 1849,
1851), Part 1, 83ff., 97; Part 2, pp. 592-595, 659. This is drawn from a work of Thorndike
on the covenant of grace which was first published in 1659. See also Allison, 117.

[42] Henry Hammond, *A Practical Catechisme* (Oxford, 1646), p. 38; Allison, 119, 121,
123-124.

[43] Allison, pp. 71, 100, 114-115.   [44] (London, 1650).

[45] Simon Patrick, *A Brief Account of the New Sect of Latitude-Men* (1662), 9-10, 14.

we sincerely design and study to obey him in all things." This new covenant of the gospel is conditional upon faith and obedience.[46]

Edward Fowler was raised to the episcopate in 1691, and like Patrick attempted an explanation of the position of the more liberal divines. In his explanation Fowler emphasized that the gospel and its duties were reasonable, indeed such that reason could have discovered, except that in the gospel these duties were better compacted together and better made available to all than they would have been by reason. Moreover, the gospel discloses "matters of fact" as well as "points of meer belief" which go beyond "Natural Religion." The gospel also gives "far greater helps to the performance of our duty," God sending "grace to assist us in well-doing" and giving us his Spirit "if we will not resist and quench it." The gospel also enforces our duty with more "perswasive Motives and Arguments" than were known before, such as the example of Christ, his pardoning of repentant sinners, and the promise of immortality. All this renders Christianity "a Religion as easie to be practised by Mankinde as can be." Christianity is then not at all a matter of obscure mysteries but a religion that has no idea "but that our Reason may admit of it, and close with it," even though some of its truths could only be known by revelation.[47]

Of justification by faith, Fowler says that moderate divines so explain it as "to include a hearty willingness to submit to all Christ's precepts in the nature of it." Imputation is described as "Those which are sincerely righteous, and from an inward living principle allow themselves in no known sin, nor in the neglect of any known duty . . . shall be dealt with and rewarded, in and through Christ, as if they were perfectly, and in a strict Legal sense so." Such faith as this is the condition of the new covenant and includes the good works of "sincere obedience to Christs [SIC] Gospel" though excluding "popish" or "Jewish" works.[48] In attacking John Bunyan as an Antinomian, Fowler again expressed these ideas about justification, and cited Baxter in support. Baxter in turn rallied to Fowler's defense against his fellow Dissenter Bunyan.[49]

[46] Simon Patrick, *A Friendly Debate Between A Conformist and a Non-Conformist* (London, 1669), 43, 12-14, 26, 46.

[47] Edward Fowler, *The Principles and Practices, of certain Moderate Divines of the Church of England, (greatly mis-understood) Truly Represented and Defended . . . In A Free Discourse between two Intimate Friends* (London, 1670), 42, 48-49, 68, 74, 86, 94, 96.

[48] *Ibid.,* 114-15, 138-39, 142, 152, 157, 162-64, 166, 175, 188.

[49] Edward Fowler, *The Design of Christianity; or, A Plain Demonstration and Improvement of this Proposition, viz. That the enduing men with Inward Real Righteousness or True Holiness, was the Ultimate End of our Saviour's Coming into the World, and is the Great Intendment of His Blessed Gospel* (1671; rpt. London, 1676), 217, 220-22; Edward Fowler, *Dirt Wipt Off: or a Manifest Discovery of the Gross Ignorance, Erroneousness and most Unchristian and Wicked Spirit of one John Bunyan, Lay Preacher in Bedford, which he hath shewed in a vile Pamphlet published by him, against The Design of Christianity* (London, 1672), 12-14; Baxter is cited on 49 and 73ff, the latter being

It is ironic that Samuel Parker should be included alongside of those Latitudinarians who expressed ideas on justification similar to Locke's because Parker was a high Tory proponent of absolute obedience to the monarchy, an advocate of a hard line with the Dissenters, who, he thought, should be answered "by the Pillory and the Whipping-Post" and "lashed into obedience," and a compromiser with the Roman Catholicism of James II, who made him Bishop of Oxford.[50] But in his virulent attacks upon the supposed Antinomianism of the Dissenters he went so far in the identification of grace with moral virtue that the poet-parliamentarian and supporter of the Dissenters Andrew Marvell resolved satirically to call him henceforth "your morality" rather than "your grace."[51] Parker excoriated the Dissenters for turning grace into an excuse for license and rebellion, but they countered by arguing that he had reduced grace to mere morality.[52] Parker responded by asserting that evangelical grace was nothing more than moral virtue "heightened by the Motives of the Gospel, and the Assistance of the Spirit," the Christian "Institution" not introducing "any new Duties distinct from the Eternal Rules of Morality." According to Parker, "The Christian Institution is not for the substance of it any new Religion, but only a more perfect digest of the Eternal Rules of Nature and Right Reason." Christ reinforced the "obligation" of these moral duties "by endearing our duty with better Promises, and urging our Obedience upon severer Penalties." Parker described faith as believing the doctrines of the gospel, and conversion as becoming "sincere Proselytes to the Gospel." For Parker, Christ pardons those who perform the conditions of the new covenant.[53]

An interpretation of justification similar to Locke's also appeared in two polemical works by William Sherlock, who was made Dean of St. Paul's after the Glorious Revolution. Sherlock maintained that the Dissenter's view of faith in and knowledge of Christ, particularly as held by the leading English Calvinist John Owen, had substituted "a kind of Amorous and Enthusiastick Devotion" for obedience to the commandments of Christ. In carrying on this debate, Sherlock argued that faith is a believing in the revealed propositions of the gospel, that there is no imputation of Christ's righteousness to the believer, that justifying faith includes obedience and good works, and that the new covenant is conditional upon faith and works. As for the mystical union with Christ of which Calvinists spoke, Sherlock denied that to be individual, arguing

---

extracts from his writings; Richard Baxter, *How Far Holiness is the Design of Christianity* (London, 1671).

[50] Samuel Parker, *A Defence and Continuation of the Ecclesiastical Polity* (London, 1671), 144; Parker, *Discourse of Ecclesiastical Polity* (London, 1670), 304-05.

[51] Andrew Marvell, *The Rehearsal Transprosed* (London, 1672), 135.

[52] Parker's chief opponent was the renowned Calvinist theologian John Owen, who rebutted Parked in *Truth and Innocence Vindicated* (London, 1669), see *The Works of John Owen, D.D.*, edited by William H. Goold, 24 vols. (London and Edinburgh, 1850-55), XIII, 414, 417-18, 420, 424-25, 431.

[53] Parker, *A Defence and Continuation*, 88, 132, 207, 211, 304-07, 314-16, 322, 343, 345.

that "the Union of particular Christians to Christ is by means of their Union to the Christian Church." "So that to abide in Christ, is to make a publick and visible Profession of Faith in Christ, to be Members of his visible Church." Furthermore, Sherlock argued, Christ came into the world to "publish such a religion, as may approve itself to our reason, and captivate our Affections by its natural charms and beauties." As for Christ loving sinners, Sherlock says: "The reason of Christs [*sic*] love to any Person is his [i.e., that person's] Holiness and Obedience."[54]

In several sermons on faith and justification Isaac Barrow, mathematician and clergyman, expressed similar notions. Faith is assent to the testimony of the gospel; it involves the resolution to do good as well as actual obedience; it includes repentance; those are justified who "seriously resolve" to live according to the gospel, such faith being imputed as righteousness; the covenant is conditional. Faith is *not* a believing that *my* sins will be forgiven, nor any enthusiastic "recumbency" upon Christ, but "nothing else, but sincere embracing Christian Religion."[55]

Joseph Glanvill, best known as one of the scientific divines associated with the Royal Society, spoke similarly. Faith "is the belief of a Testimony," that is, propositional. Justifying faith includes our moral endeavors, which will be "assisted" by God's Spirit. The fruits of God's Spirit in believers will be moral virtues, Christianity having come into the world for the "perfection of morality."[56]

When John Tillotson was appointed Archbishop of Canterbury in 1691, a proponent of Latitudinarianism had acceded to the highest office in the English Church. The same views of faith imputed for justification, faith as assent to testimony, faith including works, the conditional covenant and the assistance of grace appeared in his sermons. For him too Christianity was a republication of natural morality, only made plainer and reinforced by more explicit rewards and punishments.[57]

In spite of Locke's disclaimer that his ideas in *The Reasonableness of Christianity* were drawn simply from his interpretation of the Bible, the similarity of his views on justification to those of the Latitudinarians and Baxterians strongly suggests dependence, whether specifically through the reading of their books or generally through the absorption of ideas widely current. In the explanation of his occasion for writing *The Reasonableness of Christianity* that appeared in Locke's *Second Vindication*, he declared his familiarity with the Dissenter's debates on justification, and in that same vindication he made reference to his "little

[54] William Sherlock, *A Discourse Concerning the Knowledge of Jesus Christ* (1673; rpt. London, 1678), 7-8, 18, 21, 23-24, 88, 91, 121, 147-48, 157-58, 209, 253; see also William Sherlock, *A Defence and Continuation of the Discourse Concerning the Knowledge of Jesus Christ* (London, 1675), 19, 26-27, 120-22, 155, 273.

[55] Irene Simon, editor, *Three Restoration Divines, Barrow, South, Tillotson: Selected Sermons*, 2 vols. (Paris, 1967), I, 402, 405-06, 411-12, 414-15, 419-21, 424, 429-30, 439-40.

[56] Joseph Glanvill, *Some Discourses, Sermons and Remains* (London, 1681), 18, 23, 37-38, 66-68, 72-73, 89. [57] Simon, II, 518, 526, 535, 561-63, 566, 576, 592-93, 596.

reading" on the matter of justification in "Books of divinity" in which
he found the matter not to be explained "so fully and advantageously"
as the New Testament itself called for. But he also acknowledged that
he thought his views so common that he did not expect to receive opposition "from any one in the communion of the church of England."[58]
A few references to divines appear in the vindications and they are to
those whom one might expect: Baxter is cited once, Simon Patrick and
Tillotson each twice, and Chillingworth three times.[59]

Further evidence of Locke's dependence upon the Latitudinarians
appears in the fact of his close connections with a number of them. A
recent biographer, Maurice W. Cranston, thinks that Locke met some
of the Latitudinarian divines at the London home of Thomas Firmin,
which a number of them frequented as well as Locke. Both John Tillotson
and Edward Fowler were acquaintances of Locke. After Tillotson died,
Locke told a correspondent: "There is now scarcely anybody I can consult
about doubtful points of divinity." Fowler paid a visit to Locke when
the latter was gravely ill in 1704.[60]

Thus it would appear that *The Reasonableness of Christianity*, insofar
as it was a treatise on justification, repeated, without a great deal of
originality, an understanding of justification which had been a commonplace of Anglican Latitudinarians and Baxterian Presbyterians for more
than a generation. Although Locke's treatise tended to pull together and
even simplify a number of points which had been scattered throughout
the writings of these liberal divines, it does not appear to have been more
radical than their writings on the subject, and in some instances he spoke
more cautiously than had Parker or Sherlock, for example. Why then
did his work beget so much controversy? Part of the answer is that more
conservative Calvinists had been rebutting Latitudinarian works for a
long time, and this continued in John Edwards' attack upon Locke. But
another part of the answer lies in the way in which Locke entangled
himself in controversial matters extraneous to his main points, such as
what he had said about the epistolary literature of the New Testament
or the question whether Christianity could be reduced to a single principal
tenet. One vulnerable point in *The Reasonableness of Christianity* was
Locke's virtual denial of original sin, insofar as he interpreted Adam's
fall to have entailed only the loss of immortality and not either guilt or
any propensity to sin, and yet he was relatively unmolested over this by
his opponents.[61] He was similarly vulnerable because of the implications

---

[58] *The Works of John Locke*, VII, 18, 189.
[59] *Ibid.*, 172, 179, 252, 276, 296, 302, 362.
[60] Cranston, 126-27, 363, 386, 470. See also Aaron, 26, 29.
[61] *The Works of John Locke*, VII, 6-8; Edwards, *Some Thoughts Concerning Atheism*,
110, made note of Locke's unorthodoxy in this connection, but did not press the point;
John Milner, *An Account of Mr. Lock's Religion . . . and . . . A brief Enquiry whether
Socinianism be justly charged upon Mr. Lock* (London, 1700), 186, thought that Locke,

of his view of justification for the doctrine of the atonement, and it was
in relation to this subject that Edwards found grounds for charging Locke
with Socinianism.

Socinianism and *The Reasonableness of Christianity*

John Edwards claimed that Locke was "all over Socinianized,"[62] and
there were many particulars listed by his opponents as evidence of this,
including such things as his supposed reduction of Christian faith to one
article and his denial of the eternal torment of the damned. Naturally
suspicion of Locke's Socinianism was only abetted by Bishop Edward
Stillingfleet's claim that Locke's denial of innate ideas and ideal "substances" in his *Essay* had undercut the only proper basis for the defense
of the Trinity, but Stillingfleet never said that Locke actually was an
Antitrinitiarian.[63] Locke in turn vehemently denied any Antitrinitarian
intent.[64]

There was a better basis however for the accusation that Locke held
a Socinian view of the atonement in denying, as he did, that Christ's
death was a propitiatory sacrifice making satisfaction for God's requirement of the punishment of sinners. This issue was central to Edward's
assault upon Locke. In the controversies over justification, both between
the moderate and strictly Calvinist Dissenters and between churchmen
and dissenting Calvinists, the issue of the atonement of Christ had been
important, with the conservative Calvinists claiming that the "moralist"
view of justification without any imputation of Christ's righteousness to
the believer removed Christ's death from any integral connection with
salvation at all, and was hence downright Socinianism. Those Calvinists
who tended to Antinomianism thought that salvation by Christ necessarily involved a real "exchange of persons" between Christ and the
believer, so that Christ was made "sin" and a "curse" in the believer's

---

like the Socinians, denied original sin. While the Latitudinarians generally minimized
original sin, they did not altogether deny that there was some corruption and either moral
weakness or tendency to sin entailed in Adam's fall. For example, for Tillotson's view,
see Simon, II, 590; Cf, R. Buick Knox, "Bishops in the Pulpit in the Seventeenth Century:
Continuity and Change," in *Reformation, Conformity and Dissent: Essays in honour of
Geoffrey Nuttall* (London, 1977), 101: "Tillotson had no place for a doctrine of original
sin. . ." Jeremy Taylor, on the other hand, had been accused of a Pelagian view of sin.
Much later (1740) the Presbyterian John Taylor expressed a view of Adam's fall similar
to that of Locke, Griffiths, 142.

[62] Edwards, *Some Thoughts Concerning Atheism*, 113.

[63] Edward Stillingfleet, *A Discourse in Vindication of the Doctrine of the Trinity*
(London, 1697), 239ff; Edward Stillingfleet, *The Bishop of Worcester's Answer to Mr.
Locke's Letter* (London, 1697), 3-7; Edward Stillingfleet, *The Bishop of Worcester's Answer
to Mr. Locke's Second Letter* (London, 1698), 4, 55. See also Robert Todd Carroll, *The
Common-Sense Philosophy of Religion of Bishop Edward Stillingfleet, 1635-1699* (The
Hague, 1975), 86-100, 137-142.

[64] *Works of John Locke*, IV, 4, 13, 30, 68, 95-96, 156, 163, 196-99.

stead, and this very point was a prominent issue in the Dissenter's debate which had stimulated Locke's investigation of justification. A survey of the theological conflicts of the Restoration age could easily lead to the conclusion that the main thing meant by "Socinianism" in those controversies was the denial of the satisfaction of Christ.[65]

Edwards first took note of Locke's book (he did not yet know the author's identity) in *Some Thoughts Concerning the Several Causes and Occasions of Atheism, Especially in the Present Age*, which was published in the same year (1695) as Locke's treatise. Edwards noted that Locke had left out of his account of Christian essentials such "Grand Heads of Christian Divinity" as "Reconciliation by Christ's Blood," "the efficacy of his Death, the full Satisfaction thereby made to the Divine Justice, and his being made an All-sufficient Sacrifice for Sin."[66] This work was followed by *Socinianism Unmask'd* in 1696 and *The Socinian Creed* in 1697. In the first of these, Edwards argued that Locke's reduction of Christianity to belief in the Messiah made Christ's satisfaction unnecessary and declared that Locke "gave proof of his being Socinianiz'd by his utter silence about Christ's satisfying for us, and purchasing Salvation by vertue of his Death."[67] By his third treatise Edwards knew that Locke was his opponent, and he had also seen Locke's defence, but he still charged Locke with denying that the death of Christ was a satisfaction and propitiation.[68]

Thomas Burnet, in a more temperate attack upon Locke, nonetheless repeated the same point: Locke "overthrows the Notion of our Saviour's redeeming us from an Eternity of Torments," . . . "destroys in great measure the Doctrine of Christ's Satisfaction," and he makes faith in Christ to be only faith in his messiahship, not in his character as the mediator who "through the Merits of his Satisfaction" "redeemed us from Eternal Misery."[69]

[65] The most notable defenses of the anti-Socinian position on the satisfaction of Christ were made by John Owen, see Wallace, (*op. cit.*, n. 16 above), 152-53; Stephen Lobb, *A Report of the Present State of the Differences in Doctrinals, between Some Dissenting Ministers in London, In a Letter to a Friend in the Country* (London, 1697), shows how important the strict Calvinists considered the question of the atonement to be in the debate over justification, see sig. A2ʳ, pp. 4-6, 8. Lobb thought that the issue of whether or not in the atonement there was a real exchange of persons between Christ and believers was "the very hinge on which the Controversie between the Orthodox and Socinians doth turn." He also thought that the Presbyterian Daniel Williams denied this exchange. He repeated this and coupled Williams with Baxter in *An Appeal . . . About the Great Doctrine of Christ's Satisfaction . . . Against Socinianism* (London, 1698), 2, 61-62.

[66] Edwards, *Some Thoughts Concerning Atheism*, 110.

[67] John Edwards, *Socinianism Unmask'd. A Discourse Shewing the Unreasonableness of a Late Writer's Opinion Concerning the Necessity of only One Article of Christian Faith; and of his other Assertions in his late Book, Entituled, The Reasonableness of Christianity* (London, 1696), 4; see also 13-15, 94-101.

[68] Edwards, *The Socinian Creed*, 69, 120.

[69] Thomas Burnet, *Animadversions on a late Book Entituled the Reasonableness of Christianity as delivered in the Scriptures* (Oxford, 1697), 3, 51, 57, 59.

A third critic of Locke, John Milner, found many elements in *The Reasonableness of Christianity* to be Socinian, not least its implications for the doctrine of the satisfaction of Christ.[70] Milner was one of the nonjurors, those high Anglican clergy who refused to take the oath of allegiance to William and Mary. Locke in turn rebutted the charge of Socinianism by clarifying his understanding of the atonement. His *First Vindication* dealt extensively with this question, Locke arguing that he had said in *The Reasonableness of Christianity* that Christ restored humankind to the possibility of salvation after the sin of Adam, and so Christ did purchase life and salvation by his death. As to whether this death was a "satisfaction," Locke maintained that controversial matters such as the question of satisfaction were not part of the fundamental articles of the Christian religion. The satisfaction of Christ, he continued, is not included in the Apostle's Creed, and is not one of the articles laid down by Christ and the apostles as essential to be believed in order to be a Christian. "I only set down the Christian religion as I find our Savior and his apostles preached it," which is, that God, "out of his free grace, proposed a new law of faith to sinful and lost man."[71] His *Second Vindication* did not deal so centrally with the atonement as the first, but the subject recurred there too. For example, Locke defended himself against Edwards' charge that, like the Jesuits in China, he had dissembled the sufferings of Christ.[72] Locke also contended in the *Second Vindication* that "there is not any such word in any one of the epistles, or other books of the New Testament, in my Bible, as satisfying, or satisfaction made by our Saviour; and so I could not put it into my Christianity as delivered in the Scripture," and in replying to Edwards, "if mine be not a true Bible, I desire you to furnish me with one that is more orthodox." Furthermore, Locke wrote, "if it be necessary to name the word Satisfaction, and he that does not so is a betrayer of Christianity, you will do well to consider, how you will acquit the holy apostles from that bold imputation." Locke did acknowledge, however, that Christ was "offered up," fulfilling a sacrificial work of redemption,[73] but of course such a formulation fell far short of what strict Calvinists considered orthodox. Samuel Bold, Locke's eager defender on this and other matters, also denied that Locke's view of the atonement was Socinian.[74]

Locke's interpretation of the atonement, in spite of its sketchiness, falls roughly into that type of theology of the atonement which is usually called the "moral influence" doctrine. Such a doctrine of the atonement fits well his moralistic interpretation of justification as a whole and is

---

[70] Milner, *An Account of Mr. Lock's Religion*, 22-24, 37, 72, 152, 179-88.

[71] *Works of John Locke*, VII, 162-64, 166-68, 175-76.

[72] *Ibid.*, 166.

[73] *Ibid.*, 267-68.

[74] Samuel Bold, *A Collection of Tracts, Publish'd in Vindication of Mr. Lock's Reasonableness of Christianity . . . and of his Essay, Concerning Humane Understanding* (London, 1706), 47 of *A Short Discourse* and 87 of *Observations on the Animadversions*.

also of such a sort as would appear to his contemporaries as "reasonable." The Latitudinarian Anglicans and the Baxterian Dissenters held a similar view of the atonement.[75] But for doing so, they too were accused of Socinianism.

A number of conclusions can be drawn from this analysis of Locke's treatise on *The Reasonableness of Christianity* and its context in the religious disputes of late seventeenth-century England. Though hitherto overlooked, justification was the principal subject of Locke's treatise and it was treated in relation to the disputes about that topic, disputes which had gone on for more than a generation among both Dissenters and Anglicans. In his opinions that faith was assent to propositions, that it was faith itself which was imputed as righteousness, that justifying faith included works, that the new covenant was conditional, and that grace was primarily assistance, Locke had departed radically from Reformation Protestantism. However, he shared these departures from earlier orthodoxy with a large company of Anglican Latitudinarians and Baxterian Dissenters. The same could be said for Locke's view of the atonement, and it was especially because of his rejection of the necessity of Christ's making satisfaction for sin that he was widely accused of Socinianism. These views of justification and atonement, which he shared with the Latitudinarians, he and they regarded as an eminently reasonable understanding of the content of Christian revelation. Furthermore, Locke's version of these doctrines was dependent upon the ideas of Baxter and the Latitudinarians, although he chose to stress the importance of his study of the Bible alone in forming his opinions.

In sum, Locke should be placed in the midst of other liberal Christians in England during the generation after the Restoration. He was a major and influential, if not very original, formulator of the Latitudinarian and later "rational Christian" interpretation of Christian revelation. His firm adherence to a belief in revelation sharply separated him from Deism, but he was more sympathetic to Dissent and less fearful of Socinianism than were his ecclesiastical partners in Latitudinarian theology. And if important elements in his thought constituted some sort of half-way house towards either Unitarianism or Deism, he was in good company with a number of prominent bishops of the Church of England.

The George Washington University.

[75] Richard Baxter, *An Appeal to the Light* (London, 1674), 1-2; Baxter, *Aphorisms of Justification*, 111-12, 115; Richard Baxter, *Catholick Theologie* (London, 1675), 66-67; Daniel Williams, *Gospel-Truth Stated and Vindicated*, sigs. A4ᵛ −5ʳ, pp. 7-8, 10, 16, 24, 33, 40; Sherlock, *A Discourse Concerning the Knowledge of Jesus Christ*, 12, 28, 33; Allison, 192, observes that those whom he calls "moralists" gave to the atonement the significance of moral example. One Anglican theologian sometimes considered a Latitudinarian, Edward Stillingfleet, did defend Christ's satisfaction against Socinianism just as he defended the dogma of the Trinity, *Two Discourses Concerning the Doctrine of Christ's Satisfaction* (London, 1700), 171.

Chapter XII

LEIBNIZ ON LOCKE AND SOCINIANISM

By Nicholas Jolley

In October 1709 Leibniz happened to tell an academic correspondent, Bierling, that he found Locke's philosophy unsatisfactory.[1] Bierling confessed surprise, since he admired Locke, and he asked Leibniz to explain the grounds of his dissatisfaction.[2] This challenge drew from Leibniz one of his best brief statements of his verdict on Locke as a philosopher; in one paragraph Leibniz manages to compress many of the criticisms which are familiar to readers of the *Nouveaux Essais*. If Locke had thought harder about the distinction between necessary and contingent truths, we are told, he would have realized that the former can only be proved by principles latent in the mind. According to Leibniz, Locke also fails to appreciate that ideas such as being, substance, and unity are innate, since the mind is innate to itself. As in the *Nouveaux Essais* Leibniz encapsulates this criticism in the tag on which his fame as a critic of Locke largely rests: "Nothing is in the understanding which was not previously in the senses, except the understanding itself." But the remark which Leibniz then proceeds to make has received far less attention than it deserves:

Many other things could be criticized in Locke, since he also undermines the immaterial nature of the soul. He inclined to the Socinians (as also his friend LeClerc), whose philosophy of God and mind was always poor.[3]

In this paper I wish to analyze this statement in the light of an important, recently published essay by Leibniz on Socinian metaphysics. The effect of discovering what Leibniz meant by this remark to a forgotten German academic is to compel a complete reappraisal of the nature and purpose of his critique of Locke.

Today Socinianism is an obscure heresy which belongs to the history of theology, but in Leibniz's age, particularly during the period of his involvement with Locke, it was very much a live issue. To say of a writer that he was a Socinian was a serious, even a dreaded accusation, and Locke himself disowned the label vigorously. At first sight the charge of Socinianism in such a context is puzzling, for it is not obvious how it could apply to the philosophy of the *Essay Concerning Human*

---

[1] 24 October 1709, *Die Philosophischen Schriften von G. W. Leibniz*, ed. C. I. Gerhardt (Berlin, 1875-90), VII, 487, cited below as "Gerhardt." Translations from Leibniz texts are my own.

[2] Undated, LBr 67, Bl. 5, Niedersächsische Landesbibliothek, Hanover.

[3] The date, 19 Nov. 1709, is deleted. Gerhardt VII, 488-89.

Understanding. It is true that it was not only on the basis of his explicitly religious writings that Locke was accused of heterodoxy by his contemporaries, and Leibniz was not the first to claim that the *Essay* was tainted with Socinianism: Locke's destructive analysis of the concept of substance was interpreted by Bishop Stillingfleet as a covert attack on the doctrine of the Trinity.[4] Socinianism is certainly a difficult term to define with precision: it is an open-ended concept which covers a range of doctrines and attitudes. The essential elements of Socinianism are usually taken to be a denial of the Trinity and of the divine Incarnation, but the term was also used to indicate heterodox positions on other articles of the Christian faith. Thus when Locke faced the charge as a result of the *Reasonableness of Christianity,* his antagonist cited as proof his denial of the doctrine of original sin and his silence on Christ's satisfaction and atonement.[5] If the term is not easy to define, however, its scope is generally confined to revealed theology. But the present context makes it clear that it is not revealed theology but natural theology and metaphysics which Leibniz has in mind when he accuses Locke of inclining to the Socinians.

When Leibniz told Bierling that Locke had Socinian tendencies, Socinian philosophy was very much in the forefront of his thoughts. A year previously Leibniz had come into possession of a manuscript copy of a Socinian treatise on metaphysics by Christoph Stegmann,[6] and it was probably around 1709-10 that he wrote the important critique of that work which he entitled *Ad Christophori Stegmanni Metaphysicam Unitariorum.*[7] Leibniz's particular interest in Socinian doctrines at this time is almost certainly connected with the composition of the *Théodicée;* for Socinianism offers a radically opposed set of solutions to the problems of divine justice which Leibniz tackled in that work. In the interests of preserving divine justice, for instance, the Socinians felt compelled to deny that God had foreknowledge of events. As we shall see, many of Stegmann's metaphysical positions seem to have been thought out with a view to providing a philosophical basis for the characteristic tenets of Socinian theology.

Leibniz may have made a special study of Socinian philosophy in

[4] E. Stillingfleet, *Discourse in Vindication of the Doctrine of the Trinity* (London, 1697), X. On Socinianism: H. J. MacLachlan, *Socinianism in Seventeenth Century England* (Oxford, 1951).

[5] J. Edwards, *The Several Causes and Occasions of Atheism* (London, 1695).

[6] *Christophori Stegmanni Rupinensis Marchichi Metaphysica repurgata,* Lognitzi Ipsis kalend. Januar. MDCXXXV. Manuscript copy corrected in Leibniz's hand. LH IV, I, 9, Bl. 1-57, Niedersächsische Landesbibliothek, Hanover. On the German philosophical background: L. W. Beck, *Early German Philosophy: Kant and his Predecessors* (Cambridge, Mass., 1969).

[7] N. Jolley, "An Unpublished Leibniz MS on Metaphysics," *Studia Leibnitiana,* 7, 2 (1975), 161-89.

1709-10, but he had long been familiar with their doctrines. It would thus be quite wrong to suppose that Leibniz's remark to Bierling simply reflected his current preoccupations, and was to that extent irrelevant to an understanding of the *Nouveaux Essais*. Even Stegmann's treatise had been known to him from an early age, and from the first his estimate of it had been hostile. In 1691 Leibniz had told Ernst von Hessen-Rheinfels how he had encountered Stegmann's treatise in manuscript while von Boineburg was his patron (c. 1669-70).[8] This remark is echoed in the *Ad Christophori Stegmanni* itself, where Leibniz explains that the paper was essentially a revised version of some notes he had made in his youth.[9] More relevantly for our own purposes, there are disparaging references to Stegmann in Leibniz's writings on Locke. In the *Nouveaux Essais*, for instance, Stegmann's *Metaphysica repurgata* is cited in the course of a discussion of the grounds of assent to the propositions of revealed religion.[10]

Early in the *Ad Christophori Stegmanni Metaphysicam* Leibniz vividly describes the essential character of his quarrel with Socinian philosophy. Leibniz complains that the Socinians have introduced:

a certain attentuated ("extenuatam") philosophy in which scarcely anything outstanding and sublime survives, God himself is almost reduced to the status of creatures and our mind degenerates into the nature of matter. . . . And much more generous seem to me to have been the opinions of Pythagoras and Plato who recognized that souls are incorporeal and immortal by their own nature, and that there is a supreme mind governing all things with great wisdom.[11]

This statement is quite clearly an elaboration of Leibniz's remark to Bierling, but there are also verbal echoes of some of his other characterizations of Locke. The reference to Plato is particularly significant. In his later years Leibniz's admiration for Plato increased, and he more and more came to stress the affinities between Plato's philosophy and his own; Leibniz speaks with special sympathy of the Platonic doctrines of reminiscence and the transitory nature of matter. When Leibniz writes about Locke, the contrast with Plato is repeated in a way that strikingly recalls this passage in the *Ad Christophori Stegmanni Metaphysicam*. To several of his correspondents Leibniz described the debased nature of Locke's philosophy in almost identical terms without specifying the doctrines which earned it such an unfavorable description. His account of Socinian metaphysics allows us to see the point of such comments. To Jaquelot, for instance, Leibniz writes that Locke: "minimizes too much the generous philosophy of the Platonists: . . . and puts in its place opinions

---

[8] 10? Jan. 1691, *G. W. Leibniz: Sämtliche Schriften und Briefe*, ed. German Academy of Sciences (Darmstadt, 1923-), I, VI, 159-60, cited below as "Academy.'
[9] 31-33, Jolley, "Unpublished Leibniz MS," 177.
[10] XV, XVIII, Academy VI, VI, 497. Cf. *Compte rendu*, Academy VI, VI, 17
[11] 19-22; 28-31, Jolley, "Unpublished Leibniz MS," 177.

which abase us and may even do mischief in ethics."[12] To Remond ten
years later he wrote that Locke "has some sort of superficial metaphysics,"[13] and in a letter to Hansch the contrast with Plato recurs:

The innate ideas of Plato . . . are much to be preferred to the tabula rasa of
Aristotle, of Locke, and other more recent philosophers who philosophize
exoterically.[14]

There are thus excellent grounds for believing that Leibniz had
Stegmann's treatise in mind when he accused Locke of inclining to the
Socinians. Such an identification is suggested not merely by chronology
but also by the striking verbal parallels between Leibniz's comments on
Locke and on the debased philosophy of the Socinians as exemplified by
Stegmann's metaphysics. Yet the fact that Leibniz should have seen fit
to connect the two works is surprising, and no doubt tells us more about
the nature of Leibniz's interest in other philosophers than about Locke
himself. Despite its heterodoxy on central issues, Stegmann's *Metaphysica repurgata* is a work written in the Scholastic tradition with which
Locke had broken; indeed it is the kind of traditional metaphysics of
which Locke tended to be contemptuous and which he devoted so much
energy to opposing.

The gulf that divides Locke from Stegmann becomes apparent if we
consider their treatment of the topic which prompted Leibniz to compare
them. According to Leibniz, the common element in Locke and Stegmann is their materialism. However, Stegmann's case for materialism is
couched in markedly traditional terms: it depends on the concepts of
form and matter which have their origin in Aristotle. Stegmann seeks to
prove that matter and form are principles of every being by arguing that
matter gives a common nature, form a distinct nature to things;[15] he
rejects the Aristotelian doctrine that matter is the principle of individua-
tion. One might expect that Stegmann would develop his argument by
claiming that the soul is a substance, and is therefore matter and form by
definition. But in fact he asserts that the soul is an accident inhering
in the body as a subject, and this prompts Leibniz to object that this
opinion is merely asserted when it should have been proved:

He says that the soul is an accident, in almost the same way that some speakers

---

[12] 28 April 1704, Gerhardt III, 474.
[13] 14 March 1714, *ibid.,* 612.
[14] *De Enthusiasmo Platonico,* 25 June 1707. *G. G. Leibnitii Opera Omnia,* ed.
L. Dutens (Geneva, 1768), II, 223, cited below as "Dutens." In the first draft
of this letter Leibniz refers to Locke without actually naming him: "Longe ergo
praeferendae Platonis ideae innatae et recte intellecta reminiscentia, tabulae rasae
Aristotelis et recentiorum quorundam humilius philosophantium." 23 June 1707,
LBr 361, Bl. 15, Niedersächsische Landesbibliothek, Hanover.
[15] 150-54, Jolley, "Unpublished Leibniz MS," 182.

in Plato's *Phaedo* said that the soul is harmony. But he nowhere proves this opinion of his.[16]

It was this thesis above all which must have reminded Leibniz of Locke: in the *Essay* and in controversy with Stillingfleet Locke suggested that thought might be a modification of material substance.[17]

There is a certain superficial resemblance between Stegmann's thesis that the soul is an accident inhering in the body as a subject and the position that Locke defended against Stillingfleet. But the resemblance is only superficial, and the fact that Leibniz seriously thought it worth pointing out provides a key to his own reading of Locke; it may also explain the force of the word "inclined" in his remark that Locke inclined to the Socinians. One obvious difference between the works of Locke and Stegmann is that whereas the former treats philosophy according to the "plain historical method," the latter proceeds in the manner of a Scholastic disputation: each topic is treated formally in a series of definitions, objections, and replies. It is thus difficult to make sense of the author's professed hostility to Scholastic metaphysics, at least as far as the form of argument is concerned. Indeed, if Leibniz regards this treatise as a representative example of Socinian philosophy, his own emphasis on their rejection of Scholasticism is puzzling:

In the desire of distancing themselves from the Scholastic theologians, they overturn everything great and sublime in Theology.[18]

Certainly the alienation from Scholastic theology did not extend to the procedure of argument. But though the contrast in the method of exposition is striking, it is not the essential difference between Locke and Stegmann; moreover, this stylistic contrast is covered by Leibniz's own distinction between the "exoteric" and the "acroamatic" way of writing, and his frequent observation that the *Essay* belongs to the former genre.[19] The chief difference between Locke and the Socinian treatise, which renders the parallel so seemingly implausible, is one that Leibniz hardly recognized. Stegmann's treatise is a metaphysics, as its title suggests; Locke's *Essay* is not. The fact that Leibniz does not seem to have understood this reveals the degree to which he interpreted Locke in terms of his own philosophical bias.

Stegmann may not succeed in proving that the soul is material, but he does advance it as a positive metaphysical doctrine. By contrast, the

[16] 186-88, *ibid.*

[17] *John Locke: An Essay Concerning Human Understanding,* ed. P. H. Nidditch (Oxford, 1975), IV, III, 6. Subsequent references are to this edition. Cf. Locke, *Letter to the Bishop of Worcester* (London, 1697).

[18] Leibniz to LaCroze, 4 Dec. 1706, LBr 517, Bl. 104, Niedersächsische Landesbibliothek, Hanover; Dutens V, 482. Incorrectly dated by Dutens.

[19] E.g., *Nouveaux Essais,* Preface, Academy VI, VI, 48.

form in which the thesis interests Locke is epistemological. In the *Essay*
the argument which so offended Leibniz and many of his contemporaries
occurs simply as an illustration of the extent of human knowledge. Locke
devotes so little space to the issue that it seems to have escaped Leibniz's
attention when he first read the *Essay*.[20] The argument is strictly subservient to his chief design in the Fourth Book of analyzing the nature of
knowledge and is at least consistent with his general theory. According
to Locke, knowledge consists in the perception of the agreement or disagreement of ideas. But in the case of the ideas of matter and thought,
no such disagreement can be perceived, and hence we cannot know that
matter and thought are incompatible:

> We have the *Ideas* of *Matter* and *Thinking,* but possibly shall never be able
> to know, whether any mere material Being thinks, or no.[21]

Locke's position is not free from ambiguities. Thus it is not clear whether
he thinks that our inability to perceive conceptual connections here is a
logical or contingent affair. Locke may be saying that though the concepts of thought and matter are not logically inconsistent, materialism is
not really a subject for *a priori* reasoning at all: it is rather a subject for
empirical research. On the other hand, Locke's reference to the mathematical example of squaring the circle in the immediately preceding
passage points in the opposite direction: it suggests that for Locke our
lack of *a priori* knowledge is a contingent limitation which could be overcome once we found the intermediate ideas.[22] If that is Locke's position,
then he lays himself open to the objection that a proper analysis of the
ideas of matter and thinking does reveal their incompatibility. This is
the essence of Leibniz's reply: though he thinks Locke's general criteria
of knowledge are too stringent, he holds that the soul's immateriality
can be known inasmuch as it can be proved *a priori*. But whereas for
Leibniz the proof of this claim is the foundation for a metaphysics, for
Locke the nature of the soul arises simply as a topic in the theory of
knowledge.

  Despite the ambiguities of Locke's position, it is surely clear that his
main contention is a negative one. Whatever conceptual difficulties are
involved in supposing that matter might think, they are no greater than
those which dualism of the Cartesian type presents: each hypothesis
involves something "dark and intricate," and there is no good ground
for deciding in favor of one or the other:

> . . . it becomes the Modesty of Philosophy, not to pronounce Magisterially,
> where we want that Evidence that can produce Knowledge.[23]

---

[20] Leibniz's first paper, *Quelques Remarques sur l'Essay* (1695?, Academy VI,
VI, 4-9), does not mention this doctrine.   [21] *Essay,* IV III 6.
  [22] G. Buchdahl, *Metaphysics and the Philosophy of Science* (Oxford, 1969),
198.   [23] *Essay,* IV III 6.

However, when Leibniz cites Locke's argument he takes no notice of its epistemological context, and thus he converts a claim which in Locke is primarily one about knowledge into a positive metaphysical thesis. It is symptomatic of this change of emphasis that he sometimes misrepresents Locke by ignoring his essentially negative conclusion. Often, it is true, he is careful to recognize that Locke is less than dogmatic. In the Clarke correspondence the tentative character of the claim is clearly acknowledged: "Mr. Locke and his followers ('sectateurs') suspect at least that souls may be material and naturally perishable,"[24] and in a letter to Isaac Jaquelot he complains that Locke leaves the soul's immateriality doubtful.[25] Writing to Sebastian Kortholt three years later he says that Locke believes that matter may be able to think.[26] On other occasions, however, Leibniz does not do justice to the form of Locke's claim; he criticizes it without paying any attention to its hypothetical character. In correspondence with Thomas Smith, for instance, Leibniz simply asserts that Locke reduces mind to the level of matter:

Therefore I was unable to approve certain thoughts about the human mind of Locke's, certainly a clever man, who depressed its nature and elevated that of matter, because he did not sufficiently examine the sources of either.[27]

In his own private, random remarks which preface the first draft of the *Nouveaux Essais,* Locke's argument is represented, or misrepresented, in equally positive terms:

The author's philosophy destroys what appears to me most important, namely that the soul is imperishable, whereas according to him a miracle is necessary to make it endure.[28]

It is probably in part as a way of recognizing the essentially negative character of Locke's claim that Leibniz confines himself to the modest assertion that Locke inclined to the Socinians; this is his manner of doing justice to the epistemological framework of the original argument. But we have seen that at other times Leibniz is not so scrupulous, and he writes as if Locke positively asserted the materiality of the soul; the hypothetical nature of the claim is completely discounted, and in this way the *Essay* is assimilated to the explicitly metaphysical thinking of the Socinian writer Stegmann. And this suggests that for Leibniz Locke's epistemological enquiry is not a genuine, autonomous enterprise: it is rather a blind for his real concern, which is to insinuate a Socinian metaphysics.

[24] Nov. 1715, Gerhardt VII, 352.   [25] 28 April 1704, Gerhardt III, 473.
[26] 18 Aug. 1707, Dutens V, 304-05.
[27] "Itaque nec Lockii ingeniosi quidem Viri de Mente cogitata quaedam probare potui, qui naturam ejus depressit, materiae extulit; utriusque fontibus non satis exploratis." 2 September 1707, LBr 872, Bl. 102, Niedersächsische Landesbibliothek, Hanover.
[28] Academy VI, VI, 48n.

Leibniz's tendency to treat Locke's claim as a metaphysical thesis may have a further explanation connected with a feature of Locke's own text. In the discussion in IV.III of the *Essay* Locke does seem to advance one positive epistemological claim: he suggests that we can at least be sure that thought is not within the natural powers of matter. Locke justifies his skeptical attitude towards dualism by appealing to God's omnipotence: although thought is not explicable in mechanical terms, we cannot be certain that God has not simply "superadded" to some system of matter a power of thinking. It is tempting perhaps for us to read Locke's reference to God as metaphorical in this context: in terms of the contemporary state of knowledge of body it is not possible to understand how matter could produce thought, but there is no *a priori* reason why this process should not be made intelligible in the light of future research and more sophisticated modes of explanation. This interpretation may appear attractive, but it is certainly not the way in which Leibniz reads Locke: he takes Locke's appeal to God's power *au pied de la lettre*. For Leibniz, the significant feature of Locke's discussion is the admission that thought is not a natural property of matter, and for him this means that thought could only be annexed to matter by a miracle.

Leibniz's belief that Locke's position implies a miracle throws more light on the parallel with the Socinian treatise. If thought were annexed to matter by a miracle, it could only persist by a perpetual act of divine recreation: God would need to intervene constantly to keep thought going. This is the logic of Leibniz's claim that by reducing mind to matter Stegmann destroys the soul's natural immortality:[29] and we have seen that he often makes similar remarks about Locke. To say that the soul is immaterial and to say that it is naturally immortal may appear independent propositions, but in fact for Leibniz they are interderivable: the soul is naturally immortal if, and only if, it is immaterial. Because of the paradoxes of the continuum, only immaterial substances can be simple, and since death consists in the dissolution of parts, they are incapable of natural extinction.[30]

The equation of immateriality with indestructibility is so fundamental to Leibniz's metaphysics that he does not always feel the need to argue for it or even explain it; for this reason he sometimes refers to Locke's doctrine as a denial of the soul's immateriality and sometimes as a denial of its natural immortality. To argue, as Locke and the Socinians do, that the soul is an accident inhering in the body as a subject, is to render it naturally mortal:

However, I confess that I believe that the immortality of the soul would be

---

[29] 25, Jolley, "Unpublished Leibniz MS," 177.

[30] For a valuable study of Leibniz's attitude to materialism: M. Wilson, "Leibniz and Materialism," *Canadian Journal of Philosophy* 3, 4 (1974), 495-513. She does not discuss Leibniz's critique of Locke in this connection.

very improbable, if one destroyed its immateriality, and if sensation ("senti-ment") could be produced and destroyed in matter as one of its modifications. After that it would need a miracle to make it subsist or revive. That is also what the Socinians claim; but such principles cannot fail to render the thing suspect to people of good sense.[31]

At first sight this argument may seem inconsistent with Leibniz's meta-physics, for one of his doctrines is that the body as well as the soul is conserved after death. But in fact Leibniz simply represents the position of his antagonists in the most unfavorable light. He takes advantage of Locke's admission that thought cannot be derived from the essence of matter to suggest that in that case it would no more survive death than any other inessential modification. Leibniz's theory allows for the trans-formation of the body in order to accommodate the fact that it is not the same material particles which are conserved. Thus though Locke's theory might have received a more charitable interpretation, it must be conceded that the formal inconsistency is only apparent.

Leibniz's identification of immateriality with indestructibility helps to explain why he should object so strongly to any suggestion that matter might think. In terms of his metaphysics, especially where it touches on his dynamics, it may seem difficult to justify his suspicions of such a theory. The concept of matter is hardly straightforward or unambiguous for Leibniz. Indeed it is impossible to speak of one Leibnizian conception of matter. Russell argued that at least five senses of the term could be distinguished in Leibniz.[32] Certainly there is one sense in which Leibniz's own theory of matter approaches the opinion he is attacking. Leibniz's dynamics compelled him to recognize an active element in matter which he termed "force," and in this sense matter is essentially active. Moreover, the dynamical concept of force is correlated on the metaphysical level with the active element of the monad, that is, with its clear and distinct perceptions. Leibniz was forced to admit the complexity of the issue on his principles in a letter he wrote to Burnett soon after he encountered Locke's theory:

What is essentially passive could not receive the modification of thought without receiving at the same time some substantial active principle which is joined to it: and as a consequence matter taken by itself could not think, but nothing prevents the principles of action or of unity which are found every-where in matter and which already envelop essentially a manner of perception, from being elevated to that degree of perception which we call thought.[33]

Thus it is only when taken in the sense of prime matter, which means

---

[31] Leibniz to Burnett, 6 July 1706, Gerhardt III, 311. Cf. *Nouveaux Essais* Preface, Academy VI, VI, 67-68.

[32] *A Critical Exposition of the Philosophy of Leibniz* (London, 1900), 75 Cf. C. D. Broad, *Leibniz: An Introduction* (Cambridge, 1975), 89.

[33] Undated, Gerhardt III, 261.

the purely passive qualities of impenetrability and inertia, that it is non-sense to say that matter might think: it is this sense which Leibniz has in mind when he speaks of "matter taken by itself": yet, as he recognizes, this concept is a pure abstraction.

Once it is realized that immateriality implies indestructibility the vehemence of Leibniz's hostility to Locke's views becomes much easier to understand. In other words, his stance is only fully intelligible in terms of his natural theology. If to say that the soul is material means that it is naturally perishable, then on Leibniz's theory its immortality is highly improbable. Indeed, orthodox theology can only be salvaged at the cost of having recourse to the miraculous, and Leibniz's dislike of such modes of explanation is well known. The necessity of explaining phenomena in terms of their natural properties is a methodological principle on which he insists emphatically in the Preface to the *Nouveaux Essais*. But if Leibniz objects to a materialist theory of the mind because it entails recourse to the kingdom of grace, another serious objection arises from his theory of identity.

In his treatise Stegmann admits that a materialist doctrine of the soul has consequences for the Christian dogma of the general resurrection. If the soul is an accident of the body, then the resurrection can only be interpreted in terms of God's creation of new bodies and souls. Stegmann argues that there is no difficulty in such a supposition.[34] A similar claim is actually made by Locke in a passage where he attempts to vindicate the suggestion that matter might think from the charge of contributing to skepticism and impiety:

All the great Ends of Morality and Religion, are well enough secured, without philosophical Proofs of the Soul's Immateriality; since it is evident, that he who made us at first begin to subsist here, sensible intelligent Beings, and for several years continued us in such a state, can and will restore us to the like state of Sensibility in another World, and make us capable there to receive the Retribution he has designed to Men, according to their doings in this Life.[35]

It is obvious that such a theory is likely to pose problems concerning personal identity. In this passage Locke skates over the issue, using the personal pronoun confidently. But once it is argued that immortality does not consist in the persistence of the same substance, it is natural to ask how personal identity is guaranteed. This is precisely Leibniz's objection to Stegmann's thesis that immortality will involve the creation of new souls and new bodies:

It turns out at last that he asserts that completely new men in respect of body

[34] *Metaphysica repurgata*, LH IV I 9, Bl. 15, Niedersächsische Landesbibliothek, Hanover.

[35] *Essay*, IV III 6.

and soul will arise at the resurrection. From which it is not clear how the happiness or unhappiness of those men may belong to us.[36]

For Leibniz personal identity through time consists in the persistence of the same immaterial substance. Once this is removed, it is impossible to say that a resurrected person is the same as one before death: in fact it is improper to speak of resurrection at all in such a case. For Leibniz, then, it can have seemed no coincidence that Locke denies that personal identity involves any reference to substance, and that he interprets it instead in terms of consciousness.[37] The Lockean doctrine of personal identity must have appeared to Leibniz as designed to meet the consequences of casting doubt on the soul's immateriality: it is an attempt to answer the objection which his explicit treatment of the issue ignores. In this way we can see part of what Leibniz means when he claims that Locke overturns the principles from which the soul's immortality can be proved.[38] Locke's theory of personal identity is required by his suggestion that matter might think. The two doctrines hang together, in Leibniz's eyes, as part of a strategy for insinuating a Socinian metaphysics.

According to Leibniz, then, Locke's suggestion that matter might think is tantamount to an attack on personal immortality, for this can only depend on the identity of the same substance. But if this theory is the chief basis for his charge against Locke, we must remember that in our initial quotation Leibniz also mentions the philosophy of God. In his characterizations of Socinian metaphysics it is their teaching about God no less than their doctrine of the mind which Leibniz criticizes. The scope of this criticism is not always constant. In some of his references to the Socinians' philosophy Leibniz instances simply their denial of God's prescience of future events; this is the only aspect of the Socinians' doctrine of God which he mentions in the account of their distinctive natural theology he wrote for LaCroze.[39] But in Stegmann's treatise the attack on divine omniscience is extended to a denial of all aspects of God's infinity, and since he claims that every being consists in the two components of matter and form, even the incorporeality of God is challenged.

Leibniz's attack on Socinian philosophy thus has two prongs, but it is difficult to see how his strictures about their doctrine of God could be made to stick on Locke. At no point in the *Essay* does Locke explicitly deny God's providence, and he is emphatic in maintaining that God is incorporeal. It may be thought that Locke's remoteness from the Socinians on this issue is another reason why Leibniz limits himself to saying that Locke "inclined" to the Socinians, and it is true that it is their

[36] 188-91, Jolley, "Unpublished Leibniz MS," 183.
[37] *Essay,* II XXVII.
[38] Leibniz to Kortholt, 18 Aug. 1707, Dutens V, 304-05.
[39] 4 Dec. 1706, Dutens V, 479-84.

common ground on the nature of the soul which he chooses to emphasize. If Leibniz's remark to Bierling were an isolated occurrence, there might be some reason for not paying it too close attention. But Leibniz also mentions Locke's philosophy unfavorably in a letter to Malebranche where he states that the refutation of Locke is one of the subsidiary themes of the *Théodicée:*

I have also tried to combat in passing certain lax philosophers, like Mr. Lock, M. LeClerc, and their like, who have false and base ideas of man, the soul, the understanding, and even the Divinity, and who treat as chimerical everything which goes beyond their popular and superficial notions.[40]

In the remainder of this paper I shall argue that there are indications that for Leibniz even Locke's philosophy of God is not free from suspicion of heterodoxy. The evidence here is cumulative: that Leibniz found fault with the Lockean God is more a matter of inference than of explicit statement.

The Socinian argument for the denial of God's infinity is that if God were infinite, he could not be known.[41] According to Leibniz, such an argument could only arise from ignorance of mathematics; mathematics deals with infinite series the magnitude of which can be known; thus the infinite can be known although it cannot be understood.[42] Locke does not argue along these lines, for he acknowledges that God is incomprehensibly infinite.[43] But for Leibniz Locke shares with the Socinians a mistaken analysis of the concept of infinity. As early as his first paper on the *Essay* Leibniz had taken issue with Locke for holding that in strictness the concept of infinity applies only to quantity,[44] and he returns to this thesis in the *Nouveaux Essais.* Against Locke Leibniz argues that infinity is predicated not more figuratively, but only less directly of the qualitative attributes of God:

Philal. When we apply our idea of infinity to the first being we do it originally in respect of his duration and ubiquity, and more figuratively with regard to his power, wisdom, goodness and his other attributes.

Theoph. Not more figuratively but less immediately, because the other attributes make their size known in respect of those into which the consideration of parts enters.[45]

Here the theological dimension of Locke's argument emerges quite clearly. To suggest that infinity strictly applies only to quantity is in

---

[40] Undated, Gerhardt I, 361.
[41] Stegmann, *Metaphysica repurgata,* V: "In quo de Unitate sive Finitate et Compositione," LH IV I 9, Bl. 32, Niedersächsische Landesbibliothek, Hanover.
[42] 281-85, Jolley, "Unpublished Leibniz MS," 185.
[43] *Essay,* II XVII 1.
[44] *Quelques Remarques,* Academy VI, VI, 7.
[45] II, XVII, Academy VI, VI, 157.

effect to deny that it really makes sense to speak of the infinity of God's qualitative attributes: in this way Locke appears to undermine God's omniscience, and thus to sympathize with the Socinian doctrine of God.

For Leibniz, Locke's thesis that infinity can in strictness be predicated only of quantity arises from his failure to realize that the true idea of the infinite is the absolute.[46] For Leibniz, as for other seventeenth century metaphysicians, the idea of infinity is positive, and is logically prior to the finite which implies limitation: it is an innate idea, since it cannot be derived from the experience of finite quantities. Leibniz does not accuse Locke of the grossest mistakes concerning the idea of infinity: he is aware that even Locke realizes that the idea of an infinite quantity is an absurdity, a notion which implies a contradiction. But because Locke thinks that the idea of infinity is negative, he misunderstands the nature of even those infinite attributes of God which have an immediate relation to quantity. Locke does not recognize that the true concept of infinity is prior to all composition, and for this reason he conceives of the infinite as a whole which consists of parts. The immensity and eternity of God are identified with infinite space and time. In Leibniz's eyes, such an equation implies an unworthy conception of the deity.

In reality, Locke's statements about God's relation to time are hard to interpret and seem to point in different directions. But at least his analysis of infinity as a negative concept formed by the repetition of parts leads him to identify God's eternity with sempiternity (infinite duration). In this he is in agreement with Stegmann who claims that God is subject to time. Stegmann's insistence on this point is clearly motivated by a desire to find a philosophical justification for denying to God a knowledge of future contingent events: indeed his account of God's relationship to time seems specifically designed to buttress this essential thesis of the Socinian theodicy. Stegmann thus opposes the tradition deriving from Boethius which interprets God's eternity as a *totum simul*—the simultaneous possession of the whole of time. In Leibniz's view, Stegmann's attack is directed against a parody of a serious philosophical position:

He imputes to others a ridiculous opinion, as if they thought that God is simultaneously in all moments, or ('seu') is at this moment in all moments, and by this means all moments coexisted with this moment. It is true that God exists in any moment of time whatever, but he does not depend on moments of time, since they themselves depend rather on God. That past or future events are now present to God must be interpreted in a rational manner, lest they are said simultaneously to be, as present, and not to be, as future. However, they are known to God as if they now existed, and he decreed at once about the totality of things from eternity, as if they were separated by no intervals of time.[47]

Leibniz may be wrong to think that Stegmann is attacking a straw man,

---

[46] *Ibid.*   [47] 241-49, Jolley, "Unpublished Leibniz MS," 184.

but in his view the attack misfires because the true concept of God's eternity is neither the *totum simul* nor infinite duration. As in the *Nouveaux Essais* Leibniz insists that God's eternity implies necessary existence:

The author says that eternity is time boundless on all sides or duration in every way infinite. This can be excused, provided it is observed that eternity, when ascribed to God, means something more, that is, the necessity of existing. Thus God is not affected by the flux of time, as creatures are, who lack the necessity of existing and always depend on something else.[48]

Leibniz's strictly atemporal conception of eternity is entailed by his theory that space and time are simply relations among the phenomena, and that the phenomena are themselves dependent on God. Of course this conception is not without its own difficulties. Indeed, even its polemical adequacy as an answer to Stegmann is doubtful. Although atemporal existence may be compatible with omniscience, Leibniz could hardly claim that his God has *foreknowledge* of future events: events can only be future for someone located with the temporal framework, which God, by definition, is not. Yet it is just such foreknowledge which Leibniz accuses the Socinians of destroying. Perhaps Leibniz might have answered Stegmann more effectively if he had invoked his distinctive metaphysical doctrines. Stegmann seems to assume that existence in time automatically excludes knowledge of future events; yet on one interpretation Leibniz's metaphysics implies that there is no such incompatibility: the monad knows everything, although confusedly. It is understandable perhaps that Leibniz should not invoke his more esoteric doctrines in a polemical context, and certainly, without the benefit of Leibnizian metaphysics, it is difficult to see how temporal existence and omniscience can be reconciled. Unlike Stegmann, Locke explicitly professes his belief in divine omniscience, but he makes no attempt to explain how it is possible if God exists in time.[49] Thus Leibniz could claim that Locke's equation of eternity with sempiternity prepares the ground for the denial of divine foreknowledge, even if it does not actually entail it.

Because of his defective analysis of the concept of infinity Locke undermines the infinite qualitative attributes of God, and he interprets His infinity in a way which suggests that He has parts. However, this is not the only aspect of Locke's teaching about God which appears suspect to Leibniz: Leibniz also seems to have discovered materialist implications for the divinity in Locke's theory of substance.

We have seen that Stegmann argues for materialism in general from the premise that form gives a distinct nature, matter a common nature to things. With the first claim Leibniz is in substantial agreement, since his

---

[48] 225-29, *ibid.*, *Nouveaux Essais*, II XVII, Academy VI, VI, 159.
[49] *Essay*, II XV 12, II XVII 14-22.

theory of complete concepts implies that no two individuals share exactly the same form. However, Leibniz does criticize the claim that matter gives a common nature to things:

> But this again had to be proved. For two things may have this in common that they are both beings or things, although they have no common matter. And it is just as if someone maintained that extension and time have some common matter because they have this in common, that they are something real, inasmuch as quantity is predicated of them, and they are continuous.[50]

It is perhaps strange to find Leibniz using just these examples since he really believes that space and time are not things at all but relations. But the point of the argument is clear: to say that two things belong to the same logical category—in this case, substance—is not to say that they share the same physical stuff. Significantly, Leibniz deploys precisely the same argument against Locke in the Preface to the *Nouveaux Essais* where he accuses him of failing to distinguish between the physical and the logical genus:

> Thus time and space are very heterogeneous things, and one would be wrong to imagine I know not what real common subject which had only continuous quantity in general and the modifications of which were the source of time or space.[51]

Of course, the fact that Leibniz finds occasion to use the same argument against both Locke and Stegmann does not mean that the target is necessarily the same in both bases. Though Leibniz employs it against Stegmann as a means of refuting the assertion that all substances are material, he might find a quite different use for it in arguing against Locke. But this is not the case. In the Preface to the *Nouveaux Essais* this argument is directed against Locke's defence of the thesis that matter might think as he presented it in the Stillingfleet controversy. But the mention of space suggests that Leibniz is also picking up an idea of Locke's which receives only a passing mention in the dialogue of the *Nouveaux Essais*.

In II, XIII, 18 of the *Essay* Locke discusses the issue of whether space void of body can properly be termed a substance. Locke's intention in this passage seems clear: his aim is to show that the question is an improper one by criticizing the concept of substance itself. To expose the emptiness of the concept Locke confronts his reader with a dilemma, and argues that either alternative entails unacceptable consequences. If the term "substance" has the same sense when applied to objects as different as God, spirit, and body, then, Locke argues, we must accept what he terms the "very harsh doctrine" that God, spirits and body differ only as modifications of the same matter. On the other hand, Locke thinks that to concede that "substance" has a different sense in the three cases will involve us in confusion. The point which Locke is making

[50] 152-56, Jolley, "Unpublished Leibniz MS," 182.   [51] Academy VI, VI, 64.

here may well be an anti-Cartesian one; in the *Principia Philosophiae* Descartes begins by defining substance as something independent, "nothing other than a thing existing in such a manner that it has need of no other thing in order to exist."[52] But Descartes immediately confesses that in this sense only God is a true substance, and is thus forced to admit that "substance" does not apply univocally to God and created things.

Leibniz agrees with Descartes on occasion, and claims that his position is the only possible alternative to Spinozism.[53] So Leibniz could answer Locke by conceding that "substance" is ambiguous, yet take issue with his claim that this necessarily leads to confusion. In fact, Leibniz's reply is rather different. Significantly he focusses all his attention on one half of the dilemma and adumbrates the criticism which he makes more explicit in the Preface to the *Nouveaux Essais:*

Philal. However, to know if space is a substance, it would be necessary to know in what consists the nature of substance in general, but in that there is some difficulty. If God, finite spirits and bodies participate equally in one and the same nature of substance, will it not follow that they differ only by the different modifications of this substance?

Theoph. If that consequence were valid, it would also follow that God, finite spirits and bodies, equally participating in the same nature of being, differed only by the different modifications of this being.[54]

By ignoring one half of the dilemma which Locke poses, Leibniz contrives to eliminate all Locke's statements which show that his real purpose is to expose the emptiness of the concept of substance. Leibniz's account of Locke's position does not even suggest that his argument takes the form of a dilemma. Thus in the light of the Preface, it seems clear that Leibniz understands Locke to be embracing the "very harsh doctrine" that God, spirits, and body differ only as modifications of the same physical substance. In other words, Leibniz understands Locke's thesis to be not a critical but a metaphysical one: Locke implies that even God is material.

By following Leibniz's own indications, we can detect signs that Locke's philosophy of God is not excluded from the charge of theological heterodoxy. It may be objected that Locke emphatically maintains that God is incorporeal; indeed in one place he claims that it is no less than a contradiction to suppose that the eternal, thinking being could be material.[55] But we need only remember that Locke is notoriously inconsistent on the subject of the soul's immateriality to realize that this objection is not compelling. Indeed, the fact that Locke's official teaching about God was in conflict with the implications of his other arguments

---

[52] I, LI, *Descartes: Philosophical Writings*, eds. G. E. M. Anscombe and P. Geach (London, 1975), 192.

[53] *Entretien de Philarète et d'Ariste*, Gerhardt VI, 582.

[54] *Nouveaux Essais*, II XIII, Academy VI, VI, 150.   [55] *Essay*, IV III 6; IV X.

would not count against Leibniz's view that his philosophy was insidious: on the contrary, it would tend to confirm it. But it would be a mistake to overemphasize those aspects of Locke's philosophy which might be seen as tending to subvert the infinity of God's perfections on the one hand and his incorporeal nature on the other. If, in his letter to Bierling, Leibniz instances the Socinian philosophy of God, this is at least in part because the question of the soul's nature has consequences for the divine attributes: in particular, it reflects on God's justice.

Leibniz sometimes writes that theology is a sort of divine jurisprudence which explain the laws of our fellowship with God.[56] The force of this remark can be understood from an illuminating passage in the *Ad Christophori Stegmanni Metaphysicam*. Here we can see how the issues of the soul's immateriality and divine justice were related in Leibniz's mind:

For when you at once take away from God his universal providence and from our mind its immortal nature, you will hardly expect from God those things which proclaim supreme wisdom and justice; or protract the hope of living beyond present death by which the perturbations of this life are reduced to a better state.[57]

This makes it clear that Leibniz thinks of both doctrines which he attributes to the Socinians as tending to subvert God's justice. The line of reasoning here is perhaps a little elliptical, but it is possible to reconstruct the stages of the thought. The argument from the denial of God's providence of contingent events seems to rest directly on the assumption of an interdependence among the divine perfections: thus to deprive God of one of his perfections, namely, his omniscience, is to render less plausible his possession of other perfections, like justice. Ironically a doctrine which is obviously introduced to save the divine justice from the consequences of admitting predestination appears to Leibniz to militate against it. In correspondence with Ernst von Hessen-Rheinfels, Leibniz himself admitted that this was the whole point of the Socinian doctrine.[58]

The argument from the soul's immortality is more complex. When Leibniz speaks of divine justice he is of course thinking of a system of rewards and punishments in an afterlife, as the passage itself makes clear. The distribution of such compensatory awards is dependent on the survival of the same immaterial substance. In Leibniz's view, any attempt to find an alternative explanation of such survival runs into problems over identity. We have already seen how Leibniz countered Stegmann's theory of the creation of new men on the day of judgment by asking how their happiness or unhappiness could concern us: it would not be we who were being punished but some wholly new beings. Thus the Socinian

[56] E.g., *G. W. Leibniz: Textes Inédits*, ed. G. Grua (Paris, 1948), I, 241.
[57] 24-28, Jolley, "Unpublished Leibniz MS," 177.
[58] Undated, Gerhardt II, 18; and 10? Jan. 1691, Academy I, VI, 159-60.

denial of the soul's natural immortality appears as a direct threat to the system of eternal rewards and punishments which is essential to the Leibnizian theodicy. But even if the philosophical objection from the nature of identity could be overcome, the Socinian theory would still undermine confidence in divine justice. For in Leibniz's view the doctrine that the soul is immortal only by grace implies that God does not operate according to the natural order: in other words, it casts doubt on his supreme wisdom. Again, as on the former argument, any challenge to one of his perfections is a challenge to his others as well. By calling into question any of God's perfections, the Socinian theory jeopardizes the one it is most anxious to maintain, namely the divine justice. Behind Leibniz's whole argument is the assumption that God's wisdom consists in acting according to a natural order which it is in the power of human reason to discover. The issues which Leibniz was to debate with Clarke are already foreshadowed in such arguments: it is not surprising that he opened that controversy with a side-glance at Locke.[59]

Leibniz was sometimes careful to remark that the demands of theological orthodoxy should not be allowed to interfere with the freedom of philosophical speculation: in the *Echantillon des Réflexions sur l'Essay*, for instance, he protests that he has no wish to mingle theological arguments with philosophical ones.[60] But even though he regards his metaphysics as a self-supporting structure, he rarely loses an opportunity of pointing out its convenience for orthodox theology. The independent validity of his philosophy does not prevent him from justifying it in terms of its theological advantages. Indeed, he sometimes claims that his metaphysics is the unique guarantee of Christian orthodoxy against heterodox systems like Spinozism.[61] The Socinian charge against Locke reminds us of the persistence of the concern with theodicy throughout Leibniz's writings. As Baruzi has said, the issue of theodicy was not one which occupied Leibniz for a day to be later dropped: on the contrary, throughout his life it was his constant ambition to write a theodicy.[62] The *Essais de Théodicée* must not be regarded as his first attempt at this task. Although the doctrines of Locke's *Essay* may be refuted by strictly philosophical arguments, not the least reason for supposing the doctrines invalid is that they are incompatible with the nature of divine justice. Leibniz's critique of the *Essay* is hardly less theologically motivated than the earlier *Discours de Métaphysique* or the later *Essais de Théodicée*. As he himself said of his critiques of other philosophers, including Locke, "I start as a philosopher but I finish as a theologian."[63]

Christ's College, Cambridge.

[59] Nov. 1715, Gerhardt VII, 352.   [60] Academy VI, VI, 16.
[61] Leibniz to Bourguet, 22 March 1714, Gerhardt III, 567.
[62] J. Baruzi, *Leibniz et l'Organisation Religieuse de la Terre d'après des Documents Inédits* (Paris, 1907), 195.
[63] E. Bodemann, *Die Leibniz Handschriften der königlichen öffentlichen Bibliothek zu Hannover* (Hanover, 1890), 58.

Chapter XIII

THE ANGLICAN RESPONSE TO LOCKE'S THEORY OF PERSONAL IDENTITY

By R. C. TENNANT

The theological importance of the concept of personal identity has been recognized from patristic times.[1] The present essay takes an eighteenth-century version of John Locke's theory and traces the way in which a group of Anglican churchmen redefined it, using it to maintain the doctrines of redemption and revelation. Much detailed research in church history remains to be done before charting properly the development of this idea in the intellectual, spiritual, and literary culture of eighteenth- and nineteenth-century Britain. This essay is intended to sketch in broad outlines the purely intellectual aspects of a system of thought which, laid down chiefly in the 1730s and 1740s, increased in influence steadily until their fruition in the first decades of the nineteenth century. References will be restricted as far as possible to major writers and well-known works.

The meaning of the term "personal identity" broadened as the concept of freedom developed. The continued extension of the meaning of personal identity, which has been termed Romantic,[2] had its origin in a confusion in Locke's own thought. He added the chapter "Of identity and diversity" (II.xxvii) to the second edition (1694) of the *Essay Concerning Human Understanding*. In that chapter, whatever its internal fallacies, Locke argues that, whereas the identity of dead objects and soulless living things is readily determined (by one of two criteria, same numerical substance or same "living organized body,"[3] the identity of a rational creature is established only by the sameness of consciousness of its own history. Locke sets up this doctrine in order to draw the conclusion that punishment at law is just

---

[1] See Russell Coleburt, "Principle of Identity: Philosophical Problem and Theological Mystery," *Downside Review*, **96**, no. 323 (April 1978), 132-43, *passim*.

[2] A recent work, *The Mysteries of Identity* by Robert Langbaum (New York, 1977), contains much interesting literary criticism of writers from Wordsworth to Beckett, and, while no sharp definition of terminology is achieved, it does show how political radicals used, and conservatives were disturbed by, the question of identity over 150 years. For the relation of modernist symbolism to Romanticism see P. N. Furbank, *Reflections on the Word 'Image'* (London, 1970), e.g., 34-48; also Michael Hamburger, *The Truth of Poetry* (London, 1969), Chaps. 3, 4, 6.

[3] *Essay*, II.xxvii.7. All quotations from Locke, unless otherwise noted, are from *An Essay Concerning Human Understanding*, ed. John W. Yolton (London, 1961; revised ed., 1974). Yolton's, *Locke and the Compass of Human Understanding* (Cambridge, 1970), 149-58, provides an excellent commentary on the theory of personal identity. See also J. D. Mabbott, John Locke (London, 1973).

only when the criminal can remember his crime, except in special circumstances where the judiciary "cannot distinguish what is real, what counterfeit" in testimony regarding memory.[4] Even for Locke earthly justice, where only the *fact* can be proved, is "natural" and Hobbist, retributive and not regenerative.

But in the Great Day, wherein the secrets of all hearts shall be laid open, it may be reasonable to think no one shall be made to answer for what he knows nothing of, but shall receive his doom, his conscience accusing or excusing him (II.xxvii.22).

It must be insisted that Locke's aim is to define "person" in a legal sense within a Protestant latitudinarian society (e.g., II.xxvii.26). As in his political work and *The Reasonableness of Christianity*, he wishes to encompass all conduct within the conscious acceptance of personal responsibility: neither God with his omniscience nor the State with its history and public records can justly violate the individual's conscience.

Despite Locke's forthright political formulation of personal identity, which, unlike that which Norris and Berkeley developed from Malebranche, had no contact with the third- and fourth-century disputes about *prosopon* and *homoousios/homoiousios*, the theory has an ambiguous nature in the *Essay*. In *Essay* IV.ix, Locke gives the ontological environment of his theory and this persists in the subsequently composed "Of identity and diversity." The linguistic errors involved in bringing together the ontological and the forensic were exposed by Hume,[5] and the resulting loose ends ensured that for almost a century the issue flourished within the parameters of Locke's secular philosophy. The resulting denigration of the will and the consequences of rendering the self passive (e.g., the "sentimental" and "gothick" schools of literature with their special mode of manipulating the unresisting reader's states of mind) have been charted in E. L. Tuveson's *The Imagination as a Means of Grace* (Berkeley, 1960). Locke inextricably links and confuses the two issues, forensic and ontological (e.g., II.xxvii.18). *Essay* II.xxvii.26 is phrased carefully: "whatever past actions [the person]

---

[4] Since admission of guilt without prosecution evidence was not sufficient for conviction, Locke's extreme radicalism in attempting to align the judicial and the ethical can be appreciated. In practise a majority of cases would be resolved within the provisions of Locke's "special circumstances." This is unjustly arbitrary in Locke's own terms because the "person," if not the "I" (II.xxvii.20), may not be identical in a man with a blank in his memory, so that the court may legitimately inflict suffering on the innocent: a crucial reminiscence of Hobbes whose cardinal social emotion is fear (e.g., *Leviathan*, Chaps. 27, 28), and who unflinchingly recognizes the legitimacy of the commonwealth's use of violence on its internal enemies, and even its local priority over a strictly objective justice.

[5] David Hume, *A Treatise of Human Nature*, ed. Selby-Bigge and P. H. Nidditch (2nd ed., Oxford, 1978), 261 f.

cannot reconcile or appropriate to that present *self* by consciousness, it [cannot be] concerned in. . . ." The word *reconcile* is especially significant since it implies a grasp of the ontological extent of a person in terms of fitness to an ideal conception of that person, be it moral or aesthetic, and a judgment about a past action's harmony with that conception. Locke makes provision, apparently, for such psycholog- ical mechanisms as repression (of historical but unpalatable actions), translating them into pleas of diminished responsibility, temporary in- sanity, and so on. Such a faculty, flourishing within a being, cannot itself be the person it is examining, which has in any case been previ- ously defined as the awareness of a set of ideas. The fallacy of this effectual regression is a point which Butler will later be shown to have identified. Defending this uneasy compromise, Edmund Law, a de- voted disciple, was pushed into an extreme position:

Personality [is] solely a creature of society, an abstract consideration of man, necessary for the mutual benefit of him and his fellows *i.e.* a mere forensick term; and to enquire after its criterion or constituent, is to enquire in what circumstances societies or civil combinations of men have in *fact* agreed to inflict evil upon individuals, in order to prevent evils to the whole body from any irregular member.[6]

Again he writes that personal identity "is an *artificial* distinction, yet founded in the nature, but not the *whole* nature of man" (*ibid.*, 21). Once society has defined personality it leaves subjective experience (the essence of identity) free and unfettered.

There are other crucial false assumptions. One, presumably a weakening before the prevailing neo-Platonism, is that the soul was co-extensive with consciousness; secondly, that formal limiting fac- tors such as the impossibility of two objects sharing the same space/ time locus or inception begs the question of identity (II.xxvii.1; see Mabbott, 58), a fateful mistake when considering the relation of soul and body; thirdly, that one proof of continued existence was an or- ganization, or, in less temporal terms, a pattern (e.g., Mabbott, 60). In some cases the identification and solution of such problems were beyond the power of eighteenth-century philosophy, but Berkeley, for example, circumvented all these by his less analytic procedure. As Berkeley himself said, such shortcomings lost hold of Locke's philosophy on things and transferred much attention instead to the study of linguistic behavior (see *Alciphron*, Dialogue IV; Hume, *Treatise*, 253 ff.).

In English religious thought, Locke is original because he formu- lates personal identity as a matter of the grammatical first person and assumes a community and similarity among men which require that proofs of identity be advanced only for this first person. If this were

---

[6] Edmund Law, *A Defence of Mr. Locke's Opinion Concerning Personal Identity* (Cambridge, 1769), 10 f.

not so, he would have to deal with conscious lies as well as loss of memory. In his critique of Locke's theory R.I. Aaron objects that,

> The very fact that we say 'He has now forgotten that he did so-and-so, yet he *was* the person who did it' . . . points to the conclusion that we have other criteria for determining personal identity than the one Locke mentions.[7]

For Locke "we" can make no statement about "his" identity, not having access to "his" memory: the interesting impossibility is to say "*I* have forgotten X, and yet I did it," identity of person being an affair of the psychological concept, consciousness, an accretion of ideas in the mind's *tabula rasa*. The debate about how a model may be constructed to demonstrate continuity of identity through a series of imperfect memory states, whether considered by H. P. Grice in this century or Edmund Law in the eighteenth, has little contact with the issue as Locke himself *conceived* it, and the problematic introduction of words like *continuity, series,* and *states,* heavily criticized by Hume and recently by Jonathan Bennett, should not be imputed directly to Locke but to those interpreters who had to grapple with his ambiguities.[8] For Locke himself the impossibility of "I have forgotten X, and yet I did it" resides in his effective refusal (no longer logical) to accept as authoritative statements of fact and idea (political, theological, or even revelatory) not immediately available (through the consciousness which forms identity) to the conscience. It is a safeguard of human rights.

Locke's latitudinarian Protestantism made direct attacks on Anglican doctrine, as shown by the deistic use of the *Essay* by Toland, Shaftesbury, and their followers, by his confining God's exercise of authority to what was "reasonable" and according to the individual's conscience before the Judgment Seat,[9] and above all, by the con-

---

[7] R. I. Aaron, *John Locke* (3rd ed., Oxford, 1971), 152. It might be objected that Locke himself would not wish to seek "criteria for determining personal identity" and certainly he distinguishes between the types of problem presented by personal identity and "identity of man" (II.xxvii,6,7,9), himself offering no formal criteria of the former. It must be pointed out, however, that all of Locke's early critics and disciples treat personal identity as a criterion question, whether Hume (e.g, *Treatise,* 261-62); Edmund Law (see above); minor controversialists such as Henry Felton (see n. 16 below); William Lupton, *The Resurrection of the Same Body* (Oxford, 1711), 15, or William Stephens, *The Catholic Doctrine Concerning the Union of the Two Natures in the One Person of Christ* (Oxford, 1719), 8, and *The Divine Persons One God by an Unity of Nature* (Oxford, 1722), 18-19; and, of course, the group under examination in the present essay, especially Stillingfleet, Berkeley, and Butler. What is under review here are interpretations of Locke rather than his own work directly.

[8] See H. P. Grice, "Personal Identity," *Mind,* **50,** no. 200 (Oct. 1941), 330-50 (also H. H. Price, *Hume's Theory of the External World* (Oxford, 1940); J. D. Mabbott, *John Locke* (London, 1973), 60 ff.; D. Wiggins, *Identity and Spatio-Temporal Continuity* (Oxford, 1967); A. G. N. Flew, "Locke and the Problem of Personal Identity," *Philosophy,* **26,** no. 96 (Jan. 1951), 53-68; Edmund Law, *A Defence of Mr. Locke's Opinion Concerning Personal Identity* (Cambridge, 1769); Jonathan Bennett, *Locke, Berkeley, Hume. Central Themes* (Oxford, 1971), 341 ff.

troversy with Edward Stillingfleet, Bishop of Worchester, about the immateriality of the soul. Locke perhaps did believe that the soul was immaterial, but as a philosopher he could only regard the doctrine as unintelligible.[10] Stillingfleet linked Locke with Toland as a deist, and *The Bishop of Worcester's Answer to Mr. Locke's* [first] *Letter* (London, 1697), written in reply to Locke's *Vindication* of himself, is the central document in the controversy. He prepares the way for Berkeley in his perception (9-23) that Locke requires a mysterious "*Substratum to support Accidents*" (17), implying that the spirit is not an immaterial substance but merely a quality of matter (48-49). "You grant that you have not proved, nor upon your principles can it be demonstratively proved, that there is an Immaterial Substance in us that thinks" (49). The effect is to deny revelation, miracles, and the survival by the soul of physical death and to raise the problem of exactly what (or what sort of personal identity) is resurrected for Judgment. Furthermore, Locke is tacitly inviting people to separate (orthodox) faith and (philosophical) reason, within an anti-evangelical ethos Historically, this was disastrous for the Church, and Locke was unable to reply satisfactorily to the charges.

Whatever his day-to-day beliefs, Locke was anti-Christian in the impact his work made on eighteenth-century thought.[11] To give a random example, when the Rev. Walter Harte (tutor to Chesterfield's illegitimate son) wrote,

> True wit and religion are but one
> Though some pervert 'em, and ev'n most have none.[12]

[9] Locke's heterodox influence may be observed in Edward Young's poem *The Last Day*, which lacks a sense of the reality of the Fall and the damnation of Satan largely on Lockean grounds. See R. C. Tennant, *The Poetry and Religion of Christopher Smart* (unpublished London Univ. Ph.D. thesis, 1977), 7 f.

[10] See R. I. Aaron (*op. cit.*), 147.

[11] This paragraph was influenced by Richard Ashcraft's "Faith and Knowledge in Locke's Philosophy" in J. W. Yolton, ed., *John Locke: Problems and Perspectives* (Cambridge, 1969), 194-223. Ashcraft is convincing about the sincerity of Locke's religious motives, but I find Locke theologically naive and destructive. Moreover, one of the major figures of the present essay, William Law, gave a classic argument against the sufficiency of sincerity in his controversy with Benjamin Hoadley, a member of the Locke-centred latitudinarians. See Law's *The Bishop of Bangor's Late Sermon, And His Letter to Dr. Snape in Defence of It, Answer'd* (London, 1717), 5 and *passim*. In the mid-nineteenth century Locke's epistemology was still a conceptual hindrance. See J. M. Cameron, "Newman and the Empiricist Tradition," in J. Coulson and A. M. Allchin, eds., *The Rediscovery of Newman* (London, 1967), *passim*, esp. 82 ff and 94 ff; and J. H. Newman, *An Essay on the Development of Christian Doctrine*, ed. J. M. Cameron (Harmondsworth, 1974), 36-41. A general survey of Locke's connection with the religious life of his day is found in J. W. Yolton, *John Locke and the Way of Ideas* (Oxford, 1956). In this essay I imply that deistic beliefs are *ipso facto* anti-Christian. While one finds arguments concerning the ultimate usefulness of deism to Christian spirituality it must be admitted that any such benefits did not accrue until the nineteenth century. See F. R. Tennant, *Philosophical Theology* (Cambridge, 1928, 1930), e.g., Vol. 2, Chap. VIII, *passim*.

[12] Walter Harte, *An Essay on Painting:* in R. Anderson's *Poets of Great Britain*,

he provides a case of Locke-inspired deism. For Harte, "wit" meant
synthetic play upon sense data. Its equation with religion, therefore,
entails the exclusion of revelation, and the final "ev'n most have
none" recalls Christopher Smart's criticism of Locke (from *Essay*
IV.x.1):

For Lock supposes that an human creature, at a given time may be an atheist
i.e. without God, by the folly of his doctrine concerning innate ideas.

In this case, closely related to the nature of personal identity, redemption would not be available to each soul. Again, Locke's theory
of ideas provoked Addison's famous image of the disconsolate knight
deprived of secondary qualities "upon the finishing of some secret
Spell": the fear is that God has the theoretical resource of withdrawing his grace, withholding his love.[13] One may well ponder the naivety
of a writer who is angered by the hostile reaction to his effective
denial of the soul's immateriality and who (e.g., *Essay* IV.iii.6) can
advance arguments about the uncertainty of doctrine which had to
wait for a Coleridge and a Newman for resolution. His interventions
were deeply disturbing; his theories helped promote Unitarianism and
Socinianism.

Joseph Priestley, "the author of the modern Unitarianism" (see S.
T. Coleridge),[14] displayed an unmodified Lockean theory of personal
identity as late as 1777 in his *Disquisitions relating to matter and
spirit* (§ XIII, 155-66) which appears to have led directly to his assertion of the resurrection of the soul (admittedly as part of an un-
Lockean "same body") and even, in his tract, *A General View of the
Arguments for the Unity of God* (1783), to his denial of Christ's
divinity.

Simply because of its heterodox tendency, however, Locke's
identity theory became the focus of critiques by a group of what J. H.
Newman was to call Anglo-Catholics.[15] Within the narrow limits of
the present essay the use of a term like "group" is inevitably contentious, even though it is common knowledge that its members were,
for the most part, personally acquainted with one another and that
mutual awareness through publications was at a high level. In this
group the chief writers to attempt the problems raised by Stillingfleet
were George Berkeley, Joseph Butler, and William Law who each,

---

Vol. 9 (Edinburgh, 1794), 823, col. 1. The quotation from Smart below is from
Jubilate Agno, ed. W. H. Bond (London, 1954), fragment B2. 396.

[13] Joseph Addison, *Spectator* 413; cf. E. L. Tuveson, *The Imagination as a Means
of Grace: Locke and the Aesthetics of Romanticism* (Berkeley, 1960), Chap. V, esp.
108 ff.

[14] S. T. Coleridge, *Table Talk*, June 23, 1834.

[15] See also W. E Gladstone, *Studies Subsidiary to the works of Bishop Butler*
(Oxford, 1896), 108 ff.

especially the latter two, had a wide influence among evangelicals, and who may even be described as mystics: that is, they knew by personal experience the suprarational, non-linguistic character both of direct communion between the soul and God and of the understanding of the redemptive scheme. Their work reflects this, and having a conception of the limits of reason also made them accomplished, even great, controversialists (e.g., *Alciphron, Analogy, Letters to the Bishop of Bangor*, respectively).

At first this counter-attack was mounted in legalistic terms. Henry Felton, an Oxford divine, was an early champion of the Church. He pointed out that "person" in the Scriptures was not an affair of the consciousness nor of the soul but of man's standing or being in the world: "no respecter of persons." He quotes the legal definition of the word and remarks that the persons of the Trinity are distinguished in respect not of their essence but of their actions and functions. "Person [is] an *Intelligent Compound Being* as Man, which makes the *Body* a Part of the *Person* as much as of the *Individual*." [16] The forensic nature of identity is admitted, but the criteria are from the accretions of common law, as later in Burke, and not from ontological first principles. "In common Acceptation *Person* is very properly apply'd to the *characters* and *Offices* of Men in all their Transactions, *Sacred* or *Civil, Public* or *Private* . . ., this hath no Relation to the *Intelligent Being abstracted* from the *Body* . . ." (*ibid.*, 7). The religious flourishes within the life of society; it does not wait outside for an invitation to enter and transform, for the person is always related directly to its status in God. Locke, by contrast, writes from within a tradition of analytic radicalism.[17]

The movement under review resembled this conservative appeal to existing legal definitions in the emphasis put on the social and the divine at the expense of the individual, but was more incisive and contemporary in its conceptions. These first emerge in the works of John Norris, the earliest published critic of Locke's *Essay*[18] and a

[16] Henry Felton, *The Resurrection of the same Numerical Body, and its Reunion to the same Soul . . . A Sermon Preached on Easter-Monday, 1725*. Reference to the second edition, published by Benjamin Motte (London, n.d.), 6-8.

[17] For the contrast between the radical (the Milton to J. S. Mill line) and the conservative (e.g., Newman and Arnold) on related matters, see Northrop Frye, "The Problem of Spiritual Authority in the Nineteenth Century" (1964), rpt. in his collection *The Stubborn Structure* (London, 1970), 241-56. See also J. H. Newman, *Essay on Development*, 111-13, quoting Guizot. For Felton's arguments see *op. cit.*, 9-13 and his *Discourse Concerning the Universality and Order of the Resurrection* (London, 1733), 12 ff. His sermon *The Scripture Doctrine of the Resurrection as it stood before the Law* (Oxford, n.d. [1734-5]), *passim*, is also relevant.

[18] John Norris, *Cursory Reflections upon a Book call'd, An Essay Concerning Human Understanding* (London, 1690). The editor of the Augustan Reprint Society's 1961 republication (no. 93), Gilbert D. McEwen, notes that "This earliest [of all published] criticism is unusual in that it questions Locke's epistemology rather than his ontology" (4).

neo-Platonist disciple of Malebranche. His constant theme was the necessity of trusting in divine revelation. "Faith as *Faith* has no *regard* to Evidence . . . and Faith as *Divine* has no *need* of it.[19] In his popular *Account of Reason and Faith* (1697, with twelve further editions by 1740) he uses Locke's model of the human mind (e.g., chapter 1, "Reason") but denies ideas and the combinative faculty any high importance, the person finding itself in the intuition of God and of the role of its will in redemption. He anticipates Berkeley, another student of Malebranche,[20] with his doctrine that man's prelapsarian "positive immortality" was by a particular, sustained act of divine will[21]:

[It] does no way follow, that because we existed a little before, we shall therefore exist now; or that because of our existing now, we shall exist afterwards, there being no necessary Connexion between the Moments themselves, whereof our Duration is made up. If therefore we do exist in several Instants or *Nows* of Time, this must be from some Cause which conserves us, and as it were gives us being in every one of those *Nows* or *Moments*.[22]

Norris also notes that the "*Permanency* and *Immutable Stability* of simple Ideas" is proof of their being in God and that " 'Tis highly rational to believe that we Know and Perceive *Now* after the same manner, though not in the same degree, as we shall *hereafter* in Heaven" (*Reason and Religion*, 207, 216). Thus he has gathered much of the material used subsequently by the movement, to whose members his works were well known.

We must now consider George Berkeley, the movement's central figure, whose ideas were not seriously modified by his colleagues and

[19] John Norris, *An Account of Reason and Faith, in Relation to the Mysteries of Christianity* (1697), Chap. 2, Sect. 23. Quoted from the 13th ed. (London, 1740). Compare S. T. Coleridge: "*Evidences* of Christianity! I am weary of the word. Make a man feel the *want* of it; rouse him, if you can, to the self-knowledge of his *need* of it; and you may safely trust to its own Evidence" (*Aids to Reflection* [London, 1825], 272). Neighboring passages speak of "an increasing unwillingness to contemplate the Supreme Being in his *personal* attributes" (270) and "an inward withdrawing from the Life and Personal Being of God" (271). It was this tendency, clearly operative by the 1730's, which motivated a reaction by the movement being discussed. The passage from Coleridge is quoted in Basil Willey's important *Samuel Taylor Coleridge* (London, 1972).

[20] *Vide* A. A. Luce, *Berkeley and Malebranche* (London, 1934).

[21] John Norris, *A Philosophical Discourse Concerning The Natural Immortality of the Soul* (London, 1708), Part I, 16-17.

[22] John Norris, *Reason and Religion: or, the Grounds and Measure of Devotion, Consider'd from the Nature of God, and the Nature of Man* (London, 1689), Part II, Contemplation I, §XI, 172 f. This somewhat Cartesian paragraph anticipates the publication of Locke's *Essay* II.xxvii (although Norris may have had special access to Locke's through a common patron, Lady Masham of Oates, *v. Cursory Reflections*, ed. McEwen, 2) and states clearly a major logical objection to Locke's theory, as presented later by Hume (*Treatise* II. IV. VI, 252 ff. See also H. H. Price, *op. cit.* 38 ff. and D. Wiggins, *op. cit., passim.*)

will therefore not be criticized within this essay.[23] The three points educed from Norris above—the role of the will, the fallacy of believing that sequence entails identity, and the sameness in kind of earthly and heavenly perceptions—are all observed to be central in Berkeley, with the addition of a denial that consciousness comprizes identity.

At the end of his last substantial work, *Siris* (1744), §§341-349, Berkeley writes of the platonic universal mind or deity, drawing the comment from Fraser, that "Here we find ourselves returning into Berkeley's early philosophy of spiritual or personal phenomenalism—a universe of 'ideas' or 'phaenomena', ultimately dependent upon Persons" (Fraser, II, 352); and indeed it is in the earlier, more purely philosophical works, *PC, TV* and *PK*, that the theory is developed which underpins the theology of Berkeley and the movement. Let us first consider the essential passivity of the human personal identity.

For Locke, the prime fact about a "person" was that it was conscious of its manipulation of ideas (*Essay* II.xxvii.9), the building-blocks of reason, which accumulated as (analogical) evidence of the existence and nature of God.[24] Being conscious of this thinking process, the "person" guarantees the self's responsibility for its actions and tends to be regarded as a real agent, or an aspect of one.[25] Berkeley took the opposite view, as in *PK*.

All our ideas, sensations, notions, or the things which we perceive . . . are visibly inactive—there is nothing of power or agency included in them. So that one idea or object of thought cannot produce or make any alteration in another . . . whence it plainly follows that extension, figure, and motion cannot be the cause of our sensations (§25). But, whatever power I may have over my own thoughts, I find the ideas actually perceived by Sense have not a like dependence on my will. When in broad daylight I open my eyes, it is not in my power to choose whether I shall see or no . . . (§29).

This leads Berkeley to separate the will and the understanding (e.g., *PK* §27), the latter being the reception of ideas. Of the former he writes:

---

[23] All references to Berkeley are to the edition by T. E. Jessop and A. A. Luce, unless A. C. Fraser's edition (Oxford, 1871) is named. *PC = Philosophical Commentaries, TV = New Theory of Vision, PK = Principles of Human Knowledge.*

[24] "Analogy": not as in Joseph Butler, whose method is founded on mystical perception of divine immanence, however well disguised by the vocabulary he employs, but, Jessop indicates (*Alciphron*, 14), as in Bishop Peter Browne, follower of Locke and provost of Berkeley's college, whose concept of analogy is criticized on somewhat mystical grounds in *Alciphron* IV.

[25] *Vide* J. W. Yolton, *Locke and the Compass of Human Understanding*, 141.

The words *will* . . ., *soul, spirit*, do not stand for different ideas, or, in truth, for any idea at all, but for something which is very different from ideas, and which, being an agent, cannot be like unto, or represented by, any idea whatsoever. (*loc. cit.*)

In this last passage the ellipsis represents the suppression after the first edition of the words *"understanding, mind."* It will be noted that Berkeley realized his slip and wished to emphasize that it was the *active* principles which were beyond ideas: those which, being active, were divine. This shows a sharpening of theological urgency.

The will, then, is active: it can make and unmake ideas (*PK* §28), but it cannot compete with the involuntary sense-ideas which have an unmatched constancy and strength. The conclusion is readily achieved that sense-ideas are willed by God. As early as *PC* Berkeley had noted, "Qu: Whether Identity of Person consists not in the Will" (194a: he decided it did not), and "Doctrine of Identity best explain'd by Takeing the Will for Volitions, the Understanding for Ideas. The difficulty of Consciousness of wt are never acted etc solv'd thereby" (681). Yet it is not the will which is the principle of identity for Berkeley. In *Siris*, as Fraser remarks (II, 252), Berkeley adopts an Augustinian trinity of Being: *to hen* (personality), *logos* (intellect), and *psyche* (spirit); of *to hen* Fraser writes, "This abstract personality seems to exclude conscious intellect or mind, to which it is assumed to be prior" (*loc. cit.*). It corresponds, in fact, to the passively received ideas in man, his basic fabric, the human analogy of God the Father.

Berkeley arrived at this conclusion by way of his work on vision.

Qu: wherein consists identity of Person? not in actual consciousness, for then I'm not the same person I was this day twelvemonth, but while I think of wt I then did. Not in potential for then all persons may be the same for ought we know (*PC*, 200).[26]

It is revealing that he goes from here to discuss vision.

A meer line or distance is not made up of points, does not exist, cannot be imagin'd or have an idea fram'd thereof no more than meer colour without extension (*PC*, 253).

Berkeley continually argued against abstraction and reification, in *PC, TV, PK de Motu, The Analyst*, and elsewhere.[27] By analogy with *TV* and *PC*, 253 one may say that just as a line in vision is not a series of points so identity is not a series of perceptions; both would be purely hypothetical. Hume points out that even the *feeling* that I exist

[26] Further evidence that Berkeley was understood to deny the consciousness/ identity equation is provided by Edmund Law (*op. cit.*, 22n).

[27] P. N. Furbank, *op cit.*, 16-19, has recently maintained the Berkeleian position against A. D. Nuttall's advocacy of Locke in his account of the imagination within aesthetics.

proves the existence of nothing more than the feeling itself.[28] The connection between this fallacy and Locke's identity theory was extended into "sentimental" ethics by Shaftesbury and various "minute philosophers." Since its fallaciousness had been mentioned by Norris in 1689, its subsequent acceptance must have been infuriating, which possibly accounts for Berkeley's unusual vehemence against Shaftesbury (e.g., *Alciphron*, 9). As an alternative to Locke, Berkeley's *esse est percipi* principle locates personal identity in the same theoretical structure as actual existence: both are created and sustained by the voluntary and attentive perception of God (the Father). A person is not identified by its own consciousness (especially memory), nor by its creator's, but by the divine *act* of creation.

The final characteristic of Berkeley's concept of personal identity is its connection with the rejection of causality. We will not survey this aspect of his thought, which is closely connected with the assaults on reification in *de Motu* and *The Analyst*, but it may be noted that where it occurs it is often related directly to metaphysical and even theological concerns. The "constant uniform working" of the creative divine perception "is so far from leading our thoughts to Him, that it rather sends them wandering after second causes" (*PK*, §32). Those in greatest danger are the intellectuals, the "minute philosophers" whose faith and trust in "the goodness and wisdom of that Governing Spirit whose Will constitutes the law of nature" (*loc. cit.*) is inadequate. Natural laws, as Fraser remarks (I, 171n) are of an arbitrary character; God is not bound by them as he is in Shaftesbury's *The Moralists*. "The set rules or established methods wherein the Mind we depend on excites in us the ideas of sense, are called the *laws of nature;* and these we learn by experience . . ." (*PK*, §30). Berkeley obviously weighed his words very carefully here. Marc-Wogau has established the importance in his thinking of trusting in God, and presumably he was prepared to accept the merely philosophical loose ends entailed at this point.[29]

An early writer influenced by Berkeley was his American friend, Samuel Johnson D.D., who covered in his *Elements of Philosophy*[30] much of the above ground, being particularly interested in Berkeley's ontology (162 ff.). While assuming this, however, Johnson gave (58) a prior account of personal identity in a précis of Locke, the inaccuracy and irrelevance of which remind us of the extent to which Berkeley had removed the theory from its home in liberal politics to the orbit of mysticism. Berkeleian thought is a totality and a unity, referring at every point to the strictly suprarational immanence of the deity. The

[28] See R. W. Church, *A Study in the Philosophy of Malebranche* (Port Washington, New York, 1970), 51 ff. esp. 52.

[29] K. Marc-Wogau, "The Argument from Illusion and Berkeley's Idealism" (1957); rpt. in *Locke and Berkeley Critical Essays*, eds. C. B. Martin and D. M. Armstrong, 345 ff.

largely unspiritual Johnson retains the desire, inherited both from rhetoricians and from natural philosophers (e.g., John Ray and Cotton Mather), to create hierarchy, ascending from dead elements through the chain of being to moral and spiritual values. Berkeleian doctrine being inapplicable here, Johnson goes to Locke rather than transform his cast of thought.

The points raised above are not a random collection, for together they meet some of the difficulties in Locke's account of personal identity, and while they follow the general trend in ignoring the limited scope of its ontology, they do make for a theory of personal identity which is both stronger and better fitted to the uses of Christianity. The will is seen in more immediately human terms, Locke's effective ignoring of the after-life is at least potentially set aside, and the theory is tautened and simplified by the removal of the illogicalities and superfluous layers of ideas mentioned in the first pages of the present essay. Above all, Berkeley's reformulation puts aside the analytic mode by the *esse est percipi* principle, for things are conceived whole by God in every instant. Thus the tone is set for the rest of the group: the foundations of this doctrine are in mystical experience rather than metaphysical reasoning.

This claim is borne out by the treatment of the issue by David Hume in his *Treatise of Human Nature*. Hume's two references to Berkeley in the *Treatise* (17) and the *Enquiry concerning human understanding*[31] are both related to personal identity: they concern Berkeley's opposition to abstract ideas, as illegitimate generalizations from particulars, and thus underpin his skeptical conclusions about the roles of memory and consciousness within the theory, since they involve the concept of sequence. Hume's destruction in the *Treatise* of current formulations of the theory attracted little if any contemporary attention, but it is important here because of its connection with Berkeley. In the "Appendix" Hume appears to recoil somewhat from the skepticism of the main text (I.IV.VI) and quotes two principles of perception which, he confesses, he believes but "cannot render consistent" (636). However, the fact that halfway down the same page and in the same note he "*take[s] this opportunity*" (my italics) of admitting as an error his use of a geometrical account of the perception of distance (cf. *TV*, §XII ff.), reminds one that his previous confession is an ironical, skeptical glance at Berkeley whose mysticism was the agent of reconciliation when faced with the same prob-

---

[30] Page references to the 3rd edition (London, 1754). A first version of this work was published in 1746.

[31] David Hume, *An enquiry concerning human understanding*, ed. L. A. Selby-Bigge (2nd ed., Oxford, 1962), 155.

lem. The *Enquiry* makes this irony clear, for Berkeley is there alleged to "form the best lessons of scepticism . . . Bayle not excepted" (155n) because of the importance he gives to faith merely as faith. What Hume the philosopher satirized, Berkeley the theologian would accept simply on that ground.

Joseph Butler, an acquaintance, perhaps a friend, of Berkeley,[32] made his contribution to the issue in a dissertation "Of Personal Identity" appended to *The Analogy* (1736),[33] significantly an excision from his first chapter, "Of a future life." It is notable that he carries over Berkeley's concept of reason and imagination from the fourth of the *Dialogues* (*Analogy*, 84-85); reason, in human terms, is calm and natural, the fabric of God's creatively willed perception, while imagination, "that forward, delusive faculty ever obtruding beyond its sphere" (*loc. cit.*), is the inconstant and undisciplined human equivalent. Moreover, Butler gives (e.g., 88-90) a classic statement of the mind/body distinction, and by separating the sensory apparatus from the perceiving mind he relaxes Locke's identification of mind with percepts and allows the mind (or soul) to employ its will upon *making use* of percepts. Thus Butler argues that while accepting revelation could be a redemptive activity, so also could accepting sense-data: he brings a deist strategy (*v.* Tuveson, *passim*) into orthodox Christianity, while simultaneously minimizing the purely ethical, in direct contradiction of his chief target, Shaftesbury[34]: "The true notion or conception of the Author of Nature is that of a master or governor, prior to the consideration of his moral attributes" (*ibid.*, 103). Furthermore, since for Butler analogy and probability are the "very guide of life" for "beings of limited capacities" (73), they are a confession at once of Berkeleian total dependence on God and of total security of trust in God. The poet Christopher Smart, much influenced by Butler and Berkeley, frequently demonstrates this dependency and trust, serenely writing what Locke would find outrageously cynical,

> Thou God of goodness and of glory, hear!
> Thou, who to lowliest minds dost condescend,
> *Assuming* passions to enforce thy laws,
> Adopting jealousy to prove thy love . . . (my italics).[35]

[32] See *Alciphron*, 7 n. Bishop Thomas Secker writes to Berkeley of "our common friend, Dr. Butler." Secker himself was on the fringes of the movement.
[33] All references to Butler, unless otherwise stated, are to the Bohn's Standard Library edition of the *Analogy* and *Sermons* (London, 1889).
[34] See R. C. Tennant, *The Poetry and Religion of Christopher Smart*, ch. 1, Sect. V, for an account of Butler's anti-Shaftesbury strategy.
[35] C. Smart, *On the Goodness of the Supreme Being* (Cambridge, 1756), 13-14.

All this bears on the idea that the formal structure of personality is the central fact of orthodox redemptive Christianity. It is supported by Butler's brief essay "Of personal identity." Here he responds to Locke's provision (*Essay* II.xxvii.6, *etc.*) that a person may be successively "united" to different bodies, by pointing out that the effect may be (as with Shaftesbury) "to render the inquiry concerning a future life of no consequence at all to use the persons who are making it" (329). His essay was accused by Vincent Perronet of playing on different meanings of "person" at the expense of a proper treatment of its subject,[36] but in fact he assumes Berkeley's critique and offers a complementary version adapted to his own needs.

One should really think it self-evident, that consciousness of personal identity presupposes, and therfore cannot constitute, personal identity; any more than knowledge, in any other case, can constitute truth, which it presupposes . . . [Present] consciousness of past actions . . . is not necessary to our being the same persons who performed those actions . . . (329).

Thus is personal identity divorced from consciousness.[37]

The only element of the theory developed by Norris and Berkeley which is not obviously present in Butler is the notion of God's steady, creative perception, but even here he offers his own version. He relies on a form of Locke's "same organization" argument to prove continuity of object (grammatical and material) in a series of statements, "I perceive a tree," and transfers this to "I perceive my self," by-passing the problem of consciousness which is present only in the inessential grammatical subject, which, for all he is prepared to argue, may well be Shaftesbury's flickering consciousness.[38] He also uses this tactic to prove, against Locke, that the soul is an immaterial substance (333-34). However, Butler is a subtle and original thinker

---

[36] Vincent Perronet, *A second vindication of Mr. Locke, Wherein his Sentiments relating to Personal Identity Are clear'd up from some Mistakes of The Rev. Dr. Butler* . . . (London, 1739), 5 *et passim*.

[37] This is the chief locus of Hume's contact with Butler on identity. Hume exposes the fallaciousness of believing that the feeling that one exists proves anything about identity (*v.* n. 27 above) which is a restatement of Butler's point about knowledge presupposing truth. Both are arguments against the *cogito ergo sum* type of hypothesis. Hume had almost certainly read the *Analogy* when he composed the *Treatise*'s appendix (see: W. E. Gladstone, *op. cit.*, 133; E. C. Mossner, *The Life of David Hume* [London, 1954], 110 ff.). He there offers further critiques of Locke and Berkeley, but does not challenge Butler, whom he respected: "I am told that Dr. Butler has everywhere recommended [my *Political Essays*], so that I hope they will have some success," he wrote to Kames (Gladstone, *loc. cit.*). Hume's religion of man relies upon the authority of natural truth; Butler's Anglo-Catholicism adds the idea that the structure of the Church is analogous to such truth.

[38] Shaftesbury, *Miscellany* IV, Chap. 1, in *Characteristics*, ed. J. M. Robertson (Indianapolis and New York, 1964), II, 275.

who prefers not to advertize his qualities. While his arguments reveal his awareness, and use, of Berkeley's revelation of the purely linguistic nature of much metaphysical argument, his elimination of the grammatical subject from his version of the theory effectively rewrites "I perceive my self," *via* ". . . perceives my self," and "my self is perceived." The lack of a perceiver simply recalls Berkeley's observation that agents cannot be presented as ideas to our (passive) minds (*PK*, §27); at this superficially unpromising point, too, Butler's thought is fully aligned with the movement's basic commitment to the mystical in Christianity.

Of a piece with the above-mentioned subtlety, and contributing to Butler's conception of the Church, is a very important consequence of his thinking on personal identity: the use of the theory to argue against the polarity of interested and disinterested actions which was characteristic of the more cynical—and "sentimental"—ethical writers. Butler often refers to this polarity (e.g., Sermon XI, "Upon the love of our neighbour"), but it is merely a manner of speaking for him. When "me," "you," and "tree" have the same ontological status, the possibility re-emerges of good actions including self-interested ones; a comfortable doctrine, but one which discourages false pride, romantic agonies, and antinomianism, and allows that the Self too may be the object of cherishing (e.g., 382). It is the strength of spirituality underlying his works, and not only their intellectual power, which ensured that no subsequent thinker of any accomplishment was properly to be called a deist, and thus made Butler's influence on the English Church so profound and enduring.

The last writer to be considered is William Law, outside the Anglican communion, as a non-juror, but profoundly influential in the Church of England, at least posthumously, as well as in evangelical and pietist circles. The flourishing of the movement we have been considering, at least in the mid-eighteenth century, would largely be found, apart from the Butler circle, in Law's sphere of influence, which included the poet John Byrom, the natural philosopher George Cheyne, the psychologist David Hartley, and the novelist Samuel Richardson.

For William Law the idea of personal identity was essential for redemption and revelation, the great truth of the spiritual and the natural man. His last work, *An Humble . . . Address to the Clergy* (London, 1761) teaches that a "continual and immediate Inspiration of the Spirit" (39) was the necessary condition for the personality and for all activity, whether good (9) or, if the will rejects God, evil. The "natural" self, the quirky and individual personality of the unregenerated man, is the result of the latter (33 f.): the will creates sensory chimeras which challenge the calm and normative person created and sustained by God. The reason and fancy must therefore be denied, i order that the true state of grace, aesthetically contemplative and ecstatic, may be achieved (55 ff.).

This state of grace is the chief subject of the religious poetry of Christopher Smart, one of Law's greatest followers.[39] In Hymn XIII, "St. Philip and St. James," for example, he dramatizes the two saints' regeneration in aesthetic terms: first they pray for redemption and then, between stanzas, it is achieved, and serene statement changes to joyful imagery (stanzas 9, 10):

> Pray'r and praise be mine employment
>   Without grudging or regret,
> Lasting life, and long enjoyment,
>   Are not here, and are not yet.
>
> Hark! aloud the black-bird whistles,
>   With surrounding fragrance blest,
> And the goldfinch in the thistles
>   Makes provision for her nest . . .

As with Berkeley a lively and penetrating perception of beauty is equated by Law and Smart with being in God, in contradistinction to the anxious theorizings of man without God.

Law's ontology is virtually borrowed directly from Berkeley. Here, in the pre-lapsarian universe, is the *esse est percipi* principle, in Byrom's versified paraphrase of the first part of Law's *Spirit of Prayer*: the angels might

> Call forth its Wonders, and enjoy the Trance
> Of Joys perpetual thro' its whole Expanse:
> Ravishing Forms arising without End
> Would, in Obedience to their Wills, ascend;
> Change, and unfold fresh Glories in their View
> And tune the *Hallelujah* Song anew.[40]

This divine creativity (of objects of praise) is in man also, as with Berkeley, but in the unregenerated man works evil. His reason, "the *Flesh,* or the *Carnal Man,*"[41] produces aberrations. The essence of salvation is to remember the passivity of all such objects and the uniquely active and unanalyzable nature (compare Berkeley, *PK* § 27) of man's fragment of divine will.

[39] Quotations from Norman Callan's edition of Smart's *Collected Poems* (London, 1949), II, 814-15. For the intellectual and religious background of Smart's poetry, see Christopher Devlin, *Poor Kit Smart* (London, 1961); Moira Dearnley, *The Poetry of Christopher Smart* (London, 1968); and R. C. Tennant, *The Poetry and Religion of Christopher Smart.*

[40] J. Byrom, *An Epistle to a Gentleman of the Temple* (London, 1749), 9.

[41] W. Law, *Humble Address* (London, 1761), 53. The pages around this contain a lucid and definitive statement of his version of the theory, towards which he was working in his Boehme–influenced *The Spirit of Prayer* (London, 1749) and *The Spirit of Love* (London, 1752).

Our Will and Thoughts . . . must have *Self-motion* and *Self-direction*, because they came out of the Self-existent God. They are eternal, divine Powers, that never began *to be*, and therefore cannot begin to be in Subjection to any Thing.[42]

For William Law the self was not consciousness but the whole man, which had to be transformed to ally itself at all points with God's nature, to which it was formally analogous.

The Creation . . . of a Soul, is not the Creation of Thinking and Willing . . . but it is the Bringing of *Powers* of Thinking and Willing out of their *Eternal State* in the One God, into a *Beginning State* of a Self-conscious Life, distinct from God . . . (*ibid.*, 12).
The Soul . . . must have the *Nature* and *Likeness* of God in it, and is . . . so much of the *Divine* Nature become creaturely existing (*ibid.*, 2-3).

One might say that for Law man had two choices, the Berkeleian salvation or the Lockean damnation; in the latter case the nature of reason is misunderstood and so cannot without formal preparation will its regeneration and the blotting-out of its personality by the epiphany of the true soul. "The *Principle* of Action in Spiritual Substances, is or ought to be, that Essential one of REUNION with the Origin of their Being. . . ."[43]

For Law personal identity is neither consciousness nor substratum but a complex of percepts exhibited by God and either directed by the person's fragment of divine will back to God or given over in evil to the fanciful manipulations of Lockean reason. Because of his greater involvement with evangelism Law is more analytical than Berkeley: the person is seen less as a substance and more as a node of redemptive mechanisms; like the whole of creation, its mode of existence is purely teleological. In a fine phrase Byrom writes of "these temporary skies" (*op. cit.*, 14): creation is a phase in the *explicatio* of the Spirit, and reason itself is merely local too.[44] It is this understanding of the nature of personal identity which enabled the movement to state with renewed force the idea that God indeed acts to save, if invited, but not to damn.

> He made no *Hell* to place his Angels in;
> *They* stirr'd the Fire that burnt them, by their Sin:

[42] Law, *An Appeal to all that Doubt* . . . (London, 1742), 9.

[43] George Cheyne, *Philosophical Principles of Religion, Part II* (London, 1715) 4. Cheyne covered some of the ground before Law started publishing, but became the younger man's disciple. Many similar passages from Law could be quoted.

[44] "So tho *Self-evidence* excludes *Reason*, yet all *Demonstration* becomes at length *self-evident*," wrote John Toland in *Christianity Not Mysterious* (1696; ed used, London, 1702), 14. There has been no space in this essay to set out the intricat relationship between deism and Anglican mysticism and the latter's ultimate benefi from this relationship.

The Bounds of Nature, and of Order, broke,
And all the Wrath that follow'd them awoke.[45]

I have hinted at this group's intimations of nineteenth-century Anglo-Catholicism more freely, perhaps, than there has been space to justify in this essay. However, the Oxford movement itself recognized these men as among the chief of their forerunners. The modified theory of personal identity ensured a generally Catholic attitude, especially regarding the conditions of redemption and the relation of ethics to revealed religion. In the Romantic period, the reputation of William Law as a spiritual and holy man was revived, Butler's works became set texts at Oxford, and theologically Berkeley represented, at the very least, a native anticipation of German thought; Coleridge, of course, named a son after him. It would be possible to show that the revival of the movement was not in fact merely a resurrection in the Coleridge and Keble circles but rather that the movement continued actively from the 1730s to the 1850s and even beyond. J. H. Newman's theory of doctrinal development within Catholic Christianity, for example, depends on a theory of identity closely similar to that under discussion, and he recognized it. Although Newman had limitations as a student of eighteenth-century thought, it enabled him to reassert the primacy of faith and love. In a passage which links Berkeley and Butler he writes:

It is faith and love which give to probability a force which it has not in itself. Faith and love are directed towards an Object; in the vision of that Object they live; it is that Object, received in faith and love, which renders it reasonable to take probability as sufficient for internal conviction. Thus the argument from Probability, in the matter of religion, became an argument from Personality, which in fact is one form of the argument from Authority.[46]

Here Newman penetrated to the heart of this movement's understanding of a crisis of faith from which came a renewed spirituality and an extension of the grounds of Church authority, the latter an issue especially problematic for the Church of England. The exploration of personality and its being in God could now be seen not merely as a mystical supplement to faith but as a foundation of rational and loving worship, an activity, like reading the Scriptures, which could be closely defined and therefore controlled in its scope and established by distinctively Anglican forms of both faith and scholarship.

Addison Institute for Adult Education, London.

---

[45] Byrom, *op. cit.*, 12, see Law, *Appeal*, 88 f.
[46] J. H. Newman, *Apologia pro vita sua* (London, 1873), 19.

Chapter XIV

THE SEPARATION OF REASON AND
FAITH IN BACON AND HOBBES, AND
LEIBNIZ'S *THEODICY*

BY JEFFREY BARNOUW

Insistence on the separation of reason and faith has played diverse roles in a variety of religious and scientific attitudes. The present essay traces the delineation and use of the separation in a line of thinkers who show marked continuity with the approach established by Ockham. Ockham's way of ensuring that inquiry and piety, the claims of knowledge and those of belief, would not interfere with one another was developed by Bacon and then by Hobbes in definition and defense of the endeavors of modern science. That a similar approach to the relation between reason and faith can be found in Leibniz is more striking, since Leibniz—above all, in his *Theodicy*—overtly emphasizes the harmony and mutual support of reason and faith and might even be taken as reaffirming a form of rational theology. To recognize Leibniz's affinity with Bacon and Hobbes in this respect may overturn certain widespread assumptions in intellectual history and should contribute to our understanding of the *Theodicy*.

1. *Introduction*—In *The Dissolution of the Medieval Outlook* Gordon Leff stresses the importance of distinguishing three philosophical views that are often thrown together: nominalism, what he calls ''an Ockhamist standpoint,'' and finally, ''the belief in the inherent uncertainty and contingency of all existence, other than God's.''[1] This last belief was common property of almost all Christian thinkers in the fourteenth century. It may have reflected a reaction to the 1277 condemnation in Paris of all manner of theses that advocated the naturalist determinism of the ''de-neoplatonized'' Arabic Aristotle of the arts faculty, but the belief in the contingency of existence was traditional and goes back to Augustine's doctrine of grace and predestination. The ''inherent contingency of creation'' meant ''that however necessary the laws that God had ordained for this world were, they were only conditionally necessary on God's

---

[1] Leff, *The Dissolution of the Medieval Outlook* (New York, 1976), 12. Subsequent page references to this book will be given in parentheses within the text. Hans Blumenberg has also dealt in an interesting way with the Scholastic recourse to God's *potentia absoluta* (as opposed to *ordinata*) to establish the basic contingency of the created world, although in calling it ''nominalist'' (and identifying Ockhamism with nominalism) he perpetuates what Leff shows to be misleading views. See Blumenberg, *Die kopernikanische Wende* (Frankfurt, 1965), 19, 35 ff., 60 ff., 74 ff., 98.

having willed them and not by any unqualified absolute necessity of
their own'' (13).

The contingency of creation reflects God's absolute power to do
whatever is logically possible, and logical recourse to His omnipotence serves to separate the sphere of contingent necessity from that
of absolute necessity where the contrary implies a contradiction. As a
result, God cannot be thought of as necessitated by anything created,
and, conversely, man is incapable of necessary knowledge of fact or
existence. The certainties which had been ''adduced from a necessitarian order'' in the Greco-Arabian thinking characteristic of the
Paris arts faculty before the Condemnations of 1277 ''became with
Duns Scotus and above all Ockham merely probabilities'' (29). This
was not, however, a repetition of the classical split between merely
probable knowledge of the changeable realities of the phenomenal
(sublunary) and practical spheres, on the one hand, and science conceived, on the other hand, as necessary knowledge of things that
could not be otherwise and thus could be known in their essence.

For, beginning with Duns Scotus and culminating in Ockham, the
very definition of knowledge was transformed. In effect, recourse to
God's omnipotence cut nature free to be taken as given, ''positive'' in
the sense of posited by God's will, and with Ockham this came to
mean free not only from Arabic-Aristotelian determinism but also
from the hypostatized ontological categories of Greek rationalism. An
empiricism based on the immediate intuition of sense was elaborated
in terms of a conception of rationality and truth that was logical
instead of ontological. The power of the shift in approach was revealed only when Ockham, breaking radically with Scotus, affirmed
''the exclusively individual nature of all being'' (57). Logic and universality were correspondingly linked with human language. One
result of this shift was to center the conception of knowledge in the
human mind and its relations with the world of experience, an
affirmation of contingency which worked to alleviate existential
uncertainty and to clarify the sense of dependence on God.

Once the exclusively individual nature of existence or the unattainability of
universal being was accepted, the world became at once a more knowable
and a less perplexing place. The ingenuity that had for so long been ex-
pended upon reconciling individuals with their universal natures could instead be redirected to exhibiting the ways in which singular things can be
described by universal words.(15)

For Ockham, ''knowledge of existence alone constituted evident
knowledge, which meant, since all existence was individual, that individual existence was the source of all proper knowledge.'' However, this did not lead him to deny any epistemological status to
universals, which for Leff is ''the way of nominalism.'' Rather, ''re-

ducing the concepts, terms and propositions comprising all logical discourse to their individual import.'' Ockham accepted ''their universality as inseparable from all such discourse and necessary, i.e., demonstrative knowledge'' (58). A newly valued empirical probable knowledge of the natural world was thus integrated with truth and universality, conceived as the properties of propositions and language. Even with the relative absence of mathematical and experimental aspects, Ockham's position anticipated the guiding conceptions of the scientific revolution of the seventeenth century, particularly its British component as elucidated in the interpretations of Bacon and then Hobbes.

The continuity between Bacon's and Hobbes's ideas of science is based in a shared awareness of the essential connection between experience deliberately undertaken and rational insight into causal processes. Whereas passive ''prudential'' experience must infer from given effects to possible, conjectural causes, reflective experience or experiment can conclude from given ''causes'' to possible, makeable effects. Conscious correlation of cause-and-effect and means-and-end relations in the process of inquiry leads to the method that allows for the integration of evidence and truth, the transition of empirical to logical necessity and the reckoning of consequences in propositions.[2]

In contrast to Hobbes, the Christian virtuosi of the Royal Society not only vulgarized Bacon's concern with utility as a criterion for cognition and exaggerated his idea of compiling natural histories (at the expense of his rationalist insistence on the discovery of laws or Forms, that is, deep-seated systematic causes), they also sacrificed the Baconian scope of ''natural philosophy'' and its culmination in human science. The idea that science can support religion played a restrictive role here that needs further research. One aspect is the rejection of the Ockhamist tendency which had been renewed by their ''mentor'' Bacon, the strict separation between natural and revealed knowledge, with a resulting attenuation of the Baconian restriction of the roles of reason and of inference from natural experience in our consideration of God's attributes and intentions.

As Leff writes, in Ockham's time ''there was a virtual abandonment of a systematic attempt at a natural theology in the thirteenth-century sense of finding natural reasons for revealed truths. Instead the stress was upon their natural unknowability and dependence upon God's will'' (16). Denial of an *a priori* rational approach to knowledge of contingent nature thus corresponded to rejection of rationalist theol-

---

[2] See my essays, ''Bacon and Hobbes: The Conception of Experience in the Scientific Revolution,'' *Science/Technology and the Humanities*, 2 (1979), 92-110; and ''Vico and the Continuity of Science: The Relation of his Epistemology to Bacon and Hobbes,'' *Isis*, 71 (1980), 609-20.

ogy on the grounds that reason should not be misused to support or justify what must be taken on faith. A prime example of the use of this separation of contingent natural and positive revealed knowledge is Ockham's treatment of problems relating to—as the title of one of his works reads—*Predestination, God's Foreknowledge, and Future Contingents*. In this work he sustains the possibility of necessity in natural knowledge and of human freedom and responsibility. We shall return to this work for its pertinence to Leibniz's *Theodicy*, but first we must see how this Ockhamist tradition, carried forward in Bacon and Hobbes, is opposed in crucial respects to the tendencies toward natural religion associated with the publicists, prelates, and virtuosi of the Royal Society.

No unilinear historical continuity is intended here. Between Ockham and Bacon, the Reformation, particularly in its Calvinist forms, enters the intellectual force-field to give new direction and meaning to the tendency that might be broadly called "separationist." This added impetus to, but also deflected, impulses coming from Ockham in ways that cannot be gone into here. At the other end of the development, too, there are important and relevant continuities from Bacon to Boyle and from Hobbes to leading ideas of certain deists. Still, the links between Bacon and Hobbes and their shared opposition to "natural religion" tendencies (including those associated with the Royal Society) have been neglected by intellectual historians, resulting in a basic distortion of the spectrum of attitudes that defined the seventeenth and early eighteenth centuries. Gauging the position of Leibniz is a case in point.

2. *Bacon and Hobbes*—In considering Bacon this brief essay must concentrate exclusively on the early and presumably well-known *Advancement of Learning*. Toward the beginning Bacon sets out three essential limitations of human knowledge that must be observed in order "that it may comprehend all the universal nature of things." The third of these is "that we do not presume by the contemplation of nature to attain to the mysteries of God," for "if any man shall think by view and inquiry into these sensible and material things to attain that light whereby he may reveal unto himself the nature or will of God, then indeed he is spoiled by vain philosophy." Contemplation of God's creatures and works produces not knowledge of God, "but wonder, which is broken knowledge."[3]

Bacon goes on to defend inquiry into second causes, which does not lead away from "devout dependence upon God which is the first cause," for deeper inquiry can lead man to see "the dependence of

---

[3] Francis Bacon, *Selected Writings*, ed. Hugh G. Dick, (New York, 1955), 163 f. Subsequent page references are given within the text.

causes and the works of Providence" so that "he will easily believe that the highest link of nature's chain must needs be tied to the foot of Jupiter's chair." In its caution this assurance stops well short of an argument from design. The stronger argument by far is that "God worketh nothing in nature but by second causes," and it would be unworthy to "lie for God" by denying their reality. He concludes this section by stressing the need to search as deeply as possible into the twin books of God's word and God's works, divinity and philosophy, adding "only let men beware . . . that they do not unwisely mingle or confound these learnings together."

For Bacon, the Scriptures reveal the will of God, and creatures express God's power. Knowledge of the latter is thus "a key unto the former; . . . chiefly opening our belief, in drawing us into a due meditation of the omnipotency of God, which is chiefly signed and engraven upon his works" (200). It was already established as a *topos* (found in other, fragmentary writings of Bacon) that creation told not only of God's power but also of God's wisdom and benevolence, though the two latter attributes are omitted—I would say, deliberately avoided—here.

In Book II Bacon takes up "Divine Philosophy or Natural Theology," one of the three main divisions of philosophy (Divine, Natural, and Human), defining it as "that knowledge or rudiment of knowledge concerning God which may be obtained by the contemplation of his creatures. . . . The bounds of this knowledge are, that it sufficeth to convince atheism, but not to inform religion; . . . because no light of nature extendeth to declare the will and true worship of God" (250). In this context Bacon grants that contemplation of nature can serve "to induce and inforce the acknowledgement of God, and to demonstrate his power, providence, and goodness," but he adds, "on the other side, out of the contemplation of nature, or ground of human knowledges, to induce any verity or persuasion concerning the points of faith, is in my judgment not safe: *Da fidei quae fidei sunt.*" This "field of learning" suffers not from any deficiency but from excess, Bacon says, and he has only taken it up "because of the extreme prejudice which both religion and philosophy [have] received and may receive by being commixed together; as that which undoubtedly will make an heretical religion, and an imaginary and fabulous philosophy."

Bacon offers an example of what he means by the latter when he criticizes Plato's and Aristotle's "handling of final causes mixed with the rest in physical inquiries," which "hath intercepted the severe and diligent inquiry of all real and physical causes, and given men the occasion to stay upon these satisfactory and specious causes, to the great arrest and prejudice of further discovery" (259). Resort to final causes satisfies psychological needs which Bacon considers weak-

nesses that can be counteracted in and through a "natural philosophical" attitude, one which resists the appeal that underlies the argument from design in its teleological form. Accordingly, he endorses a
classical materialist conception of nature:

. . . the natural philosophy of Democritus and some others, who did not
suppose a mind or reason in the frame of things, but attributed *the form
thereof able to maintain itself to infinite essays or proofs of nature*, which
they term *fortune*, seemeth to me (as far as I can judge by the recital and
fragments which remain unto us) in particularities of physical causes more
real and better enquired than that of Aristotle and Plato. (260, Bacon's
emphasis.)

This projection of the progressive experimental method into the
process of nature itself, thereby construing it as developmental and
productive of its own "form" (that is, regularities or lawfulness), is
Bacon's own interpretation and, indeed, points to a conception beyond the range of most of his own ideas on nature. But, for our
purposes, it shows clearly the depth and consistency of Bacon's rejection of final causes in physics, to the extent that natural inquiry can
provide no information or confirmation of divine intention or even
purposive, providential deity. Bacon's perspective cuts deeper than
the rejection of anthropocentric teleology which would make man the
final cause or intended beneficiary of natural processes. In fact, his
treatment of teleology in the context of his critique of the wish-
fulfilling aspects of metaphysical systems suggests that anthropocentric bias underlies the construction of nature by use of final causes
even when man is not overtly referred to. Anticipating Kant to an
extent, Bacon refers all teleology to a human perspective and thus
relegates inquiry into final causes to metaphysics, strictly separated
from inquiry into "real and physical ones" in natural philosophy or
"Physic."

With his insistence on the separation of philosophy and divinity,
whether the latter term is taken to refer to "natural theology" ("divine philosophy") or to what he calls "inspired" or "sacred theology" based on revelation (in either case this separation represents an
exception to Bacon's "rule, that all partitions of knowledge be accepted rather for lines and veins, than for sections and separations"
[268]), Bacon stands in opposition to the characteristic approach of
Boyle and of the Royal Society generally. But where he dips into
"Metaphysic" to consider the relation of providence to nature, as a
way of correlating two perspectives, Bacon provides a model that
was to be broadly exploited by Boyle[4]:

---

[4] For Boyle, see the selections in Marie Boas Hall, ed., *Robert Boyle on Natural
Philosophy* (Bloomington, 1965), 142-53, esp. 146, 151 ff.

For as in civil actions he is the greater and deeper politique, that can make other men the instruments of his will and ends and yet never acquaint them with his purpose, so as they shall do it and yet not know what they do, than he that imparteth his meaning to those he employeth; so is the wisdom of God more admirable, when nature intendeth one thing, and providence draweth forth another, than if he had communicated to particular creatures and motions the characters and impressions of his providence. And thus much for Metaphysic; the later part whereof I allow as extant, but wish it confined to its proper place (261).

As he had made clear in the preceding sentences, Bacon means that nature does not ''intend'' anything, even with regard to the functioning of parts of the human body: there is only ''consequence'' for physics where metaphysics construes ''intention.'' Teleology can be seen as ''making use of'' efficient causality in the sense that providence is a perspective that gives natural happenings a new significance.

Whether the analogy with the shrewdness of a *politique* really makes God's wisdom more admirable for Bacon is questionable. Just as this providential *topos* was later adapted, in Milton, Vico, or Adam Smith, as a relation which might eventually be absorbed and collapsed into aware and answerable human prudence, so where Bacon considers the spectrum of political constitutions in the *Advancement of Learning* ''that which approacheth nearest to the similitude of the divine rule'' is at the other extreme from the politique and is explicitly contrasted to the mere command of ''deeds and services'' and even of the wills of men: ''a commandment over the reason, belief and understanding of man, which is the highest part of the mind, and giveth law to the will itself, . . . lawful sovereignty over men's understanding, by force of truth rightly interpreted'' (217). Here in man's ethical relationship to divine power there are the seeds of a claim to a central role for reason in religion that are largely ignored in the ''natural religion'' emphasis of deism and better developed in Milton's supposed ''theodicy'' than in Leibniz's.

Bacon does not follow up any such possibilities, however, when he turns to ''sacred Theology'' or ''Divinity'' toward the end of the *Advancement of Learning*: ''As we are to obey his law though we find a reluctation in our will, so we are to believe his word though we find a reluctation in our reason'' (378). His reasons for this position emphasize the elements of confidence in and obedience to authority implicit in ''revealed knowledge'': ''For if we believe only that which is agreeable to our sense, we give consent to the matter and not to the author; which is no more than we would do towards a suspected and discredited witness.'' Bacon goes so far as to assert that such belief is ''more worthy'' than knowledge of the sort ''now'' accessible to us, for ''in knowledge man's mind suffereth from sense, but in belief it suffereth from spirit, such one as it holdeth for more authorised than itself, and so suffereth from the worthier agent." Bacon devotes his greatest efforts to combatting this attitude within the sphere of natural knowledge, but that does not mean that his use of it in supporting the separate consideration of revelation is insincere.

One consideration that gives credibility to Bacon's position on revelation is the point he draws in this context from the idea that the heavens declare the glory but not the will of God. To know God's will men must turn to Scripture. This holds, he says, "not only in those points of faith which concern the great mysteries of the Deity, of the Creation, of the Redemption, but likewise those which concern the law moral truly interpreted, . . . [which] is a voice beyond the light of nature" (379). He makes his point by means of two nice distinctions:

the light of nature is used in two several senses: the one, that which springeth from reason, sense, induction, argument, according to the laws of heaven and earth; the other, that which is imprinted upon the spirit of man by an inward instinct, according to the law of conscience, which is a sparkle of the purity of his first estate: in which later sense only he is participant of some light and discerning touching the perfection of the moral law: but how? sufficient to check the vice, but not to inform the duty. So then the doctrine of religion, as well moral as mystical, is not to be attained but by inspiration and revelation from God. (*Ibid.*)

In sum, Bacon feels that "the true limits and use of reason in spiritual things, as a kind of divine dialectic," have not been "sufficiently enquired and handled," with the result that people persist in the twin errors of "demanding to have things made more sensible than it pleaseth God to reveal them," and being "scandalized at a show of contradiction" (381). It seems clear that Bacon does not consider Divinity a form of learning which is susceptible of "advancement." A wholly different attitude and approach apply here from his "moral psychology" of science,[5] though with the same ultimate end in mind: he insists on the positivity of revelation because its acceptance would "be an opiate to stay and bridle not only the vanity of curious speculations, wherewith the schools labour, but the fury of controversies, wherewith the church laboureth" (382).

This last reference should remind us that already for Bacon the context of discussion about relations between "Divinity" and "Philosophy" was marked by the religious and political struggles that were to lead into the Puritan or real English Revolution. Bacon contrasts the proper spirit of inferences from revelation "in opinions and counsels, not in positions and oppositions," to a growing "prophetic

---

[5] See my essay, "Active Experience vs. Wish-Fulfillment in Francis Bacon's Moral Psychology of Science," *The Philosophical Forum*, 9 (1979), 78-99.

tendency: "men are now over-ready to usurp the style *Non ego, sed Dominus,* and not so only, but to bind it with the thunder and denunciation of curses and anathemas. . . ." Insistence on the separation of revealed knowledge from empirical and rational knowledge reflected an attitude toward the relations between church and state which could be considerably modified after the Restoration and even more after the Glorious, or so-called English, Revolution.

Puritanism can in general be thought of as promoting its own version of the separation of revelation and rationality which in some cases corresponded to theocracy but in other cases supported a strong sense of the inwardness and individuality of piety which must keep itself disengaged from external, and particularly political, organization and engagement. The strife between Laud and the Puritans can be seen as extending the theological differences between Arminian and Calvinist, which centered in the issues of Predestination and Grace, but Laud was himself wary of giving reason too large a role in the articulation or justification of belief and authority. It was apparently the Cambridge Platonists who broke with the one position shared by all the conflicting parties, the separation of religion and philosophy, although they could in this respect also reclaim the legacy of Richard Hooker. From the Cambridge Platonists this new or revived attitude spread through the Latitudinarians and gave a generally underestimated or neglected unBaconian aspect to the approach to relations of reason and faith characteristic of the Royal Society. While reflecting a political settlement based on compromise, in 1660 as in 1688, this attitude also is evidence of a general decline of concern with the issues of Predestination and Grace, Redemption and Salvation.[6]

In 1662 the Act of Uniformity was reinforced by letters from Charles II to the Archbishops containing directions for preachers, from which Cragg quotes: "None are in their sermons to bound the authority of sovereigns, or determine the differences between them and the people; nor to argue the deep points of election, reprobation, free will, etc."[7] With the waning of interest in the latter, the imperative character of the former was diffused. In this way Hobbes's ideas on the relation of church and state, revelation and reason, though social and political developments tended to lessen their distance from prevailing realities, came to be seen as unwelcome reminders of harsher times. This was a contributing factor to the widespread overt

---

[6] G. R. Cragg, *From Puritanism to the Age of Reason* (Cambridge, 1950); Richard S. Westfall, *Science and Religion in Seventeenth-Century England* (Ann Arbor, 1973); and S. L. Bethell, *The Cultural Revolution of the Seventeenth Century* (London, 1951).

[7] Cragg, *op. cit.*, 33.

eclipse of Hobbes which extended into the eighteenth century, and this brought with it the loss of essential aspects of the Baconian legacy.

In his article on "Deism" in the *Encyclopedia of Philosophy*, E. C. Mossner writes: "Bacon had enunciated the principle of a rigid dichotomy between science and religion which, on the whole, was adhered to during the seventeenth century. Indeed, science was more generally used as a bulwark for Christianity than the reverse" (II, 330). What is obliterated in the obscurity of this transition, masked by a paradoxical "indeed," is the historically significant and potent idea that such support in effect sapped, or at least endangered, the foundations of faith. While Hobbes's reputation for piety is not great, it must be confessed that it was he who most ably carried forward this line of Ockhamist and Baconian reasoning. Leaving aside, in this instance, the larger issues of Hobbesian epistemology and Erastianism, let us concentrate on the logical separation of faith and reason in a work well suited to exemplify it.

In his critique of Thomas White's *De Mundo*, which only in 1976 became available in English, Hobbes confronts a work of rationalist theology that attempts to construe Galilean science as a confirmation and reinforcement of Catholic belief. He comments, for example, on White's treatment of the existence in space of incorporeal substances:

> But since it cannot be known by natural reason whether any substances are incorporeal, what has been revealed supernaturally by God must be accepted as true. This is the way, therefore, in which Christians, bowing to the authority of Holy Scripture, not to the reasonings of philosophers, have classed substances; but to do so constitutes a tenet of faith, not of knowledge. Those who bring the matter forward for discussion cannot explain how substances can exist in this fashion and yet not be situated anywhere; so such people do not confirm the Christian faith, but weaken it. Indeed, it is natural for many to consider as false what someone tries to prove true, but cannot.[8]

As Collins later was said to remark, no one had doubted God's existence until Clarke undertook to demonstrate it in his Boyle lectures.

Where White claims to establish "that the existing world is the best of those creatable," Hobbes shows that this assertion can be taken to mean either "that He called all things good because they pleased him as God, or because He created them to His own lik-

---

[8] Hobbes, *Thomas White's 'De Mundo' Examined*, trans. Harold Whitmore Jones (London, 1976), 54; cf. 341, 351 *et al.* Subsequent page references are given within the text. See my review in the *Review of Metaphysics*, **32** (Dec. 1978), 361 ff.; and "Materialism and Freedom," *Studies in Eighteenth-Century Culture*, **7** (1978), 93-212, esp. 197, 209 ff., nn. 7 and 16.

ing . . . not because they had to please the men who were to conduct disputations concerning them." As to the basis of God's judgment or motivation. Hobbes confesses his ignorance and insists that terms such as "pleasing" are incomprehensible as applied to God. "It suffices, therefore, that God created this world and not another one. From this we gather that no other world has pleased him more. If anyone philosophizes beyond this point, he speculates beyond his own powers of comprehension" (391).

Against White's argument that God could not have created the world without reason, Hobbes stresses the difference which we have to assume between divine "will" and human will, and he maintains that God's creation resulted from free-will. If God's will had to be moved by a cause, this must have pre-existed creation; White's approach is best suited for denying the possibility of creation (386). White holds that beings are the offspring of "Divine Ideas" in God's mind, which Hobbes counters in Ockhamist fashion, seeing it as a denial of divine omnipotence (393 f.). "Purpose" (*finis*) cannot mean with regard to God what it means for man, and thus philosophy cannot show that God founded the world for a purpose. Analogously, "what emerges from nature takes place by necessity, not by design" (401).

Corresponding to the separation of knowledge and faith is a "negative theology" in which all that can be asserted of God positively is that "He is," other terms being applied only negatively ("incomprehensible," "infinite") or metaphorically (as in the Bible's ascribing rest and motion to him—although Hobbes resists the implication that God could be idle in any sense). Speech about God's attributes in each case says, and is meant to say, something about the speaker rather than God and, above all, shows that the speaker honors God in the only way he can (321, 417). This is part of Hobbes's way of dealing with the problem of theodicy (434):

we may reverently and as Christians say of God that He is the author of every act, because it is honorable to do so, but to say 'God is the author of sin' is sacrilegious and profane. There is no *contradiction* in this matter, however, for, as I said, the words under discussion are not propositions of people philosophizing but the actions of those who pay homage. A contradiction is found in propositions alone.[9]

In sum, Hobbes's conviction is "that those who worship no god but the one they do understand are not Christians; and that those who

[9] The eventual result of the double-truth theory can be discerned here: the truths of faith are "saved" into meaninglessness. As a consequence of their exclusively subjective affective reference and significance, they "do not signify." Whether this is already a part of the intention of Paris arts faculty Averroists like Siger of Brabant, or Ockham or Pomponazzi, it may be taken to be so in Hobbes's case.

think they can demonstrate any attribute of something [or Him] they do not comprehend are not philosophers" (326).

The consequence of Hobbes's position would be to call into question not only the tenuous hybrid "Christian deism" but also natural religion insofar as it purports to establish more than the simple existence of a creative "will" that has no principle. Other parts of Hobbes's work, particularly the construction and use of Scripture in *Leviathan*, display a far more critical relation to Revelation, but even here Hobbes is often mainly intent on disengaging what he sees as adventitious Greek metaphysics ("incorporeal substances") from the literal, naturally materialist, level of the text. In recognizing and exerting the concern of reason with the content of what is to be believed, if not the grounds of belief, and especially in his anti-metaphysical use of historical consciousness, Hobbes contributes to critical tendencies that fed into deism. But if we take "natural religion" to be an essential element of deism, we must recognize that the general bent of Hobbes's thought is not congenial to deism. In Chapter 12 of *Leviathan*, "Of Religion," more than anticipating Hume's "Natural History," Hobbes analyzes "the Naturall seed of *Religion*": "Opinion of Ghosts, Ignorance of second causes, Devotion towards what men fear, and Taking of things Causal for Prognostiques."

There is a fundamental opposition between natural religion and the approach that bases the separation of reason and faith, and concomitantly the contingency of the creation or natural world, in the omnipotence of God's will. The Ockhamist or, more broadly, separationist approach tends to undermine inference from nature to the attributes of God considered positively. Of course, natural religion was not originally oriented exclusively or even primarily toward "nature's god" but went back to principles of piety supposedly inherent in human nature. The five fundamental truths of Herbert of Cherbury reflected man's ethical and existential uncertainties:

1) that God exists; 2) that it is a duty to worship Him; 3) that the practice of virtue is the true mode of doing Him honour; 4) that man is under the obligation to repent of his sins; 5) that there will be rewards and punishments after death.[10]

Although this catechism of "natural piety" involves an element of comparative religion, it is essentially a distillation of Christianity.

Natural religion came to be defined, however, in terms of the relation to the god, or conception of god, that can be known exclusively through the natural use of reason, apart from revelation, and

---

[10] Cragg, *op. cit.*, 137. Other versions of Herbert's five basic truths include reference to rewards and punishments in this life as well.

this reinforced a shift of emphasis to "nature's god." The new focus tended even to absorb the ethical and existential concerns, as problems of predestination and grace gave way to or faded into questions about the compatibility of divine foreknowledge (or determinism) and human freedom. The hopeful dependence of prudence on the interventions of particular providence disappeared in reliance on the rationality of the workings of "general providence." But reference of natural contingency to divine will did not completely disappear in such rationality.

3. *Leibniz*—In a characteristic passage of the "Discourse of the Conformity of Faith with Reason," which forms the preliminary essay of the *Theodicy*, Leibniz writes:

> Now we have no need of revealed faith to know that there is such a sole Principle of all things, entirely good and wise. Reason teaches us this by infallible proofs; and in consequence all the objections taken from the course of things, in which we observe imperfections, are only based on false appearances. For, if we were capable of understanding the universal harmony, we should see that what we are tempted to find fault with is connected with the plan most worthy of being chosen; in a word, we should *see*, and should not *believe* only, that what God has done is the best.[11]

Such is Leibniz's vindication of God with respect to the existence of evil. In some respects it may seem deistic, but it also reveals affinities with the separationist line of thinking common to Scotus and Ockham, Bacon and Hobbes.

Leibniz's *Theodicy* is framed as a response to positions taken by Pierre Bayle "wherein religion and reason appear as adversaries, and where M. Bayle wishes to silence reason, after having made it speak too loud: which he calls the triumph of faith" (63). But Leibniz maintains that Bayle's "triumph of faith" is in effect often "a triumph of demonstrative reason against apparent and deceptive reasons . . . [For] the objections of the Manichaeans are hardly less contrary to natural theology than to revealed theology" (98). Bayle "declares himself against reason, when he might have been content to censure its abuse . . . [and he] thinks that human reason is a source of destruction and not of edification" (99). Nonetheless, Leibniz comes to suggest, toward the end of the preliminary discourse, that Bayle's opinions are "not fundamentally so remote from mine as his expressions" (120).

This recognition of affinity expresses more than simply the conciliatory aspect of Leibniz's edificatory conception of reason. Simi-

---

[11] Leibniz, *Theodicy: Essays on the Goodness of God, the Freedom of Man and the Origin of Evil*, trans. E. M. Huggard, (New Haven, 1952), 98. Page references to the translation will be given in the text, and I have tried to describe the location of passages referred to for readers using the original text. Here §44.

larly Leibniz chooses to conclude the third and final part of the
Theodicy proper with a continuation of the *Dialogue on Free Will*, by
Lorenzo Valla, who also insisted on the incommensurability of reason and faith, in some ways closer to Ockham than to other Italian
humanists. Leibniz's constructive use of reason, in both senses of
"constructive," is intended to support or reinforce faith by erecting a
parallel structure. In the last paragraph of Part I of the *Theodicy*
Leibniz sums up his approach:

> But, in fine, all these attempts to find reasons, where there is no need to
> adhere altogether to certain hypotheses, serves only to make clear to us that
> there are a thousand ways of justifying the conduct of God. All the disadvan-
> tages we see, all the obstacles we meet with, all the difficulties one may raise
> for oneself, are no hindrance to a belief founded on reason, even when it
> cannot stand on conclusive proof . . . (p. 181) [. . . n'empêchent pas qu'on
> doive croire raisonnablement, quand on ne le saurait pas d'ailleurs
> démonstrativement . . .].

Theodicy in this sense is a form of ideal casuistry which "saves the
appearances" not so much of temporal events as of the rational content of belief that seems to be continually contradicted by what happens in the world.

The basis for Leibniz's arguments supporting "reasonable belief"
is the principle of sufficient reason, and more particularly its variant
form, the principle of the best. That nothing happens without a reason, that there is no effect without an adequate cause, is the principle
of sufficient reason as it is applied to experience. Leibniz applies it as
well to the *existence* of things and of the world as a whole, and thus,
by referring it to divine motivation, gives the principle a purposive or
teleological cast. Extending the idea that there can be no action without a sufficient motive, the principle of the best states that a will
naturally follows that which seems best. As applied to God who
knows what is best, i.e., who cannot be misled like man by merely
apparent good, and who creates the world by willing it, the principle
of the best is not psychological but ontological. Or rather, knowing
from the conception of God's nature that God does and chooses what
is best, we can make inferences about the existing world. The very
fact that it exists tells us that it is the best possible.

I do not intend to try to make this part of Leibniz's argument seem
plausible. If we can understand its logic, however, I think we may
come to find significant the application of the principle of sufficient
reason to the natural, "created" world. In turn, the relation of his
conception of human motivation and endeavor to the objective order
of the moral world or general providence may cast a more appealing
light on his idea of theodicy. Paradoxically, it is the parallel treatment
of divine will in terms of the principle of sufficient reason, i.e., the

principle of the best, that has seemed to most readers, following Arnauld, Bayle, and Clarke, to put Leibniz in the category of "deist."

Leibniz's characterization of freedom, human and divine, hinges on a distinction between two kinds of necessity. He introduces this argument, in the second paragraph of the preliminary discourse, in a way that is reminiscent of Scotus and Ockham, by distinguishing two sorts of "truths of reason." First, there are eternal truths, which are absolutely necessary since their opposite (i.e., negation) is impossible (implies a contradiction); this absolute necessity is also called "logical," "metaphysical," or "geometrical" necessity. Second, there are also

others which may be called 'positive', because they are the laws which it has pleased God to give to Nature, or because they depend upon those. We learn them either by experience, that is, *a posteriori*, or by reason and *a priori*, that is, by considerations of the fitness of things [*convenance*] which have caused their choice. This fitness of things has also its rules and reasons, but it is the free choice of God, and not a geometrical necessity, which causes preference for what is fitting and brings it into existence (74).

Choice *is* determined by the "*moral* necessity" of His choosing the best, so where Leibniz concludes "that physical necessity is founded on moral necessity," he varies the late-Scholastic argument from God's omnipotence to the contingency of nature.

"It is this physical necessity that makes order in Nature and lies in the rules of motion and in some other general laws which it pleased God to lay down for things when He gave them being." Truths drawn from experience which are not logically necessary or strictly demonstrable are thus only probable (*vraisemblable*), and Leibniz suggests that they therefore have no force against faith.[12] This would also qualify the support of faith which arguments from apparent design in nature could provide, but that is not characteristic of Leibniz's approach. Even with respect to nature, he reasons rather from the imperfection of the world we experience.[13] In a similar way, physical and moral evil, suffering and injustice, are undeniably present in the world. Leibniz does not seek to explain them away, to deny that they are evils. He rather attempts to show their moral necessity in the

[12] See §§ 3, 20, and 21 of the preliminary discourse, pp. 75, 86 f., and the discussion of moral certainty and of "explanation" as opposed to "understanding," below, at n. 15.

[13] See, e.g., his early demonstration "That Corporeal Phenomena Cannot be Explained without an Incorporeal Principle, That Is God," the first part of the "The Confession of Nature Against Atheists," in Leibniz, *Philosophical Papers and Letters*, ed. Leroy F. Loemker (Dordrecht, 1969), 109 ff.

world which God has created, that is, chosen from among all possible worlds as the one most worthy of existence.

For Leibniz, the reference to God's pleasure is the very opposite of irrationalist voluntarism. The notion of God's arbitrary will, above reason and reasons, which is often wrongly attributed to Ockham, for whom the distinction between God's will and reason is an artificial one, *is* suggested by various passages in Descartes. Against this view Leibniz maintains that God's choice is morally necessitated by his nature which can include neither caprice nor indifference. He necessarily knows and chooses the best, but his choice is free because all the less perfect configurations of good and evil which he did not choose were nonetheless possible. Only a metaphysical, logical, geometrical, or absolute necessity, the opposite of which is impossible, would pose a danger to freedom. For God to be able to choose less than the best would conversely be an imperfection and a contradiction of the very idea of a divine will.

Leibniz thus denied God a supposed "freedom of indifference" or power of acting without motive or reason, which in His case means without acting for the best. God's freedom is thus, in one sense, truly indistinguishable from his wisdom and his benevolence (understood as general providence). Leibniz does, however, distinguish His will from His intelligence in order to account for the existence of evil in the world. God's will, of itself, tends only toward the good, while in its eventual choice it has to allow the existence of some evil as entailed in the greatest compossibility of goods as fixed in their eternal ideas in God's intelligence. In his reliance on the "eternal ideas" Leibniz continues the approach of Scotus which was undermined by Ockham's conceptualism. In a similar way, the conception of God's freedom as morally necessitated to choose the best is restrictive because it depends on the assumption of an objective ("eternal") differentiation and hierarchic scale of goods existing apart from any will, a pervasive premise that was challenged by the Hobbesian idea of will which Leibniz follows in most other respects.

To better understand Leibniz's explanation for the existence of evil in the best of all possible worlds, we must advance from the distinction between God's intelligence and will to that between "antecedent" and "consequent" will, a distinction which he explicitly takes from "Thomas, Scotus and others" and uses to elaborate Hobbesian concepts of will and deliberation.[14] The consequent will, also

---

[14] I argued for the substantial continuity between Hobbes and Leibniz with regard to conative psychology and the analysis of deliberation on the model of mechanics in a paper given at the 1977 meeting of the American Society of Eighteenth-Century Studies in Victoria, "Leibniz's Response to Locke, and the Legacy of Hobbesian

called "final" or *décrétoire*, "results from the conflict of all the antecedent wills," that is, from their competition and mutual correction
as well as from their confluence, just as "in mechanics compound
movement results from all the tendencies that concur in one and the
same moving body." Antecedent wills are tendencies to overt action,
which Hobbes comprehended under the title of *conatus*, endeavor or
urge or drive. Leibniz characterizes the willing process here as culminating ("*ad summum conatum*") in the consequent will, for which
"this rule obtains, that one never fails to do what one wills, when one
has the power" (136 f.).

"Thence it follows that God wills *antecedently* the good and *consequently* the best," but the best necessarily includes some evils.
Leibniz thus generalizes the scholastic argument that God antecedently wills the salvation of all but must leave many to damnation in
His consequent will. More relevant than the traditional theological
reference is the question whether the conception of creation according to the principle of the best provides an adequate idea of God as
creator. To some it has seemed that He disappears more completely
here than in the reduction to an otherwise unspecifiable "first
cause." "As all the possibles are not compatible together in one and
the same world-sequence," Leibniz's thought runs, the creation can
be thought of as "a struggle between all the possibles, all of them
laying claim to existence, and those which, being united, produce the
most reality, most perfection, most significance carry the day" (253).

The conflict and convergence of motives leading up to action,
itself modelled on the parallelogram analysis of forces drawn from
Galilean mechanics, is taken as the model of creation, establishing
that there is "sufficient reason" for the world that was chosen. This is
not a merely logical problem of a maximum of compossibility, for
God's mind is presupposed as committed to the principle of the best.
This struggle "can only be a conflict of reasons in the most perfect
understanding, which cannot fail to act in the most perfect way, and
consequently to choose the best." This is the only consistent and
worthy conception of divine freedom, according to Leibniz.

Empiricism," which I hope to develop for publication. See, for now, the essay cited
in n. 8.

Leibniz credits the distinction of "antecedent" and "consequent will" "to
Thomas, Scotus and others" in the penultimate paragraph of the preface, in §24 of
the Latin synopsis "Causa Dei" appended to the *Theodicy*, and in some detail in the
"Abrégé de la Controverse" which follows Part III where he imitates a Scholastic
mode of presentation. In the *Theodicy* proper the distinction is taken up in §§22 f.
(quoted in my text), 43 (where the analogy to human will, as resultant of a summation
of inclinations, is made explicit), 80, 84, 114, 116, 119, 162, 209, 222, 236, and 282.

The rationality that is realized in creation is thus rooted not in self-evident, logically necessary relations but in what is fitting according to an overall system of compatible possibilities which can never be wholly accessible to human beings. To recognize the sufficient reason of the existence of anything or everything is an act of acknowledgment or rational faith, but not of knowledge. Also, the use of reason of the existence of anything or everything is an act of acknowledgment or rational faith, but not of knowledge. Also, the use of which can be proved *a priori*, or by pure reason, can be comprehended." *Comprendre*, in this sense, implies "absolute certainty," and Leibniz contrasts it accordingly to the externality of *expliquer* (76):

Mysteries may be *explained* sufficiently to justify belief in them; but one cannot *comprehend* them, nor give understanding of how they come to pass. Thus even in natural philosophy we explain up to a certain point sundry perceptible qualities, but in an imperfect manner, for we do not comprehend them.[15]

Faith, arrived at through reason as well as revelation, is positive knowledge, to be taken as given, just as immediate sense perception is. The distinction between "knowing that" and "knowing how" something happens or is the case, which Leibniz also relates to the Aristotelian distinction between "knowing that" and "knowing why" or knowledge (by way) of causes, is crucial to Leibniz's view of how reason can support faith. In paragraph 85 of the preliminary discourse he points out that where Bayle says explanation of mysteries is impossible, Bayle means such "as would penetrate to the

[15] Here in §5 of the preliminary discourse Leibniz develops Hobbes's conception of "understanding" (*intellectio*), which can be traced back to Ockham and Aristotle, in a way that emphasizes its contrast with positive or immediate knowledge. As the reference to natural philosophy shows, sense is a form of positive knowledge, to be taken as given (like revelation), without the possibility of insight into its cause, the why or the how. In the scientific revolution of the seventeenth century, particularly as interpreted by Bacon and Hobbes, it was recognized that necessary or demonstrative knowledge, knowledge (by way) of [*per*] causes, could be integrated into experience, and not only in mathematical physics. Although it may at first sight seem quite different, Leibniz's distinction between *comprendre* and *expliquer* is close kin to Dilthey's between *Verstehen* and *Erklären*. "Understanding" works with relations given in experience, while "explanation" must depend on hypothetical causal connections. Vico also develops this conception of *intellectio* through its link to *operatio* and points the way to a different extension of the scope of science as knowledge of causes. See the second paper cited in n. 2 above. For Hobbes on *intellectio* see *Thomas White's 'De Mundo' Examined*, 52 (where *intelligere* is misleadingly translated as "perceive"), 257, 307, 376, and 382, as well as the review cited in n. 8. For Leibniz, see Vittorio Mathieu, "Wissenschaft und Wirksamkeit bei Leibniz," *Akten des II. Internationalen Leibniz-Kongresses,* Vol. IV (Wiesbaden, 1975), 147-55, and my review essay on the volume, in *Eighteenth-Century Studies*, Vol. 12, no. 3 Spring 1979), 433-38.

how," but that this is not necessary for replying to objections against faith, which equally lack "absolute certainty." In the next paragraph he lists a number of writers who have undertaken to explain the *how* and "plunged too far into the explanation of the Mysteries" (122). Included in this number is "the Englishman Thomas Albius," that is, the Thomas White whose *De mundo* was "examined" by Hobbes.

Leibniz derives the contingency of nature from the principle of sufficient reason operative in God's consequent will or act of creation, which constitutes a sort of compromise between recourse to divine omnipotence and his subsumption of natural events to an absolute causal necessity. The fact that other worlds are logically, if not "morally," possible is a technical guarantee of God's freedom. He is not constrained in his choice of the best by the principle of contradiction. But more positively, Leibniz maintains that moral necessity, far from conflicting with human or divine freedom, makes it possible or meaningful, with the argument that reasons or motives "incline without necessitating." Like Hobbes, and later Hume, Leibniz holds that the practical basis of spontaneity and moral responsibility is the reliability of moral determination or causality in the application of the principle of sufficient reason to human action.

At one point, in Proposition XIII of the "Summary of the Discourse of Metaphysics" (1686), which he sent to Arnauld, Leibniz claimed that human events "however certain are nevertheless contingent, being based on the free choice of God and of His creatures. It is true that their choices always have their reasons, but they incline to the choices under no compulsion of necessity." [16] We need not be concerned here with the question whether the conception of moral necessity as "inclining" the will not only as "antecedent" or *inclinatoire* (as he says in the appendix to the *Theodicy*, the Latin synopsis "Causa Dei") but also as "consequent" and acting allows for an adequate conception of human or divine freedom. Suffice it to say that Leibniz defined spontaneity as acting from one's own motives, [17] that the immanence of the motives did not inhibit them from

---

[16] Leibniz, *Selections*, ed. Philip P. Wiener (New York, 1951), 305. In the supporting argument Leibniz distinguishes "the certain" from "the necessary" and adds, "the connection of sequence is of two kinds: the one, absolutely necessary, whose contrary implies contradiction, occurs in the eternal verities like the truths of geometry; the other is necessary only *ex hypothesi*, and so to speak by accident, and in itself it is contingent since the contrary is not implied. This latter sequence is not founded upon ideas wholly pure and upon the pure understanding of God, but upon his free decrees and upon the processes of the universe" (306). It follows "that that which happens conformably to these decrees is assured, but that it is not therefore necessary" (307).

[17] See, e.g., § 15 of Leibniz's answer to Clarke's Fourth Reply (in Leibniz, *Selections*, 241): ". . . properly speaking, motives do not act upon the mind, as weights do upon a balance; but it is rather the mind that acts by virtue of the motives, which

being in turn determined by the properties of objects, and that freedom in the full sense was an integration of such spontaneity and reflection or deliberation, as Aristotle and Hobbes had held.

There is, however, one final problem more relevant to the present topic that is implied in the connection between the contingency of human events and "the free choice of God and of His creatures." Does human freedom bring with it a contingency beyond that of natural events, and, if so, does this affect divine prescience or providence? Ockham had maintained "that a created will follows a divine ordinance or determination not necessarily but freely and contingently" and "that no revealed future contingent comes to pass necessarily,"[18] which leads him to deny foreknowledge of human action:

when something is determined contingently, so that it is still possible that it is not determined and it is possible that it was never determined, then one cannot have certain and infallible cognition based on such a determination. But the determination of the divine will in respect of future contingents is such a determination. . . . Therefore God cannot have certain cognition of future contingents based on such a determination.

From this he concludes, however, "that it is impossible to express clearly the way in which God knows future contingents. Nevertheless it must be held that He does so, but contingently." The conjunction of empiricist and separationist approaches is stated even more clearly in another text where Ockham insists on the limits of the fallen mind:

L. . . . I say it is to be held indubitably that God knows all future contingents certainly and evidently. But to explain this clearly and to describe the way in which He knows all future contingents is impossible for any intelligence in this [present human] condition.
M. And I maintain that the Philosopher [Aristotle] would say that God does not know some future contingents evidently and certainly, and for the following reason. What is not true in itself cannot be known at a time at which it is not true in itself. But a future contingent absolutely dependent on a free capacity [i.e., a created will] is not true in itself. . . .

---

are *its dispositions* to act. And therefore to pretend, as the author [Clarke] does here, that the mind prefers sometimes weak motives to strong ones, and even that it prefers that which is *indifferent* before *motives*: this, I say, is to divide the *mind* from the *motives*, as if they were *outside the mind*. . . ." This key to Leibniz's conception of spontaneity might, rightly understood, unlock the otherwise perplexing aspects of his monadology and "pre-established harmony" that concern the self-contained quality of the mental processes of knowing and motivation.

[18] William Ockham, *Predestination, God's Foreknowledge, and Future Contingents*, trans. Marilyn McCord Adams and Norman Kretzmann (New York, 1969), 40, 44. The quotations following are from 49 f. See the Introduction, 18 f., for Ockham's idea of God's "antecedent will" that all should be saved.

In sum, the most that can be said is that "just as [a future contingent] contingently will be, so God contingently knows that it will be."[19]

Leibniz argues for the compatibility of human freedom and divine predetermination and foreknowledge involved in creation as the choice of the best of possible worlds by use of a concept of "hypothetical necessity" or "consequential necessity" which is akin to moral necessity and opposed to absolute necessity. Hypothetical necessity is close to Ockham's sense of contingency insofar as Leibniz holds God has foreknowledge of our actions only through foreknowledge of their sufficient reasons, our motives. These follow equally from the principle of sufficient reason operative in God's creative act or will. In effect, the coherence of Leibniz's position depends on the strict separation (and ideally maintained concomitance) of the different levels or kinds of causation or purposiveness.

Just as Bacon would allow for consideration of final causes in metaphysics as long as the teleological perspective does not interfere with inquiry into the "real" causes of physics or any branch of "natural philosophy," so Leibniz's use of the recourse to God's will or purpose depends on affirming its rationality and benevolence only in general, or formally, and without specific reference to the good of man or individuals. As Ockham wrote, "There is no way in which this argument can be resolved as long as one supposes that predestination and foreknowledge are real relations."[20] In his "Discourse on Metaphysics," immediately after stating that his "opinion is that God does nothing for which He does not deserve to be glorified" and thus could not act without sufficient reason, Leibniz supports Proposition IV: "That love for God demands on our part complete satisfaction with and acquiescence in that which He has done."[21] In the course of supporting this idea Leibniz expresses a stipulation which shows most clearly how both God's predetermination and the idea of it are to be related to human spontaneity:

I mean this acquiescence in regard to the past; for as regards the future one should not be a quietist with the arms folded, open to ridicule, awaiting that which God will do. . . . It is necessary to act conformable to the presumptive will of God as far as we are able to judge of it, trying with all our might to contribute to the general welfare. . . .

This acquiescence in God's will as revealed in the outcome of past actions is, as the next paragraph makes evident, a general confidence

---

[19] From *Ordinatio*, Distinction 38, i.e., the first book of his *Commentary on the Sentences* of Peter Lombard, in an appendix to *Predestination*, 88 ff.

[20] *Predestination*, 36.

[21] *Selections*, 294. The rejection of the fatalist "lazy reason" or sophism of the ancients in §IV is a recurrent motif in the *Theodicy*. See Leibniz, *Confessio philosophi*, trans. and ed. Otto Saame (Frankfurt, 1967), 69 ff., 109 ff., 168.

that all happens for the best, which, as faith, is rooted in the distance between our reason and God's: "To know in particular, however, the reasons which have moved Him to choose this order of the universe, to permit sin, to dispense His salutary grace in a certain manner—this passes the capacity of a finite mind" (295). We must reject the idea of an arbitrary or "despotic" God on the basis of the "moral necessity" of how God must be. But we cannot presume to know His reasons or reasonableness in particular; indeed, He cannot be thought to have particular reasons or "wills," according to the *Theodicy*, but only a general one. Early in the Preface to the *Theodicy* Leibniz reveals that it is this assurance, confidence, faith, or metaphysical optimism that sustains men's endeavors:

Whether one succeeds therein or not, one is content with what comes to pass, being once resigned to the will of God and knowing that what He wills is best. But before He declares His will by the event one endeavours to meet it[22] by doing that which appears most in accord with His commands. When we are in this state of mind, we are not disheartened by ill success . . . (52).

Vindication of the ways of God is meant to nurture trust and hope as the context of ongoing efforts. We can only be reconciled to God's will, as expressed in the result of past actions, in Leibniz's view, if we have the moral certainty that what happens is indeed for the best. This conviction is attained by rational faith which entails a rejection, or severe qualification, of reasoning from empirical event to the purposes or attributes of God. Far from seeking to establish the reality of providence or God's justice by a rational construction of experience, Leibnizian theodicy relies on formal rational argument in order to justify the persistence of moral striving even in the face of apparent futility.

The predetermination that is implied in divine foreknowledge, or in the overall concatenation of those possibilities God chose to realize in creation, involves only a "hypothetical necessity" in which what is going to happen cannot be divorced from the actions which will really bring it about. As applied to human motivation, the principle of sufficient reason or of the best does not conflict with but characterizes human freedom. As applied to divine motivation, the same principle cannot conflict with human freedom because it characterizes a different order of causality or purpose. Leibniz's defense of God as a reasonable, not willful, being thus depends essentially on the implicit separation of divine reasons and rationality from human experience and inquiry.

Boston University.

---

[22] Huggard (n. 11 above) translates "rencontrer" by "to find it out."

Chapter XV

HUME AND THE RELATION OF SCIENCE TO RELIGION AMONG CERTAIN MEMBERS OF THE ROYAL SOCIETY

BY JAMES E. FORCE

From the date of its second charter on April 22, 1663, one of the announced goals of the Royal Society of London for Improving Natural Knowledge was to illustrate the providential glory of God manifested in the works of His Creation. The Charter states the Society's purposes: "studia ad rerum naturalium artiumque utilium scientias experimentorum fide ulterius promovendas in Dei Creatoris gloriam & generis humani commodum applicanda sunt." [1]

Despite this announced goal, recent scholarship has shown the impossibility of linking members of the early Royal Society with any particular set of religious beliefs. The early Society contained adherents to a variety of sects including Puritans ejected from ecclesiastical office, converts to Catholicism, Anglican courtiers and country gentlemen, Presbyterian Royalists, incipient Latitudinarians, and even two deists. [2]

Nevertheless, some of the most prominent natural philosophers of the early Society, such as Robert Boyle, John Wilkins, Walter Charleton, and Isaac Newton, went to great lengths to demonstrate the religious utility of the approach to natural philosophy institutionalized in the Royal Society. Scholars as diverse in approach as David Kubrin and Michael Hunter have documented the providentialist basis of the natural philosophy of many early Fellows. [3] These early Fellows grappled with the relationship between the world of mechanical nature and the providential deity of Christianity and, in fulfillment of one of the explicitly charted goals of the Society, added a comprehensive scientific theism to the original experimental framework of the Society.

[1] Thomas Birch, The History of the Royal Society, 4 vols. (London, 1756-57), I, 221-30. The first Royal Charter was granted in July, 1662, when the title of "Royal Society" was conferred. This official sanctioning was preceded by a year and a half of Wednesday afternoon meetings at Gresham College, London, attended by twelve people including John Wilkins, who was appointed Chairman, and Robert Boyle.

[2] L. Mulligan, "Anglicanism, Latitudinarianism and Science in Seventeenth Century England," Annals of Science, XXX, No. 2 (June 1973), 218. See also Charles Webster, The Great Instauration: Science, Medicine and Reform, 1626-1660 (New York, 1976), 496, and Michael Hunter, Science and Society in Restoration England (Cambridge, England, 1981), Ch. 7.

[3] David Kubrin, "Newton and the Cyclical Cosmos: Providence and the Mechanical Philosophy," Journal of the History of Ideas, XXVIII (1967), 325-46; cf. Michael Hunter, Science and Society in Restoration England, Ch. 7. The classic work in this field remains Richard S. Westfall, Science and Religion in Seventeenth-Century England (New Haven, 1958.) See also Michael Macklem, The Anatomy of the World (Minneapolis, 1958.)

Beginning in about 1720, however, there arose within the Society a significant group of radical deists clustered around Martin Folkes who, in 1974, succeeded Hans Sloane as President of the Royal Society. According to the Newtonian cleric, William Stukeley, F.R.S., in 1720 Folkes started an "infidel Club" and began "propagating the Infidel System." Folkes was so successful in preaching the "infidel System" that he "made it even fashionable in the Royal Society, so that when any mention is made of Moses, of the deluge, of religion, scriptures, &c., it generally is received with a loud laugh." [4]

If Stukeley is correct the orientation to science in the service of religion on the part of many Fellows of the Society underwent a significant change between 1720 and 1741, and it may not be too great an exaggeration to refer to two different eras of the Society. During the first era beginning with its second Royal Charter in 1663, many of the most active (though by no means all) of the religiously diverse early Fellows pursued the goal of illustrating how the advancement of natural philosophy demonstrated the providential glory of God the Creator. With the emergence of Folkes as a power within the Society in the 1720's a second era begins in which many (though by no means all) Fellows of prominence within the Society scorn the expressly apologetic goal of the second Charter. According to Stukeley, Folkes "chuses the Councel & Officers out of his junto of Sycophants that meet him every night at Rawthmills coffee house, or that dine with him at the Miter, fleet street." [5]

How unpopular Hume would have been in the "first" era of the Royal Society will become evident as I examine in detail his religious skepticism in the light of the apologetic concerns of that group. Hume was not a member of the Royal Society and there is no evidence that Hume specifically aimed at the destruction of the comprehensively articulated scientific theism of the "first" era of the Royal Society. Nevertheless, that is precisely what he achieved with his rebuttal of every aspect of their many-faceted apologetic position concerning the relationship between general and special providence as developed during some eighty years of religious propagandizing by members of the "first" Royal Society.

To understand fully how Hume's own religious skepticism can profitably be read as a critique of the "first" Royal Society's entire apologetic program, it is necessary first to examine the theoretical legacy regarding the concepts of general and special providence in the thought of the scientist-theologians of the "first" Society. Latent in the thought of Wilkins, and more explicit in some of his colleagues such as Boyle, is a conflict between a purely mechanistic conception of the cold, mathematically calculable order of nature and natural law *and* a traditional Christian conception of a specially provident deity active daily in the

---

[4] William Stukeley, *Family Memoirs of the Rev. William Stukeley* (London, 1880), Vol. I, "The Commonplace Book, 1720," 100.   [5] *Ibid.*

governance of His creation and powerful enough to set aside the laws of nature through miracles. Accordingly, in Section I, I examine the roots of this problem in the work of some of the founding members of the "first" Society, how Newton inherited this problem, and how, aided by some of his disciples, most notably Richard Bentley and Samuel Clarke, he attempted to solve it.

In Section II, I examine Hume's skeptical critique of religious proofs in the light of the effort by some members of the "first" Royal Society to balance naturalism and supernaturalism. By viewing the essay "Of Miracles" and "Of a Particular Providence and a Future State" against the context of the total apologetic perspective established during the roughly eighty years of the "first" Society's existence, I show why the attempts by these apologists were doomed to fail, i.e., why Hume's critique succeeds, and also why the two essays are logically related as parts of a co-ordinated attack on general and special providence as these concepts had emerged from the apologetic anvil of the scientist-theologians of the "first" Royal Society.

I. Balancing God's "General Providence" Against His "Special Providence" in Apologetics of the "First" Royal Society 1662-1741

A. The Christian *Virtuosi*—The Royal Society from 1662 to 1703

From the beginning of the Royal Society some founders had argued that natural philosophy leads man to God, not away from Him. Many of the Christian *virtuosi* responsible for founding the Royal Society insisted that their scientific inquiries into the operations of the laws of nature would be the strongest buttress for religion. In a series of apologetic books and pamphlets the scientist-theologians maintained that a scientific study of nature reveals two specific kinds of divine direction and control of created nature, i.e., two types of divine providence. A study of nature shows both "general providence" and "special providence." [6]

"General providence" refers to God's action in the original creation of nature. In the beginning, God created the material frame of nature *and* He structured it to function in obedience to the laws of nature which He also created. In contrast to this original creative act of general providence is "special providence" which refers to a particular act of direct divine intervention that cancels or contravenes the ordinary course of natural operations. The historical record of the Bible reveals in accom-

---

[6] This seminal distinction of two subspecies within the broad concept of divine providence appears in the modern period in *De Veritate* (Paris, 1624), 213, by Lord Herbert of Cherbury. He was rightfully regarded in the mid-eighteenth century as one of the founders of the deist movement because, after distinguishing between the two types of providence, he eliminates special providence as revealed in Scripture. At least, he lays down such stringent rules for authenticating such reports that the Bible is virtually excluded as a source of knowledge about God.

plished miracles and fulfilled prophecies God's continued beneficent care and governance of the natural world through acts of special providence. The chief apologetic problem of the early Royal Society was to save the notion of a specially provident God who can miraculously intervene in His creation (or prophetically advertise a specially provident act for completion at some later date) and the increasingly detailed elaboration of nature as an undeviating clockwork mechanism illustrative only of God's general providence and contrary to a miracle-working, prophecy-fulfilling, specially provident God as found in the Bible. In striving to retain both a generally provident celestial watchmaker and the specially provident God of revelation fully capable of miraculous intervention in the regular course of nature, the Christian *virtuosi* of the later seventeenth century and the Newtonians of the early eighteenth articulate what may be styled the unofficial apologetic position of the Royal Society during its first eighty years of existence (1660 to 1741), the period of what I call the "first" Royal Society.[7]

The early apologist-scientists in the Royal Society sought to institutionalize the design argument to demonstrate God's general providence while simultaneously maintaining that God is also capable of a direct interruption of the orderly operation of the machine of nature in miraculous or prophetically advertised acts of special providence.

John Wilkins, Chairman of the historic meeting on November 28, 1660, when the decision was made to establish a Society of Experimental Philosophy, maintained a rigid model of the machine of nature which operates undeviatingly in accord with the natural law designed by a generally provident creator.[8] Nevertheless, God has the specially provident power to alter the regular course of (generally provident) natural

[7] Of course, some writers in the Society tended to overemphasize one aspect of divine providence at the expense of the other. Sir Kenelm Digby (1603-1665), for example, limits God's role to that of a generally provident creator and has done with it. In the beginning, God built and programmed the great machine of nature. For Digby, God's generally provident ordering of nature is revealed by observation of the chain of necessary mechanical causes "built in" to the machine of nature by God at creation and left to run on its own ever since. In Digby's view, general providence excludes special providence; his God is truly a Dieu fainéant. See Sir Kenelm Digby, *Observations upon Religio Medici* (Oxford, 1909), 10. Though continually involved with the Royal Society from its first formal meetings in 1660, Digby did not attend meetings with very great regularity. In contrast, some of the people most active in the early life of the society are precisely those who attempt to synthesize a God who is both specially *and* generally provident, e.g., Charleton, Wilkins, and Boyle. These men were part of what Charles Webster terms an "active nucleus" which sustained the early Royal Society. See Webster, *The Great Instauration: Science, Medicine and Reform, 1626-1660,* 90-2. (See note 2, above.)

[8] John Wilkins, *Of the Principles and Duties of Natural Religion* (London, 1683), 402. Henry Lyons, *The Royal Society, 1660-1940: A History of its Administration under its Charters* (New York, 1968), 10.

law in specially provident, supernatural acts. There is no creature not directly under His special, as well as His general, providence.[9]

Dr. Walter Charleton, another of the most active of the early fellows of the Society, attempted, like Bishop Wilkins, to retain a notion of God who exercises both sorts of providence. According to Charleton, just as God created the frame of nature and the order of natural law in an act of general providence, "so He can alter her and tune all her strings in accord with His will." [10]

Robert Boyle, the most renowned of all the *virtuosi,* attempted to synthesize the idea of a specially provident, miracle-working God with the model of a maintenance-free, mechanical-atomistic, world machine created at a single stroke of general providence a long time ago. Boyle actively espoused the design argument to emphasize the role of God as the generally provident creator of order and regularity as observed in the operations of natural law.[11] But Boyle was a Christian virtuoso who believed in the special providence of God to work miracles in spite of the case he makes for thinking of God solely as a generally provident creator. In his *Christian Virtuoso,* Boyle tried to make room in his clock-work universe designed by a generally provident God for God's contraventions of the orderly operation of nature through specially provident miracles. For Boyle, miracles are absolutely necessary to support Christianity.[12] Furthermore, Boyle specifically designates fulfilled prophecies as miraculous signs of God's special providence because they "are supernatural things; and as such (especially their author and design considered) may properly enough be reckoned among miracles." [13]

Finally, in his *History of the Royal Society,* Bishop Sprat is quick to emphasize the contributions of the Society's members in demonstrating God's general providence by means of the design argument.[14] But Sprat is just as quick to point out that in no way does the new natural philosophy of the Society militate against belief in God's acts of miraculous special providence. On the contrary, an "Experimental Philosopher" of the Society who "familiarly beholds the inward workings of things" will strengthen belief in God's true miracles by exposing fraudulent, enthu-

---

[9] Wilkins, *Of the Principles and Duties of Natural Religion,* 130.

[10] Walter Charleton, *Darkness of Atheism* (London, 1652), 127. Charleton argues that if God's providence is not special, as well as general, then it would be a maimed and feeble thing. *Ibid.,* 137-52, 217, 329.

[11] It is Boyle, as Professor Westfall has pointed out, who earnestly adapts Cicero's machine analogy to the service of the demonstration of God's general providence. *The Works of the Honourable Robert Boyle,* ed. Thomas Birch (London, 1744), 5 vols. *Some Considerations Touching the Usefulness of Experimental Natural Philosophy,* 1:446a. See also Richard S. Westfall, *Science and Religion in Seventeenth Century England* (Ann Arbor, 1973), 75 and Ch. 4 passim.

[12] Robert Boyle, *The Works, op. cit.,* V, 526.   [13] *Ibid.*

[14] Thomas Sprat, *History of the Royal Society* (London, 1667), 349.

astic, "Holy Cheats." [15] All this comes in a section entitled "Experiments
ill not destroy the Doctrine of Prophecies, and Prodigies." [16]

These earliest fellows of the "first" Royal Society bequeathed to their
iccessors the notion of a mechanical frame of nature obedient to the
ws of nature established by God's general providence and the notion
f a still active, specially provident, but not totally inflexible, mechanism.
ut there is a tension between the two sorts of providence. The more
etailed and defined the picture of the natural and mechanical order of
eneral providence becomes, the less room there appears to be for specially
rovident divine intervention. This dangerous tendency is echoed in the
epeated warnings of Wilkins, Boyle, and Sprat to be cautious when
eciding whether to believe in reports of miracles, especially recent ones.
Miracles may have indeed happened once long ago; they will probably
appen again. But they do not happen often. According to Wilkins, it is
mply "not reasonable to think that the universal laws of nature, by
which things are to be guided in their natural course, should infrequently
r upon every little occasion be violated or disordered." [17]

Newton and his followers in the next generation of the "first" Royal
ociety continue to labor to preserve both kinds of divine providence.

B. The Newtonian Synthesis of General and Special Providence

By 1703, when Newton was elected President of the Royal Society,
ie Society's apologetic ideology *generally* reflected Newton's personal
iew that his own scientific theories provided, through the design ar-
ument, a solid foundation for demonstrating a generally provident deity.
'he first to utilize the Newtonian discovery of the law of gravity to
emonstrate God's general providence was Richard Bentley in the 1692
Boyle Lectures. [18] In the second edition of the *Principia* (1713), Newton

---

[15] *Ibid.*, 360.   [16] *Ibid.*, 358-62.

[17] John Wilkins, *Of the Principles and Duties of Natural Religion*, 130. Sprat, too,
ounsels extreme caution regarding modern reports of specially provident divine inter-
ention, although he does not absolutely exclude the possibility that they may be true,
History of the Royal Society, 359-60. Boyle, too, worries about the enthusiasm to believe
1 divine special providence. Though he insists that miracles do happen, we must not
onfuse our ignorance of some mechanical operations established by God's general prov-
lence with such prodigies; *A Free Inquiry into the Vulgarly Received Notion of Nature*,
1 *The Works, op. cit.*, IV, 339a.

[18] Newton exchanged a series of letters with Bentley beginning five days after Bentley's
nal lecture. Bentley's adaptation of Newton's discovery of the law of gravity to the
lustration of a generally provident creator-architect occurs in the last three published
ersions of these lectures separately entitled "A Confutation of Atheism from the Origin
nd Frame of the World" in *A Defence of Natural and Revealed Religion: Being a
Collection of the Sermons Preached at the Lecture founded by the Honourable Robert
Boyle, Esq; (From the Year 1691 to the Year 1732)*, 3 vols., edited by Sampson Letsome
nd John Nicholl (London, 1739), I, 1-11. In his letters to Bentley, Newton indicates
hat he is delighted with Bentley's application of his "systeme" to the support of belief
1 a generally provident deity skilled in geometry and physics. Newton himself equivocates
bout whether the direct cause of gravity is material or immaterial but Bentley, along

himself set out the creator-architect deity of general providence in his famous "General Scholium."

Newton also used this statement of the design argument for his inferential leap to a specially provident deity. After his eloquent description of the solar system and his conclusion that "This most beautiful system of the sun, planets, and comets, could only proceed from the counsel and dominion of an intelligent and Powerful Being," Newton emphasized the specially provident nature of a God who sternly governs his generally provident creation: "This Being governs all things . . . as Lord over all; and on account of his dominion he is wont to be called *Lord God* . . . or Universal Ruler; for God has a respect to servants; and *Deity* is a dominion of God . . . over servants." [19]

The Newtonians attempt, when they adhered to Newton, to preserve both the mathematically competent, generally provident mechanic of the design argument with the specially provident God who daily exercises dominion over His created servants down to the last sparrow's last flight. In the system of theism worked out by some of Newton's followers, God usually displays his special providence through miracles and fulfilled prophecies.

Miracles. —The original creation of gravity demonstrates God's general providence but its continuous operation since that point reveals His special providence. God's sustained preservation of the order of nature and natural laws demonstrates divine special providence because of the very nature of gravitational attraction. Newton even claims that "a continual miracle is needed to prevent the sun and fixed stars from rushing together through gravity." [20] This point is echoed by such an important Newtonian disciple as Samuel Clarke.

Newton tends generally to discount the traditional conception of miracles held by Boyle, Wilkins, and some of the other founders of the Royal Society. A miracle is not a transgression of natural law. Rather, the sustained operation of natural law is itself a miracle and illustrative of divine special providence. Newton observes that miracles in the traditional sense are simply misunderstandings on the part of the vulgar.

---

with most of Newton's other disciples, reiterates that the cause of gravity is immaterial, divine power. There is highly probable evidence that Newton participated in handpicking Bentley to be the first Boyle Lecturer with the executors of Boyle's will, especially Pepys (at one time a President of the Royal Society) and Evelyn. See H. Guerlac and M. C. Jacob, "Bentley, Newton, and Providence," *Journal of the History of Ideas,* **30**, No. 3 (July-Sept., 1969), 318.

[19] *Sir Isaac Newton's Mathematical Principles of Natural Philosophy,* trans. A. Motte, rev. and ed. Florian Cajori (Berkeley, 1934), 543.

[20] *The Correspondence of Isaac Newton,* 7 vols. (Cambridge, 1959-77); the first three volumes were edited by H. W. Turnbull, III, 336.

They "are not so called because they are the works of God, but because they happen seldom and for that reason excite wonder."[21] It is his view about the possibility of a cessation or interdiction of natural law that leads Newton to his hermeneutic method for interpreting such scriptural accounts as, for example, the creation. Moses was popularizing, i.e., he was "accom[m]odating his words to the gross conceptions of the vulgar,"[22] and not giving a "philosophical" account in terms of mechanical causes. At least one Newtonian philosopher who engaged in controversies on behalf of his mentor, Samuel Clarke, nevertheless insists on the possibility of miracles. Clarke points out in his correspondence with Leibniz that one of the chief issues between Leibniz and the Newtonians is the Newtonians' insistence on the possibility of specially provident divine intervention in the universe. It is precisely because the Newtonians insist that God can and does providentially direct and govern his creation as the Lord God, even to the point of direct intervention in the operation of natural law, that Leibniz levels against them the charge of reducing God to an inferior clock repairman. According to this Newtonian doctrine, scoffs Leibniz, "God Almighty wants to *wind up* his watch from time to time: otherwise it would cease to move. He had not, it seems, sufficient foresight to make it a perpetual motion."[23]

Clarke replies that Leibniz misunderstands the nature of providence due to his doctrine of pre-established harmony which leaves God without "dominion" after the generally provident act of creation. It redounds to the greater glory of his generally provident workmanship that God fabricated the universe to be under his continuous, specially provident governance. Clarke argues that, for the Newtonians, "the wisdom of God consists, in framing originally the perfect and complete idea of a work, which begun and continues, according to that original perfect idea, by the continual uninterrupted exercise of his power and government."[24]

Clarke is not absolutely unequivocal about the nature of the phenomenon of gravity as a manifestation of God's continual uninterrupted exercise of his specially provident dominion over nature. When Leibniz ridicules the Newtonian conception that the everyday operation of gravity is a specially provident miracle,[25] Clarke replies that a miracle is only what is unusual in nature and so, because the operation of gravity is

[21] *Sir Isaac Newton's Theological Manuscripts,* ed. H. McLachlan (Liverpool, 1930), 17.

[22] See Newton's correspondence with Thomas Burnet on this point in *The Correspondence, op. cit.,* II, 331.

[23] "Mr. Leibnitz's First Paper," In *The Leibniz-Clarke Correspondence,* ed. H. G. Alexander (New York, 1956), 11. See also *Leibniz Selections,* ed. Philip P. Wiener (New York, 1951), 216.

[24] "Dr. Clarke's Second Reply," *The Leibniz-Clarke Correspondence,* 22.

[25] "Mr. Leibnitz's Third Paper," *Ibid.,* 29-30; "Mr. Leibnitz's Fourth Paper," *Ibid.,* 2-3; "Mr. Leibnitz's Fifth Paper," *Ibid.,* 91-5. Cf. Wiener, *op. cit.,* 227-8, 235, 275-8.

regular and constant, " 'tis no miracle, whether it be effected immediately by God Himself, or mediately by any created power."[26] But, in his Boyle Lectures, Clarke states of gravity that it results from a cause "superior to matter *continually* exerting on it a certain force or power" and thus that the world depends "every moment on some superior being, for the preservation of its frame."[27] Clarke believes ultimately, if reluctantly, that a miracle "is a work effected in a manner unusual or different from the common and regular method of Providence by the interposition either of God Himself, or some intelligent agent superior to man. . . ."[28]

The Newtonians thus use miracles in two senses to demonstrate God's special providence. First, God's continuous act of preserving the natural world is specially provident. But, when pressed by Leibniz about the Newtonian reduction of God to an inferior clock repairman or when considering reliable Scripture reports of phenomena for which there is no mechanical explanation, they accept miracles in the traditional sense as proof of God's continuous special providence.

Prophecies. —Ultimately, however, fulfilled prophecies become an even more important tool than miracles for demonstrating God's special providence in the apologetics of the "first" Royal Society. Fulfilled prophetic predictions tidily demonstrate the messiahship of Christ and reveal, once and for all, the hand of a specially provident deity continuously active in His creation. At the same time, fulfilled prophecies seem to avoid the dilemma of how it is possible for the generally provident order of natural law to be suspended in a specially provident miraculous act and also to avoid the problem of spurious miracles.

Locke,[29] Newton,[30] and Newton's successor at Cambridge, William Whiston, use the many instances of apparently fulfilled prophetic predictions recorded in the Bible to supplement the design argument of natural religion, to round it out, and draw from the total package the special, as well as the general, providence of God. Newton, for example, claims that "giving ear to the Prophets is a fundamental character of the

---

[26] "Dr. Clarke's Third Reply," *The Leibniz-Clarke Correspondence*, 35.

[27] Clarke, *Works*, 2:601. Cited by H. G. Alexander in his Introduction to *The Leibniz-Clarke Correspondence*, xx.

[28] Clarke, *A Discourse Concerning the Unchangeable Obligations of Natural Religion, and the Truth and Certainty of the Christian Revelation, Being Eight Sermons Preached at the Cathedral Church of St. Paul in the Year 1705* in *A Defence of Natural and Revealed Religion*, II, 165. As in the case of Bentley and probably also that of William Whiston, it seems reasonable to assume that Newton may have played some role in Clarke's Boyle Lectures though there is no direct evidence that he did so. See Note 32 below.

[29] Locke writes that the miracles of Jesus are significant only because they are predicted in Biblical prophecy. See his work *The Reasonableness of Christianity as Delivered in the Scriptures* (London 1695), 55.

[30] Newton agrees that "the events of things predicted many ages before will then be a convincing argument that the world is governed by *providence*." *Observations Upon the Prophecies of Daniel and the Apocalypse of St. John* (London, 1733), 252.

true Church. For God has so ordered the Prophecies, that in the latter days *the wise may understand, but the wicked shall do wickedly, and none of the wicked shall understand.* Dan. xii. 8-10."[31]

Just as Newton (in all likelihood) utilized the Boyle Lectures as a platform to publicize how his "systeme" demonstrates God's general providence through Bentley's 1692 lectures, so, too, he apparently utilized the same platform to demonstrate God's special providence as revealed in lists of fulfilled prophecies, e.g., in Whiston's 1707 Boyle Lectures, *The Accomplishment of Scripture Prophecy.* In these lectures, which were probably suggested by Newton[32] and which were dedicated to the Archbishop of Canterbury, Thomas Tenison, Whiston argued, for example, that the war with the French represented proof of God's special providence because it was an "Accomplishment" of an event predicted in Scripture.

During the first eighty years of the Royal Society, the chief apologetic aim of these scientist-theologians was to balance general and special providence. The Newtonians finally achieved synthesis of the two. The Newtonian version of the design argument demonstrates a generally provident deity who first created the universe and the laws of nature and then, "miraculously," i.e., continuously, preserved that creation. The argument from fulfilled prophecy discloses, through its list of prophetically revealed predictions which had come true, a specially provident deity active in governing His creation directly and gave clues for the wise concerning the future course of human and natural history. This argument was particularly emphasized by the Newtonians of the "first" Royal Society.[33]

[31] *Ibid.,* 14.

[32] This point at least seems probable in the light of Guerlac's and Jacob's picture of Newton's influence upon the executors of Boyle's will in picking Bentley as the inaugural lecturer and given Newton's evident interest in the selection of Whiston. There is, however, no direct evidence that Newton intervened to help get Whiston appointed as Boyle Lecturer. Whiston does state that his topic for his series of lectures was originally suggested by Newton himself. In the midst of a long passage in his *Memoirs* concerning the "ludicrous" skepticism engendered by the allegorical or figurative method of interpreting Scripture (in contrast to Whiston's and Newton's "literalistic" hermeneutic method), Whiston complained that the allegorical method was so entrenched that even such "learned men as bishop *Chandler,* and *Dr. Clarke,* made use (of it): till I, upon Sir *Isaac Newton's* original suggestion, shewed them the contrary" (98). The work in which Whiston attacked Clarke and Chandler appeared in 1725. It was an appendix to the 1708 Boyle lectures. Thus, it seems probable that Whiston's Boyle Lecture series topic was first suggested by Newton. If so, Guerlac's and Jacob's contention that Newton utilized the public platform to promulgate by proxy his views on controversial religious questions is strengthened. See also Whiston, *A supplement to the Literal Accomplishment of Scripture Prohecies* (London, 1725), 4-5.

[33] Whiston was not a Fellow of the Royal Society. Newton was a total dictator in the Royal Society in his years as President from 1701 to 1727. He endorsed only those who agreed with his views. Eventually, Newton even had a quarrel with Whiston, his hand-picked successor at Cambridge. In 1720, Sir Hans Sloane and Edmund Halley

II. Hume's Critique of the Synthesis of General and Special Providence

A. The "Second" Era of the Royal Society, After 1741

Some of the members of the "first" Royal Society sought to promote their conception of generally provident nature and regular natural law while also retaining God's special providence via miracles and/or prophecies. But with the retirement of Sir Hans Sloane, from the post of President and the subsequent election of Martin Folkes, the apologetic stance of the first eighty years of the Society was, to some degree, apparently abandoned. William Stukeley, a close friend of Newton and Whiston and rector of St. George's, Bloomsbury, and Fellow of the Royal Society, recorded the nature of Folkes' palace revolt against the apologetic goals of the "first" Society. Folkes, according to Stukeley, packed the Council of the Society with his mockingly deistical friends. "From that time he has been propagating the infidel System with great assiduity, & made it even fashionable in the Royal Society, so that when any mention is made of Moses, of the deluge, of religion, scriptures, &c., it generally is received with a loud laugh."[34]

The secularization of the Royal Society was undoubtedly gratifying to Hume who was friendly with Dr. Thomas Birch, an historian and man of letters who served actively as Secretary from 1751 to 1765, and, of course, with Sir John Pringle (Hume's friend and doctor during Hume's

---

proposed Whiston for membership in the Royal Society, but Newton blocked Whiston's election by threatening to resign as President, an action prompted by the conflict between two strong wills. Whiston writes that "if the reader desires to know the reason of Sir *Isaac Newton's* unwillingness to have me a member, he must take notice, that as his making me first his deputy, and giving me the full profits of the place brought me to the heads of the colleges in *Cambridge,* made me his successor; so did I enjoy a large portion of his favor for twenty years together. But he then perceiving that I could not do as his other darling friends did, that is, learn of him, without contradicting him, he could not, in his old age, bear such contradiction; and so he was afraid of me the last thirteen years of his life. . . . He was of the most fearful, cautious, and suspicious temper, that I ever knew." Whiston, *Memoirs,* 2nd ed., 2 vols. (London, 1753), I, 250-51. Although allowed to present his papers before the Society whenever he pleased, Whiston was never admitted as a Fellow due to Newton's personal enmity in later years. Nevertheless, Whiston's views on the importance of prophecy for demonstrating divine special providence were shared by Newton and repeated by so many Fellows of the Royal Society that I feel justified in using his texts to illustrate the unofficial apologetic position of the "first" Royal Society. For accounts of Newton in his later years as President of the Royal Society, see Christopher Hill, *Change and Continuity in 17th Century England* (London, 1974), Ch. 12, "Sir Isaac Newton and His Society," and Frank E. Manuel, *Freedom from History and Other Essays* (London, New York, 1972), Ch. 7, "Newton as Autocrat of Science."

[34] William Stukeley, *Family Memoirs of the Rev. William Stukeley, M. D.* (London, 1880), Vol. 1, "The Commonplace Book, 1720," 100. Folkes was Vice-president of the Royal Society while Newton was President and chaired many meetings in Newton's absence. His influence within the Society predates his own election to the Presidency by a considerable period.

final illness) who was President from 1772 until 1778.[35] The institutional shift in the "second" Society divorcing religion from science seems to have been accomplished within the Society itself more through ridicule and mockery than as a result of explicitly argued tracts and pamphlets. For such arguments against the attempt by apologists of the "first" Society to balance God's general and special providence, we must look to David Hume.

B. Hume's Critique of the "First" Royal Society

Mossner is correct that Hume's essays "Of a Particular Providence and a Future State" and "Of Miracles" ought to be read together.[36] These two essays, which first appear in print in 1748, constitute a co-ordinated assault on the synthesis of general and special providence as developed by the Newtonians of the "first" Royal Society. In undermining the design argument in "Of a Particular Providence and a Future State" (as well as in his more leisurely attack in the *Dialogues*) Hume is attacking the idea of a generally provident God as a *certain* inference in an argument which proceeds to infer the nature of the cause of the universe based on observed effects. In the essay "Of Miracles" Hume attacks the idea of a specially provident God who directly intervenes in the regular course of nature in miracles, which he defines as violations of natural law. Hume explicitly widens his attack in his essay to include prophecies, the chief argument utilized by the Newtonians of the "first" Royal Society for demonstrating God's special providence.

(1) General Providence and Hume's Essay

Hume's essay "of a Particular Providence and a Future State" is designed to show that the inference to a generally provident creator-designer from the "order" exhibited in the phenomena of nature is only speculative and no more certain than any other hypothetical account of natural order. Hume means by the "particular providence" of the title the specific and unique act of the creator in designing the apparent order observed in nature. He thus uses the phrase in the sense outlined above of "general providence" and not in the sense reserved for specific (or particular) acts of nature-transcending special providence.

Hume argues in the second part of the essay that the denial of the certainty of the general providence of God as the cause of nature has no effect on the conduct of society.[37] Whether the uneducated masses need an establishment religion to preserve the order of society is a much disputed question in the Enlightenment and Hume is anxious to refute

---

[35] Ernest C. Mossner, *The Life of David Hume,* 2nd ed. (Oxford, 1980), 590-1.

[36] *Ibid.,* 286.

[37] Hume, *An Enquiry Concerning the Human Understanding,* Section XI, "Of a Par-ticular Providence and a Future State," in *Enquiries Concerning Human Understanding and Concerning the Principles of Morals,* ed. L. A. Selby-Bigge, rev. P. H. Nidditch Oxford, 1975), 135 ff.

the claim for the necessity of establishment religion as a social policeman of the kind apparently envisioned by Stukeley who blames murder and thievery on the "discountenancing" of religion. But Hume's essay goes further and undermines the basic causal inference from the "order of work" to the "forethought of the workman." In reasoning from effects to causes, Hume argues that the inferred causes must be proportioned precisely to the observed effects.[38] But the "religious hypothesis" of a generally provident creator-designer is only one possible way among many for explaining observed phenomena, both physical and moral. If we insist that the cause of nature be suited precisely to the effects found in nature, then the only possible rational result is confusion and doubt.[39] By all means, Hume counsels, draw whichever of the possible inferences about the cause of nature you wish but recognize its dubious nature and allow freedom to others to draw different inferences, especially because such speculations have no effect on the morals of society. "But here," says Hume, "you ought to rest."[40]

In casting doubt on the inference of the design argument to a generally provident creator-designer, Hume attacks one of the fundamental arguments of the "first" Royal Society. Even more important, however, is the relationship between this familiar argument and the essay "Of Miracles" which attacks the corollary concept of a specially provident God who directly transgresses the regular course of nature through miracles.

(2) The Attack on Special Providence in the Essay "Of Miracles"

As in the *a posteriori* inference from effect to cause, so, too, in the case of miracles, "A wise man proportions his belief to the evidence."[41] The evidence for miracles is incompatible with the laws of nature as established by experience.[42]

In the first section, Hume concentrates on the conflict between each individual's experience of the laws of nature and a miracle. Although Hume considers causation rationally undemonstrable he does recognize a regularity of succession in practical human experience. Laws of nature, for Hume, are established because of universally firm and unalterable human experience of such a succession of events. A miracle, however, is by definition "the violation of the laws of nature."[43] Because a miracle

---

[38] "If the cause be known only by the effect, we never ought to ascribe it to any qualities, beyond what are precisely requisite to produce the effect." *Ibid.*, 136.

[39] In the face of such complicated subjects, Hume inquires, "Why torture your brain to justify the course of nature upon suppositions, which for aught you know, may be entirely imaginary, and of which there are to be found no traces in the course of nature?" *Ibid.*, 139.   [40] *Ibid.*

[41] Hume, *An Enquiry Concerning the Human Understanding,* Section X, "Of Miracles," 110.   [42] *Ibid.*, 112.

[43] *Ibid.*, 114. Cf. Philip P. Wiener, "The Peirce-Langley Correspondence and Peirce's Manuscript on Hume and the Laws of Nature," *Proceedings of the American Philosophical Society* XCI (1947), 201-228.

is a violation of that for which we have "a firm and unalterable" experience, the evidence for a miraculous event must be of a degree of strength which is impossible to obtain. The more miraculous an event appears to be, the more contrary to the normal sequential experience of universal natural law, and consequently, the less believable it is.

Hume acknowledges the possibility of apparent exceptions to natural law but argues, with the example of the subcontinental Indian's ignorance of the freezing of water in cold climates, that such "exceptions" are due only to limited experience. They are not really violations of the law of nature but result from a lack of experience of the regularity with which water freezes below a certain temperature.

To believe in a miracle requires evidence that is impossible to obtain because it runs counter to our unalterable experience to the contrary. And when one considers how open to deception and error are the historical testimonies of such prodigies, the "plain consequence" is "That no testimony be of such a kind, that its falsehood would be more miraculous, than the fact, which it endeavours to establish."[44]

In the second section of this essay, Hume examines the sorts of testimony upon which the credibility of miracles is founded to see if there are any testimonies which satisfy the criterion that their falsity would be a greater miracle than the miracle which the testimony purports to establish in the first place. Hume finds no examples where the falsity of such testimony is more miraculous than the event it is used to confirm, especially because none of the testimony originates with hardheaded, Enlightened Scotsmen. In the penultimate paragraph, Hume concludes with his famous direct reference to the miracle stories of the Bible:

I desire any one to lay his hand upon his heart, and after a serious consideration declare, whether he thinks that the falsehood of such a book, supported by such testimony, would be more extraordinary and miraculous than all the miracles it relates; which is, however, necessary to the measure of probability above established.[45]

What has heretofore been largely neglected in the voluminous discussion of the essay "Of Miracles" is the last paragraph. In this paragraph, Hume drops a bombshell which exposes the futility of the Newtonians who attempt to retain the Biblical God of special providence via the argument from fulfilled prophecies. Hume says, "What we have said of miracles may be applied, without any variation, to prophecies: and indeed, all prophecies are real miracles, and as such only, can be admitted as proofs of any revelation."[46]

---

[44] *Op. cit.,* footnote 41 above.
[45] *Ibid,.* 130.
[46] *Ibid.* Most of Hume's contemporaries fail to perceive the application of the attack on miracles to prophecies, most notably Dr. Johnson. See James E. Force, "Hume and Johnson on Prophecy: The Context of Hume's Essay 'Of Miracles'," *Journal of the History of Ideas* **43**, No. 3 (July-Sept., 1982), 463-75.

Hume is here pointing to the fact that the only sense of prophecy which signifies a specially provident deity is the ability of the prophet, empowered by God, to transcend the limits of his human nature and to foretell future events. In this sense, prophetic insight or ability transcends merely human predictions such as those made by scientists and soothsayers. To be truly significant of God's special providence, a prophet must derive his ability to see into the future from God. A prophecy, in this sense, must be, as Locke noted, a miraculous event which transgresses the ordinary course of natural law. The prophetic predictions of Old Testament prophets may be divided into two sub-categories: (1) those which interpreters claim already to have been fulfilled in history (historical prophecies); and (2) those which interpreters claim have not yet come to pass (future prophecies, e.g., the millennial prophecies of *Daniel* and the *Revelation of St. John.*)

William Whiston's primary contribution to a comprehensive, fully articulated Newtonianism is his extension of the empirical method of Newton and the Royal Society into the realm of interpreting prophetic predictions uttered by divinely inspired prophets. A scientific exegete can examine the genuine documents containing the prophetic prediction and the evidence from historical testimony for its completion or non-completion. Feigned hypotheses have no place in the science of Biblical interpretation where, as in the physical sciences, the experimental method must reign supreme. Whiston claims that the interpretation of the historical evidence from the Bible is simply another application of the method of Royal Society natural philosophers, of judges, and of physicians. As a result of this common-sense approach from "Matters of Fact and Experiment," Whiston believes that "genuine Christianity" is more firmly established.[47]

Regarding those "future" prophecies which remain unfulfilled in history, the Newtonian exegete does not have nearly the degree of certainty he has in interpreting the already completed "historical" prophetic predictions. Whiston states that the purpose of his 1707 Boyle Lectures is "to discourse of the ancient Predictions and Prophecies contain'd in Scripture . . . to shew the completion and fulfilling of them whose periods are already past." Whiston hints that this examination of the completed "historical" prophecies in his Boyle Lectures, entitled *The Accomplishment of Scripture Prophecies,* was first suggested to him by Isaac Newton.[48] Because Biblical interpreters are not themselves divinely inspired prophets miraculously empowered by God to foreknow the future, the completion

---

[47] Whiston, *A Supplement to the Literal Accomplishment of Scripture Prophecies* (London, 1725), 5-6.

[48] Whiston, *The Accomplishment of Scripture Prophecies, Being Eight Sermons Preach at the Cathedral Church of St. Paul, In the Year MDCCVII. At the Lecture Founded b Robert Boyle Esq.* (London, 1708), 6, and *Memoirs,* 1:98.

532   JAMES E. FORCE

of the as yet unfulfilled "future" prophecies exceeds the scope of their powers of exegesis.

Nevertheless, the scientific Biblical interpreter has justification, or as Whiston states, "good reasons," to expect "the completion of those other prophecies whose periods are not yet come."[49] Although Newton is extremely cautious, especially in his later years, in trying to predict the actual times and means for the accomplishment of "future" prophecies, with Whiston he has "good reasons" to hope that they will be completed:

There is already so much of Prophecy fulfilled, that as many will take pains in this study, may see sufficient instance of God's providence; but then the signal revolutions predicted by all the holy Prophets, will at once both turn men's eyes upon considering the predictions, and plainly interpret them. Till then we must content ourselves with interpreting what hath already been fulfilled.[50]

Viewed next to this aspect of the Newtonian context, it is now perhaps more evident why Hume's claim that his argument against miracles also applies to prophecies is not an idle, uncomplicated remark when it was first published in 1748 in his *Philosophical Essays concerning Human Understanding* (retitled by Hume in 1758 as *Enquiry concerning Human Understanding.*) The Newtonians were eager to promote the argument from prophecy because it seemingly evaded the tension between a strong conception of generally provident natural order and law *and* the specially provident power of the creator to break that law. While emphasizing the empirical and repeatable nature of the "science" of Biblical interpretation, most of the Newtonians (though not all) tended to ignore the fact that the essential nature of an Old Testament prophecy was viewed as necessarily miraculous and involved a break or suspension of the laws of nature which empowered a human being to foreknow the future. So long as the necessarily miraculous nature of prophecy was ignored, the tension between naturalism and supernaturalism, between Newton's God and Newton's physics, was evaded.

But Hume permits no such ambiguity or evasion. He understands that for a completed "historical" prophecy to be demonstrative of special divine providence, it must be miraculous, which renders it automatically unbelievable. Completed "historical" prophecies offer no resolution to the tension between the traditional, specially provident, Christian God and the concept of the rigid, unbreakable laws of nature established by general providence. If one understands them properly, then completed

---

[49] Whiston, *The Accomplishment of Scripture Prophecies*, 1. In addition to this work and the work cited in Note 47, Whiston has lists of completed "historical" prophecies, as well as a sprinkling of unfulfilled "future" prophecies in his *The Literal Accomplishment of Scripture Prophecies* (London, 1724), and the second volume of the second edition of his *Memoirs* which bears the subtitle *To which are added his Lectures on the late Remarkable Meteors and Earthquakes, and on the Future Restoration of the Jews.*

[50] Newton, *Observations Upon the Prophecies*, 252-53.

prophecies are like other miracles which violate natural law as established in the course of human experience. As such, fulfilled "historical" prophecies are simply too implausible to be believed.

Part 2 of the essay "Of Miracles" may profitably be read as the completion of Hume's case against the Newtonian Biblical interpreters. There, Hume discredits the historical evidence which exegetes utilize to establish either the occurrence of miracles or, what amounts to the same thing, the completion (or "accomplishment") of prophetic predictions. Hume would not have believed a word of Whiston's carefully compiled catalogs of fulfilled prophecies because the completions are invariably contained in the same historical document as the prophecies themselves and are not, therefore, trustworthy and because, precisely, these so-called fulfillments or completions *do* appeal to the vulgar, un-Enlightened, non-Scottish ancients.

At a single stroke, Hume, as a philosophical historian, does away with the "science" of Biblical interpretation.[51] As long as the Bible contains any miracle stories founded on human testimony and as long as it contains any stories of historically completed prophetic predictions beyond the capacity of scientific reason or of chance utterances to predict, it will be too implausible to be believed. For similar reasons, in the *Dialogues concerning Natural Religion,* Hume dismisses "future" proph-

---

[51] Antony Flew, in his "Parapsychology: Science or Pseudo-Science?", *Pacific Philosophical Quarterly* (1980), 100-14, states and illustrates why parapsychology ought to be classified as a pseudoscience and how Hume's argument against miracles applies to the data of parapsychological experimentation. Parapsychology is defined as the study of psi-phenomena which includes psi-kappa phenomena (psycho-kinesis, movement by the mind) and psi-gamma phenomena (clairvoyance, mind communicating to mind; telepathy, matter communicating to mind.) The most important aspect of psi-gamma phenomena, in the context of the present essay, is precognitive, psi-gamma phenomena. The subject of an experiment involving pre-cognitive, psi-gamma phenomena will receive or produce or derive information from outside (through clairvoyance or telepathy) normally referring only to the future. For example, Astrologers who claim to derive their advance information "from the stars" claim to be pre-cognitive paranormals. Hume's argument applies to pre-cognitive, psi-gamma phenomena because "any piece of work claiming to show that psi-phenomena have occurred is in effect a miracle story." Flew concludes that "This means that we have to interpret and assess the available evidence in light of all we know, or think we know, about what is probable or improbable, possible or impossible. But now . . . psi-phenomena are implicitly defined in terms of the violation of some of our most fundamental and best evidenced notions of contingent impossibility. So, even before any Humian allowance is made for the special corruptions afflicting this particular field, it would seem that our historical verdict will have to be, at best, an appropriately Scottish, and damping: 'Not proven'." (108.) The effect of Flew's analysis is to show that all stories of paranormal precognition—from the predictive utterances of soothsayers and astrologers to the predictions of the Old Testament Prophets—are undercut by Hume's argument. I am indebted to Professor Flew for this article and this insight. My point is that Hume understands that his argument applies at least to Biblical prophecies.

ecies as well as "historical" prophecies as simply beyond our human experience and, hence, capacity to know:

When we carry our speculations into the two eternities, before and after the present state of things; into the creation and formation of the universe; the existence and properties of spirits; the powers and operations of one universal spirit; omnipotent, omniscient, immutable, infinite, and incomprehensible: We must be far removed from the smallest tendency to scepticism not to be apprehensive that we have here got quite beyond the reach of our faculties.[52]

III. Conclusion—Hume is the only writer in the eighteenth century to mount careful critical attacks upon all the separate elements of the "first" Royal Society's elaborate synthesis of general and special providence. The deist Woolston attacked miracles.[53] The deist Collins attacked prophecies in a protracted controversy with Whiston. Wits and satirists such as Whitehead, Gay, Swift, and Walpole savaged the providentialist interpretation of such natural phenomena as comets, eclipses, and, especially, earthquakes[54] although none dared to challenge the design argument directly. Hume, too, is capable of devastatingly witty ridicule of the willingness on the part of the general public to accept providentialist explanations for natural events such as the London earthquakes of 1750. Hume satirizes such religious enthusiasm in a letter about the minor 1750 earthquakes to his friend, Dr. John Clephane:

I think the parsons have lately used the physicians very ill, for, in all the common terrors of mankind, you used commonly both to come in for a share of the profit: but in this new fear of earthquakes, they have left you out entirely, and have pretended alone to give prescriptions to the multitude. . . . I see only a Pastoral Letter of the Bishop of London where, indeed, he recommends certain pills, such as fasting, prayer, repentance, mortification, and other drugs, which are entirely to come from his own shop. And I think this is very unfair in him and you have great reason to be offended; for why might he not have added, that medicinal powders and potions would also have done service? The worst is, that you dare not revenge yourself in kind, by advising your patients to have

[52] Hume, *Dialogues Concerning Natural Religion*, ed. Norman Kemp Smith (Indianapolis, 1947), Part 1, 134-35.
[53] In this attack on miracles, Woolston actually does mention very briefly that prophecies are miraculous, i.e., that they cannot "be given forth by human Foresight. . . ." See *A Discourse on the Miracles of Our Savior, In View of the Present Controversy between Infidels and Apostates* (London, 1727), 15-6.
[54] For a brief account of the furore caused by the very slight London earth tremors in 1750, see G. S. Rousseau, "The London Earthquakes of 1750," *Journal of World History* 11, no. 3 (1968), 436-51. Recently Maxine Van de Wetering has traced the providentialist interpretation of earthquakes in the sermons of American Puritans in the first half of the seventeenth century in her article, "Moralizing in Puritan Natural Science: Mysteriousness in Earthquake Sermons," *Journal of the History of Ideas* 43, no. 3, (July-September, 1982), 417-38.

nothing to do with the parson; for you are sure he has a faster hold of them than you, and you may yourself be discharged on such an advice. You'll scarcely believe what I am going to tell you; but it is literally true. Millar had printed off some Months ago a new edition of certain philosophical Essays [i.e., the second edition of the *Philosophical Essays concerning Human Understanding*] but he tells me very gravely, that he has delay'd publishing because of the Earthquakes.[55]

Hume is the only writer, however, who combines such off-hand raillery with serious attacks on miracles, prophecies, and the inference of the design argument to a generally provident deity. Hume's familiar religious skepticism takes on a new dimension when viewed in the context of the efforts by certain members of the "first" Royal Society, especially by Newton and his followers, to balance general and special providence.

Hume's attack on prophecies not only rules out specially provident divine intervention in world history; it also secularizes history. Hume removes more than a specially provident deity when he points out that it exceeds the capacity of human beings to predict the future and that such miracles are, in principle, unbelievable. He also removes the anticipations of the future course of history in which the Newtonians of the "first" era of the Royal Society so ardently believe. Of Newton's own attempt to interpret "historical" prophecies and to give us hope for the completion of those yet unfilfilled in his *Observations Upon the Prophecies of Daniel and the Apocalypse of St. John,* Hume, the Newton of the mind, notes that we "never should pronounce the folly of an individual, from his admitting popular errors, consecrated by the appearance of religion."[56]

When seen in the context of the apologetic concerns of the members of the "first" Royal Society, the sweeping nature of Hume's rejection of their synthesis of general and special providence is striking. Hume disconnects the frame of nature from a generally provident creator-designer and then eliminates any continuous, specially provident divine participation in the external world. Simultaneously, he eliminates the prophetic past and the prophetic future. In his coordinated attack on all the facets of the apologetic position of the "first" Royal Society, Hume far exceeds the casual ridicule of the scoffing dilettantes and the limited criticism of the deists. By 1750, few members within the "second" era of the Royal Society couple scientific research into physical phenomena with religious apologetics.

When viewed in this context, we see Hume as himself a prophet of our own secular era. It is his vision of our modern secular world in which

[55] Hume to Dr. John Clephane, April, 1750, in *The Letters of David Hume,* ed. J. Y. T. Greig, 2 vols. (Oxford, 1932), I, 141.
[56] Hume, *The History of England, from the Invasion of Julius Caesar to the Revolution in 1688,* 8 vols., (London, 1782), VI, 196-97.

humanity is disconnected from God and God is disconnected from human history which constitutes Hume's uniqueness.[57]

University of Kentucky

[57] I have incurred many debts to individuals and to institutions in the course of preparing this article. I wish to thank members of the Hume Society who sat through an earlier version of this paper at the 1981 Dublin meeting, especially David Fate Norton and Richard H. Popkin. Material support over the period when this article was written was provided by, in part, The NEH Summer Stipend, the University of Kentucky Faculty Research Grant, the University of Kentucky Summer Research Fellowship, and the William Andrews Clark Memorial Library Short-Term Fellowship. Professor Simon Varey of the University of Utrecht provided many helpful criticisms as did the referees for this journal.

PART THREE

LOCKE AND SCIENCE

Chapter XVI

LOCKE'S REJECTION OF HYPOTHESES ABOUT SUB-MICROSCOPIC EVENTS

By R. M. Yost, Jr.

In this essay I shall try to establish the proposition that: unlike many scientists and philosophers of the seventeenth century, Locke did not believe that the employment of hypotheses about sub-microscopic events would accelerate the acquisition of empirical knowledge.

In order to avoid certain easy misconstructions of this statement, I shall have to say a word or two about the meanings of the terms " sub-microscopic " and " empirical knowledge." Roughly speaking, " sub-microscopic " will be used as an abbreviation of the phrase " so small as to be imperceptible by the most powerful known instruments." So far as terrestrial events are concerned, it is an antonym of " observable," which will be used as an abbreviation of the phrase " perceptible with some known instrument or with the naked eye." Thus, according to these rough definitions, the activities of molecules or atoms are examples of sub-microscopic processes, whereas the activities of the protozoa in a drop of water or of football players on a playing field are examples of observable processes. By " empirical knowledge " I do not mean propositions about the world which are known with theoretical certainty. The term will be used to denote well-founded propositions which describe how kinds of observable objects behave under various circumstances. For example: " After being in the presence of a loadstone, a piece of iron will acquire magnetic powers," " Sound will not travel in a vacuum," " Aqua fortis dissolves silver but not gold," " A cold regimen will recover a smallpox patient faster than a hot regimen." A piece of empirical knowledge is usually a recipe which tells us how to induce a certain property on some specified kind of thing. Empirical knowledge is not what Locke called " Knowledge " in the fourth book of his *Essay Concerning Human Understanding;* for in that place " Knowledge " referred only to propositions which are known with theoretical certainty.

The argument for the proposition stated above will fall into two parts. *Part I* will contain an explanation of the manner in which hypotheses about sub-microscopic events were expected, in the seventeenth century, to speed the acquisition of empirical knowledge. In *Part II* it will be shown that there are good grounds for believing that Locke did not share this expectation.

Part I

The belief in the fruitfulness of hypotheses about sub-microscopic events contained the following four important points: (1) most, if not all, observable events are dependent upon sub-microscopic events; (2) if one could discover the nature of sub-microscopic events, one could discover the powers of things faster than one could by merely looking for brute correlations among observable events; (3) the fact that an event is sub-microscopic does not prevent our knowledge of it from helping us to control observable events; and (4) there were grounds for supposing that the nature of sub-microscopic events are discoverable. I shall now reconstruct, as plainly and briefly as I can, a meaning which many seventeenth-century scientists and philosophers would attach to these four statements.

(1) In order to explain the first point, let us consider, as an example, the softening of egg-shell in vinegar. Before placing egg-shell in vinegar, one can feel the hardness and rigidity of the shell; and after it has been in vinegar for some time, one can feel its softness and flexibility. One can also see and taste the vinegar. The vinegar is said to cause the egg-shell to become soft. Presumably, this correlation between vinegar and the softening of egg-shell was simply stumbled upon, and was regarded for a long time as a brute fact, not as a special case of some other correlation or law. But science has generally tried to show that seemingly independent, irreducible laws are special cases of a single law which was, for one reason or another, looked upon as more " evident," " rational," " intelligible," etc. In the seventeenth century the most advanced investigators considered the laws of mechanics to be the most " evident," " rational," etc. And thus it was that although the directly observable properties of egg-shell and vinegar are clearly not connected by mechanical laws, these investigators felt that somehow they nevertheless are.

They persuaded themselves that such a connection is possible in the following way. When the egg-shell is at a " normal " distance from the eye, say at arm's length, its surface appears to be continuous. When the egg-shell is brought as close as the eye can focus, it has a new appearance, revealing bumps and pores. If a microscope is used, the egg-shell has still another appearance, containing far more differentiations. It was inferred that as more powerful microscopes were invented, one could become aware of even more complex and highly organized appearances. Generally, it was believed that for each natural object there is a series of appearances, graded according to increasing complexity; and that, within a given series, the number of appearances of which one could become aware depends upon the contemporary skill at making optical instruments.[1]   To say, at a given time, that a series has imperceptible appearances is to say, in part, that one could become aware of more and more highly differentiated appearances as one acquired better and better instruments.   To be sure, some objects, such as filtered vinegar, did not yield more complex appearances with the application of seventeenth-century microscopes; but this could be explained by saying that the appearances of the vinegar become complex more slowly than those of the egg-shell series.

At this point a hypothesis was made concerning certain very remote, imperceptible, and highly complex appearances of the egg-shell and vinegar.   It was supposed that when we observe the action of vinegar on egg-shell at a normal distance, we could, if we had sufficiently powerful microscopes, notice an appearance of interaction and meshing which resembles the sort of appearance, noticeable with the naked eye, which we ordinarily call " the appearance of an operating mechanism." The principles of mechanics were first suggested and tested by normal appearances, e.g., Galileo's experiments.   And although most normal changes do not resemble mechanical changes, it was supposed that all sub-microscopic changes do, i.e., obey the principles found to hold in appearances of observable mechanical changes.[2]

[1] The series is generated by what Professor H. H. Price called the Principle of Specific Detail in his *Perception*, p. 225.

[2] There is an abundance of passages where this supposition was asserted or implied.   Since it is not practicable to list them all, I shall mention only some of the more striking ones.   Descartes *Oeuvres,* ed. Adam and Tannery (Paris, 1897–1910), IX, *Principes,* 319–322.   Glanvill, *The Vanity of Dogmatizing,* reproduced from the edition of 1661 (New York, 1931), 5ff.   Boyle, *Works,* ed. Thomas Birch (London, 1772), II, 191f.; III, 13 and 29ff.; IV, 71ff.; V, 2.   Newton, letter to Boyle in Sir David Brewster's *Memoirs* (London, 1855), I, 414ff. (also printed in *Boyle,* I, cxii–cxvii); and *Opticks,* 4th ed. (London, 1730; reprinted 1931), 394f.   Since each of these passages is fairly long, I shall quote only a part of one of them, namely, *Boyle,* IV, 71ff.

Boyle said there that " both the mechanical affections of matter are to be found, and the laws of motion take place, not only in the great masses, and the middle sized lumps, but in the smallest fragments of matter; and a lesser portion of it being as well a body as a greater, must, as necessarily as it, have its determinate bulk and figure: and he, that looks upon sand in a good microscope, will easily perceive, that each minute grain of it has as well its own size and shape, as a rock or mountain. . . . And though nature . . . be wont to work with much finer materials, and employ more curious contrivances than art, (whence the structure even of the rarest watch is incomparably inferior to that of a human body;) yet an artist

Moreover, it was supposed that in the series of appearances belonging to an object, if the sub-microscopic appearances change, then all the less complex appearances of the series also change.[3]

The connection between changes of appearances within the same series is, of course, not *directly* mechanical. No one ever supposed that an element in an appearance of one level "impinges" upon an element in an appearance of another level.[4] Nevertheless, the con-

---

himself, according to the quantity of the matter he employs, the exigency of the design he undertakes, and bigness and shape of the instruments he makes use of, is able to make pieces of work of the same nature or kind of extremely differing bulk, where yet the like, though not equal art and contrivance, and oftentimes motion too, may be observed. . . . And therefore to say, that though in natural bodies, whose bulk is manifest and their structure visible, the mechanical principles may be usefully admitted, that are not to be extended to such portions of matter, whose parts and texture are invisible; may perhaps look to some, as if a man should allow, that the laws of mechanism may take place in a town clock, but cannot in a pocket-watch. . . . the mechanical philosopher being satisfied, that one part of matter can act upon another but by virtue of local motion, or the effects and consequences of local motion, he considers, that as if the proposed agent be not intelligible and physical, it can never physically explain the phaenomena; so, if it be intelligible and physical, it will be reducible to matter."

[3] Many writers expressed or implied this supposition, e.g., Descartes, *Oeuvres*, IX, *Principes*, 315f. But Boyle's expressions of it were perhaps the clearest and most detailed. In many places he remarked on the fact that changes in the close-range appearances of a thing can permanently change its long-range appearances. For example, he noted that "sometimes a slight and almost momentary mechanical change will seem to over-rule nature, and introduce into a body the quite opposite quality to that she had given it: as when a piece of black horn is, only by being thin scraped with the edge of a knife, or a piece of glass, reduced to permanently white shavings" (*Boyle*, IV, 234. See also *Boyle*, III, 67). And he extended this principle to sub-microscopic appearances. Speaking specifically, he said in one place, "since we see that in the same parcel of metalline matter which a little before was true and pure gold, by having some few of its parts withdrawn and the rest transposed or otherwise altered in their structure . . . or by both these ways together, the form of gold, of that peculiar modification which made it yellow, indissoluble in aqua fortis, &c. is abolished; and from the new texture of the same matter there arises that new form or convention of accidents, from which we call a metal silver " (*Boyle*, III, 97). Speaking generally, he said, "when it happens that there is a strict connexion betwixt that modification of matter which is requisite to exhibit one phaenomenon, and that from which another will necessarily follow; in such case we may not only grant, but teach, that he, who by a change of its texture gives a portion of matter the former modification, does likewise qualify it by the same change to exhibit the congruous phaenomenon; though one would not perchance suspect them to have any such dependence upon one another " (*Boyle*, III, 294).

[4] This statement does not assert that nobody in the seventeenth century held a version of the causal theory of perception. For views of this sort were held by Descartes, Boyle, Locke, and Newton. But for the sake of simplicity, I have de-

ections between different levels of appearances were believed to be
egular and orderly rather than capricious.   For example, everyone
s confident that whenever, at close range, individual stalks of wheat
ppear to oscillate in a breeze, the whole wheat field, from a distance,
vill appear to be traversed by wave trains.

(2) I now pass to the second point.   If one had a plan, or blueprint, of the sub-microscopic structure of an elementary bit of egg-
shell, and if one had similar blueprints of elementary bits of many
ther substances, $S_1, S_2, \ldots$, then, by means of mechanical principles,
ne would be able to predict how the structure of an elementary bit
f egg-shell and that of an elementary bit of any other substance S_k
vould alter one another when the two bits come in contact; and, by
means of the non-mechanical correlations between appearances at
lifferent levels, one would be able to tell how egg-shell and S_k would
ppear to the normal eye after their sub-microscopic structures had
been altered.   This situation may be illustrated in the following way.
Suppose that a visitor from Mars were to observe, always from a dis-
ance, the operations of an all-purpose vacuum cleaner.   Until some-
body began to use the vacuum cleaner, the man from Mars would
aave no way of telling what its powers are.   However, as soon as it
vas used to suck up dust, the Martian would know that the ability
o suck up dust is one of its powers.   And as soon as it was used to
pray paint, the Martian would know another of its powers.   In this
vay, as circumstances permitted, he would *gradually* learn that it can
suck up dust, spray fluids, sand-blast, drill holes, polish surfaces, etc.
But if he were supplied with a blueprint of the machine and a cata-
ogue of its attachments, and if he knew certain basic physical principles, he could compute its powers immediately.   He could deduce
hem " in sheaves " instead of slowly discovering them one by one.
And assuming that he knows how the appearances of things vary with
heir distance from an observer, he could tell, without ever examining
he machine at close range, how its operations would appear from a
distance.[5]

---

iberately avoided any reference to this, or any other, theory of perception.   Moreover, I have tried to avoid committing myself to any metaphysical view, such as
phenomenalism or realism, or imputing such a view to any seventeenth-century
writer.   My use of the word "appearance" is intended to be entirely neutral with
respect to any of these points of view.   I think this usage is legitimate, since all
theories of perception must admit and attempt to account for the known facts
about the sensible appearances of things.

[5] This point is implied in Boyle's penetrating analysis of the nature of a power
or dispositional property, in which he selects as a paradigm the power of a key to

(3) The third point raises the question, If we succeeded in discovering the kinds of events that occur in the sub-microscopic world, would this knowledge enable us to control them? This problem arises because the only appearances we can alter directly by manipulation are observable ones. Even if the sub-microscopic states of things were known, they could not be controlled, unless there were some principles which described how they are affected by alterations of observable appearances. Without such principles, a knowledge of sub-microscopic events would be like a knowledge of astronomy, in that although it might allow us to predict certain observable events, it would not allow us to control them. Yet many seventeenth-century scientists agreed that one of the primary values of science is the power it gives us to control everyday events.[6]

---

open a lock. See *Boyle*, III, 18ff. But the point is stated more succinctly by Hooke and Huygens. Hooke said that from a knowledge of sub-microscopic events " there may arise many admirable advantages, towards the increase of the Operative, and the Mechanick Knowledge, to which the Age seems so much inclined, because we may perhaps be inabled to discern all the secret workings of Nature, almost in the same manner as we do those that are the productions of Art, and are manag'd by Wheels, and Engines, and Springs, that were devised by humane Wit " (*Micrographia* [London, 1665], Preface). The same view is expressed in Hooke's *The Posthumous Works of Robert Hooke*, ed. Richard Waller (London, 1705), 47. In his *Treatise on Light*, Huygens formulated many hypotheses about sub-microscopic events in order to explain the behavior of light. But he was not content merely to *explain;* in the preface to that work he intimates that " one can imagine and foresee new phenomena which ought to follow from the hypotheses " and that " the fact corresponds with our prevision " (*Treatise on Light* [1690], tr. Sylvanus P. Thomson [London, 1912], vii). See also Glanvill, *Vanity of Dogmatizing*, 179f.

[6] Even Descartes explicitly adopted this idea; in his *Principes* he said: " je croiray auoir assez fait, si *les causes* que j'ay expliquées sont *telles que tous les effets qu'elles peuuent produire se trouuent* semblables à ceux que nous voyons dans le monde, *sans m'enquerir si c'est par elles ou par d'autres qu'ils sont produits.* Mesme je croy qu'il est aussi vtile pour la vie, *de connoistre des causes ainsi imaginées, que si on auoit la connoissance des vrayes:* car la Medecine, Les Mechaniques, & generalement tous les arts à quoy la connoissance de la Physique peut seruir, n'ont pour fin que *d'appliquer tellement* quelques corps sensibles *les vns aux autres, que, par la suite des causes naturelles, quelques effets sensibles soient produits; ce que nous ferons tout aussi bien, en considerant la suite de quelques causes ainsi imaginées, bien que fausses, que si elle estoient les vrayes, puis que cette suite est supposée semblable, en ce qui regarde les effets sensibles* " (*Oeuvres*, IX, *Principes*, 322; see also IX, *Principes*, 123). Boyle's expressions of this idea are too numerous to mention. By way of example, however, it may be pointed out that in the *Sceptical Chymist* (*Boyle*, I) he repeatedly rejected the speculations and explanations of the spagyrists and hermetics because they did not tell him precisely what to do in order to induce a given property on a given kind of object. He even wrote an essay entitled *The Usefulness of Experimental Philosophy* (*Boyle*, III). It remained for

Some such principles were presupposed in a good deal of seventeenth-century science. The following principle was perhaps the most widely used. It was assumed that if a normal observable appearance is characterized by pushing or impact, then all the closer range appearances of the series to which it belongs, including the imperceptible ones, will also be characterized by pushing or impact. Thus, it was believed that whenever one observes a spoon pushing sugar around in a cup of tea, one could, if a sufficiently powerful optical instrument were applied, observe another case of pushing, namely, the pushing of sub-microscopic bits of sugar by sub-microscopic bits of spoon. This principle indicated what one could do, guided by observable appearances, in order to stir up the elementary, sub-microscopic bits of two substances and to bring them into contact with one another. If the sub-microscopic mechanisms of two substances, *e.g.*, egg-shell and vinegar, will engage, or mesh, under normal conditions, then in order to make them mesh, one has only to produce the observable situation that would ordinarily be described as stirring egg-shell around in vinegar.

If this principle about the appearances of pushing and impact had been explicitly considered, it would probably have been regarded as self-evident. But its analogues for color, smell, and so forth, which *were* explicitly considered, were believed to be false. For example, if one could change the color of a dye from violet to red, it was not believed that there was any change of color in the corresponding sub-microscopic events. However, many held that although sub-microscopic events are not characterized by hotness, yet by heating a substance, guided by observable appearances, the velocity of its elementary, sub-microscopic bits could be increased. And sometimes, it was held that if an observable appearance is of the sort we should call " chemical," *e.g.*, an appearance of dissolution or combustion, then all the closer range appearances of the series to which it belongs would be of this sort.[7]

Hooke to give the liveliest expression of the idea. He said: " The Business of Philosophy is to find out a perfect Knowledge of the Natures and Properties of Bodies, and of the Causes of Natural Productions, and this Knowledge is not barely acquir'd for it self, but in order to the inabling a Man to understand how by the joyning of fit Agents to Patients according to the Order, Laws, Times, and Methods of Nature, he may be able to produce and bring to pass such Effects, as may very much conduce to his well being in this World, both for *satisfying his Desires,* and the relieving of his *Necessities* " (*Post. Wks.,* p. 3).

[7] Boyle sometimes seemed to hold this view, although he generally held that the ultimate sub-microscopic events are purely mechanical. For example, he suggested

We have seen that if one knew sub-microscopic mechanisms, and had computed the powers of things from them, one could, by assuming the principle about pushing and impact, achieve a high degree of control over his everyday world. But many substances do not react under normal conditions, or under any circumstances known in the seventeenth century. The method of making such substances react appeared to require far more refined techniques and principles than the rough and ready practice of mixing or heating them. This difficulty can be seen more clearly, perhaps, by considering the following hypothetical case. Suppose that one knew the principles of mechanics, the sub-microscopic mechanisms of egg-shell and of a certain acid, and some principles permitting one to infer the observable appearances of egg-shell and the acid from their sub-microscopic states. Suppose further that from this information one could deduce that: (i) under normal conditions the two mechanisms will not mesh, (ii) they would mesh if the mechanism of the acid were adjusted in a certain way, and (iii) as a result of meshing, the egg-shell's observable properties of hardness and rigidity would be replaced by softness and flexibility.   Then if, on some occasion, one observed egg-shell to turn soft and flexible in the presence of this acid, one might infer that the sub-microscopic mechanism of the acid somehow or other had been suitably adjusted. One would thus understand why events of this kind occur. But one would not be able to control them until one could bring about or prevent the necessary adjustment by one's own actions.

In this case, the task is to adjust the mechanisms of all the elementary bits contained in a sizable quantity—a quart, say—of this acid. But in other cases, such as biological ones, the task might be to adjust a single sub-microscopic mechanism. It was held that a slight adjustment to the sub-microscopic mechanism of an organ or of a seed would cure a disease or alter the growth-pattern of a plant.

But, generally speaking, no principle was known that would indicate how one could adjust at pleasure the mechanism of an elementary, sub-microscopic bit. Yet many thought that some day such principles might be discovered and that they would prove to be of tremendous advantage. They would make the difference between an

that since spirit of hartshorn can be observed to dissolve mucus, it will dissolve the sub-microscopic bits of mucus which, he believed, sometimes clog certain sub-microscopic conduits and strainers in the human body and thereby cause disease. See *Boyle*, II, 192.

ability to stir up a barrelful of clocks with a pole and an ability to set
the alarms of the clocks for 6:00 a.m.[8]

(4) There were two main grounds for the widespread optimism
that the nature of sub-microscopic events would eventually be discovered. One was the rapid improvement of optical instruments.[9]
The other was the belief that the existence and nature of insensible
causes could be inferred from the existence and nature of sensible
effects. To take a very simple and ancient example. If one throws
a large handful of gravel at a small sail, it will belly and tug at its
lines. But if one sees a sail belly and tug at its lines, and sees no
gravel, one infers that something like small, imperceptible gravel is
striking the sail.[10]

[8] It was often *conjectured*, however, that certain observable activities are correlated with certain adjustments of sub-microscopic corpuscles, and that whenever
these adjustments occur, the corpuscles acquire powers which they did not have
before. Boyle, for example, thought that there are some bodies whose non-corrosive
sub-microscopic corpuscles can be so adjusted that they will become corrosive. If
one were to act in such a way that these bodies appear to be immersed in a flame,
then, Boyle conjectured, the sub-microscopic corpuscles of the fire would cause the
sub-microscopic corpuscles of the bodies to " rub one another into the figure of little
sharp blades," or to split " some solid parts into sharp or cutting corpuscles," or to
unsheath some parts which had been sharp all along, thereby making them corrosive
(*Boyle*, IV, 315f.). See also *Boyle*, I, 582.

[9] In the preface to his *Micrographia*, Hooke said: " It seems not improbable,
but that by these helps [*i.e.*, improved optical instruments] the subtilty of the
composition of Bodies, the structure of their parts, the various texture of their
matter, the instruments and manner of their inward motions, and all the other
possible appearances of things, may come to be more fully discovered." See also
his *Post. Wks.*, pp. 15ff. And in his *Opticks*, Newton seemed confident that " it is
not impossible but that Microscopes may at length be improved to the discovery
of the Particles of Bodies on which their Colours depend, if they are not already in
some measure arrived to that degree of perfection. For if those Instruments are
or can be so far improved as with sufficient distinctness to represent Objects five or
six hundred times bigger than at a Foot distance they appear to our Naked Eyes,
I should hope that we might be able to discover some of the greatest of those Corpuscles. And by one that would magnify three or four thousand times perhaps
they might all be discover'd, but those which produce blackness " (261).

[10] Descartes: " en mesme façon qu'*vn horologier* . . . , en voyant *vne montre
qu'il n'a point faite*, peut ordinairement juger, de quelques vnes de ses parties qu'il
regarde, quelles sont toutes les autres qu'il ne voit pas: ainsi, en considerant les
effets & les parties sensibles des corps naturels, j'ay tasché de connoistre quelles
doiuent estre celles de leurs parties qui sont insensibles " (*Oeuvres*, IX, *Principes*,
322). Hooke: " The Internal Motions also of Bodies may be discover'd by various

This completes the account of those ideas which, I believe, made it appear plausible to many seventeenth-century scientists that one could discover the powers of natural bodies more quickly by making judicious hypotheses about sub-microscopic events than by merely looking for correlations among observable events.

Part II

In *Part II* I shall try to show that Locke had very little, if any, enthusiasm for the program of investigation explained in *Part I*. We shall find, I think, that he would assent to the first three points of the program, but would reject the fourth.

Before going on to consider his views on each of these points, it will be well to set down here a few prefatory remarks. Unhappily, the evidence for the thesis of this Part does not constitute a crisp, absolutely conclusive case. There are at least two reasons for this. First, Locke never wrote a treatise or even a chapter that was devoted exclusively to the methods of empirical science. Hence, the evidence for my thesis must consist of *obiter dicta*. Secondly, he often used words in ways that were vague, ambiguous, or too general. One might be inclined to say here that all this would be quite understandable if Locke had never thought very much about the methods of science; and if he had not, then there would not be much point in trying to discover his opinions on the subject. But in point of fact, this was one of his main interests throughout most of his life. He was very well acquainted with the science and scientists of his time, and he carried out several investigations himself. It is therefore likely, I think, that he thought a good deal about the methods of empirical science and had well-considered opinions concerning them. And since, in addition, his opinions were highly respected by many of the best scientists of his day, it is of some interest to see that he did

Effects, such as those of Fermentation, Heat, Corruption, Generation, Growth, Decay, Dissolution, Coagulation, and the like, from the accurate Observation of divers of which compared with several other Circumstances, may be very well collected the Degree, Nature and Manner of Internal Motions " (*Post. Wks.*, 15). However, on p. 61 of this work Hooke recognized that the chain of inferences would often have to be very long and intricate; and although he promised to devise a method of constructing them, there is not, according to Waller (*Post. Wks.*, p. 7 and p. 65), any record of his having done so. Newton thought that " the bigness of the component parts of natural Bodies may be conjectured by their Colours "; and, dispensing with *general* descriptions, he made the highly *specific* statement that the diameter of a corpuscle having the same density as glass and reflecting " green of the third Order " is " 16¼/10000 parts of an Inch " (*Opticks*, 255).

not share their enthusiasm for the method of investigation explained in *Part I.* I turn now to an account of Locke's views on each of the four points described in that Part.

(1) Locke believed that most, if not all, observable events are dependent upon sub-microscopic events. More exactly, he believed that each set of observable properties connoted by a species-name is correlated with a certain specific kind of sub-microscopic corpuscular mechanism.

There are many passages in Locke's works which assert or imply this view. The following are two fair samples. With regard to a specific case he said: " supposing the nominal essence of gold to be a body of such a peculiar colour and weight, with malleability and fusibility, the real essence is that constitution of the parts of matter on which these qualities and their union depend; and it is also the foundation of its solubility in *aqua regia* and other properties, accompanying that complex idea." [11] Speaking generally, he said: " *insensible corpuscles* . . . [are] the active parts of matter, and the great instruments of nature, on which depend not only all their secondary qualities, but also most of their natural operations." [12] For Locke this implied the statement that for every appearance of an observable change, we could, with sufficiently powerful instruments, become aware of an appearance of a correlated sub-microscopic *mechanical* change. In fact, the notion of the series of appearances associated with an object was virtually explicit in Locke's mind. His man with the adjustable " microscopical eyes " would become acquainted with all the members of such a series if he were to look at an object and run the controls of the eyes through the full range of adjustments. In Locke's words:

For how much would that man exceed all others in knowledge, who had but the faculty so to alter the structure of his eyes, that one sense, as to make it capable of all the several degrees of vision which the assistance of glasses (casually at first lighted on) has taught us to conceive? What wonders would he discover, who could so fit his eyes to all sorts of objects, as to see when he pleased the figure and motion of the minute particles in the blood, and other juices of animals, as distinctly as he does, at other times, the shape and motion of the animals themselves? [13]

[11] *Essay Concerning Human Understanding*, Book III, chapter 6, paragraph 6. All references to the *Essay* apply to A. C. Fraser's edition, and each of them will be indicated by means of three numbers, designating respectively the proper Book, chapter, and paragraph.

[12] IV.3.25.   [13] II.23.13.

And again:

Had we senses acute enough to discern the minute particles of bodies, and the real constitution on which their sensible qualities depend, I doubt not but they would produce quite different ideas in us: and that which is now the yellow colour of gold, would then disappear, and instead of it we should see an admirable texture of parts of a certain size and figure.[14]

(2) Locke also believed that *if* one had a knowledge of the laws of mechanics (or physics), the correlations between sub-microscopic and observable appearances, and the blueprints of the specific sub-microscopic engines corresponding to observable species, one could then compute both the observable and sub-microscopic powers of natural bodies, *i.e.*, one could "grasp at a time whole sheaves, and in bundles comprehend the nature and properties of whole species together."[15] This view is expressed in the following two familiar passages:

Did we know the mechanical affections of the particles of rhubarb, hemlock, opium, and a man, as a watchmaker does those of a watch, whereby it performs its operations; and of a file, which by rubbing on them will alter the figure of any of the wheels; we should be able to tell beforehand that rhubarb will purge, hemlock kill, and opium make a man sleep: as well as a watchmaker can, that a little piece of paper laid on the balance will keep the watch from going till it be removed; or that, some small part of it being rubbed by a file, the machine would quite lose its motion, and the watch go no more. The dissolving of silver in *aqua fortis*, and gold in *aqua regia*, and not *vice versa*, would be then perhaps no more difficult to know than it is to a smith to understand why the turning of one key will open a lock, and not the turning of another.[16]

Could we begin at the other end, and discover what it was wherein that colour consisted, what made a body lighter or heavier, what texture of parts made it malleable, fusible, and fixed, and fit to be dissolved in this sort of liquor, and not in another;—if, I say, we had such an idea as this of bodies, and could perceive wherein all sensible qualities originally consist, and how they are produced; we might frame such abstract ideas of them as would furnish us with matter of more general knowledge.[17]

(3) Like Boyle, Hooke, *et al.*, Locke attached very great importance to the enlargement of human control over nature.[18] In order

---

[14] II.23.11. See also III.6.3.   [15] IV.12.12.

[16] IV.3.25.   [17] IV.6.10. See also IV.6.11.

[18] Expressions of this valuation can be found in many of Locke's writings. See, for instance, IV.12.11. Earlier expressions, dated 1677 and 1669, can be found, respectively, in Lord King's *Life of John Locke* (London, 1830), I, 163f., and in

to achieve control over nature, one must know how each kind of objects will change when subjected to various conditions. And so far as human beings are concerned, a kind of objects is determined solely by their observable appearances.[19] Locke asserted over and over again that it is precisely this kind of information—although this kind of information can never be certain, and therefore can never be " Knowledge " in Locke's stricter sense—which people ought to seek when they are inquiring into the powers of natural objects.[20] Finally, he said that a knowledge of sub-microscopic events, by whatever means it may have been obtained, will do us no good at all if it cannot be used to help us in our business with objects as they appear to us in everyday life.[21] Such a knowledge would do us good only if it enabled us to avoid dangers, remove unpleasant situations, and produce pleasant ones.

Locke evidently did admit that in some simple cases one could act in such a way as to produce certain desired sub-microscopic states. For example, by rubbing two sticks together one could increase the velocities of the sub-microscopic corpuscles of the sticks, and as a result the temperature of the sticks, which is a macroscopic quality, would increase.[22] But there are exceedingly few places where he deliberately considered the possibilities of interfering with sub-microscopic mechanisms so as to produce desired observable qualities. The reason for this is, I think, that he generally denied the possibility of discovering, either certainly or probably, the *specific* sub-microscopic mechanisms that correspond to observable species. We turn now to this point.

(4) The evidence that Locke denied this possibility is of two sorts: a) direct and b) indirect. The direct evidence consists of (i) statements which assert that we can never " see " sub-microscopic mechanisms, and (ii) statements which assert that their specific natures can never be inferred with a high degree of probability, *i.e.,* reliably guessed at, from observable phenomena. The indirect evidence consists of statements which assert the proper way to conduct empirical research and which he would not have written down if he had believed that we could reliably infer the nature of sub-microscopic mechanisms from observable phenomena.

H. R. Fox Bourne's *Life of John Locke* (London, 1876), I, 223–226. Fox Bourne asserts that Locke's *primary* interest in philosophy and science was utilitarian; see Fox Bourne's *Life*, I, 360 and II, 54. The same opinion is asserted by R. I. Aaron in his *John Locke* (Oxford, 1937), 312f.

[19] This is one of the principal theses of Book III of the *Essay*.

[20] *E.g.:* IV.3.9 and IV.3.16.   [21] II.23.12.   [22] IV.16.12.

a) I shall consider the direct evidence first.

(i) Although Locke was aware of the advances that had been made in microscopy,[23] he apparently did not think that one could ever see, more or less directly, the specific corpuscular mechanisms corresponding to observable species. This belief is expressed, I think, by his frequent statements that our faculties are not suited to perceiving the "real constitutions" of things. The following statements are examples.

We having but some few superficial ideas of things, discovered to us only by the senses from without, or by the mind, reflecting on what it experiments in itself within, have no knowledge beyond that, much less of the internal constitution, and true nature of things, being destitute of faculties to attain it.[24]

Since our faculties are not fitted to penetrate into the internal fabric and real essence of bodies; but yet plainly discover to us the being of a God, and the knowledge of ourselves, enough to lead us into a full and clear discovery of our duty and great concernment; it will become us, as rational creatures, to employ those faculties we have about what they are most adapted to, and follow the direction of nature, where it seems to point us out the way.[25]

It is unlikely that repeated statements of this sort were intended to assert nothing but the obvious fact that the naked eye does not see corpuscular mechanisms when it looks at a glass of water, a gold ring, and so on. I think they were intended to assert that corpuscular mechanisms would never be " seen " with an instrument.

(ii) I do not wish to assert that, in Locke's opinion, one could make no probable inferences at all from observed to sub-microscopic events. I wish to assert only that, in his opinion, the propositions inferred would never be specific enough to allow us to compute the powers of things. As an illustration, let us consider the case of a general who is charged with defending a wooded area. Suppose his scouts give him some initial reports from which he can infer that a large body of enemy troops is approaching under concealment of the forest. But this inferred proposition is very general; it is not specific enough to enable him to estimate the powers of the approaching force. As more reports come in, he is able to infer more specific propositions. It may be that his data become so complete that he is able to infer with a high degree of reliability and exactness the different kinds of

---

[23] II.23.11, II.23.12, and II.23.26. See also the passages in his *Journal* which indicate his familiarity with the work of Leeuwenhoek and Swammerdam (King's *Life*, I, 307ff.).   [24] II.23.32.   [25] IV.12.11.

units, their strengths, the manner in which they are deployed, their equipment, and their method of supply. At this point, he can infer with a high degree of probability precisely what the enemy is capable of doing, and precisely how he can dispose and apply his defending forces so as to thwart, repulse, and destroy the enemy. In short, he can confidently commit his forces to an engagement. Locke would say that our inferences about sub-microscopic mechanisms correspond only to the inference which the general would base upon the initial reports of his scouts. He thought one could infer *something* about sub-microscopic mechanisms, but not enough to help us in making discoveries.

Sub-microscopic mechanisms, he said:

coming not within the scrutiny of human senses, cannot be examined by them, or be attested by anybody; and therefore can appear more or less probable, only as they more or less agree to truths that are established in our minds, and as they hold proportion to other parts of our knowledge and observation. *Analogy* in these matters is the only help we have, and it is from that alone we draw all our grounds of probability. Thus, observing that the bare rubbing of two bodies violently one upon another, produces heat, and very often fire itself, we have reason to think, that what we call *heat* and *fire* consists of a violent agitation of the imperceptible minute parts of the burning matter.[26]

But with regard to most other physical properties, and with regard to all chemical, botanical, and zoological properties, he said that we have no idea at all of the *specific* corresponding sub-microscopic mechanisms, and that we have virtually no prospect of getting any. In the particular case of gold he said that the sub-microscopic mechanism from which its properties " flow " is something which,

when I inquire into it and search after it, I plainly perceive I cannot discover: the furthest I can go is, only to presume that, it being nothing but body, its real essence or internal constitution, on which these qualities depend, can be nothing but the figure, size, and connexion of its solid parts; of neither of which having any distinct perception at all can I have any idea of its essence: which is the cause that it has that particular shining yellowness; a greater weight than anything I know of the same bulk; and a fitness to have its colour changed by the touch of quicksilver. . . . I have an idea of figure, size, and situation of solid parts in general, though I have none of the particular figure, size, or putting together of parts, whereby the qualities above mentioned are produced.[27]

In the particular case of sage and hemlock he said of their properties that we cannot " so much as guess, much less know, their manner of

26 IV.16.12.   27 II.31.6. See also III.10.19 and IV.6.5.

production." [28]   And after saying that the sub-microscopic mechanisms of minerals must be so complex, and our clues concerning them
so slight, that it is futile to try to imagine what they are, he added:
" And yet how infinitely these come short of the fine contrivances and
inconceivable real essences of plants or animals, every one knows." [29]

Speaking generally, Locke said that the observable clues are so
scanty that there is no hope of making good guesses about *any* kind
of specific sub-microscopic mechanisms. The clearest of these statements is the following one.

Our faculties carry us no further towards the knowledge and distinction of
substances, than a collection of *those sensible ideas which we observe in
them;* which, however made with the greatest diligence and exactness we
are capable of, yet is more remote from the true internal constitution from
which those qualities flow, than, as I said, a countryman's idea is from the
inward contrivance of that famous clock at Strasburg, whereof he only sees
the outward figure and motions.   There is not so contemptible a plant or
animal, that does not confound the most enlarged understanding. . . . The
workmanship of the all-wise and powerful God in the great fabric of the
universe, and every part thereof, further exceeds the capacity and comprehension of the most inquisitive and intelligent man, than the best contrivance of the most ingenious man doth the conceptions of the most ignorant
of rational creatures.[30]

[28] IV.3.26.

[29] III.6.9. It is instructive to contrast Locke's pessimism in this matter with
Hooke's optimism, which is expressed in the following passage. " There may be
also a possibility of discovering the Internal Motions and Actions of Bodies by the
sound they make, who knows but that as in a Watch we may hear the beating of
the Balance, and the running of the Wheels, and the striking of the Hammers, and
the grating of the Teeth, and Multitudes of other Noises; who knows, I say, but
that it may be possible to discover the Motions of the Internal Parts of Bodies,
whether 'Animal, Vegetable, or Mineral, by the sound they make, that one may
discover the Works perform'd in the several Offices and Shops of a Man's Body, and
thereby discover what Instrument or Engine is out of order, what Works are going
on at several Times, and lie still at others, and the like; that in Plants and Vegetables one might discover by the Noise the Pumps for raising Juice, the Valves for
stopping it, and the running of it out of one Passage into another, and the like
I could proceed further, but methinks I can hardly forbear to blush, when I con
sider how the most part of Men will look upon this: But yet again, I have thi
Incouragement, not to think all these things utterly impossible, . . . that as th
thinking them impossible cannot much improve my Knowledge, so the believin
them possible may perhaps be an occasion of taking notice of such things as anothe
would pass by without regard as useless " (*Post. Wks.*, 39).

[30] III.6.9. See also IV.6.11; *The Works of John Locke*, 9 vols., 12th ed. (Lon
don, 1824), III, 77f. and VIII, 182.

b) So much for the direct evidence. I shall now consider the indirect evidence. In IV.3.25, it will be recalled, Locke said that if one could *know* the internal mechanisms of hemlock and men as well as a watchmaker *knows* the internal mechanism of a watch, then one could *know* without trial that hemlock will kill men. But he affirmed over and over again that one can never *know*—in his strict usage of this term—either real essences or instructive universal propositions about bodies; and he concluded " it lost labour to seek after it." [31] One must be content with and seek after probabilities.[32] Now it seems quite plain that if one could get probable knowledge about the specific internal mechanisms of hemlock and men, one could also get probable knowledge about those powers of hemlock which can affect men. It therefore seems extremely likely to me that if Locke had believed it possible to get probable knowledge of *specific* sub-microscopic mechanisms—specific enough to permit one to " read off " the hitherto unknown powers of observable things—he frequently would have urged investigators to seek it.

But there is no passage in which Locke unequivocally recommended this. Whenever he spoke of the methods of increasing empirical knowledge, he recommended the " historical " method, not the " speculative " or " hypothetical " method.[33] The " historical " method consisted chiefly in classifying a subject in a convenient way, subjecting the materials under each heading to certain reagents and conditions, and observing the results. This was the method of trial, experiment, observation, and inference to observable but unobserved cases by means of " wary analogy." To be sure, this method employed hypotheses, but they were hypotheses about correlations of observable qualities and did not refer to sub-microscopic mechanisms. I have collected below the bulk of Locke's *explicit* statements about the method of inquiry proper to empirical science.

Concerning the causes of the several effects which " come every day within the notice of our senses," he said,

we can go no further than particular experience informs us of matter of fact, and by analogy to guess what effects the like bodies are, upon other trials, like to produce.[34]

---

[31] IV.3.29. See also IV.3.26 and the latter half of IV.6.   [32] IV.11.10.

[33] The distinction between these two methods was made by several seventeenth-century authors. For a general account see *Boyle*, I, 662ff.; for specific examples of strictly " historical " investigations, see *Boyle*, IV, 595ff. and 795ff. See also Hooke, *Post. Wks.*, 61.   [34] IV.3.29.

128   R. M. YOST, JR.

Concerning our empirical knowledge of substances, he said:

Possibly inquisitive and observing men may, by strength of judgment, penetrate further, and, on probabilities taken from wary observation, and hints
well laid together, often guess right at what experience has not yet discovered to them.[35]

And,

the general propositions that are made about substances, if they are certain,
are for the most part but trifling; and if they are instructive, are uncertain,
and such as we can have no knowledge of their real truth, how much soever
constant observation and analogy may assist our judgment in guessing.[36]

The following two passages are taken from a chapter in the *Essay*
entitled *Of the Improvement of Our Knowledge.*

I deny not but a man, accustomed to rational and regular experiments, shall
be able to see further into the nature of bodies, and guess righter at their
yet unknown properties, than one that is a stranger to them. . . . This way
of *getting and improving our knowledge in substances only by experience
and history,* which is all that the weakness of our faculties in this state of
mediocrity which we are in in this world can attain to, makes me suspect
that *natural philosophy is not capable of being made a science* . . . . Experiments and historical observations we may have, from which we may draw
advantages of ease and health, and thereby increase our stock of conveniences for this life; but beyond this I fear our talents reach not, nor are our
faculties, as I guess, able to advance.[37]

Where our inquiry is concerning co-existence, or repugnancy to co-exisᵥ,
which by contemplation of our ideas we cannot discover; there experience,
observation, and natural history, must give us, by our senses and by retail,
an insight into corporeal substances. The knowledge of *bodies* we must get
by our senses, warily employed in taking notice of their qualities and operations on one another.[38]

[35] IV.6.13.

[36] IV.8.9. The term " analogy " which occurs in this passage and in the second
passage previous to it does not refer to inferences which proceed from observed data
to sub-microscopic events. Its meaning is explained in his *Conduct of the Understanding,* where he said: " Analogy is of great use to the mind in many cases, especially in natural philosophy; and that part of it chiefly which consists in happy and
successful experiments. But here we must take care that we keep ourselves within
that wherein the analogy consists. For example, the acid oil of vitriol is found to
be good in such a case, therefore the spirit of nitre or vinegar may be used in the
like case. If the good effect of it be owing wholly to the acidity of it, the trial may
be justified; but if there be something else besides the acidity in the oil of vitriol
which produces the good we desire in the case; we mistake that for analogy, which
is not, and suffer our understanding to be misguided by a wrong supposition c
analogy where there is none " (*Works,* II, 388). See also III.6.8, and King's *Life*
I, 226.   [37] IV.12.10.   [38] IV.12.12.

Finally, it will be instructive to consider Locke's opinions on the proper method of research in the science he knew best, namely, medicine. In a fragment entitled *Ars Medica,* written in 1669, he rejected all attempts to advance medicine by trying to discover " the hidden causes of distempers, . . . the secret workmanship of nature and the several imperceptible tools wherewith she wrought," believing these matters to be " utterly out of reach " of man's apprehension.[39] In a fragment entitled *Anatomica,* dated 1668, Locke even rejected the detailed study of anatomy as an aid to medical research, giving the following reason.

All that anatomy can do is only to show us the gross and sensible parts of the body, or the vapid and dead juices, all which, after the most diligent search, will be no more able to direct a physician how to cure a disease than how to make a man; for, to remedy the defects of a part whose organical constitution, and that texture whereby it operates, he cannot possibly know, is alike hard as to make a part he knows not how is made.[40]

These fragments were written during his early collaboration with Dr. Sydenham. In 1693, after Sydenham's death, Locke wrote a letter to a Dr. Molyneux which contained his final opinions on the methods of medical research. In this letter he rejected, along with many other hypotheses, the main hypothesis about imperceptible events that Sydenham had employed, namely, the doctrine of humors.[41] But he accepted Sydenham's "historical" method, which was, simply, "nicely to observe the history of diseases in all their changes and circumstances." And he added:

What we know of the works of nature, especially in the constitution of health, and the operations of our own bodies, is only by the sensible effects, but not by any certainty we can have of the tools she uses, or the ways she works by. So that there is nothing left for a physician to do, but to observe well, and so, by analogy, argue to like cases, and thence make to himself rules of practice.

Hypotheses in medicine, if they are used at all, should be used only as aids to the memory; they should be relied on only as " artificial helps to a physician, and not as philosophical truths to a naturalist." [42]

---

[39] *Ars Medica* is reproduced in its entirety by Fox Bourne in his *Life,* I, 223–226.   [40] Fox Bourne's *Life,* I, 228f.

[41] For an example of Sydenham's use of the doctrine of humors, see *Medical Classics,* vol. IV (Baltimore, 1939–1940), 364f. and 370. For an example of Sydenham's clinical disease-histories, see 314f.   [42] *Works,* VIII, 463–465.

The foregoing passages constitute Locke's principal *explicit* utterances on the question of the proper method of research in the empirical sciences. So far as I know there is no clear-cut statement in Locke's published works which asserts the fruitfulness of employing hypotheses about the specific sub-microscopic mechanisms of material objects.[43] And this implies, as I said at the beginning of this section, that in Locke's opinion there was little, if any, hope of getting well-founded knowledge about them.

I append here a brief summary of this essay, and a final clarifying remark. In *Part I*, I showed that in the opinion of many seventeenth-century scientists and philosophers, a careful use of hypotheses about sub-microscopic events would accelerate the acquisition of empirical knowledge. This opinion was broken down into four main points: (1) the everyday appearances of things depend upon sub-microscopic events; (2) the powers of sub-microscopic mechanisms can easily be computed; (3) the fact that such mechanisms are sub-microscopic would not render knowledge about them, if we had it, useless; and (4) there was good reason for believing that knowledge about sub-microscopic mechanisms, even though it be only probable, was obtainable. In *Part II*, I showed that Locke would agree with the first three points, but would dissent from the fourth one; and that he rejected the use of hypotheses about sub-microscopic mechanisms as a means of research in the empirical sciences.

Now for the final clarifying remark. Locke believed it was impossible to discover *necessary connexions* among observable events. But it was not my purpose to show this.[44] Many of the leading scientists concurred in this belief.[45] But they differed from Locke when they believed that a judicious use of hypotheses about sub-microscopic events would speed the discovery of well-founded, though not theoretically certain, knowledge about the observable world. My purpose was to show that Locke disagreed with them on this point.

University of California at Los Angeles.

---

[43] The only plausible exception I know of is the last sentence of IV.16.12. But it is so closely connected with his speculations about the continuity of the Great Chain of Being that I cannot regard it as a decisive exception to the opinion clearly stated in so many other passages.

[44] This belief of Locke's has been pointed out with great emphasis by several commentators, notably Prof. John Dewey ("Substance, Power, and Quality in Locke," *Philosophical Review*, XXXV, 1926, 22–38).

[45] See *Boyle*, IV, 77; Huygens' *Treatise on Light*, vi` and vii; and Newton' *Principia, Rules of Reasoning in Philosophy* and *General Scholium*.

Chapter XVII

THE NATURE AND SOURCES OF
LOCKE'S VIEWS ON HYPOTHESES

By Laurens Laudan

It has often been assumed that John Locke was primarily an
epistemologist with only a casual and superficial interest in the physical sciences. Despite the fact that he studied medicine and spoke
glowingly of figures like Newton and Boyle,[1] Locke's *Essay* seems—
at least on the surface—to be concerned with the epistemology of
common sense rather than with the logic and methods of science.
Philosophers, by reading history backwards, have written as if Locke
accepted the view of Berkeley and Hume that the empiricist philosophy should not be based on a "scientific" metaphysics. Furthermore,
in so far as the *Essay* does deal with scientific matters, it usually
seems to treat them with derision and condescension. Consequently,
some commentators have inferred that Locke was an opponent of the
Corpuscular philosophy which dominated the physics of his day and
have viewed his *Essay* as an attempt to develop a theory of knowledge
with no Corpuscularian, or other quasi-scientific, bias. They suggest
that Locke was opposed not only to the atomic hypothesis, but to the
use of virtually all hypotheses in science. Those commentators who do
not explicitly attribute an anti-hypothetical view to Locke generally
leave unmentioned his remarks about scientific method, as if meta-
science was foreign to the spirit of the *Essay*.[2] Recently, however,
Maurice Mandelbaum has pointed out not only that Locke was sympathetic to the Corpuscular program, but that an atomic view of
nature is essential to Locke's epistemology and metaphysics.[3] Rather
than read Locke in the light of Berkeley's criticisms, Mandelbaum
urges us to approach the *Essay* with the atomic theories of Boyle and
Newton in mind. It is surely as important to understand Locke in
terms of his contemporaries and predecessors as it is to view him as a
forerunner of Berkeley.

[1] In a classic piece of understatement, Locke speaks of himself as an "under-
labourer" to the scientists Boyle, Sydenham, Huygens, and "the incomparable Mr.
Newton" (*Essay*, ed. A. C. Fraser [Oxford, 1894], I, 14).

[2] Among those who have taken the above interpretation of Locke, the most
prominent are probably R. I. Aaron, *John Locke* (Oxford, 1955), J. Gibson, *Locke's
Theory of Knowledge* (Cambridge, 1960), and J. W. Yolton, *John Locke and the
Way of Ideas* (Oxford, 1956).

[3] Mandelbaum. *Philosophy, Science and Sense Perception* (Baltimore, 1964),
.-60. I can do no better than cite Mandelbaum's own summary of his thesis: "The
conclusion which I wish to draw . . . is that Locke, throughout his career, was an
atomist, and that he accepted both the truth and the scientific usefulness (or, at
least, the scientific promise) of the corpuscular, or new experimental, philosophy"
(*Ibid.*, 14).

In this paper, I want to build upon Mandelbaum's analysis by looking carefully at the theory of scientific method implicit in the *Essay*. For if Mandelbaum is right that Locke was vitally concerned with corpuscular physics, then we have every reason to expect that the *Essay* will provide guidelines for the way in which Locke—a lifelong scientist himself—wanted to see science develop. Although it is hoped that this paper will substantiate Mandelbaum's reading of Locke as a corpuscularian, from a slightly different point of view, its primary aim is to ascertain Locke's attitude on the rôle of hypotheses in science. The bearing of this latter problem on Mandelbaum's thesis should be clear; if Locke was as anti-hypothetical as most writers have made him out to be, then he could not conceivably have embraced so hypothetical a theory as the atomic one. Conversely, if Locke was sympathetic to the use of hypotheses in physics, then it would not be surprising if he adopted the corpuscular philosophy as enthusiastically as Mandelbaum maintains he did.

Perhaps the best place to begin is in response to one of the most detailed studies of Locke's methodology; namely, that conducted by Professor Yost.[4] In his lengthy analysis of the methodology of the *Essay*, Yost comes to the conclusion that Locke was not only sceptical about the scientific value of the atomic philosophy, but that he objected—on methodological grounds—to all scientific theories which employed hypotheses about unobservable events or objects. More specifically, Yost claims that "unlike many scientists and philosophers of the XVIIth century, Locke did not believe that the employment of hypotheses about sub-microscopic events would accelerate the acquisition of empirical knowledge."[5] Yost insists that while Locke allowed, albeit grudgingly, the use of hypotheses about observable events, he was categorically opposed to all hypotheses dealing with the behavior and properties of unobservable forces and atoms. He contrasts Locke's views on this subject with those of such XVIIth-century atomists as Boyle and Descartes, who encouraged the use of hypotheses about unobservable events. Yost suggests that Locke's anti-hypotheticalism was a radical departure from the hypothetical methodology which accompanied the atomism of his contemporaries. But Yost's analysis seems to overlook many of Locke's crucial pronouncements on methodology and to obscure the meaning of others. For not only did Locke look favorably on many uses of the hypothetical method, but in doing so he was solidly in, rather than aligned against, the corpuscularian tradition. To develop this argument, I shall work in two directions. To begin with, I want to determine precisely what Locke's attitude towards sub-microscopic hypotheses was. I shall then turn to consider his debt to the corpuscular philosophers who preceded and influenced him.

[4] R. M. Yost, Jr., "Locke's Rejection of Hypotheses about Sub-Microscopic Events," *JHI*, XII (1951), 111–30.   [5] *Ibid.*, 111

The casual reader of Locke's *Essay* invariably comes away from that volume with the firm suspicion that Locke was uniformly pessimistic about the natural sciences. Apart from the general scepticism which forms the dominant motif of the fourth book of the *Essay*, there are numerous specific passages which reinforce this impression. Thus, Locke asserts:

As to a perfect science of natural bodies, . . . we are, I think, so far from being capable of any such thing, that I conclude it lost labour to seek after it.[6]

If it is ill-conceived even to attempt to develop a science of mechanics, how hopeless must the situation be for other branches of scientific inquiry? Elsewhere, he writes that "scientifical" knowledge of nature is forever out of our reach.[7] Or again, he sadly proclaims that mechanics must not "pretend to certainty and demonstration," and that there can never be a "science of bodies" (*Ibid.*). Locke's pessimism seems especially pronounced whenever he discusses the corpuscularian program for explaining the observable world in terms of the motion and concretions of unobservable atoms. Thus,

Because the active and passive powers of bodies and their ways of operating, consisting in a texture and motion of parts which we cannot by any means discover. . . .[8]

Or,

doubt not but if we could discover the figure, size, texture, and motion of the minute constituent parts of any two bodies, we should know *without trial* several of their operations upon one another. . . . But whilst we are destitute of senses acute enough [to perceive such corpuscles] . . . we must be content to be ignorant of their properties and ways of operations.[9]

Passages like these have disposed many historians to interpret Locke both as an anti-hypotheticalist and as an opponent of corpuscularism. But in fact Locke was neither of these. To see the flaws in caricaturing Locke as an anti-hypotheticalist, we need only recall that he devoted an entire section of the fourth book of the *Essay* (iv, 12, §13) to the true use of hypotheses" and that he frequently spoke as if the phenomena of the visible world ultimately derived from interactions at the corpuscular level.[10] But if such remarks indicate Locke's accept-

[6] *Essay concerning Human Understanding*, iv, 3, § 29.

[7] *Ibid.*, iv, 3, § 26. Cf. also iv, 12, § 10.   [8] *Ibid.*, iv, 3, § 16.

[9] *Ibid.*, iv, 3, § 25. Italics added. Elsewhere, he writes: "Thus, having no ideas the particular mechanical affections of the minute parts of bodies, that are within our reach and view, we are ignorant of their constitutions, powers, and operations. . . ." *Ibid.*, iv, 3, § 15.

[10] As one of the numerous passages where Locke overtly takes a corpuscular view, consider his remark that heat and cold are "nothing but the increase or diminution of the motion of the minute parts of our bodies, caused by the *corpuscles* of other body" *Ibid.*, ii, 8, § 21 (Italics added). Cf. also his *Elements of Natural*

ance of the hypothetical method, we are confronted, when we compare them with *obiter dicta* like those cited above, with an obvious tension between Locke's simultaneous denunciation and acceptance of hypotheses.

To resolve this apparent contradiction, we need only invoke Locke's pivotal distinction between knowledge and judgment. Knowledge, for him, is based on a true and infallible intuition of the relation of ideas. To know that a statement x is true is to perceive that we could not conceive things to be other than the state of affairs which x specifies. In this way, we "know" the truth of mathematics. But we do not "know" anything about the physical world. Many statements the scientist makes may be highly probable, but they are not indubitably true and, because of this deficiency, are not in the domain of knowledge. When Locke says that we cannot "know" anything about the "minute parts of bodies," he is using knowledge in this technical sense. Since science is the name given to the body of our knowledge, natural philosophy can never be "scientifical." [11] But Locke was not so imprudent as to restrict our discourse rigidly to strictly "scientific" statements.[12] He recognized clearly that one can say some informative and highly probable things about the physical world. Such statements belong, however, not to knowledge, but to *judgment:*

The faculty which God has given man to supply the want of clear and certain knowledge, in cases where that cannot be had is *judgment:* whereby the mind takes . . . any proposition to be true or false, without perceiving a demonstrative evidence in the proofs.[13]

The physicist may be able to make many very likely statements but "the highest probability amounts not to certainty; without which there can be no true knowledge" (*Ibid.*, iv, 3, §14). Knowledge, then

Philosophy: "By the figure, bulk, texture, and motion of these small and insensible corpuscles, all the phenomena of bodies may be explained."

[11] "Therefore I am apt to doubt that how far soever human industry may advance useful and experimental philosophy in physical things, scientifical [knowledge] will still be out of our reach. . . ." *Ibid.*, iv, 3, § 26.

[12] Locke expresses himself thus: "The understanding faculties being given to man, not barely for speculation, but also for the conduct of his life, man would be at a great loss if he had nothing to direct him but what has the certainty of true knowledge. For that being very short and scanty, as we have seen, he would be often utterly in the dark, and in most of the actions of his life, perfectly at a stand, had he nothing to guide him in the absence of clear and certain knowledge. He that will not eat, till he has the demonstration that it will nourish him; he that will not stir, till he infallibly knows the business he goes about will succeed, will have but little else to do, but to sit still and perish" (*Ibid.*, iv, 14, § 1). Again, he remarks: "How vain, I say, is it to expect demonstration and certainty in things not capable of it, and refuse assent to very rational propositions . . . because they cannot be made out so evident, as to surmount even the least . . . pretence of doubting" (*Ibid.*, iv, 11, § 10).

[13] *Ibid.*, iv, 14, § 3.

consists in those statements which are already clearly and distinctly perceived to be true; judgment consists of all those statements which are merely probable or conjectural. "Judgment is the presuming things to be so, without perceiving it." [14]

Having decreed that judgment deals with probable statements, Locke proceeds to argue that there are two sorts of such statements: (1) those dealing with strictly observable phenomena, or "matters of fact," and (2) speculations dealing with unobservable phenomena.[15] Locke then turns his attention to the second sort of probable statement, viz., speculations about unobservables. Wielding again the logician's axe to split hairs, he argues that there are two types of such speculations: (1) conjectures about purely spiritual beings (e.g., angels, demons, etc.) and (2) hypotheses about the unobservable causes of such natural phenomena as generation, magnetism, and heat.[16] Locke's remarks on this second class are particularly of interest to our argument.

Suppose, Locke reasons, that we want to understand the ultimate nature of heat. Because we do not clearly perceive, or even dimly observe, the causes of heat, we cannot claim to "know" anything about it.[17] All we can hope to pronounce are probable statements about its nature and causes. Since Locke believes that any tentative explanation of heat will be couched in terms of the behavior of unobservable corpuscles, he insists that observation can tell us nothing directly about the behavior of the heat-producing atoms. How then can we formulate any useful hypotheses at all? Locke's answer is straightforward: by conceiving submicroscopic corpuscles on the analogy of bodies which we do perceive, viz., we must picture the smallest particles as miniature instantiations of the gross objects of perception. Indeed, "in things which sense cannot discover, analogy is the great rule of probability" (Ibid.). In the case of heat, the analogy we should make is obvious:

Thus, observing that the bare rubbing of two bodies violently upon one another, produces heat, and very often fire itself, we have reason to think that what we call heat and fire, consists in a violent agitation of the imperceptible minute parts of the burning matter (Ibid.).

We must resort to analogies and models in conceiving the nature of

[14] Ibid., iv, 14, § 4.
[15] ". . . the propositions we receive upon inducements of probability are of two sorts, either concerning some particular existence, or, as it is usually termed, matter of fact, which, falling under observation, is capable of human testimony, or else concerning things, which being beyond the discovery of our senses, are not capable of any such testimony" (Ibid., iv, 16, § 5).
[16] Cf. Essay, iv, 16, § 12.
[17] ". . . effects we see and know; but the causes that operate, and the manner they are produced in, we can only guess and probably conjecture." Ibid., iv, 16, § 12.

submicroscopic events because, since our conjectures about them cannot be directly verified, the only reason we have for believing them to be even probable is that "they more or less agree to truths that are established in our minds" and because such conjectures are at least compatible with "other parts of our knowledge and observation" (*Ibid.*). "Analogy," he notes, "in these matters [viz., relating to unobservable events] is the only help we have, and it is from that alone we draw all grounds of probability" (*Ibid.*).

It was a basic tenet of Lockean epistemology that all our ideas of external objects derive from sensation. Thus, it was perfectly natural for him to insist that our ideas about unobservable corpuscles must be based on, and derived from, ideas which visible bodies impress on our senses. He would undoubtedly have been delighted with the kinetic theory of gases because it takes macroscopic objects as models for submicroscopic phenomena.

These remarks about analogy-based hypotheses dealing with submicroscopic events are not merely a grudging concession Locke makes to his scientific colleagues. On the contrary, he insists that the enunciation of analogical hypotheses is the most productive and theoretically fertile method which the sciences possess:

This sort of probability, which is the best conduct of rational experiments, and the rise of hypothesis, has also its use and influence; and a wary reasoning from analogy leads us often into the discovery of truths and useful productions, which would otherwise lie concealed.[18]

Having said as much, we can see how misleading Yost's remark is that Locke's "method employed hypotheses, but they were hypotheses about correlations of observable qualities and did not refer to submicroscopic mechanisms." [19] Equally untenable is Yost's view that Locke "thought that one could infer *something* about submicroscopic mechanisms, but not enough to help us in making discoveries." [20] In the passage cited above, Locke explicitly states that the use of corpus-

[18] *Ibid.* Elsewhere he writes that an accomplished experimenter can often make valuable hypotheses: "I deny not but [that] a man, accustomed to rational and regular experiments, shall be able to see further into the nature of bodies, and guess righter at their yet unknown properties, than one that is a stranger to them; but yet, as I have said, this is but judgment and opinion, not knowledge and certainty . . . [hence] *natural philosophy is not capable of being made a science*" (*Ibid.*, iv, 12, § 10). Again, he notes: "Possibly inquisitive and observing men may by strength of judgment, penetrate further, and, on probabilities taken from wary observation and hints well laid together, often guess right at what experience has not yet discovered to them. But this is but guessing still; it amounts only to opinion, and has not that certainty which is requisite to knowledge" (*Ibid.*, iv, 6, § 13).

[19] Yost, *op. cit.*, 127.

[20] *Ibid.*, 125. Further on, Yost puts it this way: "Speaking generally, Locke said that the observable clues are so scanty that there is no hope of making good guesses about any kind of specific submicroscopic mechanisms" (*Ibid.*, 126).

cular hypotheses could lead us "into the discovery of truths, and useful productions." Elsewhere, he writes that "hypotheses, if they are well made, are at least great helps to the memory, and often direct us to new discoveries." [21] Yet another misleading claim in Yost's paper is his assertion that Locke never mentioned the hypothetical method "whenever he spoke of the methods of increasing empirical knowledge." [22] The same passage cited above stands as an obvious counterexample to this statement.

In enunciating his hypothetical account of scientific explanation, Locke likened nature to a clock whose external appearances (e.g., hands moving, wheels grinding, etc.) are visible but whose internal mechanisms are forever excluded from view. The scientist's conception of nature is even "more remote from the true internal constitution" of the physical world than a "countryman's idea from the inward contrivance of that famous clock at Strasburg, whereof he only sees the outward figures and motions." [23] If we knew the "mechanical affections of the particles" of bodies, "as a watchmaker does those of a watch," [24] then we would not need to make hypotheses, but could have infallible, first-hand knowledge of nature's mechanisms. But because we can never get inside of nature's clock, we must be content to hypothesize about the possible arrangements of its parts on the basis of its external cortex.

Though Locke believed that scientific explanations should be based on hypotheses about corpuscular events, he insisted that the scientist should be very circumspect in his use of such hypotheses. Hypotheses must never be called "principles," because such an honorific title makes them sound more trustworthy than they are.[25] Furthermore, we should never accept an hypothesis unless we have carefully examined the phenomena which it is designed to explain, and even then only if the hypothesis saves all the phenomena efficaciously. Locke is quite sensitive to the dangers of an unbridled hypothetical method and he often warns us against its excesses. Thus, one of the major sources of error which he cites is the clinging tenaciously to preconceived hypotheses and prejudging the facts on the basis of those hypotheses.[26] But it is a mistake to say that Locke's critique of the extravagant

[21] *Essay*, iv, 12, § 13. He prefaces the quoted passage by an endorsement of hypotheses which is quite unequivocal: "Not that we may not, to explain any phenomena of nature, make use of any probable hypothesis whatsoever" (*Ibid.*).
[22] Yost, *op. cit.*, 127.
[23] *Essay*, iii, 6, § 9. Cf. also iii, 6, § 39.   [24] *Ibid.*, iv, 3, § 25.
[25] "And at least that we take care that the name of *principles* deceive us not, nor impose on us, by making us receive that for an unquestionable truth, which is really at best but a doubtful conjecture; such as are most (I had almost said all) of the hypotheses in natural philosophy" (*Ibid.*, iv, 12, § 13).
[26] Cf. *Ibid.*, iv, 20, § 11.

exaggerations of the hypothetical method indicates his aversion to all forms of that method. At one point, Locke explicitly acknowledges that his animadversions upon hypotheses were not designed to preclude the scientist from hypothesizing, but only to make him wary about it:

But my meaning is, that we should not take up any one hypothesis too hastily (which the mind, that would always penetrate into the causes of things, and have principles to rest on, is very apt to do), till we have very well examined particulars, and made several experiments, in that thing which we would explain by our hypothesis, and see whether it will agree to them all; whether our principles will carry us quite through, and not be as inconsistent with one phenomenon of nature, as they seem to accommodate and explain another.[27]

The traditional account of Lockean methodology is certainly correct in its insistence that Locke believed we could not have *knowledge* about unobservable events; it is equally true that Locke was exceedingly scornful of those who believed one could make indubitable statements about the properties of unobservable corpuscles. But he was not opposed to the use of atomic hypotheses—or other hypotheses which invoked unobservable entities—so long as they made sense of the phenomena and were treated as merely probable judgments.

We may conclude from the foregoing discussion that Locke was neither opposed to hypotheses (if properly conceived) nor an adversary of the corpuscularians who used hypotheses about submicroscopic events. Indeed, so far as one can judge from the texts, Locke enthusiastically accepted the view that changes in the observable world are caused by, and explicable in terms of, changes on the atomic level.[28] I now want to suggest that the major features of Locke's hypothetical method, as well as many of the epistemological arguments whereby he justifies his hypotheticalism, are derived from, or at best are variations on, the methodological ideas of his corpuscularian contemporaries. In particular, I want to claim that Locke probably derived the following methodological ideas from the corpuscularists: (1) the insistence upon the provisional and tentative character of all scientific theories, (2) the view of nature as a clock whose internal mechanisms are not susceptible of direct analysis or observation, (3) the doctrine that hypotheses must be constructed on analogy with the behavior of observable bodies, and (4) the insistence, related to (3), that the hypotheses about submicroscopic events must be compatible with law

---

[27] *Ibid.*, iv, 12, § 13.

[28] For some of the relevant passages in which Locke takes a corpuscular position cf. *Essay* ii, 8, § 13–21 and ii, 21, § 75; iii, 6, § 6; iv, 13, § 16 and § 25; iv, 10, § 10; iv, 16, § 12; iv, 6, § 10 and § 14. As Locke's XIXth-century editor, Fraser, notes "It is to the 'corpuscularian hypothesis' that he [Locke] appeals in the many passages in the *Essay* which deal with . . . the *ultimate physical cause* of the secondary qualities . . ." *Essay* (ed. Fraser), vol. ii, 205n.

of nature and phenomena other than those which they were devised to explain.

(1) Though more than willing to urge the use of hypotheses. Locke was apprehensive lest merely probable conjectures be taken for immutable truths. He emphasized that hypotheses ought not be called "principles" because such a linguistic convention might make us "receive that for an unquestionable truth, which is really, at best, but a very doubtful conjecture." [29] As we have seen, he went to some lengths to stress the necessarily hypothetical character of scientific inquiry. Though it perhaps seems trivial to us to say that scientific theories are not necessarily true, it was neither so trivial nor so obvious in the XVIIth century, when scientists were still struggling with, and to some extent dominated by, Aristotle's dictum that science is infallible knowledge of nature. This doctrine is certainly evident in Descartes' *Regulae* and *Discourse* and, in adumbrated form, even in Bacon's *Novum Organum*. Locke himself shared Aristotle's view that the term "science" should only be applied to those disciplines whose principles are analytically true. It was the corpuscular philosophers who first realized that knowledge of nature was necessarily conjectural and who made it a *sine qua non* of natural science that its principles be merely probable and hypothetical. Robert Boyle, for example, wrote that scientific theories should be "looked upon only as temporary ones; which are not entirely to be acquiesced in, as absolutely perfect, or incapable of improving alterations." [30] In a similar vein, Hooke warns against treating any scientific theories as if they were indubitable:

If therefore the reader expects from me any infallible deductions, or certainty of *axioms*, I am to say for myself that those stronger works of wit and imagination are above my weak abilities. . . . Wherever he finds that I have ventur'd at any small conjectures, at the causes of the things I have observed, I beseech him to look upon them as *doubtful problems*, and uncertain ghesses [sic], and not as unquestionable conclusions, or matters of unconfutable science. . . .[31]

Another mid-century corpuscularian, Joseph Glanvill, puts the point similarly in his *Scepsis Scientifica* (1661). True philosophers, he says, "seek truth in the great book of nature, and in that search . . . proceed with wariness and circumspection without too much forwardness in establishing maxims and positive doctrines. . . . [They] propose their opinions as hypotheses, that may probably be true accounts, without peremptorily affirming that they are." [32] Like Locke after him, Glan-

---

[29] *Essay*, iv, 12, § 13.
[30] Robert Boyle, *Works*, ed. Birch (London, 1772), I, 303.
[31] R. Hooke, *Micrographia* (London, 1667), preface, n.p.
[32] *Scepsis Scientifica* (London, 1665), 44.

vill insists that all scientific principles are conjectural; there is nothing we can say with certainty about the physical world:

For the best principles, excepting divine and mathematical [precisely Locke's exceptions], are but hypotheses; within which, we may conclude many things with security from error. But yet the greatest certainty, advanced from supposal, is still hypothetical. So that we may affirm that things are thus and thus, according to the principles we have espoused: But we strangely forget ourselves, when we plead a necessity of their being so in nature, and an impossibility of their being otherwise.[33]

All three writers—Boyle, Hooke, and Glanvill—were widely read in the 1660s and 1670s, when the ideas for the *Essay* were taking shape. It is highly likely that Locke knew the works of Hooke and Glanvill and it is certain that he knew Boyle's works, as the two were close friends for more than thirty years and, as Leyden has noted, Locke "followed with interest each new publication of his friend Robert Boyle." [34] Furthermore, Locke met frequently with Boyle's scientific circle at Oxford (of which Hooke was also a member) in the 1660s, and one presumes that among the topics for conversation was the nature of scientific knowledge and the tentative character of its hypotheses. It is not unreasonable to suggest that Locke's ideas on this topic stemmed, in part, from his discussions with, and readings of, the Oxford corpuscularists who, like him, were alarmed that hypothetical systems were being passed off as infallibly true theories.

(2) We have seen that, in explaining why the Corpuscular philosophy can never be more than an hypothesis, Locke metaphorically likened nature to a clock whose internal mechanisms could never be observed. Just as we can only conjecture about the possible internal mechanisms of an unfamiliar clock, the scientist can only hypothesize about nature's hidden mechanisms. We know no more about the real natural processes than a XVIIth-century country bumpkin knew about the "famous clock at Strasburg," which was accompanied by ingenious automata of every description. This clock-analogy [35] was widely exploited among Locke's predecessors—Descartes, Boyle, Glanvill, and Power—in justification of their insistence on the necessarily hypothetical character of scientific principles.[36] Given the fact that this analogy occurred prominently in the works of several of the most important of Locke's predecessors, it is implausible that he did not borrow it, either consciously or unconsciously, from one of them.

[33] *Ibid.*, 170–171.
[34] J. Locke, *Essays on the Laws of Nature* (ed. Leyden, Oxford, 1954), 20. Maurice Cranston, Locke's biographer, records that "Locke, as Boyle's pupil, absorbed much of the Boylian conception of nature before he read Descartes and became interested in pure philosophy." *John Locke* (London, 1957), 75–76.
[35] Locke uses the analogy on at least two occasions: *Essay*, iii, 6, § 9; iv, 3, § 25
[36] The relevant texts are the following:
(1) Descartes: "It may be retorted to this, that, although I may have imagined

(3) Locke was adamant in his insistence that hypotheses about submicroscopic events must construe atoms and their properties as natural extensions of the properties of macroscopic bodies. Locke believed there was a continuity in nature such that the laws governing macroscopic phenomena must be similar to, if not identical with, the laws governing submicroscopic phenomena. One finds anticipations of this argument in Descartes, Boyle, Hooke, and Newton.

It is well known that Descartes' scientific treatises are packed with analogies: the mind as a piece of wax, light transmission as a revolving stick, light corpuscles as grapes in a vat. It is not so well

---

causes capable of producing effects similar to those we see, we should not conclude for that reason that those we see are produced by these causes; for just as an industrious clockmaker may make two watches which keep time equally well and without any difference in their external appearance, yet without any similarity in the composition of their wheels, so it is certain that God works in an infinity of diverse ways, each of which enables Him to make everything appear in the world as it does, without making it possible for the human mind to know which of all these ways He has decided to use. And I believe I shall have done enough if the causes that I have listed are such that the effects they may produce are similar to those we see in the world, without being informed whether there are other ways in which they are produced." *Principles*, Part iv, § 204.

(2) Boyle: ". . . many atomists and other naturalists, presume to know the true causes of the things they attempt to explicate, yet very often the utmost they can attain to in their explications, is, that the explicated phenomena may be produced after such a manner as they deliver, but not that they really are so. For as an Artificer can set all the wheels of a clock a going, as well with springs as with weights . . . so the same effects may be produced by diverse causes different from one another; and it will often be difficult if not impossible for our dim reasons to discern surely which of those several ways, whereby it is possible to produce the same phenomena, she has actually made use of to exhibit them." *Works*, II, 45. It should also be mentioned that Boyle likens nature not merely to any clock, but specifically to the "clock of Strasbourg" (*Ibid.*). Was this the stimulus for Locke's allusion to "that famous clock at Strasburgh"?

(3) Glanvill: "For nature is set a going by the most subtil and hidden instruments; which it may have nothing obvious which resembles them. Hence judging by visible appearances, we are discouraged by supposed impossibilities which to nature are none, but within her sphear of actions. And therefore what shews only the outside, and sensible structure of nature, is not likely to help us in finding out the *Magnalia* [i.e., inner mechanisms]. 'Twere next to impossible for one, who never saw the inward wheels and motions, to make a watch upon the bare view of the circle of hours, and index: And 'tis as difficult to trace natural operations to any practical advantage, by the sight of the cortex of sensible appearances." *Scepsis Scientifica*, 155.

(4) Power: "For the old dogmatists and notional speculators, that onely gazed at the visible effects and last resultances of things, understood no more of nature than a rude countrey fellow does of the internal fabrick of a watch, that only sees the index and horary circle, and perchance hears the clock and alarum strike in it." Henry Power, *Experimental Philosophy* (London, 1664), 193. Locke's formulation of the analogy is particularly close to Power's when he talks of a "countryman's ideas" of the clock at Strasburgh, "whereof he only sees the outward figures and motions." *Essay*, iii, 6, § 9.

known that analogy plays an important rôle in Descartes' philosophy of science as well. In the *Regulae*, for example, Descartes argued that since light is a force whose nature we cannot perceive directly, we should imagine light on the analogy of other natural forces which we do understand.[37] Again, in the *Dioptrique*, Descartes talks of the importance of analogies in understanding light.[38] But his most explicit discussion of analogies occurs in the *Principles*, which Locke undoubtedly read. There he writes:

Nor do I doubt that anyone who uses his reason will deny that we do much better to judge of what takes place in small bodies which their minuteness alone prevents us from perceiving, by what we see occurring in those that we do perceive than, in order to explain certain given things, to invent all sorts of novelties that have no relation to those that we do perceive.[39]

The sentiments of this passage are Locke's as well as Descartes'.

Boyle was the next to take up this theme. He argues that it is absurd to assume anything but that submicroscopic corpuscles obey the same laws as macroscopic bodies do. To say, for example, that the principles of mechanics apply to visible masses but not to invisible ones would be "as if a man should allow, that the laws of mechanism may take place in a town clock, but cannot in a pocket-watch." [40] For Corpuscular hypotheses to be even intelligible, they must attribute the same type of behavior to atoms as we observe taking place in perceptible bodies.

In his *General Scheme* (c. 1667), Hooke too argues for the importance of models and analogies in the construction of hypotheses: "A most general help of discovery in all types of philosophical i.e., scientific inquiry is, *to attempt to compare the working of nature in that particular that is under examination, to as many various, mechanical and intelligible ways of operation as the mind is furnisht with.*" [41]

Another of Locke's contemporaries who attaches great importance to analogy in the argument from the seen to the unseen is Newton. The third of Newton's grand methodological precepts, the *Regulae Philosophandi*, runs as follows:

[37] "If he [the scientist] finds himself . . . unable to perceive the nature of light, he will, in accordance with Rule 7, enumerate all the natural forces in order that he may understand what light is, learning its nature, if not otherwise, at least by *analogy* . . . from his knowledge of one of the other forces." *Oeuvres* (ed. Adam & Tannery), X, 395. Italics added.

[38] He says that he intends to offer "two or three comparisons, which will help us to understand it [viz., light] in the most convenient manner, in order to explain all those of its properties that experience allows us to know, and to deduce thereafter all the others which may not be so easily noticed. . . ." *Ibid.*, VI, 83.

[39] *Principles*, Part iv, § 201.   [40] *Works*, IV, 72.

[41] Hooke, *Posthumous Works*, ed. Waller (London, 1705), 61. Italics in original

The qualities of bodies which admit neither intension nor remission of degree, and which are found to belong to all bodies within the reach of our experiments, are to be esteemed the universal qualities of all bodies whatsoever . . . nor are we to recede from the analogy of Nature, which uses to be simple, and always consonant with itself.[42]

However, regardless of whether Locke borrowed his beliefs about analogies from Descartes, Hooke, Boyle, or Newton, it is clear that the use of analogical hypotheses was a basic and explicit tenet of the corpuscularism which Locke so warmly embraced.

(4) Finally, I want to consider the likely sources of Locke's belief that Corpuscular hypotheses must be compatible with "truths that are established in our minds" and with "other parts of our knowledge and observation." [43] The writer who comes most quickly to mind in this connection is Robert Boyle, who frequently emphasized that the two requirements of any sound hypothesis are that it accord both with other known laws and with observations. Boyle goes so far as to say that the function of an hypothesis is "to render an intelligible account of the causes of the effects, or phenomena proposed, without crossing the laws of nature, or other phenomena." [44] Elsewhere, he insists that a good hypothesis must "not be inconsistent with any other truth or phenomenon of nature." [45] Varying the wording yet again, he says that an hypothesis is acceptable if we can show "its fitness to solve the phenomena for which (it was) devised, without crossing any known observation or law of nature." [46] Locke's remarks in the *Essay* at iv, 16, § 12 seem to be little more than stylistic variations on this Boyleian theme.

The object of this historical exercise has not been to belittle Locke's originality nor, even more trivially, to decide "who said what before whom." It is no criticism of Locke to point out that he adhered to certain conventions of the philosophical and scientific *milieu* in which he matured. There was a cluster of beliefs—methodological as well as scientific—which many adherents of the "new philosophy" accepted; among them was the conviction that scientific knowledge was conjectural. In sharing this conviction, Locke was in distinguished company.

University College, London.

---

[42] I. Newton. *Principia Mathematica* (trans. Motte), 385. It should be pointed out that in the first edition of the *Principia* (1687), which was the only one to appear in Locke's lifetime, this principle did not appear. Newton introduced it in the 1713 edition of the *Principia*.

[43] *Essay*, iv, 16, § 12.   [44] *Works*, IV, 234.
[45] *Ibid.*, i, 241.   [46] *Ibid.*, iv, 77.

Chapter XVIII

THE WAY OF HYPOTHESES:
LOCKE ON METHOD*

BY JAMES FARR

> "[A]s every ones hypothesis is, soe
> is his reason disposed to judge . . ."[1]

The specter of empiricism no longer haunts the *Essay Concerning Human Understanding* as once it did. Thanks to historically-minded philosophers and philosophically-minded historians, the interpretation of John Locke's masterwork is at long last being spared the time-honored ritual of reading back into it the concerns of later contrivance. The spell cast by Berkeley and Hume and Russell has largely been broken. The alleged empiricist philosopher of common sense has had restored to him an epistemology devoted to vindicating its theocentric framework[2] and an understanding of the scope and methods of science.[3]

Locke's ideas about science, however, are not so clear and distinct. In the first place "science" carries no unambiguous meaning in the *Essay*. Anticipating modern usage, "science" sometimes means those empirical and theoretical investigations about nature or reality of the sort which "Mr. Newton" undertook when he revealed "new Discoveries of yet unknown Truths."[4] More frequently, however, "science" is equated with demonstrable knowledge as found only in logic or mathematics, an equation which entails that "we are not capable of *scientifical Knowledge*" of natural entities or "the several sorts of Bodies" at all.[5] A consequence

---

* For their criticisms of an earlier draft of this essay, I am indebted to Terence Ball, Mary G. Dietz, John Dunn, Larry Laudan, Clayton Roberts, David E. Soles, and John W. Yolton.

[1] *The Correspondence of John Locke*, ed. E. S. de Beer (Oxford, 1979), in eight volumes, #1501.

[2] See, for example, John Dunn, *Locke* (Oxford, 1984), ch. 3; John Dunn, "From Applied Theology to Social Analysis: The Break Between John Locke and the Scottish Enlightenment," in Istvan Hont and Michael Ignatieff (eds.), *Wealth and Virtue: The Shaping of Political Economy in the Scottish Enlightenment* (Cambridge, 1983), 119-35; David Gauthier, "Why Ought One Obey God? Reflections on Hobbes and Locke," *Canadian Journal of Philosophy*, 7 (1977), 425-46; and Richard Ashcraft, "Faith and Knowledge in Locke's Philosophy," in John W. Yolton (ed.), *John Locke: Problems and Perspectives* (Cambridge, 1969), 194-223.

[3] See, for example, Peter A. Schouls, *The Imposition of Method* (Oxford, 1980); Roger Woolhouse, *Locke's Philosophy of Science and Knowledge* (Oxford, 1971); Gerd Buchdahl, *Metaphysics and the Philosophy of Science* (Oxford, 1969); and the works cited in notes 11, 12, and 23 below.

[4] *Essay*, 4.7.3. This is also the sense of the closing chapter, 4.21.

[5] *Essay*, 4.3.26. Similar views may be found at 4.3.29 and 4.12.10.

of this ambiguity is that the demarcation between science and non-science cannot be drawn sharply. Nor can we readily determine the continuity or discontinuity which Locke thought existed between the various enterprises of the "understanding," say, medicine, natural religion, political knowledge, and the "experimental Philosophy of physical Things."[6] In short the meaning and domain of "science" in Locke's understanding of the "understanding" are not readily fixed.

These ambiguities prefigure another. The *Essay*, taken alone, wavers ambivalently between two competing methods of the understanding: (1) the method of natural history; and (2) the hypothetical method. The first method counsels "Experience, Observation, and natural History," which yield "collections of sensible qualities" perceived to coexist in the world.[7] The second forwards the use of speculations about things which lie beyond "the reach of humane Senses," wherein "we can only guess, and probably conjecture."[8] Even when these two methods assume concrete form in seventeenth century debates in natural philosophy—debates to which Locke was a distant party—his ambivalence appears to persist. On the one hand he invokes "the corpuscularian hypothesis" to explain the ultimate constituents of matter.[9] On the other hand he calls for "improving our knowledge in Substances only by Experience and History," especially where we lack "Microscopical Eyes."[10]

Taking the *Essay* alone, then, Locke's interpreters have ample textual warrant for considering him to be a champion of one or another very different "Lockean" method. R. M. Yost, John W. Yolton, and others take Locke to be a natural historian.[11] Maurice Mandelbaum, Laurens Laudan, and others take Locke to be a proponent of the hypothetical method.[12] The corpuscularian hypothesis figures centrally and intriguingly in this debate, for almost all parties concede that Locke accepted the hypothesis.[13] What remains in dispute is the bearing that Locke's

---

[6] *Essay*, 4.3.26.
[7] *Essay*, 4.12.12; 3.6.24.
[8] *Essay*, 4.16.12.
[9] *Essay*, 4.3.16.
[10] *Essay*, 4.12.10; 2.23.12.
[11] R. M. Yost, "Locke's Rejection of Hypotheses about Sub-Microscopic Events," *JHI*, 12 (1951), 111-30; John W. Yolton, *John Locke and the Way of Ideas* (Oxford, 1956); John W. Yolton, *John Locke and the Compass of the Human Understanding* (Cambridge, 1970); and John Losee, *A Historical Introduction to the Philosophy of Science* (Oxford, 1980), ch. 9.
[12] Maurice Mandelbaum, *Philosophy, Science, and Sense Perception* (Baltimore, 1964); and Laurens Laudan, "The Nature and Source of Locke's View of Hypotheses," *JHI*, 28 (1967), 211-23. Buchdahl generally shares this view in *Metaphysics*, 211-15.
[13] See, in particular, Yolton's careful and detailed discussion, in *John Locke and the Compass of Human Understanding*, 64-75. Not all parties appear to make this concession, however. Losee says that Locke "expressed no interest in entertaining hypotheses about atomic structure" in *A Historical Introduction*, 97.

acceptance had on his conception of the method of science and the human understanding. Mandelbaum and Laudan take Locke's acceptance of the corpuscularian hypothesis as consistent with his hypotheticalism, while Yost and Yolton insist that it has no bearing on his general understanding of and prescriptions for the advancement of science. In a postscript to his contribution to this debate, Laudan concludes that a great divide separates the two interpretations of Locke's understanding of science:

Unfortunately, the interpretative and exegetical divide which separates the Yost-Yolton reading of Locke from the Mandelbaum-Laudan one probably cannot be settled by further citations of "definitive" texts from the *Essay*; taken in isolation, that work provides evidence for both interpretations.[14]

This divide might yet be crossed from two directions. Laudan suggests one direction: "What may help settle the issue is to ask a larger question about where Locke fits into the major intellectual traditions of the seventeenth century."[15] The debate whether Locke is a natural historian of science or a hypotheticalist turns, then, on whether we place him in the tradition of Bacon or in the tradition of Boyle, respectively.

Discussion of "traditions" amidst the incredible novelty and fluidity of seventeenth-century science, however, may impose more order than is to be found. No one then had very steady opinions of the changing ideals of science,[16] and steady interpretations of them are not to be found today. Thus Yolton underscores Boyle's caution about hypotheses and his praise of natural history, while Mandelbaum and Peter Urbach underscore Bacon's commitments to the hypothetical method.[17] Barbara Shapiro notes that "several leading scientists of the pre-Newtonian era suggests how the Baconian research program was forging an alliance with hypothetical reasoning."[18] "The incomparable Mr. Newton"—who shared with Locke his "mystical fansies" and once, in a spell of derangement, even wished him dead[19]—was remarkably ambivalent about the problem of hypotheses versus induction in science, despite *hypotheses non fingo*.[20] In short, the voice of "tradition" is all but inaudible amidst such clamoring of diverse opinion. Locke hardly quiets matters, either,

[14] In I. C. Tipton (ed.), *Locke on Human Understanding* (Oxford, 1977), 161.
[15] *Ibid.*
[16] Margaret J. Osler, "John Locke and the Changing Ideal of Scientific Knowledge," *JHI*, 31 (1970), 3-16.
[17] Yolton, *John Locke and the Compass of Human Understanding*, 57; Mandelbaum, *Philosophy, Science, and Sense Perception*, 51; and Peter Urbach, "Francis Bacon as a Precursor of Popper," *British Journal of the Philosophy of Science*, 33 (1982), 113-32.
[18] Barbara Shapiro, *Probability and Certainty in Seventeenth-Century England* (Princeton, 1983), 49. More generally on early probabilistic reasoning, see Ian Hacking *The Emergence of Probability* (Cambridge, 1984).
[19] *Correspondence*, # #1357 and 1659.
[20] See, for example, Mandelbaum, *Philosophy, Science, and Sense Perception*, ch. 2 and I. B. Cohen, "Hypotheses in Newton's Philosophy," *Physis*, 8 (1966), 163-84.

for his praise for Bacon and Boyle and Newton and other scientific lights of his generation makes it all but impossible with any confidence or unanimity to class his ideas with those of any one of his contemporaries. And in the end Locke speaks for himself, whatever Bacon or Boyle or Newton may have said.[21]

In this essay I hope to cross this divide in another way. Setting my sights exclusively on Locke, I engage in a conceptual reconstruction of his views of the human understanding by attending to his explicit invocation of "hypotheses" and "method." In so doing, I shall look beyond the *Essay*—to Locke's other works, to his disputes in print, and to his manuscript on "method." And I shall consider contexts other than those circumscribed by debates over the corpuscularian hypothesis. When this is done—that is, when the range of texts and contexts is enlarged and perused—two general points emerge.

First, Locke recognized the indispensable *use* of "hypotheses" in the advancement of human understanding—not only in what we have come to call physics but also in optics, geology, medicine, natural religion, and politics. Indeed Locke himself advanced and pursued a number of his own hypotheses in these various contexts—all of which or none of which may be considered to be "scientific," depending on Locke's ambiguously different characterizations of "science." Second, Locke outlines a *method* for judging hypotheses. To put it briefly, hypotheses are to be compared and judged competitively, such that one hypothesis is rejected only when another with "greater light" is available to replace it; and this is determined in turn by judging the overall comparative advantage of the "whole systems" from which these competing hypotheses issue. Both points suggest a form of imaginative but disciplined inquiry which Locke could well have called his "way of hypotheses."

Locke's manuscript on "method" helps advance these points in a dramatic way. Despite its publication a century and more ago in Lord Peter King's *Life of John Locke*,[22] this remarkably important and succinct statement has surprisingly failed to figure in the debates over Locke's understanding of science.[23] Given its importance in this context, a more faithful version is introduced and printed below as an appendix. Com-

[21] Many similarities, of course, may be found. Laudan's case for the filiations between Boyle and Locke is a strong one indeed, as others have also observed. For striking comparisons with Locke in the matter of hypotheses, see Boyle's "MS Notes on a Good and Excellent Hypothesis" in M. A. Stewart (ed.), *Selected Philosophical Papers of Robert Boyle* (Manchester, 1979), 119.

[22] *Life of John Locke, with Extracts from His Correspondence, Journals, and Commonplace Books* (London, 1829). There are also editions from 1858 and 1884.

[23] This situation may finally be changing (to judge by developments which I discovered after finishing this essay). See the brief attention to Locke's manuscript in the essay by David E. Soles's, "Locke's Empiricism and the Postulation of Unobservables," *Journal of the History of Philosophy*, 23 (1985), 365-66. The concluding section of Soles's important essay complements the discussion here.

peting hypotheses, Locke tells us there, provide what little light we have "to finde truth . . . in this our darke and short sighted state."

I. When discussing "the abuse of words" in the *Essay*, Locke complains of the failure of disputants to provide definitions for their words. "If Men would tell, what *Ideas* they made their Words stand for, there could not be half that Obscurity or Wrangling, in the search or support of Truth, that there is." [24] Had Locke followed his own advice by offering a definition or suggesting what Idea it stood for, when, as often, he used the word "hypothesis," perhaps the subsequent history of dispute over his account of science and the human understanding would not have been marked by such "Obscurity or Wrangling" that there has been. But, alas, Locke never defined "hypothesis"; much less did he compose a sustained work on the hypothetical method. He left no Essay, no Treatise, no Letter on the matter. In the absence of a definition or a sustained work, students of Locke's thought must attend carefully and systematically to Locke's uses of the term "hypothesis," for such uses provide the necessary linguistic material out of which Locke's considered views may be reconstructed. This is necessary in order to avoid attributing to Locke certain views or distinctions that he did not hold and to restore the discussion about "hypotheses" to those contexts which he thought the appropriate ones.

There are two principal sorts of these contexts. The second section of this essay will attend to those contexts—which these days we would call philosophical or methodological—in which Locke reflects in very general terms on topics like maxims, probability, bottoming, and explanation. Here he makes a number of references to "hypotheses" from which we may reconstruct his views of the hypothetical method as a whole. The first section attends principally to those contexts—which these days we would call scientific or substantive—in which Locke directs his attention to actual debates over competing hypotheses in physics, geology, natural religion, and politics. Attention to both sorts of contexts takes us far and wide, but the travels are rewarding. At the end we may espy a greater unity than is often seen in Locke's account of the human understanding and the various domains of its inquiry. What he says methodologically about "hypotheses" concords with what he shows substantively about their actual use.

Although Locke provides no explicit definition of "hypotheses," what he states or implies in many contexts, in and out of the *Essay*, suggests what he has in mind. Hypotheses are probable conjectures beyond the facts of observation and experience about things, actions, events, their causes or consequences which issue from some theoretical system serving to explain known phenomena.

[24] *Essay*, 3.10.15.

Hypotheses, that is, are a species of "conjecture" or "speculation" about empirical matters which attend the inevitable human propensity to "penetrate into the Causes of Things."[25] As such, they are not, strictly speaking, a part of "knowledge" on Locke's reckoning, for knowledge means demonstrable or intuitive certainty such as found only in logic, mathematics, or (as Locke thinks) morality.[26] Rather, hypotheses exist in the "twilight of probability," wherein lies "the greatest part of our Concernment."[27] "Probability," Locke avers, is "to supply the defect of our knowledge, and to guide us where that fails, is always conversant about Propositions, whereof we have no Certainty, but only some inducements to receive them for true."[28] Such inducements to truth as we humans have in this our twilight passage "either concern some . . . matter of fact, which falling under Observation, is capable of humane Testimony; or else concerning Things, which being beyond the testimony of our Senses, are not capable of any such Testimony."[29] Since so very much lies beyond our senses, where "we can only guess, and probably conjecture," hypotheses are indispensable in the conduct of the human understanding.[30]

Hypotheses, moreover, are seldom isolated conjectures. Rather, they are usually part of "whole systems" of thought. Such systems, as Locke implies in his manuscript on "method" (appended below), are complex structures of propositions and beliefs, whether about matter or thinking, God or political order. These systems establish the relevant cognitive framework for fashioning hypotheses in the first place. Since the human understanding forms a complex and integrated structure of ideas, hypotheses add to and follow from the coherence of our knowledge as a whole. Otherwise they would be but isolated stabs in the dark and of no assistance to "our dim candle, Reason" as it attempts to illuminate the path of "our Pilgrimage."[31]

Despite its reputation as a "philosophical" classic, the *Essay* itself yields numerous references to actually debated and debatable "hypotheses" of the sort here described. Most of these references are of a general nature, and most advise approaching hypotheses warily since many are "false," none "certain," all at best "probable."[32] Especially false, Locke thinks, are those "distinct hypotheses" about "innate prac-

---

[25] *Essay*, 4.12.13; cf. 4.16.12.
[26] It is a matter of some controversy whether Locke includes sensitive knowledge as a part of genuine knowledge. Nothing discussed here, however, turns on the outcome of that controversy.
[27] *Essay*, 4.14.2.
[28] *Essay*, 4.15.4.
[29] *Essay*, 4.16.5.
[30] *Essay*, 4.16.12.
[31] *Essay*, 4.19.8; 4.14.2.
[32] *Essay*, 4.12.13; 4.16.12; 4.20.11.

tical principles," as well as virtually all the hypotheses held by "the Schoolmen and the Metaphysicians," those "great Mint-Masters" who "coin new words." [33] Indeed it is against the abuse of words of these "Mint-Masters" that Locke's frequently pejorative uses of "hypothesis" may be understood. Animal generation, magnetism, and "intelligent Inhabitants in . . . other Mansions of the vast Universe" are "hypotheses" about which Locke makes no commitments.[34] The "corpuscularian hypothesis," on the other hand, appears to enjoy Locke's full acceptance, for once we conceive of matter as composed of minute corpuscles, "it is thought to go farthest in an intelligible explication of the Qualities of Bodies; and I fear the Weakness of Humane Understanding is scarce able to substitute another." [35]

Weaker still is the human understanding when it hypothesizes about the soul: whether it be an immaterial substance or thinking matter. Warily, Locke calls it a draw:

He who will give himself leave to consider freely, and look into the dark and intricate part of each Hypothesis, will scarce find his Reason able to determine him fixedly for, or against the Soul's Materiality. Since on which side soever he views it, either as an unextended Substance, or a thinking extended Matter; the difficulty to conceive either, will, whilst either alone is in his Thoughts, still drive him to the contrary side.[36]

Locke does not remain altogether silent, however. For he seizes the opportunity offered by this stalemate of hypotheses to suggest his own, "that GOD can, if he pleases, superadd to Matter a Faculty of Thinking." [37]

For all its references to "hypotheses," the *Essay* understates Locke's use of hypotheses, and his recognition of their indispensability in the conduct of human understanding. Exploring beyond the pages of the *Essay* we discover new worlds of "hypotheses."

"Minute corpuscles" (to begin with the most controversial hypothesis of the *Essay*) emerge again and again as part of the system of mechanical philosophy to explain the ultimate constituents of matter. In the *Conduct of Human Understanding*, in *Elements of Natural Philosophy*, and in *Some Thoughts Concerning Education*, Locke allows, as he puts it in the last mentioned of these works, that "the modern Corpuscularians talk in most Things more intelligibly than the Peripateticks" when they talk

[33] *Essay*, 1.3.14; 3.10.2. Also see 3.10.14 and the chapter on "maxims" (4.7).
[34] *Essay*, 4.16.12. Also see the list compiled by Yolton in *John Locke and the Compass of Human Understanding*, 59-60.
[35] *Essay*, 4.3.16.
[36] *Essay*, 4.3.6.
[37] *Essay*, 4.3.6.

the language of "hypotheses."[38] The corpuscularian hypothesis finds another theoretical purpose in explaining perception in the *Examination of P. Malebranche's Opinion*. Against the deficient "hypothesis" of Malebranche that we see all things in God, Locke uses "my hypothesis" to explain "how by material rays of light visible species may be brought into the eye." Given our "animal spirits" (another hypothesis warily advanced in the *Essay*), we perceive "visible species" due to "the motion of particles of matter coming from them and striking on our organs."[39]

But matter—whether it be composed of minute corpuscles or whether it propagates light—does not exhaust Locke's catalogue of physical (much less other) hypotheses. This, indeed, is just the beginning. He accepted the Copernican hypothesis about planetary motions as "the likeliest to be true in itself."[40] He also accepted Newton's hypothesis of gravitational attraction, repeatedly going so far as to think it "demonstrable."[41] And in speculations about the geology of the Biblical Flood, he thought he found something fully as intelligible as gravity.

And therefore since the Deluge cannot be well explained without admitting something out of the ordinary Course of Nature, I propose it to be considered whether God's altering the Centre in the Earth for a Time (a Thing as intelligible as Gravity itself . . .) will not more easily account for Noah's Flood than any Hypothesis yet made use of to solve it.

This is not a Place for that Argument [Locke goes on] reserving to a fitter Opportunity a fuller Explication of this Hypothesis, and the Application of it to all the Parts of the Deluge, and any Difficulties can be supposed in the History of the Flood, as recorded in the Scripture.[42]

Locke never seized the opportunity he reserved for later. But his correspondents kept alive the topic of "your Hypothesis about the Deluge."[43]

Medicine—the discipline in which Locke was trained—also abounds with hypotheses, especially "distinct hypotheses concerning distinct species of diseases."[44] In these matters, and often in correspondence with

[38] *Some Thoughts Concerning Education*, section 193 in *The Works of John Locke* in ten volumes (London, 1812), IX, 185. Also see the explanatory potential of "these small and insensible corpuscles" in *Elements of Natural Philosophy* in *Works*, III, 304.

[39] *Works*, IX, 215-17. Cf. *Essay*, 3.4.10 and *Works*, III, 262-64 where Locke uses the hypothesis of "animal spirits" as the "mechanical cause" to explain certain visions individuals have in the dark.

[40] *Works*, IX, 173.

[41] *Essay*, 4.7.11; *Correspondence*, #1538; *Works*, IX, 186. This is very strong language indeed given Locke's usual strictures on what counts as demonstration.

[42] *Works*, IX, 184-85. Note well here how Locke stands by his hypothesis even against the historical account of the Flood as found in Scripture.

[43] *Correspondence*, #1865. Cf. ##1684 and 2131.

[44] *Correspondence*, #1593. In this letter Locke characterizes "general theories" as "for the most part but a sort of waking dreams."

the brothers Molyneux, Locke often rings a tocsin against "speculative hypotheses," praising instead a natural history of disease. Intimations of such complaints against "speculative theorems" and "hypotheses" can be heard as early as 1669 in the manuscript "de Arte Medica."[45] Locke's tone, however, is by no means universally dismissive, as evidenced the very next year in the 1670 fragment on smallpox, where he forthrightly adopts the "hypothesis" that "acute diseases" are inflammations that may be cured in the same way as smallpox.[46] A balanced noted is struck in "Methodus Medendi" (1678).

Once these ["specific natures" of diseases] are ascertained, then the Rules which dogmatists have built up out of their hypotheses of the humors, plethora, etc., may be very useful in applying the method or remedies, modifying them according to the patient's particular constitution.[47]

Elsewhere Locke speaks even more neutrally of the "ordinary hypothesis" of the humoral theory of disease, a neutrality well-chosen, since he advances an alternative supposition about "the archaeus being enraged," which had even less in its favor than did the ordinary hypothesis.[48] Indeed by 1692 Locke was quite aware that his hypotheses departed from medical orthodoxy. Yet they were no less reasonable on that account, since reason followed hypotheses in such matters. On the occasion of the illness of the young Lord Mordaunt, Locke confessed that

My notions in physick are soe different from the method which obteins . . . and not being of the [Royal] Colleg [of Physicians] can make noe other figure there but of an Unskillful empirick, and noe doubt anything I should offer would seeme as strange to his physitians as the way you tell me they take with him seems strange to me. But as every ones hypothesis is, soe is his reason disposd to judge both of disease and medicines.[49]

The battle between hypotheses raged in the heated arenas of natural religion and politics as well. Here too, that is, we find debates over probable conjectures beyond the facts of observation and experience, conjectures which are all the more important because they additionally concern our conduct and the prospects of our right living. Thus, even though Locke thought that we could have demonstrably certain "Knowledge of the Creator and the Knowledge of our Duty,"[50] there was much else only probable and hypothetical and so controversial. Thus his hypothesis that God might superadd thinking to matter did not long remain an innocent metaphysical speculation in the *Essay*. Indeed in John Yol-

[45] Quoted in Patrick Romanell, *John Locke and Medicine* (Buffalo, N.Y., 1984), 116.
[46] Quoted in *ibid.*, 71.
[47] Quoted in *ibid.*, 139.
[48] Quoted in *ibid.*, 104.
[49] *Correspondence*, #1501.
[50] *Essay*, 2.23.12.

ton's intricate telling of the tale of "thinking matter," its obvious flirtation
with materialism "raised a storm of protest right through to the last
years of the eighteenth century."[51] Sounding suspiciously unitarian (and
much else besides) to orthodox ears, Locke's hypothesis helped sustain
hundreds of pages of increasingly testy controversy, especially with
Thomas Burnet and Edward Stillingfleet, the Bishop of Worcester. In
defending more generally what Stillingfleet called his (Locke's) "new
hypothesis of reason," Locke stuck to his guns, saying that "it can never
be proved that there is a substantial substance in us, because upon that
supposition it is possible it may be a material substance that thinks in
us."[52] Later still, as replies and recriminations flew back and forth, Locke
tried to shift the burden of proof in matters hypothetical, saying to the
good Bishop, "I humbly conceive it would be more to your purpose to
prove, that the infinite omnipotent Creator of all things out of nothing,
cannot, if he pleases, superadd to some parcels of matter . . . a faculty
of thinking."[53] Locke's thin veneer of tact with Stillingfleet was wholly
absent when debate was not public. In the margins of his copy of Burnet's
Third Remarks Upon an Essay Concerning Human Understanding, Locke
vehemently defends his "hypothesis" against suspicions of deism.

When you have demonstrated the soule of man to be immaterial your own
hypothesis will be clear of these objections against mine, & I shall come over
to you & be clear too, if you know more than I can goe beyond probability that
it is soe. All my accusations of Philosophical Deisme let the fault of that be
what you please fall upon yourself and own hypothesis.[54]

Locke's testiness in these disputes says less about his rancorousness
than about the stakes at issue in the debate. Being lumped together with
deists, unitarians, and materialists was tantamount to being indicted as
an atheist. Indeed two years after Locke's death the "discovery of Atheism" in the *Essay* was explored at considerable length.[55] But Locke was
no atheist.[56] And while his theism was a matter of faith, he shored it up

[51] John W. Yolton, *Thinking Matter* (Minneapolis, 1983), 17. Also see the important
essay by M. J. Ayers, "Mechanism, Superaddition, and the Proof of God's Existence in
Locke's *Essay*," *Philosophical Review*, 90 (1981).

[52] *Works*, IV, 28-29, 33. Also see discussion of Locke's "hypothesis" about human
nature, 74-75.

[53] *Works*, IV, 294.

[54] Quoted in Noah Porter, "Marginalia Lockeana" (1857), reprinted in Peter A.
Schouls (ed.), *Remarks upon an Essay Concerning Human Understanding*, (New York,
1984), 49.

[55] William Carroll, *Dissertation upon the Tenth Chapter of the Fourth Book of Mr.
Locke's Essay, wherein the author endeavors to establish Spinoza's atheistic hypothesis*
(London, 1706), as noted in A. C. Fraser's edition of the *Essay* (New York, 1959),
316 n.

[56] As is well known, Locke went out of his way to exclude atheists (alongside papists)
from any act of toleration. See especially the *Letter Concerning Toleration* (New York,

with critical engagements by the way of hypotheses. In the context of making more general reflections on "method" (see appendix below), atheism was very much on Locke's mind. Recapitulating the arguments of the *Essay* against the "hypotheses" advanced by "atheists" and "the Men of Matter," Locke explodes the "direct contradictions" of those "who denie a God." These contradictions reveal themselves more clearly than ever in such claims (as Locke reconstructs them) as "thinking things were made out of unthinking things by an unthinking power." Locke brings his attack to a close, saying "these mens hypotheses" are "ridiculous when set up against the supposition of a being that had from eternity more knowledge & power than all matter taken togeather & soe was able to frame it into this orderly state of nature."

In the Preface to the *Two Treatises of Government* Locke pressed an even more dangerous adversary in the matter of hypotheses. With characteristic finality about political judgments he announced his intentions to strike a final blow against Sir Robert Filmer, for already "the King, and Body of the Nation, have since so thoroughly confuted his Hypothesis."[57] "Sir Robert's Hypothesis" attempted, unsuccessfully in Locke's judgment, to trace all extant political authorities to "Adam's Royal Authority." This was his "whole Hypothesis."[58] But it invoked an entire system of arch-royalist doctrines—patriarchalism, divine-right absolutism, and passive obedience to a *de facto* conqueror—doctrines which Locke wanted publicly renounced and abjured in 1690 in order to settle the nation after the Glorious Revolution.[59]

To all this Locke opposed "my Hypothesis," a hypothesis which invoked, again more generally, his own political system with its doctrines of consent, trust, and natural rights.[60] Locke specified a particularly striking consequence of "this hypothesis" in the closing chapter of the *Second Treatise*.[61] It is the very radical and seditious hypothesis that the people may act legitimately to resist tyrannical sovereigns who have broken their trust. Perhaps it was such sedition which caused Locke to hold his tongue about owning the hypothesis as his, at least until his executors broke the seal on his will.

1955), 52. However, in the *Third Letter Concerning Toleration*, Locke proclaimed his position against the "hypothesis for the necessity of force" against atheists in maintaining true Christian religion, as proposed by Jonas Proast. See *Works*, VI, 302. (Incidentally, the *Third Letter* is replete with references to "hypotheses," particularly chapters 5 and 10).

[57] *Two Treatises of Government*, ed. Peter Laslett (New York, 1960), Preface, 171.
[58] *Two Treatises*, 1.32; 1.78.
[59] Locke's radical demands may be found in Bodleian Library MS Locke e. 18, as edited and introduced in James Farr and Clayton Roberts, "John Locke on the Glorious Revolution: A Rediscovered Document," *Historical Journal*, 28 (1985), 385-98.
[60] *Two Treatises*, Preface.
[61] *Two Treatises*, 2.224.

Lest it be thought that in the above examples Locke uses "hypothesis" indiscriminately or equivocally in too many contexts—or that we might readily distinguish "scientific" from "non-scientific" hypotheses—it should be reemphasized that all of the hypotheses mentioned conform at least rudimentarily to the definition briefly sketched at the outset. Though they may display either speculative or practical functions in everyday life, all are probable conjectures beyond the facts of observation and experience about things, actions, events, their causes or consequences. These conjectures issue from some whole system which serves to explain known phenomena. This is evidently true of hypotheses in natural philosophy or about physical unobservables, like gravity, unextended substance, bodily humors, God's loosing Noah's flood, or His making matter think. It is also true of the hypotheses of natural religion and politics, even though they *additionally* concern human conduct and so invoke still *other* standards for our believing them worthy of acceptance. Locke's pre-Kantian sensibilities allow him to discover or forge continuities between those hypotheses in natural philosophy or about unobservable entities and those hypotheses in natural religion or about political action—even though these latter hypotheses have normative or prescriptive content, as we would put it these days.[62]

Thus, for example, the normative grounds of our obedience and the limits of our prescriptive duties are surely the stakes in the *Two Treatises*. Nonetheless, Locke's many attacks focus in good part on the causal and empirical claims embedded in "Sir Robert's Hypothesis" of Adam's royal authority. That is, Locke not only found Filmer's hypothesis normatively unacceptable as a morally binding prescription for God's creatures, but he also rejected it for harboring other deficiencies of a non-normative sort, particularly because it was premised on unknowable claims about Adam's lineage and some patently false claims about current rulers. Thus in speaking of the evidence necessary for empirically ascertaining Adam's royal authority after Babel, Locke says facetiously, "If you must find it, pray do, and you will help us to a new piece of History."[63] Of course,

---

[62] This is a methodological variant of a claim that a number of historians of science have made with regard to Locke's era. For example, M. A. Stewart reminds us in the case of Boyle that "there is no clear line at which the science of nature ends and the theology of nature begins." *Philosophical Papers of Robert Boyle*, xiii. Margaret C. Jacob makes a similar point about Newtonians and Latitudinarians at the end of the seventeenth century. Natural philosophy, natural religion, and political theory all merged. See *The Newtonians and the English Revolution, 1689-1720* (Ithaca, 1976).

[63] *Two Treatises*, 1.143; cf. 1.111. The historical or empirical status of Locke's state of nature is less clear. Hans Aarsleff follows Dugald Stewart in holding that it is itself a piece of "conjectural or theoretical history." See "The State of Nature and Human Nature," in Yolton (ed.), *John Locke: Problems and Perspectives*, 103-04. John Dunn denies this in *The Political Thought of John Locke* (Cambridge, 1969), ch. 9. For related discussion, see Richard Ashcraft, "Locke's State of Nature: Historical Fact or Moral Fiction?" *American Political Science Review*, 62 (1968), 898-915.

Locke thinks no such "new place of History" is to be discovered. So much the worse for Filmer's hypothesis. Thus Locke concludes his indictment of Filmer by observing that " 'twas his misfortune to light upon an hypothesis that could not be accommodated to the Nature of things and Human Affairs . . . and therefore must needs often clash with common Sense and Experience."[64]

Locke shores up the non-normative defenses of his own hypothesis by adducing "several examples out of History" about the contractual origins of particular civil societies or of "Men withdrawing themselves . . . and setting up new Governments in other places."[65] Some of these examples are "evident matter of fact"; others "great and apparent Conjectures" of the sort Joseph Acosta had to make in order to account for "many parts of America" in its prehistory.[66] (Beyond his explanatory efforts, Locke is also concerned to refute arguments directed to the consequences of propagating his views. "This hypothesis" does not "lay a ferment for frequent Rebellion," at least "no more than any other Hypothesis."[67] Empirically speaking, "the People" are "not so easily got out of their Old Forms."[68])

The corpuscularian hypothesis, it bears mentioning in this context, is the only hypothesis which at least *sometimes* appears *not* to conform to Locke's account—paradoxical as this might sound given all the attention to this particular hypothesis. For at least occasionally Locke intimates that his "minute particles of Bodies" might be *observable in principle* because already in practice "microscopes plainly discover to us" tiny new things "by thus augmenting the acuteness of our senses." What lies ahead, however, "if Glasses could be found, that yet could magnify them 1000, or 10000 times more, is uncertain."[69] But whatever the final judgment on the direct observability of minute corpuscles, and so of his espousal of the corpuscularian hypothesis, Locke shows himself to be a hypothetical thinker of enormous range and fertility.

Hypotheses, in short, are everywhere evident in Locke's "commonwealth of Learning."[70] They emerge, clearly labelled, in virtually all of his writings—in his major works, in his lesser works, in his published

[64] *Two Treatises*, 1.137.
[65] *Two Treatises*, 2.102; 2.115.
[66] *Two Treatises*, 2.103. Also note the counterfactual language of historical conjecture when Locke discusses early civil societies in the *Third Letter of Toleration*: "Let me ask you, Whether it be not possible that men, to whom the rivers and woods afforded the spontaneous provisions of life, . . . should live in one society . . . under one Chieftain . . . without any municipal laws, judges, or any person with superiority established amongst them. . . ." Cited in Laslett's note to *Two Treatises*, 2.108.
[67] *Two Treatises*, 2.224.
[68] *Two Treatises*, 2.223.
[69] *Essay*, 2.23.11; cf. 4.3.25.
[70] *Essay*, Epistle to the Reader.

and unpublished disputes, in the seemingly inexhaustible storehouse of reflections preserved in letters, commonplace books, notes for publication, and the margins of books. The intellectual contexts for raising and using hypotheses are as varied as the texts within which they are recorded— in physics, optics, geology, medicine, natural religion, and politics. From minute corpuscles, to thinking matter, to gravity, to the deluge, to humors, to atheism, to Adam's royal authority, to popular resistance, Locke advances or attacks one hypothesis after another. If we fail to appreciate the depth of Locke's commitments to hypotheses, we are in danger of misunderstanding his conception of the speculative and conjectural contours of the human understanding. We may also be in danger of misunderstanding his own scientific and philosophical speculations, advertised to his readers as "hypotheses," "conjectures," and "strange doctrines." [71]

II. If the *Essay* intimates but understates Locke's recognition of the *use* of "hypotheses," it likewise intimates but understates his reflections on the hypothetical *method*. To discover his views in full we must turn to his collected writings. But the *Essay*'s intimations are crucial, for there Locke records the significance he attached to the hypothetical method and the general shape of his thoughts about it.

Hypotheses—at least when "intelligible" and "well made" as the *Essay* demands—serve three essential functions for systematic human inquiry. In their "true use" they (1) prove to be "great helps to the Memory"; (2) "direct us to new discoveries"; and (3) help us to "explain any Phenomenon of Nature." [72]

Hypotheses, firstly then, are mnemonic devices. Like stenographers' short-hand or "mathematicians . . . Diagrams and Figures," [73] such devices bear their histories with them. They compress for ready remembrance the facts they contain, the causal claims they embody, or the occasions under which they were inspired. Without them science would constantly have to retake its first steps and could never proceed to new cases. Medical hypotheses, for example, "are so far useful, as they serve as an art of memory to direct the physician in particular cases." [74]

---

[71] A longer study would be required to develop this point in full. But I suspect that here is a much greater degree of coherence between what Locke says in the abstract about science and the human understanding, and what he shows in his own substantive practice than is frequently allowed. As for his self-styled "strange doctrines," see his confessions about medicine (*Correspondence*, #1501); personal identity (*Essay*, 2.27.27; also characterized as a "hypothesis" in *Works*, III, 165); and just-war enslavement excluding the seizure of property (*Two Treatises*, 2.180). For a discussion of the last of these "strange doctrines," see my " 'So Vile and Miserable an Estate': The Problem of Slavery in Locke's Political Thought," *Political Theory*, 14 (1986), 263-89.
[72] *Essay*, 4.12.13.
[73] *Essay*, 4.3.19.
[74] *Correspondence*, #1593.

Besides this use, Locke may have been intimating an even more important insight into science, as well as revealing why memory and discovery make such a natural pair of functions for him. Medicine—like other forms of systematic inquiry—often progresses when facts or symptoms which are already well documented, but otherwise insignificant or apparently irrelevant to the present state of knowledge, suddenly gain theoretical novelty and significance by being connected with other facts, symptoms, or causes of disease. In these cases, as is now being appreciated, long known facts become "novel facts" or new discoveries, despite their pedestrian inheritance.[75] Thus there is an intimate link between memory and discovery, a link made possible by hypotheses.

"The discovery of Truths" comprises the second function of hypotheses, a function denied to syllogisms and "received maxims."[76] Hypotheses "serve as clues to lead us into farther knowledge" when the testimony of our senses fail us, as our senses must with bodies remote or minute, or causes ancient or invisible.[77] This is an obvious function of hypotheses in science, as was noted by Boyle; and Locke, perhaps unfortunately, expends little effort beyond stating the obvious.[78]

In the *Conduct*, in a passage referring to the *Essay*, Locke elaborates upon what he has in mind about the third and most important function of the "true use" of hypotheses.

True or false, solid or sandy, the mind must have some foundation to rest itself upon, and, as I have remarked in another place, it no sooner entertains any proposition but it frequently hastens to some hypothesis to bottom it on; till then it is unquiet and unsettled. So much do our own very tempers dispose us to a right use of our understandings, if we would follow as we should the inclinations of our nature.[79]

The sections on "fundamental verities" and on "bottoming" remake the same point. Hypotheses, as Locke says there, provide a set of foundational principles or "fundamental truths that lie at the bottom, the basis upon which a great many others rest, and in which they have their consistency." Here our explanations may find a "place of rest and stability."[80]

The gravitational hypothesis—"that admirable discovery of Mr. New-

[75] See Elie Zahar's amendment to Imre Lakatos's view of novel facts in "Why Did Einstein's Research Programme Supersede Lorentz's?" *British Journal of the Philosophy of Science*, 24 (1973), 95-123, 223-62.
[76] *Essay*, 4.16.12; 4.7.11; 4.17.6.
[77] *The Conduct of Human Understanding* (Oxford, 1901), 95.
[78] See Boyle's view that an "excellent hypothesis" will "enable a skillful Naturalist to Foretell Future Phaenomena," in Stewart (ed.) *Philosophical Papers of Robert Boyle* 119. In this connection also see Locke's letter to Boyle in which he hopes for a speedy return to his (Locke's) health so that he may go "trudging up and down in quest of new discoveries." *Correspondence*, #335.
[79] *Conduct*, 17.
[80] *Conduct*, 95-96.

ton"—provides Locke with an illustration of this explanatory function of hypotheses.[81] A political hypothesis provides another, one which is especially instructive for understanding Locke's view of explanation as well as reinforcing the observation made in the previous section that Locke saw methodological continuities between hypothetical reasoning in natural philosophy and in matters requiring our political judgments. The more particular question of the grand seigneur's lawful right to appropriate property from his people is to be "bottomed" on the foundational hypothesis whether people are equal or not.[82] In the *Two Treatises* Locke leaves no doubts as to his own assessment of the probable truth of the hypothesis of human equality. He goes on from that hypothesis to explain how men contract to form civil society under a system of laws entrusted to a sovereign body to execute. The violation of this trust— say, by the unlawful appropriation of the people's property—becomes the basis, yet further along the chain of explanations, for explaining popular resistance. Thus, the foundational hypothesis of human equality functions as a bottom for explaining lesser hypotheses, facts, and observations.

Beyond elaborating the three functions of hypotheses, the *Essay* also intimates how hypotheses are produced or generated. In the context of discovery, as we often put it these days, "the best conduct of rational Experiments, and the rise of Hypothesis" follow "a wary Reasoning from Analogy."[83] Analogy, in other words, helps us frame possible theories about things or causes unseen or unknown on the basis of things or causes seen or known. Herein lies a mechanism for educational reinforcement, for he or she who is experienced in producing hypotheses by analogy may "guess righter" in the future.[84]

Method, however, promises and must deliver more than just an account of the "true use" and "rise" of hypotheses. Precisely because our imaginations know no bounds when speculating beyond the testimony of our senses, the human understanding needs a method to *judge*—that is, to justify, retain, modify, or reject—the hypotheses it is compelled to pursue in its search for truth. In this matter the *Essay* must be read with care and eventually with other texts in hand. To appreciate this, consider the very first reference to "hypotheses" in the *Essay*: "But he, that would not deceive himself, ought to build his Hypothesis on matter of fact, and make it out by sensible experience, and not presume on matter of fact, because of his Hypothesis, that is, because he supposes it to be so."[85]

Short work could be made of Locke's conception of method if this

---

[81] *Conduct*, 95.
[82] *Conduct*, 96.
[83] *Essay*, 4.16.12.
[84] *Essay*, 4.12.10.
[85] *Essay*, 2.1.10.

oft-quoted remark exhausted his reflections. Taken literally, the admonition "to build ... Hypothesis on matter of fact and ... sensory experience" might appear to suggest a method of simple induction or confirmation. But to go by the evidence of the *Essay* alone, Locke cannot have meant it to be taken this way. Hypotheses cannot be built literally on "sensory experience" for they are, by definition, "beyond the testimony of the senses."[86] Moreover, hypotheses and matters of fact form two logically distinct classes of probability claims.

"To build," then, must be taken in a different way, a way which endorses only some sort of empirical basis for our hypotheses. To appreciate what sort, note two important features of Locke's reflections on method. The first is his persistent theme of wariness. Science and the human understanding need a "wary induction of particulars," lest we "cram ourselves with a great load of collections."[87] What is this, Locke asks, but "to make the head a magazine of materials which can hardly be called knowledge; ... he that makes every thing an observation has the same useless plenty and much more falsehood mixed with it."[88]

The selectiveness of observation, especially to reject falsehood, gives the lie to a simple inductivist reading of Locke's intentions. If anything, Locke's wariness in matters of fact and hypothesis suggests a falsificationist message (to use the idiom of our time). In his earliest speculations in the *Essays on the Law of Nature* Locke criticizes those who do not "suffer [their notions] to be called into question."[89] Later, in the *Conduct*, he speaks more frankly still of the fallacy of "hunting after arguments to make good one side of a question, and wholly to neglect and refuse those which favor the other side."[90] Conversely, he praises those who "freely expose their principles to the test" such that "if there be anything weak and unsound in them, are willing to have it detected."[91]

Hypotheses, in short, are "built" on the facts only insofar as they "freely expose" themselves "to the test." The tests, furthermore, are not simple or easily judged, a point brought out in a second feature of Locke's reflections on method. Only "upon a due ballancing [of] the whole" may we "reject, or receive" an hypothesis, as indeed of any probable proposition.[92] But hypotheses are special probabilities:

For these and the like coming not within the scrutiny of humane Senses, cannot be examined by them, or attested by any body, and therefore can appear more or less probable, only as they more or less agree to Truths that are established

---

[86] *Essay*, 4.16.12.
[87] *Conduct*, 37, 45.
[88] *Conduct*, 60.
[89] *Essays on the Law of Nature*, ed. W. von Leyden (Oxford, 1954), 143.
[90] *Conduct*, 38.
[91] *Conduct*, 88.
[92] *Essay*, 4.15.5.

in our Minds, and as they hold proportion to other parts of our Knowledge and Observation.[93]

Thus the rational basis of our hypotheses amounts to their overall "conformity" with what else we know.[94] "Tests" or "observations"—directly or standing alone—neither "build" up nor tear down a hypothesis. "Other parts of our knowledge" also figure as some of the counterweights in our "ballancing" of the whole."

This suggests a rich and complex method for judging hypotheses, one which presses well beyond the boundaries of an imagination hedged round by induction or natural history or even simple falsificationism. But Locke presses further still in the very important manuscript on "method." The full text can be found in the appendix below; only the high points need concern us here. It is worth mentioning that Locke's reflections are strikingly modern in a number of ways, *if* one wishes to read Locke with our own contemporary conceptions ready-to-hand.[95]

Tolerance, tenacity, and an enlarged understanding of alternative hypotheses must guide our "method" along its "way to finde truth." We initially "pursue the hypothesis which seems to us to carry with it the most light and consistency." We come to judge it, however, *only after* tolerating it "as far as it will goe" along a course charted by the "whole system" from which it issues. The system also provides some prima facie reasons for thinking our hypothesis probably true. With its support we give "what light and strength" we can to our hypothesis, in the face of ostensible inconsistencies or problems.

Although objections to an hypothesis will naturally emerge, they should not be allowed to prove immediately decisive. Tenacity has its advantages. First, the "weakness of our understanding" is such that our hypothesis will always "be liable to some exception beyond our power wholly to cleer it from." (Hypothetical truths are simply like that, given that they cannot, by definition, be produced or defended by reference to direct sensory testimony, much less to "clear demonstrations.") Second, we would "loose all stability" if, upon meeting an objection, we immediately gave up our hypothesis and wildly cast about for another, perhaps eventually thinking it "indifferent" which one we believed. Third, and most importantly, since such objections as we meet are themselves usually grounded in yet other hypotheses, we must "consider upon what foundation they are bottomed, and examine that in all its parts." This examination is particularly important, for as Locke puts it elsewhere, only

---

[93] *Essay*, 4.16.12.

[94] *Essay*, 4.15.4.

[95] I have in mind those philosophers of science who suggest the need to compare in sophisticated and complex way entire research programs or traditions, in particular Imre Lakatos, *The Methodology of Scientific Research Programmes* (Cambridge, 1978); and Larry Laudan, *Progress and Its Problems* (Berkeley, 1977).

"when another hypothesis is produced wherein there are not the like difficulties" are we justly tempted to abandon our original hypothesis.[96] To put this other competing hypothesis to the test, however, is to tally its problems and objections, to press it to *its* foundations, and so be led to the "whole system" from which it issues.
Now, at last, we may judge of our original hypothesis.

To shew which side has the best pretence to truth & followers the two whole systems must be set by one another & considered entirely and then see which is most consistent in all its parts; which least clogd with incoharencies or absurdities & which freest from begd principles and unintelligible notions. This is the fairest way to search after Truth.

The search for truth, in sum, proceeds by the comparative advantage which one competing hypothesis has over another, when the whole systems from which they issue confront one another. This comparative method, as Locke puts it in the parallel paragraph in the *Essay*, prevents the natural inclination of those minds which, finding difficulties with their initial isolated hypothesis, "throw themselves violently into the contrary Hypothesis," even though it too may be "altogether as unintelligible to an unbiassed Understanding."[97] Opponents seize upon this natural inclination, thinking that if they "can finde one weak place" in another's hypothesis, then they have "got the day." But "victory no more certainly always accompanies Truth than it does Right." Truth will out by a more pacific method. In calmly and correctly judging between competing hypotheses, we must lay aside that system which is "liable to most exceptions and labours under the greatest difficulties." The alternative with the "greater light" must guide us.

This is all the light we can ever expect to have "in this our dark and short sighted state." Locke concludes his reflections on "method" not only by condemning the comparative absurdities of "these mens hypotheses" that "denie a God" but by reminding us of our incredible limits when compared with "God's knowledge and power." This is no rhetorical flourish, for God is at the center of Locke's own system. God has prepared us in this our pilgrimage with understanding enough to know ourselves, His existence, and our moral duties. Beyond that we have our senses and a method of hypotheses. Without these our state would be infinitely darker.

Appendix

In the autumn of 1694 Locke drafted a number of additions to th Essay, then barely in its second edition.[98] Locke already had plans fo

[96] In Porter, "Marginalia Lockeana," 48.
[97] *Essay*, 4.3.6.
[98] Based on the date attached to Locke's entry on "libertie" which follows the or

future editions, the fourth and last of which (published in 1700) contained a number of significant changes. Such entries as Locke made in his commonplace books and journals leading up to these changes suggest those topics most on his mind, topics often planted there because of the gentle but persistent prodding of his friend William Molyneux.[99] Besides entries on "libertie" and "understanding," Locke penned some particularly important remarks on hypotheses under the heading of "method." Another heading (but no entry) on "enthusiasm" preceded these remarks. Locke eventually added a wholly new chapter on enthusiasm to the fourth edition of the *Essay*. The manuscript remarks on "method" can be seen in altered form entering the *Essay* and the *Conduct*.[100]

Locke's entry on method was first published in 1829 (and republished in later editions) by Lord Peter King in his *Life of John Locke, with Extracts from His Correspondence, Journals, and Commonplace Books*. King, excusably given his limited aims in bringing out these materials, made no commentary on the entry, save this: "The following paper appears to be intended as a supplement to the mode of acquiring truth; it illustrates Mr. Locke's other works, and shows how deeply his mind was engaged in this particular." [101] Judged by the inattention to this entry by Locke's subsequent interpreters up to our day, it would rather appear that Lord King's *Life* has been about as dark a closet for Locke's remarks on method and hypotheses as Locke's original commonplace books (now in the Lovelace Collection at the Bodleian Library).

Locke's remarks bear so directly on our concerns that the entire long paragraph deserves to be appended here. Given its bearing, a copy closer to Locke's original is preferable to King's version. This allows me to restore two lost lines, a crossed-out item, and Locke's own spelling, capitalization, and (lack of) punctuation.[102]

Method[1]

The way to finde truth as far as we are able to reach it in this our darke & short sighted state is to pursue the hypothesis that seems to us to carry with it the most light & consistency as far as we can without

---

ɔn "method." The substance of this entry figured in a letter of Locke's to LeClerc. See note to *Correspondence*, #1798.

[99] See especially *Correspondence*, ##1579, 1592, 1609, 1622 (with discussion of 'Malebranches Hypothesis"), 1643 (with Locke's discussion of his "hypothesis" of "humane freedom"), 1652, 1655, 1685, and 1763 (with Molyneux's discussion of Locke's 'Candid Recession from your Former Hypothesis").

[100] Especially at *Essay*, 4.3.6; and *Conduct*, 19.

[101] King, *Life*, 315.

[102] I have only omitted minor items which Locke crossed out; and I have written out Locke's contractions.

[1] Bodleian Library MS Locke e. 28, f. 115-16.

raising objections or striking at those that come in our way till we have carried our present principle as far as it will goe & given what light & strength we can to all the parts of it. And when that is done then to take into our consideration any objections that lie against it but not soe as to pursue them as objections against the Systeme we had formerly erected but to consider upon what foundation they are bottomed & examine that in all its parts & then putting the two whole Systems togeather see which is liable to most exceptions & labours under the greatest difficulties. For such is the weakness of our understandings that unless where we have clear demonstrations we can scarce make out to our selves any truths which will not be liable to some exception beyond our power wholly to clear it from & therefor if upon that ground we are presently bound to give up our former opinion[2] we shall be in a perpetual fluctuation every day changeing our mindes & passing from one side to an other & we shall loose all stability of thought & at last give up all probable truths as if there were noe such thing or which is not much better think it indifferent which side we take. To this yet as dangerous as it is the ordinary way of manageing controversies in the world directly tends. If an opponent can finde one weak place in his adversarys doctrine & reduce him to a stand with difficulties riseing from thence he presently concludes he has got the day & may justly triumph in the goodness of his owne cause whereas victory no more certainly always accompanies Truth than it does Right. It shews indeed the weakness of the part attacked or of the defence of it. But to shew which side has the best pretence to truth & followers the two whole systems must be set by one another & considered entirely & then see which is most consistent in all its parts; which least clogd with incoharences or absurdities & which freest from begd principles & unintelligible notions. This is the fairest way to search after Truth & the surest not to mistake on which side she is. There is scarce any controversie which is not a full instance of this & if a man will embrace noe opinion but what he can clear from all difficultys & remove all objections I fear he will have but very narrow thoughts & find very little that he shall assent. What then will you say shall he imbrace that for truth which has improbabilities in it that he cannot master? Upon that ground what may he not entertaine? And when shall he end? This has a clear answer. In contradictory opinions one must be true that he cannot doubt which then shall he take? That which is accompanied with the greater light & evidence that which is freest from the grosser absurdities though our narrow capacitys cannot penetrate it on every side. Some men have made objections to the belief of a God & think they ought to be heard & hearkened to because perhaps noe body can unravel all the difficultys of creation and providence which are bu

---

[2] Locke here first wrote and then crossed through: "which shall quickly be reduce to perfect skepticisme. have left in our minds noe assent to any probable truth at all.'

arguments of the weakness of our understanding & not against the being of a God. Let us take a view then of these mens hypotheses & let us see what direct contradictions they must be involved in who denie a God. If there be noe God from eternity then there was noe thinking thing from eternity. For the eternal thinking thing I call God. If from eternity there were noe thinking thing then thinking things were made out of unthinking things by an unthinking power: as great an absurdity as that noe thing should produce something. If matter be that eternall thinking thing let us change that deceitfull word matter which seems to stand for one thing when it means the congeries of all Bodies & then the opinion will be that all bodies every distinct atom is in its owne nature a thinking thing. Let any one then resolve with himself how such an infinite number of distinct independent thinking things came to be of one minde & to consent & contrive togeather to make such an admirable frame as the world & the species of things & their successive continuation is. How some of them consented to lie buried for long or numberless ages in the bowels & centre of this earth or other massy globes, places certainly very uneasy for thinking beings, whilst others are delighting them selves in the pleasures of freedom & the day. Let them produce harmony beauty constancy from such a congeries of thinking independent atoms & one may I think allow them to be creators of this world & I know not why upon their own grounds they should not thinke so them selves since there is noe reason why the thinking atoms in them should not be as wise as any other in the universe for if they once allow one atom of matter to have from eternity some degrees of knowledge & power above any other they must tell us a reason why it is soe or else their supposition will be ridiculous when set up against the supposition of a being that had from eternity more knowledge & more power than all matter taken togeather & soe was able to frame it into this orderly state of nature soe visible & admirable in all the parts of it.

University of Wisconsin-Madison.

Chapter XIX

LOCKE, DESCARTES, AND THE SCIENCE OF NATURE

By H. A. S. Schankula

On 18 March 1690 (N.S.), shortly after the publication of the first edition of *An Essay concerning Human Understanding,* John Locke's friend James Tyrrell wrote to him from Oxford with news of that city's reaction to his work:

> I will let you know what, the good nature of some (of the) people of this place, have invented to disparage your booke: (one) [a Freind] told me the other day y^t he had it from one who (has) pretends to be a great Judge of bookes: y^t you had taken all that was good in it; from (Des Cartes or) divers (new) late [moderne] French Authours. not only as to the notions but the manner of connexion of them; my answer againe was. that as long as I enjoyd your conversation in England: wch was when the maine body of the booke was written; to my knowledg you utterly refused to reade any bookes upon y^t subject: that you might not take any other mens notions: and y^t you have taken another course since y^t time I did not beleive: therefore y^t [if] you have fallen upon (any other) [the notions] of others, it was by a necessary treine of thoughts: since truth being but one thing hath commonly but one way to prove it: If you have any better defence then this to make: pray let me know it; & I will make [it] for you . . . .[1]

Thus, from the very beginning, speculation was rife, partisan charges were levelled and countered concerning the nature and extent of Locke's indebtedness to Descartes and Cartesianism. This speculation has continued to the present day and has spawned a large "influence" literature. However, since this literature is large and since much of it, both positive and negative, is highly conjectural, I shall make no attempt to review it in its entirety. Instead, I shall confine myself to the works of two writers on Locke, Richard Aaron and Leon Roth.

In the 1930s Professors Aaron and Roth set out, quite independently it would seem, to re-assess and hence to supplant traditional views of the historico-philosophical relationship of Locke to Descartes and, consequently of the relationship of "the empirical school" to "rationalism."[2] They did no

---

[1] Bodleian Library, Oxford, MS. Locke c.22, fols. 86^v-87^r. The words which have placed in round brackets were deleted by Tyrrell; those in square brackets added.

[2] 1935: Leon Roth, "Note on the Relationship between Locke and Descartes, *Mind,* 44, 414-16. 1936: Richard Aaron, "Introduction" to Richard Aaron an Jocelyn Gibb, eds., *An Early Draft of Locke's Essay together with Excerpts fror his Journals* (Oxford). 1937: Leon Roth, *Descartes' Discourse on Method* (O> ford), esp. Chap. 7; Richard Aaron, *John Locke* (Oxford; 2nd ed., 1955; 3rd ed 1971). 1938: Richard Aaron, "The Limits of Locke's Rationalism." *Seventeenf Century Studies presented to Sir Herbert Grierson* (Oxford, 1938), 292-31 (amended, it is printed as Appendix IV to *John Locke,* 3rd ed., 1971, 331-51 Whenever I quote from these works, I shall give page references within my tex

agree on every point of detail.[3] Moreover, while they couched their views in the same terms, each used these terms in his own idiosyncratic way. *Prima facie,* therefore, a comparison of the views might suggest some fundamental differences of opinion. In reality, however, the two views exhibit more similarities than they do differences. Furthermore, the similarities constitute what I shall call "the Aaron-Roth thesis," the thesis currently accepted as "standard" by many students of Locke. I shall explicate the Aaron-Roth thesis and then I shall indicate how and why I think it mistaken.

In the seventh chapter of his *Descartes' Discourse on Method* Roth attempts to modify "the old view of the relationship of Locke to Descartes," namely, "that Locke represents the 'empirical' reaction against Cartesian 'rationalism' " (116). Roth would have us believe both that Locke is a Lockean, an "empiricist" critic of Cartesian "rationalism," and that he is at the same time (though not, fortunately, in the same respect) a "Cartesian" (114) and a "rationalist" (116):

The later vicissitudes of the Cartesian philosophy as a whole are displayed most strikingly in Locke. Its fundamental metaphysical position, the distinction of matter from mind, was offered by Descartes explicitly as the basis of his mathematico-physical theory of the equation of matter with extension. The whole of this is rejected by Locke, physics and metaphysics alike, and with it Descartes' well-known attempt in the ontological argument to draw the fullest consequence from the autonomy of mind. In the same way we have Locke's reiterated criticism of the very possibility of a demonstrative science of nature, a criticism which puts asunder the metaphysics and physics joined so decisively by Descartes.

And yet Locke is a Cartesian. One has only to glance at the kernel of his philosophy, the doctrine of knowledge in Book IV of the *Essay on Human Understanding,* in order to recognize its origin. The 'rules' of the *Discourse* are only repeated in Locke's account of the true method of demonstration as consisting in the 'intervention' of 'intermediate ideas', and if we couple with this Locke's stress on 'clear and distinct ideas' we have no option but to call him a Cartesian (114-115).

One wonders how Roth can say *both* that Locke absolutely repudiated Descartes' metaphysics, his science, and his philosophy of science *and* that he is, nevertheless, "a Cartesian." One wonders that the standards required for membership in that select club should be deemed so blatantly minimal. Nevertheless, that is Roth's view; or, perhaps better, it is his determined use of the term 'Cartesian.'[4]

In his *John Locke,* Aaron maintains that "Locke was *not* a Cartesian" but rather, a Gassendist or a Boylean (9, 31-35). However, just as Roth admits that Locke's "Cartesianism," his "discipleship" is "severely restricted" by his "empiricism," so too Aaron suggests that Locke's "empiricism" is modified by his "rationalism." According to Aaron:

---

[3] For example, the former affirmed while the latter denied that Locke's polemic against innate ideas was directed at Descartes.

[4] The *general* thesis of Descartes' *Discourse on Method* is that what is important (historically and, therefore, philosophically important) is his method, not his metaphysics or physics. See below, note 17.

when the long and fruitful reign of Cartesianism came to an end in intellectual Europe, writers (for instance, Voltaire and the Encyclopaedists) acknowledged Locke as its critic, though the truth is that he was only one of many critics. They hailed him as the founder of the empirical school. Confining their attention largely to the first two books of the *Essay* and neglecting shamefully the third and fourth, they created there and then the erroneous view that the two schools had nothing in common. This view prevailed until the middle of the nineteenth century, when people like Tagart and T. E. Webb in England, Hartenstein, Geil, and von Hertling in Germany discovered again the rationalist elements in Locke's thought, in a word, rediscovered the third and fourth books of the *Essay*. In our own day the pendulum is in danger of swinging too far in the other direction, for Locke is talked of as if he were a mere rationalist, owing everything to Descartes. This view is equally untrue and needs to be corrected (pp. 9-10).[5]

Starting from opposite poles, Aaron and Roth achieve a common ground; despite the different nuances of their respective uses of language, their views of the relationship of Locke to Descartes are virtually the same.

Both men oppose the two "extreme" views mentioned in the passage just quoted. Both argue that there are "empiricist" and "rationalist" elements in Locke's thought, specifically in *An Essay concerning Human Understanding*. Furthermore, both men associate Locke's "rationalism" with, principally, "(a) the conception of 'demonstration' as the end of a chain of 'intuitions,' and (b) the use made of the immediate apprehension of the 'self' "; they associate his 'empiricism' with "(c) his refusal to accept Thought as the essence of mind, (d) his parallel refusal to accept Extension as the essence of body, and (e) his severance of physics from mathematics [i.e., his denial of the possibility of a "perfect" science of nature]" (Roth, 117; see Aaron, 10-12). Finally, the two men urge upon their readers similar, though not identical, views of the nature and extent of Cartesian "influence" in the historical *development* of Locke's "empiricism" and "rationalism."

Aaron's history casts "Descartes' role" as Locke's "liberator:"

He probably began to study Descartes soon after graduation [i.e., *circa* 1656] . . . . it was Descartes who first taught Locke how to develop a philosophical inquiry intelligibly. His Oxford education had left him with a sense of despair as to the possibility of advance by way of reason. Descartes was his deliverer from this despair and pessimism (9).

Roth's history does not explicitly contradict Aaron's. However, Roth is inclined to minimize the importance of Locke's *early* reading:

Locke had made no more than an ordinary acquaintance with Descartes when he first put pen to paper and roughed out the early drafts of the Essay in 1670-1. His real and earnest study of Descartes began *after* 1671 (120).

Consequently, Roth's view of the development of Locke's "empiricism," i.e., of the above-mentioned points (c), (d), and (e), differs from Aaron's.

[5] Actually, it is difficult to determine exactly what Aaron thinks. If, in *John Locke,* Locke's "empiricism" is modified by his "rationalism," nevertheless, in "The Limits of Locke's Rationalism," "his rationalism is fundamental, empiricism being but a modification of it" (*John Locke,* 3rd ed., 1971, 351).

In general, Roth is less prepared than Aaron to concede the essential "maturity" of Locke's 1671 draft accounts of substance and of the impossibility of a "perfect" science of nature. Correlatively, he sees a greater "developmental" significance than Aaron sees in the philosophical passages published by Aaron and Gibb from the Lovelace manuscripts—especially, from the Journals for 1675-1679, the years of Locke's residence in France. "From now on [i.e., *post* 1675] we are," Roth says, "in the (anti-) Cartesian atmosphere which stimulated the emergence of the characteristic portions of the *Essay*" (123). While Aaron tends to interpret the philosophical passages as extending certain "empiricist," anti-Cartesian points already present in Drafts A and B, Roth tends to see them as original reflections on those aspects of Cartesianism to which Locke most strongly objected.

At the same time, however, both Aaron and Roth see in the philosophical passages the gradual emergence of Locke's "rationalism." Both men claim that Locke had no satisfactory theory of knowledge in 1671 and that, *post* 1671, the "mature" theory, "(a) the conception of demonstration as the end of a chain of 'intuitions,'" was taken over, more or less verbatim, from Descartes' works.

Since the truth or falsehood of this claim is crucial to an understanding of the significance of Locke's work, I wish to make explicit the details of the "developmental" view which the claim presupposes. According to Aaron:

. . . he [Locke] had no sooner finished it [Draft A] than he decided to begin again from the beginning. This is clear from the final page of the draft, which goes back to a matter considered at the outset, and reveals Locke's dissatisfaction with the opening pages. In the autumn of 1671 he tried again, this time writing his thoughts out in a neat and orderly manner and in a manuscript obviously meant for the press. But Draft B is also unfinished, and it is unfinished in respect to the very problem which Locke set out to solve, namely, that of the extent and limitations of knowledge. Its incomplete state may be due to the fact that Locke had no time to proceed with it but it is more likely that he did not then know how to finish it (pp.51-52). . . . It is not too much to say that Draft B fails entirely to inquire into the limits and extent of human knowledge, though this was the main problem which the author had set himself in 1671, as is clear from Draft A. Nor has Draft B any satisfactory theory of knowledge. With the exception of a few minor points, the all-important opening chapters of Book IV are absent in the draft. Locke was in search of a satisfactory theory of knowledge and of its object, but in 1671 he had not found it (53).

Roth (120) approves an earlier version of this passage (Aaron & Gibb, p.xxiii) and concludes that: "Theory of knowledge he [Locke] learnt from Descartes" (121). Quite clearly, Roth shares Aaron's view:

. . the opening chapters of Book IV . . . have no counterpart in the Draft of 1671 and were not, apparently, part of the original scheme. They are the product of Locke's reflections between 1671 and 1690. Locke, at first, seems to have taken knowledge itself for granted and merely inquired into its limitations. Gradually, however, he came to see that these could not be properly determined until a precise description of knowledge had been given. This accurate description of knowledge was no doubt one of the problems which concerned him during his stay in France and it was there that he found the solution he needed. . . . It was the intuitionism of Descartes, made most explicit in his *Regulae ad Directionem Ingenii*. This work was not published until 1701, but copies of it circulated amongst the Cartesians long before this. There is no evidence to show that Locke had actually seen a copy of the *Regulae*, though this is not at all impossible. But whether he was directly acquainted with it or not, he had certainly learnt its contents fully from the Cartesians, and had made the theory set forth in its pages his own. The resemblance between IV. ii of the *Essay* and some sections of the *Regulae* is remarkable (220-21).

Aaron's claim that Descartes was Locke's "liberator" rests on his interpretation of the testimony of Jean le Clerc[6] and of Damaris Cudworth Masham.[7] However, Aaron's interpretation, like his claim, is highly exaggerated and hence, misleading. A brief review of the Masham–le Clerc testimony should suffice to establish this point.[8]

According to le Clerc, Locke himself often said that he did not benefit greatly from his undergraduate training in the "old" scholastic philosophy. In fact, "il trouvoit si peu de satisfaction dans la manière, dont on y étudioit alors, qu'il eût souhaité que son Père eût pensé à toute autre chose, qu'à l'envoyer à Oxford." Initially, however, Locke did not account for his dissatisfaction by impugning the significance of the University's curriculum: "Comme il s'appercevoit que ce qu'il y apprenoit servoit peu à lui éclairer l'esprit & à le rendre plus étendu & plus juste; il s'imaginoit que cela venoit de ce qu'il n'étoit pas propre pour les études" (347). Consequently, he was for some time less than eager in his pursuit of them.

Then, however, Locke became acquainted with the "new" philosophy, both experimental and speculative: soon after Robert Boyle moved to Oxford in 1654 Locke became his friend and student; at about the same time, perhaps at Boyle's suggestion, he began to read the works of Descartes. According to le Clerc, here following Lady Masham: "Les premiers livres, qui donnerent [*sic*] quelque goût de l'étude de la Philosophie à Mr. Locke, comme il l'a raconté lui même, furent ceux de Descartes" (p.349). However, it does not follow that Locke's reading precipitated an intellectual conversion to Cartesianism; le Clerc is careful to note that Locke "ne fût pas Cartesien [*sic*]" (347) and, again following Lady Masham, "qu'il ne goutât pas tous ses sentimens" (p.349).[9]

[6] Jean le Clerc, himself a well-known author and the founding editor of the *Bibliotheque universelle et historique,* became during Locke's Dutch years (1683-89), one of Locke's closest friends.

[7] Damaris Cudworth Masham (1658-1708) was the daughter of Ralph Cudworth, the Cambridge Platonist, and the second wife of Sir Francis Masham. Locke lived with the Mashams at Oates, Sussex, during the last fourteen years of his life.

[8] Jean le Clerc published "Éloge de feu Mr. Locke" in the *Bibliothèque choisie* (Amsterdam, 1705), 342-411. In it he incorporated remarks which Damaris Cudworth Masham had made to him, at his request, in a letter dated at Oates, 12 January 1705 (Amsterdam University Library, MS. J. 57. a). The page numbers cite in the text are those of the *Bibliothèque choisie.*

[9] The Masham original (Amsterdam University Library, MS. J. 57. a) reads ". . . he very often differ'd in opinion from this writer."

The true significance of Locke's reading of Descartes, its importance in the history of his intellectual development, is found in the fact that "parce qu'en-core qu'il ne goutât pas tous ses sentimens, il trouvoit qu'il écrivoit avec beau-coup de clarté." It was the clarity of Descartes' works, not their truth, "qui lui fit croire que s'il n'avoit pas entendu d'autres Livres Philosophiques, c'étoit peutêtre [*sic*] par la faute des Auteurs, & non par la sienne" (p. 349). In short, his reading of Descartes led Locke to revise radically his initial self-estimate. He realized, as le Clerc reports, "qu'il avoit perdu beaucoup de tems, au commencement de ses études, parce qu'on ne connoissoit alors à Oxford, qu'un Péripatétisme embarrassé de mots obscurs & des recherches inutiles" (347).

If my interpretation of the Masham–le Clerc testimony is correct, then "Descartes' role" as Locke's "liberator" was far less significant than Aaron wishes his readers to believe. In fact, Locke's own statements repeatedly con-firm this view. For example, when Edward Stillingfleet, Bishop of Worcester, lumped Locke with Descartes as an advocate of a new way of certainty founded on the intuition of clear and distinct ideas, Locke replied with considerable sarcasm:

> . . . it is hard to avoid thinking that your lordship means, that I borrowed from him [Descartes] my notions concerning certainty. And your lordship is so great a man, and every way so far above my meanness, that it cannot be supposed that your lordship intended this for anything but a commendation of me to the world, as a scholar of so great a master. But though I must always acknowl-edge to that justly-admired gentleman the great obligation of my first deliver-ance from the unintelligible way of talking of the philosophy in use in the schools of his time, yet I am so far from entitling his writings to any of the errors or imperfections which are to be found in my Essay, as deriving their origin from him, that I must own to your lordship they were spun barely out of my own thoughts, reflecting as well as I could on my own mind and the ideas I had there; and were not, that I know, derived from any other original.[10]

Locke clearly acknowledged the debt which he owed to his youthful reading of Descartes, but he carefully specified the limited nature of that debt, and, more important, he explicitly denied what Aaron and Roth affirm, namely, that he had "borrowed" from Descartes "his notions concerning certainty."[11]

Admittedly, while Locke's denial strikes at the very heart of the Aaron-Roth thesis, it does not *ipso facto* destroy it: John Locke's "I am not a Cartesian" is neither more nor less self-verifying than the Pope's "I am infallible."[12] In-

---

[10] *Works* (11th ed., 1812), IV, 48-49.

[11] In "The Limits of Locke's Rationalism," Aaron actually uses the word "bor-owed" *(John Locke,* 3rd ed., 335). It is, I think, significant that in *John Locke* itself (9) he quotes Locke's acknowledgment to Stillingfleet while suppressing his denial.

[12] In an essay dated 1661 and entitled "An necesse sit dari in Ecclesia infal-ibilem Sacro Sanctae Scripturae interpretem? Negatur" (London, Public Record Office, Shaftesbury Papers, 30/24/47/33), Locke wrote: "Concesso enim dari liquem infallibilem Sacro Sanctae Scripturae interpretem, is tamen quicunque . . . uerit nihil ad enodanda fidei dubia, nihil ad stabiliendam inter Christianos pacem onferre poterit, *nisi infallibiliter doceat se esse infallibilem, quod cum ipse de se robare non potest, non enim ferendum est cuiusquam de seipso testimonium,*

deed, there is evidence to suggest that in literary and "influence" matters Locke was something less than a pathological truth-teller. In a letter addressed to Edward Clarke, dated 31 December 1686 and accompanied by the final draft version of Book 4, he claimed that

being resolved to examine *Humane Understanding,* and the ways of our knowledge, not by others' opinions, but by what I could from my own observations collect myself, *I have purposely avoided the reading of all books that treated any way of the subject,* that so I might have nothing to bias me any way, but might leave my thought free to entertain only what the matter itself suggested to my meditations. So that, if they at any time jump with others 'twas not that I followed them; and if they differ 'twas not out of contradiction, or a mind to be singular. My aim has been only truth so far as my shortsightedness could reach it, and where I have misstated it in part or in the whole I shall be glad to be set right.[13]

Locke's claim, if taken literally, is clearly and consciously false. Locke himself had reported earlier, again to Clarke, that he had spent the winter of 1683-84 "much in my chamber alone . . . busy there for the most part about my enquiry concerning *Humane Understanding.*"[14] His private papers reveal what he does not: when not busy writing, he was busy reading (in fact, re-reading) Nicolas Malebranche's *Recherche de la Vérité* and Antoine Arnauld's *Des vraies et des fausses idées.*[15]

It might be argued that if, *per impossibile,* Locke lied to his friend Clarke, it is highly likely that he lied to his adversary Stillingfleet. However, I do not think that Locke's letter to Clarke was intended to deceive, or for that matter, was capable of deceiving him. In 1685-86 Locke was preparing, at long last, to publish his *Essay.* He wanted it to be judged on the basis of philosophical merit alone but he foresaw the nature of much of the controversy that its publication would generate. To forestall such controversy, Locke suggested to his friends a "game-plan": the dissemination of the myth of his literary virginity, his innocence to the charge of any reading whatsoever. The realization of his expectation, the power of his suggestion, and, most significantly, the loyalty of his friends is attested to in James Tyrrell's answer to the charge which he reported to Locke in the letter quoted at the beginning of this paper. Tyrrell, like Clarke, clearly knew better than to answer, indeed, to "answer *againe,*" as he did. He knew that, in the twenty-odd years during which Locke wrote and re-

---

silente scriptura unde cognosci potest non facile reperio . . ." (I quote the MS. as edited by John C. Biddle, "John Locke's Essay on Infallibility: Introduction, Text, and Translation," *Journal of Church and State,* **19** (1977), 301-27; the ellipsis indicates an illegible word in the MS.; the italics are mine). I translate the italicized words (more clumsily than Biddle does) as follows: "unless he himself [the Pope] infallibly teach his own infallibility, which he himself cannot prove of himself, for no one's testimony about himself is to be tolerated."

[13] *The Correspondence of John Locke and Edward Clarke,* ed. Benjamin Rand (Cambridge, Mass., 1927), 177-78.

[14] *Op. cit.,* 117.

[15] Bodleian Library, Oxford, MS. Locke f.8, pp.2, 5-9, 33-5. I am preparing a separate paper on the extent and significance of Locke's acquaintance with the works of Malebranche and Arnauld.

wrote the various sections of the *Essay,* he had read virtually "all books" writ-ten in his century "that treated any way of the subject."[16] It is interesting to note that Tyrrell, knowing what he knew, asked Locke if he had "any better defence then this to make."

It would be ridiculous to claim that Locke's writings were uninfluenced by his reading, in particular, that he could have talked in the *Essay* of ideas of clarity and distinctness, of intuition and demonstration without having been cognizant of the roles these notions played in Cartesian literature. But this is not to say that Locke lied to Stillingfleet when he denied what Aaron and Roth affirm, namely, that he had "borrowed" these notions from Descartes. To bor-row is to take over, adopt, make use of—usually *with* permission or acknowl-edgement—something that is not one's own. I shall argue, against Aaron and Roth, that Locke's peculiar genius lies in the fact that, unlike the vast majority of his contemporaries, he did not adopt Descartes' notions concerning cer-tainty but, quite the contrary, *consciously adapted* them. I shall argue, further-more, that Locke's adaptations reflect a specific twofold aim: to provide a foundation for (or, an interpretation of) the experimental philosophy of Royal Society virtuosi such as Robert Boyle and to demonstrate the invalidity of any speculative, dogmatic philosophy, whether "old" or "new," Scholastic or Cartesian.

Four propositions are crucial to the Aaron-Roth thesis: (1) that "the open-ing chapters of Book IV . . . have no counterpart in the Drafts of 1671" (Aaron, 220); (2) that, in fact, the Drafts do not contain "any satisfactory theory of knowledge" (53); (3) that "the resemblance between" the opening chapters of Book IV "and some sections of the *Regulae* is remarkable" (221); (4) that, therefore, sometime during the years 1671-1689, probably during his French or Dutch sojourns, either "Locke had actually seen a copy of the *Regulae"* or, what is more likely, "he had certainly learnt its contents fully from the Cartesians, and had made the theory set forth in its pages his own" (220-21). In this section I shall first examine Aaron's discussion of the simi-larities and differences between Cartesian and Lockean intuition. I shall then argue that, whether or not Locke knew the contents of the *Regulae,*[17] each one of propositions (1) through (4) is false.

James Gibson suggested that Descartes intuited "simple natures," "con-ceptions" or "notions," "propositions" or "principles."[18] I have suggested, on

---

[16] The Tyrrell-Locke correspondence (Bodleian Library, MS. Locke c.22) fre-quently deals with literary matters, and from 1683 to 1691 Tyrrell himself was the custodian of a sizeable portion of Locke's library.

[17] *Regulae ad Directionem Ingenii* was first published in 1701, fifty-one years after Descartes' death and eleven years after the publication of *An Essay concern-ing Human Understanding.* Aaron, of course, recognizes the fact (10 and 220-21) but he notes, quite rightly, that several manuscript copies of the work "circulated amongst the Cartesians long before this." Then he argues that (while Locke does not once refer to such a copy in his extant manuscript papers) "it is not at all improbable . . . that he had the *Regulae* (or a note of it) beside him in writing IV. ii." Roth argues that whether or not Locke had seen a copy of the *Regulae,* its contents "are clear enough in the *Discourse on Method"* (117), a work which Locke certainly read.

[18] Locke's *Theory of Knowledge and its Historical Relations* (Cambridge, 1917), 213.

at least one occasion, that Descartes intuited (or purported to intuit) "clear and distinct ideas" containing "true and immutable natures or essences."[19] But Richard Aaron suggests that, *whatever* Descartes intuited, he intuited "pure, non-sensuous objects."

Aaron suggests that Locke's "intuition," while identical to Descartes' "as to the subjective side of the experience," is not identical to it "with regard to the objective" (224):

> With him [i.e., Descartes] Locke holds that the best instance of knowing is intuiting and that non-intuitive knowledge, for instance demonstration or indirect knowing, in so far as it is certain, contains also of necessity an intuitive element. By *intuition* is meant here a power which the mind possesses of apprehending truth . . . . it is direct and immediate . . . . Furthermore, it is infallible (221).

On the other hand:

> for Descartes the object of intuition is a pure non-sensuous object; for Locke it is a relation between certain givens of sensation or reflection or between complex ideas derived from the given (224).

Aaron's suggestion captures two important points, but it fails to capture two others. In the first place, while all objects of Lockean intuition are cognitive *relations,* (a) some cognitive relations are *not* objects either of Lockean intuition or Lockean demonstration. Secondly, while Lockean *relata* are, at base, sensuous, non-"pure" data, (b) some cognitive relations obtain *between* these data and others are features *of* them.

Locke defines knowledge as "the perception of the connexion and agreement, or disagreement and repugnancy of any of our Ideas" (4.1.2.).[20] Subsequently, he gives two different lists of the "sorts" or kinds "wherein this agreement or disagreement consists." These lists are: (A) 1. Identity, or Diversity, 2. Relation, 3. Co-existence, or necessary connexion, 4. Real Existence (4.1.3); and (B) 1. Identity and Diversity, 2. Co-existence, 3. Relation, 4.

---

[19] See my review of François Duchesneau's *L'Empirisme de Locke,* in *Dialogue,* **13** (1974), 614-19. Actually, Descartes uses the term "intuition" only in the *Regulae* and, as far as I know, in two letters, one to Mersenne, 16 October 1639 (Adam and Tannery, II, 587-99), the other to Silhon, March-April 1648 (Adam and Tannery, V, 133-39). In *Regulae* 3, 7, 11, and 12 (the statement of the rule), the objects of intuition are all propositions. In *Regulae* 6 and 12, Descartes refers to "natures" as objects of intuition. In the two letters he is concerned with intuition only as a faculty and not with its objects.

[20] I quote from the *Essay* as edited by Peter H. Nidditch (Oxford, 1975); I shall quote from Draft A as edited by Richard Aaron and Jocelyn Gibb (Oxford, 1936). I have incorporated into my text citations—of book, chapter, and section in the case of the *Essay* and of section and (Aaron and Gibb) page number in the case of Draft A. In his correspondence with Stillingfleet, Locke insists on the originality of his definition, even at the expense of exploding the myth of his literary virginity. In the second letter he states that "Nobody that I ever met with had in their writings particularly set down wherein the act of knowing precisely consisted" (*Works,* IV, 143); in the third letter he states quite specifically that Descartes did not, as he himself did, "place certainty in the perception of the agreement or disagreement of ideas" (IV, 362).

468   H. A. S. SCHANKULA

real Existence (4.3.8-9, 18, 21, and, slightly rearranged, 4.7.3). In his recent
book, John Yolton notes that the examples of (A) 3 which Locke gives in
4.1.6-7 are exclusively of co-existence, and furthermore, co-existence is a contingent agreement, a *non*-necessary connexion between ideas. Hence he concludes, quite rightly, that "necessary connexion" is redundant on list (A) and
fails to appear on list (B) precisely because " 'relation' covers all instances of
necessary connexions between ideas."[21]

List (B) is the definitive list of the sorts of cognitive relations. Yolton's
analysis of these sorts correctly emphasizes the two points (a) and (b) which,
as I have noted, Aaron's discussion does not. In the first place, (b), while the
cognitive relations of "co-existence" (i.e., *non*-necessary connexion) and "relation" (i.e., necessary connexion) obtain *between* ideas, "identity" is a feature
of all ideas and "real existence" is a feature *of* at least some.

The crucial point, however, is (a). In the face of Descartes' claim that
knowledge (i.e., certainty) is attained only through intuition and deduction,
Locke insists (e.g., in 4.3.2) that we perceive agreements or disagreements of
ideas (i.e., that we know) in *three* ways. Perceptions of identity are intuitive
and perceptions of relation (i.e., necessary connexion) are, for the most part,
demonstrative. However, perceptions of the co-existence (i.e., non-necessary
connexion) of qualities in the same subject and perceptions of the real existence of things (excluding one's self and God) are neither intuitive nor demonstrative, but rather, sensitive. Yet Locke states quite clearly that the latter two
sorts of perceptions, no less than the former, constitute knowledge.

What then of Locke's definition of knowledge? If one ignored the truth of
(a), if, in fact, one overlooked the greater part of Book 4, one could argue that
"connexion"—"agreement" and "disagreement"—"repugnancy" are sets of synonymous terms, that, in effect, Locke restricted knowledge to the intuition or
deduction of conceptual or logical necessities and contradictions. In other
words, one could argue that the Aaron-Roth propositions (4) and (3) are
true. However, if one recognized the truth and significance of (a), if one recognized that Locke's definition admits as knowledge the perception of both necessary and non-necessary connexions, logical or conceptual and factual
repugnancies, then one would understand that (4') *even if* Locke knew the
contents of Descartes' *Regulae,* he did not adopt a doctrine of certainty as consisting, *quite simply,* in *intuitus* and *deductio,* and furthermore, (3'), the
differences between the epistemology of Locke's Book 4 and that of Descartes'
Regulae are far more "remarkable" than any similarities.

To appreciate the full significance of these differences, one must relate
Locke's discussion of the sorts of knowledge to his discussions of its degrees,
extent, and reality. In particular, one must pay careful attention to Locke's
several crucial distinctions: between nominal and real essences; between trifling
and instructive propositions; between verbal (or mental) and extra-verbal
(extra-mental) or real knowledge; and finally, between real instructive knowledge which is universal and real instructive knowledge which is merely particular. At the moment, however, I shall confine myself to certain general remarks
concerning co-existence and relation.

[21] *Locke and the Compass of Human Understanding* (Cambridge, 1970),
109-110.

On the one hand, perceptions of relation obtain or are discoverable between mixed modes, those Lockean ideas which are their own archetypes, whose nominal and real essences are identical (3.5.13). Hence, perceptions of relation are, for the most part, demonstrative. And since they are, since, in Locke's words, they depend "on our Sagacity, in finding intermediate Ideas, that may shew the Relations and Habitudes of Ideas, *whose* [real] *Co-existence is not considered,* 'tis a hard Matter to tell, when we are at an end of such Discoveries; and when Reason has all the helps it is capable of, for the finding of Proofs, or examining the Agreement or Disagreement of remote Ideas" (4.3.18). However, when and where relations are perceived—in mathematics and, at least potentially, in morals—the perception (i.e., the knowledge) is "scientifical:" *certain, universal,* and *real.*

The Mathematician considers the Truth and Properties belonging to a Rectangle, or Circle, only as they are in Idea in his own Mind. For 'tis possible he never found either of them existing mathematically, i.e., precisely true, in his Life. But yet the knowledge he has of any Truths or Properties belonging to a Circle, or any other mathematical Figure, are nevertheless true and certain, even of real Things existing: because real Things are no farther concerned, nor intended to be meant by any such Propositions, than as Things really agree to those Archetypes in his Mind (4.4.6).

On the other hand, perceptions of co-existence pertain to complex ideas of substances (i.e., to collections of simple ideas of qualities). While these collections, like mixed modes, are productions of the mind, they, unlike mixed modes, refer to and are ultimately grounded in non-ideal, extra-mental realities. Furthermore, they do not capture the real essences of these realities. Thus, for example:

the nominal Essence of Gold, is that complex Idea the word Gold stands for, let it be, for instance, a Body yellow, of a certain weight, malleable, fusible, and fixed. But the real Essence is the constitution of the insensible parts of that Body, on which those Qualities, and all the other Properties of Gold depend (3.6.2).

Locke clearly *believed* that, could/did one *know* (I do not say "could/did one *observe")* the real essence of gold, one could/would demonstrate the *relation* (in the technical sense "necessary connexion") *between any one of its qualities and all the others:*

to know the Properties of Gold, it would be no more necessary, that Gold should exist, and that we should make Experiments upon it, than it is necessary for the knowing the Properties of a Triangle, that a Triangle should exist in any Matter (4.6.11).

However, one knows, one can know, only nominal essences (e.g., that collection of simple ideas: yellow, weighty, malleable, fusible, fixed). Very well then,

Could anyone discover a necessary connexion between Malleableness, and the Colour or Weight of Gold, or any other part of the complex Idea signified by that Name, he might make a certain universal Proposition concerning Gold in this respect; and the real Truth of this Proposition, That all Gold is malleable, would be as certain as of this, The three Angles of all right-lined Triangles, are equal to two right ones (4.6.10).

Unfortunately, however, "the simple Ideas whereof our complex Ideas of Substances are made up, are for the most part such, as carry with them, in their own Nature[s], no visible necessary connexion, or inconsistency with any other simple Ideas" (4.3.10). In fact, "there are so few of them, that have a visible Connexion one with another, that *we can by Intuition or Demonstration, discover the* [universal] *co-existence* [i.e., the necessary connexion] *of very few* of the Qualities [that] are to be found united in Substances" (4.3.14). Thus, our *a priori* reasoning powers are, for the most part, irrelevant and our sensory experience, crucial. Our knowledge of bodies and of spirits, unlike our knowledge of mathematical entities, cannot be what Descartes claims it can be (i.e., "scientifical," "philosophical," "perfect;" it is and will remain "experimental," "sensitive") (4.3.26, 29).

Thus far, I have argued that propositions (4) and (3) are false, propositions (4') and (3') true. In other words, Locke's distinction between the demonstrative perception or knowledge of relation and the sensitive perception or knowledge of co-existence adumbrates both his general repudiation of Descartes' epistemology and his specific repudiation of Descartes' philosophy of science. I shall now argue that the repudiation is as evident in the Drafts of 1671 as it is in the "mature" *Essay.* In other words, I shall argue that propositions (2) and (1) are false.

To begin, I shall organize my argument around the two-fold claim that, already in 1671, Locke had clearly distinguished in Draft A the four sorts of knowledge outlined in *Essay* 4.1.3 and 4.3.8-9, and furthermore, he had explicitly distinguished the various types of propositions discussed in *Essay* 4.8.2-9. I shall correlate Draft and *Essay* passages to establish the truth of this claim. And I shall suggest that these passages illuminate the interesting remark which Immanuel Kant made in the Preamble to his *Prolegomena to Any Future Metaphysics,* namely, that in reading Locke he had found "an indication" of his own distinction between analytic, synthetic *a priori* and synthetic *a posteriori* propositions.[22]

Locke's "trifling" propositions (i.e., Kant's "analytical judgments") are "barely verbal" or mental (i.e., "explicative, adding nothing to the content of knowledge"). However, they are "certain." In both the 1671 Drafts and the 1689 *Essay* Locke gives as examples of such propositions: (i) all propositions which express perceptions of identity or diversity and (ii) some propositions which express perceptions of relation.

With regard to (i), Locke says in Draft A:

That a man hath an infallible certain knowledg of universal Indentical [*sic*] affirmative propositions and others depending there upon, v.g. that what is, is. That a man hath an infallible certain knowledg of universal negative propositions where in one Idea is denied of an other, and the most generall one

---

[22] The Library of Liberal Arts edition (Indianapolis, etc., 1950), 19-20. While Kant refers to *Essay* 4.3.9 I shall suggest that the definition is even more clearly foreshadowed in 4.8.2-9.

grounded there on, viz It is impossible for a thing to be and not to be . . . (§27, p.41; see §31, p. 53).

However, he asserts that no perception of identity or diversity, no universal affirmative or universal negative proposition is "of any great moment, [n]or can [it] be said to carry any great matter of knowledg with it all that it teaches us . . . amounting to noe more then this that the same word may with great certainty be affirmd of its self without any doubt of the truth of any such propositions *and let me adde without any knowledg of any thing"* (§28, p.49). To illustrate this assertion, he adds that:

at this rate a very ignorant nay the most ignorant man in the world that can but make a proposition may make a million of propositions of whose truth he may be infallibly certain and yet not know one thing in the world the more thereby, v.g. What is a soule is a soule or a soule is a soule, a Spirit is a Spirit, a Fetiche is a Fetiche &c. These all being equivalent to that first proposition viz What is is: i.e. what hath existence hath existence, or who hath a soule hath a soule, which seems to be little better than trifleing with words, or at best is but the munkys shifting his oyster from one hand to tother, and had he but words might noe doubt have said oyster in right hand is subject and oyster in left hand is praedicate and soe might have made a self evident proposition of oyster i.e. oyster is oyster, and yet with all this not have been one whit the wiser or more knowing and that way of handleing the matter would much at one have satisfied the munkys hunger or a mans understanding and they would have improved in knowledg and bulke togeather (§28, pp. 49-50).

With regard to (ii) (i.e., those propositions "where in the predicate and subject are one conteind in the definition of the other"), Locke asserts in Draft A "that [they] are very certain and evident in them selves to the understanding but yet teach little or noe thing at all . . . and soe amount to noe more then to know what words may universally be affirmd of one an other or not" (§29, p. 50). And to illustrate this assertion, he adds:

Every man is an animal or Corpus vivens is as certain a Proposition but noe more conduceing to the knowledg of things then to say a Palfry is an ambleing Horse, or neighing ambleing animal both being only about the signification of words, and make me know but this. That body, sense, and motion or power of sensation and moveing are three of those simple Ideas that I always comprehend and signifie by the word man, and where they are not to be found togeather the name man belongs not to that thing, and soe of the other, That body sense and motion, and a certain way of goeing are four of those simple Ideas which I always comprehend and signifie by the word Palfry and where they are not to be found togeather the name Palfry belongs not to that thing (§29, p. 50).

The textual evidence is conclusive. Locke's Draft A assertions concerning (i all propositions which express perceptions of identity or diversity and (ii) some propositions which express perceptions of relation constitute the content o *Essay* 4.8.2-3 and 4-7, respectively. Indeed, Draft A, §28, pp. 49-50 and §29 pp. 50-51 survived the eighteen-year gestation period of the "mature" *Essa* almost verbatim and became, respectively, the first paragraph of 4.8.3 an all of 4.8.6.

In both the Drafts and the *Essay* Locke describes "instructive" propositions (i.e., Kant's "synthetical judgments") as extra-verbal or extra-mental ("expansive, increasing the given knowledge"), that is, "real." The interesting question, however, is this: did he, either in the Drafts or the *Essay,* recognize *both* instructive propositions which are universally certain ("synthetical judgments *a priori")* *and* instructive propositions which are not universally certain but "merely probable" ("synthetical judgments *a posteriori")?*

Prima facie, it would seem that he did not. In Draft A, §29, p. 50, he states that

all universall propositions are either Certain and then they are only verball but not instructive. Or else [they] are Instructive and then not Certain . . . .

And earlier, in §27, pp. 46-47, he stated that

all universall propositions that are certain are only verball or words applyd to our owne Ideas and not instructive: and vice-versa all universal propositions that are instructive (i.e. informe us any thing about the nature qualitys and operations of things existing without us) are all uncertain . . . .

However, in §30, p. 51, Locke makes an exception; he states that "Mathematicall universall propositions are both true and instructive because as those Ideas are in our minds soe are the things without us." Similarly, in §13, p. 26, he states that

in magnitude and number we have a certain knowledg of the truth of universal propositions because all the propertys and proportions that belong to any mathematical figure imagined in our mindes doe all belong also to and are found in the same figure without us and soe the connection of Ideas within us and their existing soe without us doe always exactly agree.

Obviously, Locke means §29, p. 51 and §27, pp. 46-47 to apply only to universal propositions concerning substances (i.e., propositions expressing perceptions of the co-existence or non-necessary connexion of qualities).

The same would seem to be true of the *Essay.* In other words, there is some evidence which suggests that Locke regarded as synthetic *a priori* the propositions of mathematics which express non-trifling relations (i.e., necessary connexions). For example, in 4.8.8 he says that:

we can know the Truth, and so may be certain in Propositions, which affirm something of another, which is a necessary consequence of its precise complex Idea, *but not contained in it.* As that the external Angle of all Triangles, is bigger than either of the opposite internal Angles; which relation of the outward Angle, to either of the opposite internal Angles, making no part of the complex Idea signified by the name Triangle, this is a real Truth and conveys with it nstructive real Knowledge.

However, the points which I wish to emphasize are: first, whether or not Locke recognized synthetic *a priori* propositions, he did recognize (indeed, he nsisted upon) a distinction between the necessary connections which constitute he content of "trifling" (i.e., analytic) propositions and the non-necessary onnections which constitute the content of "instructive" but "uncertain" (i.e., synthetic *a posteriori)* propositions; second, this recognition and insistence is as evident in 1671 as it is in 1689; third, both early and late, it is involved in and directed at Locke's assessment of "the general propositions that are made about substances." While each of these points is illustrated by Locke's remarks in Draft A, §29, pp. 50-51 (i.e., *Essay* 4,8,6, a passage which I have partially quoted), I would emphasize certain other passages in both Draft A and in the *Essay*.

In Draft A, §13, pp. 25-26, Locke says that

in such propositions wherein simple Ideas are predicated of subjects, i.e. of a collection of simple Ideas put togeather as connected in that subject we have noe farther knowledg then our senses conversant about those particulars doe or have informed us.

In other words, synthetic *a posteriori* propositions, propositions which express perceptions of the co-existence or non-necessary connexion of qualities, if particular, are either certainly true or certainly false: "as," for example, "Thomas laughd . . . The hare I saw yesterday was grey and the milke I drinke now is white." However, "when I proceed to *universall* propositions, v.g. all milke is white," the matter is quite different. *Either*
I affirme that simple Idea of any name which simple Idea I conteine in the very diffinition of that name, and then the proposition is always true but also only verball . . . .
Or else when I have observd this simple Idea to belong to all the individuals of that species that my senses have met with and then predicate it of but doe not include it in the definition of the name of that species and then the predication is real but not certainly true . . . .

Clearly, Locke's thought in Draft A is precisely the same as it is in the *Essay:*

We having little or no knowledge of what Combinations there be of simple Ideas existing together in Substances, but by our Senses, we cannot make any universal certain Propositions concerning them, any farther than our nominal Essences lead us: which being to very few and inconsiderable Truths, in respect of those which depend on their real Constitutions, the general Propositions that are made about Substances, if they are certain, are for the most part trifling; and if they are instructive, are uncertain, and such as we can have no knowledge of their real Truth, how much soever constant Observation and Analogy may assist our Judgments in guessing (4.8.9).

Aaron and Roth wished their readers to believe that while Locke rejected Descartes' "rationalist" science and philosophy of science, he nevertheless accepted his "rationalist" epistemology. However, I have established the fact that Locke did *not* accept Descartes' epistemology. Indeed, I should like to add that, both early and late, Locke rejected Descartes' science and philosophy of science *precisely because* he rejected his epistemology; furthermore, he rejected Descartes' epistemology *precisely because* he rejected his method and logic.

Locke's distinction between the necessary connexions which constitute the content of "trifling" (i.e., analytic) propositions and the non-necessary connexions which constitute the content of "instructive" but "uncertain" (i.e.

synthetic *a posteriori)* propositions provides the key to an understanding of my final point. *Essay* 4.8.9, just quoted, states the distinction:

the general Propositions that are made about Substances, if they are certain, are for the most part trifling; and if they are instructive, are uncertain.

And several other passages (e.g., *Essay* 4.6.9) help to clarify its import:

It will, no doubt, be presently objected, Is not this an universal certain Proposition, All Gold is malleable? To which I answer, It is a very certain Proposition, if Malleableness be a part of the complex Idea the word Gold stands for. But then here is nothing affirmed of Gold, but that that Sound stands for an Idea in which Malleableness is contained: And such a sort of Truth and Certainty as this, it is to say a Centaur is four-footed. But if Malleableness makes not a part of the specifick Essence the name Gold stands for, 'tis plain, All Gold is Malleable, is not a certain Proposition.

I would express Locke's meaning by saying that propositions such as "all gold is malleable" may be uttered in two different logical tones of voice. Speaking in the first tone of voice I define the meaning which I attach to the *word* gold (i.e., I analyze the content of my *idea* gold). Hence, my proposition is "trifling": certain but merely verbal or mental. On the other hand, speaking in the second tone of voice, I make a claim not about the *word* gold or the *idea* gold but rather about the *substance,* or *kind* of substances, gold, existing *in rerum natura.* My claim is (or purports to be) "instructive." However, since I do not (indeed, cannot) know the real essence, the particular constitution of the insensible particles of gold, since I do not know that, how or why all gold is (indeed, must be) malleable, my claim is not certain; it is an inductive generalization based on my "experimental" or "sensitive" knowledge of the uniform co-existence (or Humean "constant conjunction") of particular qualities in my past and present experience and, as such, it is "merely probable."

This distinction between two different logical tones of voice expresses the crucial insight which informed Locke's thought *both early and late.* Locke saw clearly the fact that many of his contemporaries confused the certainty of the first tone of voice with the instructiveness of the second. Thus, he says in Draft A, §27, p.44 that "men mistake generaly thinking such [trifling] propositions to be about the realitys of things and not the bare signification of words, when indeed they are noe thing else." And a few pages later (p.48) he adds that "a man may finde an infinite number of propositions reasonings and conclusions" of this trifling sort "in books of metaphysicks, schoole divinity, and some sort of natural phylosophy and after all know as little either of god spirits or bodys as he did before he set out." I submit that the books which Locke has in mind here were written not only by scholastics but also—in fact, principally—by Cartesians.

The Scholastics held, or so Locke thought, that it is possible, given certain 'primitive" and self-evident maxims or principles (e.g., "Whatever is, is" and "It is impossible for the same thing to be and not to be"), to deduce new actual truths about the world. Locke objected that these principles, however self-evident, are clearly "trifling" or uninstructive and, hence, that the Scholastic method of syllogistic deduction from these principles, *"ex praecognitis, et prae-concessis"* (4.7.8), is, at best, a method of logical arrangement and exposition of truths that are already known (4.7.11). He argued that a scientific method must be a *methodus inveniendi*, not a *methodus docendi* and that the logic of scientific discovery must be an informal, not a formal, one:

Would those who have this Traditional Admiration of these Propositions, that they think no Step can be made in Knowledge without the support of an Axiom, no Stone laid in the building of the Sciences without a general Maxim, but distinguish between the Method of aquiring Knowledge, and of communicating it; between the Method of raising any Science, and that of teaching it to others so far as it is advanced, they would see that those general Maxims were not the Foundations on which the first Discoverers raised their admirable Structures, nor the Keys that unlocked and opened those Secrets of Knowledge (4.7.11).

Prima facie it might be thought that Locke obviously and consciously agreed with Descartes on all these points. In fact, however, Locke's objections to Descartes' logic and method are far more serious than his objections to those of the Scholastics.

Like the Scholastics, Descartes thought it possible, given certain "primitive" truths (e.g., that the true and immutable nature of body is extension, the true and immutable essence of mind, thought), to deduce new factual truths about the world (e.g., that a vacuum is impossible, the mind, always thinking). Locke clearly believed that while the Scholastic principles were self-evident (i.e., intuitively true) but "trifling," the Cartesian principles were mere hypotheses, in fact, stipulative "nominal" definitions masquerading as statements of real essence. Consequently, he believed that while the Scholastic method of deducing from principles was a legitimate, if limited, method of teaching, the Cartesian method of deducing from true and immutable essences clearly and distinctly perceived in intellectual God-guaranteed intuitions was a *bogus* method of discovery. The deductions themselves did not (indeed, could not) *decide;* they simply *begged* any factual question at issue.

Locke's repudiation of Descartes' method and logic and his consequent repudiation of Descartes' epistemology and philosophy of science are evident in several places throughout the *Essay*. Before concluding, I should like to cite two such places: 2.1.9-21 and 4.7.12-14.

In the first place, Locke rejects Descartes' *"opinion"* that "actual thinking is as inseparable from the Soul, as actual Extension is from the Body" and, hence, "that the Soul always thinks" (2.1.9). To explain the reason for this rejection Locke says:

We know certainly by Experience, that we sometimes think, and thence draw this infallible Consequence, That there is something in us, that has a Power to think: But whether that Substance perpetually thinks, or no, we can be no farther assured, than Experience informs us . . . . The Question being about a matter of fact, 'tis begging it, to bring, as proof for it, an Hypothesis, which is the very thing in dispute: by which way one may prove any thing, and 'tis but supposing that all watches, whilst the balance beats, think, and 'tis sufficiently proved, and past doubt, that my watch thought all last night (2.1.10).

The implication of a later section (21) is obvious: had Descartes "suffered himself to be informed by Observation and Experience, and not made his own

Hypothesis the Rule of Nature," he would have followed the true, not a false, method of science.[23]

In the second place, Locke argues that if the general maxims of Scholasticism are misused, that is, if "our Notions be wrong, loose, or unsteady, and we resign up our Thoughts to the sound of Words, rather than fix them on settled determined Ideas of Things," then these maxims will serve not only "to confirm us in Mistakes" but, even worse, "to prove Contradictions." Locke then supplies this telling example:

He that with Des-Cartes, shall frame in his Mind an Idea of what he calls Body, to be nothing but Extension, may easily demonstrate, that there is no Vacuum; i.e., no Space void of Body, by this Maxim, What is is (4.7.12).

But if another shall come, and make to himself another Idea, different from Des-Cartes's of the thing, which yet, with Des-Cartes he calls by the same name Body, and make his Idea, which he expresses by the word Body, to be of a thing that hath both Extension and Solidity together; he will as easily demonstrate, that there may be a Vacuum, or Space without a Body, as Des-Cartes demonstrated the contrary (13).

Once again, the conclusion is inevitable:

. . . though both these Propositions (as you see) may be equally demonstrated, viz. That there may be a Vacuum, and that there cannot be a Vacuum, by these two certain Principles, (viz.) What is, is and The same thing cannot be, and not be: yet neither of these Principles will serve to prove to us, that any, or what Bodies do exist: for that we are left to our Senses, to discover to us, as far as they can (14).

In Locke's considered "mature" opinion, the correct method of discovery in the natural sciences (including, apparently, psychology) is not "the high priori method" of the Scholastics or, more especially, of the Cartesians; it is "the plain historical method" of Robert Boyle and his fellows in the early Royal Society of London. It is, I think, imperative to note that Locke arrived at this "mature" opinion *no later than 1671:* the words of 4.7.12-18 are found, almost verbatim, in Draft A, §27, pp.43-46.

In the course of his controversy with Edward Stillingfleet Locke had occasion to remark on the charge "That Des Cartes, a mathematical man, has been guilty of mistakes in his system."

When mathematical men will build systems upon fancy, and not upon demonstration, they are as liable to mistakes as others. And that Des Cartes was not led into his mistakes by mathematical demonstrations, but for want of them, I think has been demonstrated by some of those mathematicians who seem to be meant here [e.g., by] Mr. [Isaac] Newton [in his] Phil[osophiae] Natur[alis] Princip[ia] Mathemat[ica] l[iber] 2. §9.[24]

---

[23] Two things should be noted here: first, Locke does not mention Descartes by name; second, I have altered the tense of Locke's verbs. The sentence as he wrote it reads: "He that will suffer himself, to be informed by Observation and Experience, and not make his own Hypothesis the Rule of Nature, will find few Signs of a Soul accustomed to much thinking in a new born Child, and much fewer of any Reasoning at all."

[24] *Works,* IV, 427 & n.

The clear implication, that Descartes *did* build his system on fancy is perfectly consistent with my analysis. Locke believed, both early and late, that Descartes' foundation principles (e.g., that the true and immutable essence of body is extension) were purely fanciful, sheerly hypothetical, merely stipulative. He believed that in demonstrating the consequences of these principles (e.g., that there is no space void of body) Descartes confused a verbal certainty with an extra-verbal uncertainty (in fact, in this case, an extra-verbal falsehood). He believed, finally, that this methodological confusion is not unlike the confusion symptomatic of madness:

> *mad Men* . . . do not appear to me to have lost the Faculty of Reasoning: but having joined together some Ideas very wrongly, they mistake them for Truths; and they err as Men do, that *argue right from wrong Principles* . . . . having taken their fancies for Realities, they make right deductions from them (2.11.13).

If I am correct, if the sarcasm of Locke's repudiation of Descartes is so thinly veiled, then it is indeed odd that, historically, this sarcasm has been so scarcely noticed or, if noticed, so rarely understood. I would submit that if Locke's numerous remarks on fancy, insanity, and enthusiasm, on beasts, savages, and children, and on foreigners and madmen were read as *clues* to his lifelong estimate of Cartesianism, the analysis of this paper would prove definitive.

University of Kentucky.

Chapter XX

JOHN LOCKE AND THE CHANGING IDEAL OF SCIENTIFIC KNOWLEDGE

BY MARGARET J. OSLER

A philosophical tradition, stemming from Aristotle and including Bacon and Descartes, embodies the view that the proper aim for science is certain knowledge of the real essences of things. Two epistemological assumptions lie at the heart of this view: (1) that the world corresponds to our conceptions, and (2) that, consequently, it is possible for us to know the real natures of essences of substances existing in the world. The growth of empirical science in the seventeenth century, epitomized by the work of Robert Boyle and Isaac Newton, led to the implicit rejection of the traditional ideal for science. While writers on scientific method, including Boyle and Newton, continued to recognize the certainty of demonstration in mathematics, they regarded empirical scientific propositions as always subject to doubt in the face of further evidence. They rejected certainty as the mark of scientific knowledge in empirical matters; and they denied that we can know the inner natures or real essences of material objects, asserting that we are acquainted only with the phenomenal properties of corporeal substances. Such a blatant contradiction between the views of seventeenth-century scientists and traditional philosophy created the need for a new epistemology for experimental science, an epistemology more consistent with actual scientific practice. Conceived in the wake of the scientific achievements of the preceding century, John Locke's epistemology reflected the changing conception of scientific knowledge. Locke came to deny that certainty is an appropriate ideal for experimental science or natural philosophy and for empirical knowledge in general. He found it necessary to provide a philosophical account of knowledge more consistent with the realities of contemporary science.

In the *Posterior Analytics*, Aristotle defined scientific knowledge as certain knowledge.

> We suppose ourselves to possess unqualified scientific knowledge of a thing, as opposed to knowing it in an accidental way in which the sophist knows, when we think that we know the cause on which the fact depends, as the cause of that fact and no other, and further, that the fact could not be other than it is.[1]

Scientific knowledge for Aristotle is necessarily true; it excludes any

[1] *The Basic Works of Aristotle*, edited by Richard McKeon (New York, 1941), 11-112.

alternative. Although Aristotle insisted that scientific knowledge, properly so-called, must be demonstrative and necessary, he did, nevertheless, recognize merely probable knowledge in the sublunar world and in human affairs where objects of knowledge are subject to essential change.[2] Implicit in his claim that we possess scientific knowledge when "we know the cause on which the fact depends, as the cause of that fact and no other" is the further claim that scientific knowledge comprises knowledge of the essential natures of things; for, without such knowledge, how could we know the ultimate causes of the facts in question?

These claims continued to occupy a central role in philosophy of science well into the seventeenth century. Such disparate figures as Bacon and Descartes, neither of whom was an Aristotelian, maintained modified versions of these claims.

Although Francis Bacon is often hailed as the father of modern scientific method, his ideas are probably closer to those of the Aristotelian tradition.[3] Bacon's rejection of the Scholastic use of syllogism was based, not on a rejection of the underlying epistemological assumptions, but rather on the claim that the method of the Schools failed to lead to certain, scientific knowledge; for with uncertain premises, syllogism leads only to uncertainty. Bacon believed that the virtue of his inductive method lay precisely in the fact that it would lead men to certain knowledge of the real essences (forms) of things. In the *Great Instauration*, Bacon described the need his method fulfilled.

Now what the sciences stand in need of is a form of induction which shall analyse experience and take it to pieces, and by a due process of exclusion lead to *an inevitable conclusion*.[4]

Bacon designed his inductive method to lead to "inevitable con-

---

[2]See, for example, *Posterior Analytics, Ibid.*, 122, and *Nicomachean Ethics, Ibid.*, 1026. The characteristics of practical knowledge and knowledge of sublunar events exclude them from the class of scientific knowledge, because these kinds of knowledge do not measure up to the ideal of demonstrativeness and necessity. The rejection of the ideal of certainty for science in the seventeenth century consisted of two basic modifications of Aristotle's view: (1) an extension of the realm in which demonstrative, necessary knowledge is impossible, to include all empirical knowledge; (2) denial of the claim that demonstrative, necessary knowledge can be synthetic, e.g., Locke's claim that we have certainty only where nominal essences coincide with real essences, that is, in areas where knowledge is confined to the relations among ideas.

[3]I am indebted to the following works for this aspect of my understanding of Bacon: Robert Emerson Snow, *The Problem of Certainty: Bacon, Descartes, and Pascal* (Unpublished doctoral dissertation, Indiana University, 1967) and Henry G Van Leeuwen, *The Problem of Certainty in English Thought 1630-1690* (The Hague 1963).

[4]*The English Philosophers from Bacon to Mill*, ed. Edwin A. Burtt (New York 1939), 16. My italics.

clusions"; that is, given true premises, his method would lead to certain knowledge. Furthermore, scientific knowledge acquired by means of this method would penetrate beneath the level of phenomena and perception to the real essences or forms of the phenomena in question. It is knowledge of forms that constitutes the only genuine understanding of nature.

. . . Whosoever is acquainted with forms, embraces the unity of nature in substances the most unlike; and is able therefore to detect and bring to light things never yet done and such as neither the vicissitudes of nature, nor industry in experimenting, nor accident itself, would never have occurred to the thought of man. From the discovery of forms therefore results truth in speculation and freedom in operation.[5]

Despite Bacon's obvious differences with Aristotle, he held the same basic epistemological assumptions, namely, that scientific knowledge is certain knowledge of real essences.

Descartes joined Bacon in setting the philosophical scene for much of seventeenth-century science; and, like him, shared the Aristotelian assumptions about the nature of scientific knowledge. These assumptions are even more explicit in the writings of Descartes than they are in those of Bacon. For Descartes, scientific knowledge is certain knowledge. "Science in its entirety is true and evident cognition . . . Thus . . . we reject all such merely probable knowledge and make it a rule to trust only what is completely known and incapable of being doubted."[6] In order to escape the sceptical abyss, Descartes invoked God to guarantee the certainty of our knowledge. God is benevolent; consequently we know *"That God is not the cause of our errors."* [Principle XXIX.]

. . . *And consequently all that we perceive clearly is true* . . . Whence it follows that the light of nature or the faculty of knowledge which God has given us, can never disclose to us any object which is not true, inasmuch as it comprehends it, that is, inasmuch as it apprehends it clearly and distinctly.[7]

God's goodness guarantees that our clear and distinct ideas will provide certain knowledge of the world. Given such grounds for certainty, it is possible to extend our knowledge by employing the truth-preserving method which had served the mathematicians so well.

[5] *The New Organon*, in Burtt, *op. cit.*, 89. Bacon differed essentially from Aristotle in claiming that it is possible to acquire necessary knowledge in all regions, especially of the sublunar region.

[6] *Rules for the Direction of the Mind*, in *Philosophical Works of Descartes*, trans. Elizabeth S. Haldane and G. R. T. Ross (2 vols., New York, 1951), I, 3. [Rule I.]

[7] *The Principles of Philosophy; Philosophical Works*, I, 231. [Principle XXX.]

Those long chains of reasoning, simple and easy as they are, of which geo-
metricians make use in order to arrive at the most difficult demonstrations,
had caused me to imagine that all those things which fall under the cognizance of man might very likely be mutually related in the same fashion;
and that, provided only that we abstain from receiving anything as true which
is not so, and always retain the order which is necessary in order to deduce
the one conclusion from the other there can be nothing so remote that we
cannot reach to it, nor so recondite that we cannot discover it.[8]

By proper use of the geometrical method and certain axioms based
on our clear and distinct ideas, certain knowledge of the world lies
within our grasp. The system of the world elaborated by Descartes in
The Principles of Philosophy was presented as an example of just
how such knowledge can be acquired.

Major philosophers in the early seventeenth century continued
to maintain the Aristotelian view that the ideal towards which science
should aim is certain knowledge of the real nature of the world. The
actual practice of empirical science, as carried out by Boyle and Newton, pointed towards a very different set of epistemological assumptions as the cornerstone for scientific thought.

As practising scientists, Boyle and Newton explicitly contradicted
the traditional ideal for science. Instead of striving toward certain
knowledge of the real essences of material objects, they sought an
ordering of phenomenal experience which would enable them to
predict nature's course, regardless of whether real essences exist or
can be known. Such a drastic change in attitude toward the nature of
scientific knowledge ultimately created the need for a new set of
epistemological principles which could more adequately account for
our knowledge of the material world.

Boyle explicitly denied the Cartesian claim that the world must
correspond to human conceptions.

. . . I see no necessity, that intelligibility to a human understanding should be
necessary to the truth or existence of a thing, any more than that visibility
to a human eye should be necessary to the existence of an atom, or of a corpuscle of air, or of the effluviums of a loadstone . . .[9]

Throughout his writings, Boyle adhered to this dictum, devising
methods for acquiring knowledge about a world which does not
necessarily correspond to our conceptions and which indeed may
not be intelligible to human reason.

A large part of Boyle's work is devoted to the definition and
classification of chemical substances. Having rejected traditional
chemical doctrine which defined chemical substances (such as gold

[8] *Discourse on Method; Philosophical Works,* I, 92.
[9] Robert Boyle, *A Discourse of Things Above Reason; The Works of the
Honourable Robert Boyle,* ed. Thomas Birch (5 vols. London, 1744), IV, 44.

vitriol, etc.) in terms of substantial forms, Boyle sought to define chemical substances in a new way. For him, rejection of substantial forms amounted to the rejection of knowledge of the real essences of chemical substances. He chose instead to define chemical substances solely in terms of their operationally recognizable properties.

And if you ask men what they mean by a ruby, or nitre, or a pearl, they will still make you such answers, that you may clearly perceive, that whatever men talk in theory of substantial forms, *yet that upon whose account they really distinguish any one body from others, and refer it to this or that species of bodies is nothing but an aggregate or convention of such accidents, as most men do by a kind of agreement . . . think necessary or sufficient to this or that determinate genus or species of natural body.*[10]

If chemical substances are defined and classified solely in terms of their phenomenal properties or "accidents" and if there is no reason to assume that our conceptions of things correspond to reality, our knowledge of chemical substances will not necessarily be knowledge of their real essences. In fact, it follows as a corollary to Boyle's adherence to the distinction between primary and secondary qualities, that our knowledge of substances will not be knowledge of their inner structures, which consist of small particles of matter endowed with only a few properties (size, shape, bulk, and mobility);[11] for the secondary qualities, or accidents, which we perceive are usually quite different from the primary qualities on which they depend. Consequently, Boyle's classification of chemical substances will not yield knowledge of their real essences.[12]

Relying on empirical procedures and lacking any guarantee that the world is like our conceptions, Boyle found it necessary to evaluate propositions and theories within the framework of natural philosophy. For Boyle, the truth of a theory in natural philosophy is relative to the state of our knowledge at any given time; although a theory may be the best we can do for the moment, it lacks the certainty Descartes and Bacon sought for scientific knowledge.

That then, that I wish for, as to our systems, is this, . . . I would have such kind of super-structure looked upon only as temporary ones; which though they may be preferred before any others, as being the best in their kind that we have, yet they are not entirely to be acquiesced in as absolutely perfect, or uncapable of improving alterations.[13]

[10]Boyle, *The Origins of Forms and Qualities; Works,* II, 469. My italics.   [11]*Ibid.,* 461.
[12]Boyle developed his classification of substances to a much greater extent than indicated here, as well as having argued at great length against the various chemical traditions. (*The Origin of Forms and Qualities* and *The Sceptical Chymist.*) The important point in the context of this paper is the epistemological assumption underlying his argument, rather than the argument itself.
[13]Boyle, *Certain Physiological Essays; Works,* I, 194.

There are two main reasons why Boyle thought that our knowledge of the physical world is always subject to error and consequently lacks even the moral certainty we have in the case of theology. First, scientific theories are ultimately based on fundamental principles, such as "*ex nihilo nihil fit,*" the truth of which is by no means sure.[14] Even if the general principles and premises of our arguments were absolutely certain, the consequences we could draw from them would be less than certain; this is the second source of the uncertainty of scientific knowledge.

... The mind is so constituted, that its faculty of drawing consequences from truths is of greater extent than its power of framing clear and distinct ideas of things; so that by subtle or successive inferences, it may attain to a clear conviction, that some things are, of whose nature and properties . . . it can form no clear and satisfactory conceptions.[15]

Since we cannot trust our inferences from general premises and since we do not know whether our conceptions correspond to the world, we need criteria for testing scientific hypotheses. To fill this need, Boyle outlined criteria for what he called "good" and "excellent hypotheses," stressing the empirical nature of such hypotheses. They should, among other things, be intelligible, consistent, capable of explaining the phenomena, and consistent with all the phenomena. Moreover, they should be based on experience, should be simple, and should "enable a skillful Naturalist to foretell future Phenomena, by their Congruity or Incongruity to [them] . . .; and especially the Events of such Expts as are aptly devised to Examine it; as yt thing yt ought or ought not to be Consequent to it."[16] The recognition of the fundamental uncertainty of empirical knowledge led Boyle to discuss scientific method and criteria for determining the adequacy of scientific theories. The epistemological assumptions underlying Boyle' scientific method differ widely from those of Aristotle, Bacon, and Descartes. There is no longer any guarantee that the world corresponds to our conceptions. It is no longer possible to assume that we car acquire knowledge of the real essences of material substances; in fact, because of the nature of matter and human perception, th possibility of such knowledge is entirely ruled out.

Like Boyle, Newton presupposed a theory of knowledge which

[14]Boyle, *The Excellency of Theology; Works,* III, 432. Van Leeuwen link Boyle's distinction among degrees of certainty—metaphysical, physical, moral—with a tradition in Protestant theology which maintained that there are several levels of certainty, each corresponding to and determined by a particular kind of evidence *The Problem of Certainty,* 101f.

[15]Boyle, *A Discourse of Things Above Reason; Works,* IV, 50.

[16]Richard S. Westfall, "Unpublished Boyle Papers Relating to Scientifi Method," *Annals of Science* (1956), *12:* 116–17.

was at odds with traditional philosophy of science. The method Newton employed in the *Principia* embodies these assumptions. Newton regarded gravity as only one member of a set of active forces in nature, and the manner in which mechanics is derived in the *Principia* is a paradigm for the investigation of the laws governing all forces.[17] This method involves three major steps: the derivation of general laws or principles from empirical evidence; the extension of these principles by mathematical procedures; the deduction of as yet unaccounted for facts from the general statements of the theory. The last step results in an explanation of such facts in terms of the theory.

The process of inferring general conclusions from individual facts, Newton called "Analysis" which was, for him, logically and procedurally prior to "Synthesis" or explanation. Newton realized that inductive procedures would never lead to absolutely certain conclusions; and since, in arguing from phenomena, he believed that we are restricted to inductive procedures, he was forced to lay aside the ideal of certainty and examine ways of making inductions as strong as possible. As long as the inductive conclusion agrees with all experimental results, it may be asserted with confidence. The evidence for it is stronger when experiments of different kinds all support it. Counterevidence to the conclusion must also be based on experiments and observations.[18] Reacting to the aprioristic method of Descartes, Newton repeatedly insisted on the empirical nature of scientific statements; and he fully realized that the price for empirical grounds was the loss of metaphysical certainty.[19]

In addition to denying that the methods of natural philosophy are sufficient to achieve certainty, Newton denied that it is possible for us to discover the real or ultimate causes of phenomena. The aim of natural philosophy for him is not to ascribe occult causes to effects, but to *describe* effects by showing how they relate to the general theoretical structure. Insofar as there is such a thing as a legitimate explanation within a philosophical—as opposed to theological—

---

[17]Isaac Newton, *Mathematical Principles of Natural Philosophy, and his System of the World*, trans. Andrew Motte (1792), revised by F. Cajori (2 vols., Berkeley, 1962), I, xviii. (Hereafter referred to as *Principia*.)

[18]Isaac Newton, *Opticks* (based on fourth edition, London, 1730; New York, 1952), 404f.

[19]Newton summarized his views on inductive methods in Rule IV, at the beginning of Book III of the *Principia*: *"In experimental philosophy we are to look upon propositions inferred by general induction from phenomena as accurately or very nearly true, notwithstanding any contrary hypothesis that may be imagined, till such a time as other phenomena occur, by which they may either be made more accurate, or liable to exceptions. This rule we must follow, that the argument may not be evaded by hypothesis."* (400.)

framework, it consists in so relating the facts to be explained.[20] It is sufficient for natural philosophy to aim at describing phenomena in this manner without searching for their causes, which may lie beyond the range of human knowledge. Phenomena will remain phenomena, regardless of the status of their causes. In fact, it is epistemologically necessary for us to be content with phenomenal descriptions of the world; ultimate causes and the inner nature of material things remain beyond the realm of human knowledge. In the "General Scholium," Newton wrote:

> . . . What the real substance of anything is we know not. In bodies we see only their figures and colors, we hear only their sounds, we touch only their outward surfaces, we smell only the smells, and taste the savor; but their inward substances are not to be known either by one sense, or by any reflex act of our minds. . . .[21]

Like Boyle, Newton not only rejected the ideal of certainty for scientific knowledge, but he also rejected the traditional claim that the knowledge we seek is knowledge of the real essences of things.

Practicing scientists in the seventeenth century outgrew the strictures of traditional philosophy of science. The necessity of developing empirical methods led them to reject the old standards and old ideals—often without the aid of rigorous philosophical scrutiny. Their implicit rejection of the traditional theories of knowledge called for a new epistemology, more in line with the actual practice of contemporary science and better able to provide its conceptual foundation. The philosophy of John Locke was a major step in the formation of a new philosophy of science.

If it is a truism of Lockean scholarship that many aspects o Locke's philosophy resulted from his reaction to Descartes,[22] it i equally true, though less well-known, that Locke was deeply influenced by contemporary science, especially by the works of Boyle Newton, and Sydenham,[23] and that his theory of knowledge repre sents an effort to fill the epistemological void left by Boyle's an Newton's rejection of the Cartesian ideal of certainty in natura philosophy. Careful examination of Locke's theory of knowledg reveals the intellectual crisis underlying his views: whereas he con tinued to regard certainty as the earmark of genuine knowledge, h

---

[20]Newton, *Opticks, op. cit.*, 401f.

[21]Newton, *Principia*, 546.

[22]Cf. Richard I. Aaron, *John Locke*. (2nd ed. Oxford, 1955), 11; James Gi son, *Locke's Theory of Knowledge and Its Historical Relations* (Cambridge, 1960), 206.

[23]John Locke, *An Essay Concerning Human Understanding*, ed. A. C. Fras (2 vols., New York, 1959), I, 14. Locke's intellectual relations with Boyle, Newto and Sydenham have been well documented. See, for example, Maurice Cransto *John Locke, A Biography* (London: 1957); Kenneth Dewhurst, *John Locke (163 1704): Physician and Philosopher* (London, 1963); Fulton H. Anderson, "T

recognized that certainty was no longer a possible or an appropriate ideal for empirical science. He was consequently forced to consider new standards for evaluating scientific propositions; and in these considerations he laid a new epistemological foundation for natural philosophy.[24]

Locke's definition of knowledge reflects his insistence that we are directly acquainted only with the contents of our minds.

Knowledge then seems to be nothing but *the perception of the connexion of and agreement and repugnancy of any of our ideas.* In this alone it consists. Where this perception is, there is knowledge, and where it is not, there, though we may fancy, guess, or believe, yet we always come short of knowledge.[25]

Knowledge, then, consists only in the perception of the relations among ideas in our minds.

Locke agreed with tradition in explicitly claiming that certainty is the mark of genuine knowledge. Writing to Stillingfleet on June 29, 1697, he maintained:

. . . With me, to know and to be certain, is the same thing; what I know, that I am certain of; and what I am certain of, that I know. What reaches to knowledge, I think may be called certainty; and what comes short of certainty, I think cannot be called knowledge.[26]

There are two degrees of certain knowledge, intuition and demonstration; and they differ only in the immediacy with which we perceive the relations between ideas:

. . . sometimes the mind perceives the agreement or disagreement of two ideas, *immediately by themselves*, without the intervention of any other: and this I think we may call *intuitive knowledge*. . . . Thus the mind perceives that *white* is not *black*, that a *circle* is not a *triangle*, that *three are more* than *two* and equal to *one* and *two*. . . . this kind of knowledge is the clearest and most certain that human frailty is capable of. This part of our

nfluence of Contemporary Science on Locke's Methods and Results," *University of Toronto Studies, Philosophy*, Vol. II, no. 1, (Toronto, 1923); Patrick Romanell, Some Medico-Philosophical Excerpts from the Mellon Collection of Locke Papers," *Journal of the History of Ideas* (1964), 25: 107–16. Locke knew all of these men personally, as well as having read widely in their works.

[24]It should be pointed out that Locke continued to believe that demonstrable certainty was as possible in ethics as in mathematics. This follows from the fact that ethical ideas stand for no external archetypes. *Essay*, II, 347.

[25]Locke, *Essay*, II, 167–68. Locke defined "idea" as "that term which . . . seems best to stand for whatsoever is the *object* of the understanding when a man thinks . . . or whatever it is which the mind can be employed about in thinking." *Ibid.*, I, 32. Locke's italics.) In the first two books of the *Essay*, Locke took great pains to prove that all our ideas have their source in experience, sensation, and reflection. He sorted ideas into two major classes, simple and complex, the latter including ideas of modes, substances, and relations. *Ibid.*, I, 215–16.

[26]*The Works of John Locke* (10th ed., London, 1801), IV, 145.

knowledge is irresistible. . . . *It is on this intuition that depends all the certainty and evidence of all our knowledge . . .*[27]

Sometimes, although the mind does perceive the agreement or disagreement of two ideas, it does so only by perceiving the relations between ideas intermediate to them; where these intermediate perceptions are themselves intuitive, the procedure is called demonstration.[28] Intuition and demonstration constitute the entire storehouse of knowledge. "These two . . . are the degrees of our *knowledge*; whatever comes short of one of these, with what assurance soever embraced, is but *faith or opinion*, but not knowledge. . . ."[29]

On the basis of his definition of knowledge, Locke concluded that very little—if any—of natural philosophy ranks as knowledge, for the statements comprising it lack certainty. Most of the propositions constituting the body of natural philosophy are statements concerning substances and their attributes. Locke devoted much of the *Essay* to an explanation of why very little of our knowledge of substances is certain.

Individual substances—gold, men, chairs—are defined by their essences: " . . . Essence may be taken for the very being of any thing, whereby it is what it is."[30] Locke distinguished between two kinds of essences, real and nominal. The real essence of a material substance is its internal corpuscular structure, the primary qualities of its constituent parts which cause all its other properties. Whereas real essences exist apart from their relation to human minds, nominal essences are constructs on the basis of which we classify substances into kinds.

The nominal essence of gold is that complex idea the word gold stands for, let it be, for instance, a body yellow, of a certain weight, malleable, fusible, and fixed. But the real essence is the constitution of the insensible parts of that body, on which those qualities and all other properties of gold depend.[31]

Like Boyle's definitions of chemical substances, nominal essences do not necessarily correspond to the real essences of substances. Their constitution is arbitrary in the sense that the ideas composing them are all selected by the human mind without reference to an external archetype. Although there are real differences between substances (differences flowing from their real essences), knowledge of these differences lies beyond our capacity. All we can know are the differences in the way substances affect us, differences in the ideas produced in our minds. We name and classify substances according to their nominal essences alone. There are no external standards, no substantial forms (in the Scholastic sense) on which to mold our categories.[32]

[27]Locke, *Essay*, II, 176–77.   [28]*Ibid.*, II, 178–79.   [29]*Ibid.*, II, 185
[30]*Ibid.*, II, 26.   [31]*Ibid.*, II, 57.
[32]On January 20, 1692/93, Locke wrote to Molyneux: "This I do say, tha

The goal of natural philosophy is to learn about the properties and interactions of material substances. But our knowledge of substances is confined to their nominal essences—to their phenomenal properties, that is to say, the ideas they produce in our minds:

. . . our ideas of the species of substances being . . . nothing but certain collections of simple ideas united in one subject, and so co-existing together; v.g. our idea of flame is a body hot, luminous, moving upward; of gold, a body heavy to a certain degree, yellow, malleable, and fusible: for these or some such complex idea as these, in men's minds, do these two names of different substances, flame and gold, stand for. When we would know anything further concerning these, or any other sort of substances, what do we inquire, but what *other* qualities or powers these substances have or have not? Which is nothing else but to know what *other* simple ideas do or do not co-exist with those made up of that complex idea.[33]

In order to answer this question, we would need to know the real essence of the substance in question. But we lack knowledge of real essences, having only nominal essences at our disposal—our knowledge of substances is confined to the ideas substances produce in our minds. Experience is the only way we can discover which qualities coexist.

Knowledge of nominal essences, however, is not sufficient for discovering what other qualities the substances have. For one thing, we know of no necessary connections among the ideas we associate with the substance.

For, not knowing what size, figure, and texture of parts they are, on which depend, and from which result those qualities which make our complex idea of gold, it is impossible we should know what *other* qualities result from, or are incompatible with, the same constitution of the insensible parts of gold; and so consequently must always co-exist with that complex idea we have of it, or else are inconsistent with it.[34]

Moreover, since we do not know the primary qualities from which the ideas we have of the substance flow, we are ignorant of any necessary connection between the primary qualities and any other properties the substance may have.[35] Knowledge of the real essences of substances is beyond our capabilities. Consequently, the nature of material objects is not a possible object of certain knowledge. The stamp of the science of Boyle and Newton clearly marks Locke's theory of knowledge.

---

here are real constitutions in things from whence these simple ideas flow, which we observ'd conbin'd in them. And this I farther say, that there are real distinctions and differences in those real constitutions one from another; whereby they are distinguished one from another, whether we think of them or name them or no. But that whereby we distinguish and rank particular substances into sorts of *genera* and *species*, are not those real essences or internal constitutions, but some combinations of simple ideas as we observe in them." *Some Familiar Letters Between Mr. Locke and Several of his Friends* (London, 1708), 28.

[33]Locke, *Essay*, II, 199–200   [34]*Ibid.*, II, 200–201   [35]*Ibid.*, II, 201.

There is one more reason why we lack certain knowledge of material substances: our knowledge of their existence lacks the certainty pertaining to intuition and demonstration. Although it lacks absolute certainty, sensitive knowledge—knowledge of the existence of corporeal objects—does give us some knowledge of the material world.

There is, indeed, another perception of the mind, employed about *the particular existence of finite beings without us*, which, going beyond bare probability, and yet not reaching perfectly to either of the foregoing degrees of certainty, passes under the name *knowledge*. There can be nothing more certain than that the idea we receive from an external object is in our minds: this is intuitive knowledge. But whether there be anything more than barely that idea in our minds; whether we can thence certainly infer the existence of anything without us, which corresponds to that idea, is that whereof some men think there may be question made; because men may have such ideas in their minds, when no such things exists, no such object affects their senses.[36]

But, for Locke, a striking difference in vividness between the ideas of immediate perception and those remembered from former perceptions allows him to conclude that sensitive knowledge is a form of knowing.[37]

Sensitive knowledge lacks the scope of intuition or demonstration. It is confined to the objects producing ideas in our minds at the moment.[38] Although Locke put only limited trust in the human senses, he did not fall into total scepticism: " . . . I think nobody can, in earnest, be so sceptical as to be uncertain of the existence of those things which he sees and feels."[39] Locke defended his limited faith in sensitive knowledge on four grounds: (1) people lacking an organ of sense "never can have the ideas belonging to that sense produced in the mind"; (2) some ideas appear in our minds involuntarily; (3) "Many of those ideas are *produced in us with pain*, which afterwards we remember without the least offence"; (4) "Our *senses in many cases bear witness to the truth of each other's report* concerning the existence of sensible things without us."[40] Knowledge of particulars external to our minds does not extend very far, and it lacks the certainty pertaining to knowledge of the relations between the ideas in our minds.

The lack of certain knowledge of the material world and the lack of any guarantee that our complex ideas of substances correspond to the real nature of things led Locke to conclude that natural philosophy could never be made a science; that is to say, that its methods were incapable of producing certain knowledge.

[36]*Ibid.*, II, 185–86.   [37]*Ibid.*, II, 186–8?
[38]*Ibid.*, II, 325–26.   [39]*Ibid.*, II, 327.   [40]*Ibid.*, II, 328–3?

I deny not but a man, accustomed to rational and regular experiments, shall be able to see further into the nature of bodies, and guess righter at their yet unknown properties, than one that is a stranger to them: but yet, as I have said, this is but one judgment and opinion, not knowledge and certainty. This way of *getting and improving our knowledge in substances only by experience and history*, which is all that the weakness of our faculties in this state of mediocrity which we are in this world can attain to, makes me suspect that *natural philosophy is not capable of being made a science.*[41]

This conclusion that a science of material substances is beyond human power was a source of deep perplexity for Locke. Rather than ruling out natural philosophy and empirical knowledge in general as legitimate enterprises, he relaxed his stipulation that all knowledge must be absolutely certain: although genuine knowledge must be certain, lack of certainty does not leave us in naked ignorance. He did not succumb to the feigned scepticism which Descartes employed to establish his extreme rationalism. When we cannot *know* the truth of a proposition either by intuition or by demonstration, we can nevertheless *judge* it to be true or false.

Judgment is the thinking or taking two ideas to agree or disagree, by the intervention of one or more ideas, whose certain agreement or disagreement with them it does not perceive, but hath observed to be frequent or usual.[42]

Although we judge in the absence of certainty, we can nevertheless have good grounds on which to base the degree of assent we should grant to less-than-certain propositions; such an evaluation is made on the basis of probability.

As *demonstration* is the showing the agreement or disagreement of two ideas, by the intervention of one or more proofs, which have a constant, immutable, and visible connexion one with another; so *probability* is nothing but the appearance of such an agreement or disagreement, by the intervention of proofs, whose connexion is not constant and immutable, or at least is not perceived to be so, and is enough to induce the mind to judge the proposition to be true or false, rather than the contrary.[43]

Probability, serving to guide us where we lack certainty, has two grounds:

[41]*Ibid.*, II, 349–350. Locke expressed similar views in *Some Thoughts Concerning Education; Works*, III, 87 and 89.

[42]Locke, *Essay*, II, 409.

[43]*Ibid.*, II, 363. Locke illustrated the difference between knowing something with certainty and judging it with probability by the difference between knowing the proof of a mathematical proposition and judging it to be true, without seeing the proof, on the word of a mathematician. *Ibid.*, II, 363–64. For Locke, this difference in the ways of knowing a mathematical proposition served as a paradigm for the differences between knowing with certainty and knowing with probability generally.

First, The conformity of anything with our own knowledge, observatic and experience.

Second, The testimony of others, vouching their observation and experience

Probability provides the grounds for assertions where we fail to e tablish certainty.

Because of its empirical nature, natural philosophy can at mc yield probability. The ideal of certainty is no longer appropriate natural philosophy. But, as Locke frequently argued, the degree understanding it yields is commensurate with our capacities. If it lac the certainty sought by traditional philosophers, it is still a ve worthwhile endeavor. The study of nature gives us an opportuni to contemplate the works of God and, consequently, "gives us occ sion to admire, revere, and glorify their Author." Moreover, t study of natural philosophy leads to the improvement of mar estate, and consequently can be justified on utilitarian grounds.

He that first invented printing, discovered the use of the compass, or ma public the virtue and right use of *kin kina* [quinine], did more for t propagation of knowledge, for the supply and increase of useful commoditie and saved more from the grave than those who built colleges, workhouse and hospitals. All that I would say is, that we should not be too forward possessed with the opinion or expectation of knowledge where it is not to had, or by ways that will not attain to it: that we should not take doubtf systems for complete sciences; nor unintelligible notions for scientific demor strations.[45]

Locke's emphasis on certainty points to the intellectual cris underlying his theory of knowledge. By insisting that knowledge ar certainty are equivalent, he remained at one with the Aristotelian ar Cartesian traditions which maintained the ideal of certainty as th standard for science and for all knowledge. By recognizing, howeve that a large proportion of the assertions we make—particular about the external world—can never yield certainty or knowledge real essences, he recognized the inadequacy of the old ideal as it w challenged by Boyle and Newton. In this light, Locke can be seen having taken a major step toward providing new epistemologic underpinnings for empirical science. Locke's epistemology reflec the tensions in the changing assumptions about scientific method.

Oregon State University

[44]*Ibid.*, II, 365-66.   [45]*Ibid.*, II, 35

Chapter XXI

BOYLE, LOCKE, AND REASON

By G. A. J. Rogers

That Boyle had a considerable influence on Locke's thinking, and especially on Locke's theory of knowledge as presented in the *Essay Concerning Human Understanding*, is generally accepted.[1] Their views run remarkably parallel on many issues crucial to the production of the *Essay*, and it is clear that the influence was not comparable to, say, the influence of Plato on Aristotle, producing often a reaction to the older man's views.

But Boyle was not only influential because he emphasized empiricism in the natural sciences, as has sometimes been held.[2] Boyle was not just an empiricist; he also laid great weight on the central rôle of reason in rational enquiry. The parallels between Boyle and Locke go much further than the distinction between primary and secondary qualities in objects, though the result of Locke's following Boyle's views on this doctrine had obvious very important consequences for Locke's *Essay*. It is for this reason that F. H. Anderson's otherwise admirable account of the influence of Boyle on Locke in his *The Influence of Contemporary Science on Locke's Method and Results*[3] is inadequate. Anderson considers the connection between the *Essay* and Boyle's *Origin of Forms and Qualities*,[4] where, of course, Boyle argues for, and makes great use of, the distinction between primary and secondary qualities; but Anderson does not make any comparisons between Boyle's other works and Locke's *Essay*.

I shall show that Locke's thinking on several other topics besides the primary-secondary qualities distinction is extremely close to Boyle's, and that this is especially true of his account of reason and the possible extent of human knowledge. The similarity of their views suggests that Locke's account of knowledge as presented in Book Four of the *Essay* was well within the accepted outlook of his times, particularly when we remember the considerable popularity of Boyle's works, and the stature which he possessed as a rational theologian as

[1] E.g. J. Gibson in *Locke's Theory of Knowledge and its Historical Relations* (Cambridge, 1917), 260–261, writes: "Whilst it must remain a matter of uncertainty whether the scepticism of Glanville exerted any influence at all upon Locke, no such doubt can be felt in the case of Boyle . . ."; and R. I. Aaron writes in his *John Locke*, second edition (Oxford, 1955), 12: "The really important influence on Locke from the empiricist side was the group that gathered around Sir Robert Boyle, and which ultimately founded the Royal Society. Indeed, the most important influence of all was Boyle himself."

[2] E.g. M. Cranston in *John Locke, A Biography* (London, 1957) states: "There were two main currents which governed the development of Locke's mind. One was the unformulated *ad hoc* empiricism of Newton and Boyle and the other Royal Society virtuosi. The other was the systematic rationalism of Descartes" (265).

[3] University of Toronto Studies. *Philosophy* II, No. 1 (Toronto, 1923).

[4] First published in 1666 and reprinted in *Works* (1772) edited by T. Birch, III, –112. All references to Boyle's *Works* (London, 1772) will be to this edition.

well as a scientist. It was the earlier part of the *Essay* which made such an impact on the XVIIIth century. And this was because it was the explicit rejection of innate ideas and Locke's emphasis on the empirical basis of knowledge which appeared to be so original. But Locke's positive account of knowledge and reason, I shall argue, was neither regarded as, nor was, particularly original.

How much Boyle directly influenced Locke in personal discussions as contrasted with the parallel nature of much of their thinking is probably impossible to establish. Locke was hardly forward in acknowledging his debts to other thinkers in his published works, though he did admit to Lady Masham that it was reading Descartes which first gave him "a relish in philosophical things." [5] But a plausible argument can be made for Boyle's having had a considerable personal influence. First, Boyle and Locke were based in Oxford from 1661, when Locke took up his lectureship at Christ Church, until 1668, when Boyle went to live with his sister, Lady Ranelagh, in Pall Mall; though Locke was away for almost a year from the autumn of 1665. Secondly, we also know that during this period Locke was very much concerned with the philosophical problems which were eventually to give rise to the *Essay*. Locke's views on these matters are preserved in the series of essays on the law of nature written between 1661 and 1664.[6] It would seem very likely that as Boyle and Locke had plenty of opportunity to discuss such matters they did so, especially as the questions which the younger man was writing on were closely connected to some views held by Boyle.

But as against this it can be argued that the tone of the subsequent correspondence between Boyle and Locke does not suggest the sort of companionship between two men which was likely to encourage debate on contentious topics. The deference shown by Locke to Boyle does not suggest either that Locke seriously influenced Boyle, or that they were mutually concerned with philosophy at all. None of their letters is concerned with speculative philosophy, nor do they suggest that there was any serious philosophical interchange. Typical of the correspondence is a letter from Locke at Christ Church (Feb. 24, 1666) asking for instructions about an experiment, and closing:

Did I not know, how favourably you interpret any poor essays, and slight observations of those that are willing to learn, I should not venture to importune you with such trifles. But since my design is not (nor can ever be) to instruct you, you will permit me by all the ways I can, to assure you that I am,

Honoured Sir, Your most humble, and most obliged servant, John Locke.

[5] Mss. in the Remonstrants' Library, Amsterdam. Lady Masham to Le Clerc, 1? January 1704–5. Quoted in Fox Bourne, *Life of John Locke* (London, 1876), I, 61-62, and also Cranston *op. cit.*, 100.

[6] Now published, edited by W. von Leyden: *Essays on the Law of Nature* (Oxford, 1954).   [7] Boyle, *Works*, VI, 537

Even allowing for the deference due to the difference in their social status (Locke was especially polite to the nobility), it is clear that Locke was correctly aware of the other's then superior intellectual position. It seems, therefore, that although Boyle and Locke became acquainted whilst Boyle was in Oxford there is no direct evidence to support the view that there was ever a serious exchange of philosophical ideas. Certainly Locke attended Peter Sthael's classes on chemistry in April 1663 where, according to Wood, "he would be prating and troublesome,"[8] and Sthael was Boyle's protégé. But Wood does not say that Boyle was actually a member of these classes, and if Boyle had been a member it is fairly certain Wood would have mentioned him, as he makes a point of listing the names of people of any eminence. Nor do I know of any reason to believe that Gibson is correct in saying that "in Locke's Oxford days both he and Boyle had been members of one of those circles for discussion, of which he was so fond."[9] Perhaps Gibson is thinking of Sthael's chemistry classes referred to by Wood, but as we have seen there is reason to doubt that Boyle actually attended these.

The evidence, therefore, does not establish that Boyle and Locke did exchange philosophical thoughts. Conjecture must lead us to suppose, however, simply because their views were very similar and they were good friends, that there must have been some exchange or common source. It is also very probable that the ideas contained in Locke's *Essay* which are similar to Boyle's are in part a product of Locke's reading Boyle's works as they were published, and the sympathy which Locke had for the sorts of views that Boyle held, independently of any personal influence. That there was some influence as a result of Locke's reading Boyle is quite plain if we first consider the examples that Boyle and Locke use to illustrate a point: often they are virtually the same. That Locke had considerable sympathy for Boyle's views independently is clearly illustrated by their common dislike of the scholastic tradition of the universities, and the eagerness with which Locke awaited the publication of each of Boyle's works.[10]

At this point I wish to make some comparisons among Boyle's, Descartes', and Locke's views on perception, on the distinction between primary and secondary qualities, and on the nature of matter, to see whether Locke's position on each of these topics was Boyleian, rather than Cartesian, in tone. In talking of Boyle's views I do not wish it to be thought that I am saying that Boyle was original in holding these views. Some of them, for example, were also held by Gassendi and other early XVIIth-century thinkers.

First, we must note that Locke's empiricism is not an extreme empiricism. An extreme empiricism would be one that denied that there was anything else besides oneself and experiences; it would be

---

[8] Anthony Wood, *Life and Times of Anthony Wood* (Oxford, 1891), I, 472.
[9] J. Gibson, *op. cit.*, 265. Gibson does not cite any reference to support his remark. [10] Cf. Von Leyden, *op. cit.*, 20.

some form of idealism, and perhaps recently logical positivism has been the best example. By contrast Locke is a very conservative sort of empiricist, quite definitely committed to the existence of entities not empirically observable. The primary-secondary quality distinction patently rests on this fact. That is, Locke's empiricism states that there are minds, ideas, and physical objects independent of minds and ideas. Further, the physical objects can move around, and it is the motion of physical objects which causes us to have our ideas of physical objects. Thus he writes:

If then external objects be not united to our minds when they produce ideas therein, and yet we perceive these original qualities in such of them as singly fall under our causes, it is evident that some motion must be thence continued by our nerves, or animal spirits, by some parts of our bodies, to the brains or the seat of sensation, there to produce in our minds the particular ideas we have of them. And since the extension, figure, number and motion of bodies of an observable bigness, may be perceived at a distance by the sight, it is evident some singly imperceptible bodies must come from them to the eyes, and thereby convey to the brain some motion; which produce these ideas which we have of them in us.[11]

This account of perception which Locke gives is superficially very similar to Descartes' account in the *Dioptrics*. Descartes says:

So that you may know in more detail how the soul, seated in the brain, is able to receive through the nerves impressions of external objects. . . . I would have you conceive [nerves as] tiny fibres . . . stretching from the brain to the extremities of all parts capable of sensation. Thus the slightest touch that sets in motion the point of attachment of a nerve in these parts also simultaneously sets in motion the point of origin of the nerve in the brain; just as pulling one end of a taut string instantly sets the other end in motion. . . .[12]

But Descartes believes that the motion is "simultaneously," i.e instantaneously, transmitted, whereas Locke did not believe this Thus we find Locke writing in his *Elements of Natural Philosophy:* [1] "Light is successively propagated with an almost inconceivable swiftness; for it comes from the sun, to this our earth, in about seven or eight minutes of time, which distance is about 80,000,000 Englisl miles." Locke, then, knew that the speed of light was finite, not, a Descartes had insisted, infinite.

In other important respects the basis for Locke's theory of per

[11] *Essay Concerning Human Understanding*, Bk. II, Ch. VIII § 12. Edited by A C. Fraser, (New York, 1959), 171–172. All references to the *Essay* will be to thi edition. [12] "Dioptrics" Discourse IV. Translated by E. Anscombe and P. Geacl *Descartes' Philosophical Writing* (Nelson, 1954), 243.

[13] *Works* (7th ed., London, 1768), IV, 595. *The Elements of Natural Philosoph* was probably written by Locke when at Oates some time after 1691 (cf. H. R. Fc Bourne, *Life of John Locke* [London, 1876], II, 449). It was first published in . *Collection of Several Pieces of Mr. John Locke* (London, 1720).

ception was markedly different from Descartes'. Thus Locke's conception of the cause of most of our perceptions, i.e. physical objects, was not Cartesian. In Locke's case the fundamental particles of matter must have the properties of "solidity, extension, figure and mobility."[14] For Descartes, however, the sole property of matter is extension:

The nature of matter, or of body considered in general, does not consist in its being a thing that has hardness or weight, or colour, or any other sensible property, but simply in its being a thing that has extension in length, breadth, and depth.[15]

For Descartes, as for the Aristotelians whom he thought he was rejecting, there is no possibility of a void. Matter and space are identical. Locke explicitly rejects this view:

Those who contend that space and body are the same, bring this dilemma:— either this space is something or nothing: if nothing be between two bodies, they must necessarily touch: if it be allowed to be something, they ask, whether it be body or spirit? To which I answer by another question, Who told them that there was, or could be, nothing but *solid beings, which could not think*, and *thinking beings that were not extended?*—which is all they mean by the terms body and spirit.[16]

The basis, therefore, for Descartes' theory of perception was markedly different from that of Locke. But if we compare Locke with Boyle there are important similarities. First, let us have a look at their views on the possibility of a vacuum. In his *New Experiments Physical-Mechanical, touching the Spring of the Air* (1660) [17] Boyle points out that the "Torricellian experiment" raises the question "whether or no that noble experiment infer a vacuum?" [18] Boyle argues that there does not seem to be any single way of finding out whether or not a space is empty. There is always the possibility of some "etherial matter." But Boyle points out:

Plenists do not prove that such spaces are replenished with such a subtle matter as they speak of, by any sensible effects, or operations of it . . . but only conclude there must be such a body because there cannot be a void. And the reason why there cannot be a void, being by them taken, not from any experiments, or phenomenon of nature, that clearly and particularly prove their hypothesis, but from their notion of a body, whose nature, according to them, consisting only in extension . . . to say a space devoid of body, is, to speak in the schoolmen's phrase, a contradiction *in adjecto*. This reason, I say being thus desumed, seems to make the controversy about a vacuum rather a metaphysical, than a psysiological, question; which therefore we shall here no longer debate, finding it very difficult either to satisfy Naturalists with this Cartesian notion of a body, or to manifest wherein it is erroneous and substitute a better in its place.[19]

[14] *Essay*, Bk. II, ch. VIII, § 9, 169–170.
[15] *Principles of Philosophy*, Part II, Section IV. Anscombe and Geach, 199.
[16] *Essay*, Bk. II, ch. 13, § 16, 228. [17] *Works*, I, 1–117. [18] *Ibid.*, 37. [19] *Ib.* 38–8.

Boyle then is agnostic on this metaphysical question. Locke argues almost the same point in the probable first draft [20] of his *Essay*. Locke, however, significantly makes great use of the Cartesian notion of an idea ("idea" is a word hardly ever used by Boyle). Locke argues:

He that with Cartes shall frame in his minde an Idea of what he cals Body to be extension and cals that Idea of Extension constantly Body may easily demonstrate that there is noe *vacuum*, i.e. space without body by this universal affirmative proposition what is is. . . . But if an other shall come and make to himself an other different idea from Cartes of the thing which yet with Cartes he cals by the same name Body, and make his Idea which he expresses by the word Body to consist of Extension and Impenitrability or resistability togeather he will as easily demonstrate that there may be a vacuum or space without a body as Cartes demonstrated the contrary.[21]

Locke does not attempt here to pursue the issue one way or another; he is, as Boyle was, merely concerned to show that the existence of a vacuum—or indeed anything else (except perhaps God's existence)—was a question which could only be solved by some sort of empirical investigation. In the *Essay*, although Locke does argue that the existence of motion establishes that there is a vacuum,[22] he goes on to argue that the really important point is not "to prove the real existence of a vacuum but the idea of it" [23] because if we can have an idea of a vacuum then we can have an idea of space (i.e. an empty space), which is not identical with our idea of body, and therefore the Cartesians must be wrong in equating the two.

Boyle's positive account of perception is very close to Locke's. He argues that the sensations of color are produced by motions in the brain, sometimes caused by the motion resulting from light and sometimes a result of some other form of motion.

Colour is so far from being an inherent quality of the object . . . we shall see cause to suspect that though light do more immediately affect the organ of sight, than do the bodies that send it thither, yet light itself produces the sensation of a colour, but as it produces such a determinate kind of local motion in some part of the brain; which, though it happen most commonly from the motion whereinto the slender string of the retina are put, by the appulse of light; yet if the like motion happen to be produced by any other cause, wherein the light concurs not at all, a man shall think he sees the same colour . . .[24] [e.g., if a man is hit on the head he migh* see flashes of color].

Boyle goes to great lengths to show that motion produces sensation* of quality, e.g. colors, to establish the credibility of the thesis tha*

[20] *Locke's Essay, An Early Draft*, edited by R. I. Aaron and J. Gibb, (Oxford 1936). That there is an even earlier draft still in existence is argued for by P* Laslett in his article "Locke and the First Earl of Shaftesbury," *Mind* (1952), 89.
[21] Aaron and Gibb, *op. cit.*, 42–43.
[22] *Essay*, Bk. II, Ch. XIII, § 23, I, 233.   [23] *Ibid.*, § 24, 233–234*
[24] *The Experimental History of Colours (1663)* in *Works*, I, 671.

only matter (having the primary qualities) and motion are needed to explain why we have the sensations that we do have. That is to say, "there is a substance extended, divisible and impenetrable" [25] and motion is the "chief principle amongst second causes and the grand agent of all that happens in nature," [26] God being the first cause.

The physical basis, then, for perception in Locke and Boyle is very close. And they also agree, though this was a Cartesian position as well, that the connection between mind and body is one above man's reason to comprehend. Boyle argues that we cannot find out how the immaterial can affect the material, but we know that it does because: "if there be an effect, that we discern must proceed from such a cause, or agent, we may conclude that such a cause there is, though we do not particularly conceive how, or by what operation it is able to produce the acknowledged effect." [27] Locke more explicitly, but in the same vein, writes:

How any thought should produce a motion in body is as remote from the nature of our ideas, as how any body should produce any thought in the mind. That it is so, if experience did not convince us, the considerations of the things themselves would never be able in the least to discover to us. These, and the like, though they have a constant and regular connexion in the ordinary course of things, yet that connexion being not discoverable in the ideas themselves, while appearing to have no necessary dependence one on another, we can attribute their connexion to nothing else but the arbitrary determination of that All-wise Agent who has made them to be, and to operate as they do, in a way wholly above our weak understanding to conceive.[28]

Both Boyle and Locke recognize limits to man's understanding which they conceive as impossible to transcend. For both of them this was both a weakness and a strength. It was a position not straightforwardly in the Cartesian tradition.

What emerges from this brief comparison of Descartes, Boyle, and Locke is that in an area crucial to an empiricist account of knowledge, the account of the relation between, and the nature of, mind and matter, Locke is far closer to Boyle than he is to Descartes. Perhaps this is not surprising since both are reckoned to be empiricists as against the rationalist Descartes. Both Locke and Boyle start from experience as the basic datum, and call upon evidence to substantiate their claims in a way in which Descartes does not.

I shall now consider how far Locke and Boyle are in agreement about the nature and extent of human knowledge and the rôle of reason in acquiring knowledge. This is not such an easy comparison to make as the one made above. Boyle did not write any work comparable to the *Essay*. However, his works are filled with important

[25] *Origin of Forms and Qualities*, in *Works*, III, 14.   [26] *Ibid.*, 15.
[27] *Advice in Judging of Things Said to Transcend Reason* (1681) in *Works*, IV, 55.   [28] *Essay* Bk. IV, Ch. III, § 28, Vol. II, 221.

comments on the problem. More particularly, I shall examine Boyle's conception of reason to see if it throws any light on the *Essay*, especially Book IV.

It is usual to think of Boyle as an empiricist and Descartes as a rationalist: Locke is then represented as an empiricist strongly influenced by Cartesian rationalism. Granted that Descartes was an important influence on Locke, it is nevertheless true that most of the rationalist views which occur in Locke are also to be found in Boyle's works. The most dominant aspect of Locke's philosophy not to be found in Boyle but prominent in Descartes is based not on a rationalist's but on an empiricist's concept. This is Locke's use of the word "idea." Boyle very rarely uses the word, which perhaps adds support to his claim not to have read Descartes in detail until his own views had been formed.[29]

Boyle recognizes that there are three sorts of demonstration: metaphysical, physical, and moral. Metaphysical demonstration is "where the conclusion is manifestly built on those general metaphysical axioms, that can never be other than true; such as *nihil potest simul esse* and *non esse; non entis nullae sunt proprietates reales*, etc." [30] Physical demonstrations are those in which "the conclusion is evidently deduced from physical principles such as are *ex nihilo nihil fit; Nullo substantio in nihilum redigitur*, etc., which are not so absolutely certain as the former, because, if there be a God, he may (at least for ought we know) be able to create and annihilate substances." [31] Moral demonstrations are those "where the conclusion is built, either upon some one such proof cogent in its kind or some concurrence of probabilities, that it cannot be but allowed, supposing the truth of the most received rules of prudence and principles of practical philosophy. And this third kind of probation, yet it comes behind the two others in certainty, yet it is the surest guide, which the actions of men, though not their contemplations, have regularly allowed them to follow. And the conclusions of a moral demonstration are the surest, that men aspire to." [32]

This recognition of the possibility of moral demonstration is reminiscent of the occasion which gave rise to the *Essay*, according to

[29] *A Pröemial Essay* in *Works*, IV, 303.

[30] *Considerations about the Reconcileableness of Reason and Religion* (1675), in *Works*, IV, 182.

[31] *Ibid.* Professor A. G. N. Flew has pointed out to me that Hume makes a similar, but more far-reaching point in *An Inquiry Concerning Human Understanding*, Section XII (Library of Liberal Arts edition, 172). Hume writes in a footnote: "That impious maxim of the ancient philosophy, *Ex nihilo, nihil fit*, by which the creation of matter was excluded, ceases to be a maxim, according to thi philosophy [i.e. that 'if we reason *a priori*, anything may be able to produce any thing.'—G. A. J. R.]. Not only the will of the Supreme Being may create matter but for ought we know *a priori*, the will of any other being might create it, or any other cause that the most whimsical imagination can assign."   [32] *Ibid*

Locke's friend, James Tyrrell. In a manuscript note in his copy of the *Essay* Tyrrell explains that "difficulties" arose in discussing the "principles of morality and revealed religion." [33] We know that Locke certainly believed in the possibility of moral demonstration, for he argues, even more strongly than Boyle, that "the idea of ourselves, as understanding, rational creatures . . . would, I suppose, if duly considered and pursued afford such foundations of our duty and rules of action as might place *morality* amongst the *sciences capable of demonstration:* wherein I doubt not but from self-evident propositions, by necessary consequences, as incontestable as those in mathematics the measures of right and wrong might be made out." [34]

As Von Leyden has pointed out,[35] Locke held this position in 1663 when he wrote his essays on the law of nature, and therefore his views on this could not have been, as Passmore has suggested,[36] the result of reading Cudworth's *True Intellectual System of the Universe* (1678). But it is certainly possible that one of the influences towards this position was Boyle, with whom Locke might well have discussed this question.

But in order to carry out demonstrations there has to be the capacity to do so, and here again Locke and Boyle agree. "The innate light of the rational faculty is more primary than the very rules of reasoning, since by that light, we judge even of the lately mentioned axiom (the principle of inference) which is itself the grand principle of rating ratiocinations made by inference," [37] says Boyle. Locke echoes his words in the *Essay* where he writes:

What need is there of reason? Very much: both for the enlargement of our knowledge and regulating our assent. For it hath to do both in knowledge and opinion, and is necessary and assisting to all our other intellectual faculties, and indeed contains two of them, viz. *sagacity* and *illation.* By the one it finds out; and by the other it so orders the intermediate ideas as to discover what connexion there is in each link of the chain, whereby the extremes are held together; and thereby, as it were, to draw into view the truth sought for, which is that which we call *illation* or *inference,* and consists in nothing but the perception of the connexion there is between the ideas, in each step of the deduction.[38]

Furthermore, for both of them the understanding is viewed as analogous to the eyes. Locke writes: "For the understanding, like the eye, judging of objects only by its own sight, cannot but be pleased with what it discovers." [39] When Boyle makes the comparison he uses

[33] Cf. Fraser's note: *Essay,* "The Epistle to the Reader," 9.
[34] *Essay,* Bk. IV, Ch. 3, § 18, 208.
[35] *Op. cit.,* 55.   [36] *Ralph Cudworth* (Cambridge, 1951), 93–96.
[37] *Advice in Judging of Things said to Transcend Reason* (1681) in *Works,* IV, 460.
[38] *Essay,* Bk. IV, Ch. XVII, § 2, 387.
[39] *Essay,* "Epistle to the Reader," 8; Fraser points out that this is a favorite analogy of Locke's.

it to make the distinction drawn by Locke between intuitive and deductive knowledge.

As the understanding is wont to be looked upon as the eye of the mind, [Boyle writes] so there is analogy between them, that there are some things, that the eye may discern (and does judge of) organically, if I may so speak, that is, by the help of instruments: as when it judges of a line to be straight, by the application of a ruler to it, or to be perpendicular, by the help of a plumb-line, or a circle to be perfect by the help of a pair of compasses. But there are other things, which the eye does perceive (and judge of) immediately and by intuition, and without the help of organs or instruments; as when by the bare evidence of the perception, it knows, that this colour is red, and that other blue. . . . For thus there are some things, that the intellect usually judges of in a kind of organical way, that is by the help of certain rules, or hypotheses, such as are a great part of the theorems and conclusions in philosophy and divinity. But there are others which it knows without the help of these rules, more immediately, and as it were intuitively, by evidence of perception; by which way we know many prime notions and effata, or axioms metaphysical, etc. as, that contradictory propositions cannot both be true; that from truth nothing but truth can legitimately be deduced. . . .[40]

Boyle and Locke, therefore, were in fundamental agreement about the rôle of reason in human knowledge, and that it was a central rôle. Why is it then that this comparison has been neglected? Largely it must be for the same reason that Bk. IV of Locke's *Essay* has been neglected. His rejection of innate ideas, a notion which Boyle does not deem worth considering, and his emphasis on the importance of experience in the early part of the *Essay* have dominated the Lockean landscape. But more particularly there is in Locke a particular form of scepticism, also to be found in Boyle, which often cohabits with an emphasis on empiricism. It is this scepticism, which colored much of the new science and new thinking of the XVIIth century, that pointed away from what these men had to say about the central rôle of reason and it is this scepticism that I now wish to note.

Both Locke and Boyle recognized, quite correctly, that many of the questions to which we seek answers cannot be solved by reason alone. One such class is composed of the ontological questions that we can ask. Locke acknowledges that we can prove God's existence by demonstration and know of our own existence by intuition, but apart from these we know what things exist only by sensible experience, which does not have the certainty of intuition or demonstration. Similarly, whilst Boyle accepts the ontological argument[41] for the existence of God, he likewise is aware that empirical observation crucial to understanding the physical world around him, does not have the certainty of metaphysical truth,[42] and the existence or non-exist-

[40] *Advice in Judging of Things said to Transcend Reason, Works*, IV, 460–61.
[41] *Advice in Judging of Things said to Transcend Reason, Works*, IV, 461.
[42] Cf. *Some Considerations about the Reconcileableness of Reason and Religion Works*, IV, *passim*.

ence of an entity other than God is a question that we can only decide upon evidence. And even over God's existence Boyle constantly turns to the Argument from Design, an appeal based upon empirical evidence. Ontological questions generally, therefore, for both Boyle and Locke are a matter of evidence, and evidence from empirical sources does not have the same sort of certainty as truths of intuition and demonstration. But even if we cannot be certain by reason alone that certain entities exist, neither can we be certain that they do not exist. Locke, for example, thinks that it is probable, given the "magnificent harmony of the universe, and the great design and infinite goodness of the Architect" [43] that there is a great chain of being stretching from God to the most simple of creatures. Boyle throughout his *Advice on Things said to Transcend Reason* emphasizes the danger of negative judgments about things that we do not clearly understand.

Closely connected is the rejection by both Boyle and Locke of the importance of real essences and substantial forms. Thus Boyle argues:

The origin, Pyrophilus, and nature of the qualities of bodies, is a subject that I have long looked upon as one of the most important and useful that the naturalist can pitch upon for his contemplation. For the knowledge we have of the bodies without us, being for the most part fetched from the informations the mind receives by the senses, we scarce know anything else in bodies, upon whose account they can work upon our senses, save their qualities: for as to the substantial forms which some imagine to be in all natural bodies, it is not half so evident that there are such as it is, that the wisest of those that do admit them confess, that they do not well know them. And as it is by their qualities that bodies act immediately upon our senses, so it is by virtue of those attributes likewise that they act upon other bodies, and by that action produce in them, and oftentimes in themselves, those changes that sometimes we call alterations, and sometimes generation or corruption.[44]

Locke argues [45] that as real essences are unknowable, nominal essences are the only ones which are of importance for man and these depend upon our continual application of the same definition, based upon observation, to an object. Locke says that there are two opinions concerning the real essences of corporeal substances:

The one is of those who, using the word essence for they know not what, suppose a certain number of those essences, according to which all natural things are made, and wherein they do exactly everyone of them partake, and so become of this or that species. The other and more rational opinion is of those who look on all natural things to have a real, but unknown constitution of their insensible parts; from which flow those sensible qualities which serve us to distinguish them one from another, according as we have occasion to rank them into sorts, under common denominations.[46]

[43] *Essay*, Bk. III, Ch. VI, 68.
[44] *Origin of Forms and Qualities, Works*, III, 11.   [45] Especially Bk. III, Ch. VI.
[46] Bk. III, Ch. III, § 17, 27–28.

Similarly, Locke would have agreed with Boyle when he denies that his design in science is to illuminate ultimate causes.[47] Boyle explains that he does not have to choose between the Epicurean and Cartesian methods of explaining the elasticity of the air because his business is not "to assign the adequate cause of the spring of the air, but only to manifest, that the air hath a spring, and to relate some of its effects." [48] For Locke causation is "that which produces any simple or complex idea," [49] i.e. causation depends upon empirical factors only. Boyle's position is reminiscent of Galileo's attitude towards cause [50] and Newton's concern to steer clear of hypotheses about the ultimate causes of natural phenomena.

In conclusion, therefore, we can see from his writings that Boyle anticipated several of the key points of Locke's *Essay*. This anticipation was not confined solely to the empirical emphasis of Boyle's scientific work; it is also to be found clearly in the rationalist basis of knowledge offered by Boyle. That this has often been overlooked, and the rationalist elements of the *Essay* attributed to the influence of Descartes, has been largely because Boyle's theological, as opposed to his scientific, writings have not received all the attention that they deserve.[51] And this has been probably because Boyle's eminence in this area, so high in his own day, has since then been largely eclipsed by Locke, so that he is remembered not primarily as a philosopher or theologian but as a chemist. But like Locke himself Boyle was a man of many parts, and our present categories are largely the product of a later age.

Certainly the most important new ingredient in Locke's thinking which is not to be found in Boyle's work is Cartesian in origin. This was the notion of an idea, which had both powerful and confusing consequences.[52] But largely the *Essay* emerges, when seen beside the writings of Boyle, as a work well within the already existing English tradition. It was, of course, of considerable originality and of great importance, but it was not out of place in its surroundings. It was the most important work within an already existing tradition, not the first work of a new tradition.

University of Keele, England.

[47] This is not to say that Boyle thought that scientific investigation was not relevant to final causes. Boyle distinguished between (a) finding out the particular function of some object, e.g. the eye, where we would find out its purpose, and had a duty to do so, and (b) finding out God's ultimate purpose *in general* which is beyond man's ability. Cf. *A Disquisition about the Final Causes of Natural Things* (1688), *Works*, Vol. V.

[48] *Spring and Weight of the Air* (1660), *Works*, I, 11–12.

[49] *Essay*, Bk. II, Ch. XXVI, § 1, I, 433.

[50] Cf. *Dialogue Concerning Two New Sciences* (Dover edition), 166.

[51] Cf. Philip P. Wiener, "The Experimental Philosophy of Robert Boyle (1626–1691)," *Philosophical Review* (1932), 594–609.

[52] Cf. "Locke on the Human Understanding" by Gilbert Ryle, *John Locke Tercentenary Addresses* (Oxford, 1933) where Ryle distinguishes at least five senses in which Locke uses the word 'idea.'

Chapter XXII

LOCKE, NEWTON, AND THE CAMBRIDGE PLATONISTS
ON INNATE IDEAS

By G. A. J. Rogers

1. *The Intellectual Environment.*—There are certain features of the intellectual environment of Locke and Newton that I wish to identify. They all relate specifically to issues implicit or explicit in the outlook of the men usually referred to as the Cambridge Platonists. I shall be concerned here with certain doctrines of the Cambridge Platonists and the critics of those doctrines.

Although the full story of the impact of Platonic ideas on thinkers in the Renaissance and early modern times has still to be told there is now general agreement among scholars that this was considerable and of the greatest importance.[1] It is certainly not always easy to identify the nature of Platonism in the period partly because it was closely linked throughout the Renaissance and the seventeenth century with the magical traditions and the belief in the *Cabbala* and the *prisca theologia*.[2] There were some good intellectual reasons for these links and the whole theory is more strong and coherent than we might at first imagine. Some central doctrines of this school—there were others but they do not now concern us—were a belief in innate ideas imprinted on the mind at its first creation, and the view that these innate ideas give us knowledge of matters of religion and morals. Commitment to these positions is found in abundance in the writings of the Cambridge Platonists and has been well

---

[1] We now know that there is a continuous and powerful tradition running from the revival of interest in the views of Plato's writings in Renaissance Florence, though the astronomy of Copernicus, Kepler, and Galileo, and into the writings of Henry More, Isaac Barrow and Isaac Newton. To give a comprehensive bibliography for this would be a major (though thoroughly worthwhile) undertaking. A few of the important sources are the following: Ernst Cassirer, *The Platonic Renaissance in England* (London, 1953); Paul Oskar Kristeller, *Renaissance Thought* (New York, 1961), and *Renaissance Thought* II (New York, 1965); Alexandre Koyré, *From the Closed World to the Infinite Universe* (New York, 1957), and *Metaphysics and Measurement* (London, 1968); Frances A. Yates, *Giordano Bruno and the Hermetic Tradition* (London, 1964); John W. Yolton, *John Locke and the Way of Ideas* (London, 1956); D. P. Walker, *The Ancient Theology* (London, 1972); John Tulloch, *Rational Theology and Christian Philosophy in the Seventeenth Century* (2 vols. Edinburgh and London, 1872); J.E. McGuire and P.M. Rattansi, "Newton and the Pipes of Pan," *Notes and Records of the Royal Society* XXI (1966); C. A. Staudenbaur, "Galileo, Ficino, and Henry More's *Psychathanasia*," *JHI* 29(1968), 565-78.

[2] For a definition of the "ancient theology": Walker, *op. cit.*, 1-3.

documented.[3] I shall confine myself to two examples to illustrate the position.

In his *An Antidote against Atheism* (1653), Henry More heads Part Three of Book I "An Attempt towards the finding out the true Notion or Definition of God, and a cleare Convixtion that there is an indelible *Idea* of a *Being absolutely perfect* in the Mind of Man."[4] The idea of an absolutely perfect being, says More, "is as distinct and indelible an Idea in the Soul, as the Idea of the five Regular Bodyes, or any other Idea whatsoever." The mind of man is not "a Table book in which nothing is writ."[5] Rather, there is "an active and *actuall* Knowledge in a man."[6] "There is," said Benjamin Whichcote, often described as the founder of the Cambridge Platonists,[7] "a natural and indelible Sense of Deity, and consequently of Religion, in the Mind of Man."[8]

Such attitudes were widely canvassed and widely accepted in England in the mid-seventeenth century, particularly in Cambridge. Two men, who quite possibly had considerable influence on Newton as a young man, Henry More and Isaac Barrow, subscribed to the doctrine.[9] More's commitment we have already noted. Barrow's commitment is not a major feature of his writings but appears in his sermons. He wrote:

God our parent hath stamped on our nature some lineaments of himself, whereby we resemble him; he hath implanted in our souls some roots of piety towards him; into our frame he hath inserted some propensions to acknowledge him, and to affect him; the which are excited and improved by observing the manifest footsteps of divine power, wisdom, and goodness, which occur in the works of nature and providence; to preserve and cherish these is very commendable; a man thereby keeping the precious relics of the divine image from utter defacement, retaining somewhat of his primitive worth and integrity; declaring that by ill usage he hath not quite shattered or spoiled his best faculties and inclinations.[10]

[3] Probably the best single source is John Yolton, *op. cit.*, Ch. II.

[4] Sections of the *Antidote* are republished in *The Cambridge Platonists*, ed. C. A. Patrides (London, 1969), from which quotations will be taken unless otherwise stated. Hereafter cited as Patrides. The passage quoted is on page 217.

[5] Patrides, 222.   [6] *Ibid.*, 223.

[7] But see C. A. Staudenbaur's review article "Platonism, Theosophy, and Immaterialism: Recent Views of the Cambridge Platonists," *JHI*, 35(1974) 157-69.

[8] *The Use of Reason in Matters of Religion*, Patrides, 59.

[9] For a discussion of Newton's debt to the Platonic tradition and to Henry More in particular see J. E. McGuire, "Neoplatonism and Active Principles: Newton and the *Corpus Hermeticum*," *Hermeticism and the Scientific Revolution* (Los Angeles, 1977). See also below, and Note 22. Barrow's influence is much more problematic. D. T. Whiteside rightly stresses the lack of evidence of a strong connection between Barrow and Newton (*The Mathematical Papers of Isaac Newton* [Cambridge, 1967], I, 10, n. 25). There is, however a strong anecdotal tradition linking the two men and they certainly shared many beliefs. (Whiteside cites these sources.)

[10] Isaac Barrow, *Sermons on Various Subjects* (5 vols., London, 1823), IV, 45.

But the Platonists did not have it all their own way. Before Locke's polemic against innate ideas in the *Essay* there were other challenges. One such was Samuel Parker's *A Free and Impartial Censure of the Platonick Philosophie* (1666, second edition, 1667). Parker's work can certainly not be rated of the first rank intellectually. But it shows that the merits of the Platonic revival were a live issue in Restoration England. The book is dedicated to Ralph Bathurst, then President of Trinity College, Oxford, a man involved in the development of science at Oxford, and like Parker, a Fellow of the Royal Society. In the Dedication Parker acknowledges the great importance of rational enquiry: "Men that have laid aside the free and impartiall use of their Reasons, are just as fit for Religion as Sheep and Oxen, for they differ only in this, that the one are Brutes without Reason, and the other Brutes with it." The commitment to reason in matters of religion was common ground between Parker and those he opposed. It united the Platonists and the anti-Platonists—such as Parker, and later, as we shall see, Locke—against those whom both groups saw as opposed to reason, namely, the supporters of Enthusiasm.

Parker begins by acknowledging the merits of Platonic morality with which he has no quarrel. It is the Platonic theology that he particularly wishes to refute. He gives a brief history of Platonism down to the Platonic Academy at Florence and then gives a critical account of Plato's logic and his natural philosophy. Parker's objections to the Platonic philosophy are based largely upon its faulty method. Parker says that he prefers the method practised by the Royal Society "for they having discarded all particular *Hypotheses,* and wholly addicted themselves to exact Experiments and Observations, they may not only furnish the World with a compleat *History of Nature,* (which is the most useful part of Physiologie) but also lay firm and solid foundations to erect *Hypotheses* upon."[11] Hypotheses, he recognizes, are always likely to be "doubtful and uncertain."

Parker's worst strictures are reserved for Platonic theology: the part which relates to theory and contemplation is "monstrously darke and obscure."[12] The first fault he finds in the Platonists "is their way of resolving knowledge into its *first and fundamental Principles* in that by rejecting the Testimony and Judgement of sense in matters of Philosophy, they do but involve and perplex the Principles thereof . . . hereby the minds of men are taken off from the native Evidence of plain and palpable Truths, and are fain to ground all their knowledge upon nice and subtle Speculations. . . ."[13] So far Parker's attack upon the Platonists can be read as an attack upon a certain approach to theology, as indeed it was intended. But it is patently clear that it is also an attack on a cer-

---

[11] Parker, *Op. cit.,* 47. Quotations are from the second edition.
[12] *Ibid.,* 49.   [13] *Ibid.,* 55.

tain method of approaching the physical world. What in fact Parker is doing is advocating the method at that time gaining favor amongst the Fellows of the Royal Society and using that method as a yardstick by which to measure the method of the Platonically inclined theologians.

The remainder of Parker's work proceeds entirely in this vein. The Platonists "suppose that the Truth of all Beings consists in a conformity to their *Archetypal Ideas*, whereby they mean some General Patterns, by which all the Individuals of each Species are framed."[14] This doctrine is linked to the belief in innate ideas, because, according to the theory. in order to know the nature of man's creations the Platonist believes "that God has hang'd a multitude of these little Pictures of himself and all his creatures in every man's understanding."[15] The difference between science and opinion, according to the Platonists is that science is dependent on attending to these unchangeable ideas, and opinion is a result of "uncertain and variable reports of sense."

Parker totally rejects all the Platonic theses. General truths, such as the whole is greater than its parts, are known by experience, not by contemplating some internal idea. Even if ideas were planted in the mind this would be no guarantee of truth because false ideas can be implanted as well as true ones. The pursuit of abstract essences is entirely misconceived. He goes on to attack the link made by Platonists between Plato and Moses. The *prisca theologia* is unsubstantiated, says Parker. There is no evidence in the "writings of any agreement between the *Platonick* Philosophy and the Sacred Scriptures."[16]

Parker does not mention any of the Cambridge Platonists by name most of whom were still alive in 1666—but it is certain that he thought the book worth writing because the Platonic tradition was so much canvassed in theological and philosophical circles at the time. His particular rejection of the vocal Cabbala is especially apposite when it is remembered that in 1653 Henry More had published his *Conjectura Cabbalistica* which argued for the plausibility of the doctrine.

Any reader familiar with Locke's *Essay* will have been struck by the similarity between many of Parker's themes and those of Locke: the rejection of innate ideas, archetypes, and real essences, and the approval of the method advocated by the Royal Society are all common territory. What is important about the common links is that in Parker we see them overtly situated in the context of a rejection of Platonic philosophy. In Locke the specific position to which he is opposed is not always so easy to identify. It is, however, certain that Parker and Locke shared their outlook on Platonism, but what about Newton? Where did he stand on the epistemological issues raised by the Platonic philosophy? To this problem we shall now turn.

[14] *Ibid.*, 56.   [15] *Ibid.*, 56.   [16] *Ibid.*, 103.

2. *The Influence of Locke on Newton.*—To establish a positive influence of one thinker on another is usually a difficult and hazardous business. It is my object here to consider whether Locke had any influence on Newton in one particular respect. I wish to consider if Locke influenced Newton towards what I shall call Newton's epistemological empiricism. By this I do not mean just the fact that Newton advocated the view that natural science must be grounded in observation and experiment—what we may call his "methodological empiricism"—but the comprehensive empiricism expressed in his remark in the projected Rule V for the third edition of the *Principia, "Sed non sentio quod Idea aliqua sit innata"* ("but I do not perceive that any idea whatever may be innate"), a position which implies not only a particular methodology for science, but also has important implications for theology and morals, and, indeed, all branches of knowledge. My conclusion on this may be stated at the outset: it is quite possible that Locke did indeed have such a positive influence but that there is finally no conclusive evidence. There is, however, enough related material to make the question worthy of exploration.[17]

When Newton went up to Cambridge in 1661 there were varied intellectual forces to attract his attention: the traditional philosophy of the Schools, the new philosophies of Descartes and of Gassendi, the experimental chemistry of Robert Boyle, and the modern Platonism of Henry More and other Cambridge Platonists. References to all of these sources are to be found in Newton's early notebook preserved in the Cambridge University Library.[18] An analysis of the contents of these *Questiones quaedam Philosoph[i]cae*[19] reveals, however, that a very high proportion of the philosophical—as contrasted with the scientific—material noted has its source in the writings of Henry More; for ex-

[17] For a comparison of the epistemologies of Locke and Newton see G. A. J. Rogers, "The Empiricism of Locke and Newton," in *Philosophers of the Enlightenment,* ed. Stuart Brown (London, 1978).

[18] University Library, Cambridge, MS Add. 3996. This notebook has now been discussed by several scholars. The most important papers are: A. R. Hall, "Sir Isaac Newton's Notebook, 1661-65," *Cambridge Historical Journal,* 11(1948), 239-50; Richard S. Westfall, "The Foundations of Newton's Philosophy of Nature," *The British Journal for the History of Science,* 1(1962), 171-82. The Notebook contains notes from Aristotle's *Organon,* from his *Ethics,* paraphrasing of sections from Descartes, and from Walter Charleton's *Physiologia Epicuro-Gassendo-Charltoniana* (London, 1654) which was probably the major source for Newton's knowledge of Gassendi at this time. On this see Westfall *op. cit.,* 172, note, and J. E. McGuire, "Body and Void in Newton's *De Mundi Systemate.* Some New Sources," *Archives for the History of the Exact Sciences,* 3(1966). 224-25. Newton did not then own any of Gassendi's work. The notebook contains references to Robert Boyle, though there is not the attention given him here that there is in later notebooks, especially one for about 1690-1705, U.L.C. MS Add. 3975.

[19] Newton's title for the middle general section of U.L.C. MS. Add. 3996.

ample, many pages consist of either direct quotation or paraphrase of More's *The Immortality of the Soul*.[20] Thus the whole of the entry under the title "Of Sensation" is a paraphrase of sections of the *Immortality*, and his entry on "Memory" begins with a long quotation from the same work. Not all of the purely philosophical entries seem to be derived from More, however. Descartes's *Meditations* III appears to be the original for the paraphrase which appears at ff.83-84. But the powerful impression is that in the philosophy and theology of the notebook it is More's influence that is most patent.[21] Even the references to Gassendi, for example, do not appear to be related to matters other than issues in natural philosophy. What, if anything, does the notebook tell us about Newton's outlook on epistemology? The answer must be that it tells us very little with certainty, and what evidence there is points in contrary directions.

Let us begin with the evidence of More's influence on Newton. That More did have some influence on Newton is both widely accepted and hardly surprising.[22] It is, nevertheless, very difficult actually to document. It might even have pre-dated Newton's arrival in Cambridge, for Newton's headmaster, Stokes, in Grantham had been a pupil of More at Cambridge, and More was himself from Grantham and had attended Grantham Grammar School before going to Eton. It would not therefore be surprising if Newton soon came to know More at Cambridge. We do not know when exactly they became acquainted but there developed a friendship which lasted until More's death in 1687.[23] In this light and

---

[20] The amount of More material in the *Questiones* has not been emphasized by commentators, mainly, one supposes, because it does not bear so obviously on Newton's scientific development, but probably also because not all of the unattributed notes have been identified as originating from More.

[21] Newton owned several of More's works and they show signs of having been carefully read by him, including dog-earing and the occasional note in Newton's hand.

[22] Newton's relationship to the Cambridge Platonists has still to be properly mapped out, but that he was indebted to More on several points is generally acknowledged. Cf. Louis T. More, *Isaac Newton. A Biography* (London and New York, 1934, reptd. 1962): "The influence of More and the Cambridge Platonists on Newton's ideas of space, time, and God, was direct and important" (553). See also A. Koyré, *From the Closed World to the Infinite Universe*, esp ch. VI, IX; J. E. McGuire and P. M. Rattansi, "Newton and the Pipes of Pan," *passim*, and J. E. Power, "Henry More and Isaac Newton on Absolute Space," *JHI*, **31**, (1-70), 289-96. See also the McGuire paper cited in Note 9. Suppor for my interpretation of Newton as being fundamentally anti-platonic in epis temology but nevertheless attracted to the ontology of Platonism comes from his theological writings. Frank E. Manuel in a study based on the Yahuda manuscripts has argued that Newton was strongly opposed to Platonism in theology. Cf. *The Religion of Isaac Newton* (Oxford, 1974), 68. This suggests that Locke and Newton were even closer than is generally allowed.

[23] More bequeathed Newton a funeral ring, and was clearly fond of him.

given the high intellectual place of More and other Platonists in Cambridge during Newton's undergraduate days, it would be very surprising if More were not an influence on Newton's later accounts of God, space, and time.

But any influence in other respects is not nearly so clear. It must be remembered that More never penetrated deeply into either the natural sciences or mathematics. As with all the Cambridge Platonists his primary interests were theological. There were, therefore, clear limitations to the possible extent of his impact on Newton's mind, but the early notebook helps to fill out this picture in other ways. For Newton to have read those passages that he quotes from More he must also have read More's account of our knowledge of God, and More quite unambiguously argues that we have an innate knowledge of God's existence. There is, however, no sign of these arguments in Newton's notebook. Instead the argument for God's existence which is recorded is one that Newton was to return to throughout his life, namely, the Argument from Design. Newton sees the existence of order in the Universe as evidence of the existence of God:

Were men & beasts &c made by fortuitous jumblings of attomes there would be many parts useless in them deletions here a lump of flesh there a member too much some kinds of beasts might have had but one eye some more yn two & ye two eyes.[24]

This entry could well be a gloss on Book Two of More's *An Antidote Against Atheism,* which consists of a series of versions of the Argument from Design. But there is no further entry under "Of God," which itself suggests that even at this early stage Newton was looking for an empirical proof for the existence of God and was not attracted to any of an *a priori* nature advocated by Descartes and More. Further evidence that Newton was not at this stage strongly attracted to the existence of innate ideas are

[24] U.L.C. Ad. MS 3996 f.126. It is interesting to note that the very same argument appears in Newton's manuscripts of about fifty years later. In the course of drafting the later queries for the *Opticks* Newton wrote: "One Principle in Philosophy is ye being of a God or Spirit infinite eternal omniscient omnipotent, and the best argument for such a being is the frame of nature & chiefly the contrivance of ye bodies of living creatures. All the great land animals have two eyes in the forehead, a nose between them a mouth under the nose, two ears on ye sides of ye head, two arms or two fore legs or two wings on the shoulders & two leggs behind & this symmetry in the several species could not proceed from chance there being an equal chance for one eye for three or four eyes as for two, and so of the other members . . . " U.L.C. MS Add. 3970 f.479. This is perhaps as good an example as one is likely to get of the absorption of one man's view by another, and shows a capacity on Newton's behalf which is revealing.

his entries under "Soul."[25] Again the entries appear based upon the writings of More, but, again too, when Newton has the opportunity to refer
to innate ideas, he does not do so. They do, however, show that Newton
accepted a thoroughly dualist view of man, and a representative theory
of perception, both positions he was to maintain all his life.

The evidence of the notebook and the known association of Newton
and More suggest that while Newton followed More in his theism and
his dualism there is no positive evidence of his having accepted any kind
of doctrine of innate ideas. The evidence of the notebook, however,
should not be taken as conclusive for Newton's earlier positions, because
the lack of such entries certainly does not establish that Newton did not
subscribe to the innate-ideas doctrine. We have no knowledge at all, for
example, of how Newton would have accounted for moral knowledge—
for certainly he believed in an objective ethics, and certainly he believed
that man could know what was right and wrong. Further, we would expect that the standard undergraduate answers to questions about man's
knowledge of God and knowledge of the moral law—given in Cambridge in the decades between the Restoration and the publication of
Locke's *Essay*—would have been answers couched in terms which
appeared to imply some commitment to a doctrine of innate ideas.[26]
Equally clearly the notebook does not tell us that Newton did subscribe
to the empiricist position which he espoused in later years. In all probability Newton had not seriously considered the issue of innate ideas when
he was an undergraduate. There was no great reason for him to do so,
for major epistemological issues did not come to a head until much later,
indeed not until the publication of Locke's *Essay* in 1690. However, the
notebook does reveal, despite the influence of More and the general
intellectual atmosphere, a young man who is probably more sympathetic
to the empiricist outlook than were his mentors.

Newton's advocacy of a basic empirical approach in matters of natural philosophy was a lifelong characteristic. It finds clear expression in
his optical researches of the 1670s, in his manuscripts extending through
all his mature years, right through the manuscripts for the second and
third editions of the *Principia,* and the drafts and revisions of the *Opticks*
as well as in his published works. It is not, however, until the post-1713
period that we have clear documentary evidence of the epistemologica
empiricism embodied in the draft *Regula* V. Prior to this, Newton had
come to know Locke well and to read the *Essay.*[27]

[25] U.L.C. MS Add. 3996 ff.130-31. Newton's entries are primarily concerned
to argue for the existence of the soul as a distinct entity from the body, contrary
to Hobbes's materialism. Hobbes is in fact mentioned.
[26] Cf. Yolton, *op.cit., passim.* Cassirer, *op.cit., passim.*
[27] Cf. G. A. J. Rogers, "Locke's *Essay* and Newton's *Principia,*" *JHI,* 3
(April 1978), 217.

What exactly was Newton's reaction to Locke's major work? Once again the evidence is not substantial, but there is enough to form some parts of a picture. The only direct statement of Newton which we have on the *Essay* is that contained in his letter to Locke of 1693: "I beg your pardon . . . for representing that you struck at ye roots of morality in a principle you laid down in your book of Ideas & designed to pursue in another book & that I took you for a Hobbist."[28] Newton's later letter explained that he could not recall why he had been disparaging or even what it was he had said.

Newton was at this time mentally unbalanced, and we must for this reason be circumspect in what we may read into his remark. But it should not be dismissed out of hand.[29] There are some *prima facie* grounds for suspecting Locke of Hobbist sympathies in the *Essay,* even though ultimately they are unfounded. There were, furthermore, several reasons why a person with Newton's background might find the *Essay* objectionable. There was, first of all, the rejection of innate ideas. To anybody sympathetic to the Platonic school Locke's wholehearted rejection of this fundamental epistemological tenet could not have been welcome. Both the existence of God and the moral law were supposedly justified by reference to such ideas. But was this, in fact, the principle to which Newton objected? For two reasons it seems unlikely. First, it appears hardly the sort of objection to the *Essay* that one could forget. The whole argument of Locke's book is based on it, and if it was to this that Newton took exception then one would have expected him to say so, and not to use the circumlocution which he did.

But if it was not the rejection of innate ideas, then also surely it was not, and for the same reasons, the general empiricist principle laid down in the second book of the *Essay,* Newton was not, then, rejecting the thesis that all our ideas are the product of experience.

To what, then, did Newton object? It is here that Newton's copy of the *Essay,* which has recently been identified, and is in private possession, may indeed be able to help us.[30] It is very well known that Newton frequently turned back the corners of pages to indicate passages which particularly drew his attention. On page 157 of his copy there is a turn up which points unambiguously to the opening words of *Essay* II, XXVII,

[28] *The Correspondence of Isaac Newton* (Cambridge, 1959—   ), Vol. III, ed. by H. W. Turnbull and J. F. Scott, 280.

[29] As it has been by Frank E. Manuel, who calls Newton's remark one of several "mad accusations," *A Portrait of Isaac Newton,* (Cambridge, Mass., 1968), 219. This slip aside, Manuel's account of the relationship between Locke and Newton is generally convincing.

[30] My information on Newton's copy of Locke's *Essay* I owe entirely to Peter Laslett who has had the opportunity of examining it, and was kind enough to pass on his discoveries.

5[31] which are "Good and Evil. . . ." It appears that this paragraph at some stage drew Newton's attention. It certainly states a principle which could very well be read as committing Locke to a Hobbist position and in a way in which Newton would find unacceptable. The whole paragraph reads:

Good and Evil, as has been shewed in another place, are nothing but Pleasure or Pain, or that which occasions or procures Pleasure or Pain to us. *Morally Good and Evil* then, is only the Conformity or Disagreement of our voluntary Actions to some Law, whereby Good or Evil is drawn on us, from the Will and Power of the Law-maker; which Good and Evil, Pleasure or Pain, attending our observance, or breach of the Law, by the Decree of the Law-maker, is that we call *Reward* and *Punishment*.

It is quite possible to imagine that Newton would have read this to mean that good and evil are identical with pleasure and pain in a way which might lead him to imagine that all pleasure is good without qualification, a view which Newton's puritanism would certainly have found impossible to accept. Or, at a more profound level, he might have found the notion that the position implied that what was good and evil was somehow arbitrary, depending on the arbitrary will of the Lawmaker, whether Divine or otherwise.[32] Whatever Newton's reading of it, the passage certainly fits closely with Newton's remarks. Locke goes on in succeeding paragraphs to produce a detailed argument about the nature of moral law, which needs to be read with the paragraph quoted, and at Section 17 we have the remark "Twould make a Volume to go over all sorts of Relations: 'tis not therefore to be expected, that I should here mention them all. It suffices to our present purpose . . ." which might well be interpreted as implying that Locke hoped or intended to follow up his remarks in more detail at a later stage, which would account for Newton's comment that Locke "designed to pursue in another book."

We cannot be wholly certain that we have correctly identified the passage that troubled Newton, but the evidence is strong that this is indeed the section of the *Essay* which Newton had in mind. One can also see why he might have been reluctant to enter into a dispute with Locke over the matter. The issues raised in II XXVII (II XXVIII in later editions of the *Essay*), are complex and contentious, and indeed

[31] It is *Essay* II XXVII 5 of the first edition. In later editions this become II XXVIII 5, through the addition of the chapter "Of Identity and Diversity" after Chapter XXVI.

[32] Locke's view that the moral law is entirely dependent on the arbitrary authority of the Law Giver was the subject of attack by Thomas Burnet in his *Remarks upon an Essay Concerning Human Understanding, in a letter addressed to the Author* (London, 1697). It is possible that Newton discussed Locke Essay with Burnet. Burnet was one of the few people with whom Newton corresponded on religious matters.

resulted in Locke's being attacked by others beside Newton,[33] and Newton would no doubt have been reluctant to have become embroiled in an
argument with a man whom he no doubt admired, had just insulted, and
whom he may rightly have judged was at least his intellectual equal in
matters of philosophy and ethics.

But if this is a correct identification of Newton's criticism of the
Essay it would suggest that Newton did not have a quarrel with Locke's
major contentions. It would seem to suggest that in 1693 Newton too
accepted Locke's empiricist position. Clearly this view is only conjectural
but it has some circumstantial support. It fits with Newton's approach
to science and it anticipates a position he certainly held at a later stage.
But, it would appear to me that another reconstruction is more plausible.
This is that when Newton read the Essay he found it in general a work
with which he had great sympathy and one which argued in depth issues
into which he had not in fact himself penetrated far. In other words, the
Essay did indeed supply arguments on epistemological issues to support
positions to which he was intellectually attracted. Of Newton's intellectual attraction towards empiricism there can be little doubt, even if his
own practice often fell short of the ideal which he preached. Of his own
lack of consideration of the issues and arguments needed to support that
position his own manuscripts are a record. There are few sources prior to
about 1713 which are relevant, and there are no sustained epistemological discussions comparable to, say, Descartes' Discourse on Method or
Locke's Essay. If Newton had been genuinely struggling with such questions it is virtually inconceivable that we would not have more record of
it.

When, however, we turn to Newton's later manuscripts, particularly
to those relating to his revisions of the Principia for the third edition, and
to drafts related to successive editions of the Opticks, mostly dated from
the post 1713 period,[34] we find much of philosophical interest, and much
which reveals how close Newton's position on central epistemological
issues was to that of Locke.

Quite how close their views were may be illustrated by the following
juxtaposition of Newton's projected Regula V and comparable remarks
by Locke all contained within a short space in Book II of the Essay.[35]

[33] In the second edition of the Essay Locke attempted to meet some of these
objections. Cf. his long footnote added to II XXVIII 11 in later editions of
the Essay.

[34] It is not always easy to be sure of the date of Newton's manuscripts, but
on the basis of subject matter and handwriting fairly accurate assessments are
often possible, even without specific dates on documents. My authority for such
identification has been Dr. D. T. Whiteside.

[35] The version of the Regulae quoted is that of U.L.C. MS Ad. 3965 13 f.
19 r.

Newton. Draft Regula V

Whatever is not derived from things themselves, whether by the external senses or by the sensation of internal thoughts, is to be taken for a hypothesis.

Pro hypothesibus habenda sunt quaecunque ex rebus ipsis vel per sensus externos, vel per sensationem cogitationum internarum non derivantur.

Locke. Essay Book II

"Our observation, employed either about *external sensible objects, or about the internal operations of our minds perceived and reflected on by ourselves, is that which supplies our understandings with all* the materials of thinking. These two are the fountains of knowledge, from whence all ideas we have, or can naturally have, do spring (II.I.2)."

The understanding seems to me not to have the least glimmering of any *ideas* which it doth not receive from one of these two. *External objects furnish the mind with the ideas of sensible qualities,* which are all those different perceptions they produce in us; and the *mind furnishes the understanding with ideas of its own operations* (II.I.5).

Thus I perceive that I am thinking, which could not happen unless at the same time I were to perceive that I exist.

Sentio utique quod Ego cogitem, id quod fieri nequiret nisi simul sentirem quod ego sim.

I would be glad also to learn from these men who so confidently pronounce that the human soul or, which is all one, that a man always thinks, *how they come to know it; nay, how they come to know that they themselves think, when they themselves do not perceive it.* This, I am afraid, is to be sure without proofs, and to know without perceiving; it is, I suspect, a confused notion, taken up to serve a hypothesis, and none of those clear truths that either their own evidence forces us to admit or common experience makes it impudence to deny. For the most that can be said of it is that it is possible the soul may always think, but not always retain it in memory. And I say, it is as possible that the soul may not always think, and much more probable that it should sometimes not think, than that it should often think, and that a long while together and not be conscious to itself, the next moment after, that it had thought (II.I.18).

But I do not perceive that any idea whatever may be innate. And I do not take for a phenomenon only that which is made known to us by the five external senses, but also that which we contemplate in our minds when thinking: such as, I exist, I believe, I understand, I remember, I think, I wish, I am unwilling, I am thirsty, I am hungry, I rejoice, I suffer, etc.

Sed non sentio quod Idea alique sit innata. Et pro Phaenomenis habeo non solum quae per sensus quinque externos nobis innotescunt, sed etiam quae in mentibus nostris intuemur cogitando: Ut quod, Ego sum, ego credo, doleo, etc.

And those things which neither can be demonstrated from the phenomenon nor follow from it by the argument of induction, I hold as hypotheses.

Et quae ex phaenomenis nec demonstrando nec per argumentum inductionis consequuntur, pro Hypothesibus habeo.

If it shall be demanded then *when a man begins to have any ideas,* I think the true answer is, when he first has any *sensation.* For, since there appear not to be any *ideas* in the mind before the senses have conveyed any in, I conceive that ideas in the understanding are coeval with *sensation;* which is such an impression or motion made in some part of the body, as produces some perception in the understanding. It is about these impressions made on our senses by outward objects that the mind seems first to employ itself in such operations as we call *perception, remembering, consideration, reasoning,* etc. (II.I.23).

In Newton's manuscripts there are in fact several different versions of *Regula V.* In the papers relating to the *Opticks* there are also many remarks which are similar in both sentiment and expression. On one sheet we find Newton returning once again to the *Cogito* argument, asserting just as Locke had done, that our knowledge of our own existence is grounded on experience. Locke had written:

Nothing can be more evident to us than our own existence. I think, I reason, feel pleasure and pain: can any of these be more evident to me than my own existence? If I doubt of all other things, that very doubt makes me perceive my own existence, and will not suffer me to doubt of that. For if I know I feel pain, it is evident I have as certain perception of my own existence as of the existence of the pain I feel; or, if I know I doubt, I have as certain perception of the existence of the thing doubting, as of that thought which I call doubt. Experience then convinces us that we have an intuitive knowledge of our own existence and an internal infallible perception that we are. In every act of sensation, reasoning, or thinking, we are conscious to ourselves of our own being and, in this matter, come not short of the highest degree of certainty.[36]

And Newton wrote:

Even that celebrated Proposition *Ego cogito ergo sum* is known to us by experience. We know that we think by an inward sensation of our thoughts. And therefrom from that Proposition we cannot conclude that anything more is true then what we deduce from experience.[37]

Before this Newton had written:

For hypotheses are not to be regarded in Experimental Philosophy. Nor are we to regard Metaphysical Principles unless so far as they are founded upon experience. For all Metaphysicks not founded upon experience is Hypothetical. . . .[38]

It was a sentiment anticipated by Locke's remark that:

In the knowledge of bodies, we must be content to glean what we can from particular experiments, since we cannot from a discovery of their real essences grasp at a time whole sheaves, and in bundles comprehend the nature and properties of whole species together. . . . He that shall consider how little general maxims, precarious principles, and hypotheses laid down at pleasure have promoted true knowledge or helped to satisfy the inquiries of rational men after real improvements, how little, I say, the setting out at that end has for many ages together advanced men's progress towards the knowledge of natural philosophy, will think we have reason to thank those who in this latter age have taken another course and have trod out to us, though not an easier way to learned ignorance, yet a surer way to profitable knowledge.[39]

No doubt Locke saw Newton as one of those men.

The similarities of outlook revealed in these passages cannot be dismissed lightly. Nor can the fact that Locke's versions of them pre-date Newton's by several years. No doubt it would be quite inaccurate to attempt to depict Newton as a disciple of Locke. He was able to reach his own conclusions on intellectual questions. But the evidence that Newton found in Locke's writings powerful intellectual support cannot be dismissed.

Conclusions.—What conclusions may we draw from these comparisons between the two men? In an earlier paper I argued that we must strongly resist all those who have sought to read the *Essay* as if it were an outcome of Newton's science.[40] The evidence I have offered is such that we cannot dismiss the possibility that Locke's *Essay* encouraged Newton both in his claim to adhere to a methodological empiricism in his science and also to espouse an epistemological empiricism entirely in keeping with that argued by Locke in the *Essay*.

[36] *Essay*, IX IX 3.   [37] U.L.C. MS. Add. 3970 f.621v.   [38] *Ibi*
[39] *Essay*, IX XII 12.   [40] *loc.cit.*, note 27 abov

However, another problem is raised by my analysis of the relationship between the two men. I have suggested that Locke may well have encouraged Newton's advocacy of an empirical outlook. But both men were clearly strongly committed to aspects of empiricism before they met. The problem that remains is to account for the independent empirical approach of the two men. It is clearly beyond the scope of this paper to begin that account, but I would suggest that part of the answer, at least, is in the high regard that each man had for Robert Boyle.[41] Both owned many of his books and both were careful readers of his works. Perhaps further investigation of Boyle's influence would go some way to accounting for the common intellectual outlook of the twin founders of the eighteenth-century Enlightenment.

Finally, it must be stressed I have attempted to note some comparisons between only certain aspects of the thought of Locke and Newton. There are undoubtedly other rich fields for further investigation. Particularly is this true of their theological beliefs, where detailed comparisons may well throw future light on both their science and their theory of knowledge.

University of Keele.

[41] Boyle's influence on Locke is now widely recognized. Cf. G. A. J. Rogers, "Boyle, Locke, and Reason," *JHI*, **27** (1966), 205-16. That Boyle is more original than is often supposed I have argued in "Descartes and the Method of English Science," *Annals of Science*, **26** (1972), 237-66.

Support for research in connection with the above article was provided by a grant from the Royal Society. I am very grateful to the following for their comments on earlier versions of the paper: R. I. Aaron, A. Rupert Hall, John Harrison, Peter Laslett, D. T. Whiteside, and J. W. Yolton.

Chapter XXIII

LOCKE'S *ESSAY* AND NEWTON'S *PRINCIPIA*

By G. A. J. Rogers*

I. *Introduction.*

There is a standard picture of the relationship between John Locke and Isaac Newton which might be expressed in the following way: Locke's intellectual and philosophical attitude was molded by what he saw in the Newtonian achievement and was largely responsible for the general tone and nature of Locke's philosophical position. According to this view in the interaction between the two men Locke was the indebted partner, learning much from his younger colleague, whilst Newton learnt little, if anything, from the older man. It is indeed sometimes claimed (see below) that Newton's *Principia* completely changed Locke's intellectual stance, whilst Newton, it is assumed, was not greatly influenced by Locke at all. Such opinions of the relation between Locke and Newton are to be found amongst historians of science especially, though philosophers too, writing on the history of their subject, have sometimes been inclined to see the influence of Newton as very substantial. There are many passages in commentaries on Locke and Newton which reveal this attitude but I shall draw attention to only four, though all are recent and reflect positions held by respected scholars. The first is taken from the notes to Newton's *Correspondence,* Volume III, by H. W. Turnbull. Of Locke, Turnbull wrote: "John Locke (1632-1704), philosopher . . . He became a friend of Newton through reading the *Principia* and he early introduced its philosophical principles into his writings. . . ." The implication is clearly that there were specific Newtonian influences to be found in Locke's work and that these influences were considerable. The second example is taken from a broadcast discussion on Newton' *Principia* between I. Bernard Cohen and Peter Laslett. Locke, Laslett rightly said, read the *Principia* just after he had written the *Essay Concerning Human Understanding.* Laslett went on:

Locke, then, had written a traditional philosopher's review of the world and was preparing it for the press when he was suddenly faced with this astonishing book of the greatest intellect amongst his contemporaries and convince that he didn't understand the natural world at all. The result was, in my view

* Support for research in connection with this paper was provided by a grant from the Royal Society. I am very grateful to the following for their comments on earlier versions of this paper: R. I. Aaron, A Rupert Hall, John Harrison, Peter Laslett, D. T. Whiteside, and J. W. Yolton.

[1] *The Correspondence of Isaac Newton* (Cambridge, 1959-), Vol. III, edited by H. W. Turnbull, and J. F. Scott, 76.

that he wrote the very remarkable epistle to the reader in the *Essay on Human Understanding,* in which he says: "I am only an under-labourer. Newton, Huygens, are those who really understand the world. My function is to clear away the rubbish. This is a complete revisal of the social and the intellectual position of the philosopher. And this could be said to be historically the beginning of the two cultures. . . ."[2]

We shall turn later to a more detailed look at Laslett's statement. For the moment, let us just note that once again we have the view expressed that the *Principia* had a very substantial influence on Locke's philosophy. Once again there is no suggestion that Locke's philosophy had any influence on Newton. This general position is summarized by A. R. and M. B. Hall: Newton, they write, "is commonly regarded as furnishing the scientific substratum of Locke's philosophy."[3] It is a view from which the authors do not dissent. My fourth example is taken from John Herman Randall's *The Career of Philosophy:*

Locke's *Essay* stands with Newton's *Principia* as the fountainhead of British and French thought in the eighteenth century, as a classic illustration of the application of the Newtonian "geometrical" or "analytical" method to human nature.[4] . . . In point of fact, Locke assumed to begin with and without question the whole of Newtonian science, both its verdict on the nature of science and on the nature of the world.[5]

This paper challenges that standard view of the interaction between the two men. I show first that the influence of Newton on Locke was not nearly as straightforward or as great as it is often depicted.[5a] Second, I shall argue that there was some mutual influence, and suggest that Locke's philosophy may have had a positive influence over Newton's own thought.[6] From this there emerges a new perspective on a crucial

---

[2] Published in *The Listener* (9 December, 1971), 792.

[3] A. R. Hall and Marie Boas Hall, *Unpublished Scientific Papers of Isaac Newton* (Cambridge, 1962), 81.

[4] John Herman Randall, Jr., *The Career of Philosophy. Vol. I. From the Middle Ages to the Enlightenment* (New York and London, 1962), 595.   [5] *Ibid.,* 601.

[5a] In a second, and subsequent papers, I shall argue that there was some mutual influence, and suggest that Locke's philosophy may have had a positive influence on Newton's own thought.

[6] Recently James L. Axtell has done much to set the record straight and to add to our knowledge of the interaction between Locke and Newton. His papers on this are: "Locke, Newton, and the Elements of Natural Philosophy," *Paedagogica Europae,* I (1965), 235-45; "Locke's Review of the Principia," *Notes and Records of the Royal Society of London,* 20 (1965), 152-61; "Locke, Newton and the Two Cultures," *John Locke: Problems and Perspectives* (Cambridge, 1969); also the introduction to Axtell's edition of Locke's *Educational Writings* (Cambridge, 1968). I do not always share Axtell's conclusions, however. J. E. McGuire in his writings on Newton has also noticed that Locke may well have been an influence upon Newton's thought. Thus, in his "The Origin of Newton's Doctrine of Essential Qualities," *Centaurus,* 12 (1968), 238-39, McGuire suggests that

period of seventeenth-century thought, namely, that the effect of Locke's philosophy on the acceptability of the new science was probably more profound than is generally recognized.

Locke's most important philosophical work is, of course, his *Essay Concerning Human Understanding* and if we are to find the influence of Newton in his writings it is there that we should look. To appreciate correctly the influence of Newton on Locke's work it is absolutely vital that we are accurate about the dates when Locke wrote the *Essay* and also when he read or otherwise came to know of Newton's work. This is especially important because there has been considerable confusion in some people's mind about the relative dates of the two thinkers. First, one general point, which is obvious, but is still sometimes overlooked, is that Locke saw only the first edition of Newton's *Principia* (1687). Locke died in 1704; the second and third editions were published in 1713 and 1726, and, as is well known, there are considerable important differences between the three. Newton's other classic of science, the *Opticks*, was published in 1704, shortly before Locke's death, and too late to have any direct influence on Locke, though this is not to say that Locke was not aware of Newton's work in optics, much of which had been published in the *Transactions* of the Royal Society. It is perhaps surprising, but such elementary facts have been overlooked by writers on Locke, Newton, and the Enlightenment.[7]

Locke may well have modified Newton's views on the distinction between primary and secondary qualities. See as well McGuire, "Atoms and the 'Analogy of Nature': Newton's Third Rule of Philosophizing," *Studies in History and Philosophy o, Science*, 1 (1970), esp. 32-35.

[7] I give three examples where the lack of proper dating has led to either a fla mistake or a wrong emphasis about the connection between Locke and Newton.

Example 1. In his *Locke's Theory of Knowledge and its Historical Relation* (Cambridge, 1917, reprinted in 1960) J. Gibson, in discussing Locke's views on space, wrote: "Since the distinction between 'space in itself', as something 'uniform and boundless', and the extension of body which is presented to us in sense per ception, can hardly be regarded as the direct product of Locke's own principles it is natural to look for some external influence to account for the doctrine of the *Essay*. Now we know that Locke was a diligent student of the less mathematica portions of Newton's *Principia*, which was published in 1686, four years befor the *Essay*. We can hardly, it would seem, be wrong in connecting Locke's recentl acquired views about 'space in itself' with Newton's exposition of 'absolute spac ...'" (251). But we now know that this distinction was made by Locke as earl as 1676. It is to be found in his journal entry for March 27th. This is now pub lished in *An Early Draft of Locke's Essay, Together With Excerpts from h Journals*, edited by R. I. Aaron and Jocelyn Gibb (Oxford, 1936), 77. Gibso assumed that Locke had read the *Principia* when he wrote *Essay*, II, 15, but had not then even been published.

Example 2. In his *Isaac Newton* (Clarendon Biographies, Oxford, 1967) J. North writes: "The *Opticks*, on the other hand, was tolerably easy reading, an strangely enough, it was through this work that many had their only first-ha

To appreciate the relationship between Locke and Newton, including their mutual influence, we must clearly recognize that each wrote his most important work independently of the other. Of the influence of Locke on the *Principia* in its first edition there can be no question: we know of none, nor is it likely that any will ever be discovered. But it is not fully appreciated that the first edition of the *Essay Concerning Human Understanding* (1690) was almost equally unaffected by the *Principia*.

Leaving the production of the first edition of the *Principia* to one side, therefore, as one where there is no problem, let us turn to the writing of the *Essay*.

II. *The Production of the Essay*.

There are three drafts of Locke's *Essay* extant.[8] Following Aaron I shall refer to them as Drafts A, B, and C. Drafts A and B were written in 1671. Draft C was written in 1685. A version very nearly the same as the published edition was completed by December 1686 when Locke sent the fourth book to Edward Clarke who had already received the three earlier books. Locke was then in Holland, where he had been since 1683. He wrote to Clarke on the 31st December:

You have here at length the fourth and last book of my scattered thoughts concerning the *Understanding*, and I see now more than ever that I have reason to call them scattered, since never having looked them over all together

---

encounter with Newton's thoughts on gravitation. John Locke, the philosopher, was much influenced by it. . . ." (24). As we have noted above, the *Opticks* was not published until just before Locke's death. The ultimate source for North's view is probably the passage from Desaguliers, quoted p. 7. See also note 31 below.

Example 3. Jonathan Bennett, in his *Locke, Berkeley, Hume. Central Themes* Oxford, 1971) writes: "Locke inherited from Descartes, or borrowed from Newton and Boyle, a distinction between 'primary' and 'secondary' qualities" (89). The distinction is made by Locke as early as 1671 (cf. *An Early Draft,* 73-74). There is no reason to believe that Locke was influenced by Newton at all in his formulation of the distinction.

8 The earlier 1671 Draft (Draft A) is in the Houghton Library, Harvard University. The later 1671 Draft (Draft B) is in the Bodleian Library. The draft of 1685 is in the Pierpont Morgan Library in New York. There is a different version of the first draft in the Shaftsbury Papers in the Public Record Office. (Cf. Peter Laslett in *Mind* [Jan. 1952], 89-92.) On all of these drafts see Aaron, *John Locke* (Third edition, Oxford, 1971), 50-73. Draft A has been published in *An Early Draft of Locke's Essay Together with Excerpts from his Journals,* edited by R. I. Aaron and Jocelyn Gibb (Oxford, 1936). Draft B has also been published as *An Essay Concerning the Understanding, Knowledge, Opinion, and Assent,* edited by Benjamin Rand (Cambridge, Mass., 1931). Draft C has not yet been published, but is to be included in the forth-coming volume *Drafts for An Essay Concerning Human Understanding,* edited by Peter H. Nidditch in *The Clarendon Edition of the Works of John Locke* series.

till since this last part was done, I find the ill effects of writing in patches and at distant times as this whole essay has been.[9]

We do not possess the draft which Clarke received from Locke.[10] But Draft C does tell us quite a lot about the composition of the *Essay* in its later stages even though it is a draft of only the first two books. What it indicates in a very clear way is that on substantial points the published work argued the same position as that put forward by Locke in 1685. There are differences, some of them of considerable interest. But the differences which do exist show no sign at all of the impact on Locke of reading Newton's *Principia*. The only recognition accorded Newton in the first edition of the *Essay* is in the famous "Epistle to the Reader" where Locke clearly places Newton as the greatest among contemporary scientists.

That Locke does not accord Newton any other recognition shows that whilst he was revising the *Essay* for publication Locke was not at all inclined to alter it to take account of the *Principia*.[11] In no way did Locke feel that Newton's work called into question any parts of his major arguments. Nor can Locke's attitude be explained by either his unfamiliarity with, or lack of understanding of, the *Principia*. (Both of these points are taken up below.) If there are any conflicts between what is said in the *Essay* and what is said in the *Principia* then it is fairly safe to assume that either Locke did not notice them or he did not believe that they were worth following up. There is in fact only one major point of potential conflict in the two books and that is in the respective treatment each gives to the notions of space and time. Locke never accepted Newton's absolutist position on space.[12] It is a sign of some of the very

[9] *The Correspondence of John Locke and Edward Clarke*, ed. Benjamin Rand (London, 1927), 177.

[10] Here I follow Aaron in believing that Draft C as we have it was not the draft which Clarke received from Locke. It is likely that Draft C never reached England. Cf. Aaron, *John Locke*, 57.

[11] We know that Locke was indeed revising the *Essay* as late as 1689 for that is the date which appears in *Essay*, II, XIV, 30. The passage reads: "Hence we see that some men imagine the duration of the world from its first existence to this present year 1689 to have been 5639 years. . . ." (Quotations from the *Essay* will either be from the first edition of 1690, as this one is, or from the Everyman edition edited by John W. Yolton [London, 1961], 2 vols.) Since commencing work on this paper the Clarendon Edition of Locke's *Essay*, edited by P. H. Nidditch has been published and it has proved an invaluable guide to the *Essay* and its history. In Draft C Locke had written: "Hence we see that some men imagin ye duration of ye world from its first existence to this present year 1671 to have been 561 years. . . ." Cf. also Draft B § 120. It is odd that Locke does not make the right correction to the figure for the duration of the world.

[12] Aaron (*op. cit.*, 156f.) has already drawn attention to the fact that it wrong to view Locke's account of space as Newtonian, and he rightly place important weight on the discussions of space in the drafts of the *Essay* and

different intellectual influences on each of them in their formative years. Put simply, Newton was much more strongly influenced by the Cambridge Platonists, and Platonic views generally, than Locke was. Indeed Locke was consistently strongly and overtly hostile to a very great deal of the Platonism that he currently found.[13] This difference between the two men and its importance for an understanding of their relationship will be explored below in section VII. One further comment only is in order here. It is that once again it is vital that it is remembered that Locke saw only the first edition of the *Principia,* for in it the only discussion of absolute space and time is in the Scholium added to Definition VIII. That discussion is comparatively austere. The full metaphysical and theological implications of Newton's views on space and time were only clearly brought out in the General Scholium of the second edition of 1713. It was Newton's remarks in this section of the *Principia* which were to be the main source for the exchanges on absolute space and time in the Leibniz-Clarke correspondence of 1715-16. From this we can see that from Locke's reading of the *Principia,* prior to his completion of his preparation of the *Essay* for the press, he did not have much evidence from which he might draw the conclusion that a great deal might turn on the differences between his own and Newton's views on space and time.[14] What Locke would have undoubtedly gathered from his reading of the *Principia* was that Newton did not at all subscribe to the view of

Locke's journals. Another potential point of conflict was not apparent from the first edition of the *Principia.* That was their differing views on the primary-secondary quality distinction. This topic would require a separate paper, but see McGuire's paper cited in Note 6. In the first edition of the *Principia* Newton does not include what in the second edition was to become Rule III.

[13] On this see G. A. J. Rogers, "Locke, Newton, and the Cambridge Platonists on Innate Ideas," *JHI* (April 1979).

[14] In the Scholium to Definition VIII Newton begins: "Hitherto I have laid down the definitions of such words as are less known, and explained the sense in which I would have them to be understood in the following discourse. I do not define time, space, place, and motion, as being well known to all. Only I must observe, that the common people conceive those quantities under no other notions but from the relation they bear to sensible objects. And thence arise certain prejudices, for the removing of which it will be convenient to distinguish them into absolute and relative, true and apparent, mathematical and common." *Mathematical Principles of Natural Philosophy,* Andrew Motte's translation revised by Florian Cajori (Berkeley and Los Angeles, 1934), 6. It might be said that, roughly, Locke's view of space and time was, and remained, the view of the "common people." Whether the common people were wrong was to be much debated in the ensuing centuries. It is of some significance that Locke's notes, which he made in September 1687 and March 1688, and which are preserved in the Bodleian Library Mss. Locke c.33, fols. 19-20 and c.31 fols. 99-100) make no reference to Newton's commitment to absolute space and time. An account of the differing views of Locke and Newton on space and time, and their import, is something that I plan to give elsewhere. Dr. D. T. Whiteside has pointed out to me that the commitment to

Descartes that matter and space were the same thing. It was just one among very many positions which they held in common.[15]

III. *Locke's Scientific Background.*[16]

We can say with confidence that the first edition of Locke's great work was not in any sense influenced by Newton. But what then of Laslett's statement that reading the *Principia* convinced Locke that he did not understand the natural world at all? (Quoted above, Section I). The fact is that Laslett offered us no evidence for this view. It is my belief that the evidence points in another direction. The fact is that Locke was acknowledged by his contemporaries to be an excellent and learned *virtuoso*. By the 1680's he had behind him a substantial record in scientific activity. It is not my intention to give a detailed account of Locke's many scientific qualifications, but some key points are these. Locke had been educated at Oxford just at the time when that university was very much concerned with the new science centered on the group around John Wilkins at Wadham College. Locke went up to Christ Church in 1652. In the years that he was there he was to become well acquainted with many of the very great scientists of the seventeenth century including Robert Boyle, John Wilkins, Thomas Willis, John Wallis, Robert Hooke, David Thomas, and Richard Lower. More important still, he was to become a collaborator with some of the most distinguished. From Locke's notebooks of the period we learn that even as an undergraduate he was beginning to take a keen interest in experimental physiology, probably through the influence of the physician Richard Lower.[17] His interest in medicine developed rapidly; he attended the lectures of Thomas Willis and seriously considered taking up medicine professionally. Later

---

absolute space pervades the whole mathematical substratum of Book I of the *Principia*. It is true that Locke's apparent failure to grasp this may well point to a failure on his part really to understand the *Principia*, at least at his first reading.

[15] Locke's views on this see especially Essay II, XIII 12-16. Newton's views on matter were not clearly formulated in the first edition of the *Principia*. Rule III of the *Regulae* of the second edition has no corresponding hypothesis in the first edition, but Newton's rejection of the Cartesian position is manifest, and was of long standing. It is, for example, powerfully present in his paper *De Gravitatione et Aequipondio Fluidorum*, probably written between 1664 and 1668. Cf. A. R. Hall and Marie Boas Hall, *Unpublished Scientific Papers of Isaac Newton* (Cambridge 1962), 89-121.

[16] There has in recent years been much important work done on the scientific background to Locke's thought. Particularly relevant are: Maurice Cranston, *John Locke. A Biography* (London, 1957), Kenneth Dewhurst, *John Locke* (1632-1704): *Physician and Philosopher. A Medical Biography* (London, 1963); the many articles by Dewhurst on Locke's medical researches too numerous to list here; the three articles by Axtell already cited.

[17] Bodleian Library, MS Locke e4.

he was to collaborate with Lower when the latter was making some of his most important experiments,[18] and later still Locke was to collaborate with Thomas Sydenham.[19] Locke, indeed, was a distinguished physician, but his interest in science was by no means confined to medicine. Medicine required chemistry and this Locke set out to master. Through his interest he soon became acquainted with Robert Boyle and by 1663 they were actively working together on scientific projects. Boyle's *Memoirs for the Natural History of the Humane Blood* (1683-4) is addressed to "the very Ingenious and Learned Doctor J. L."[20] Later Newton and Locke were to be of mutual assistance in chemistry. When Newton showed interest in an experiment of Boyle's involved some "red earth" Locke sent him some, more, in fact, than Newton required. Newton wrote to Locke:

You have sent much more earth than I expected. For I desired only a specimen, having no inclination to prosecute the process. For in good earnest I have no opinion of it. But since you have a mind to prosecute it I shall be glad to assist you all I can. . . .[21]

There is undoubtedly a question-mark over Locke's early mastery of mathematics, physics, and astronomy. Although Fox Bourne reports Locke as having attended lecture courses by both John Wallis and Seth Ward,[22] we have no clear evidence of how much Locke really knew in these areas. Axtell, however, has gone a long way to establishing that Locke was capable of following much of the *Principia* when it was first published[23] and has certainly supplied sufficient evidence for rejecting the traditional picture of Locke as a man totally ignorant of the mathematical sciences. It is often taken as conclusive evidence of Locke's lack of mathematical knowledge that he is said to have consulted Huygens as to whether the proofs in the *Principia* were mathematically sound.[24] But in the light of Axtell's work this allegation must surely be treated with caution. It is well worth remembering that several other contemporaries of Newton admitted they could not follow all his mathematics, and some of those were mathematicians. David Gregory, later to be Professor of Mathematics in Edinburgh, wrote to Newton in September 1687 congratulating him on the *Principia,* but noting that "few would understand

---

[18] Cf. Dewhurst, *op. cit.,* 13-14.   [19] *Ibid.,* 34 ff.
[20] On this see Dewhurst, "Locke's Contributions to Boyle's Researches on the Air and on Human Blood," *Notes and Records of the Royal Society,* 17 (1962), 98-206.
[21] Newton *Correspondence.* III, 215. The letter was written on 7 July, 1692.
[22] Cf. H. R. Fox Bourne, *The Life of John Locke,* 2 vols. (London, 1876), I, 44ff., 55.
[23] See esp. Axtell's "Locke, Newton, and the Two Cultures," 175ff.
[24] The most usually cited source for this, almost certainly true, story is J. T. Desaguliers, *Experimental Philosophy* (1763), I, viii.

it."[25] Gilbert Clarke, another mathematician, wrote in the same month to Newton "I confess I do not as yet well understand so much as your first three sections."[26] In December of the same year John Craig (d. 1731), yet another mathematician, wrote to a friend that he found understanding the *Principia,* "no small trouble."[27] In the light of all this, Axtell is surely correct to emphasize the positive side of Locke's achievement in coming to grips with the *Principia,* probably writing a clear and accurate, if necessarily superficial, review of it within a few months, and returning to it later to tackle more obstruse sections.

If the first edition of the *Essay* gives us no real sign of the positive impact of the *Principia* on Locke then in truth it cannot be maintained that subsequent editions are over-burdened with references to Newton's work or to positions which presuppose his discoveries. In the second edition of 1694, in the chapter *Of Maxims* of the fourth Book, Locke added a substantial section on the use of maxims which includes the following:

They [i.e., maxims] are not of use to help men forwards in the advancement of sciences, or new discoveries of yet unknown truths. Mr. *Newton,* in his never enough to be admired book, has demonstrated several propositions, which are so many new truths, before unknown to the world, and are further advances in mathematical knowledge; but, for the discovery of these, it was not the general *maxims, What is, is;* or, *The whole is bigger than a part,* or the like that helped him. These were not the clues that led him into the discovery of the truth and certainty of those propositions. Nor was it by them that he got the knowledge of those demonstrations, but by finding out intermediate *ideas* that showed the agreement or disagreement of the *ideas,* as expressed in the proposition he demonstrated. . . .[28]

Here Locke uses the mathematics of the *Principia* to support a general point he wishes to make, and indeed which he had made in the first edition, against all those who wish to claim that knowledge is dependent on having knowledge of general maxims—a thesis that Locke was bound to reject as he grounded all knowledge in experience of the particular.

We have to wait until the fourth edition of the *Essay,* in 1700, before we find another clear example of the impact of the *Principia* on Locke's *Essay.* In Book II, Chapter VIII, Section 11, Locke in the earlier editions had written:

The next thing to be considered, is, how *Bodies operate* one upon another

---

[25] Newton, *Correspondence,* II, 484.　　　　　　　　　　[26] *Ibid.,* 485

[27] *Ibid.,* 501. I. Bernard Cohen in his *Introduction to Newton's 'Principia'* (Cambridge, 1971) suggests that Newton may have had Locke specifically in mind when he wrote an emendation which he contemplated making to the introductory paragraph of Book III of the *Principia.* It is possible that Cohen is right but there were so many eminent men who could not follow all of Newton's proofs that the suggestion seems unlikely. Cf. *op. cit.,* 147-48.

[28] *Essay,* IV, VIII, 11. Yolton edition, II, 199-200.

and that is manifestly *by impulse,* and nothing else. It being impossible to conceive, that Body should operate on what it does not touch, (which is all one as to imagine it can operate where it is not) or when it does touch, operate any other way than by Motion.

In the fourth edition this was changed to:

The next thing to be considered is, how bodies produce ideas in us; and that is manifestly *by impulse,* the only way which we can conceive bodies operate in.

The generalization about the ability of bodies to operate without contact has disappeared.

The explanation for this change is to be found in Locke's third letter to Bishop Stillingfleet. It reveals a way in which Newton's book played a part in modifying Locke's ideas. But it does not reveal a fundamental reappraisal. Rather it shows that Newton's book added further confirmation of a general position to which Locke already subscribed. The general position was that one cannot determine *a priori* what the powers of objects are except where there is a contradiction implied. Locke wrote:

. . . You ask, how can my idea of liberty agree with "the idea that bodies can operate only by motion and impulses?" Answ. By the omnipotency of God, who can make all things agree, that involve not a contradiction. It is true I say, "that bodies operate by impulse and nothing else." And so I thought when I writ it, and can yet conceive no other way of their operation. But I am since convinced by the judicious Mr. Newton's incomparable book, that it is too bold a presumption to limit God's power, in this point by my narrow conceptions. The gravitation of matter towards matter, by ways inconceivable to me, is not only a demonstration that God can, if he pleases, put into bodies, powers and ways of operation above what can be derived from our idea of body, or can be explained by what we know of matter, but also an unquestionable and everywhere visible instance, that he has done so. And therefore in the next edition of my book, I shall take care to have that passage rectified.[29]

The third letter was published in 1699, the year before Locke's alterations appeared in the *Essay.*

The examples show that the *Essay* was not seriously altered by Locke as a result of his reading and comprehension of the *Principia.* It is a point of some weight for a full appreciation of the *Essay's* significance. In so far as the approaches to science and knowledge revealed in the *Essay* and the *Principia* are the same, certainly with respect to all the editions of the *Essay* and the first edition of the *Principia,* then this is because their authors shared a common outlook rather than because one was greatly influential on the other. To suggest, as some have done, that

---

[29] *The Works of John Locke,* 7th ed. (London, 1768), I, 754.

the *Principia* was immediately influential because we can recognize its impact on the *Essay* is totally to misunderstand the background of both works and it leads to a wrong appraisal of the place which the *Essay* occupies in seventeenth-century thought.[30]

Let us now return to Laslett's suggestion that Locke was convinced by his reading of the *Principia* that he really did not understand the natural world at all. We may surely grant that an inability to follow all of the mathematics of the *Principia* is not in itself reason to suppose that Locke would feel that he did not understand the natural world. We must of course recognize that there are degrees of comprehension, and that there are two different things to be understood, the world itself, and Newton's account of it. It is, I believe, certain that Locke felt he understood the natural world a good deal better after reading the *Principia*, even though, as no doubt he would have gladly conceded, he had neither tried nor been able to follow all of Newton's mathematics. Here the wording of Desaguliers' account of Locke's consultations with Huygens is relevant. The passage reads:

The celebrated Locke, who was incapable of understanding the 'Principia' from his want of geometrical knowledge, inquired of Huygens if all the mathematical propositions in that work were true. When he was assured that he might depend upon their certainty, he took them for granted, and carefully examined the reasonings and corollaries deduced from them. In this manner he acquired a knowledge of the physical truths in the 'Principia', and became a firm believer in the discoveries which it contained. In the same manner he studied the treatise on 'Optics', and made himself master of every part of it which was not mathematical.[31]

It is almost certain that this is the source for the view that Locke was a keen student of the *Opticks*, even though, as we have already seen, it did not appear until shortly before his death. But that apart, one very inter-

---

[30] Despite my admiration for his important contributions to a correct understanding of the relation between Locke and Newton I cannot therefore agree with Axtell's judgement that in the *Essay* "there is considerable evidence—both internal and external—that Locke was deeply influenced by Newton's achievements, but especially by the whole methodology that lay behind the Newtonian synthesis." ("Locke's Review of the *Principia*," 159-60.) It is sometimes suggested that the really important effect of the *Principia* on Locke was that it made him aware of the power of mathematical deduction, and therefore of deduction generally. I can find no support for this in the *Essay*, and evidence to the contrary. Those passage in the *Essay* where Locke speaks of the power of deductive knowledge are often clearly anticipated in drafts of the *Essay* written in 1671. Thus in *Essay* IV, II, 9-14, Locke says that "demonstration" (i.e., deductive reasoning as exhibited in geometry) can be carried into other areas. This argument is anticipated in Draft B, § 45 and 46.

[31] As well as in the Desaguliers reference, already cited in Note 24, the story is reported in Sir David Brewster's *Memoirs of the Life, Writings, and Discoverie of Sir Isaac Newton*, 2 vols. (Edinburgh and London, 1815), I, 339.

esting facet of the story is that Locke is reported as consulting Huygens about only the *mathematics* of the *Principia* and not about any other aspect of the work. As is well known, Huygens was not wholeheartedly a supporter of Newton.[32] His attitude, along with other Cartesians, anticipated that of Leibniz in several particulars. But Locke was clearly not prepared to accept Huygen's verdict on the work. Rather, he sat down to study it, and, the mathematics granted, to assess it for himself.[33]

What exactly was Locke's reaction to the *Principia* when he first read it? We have several clues, but none of them suggest any kind of major reappraisal on Locke's part. We have already seen that the draft of the *Essay* received no important changes. But we also have what is almost certainly Locke's review, written in 1688. The review begins by indicating that Newton's book is part of a recent, but already established, approach, namely the geometricizing of mechanics. The *Principia*, Locke was saying, was not new in terms of its method, but it was new in terms of the depth to which that method had been taken, and although there are some innovations of method in the *Principia*, Locke's general point is surely sound. But it is worth emphasizing that the development of such a geometrical method was, as we have already seen, an aspiration which Locke held prior to his reading the *Principia*. (See Note 30 above.) In his review by quoting the Scholium to *Principia* Book I, Proposition LXIX, Locke also makes a point of the fact that Newton did not mean by attraction anything other than:

l'effort que font les corps, pour s'approcher l'un de l'autre, soit que cet procède, ou de l'action des corps qui tendent l'un vers l'autre, ou qui se choquent réciproquement par les corpuscules qu'ils exhalent; soit qu'il se fasse par l'action de l'Ether, par celle de l'air, ou de quelque autre milieu sensible, ou insensible, dans lequel ces corps nagent, & qui les pousse l'un contre l'autre. Je me sers, dans le même sens général, du terme d'impulsion.[34]

---

[32] Huygens' attitude towards the *Principia* was judicial in his *Discours sur la cause de la Pesanteur* (1690) but he was less polite in a letter to Leibniz. Cf. *Oeuvres complètes de Christiaan Huygens publiées par le Société hollandaise des Sciences* (The Hague, 1888-1950, 22 vols.), IX, 538.

[33] When Locke first read the *Principia* in 1687, he was in Rotterdam. Huygens was also then in Holland, and it is probable that they met there. It is possible that they first met much earlier, in 1677, when they were both in Paris. It may be objected that what is not possible is to understand the *Principia* without understanding the mathematics, for the simple and sufficient reason that it is a work of mathematics and nothing else. It must, however, be remembered that Desaguliers was himself attempting to show that it *was* possible to understand Newton's philosophy without understanding mathematics, and he tells the story about Locke precisely to illustrate that possibility.

[34] *Bibliothèque Universelle & Historique de l'Année 1688*, 439. The review which covers pages 436-450 is over 2000 words in length. For contrasting assessments of it see Axtell, "Locke's Review of the 'Principia'," cited in Note 6, and Cohen, *An Introduction to Newton's 'Principia'*, cited in Note 27, 145-47. Although

This underlines the fact that Locke was well aware that Newton was basing his argument on what he took to be well established empirical concepts, once again entirely in keeping with the empiricist approach of Locke himself.

The suggestion is, therefore, that what Locke found in the *Principia* was the exemplification of a method to which he himself already subscribed. He already believed that a combination of observation, generalization or induction, and deduction was the only route to knowledge of nature and that the *Principia* exhibited just that method in its most fruitful manner.[35] It was thus perfectly natural for him to turn to it as an example when he wished to stress that, contrary to the Ramist tradition, but entirely in keeping with that of Bacon, there was a great difference between "the method of acquiring knowledge and of communicating, between the method of raising any science and that of teaching it to others as far as it is advanced."[36] It was not on maxims that Newton's science rested, said Locke, but on showing by a chain of related ideas how one idea was necessarily connected to another.

Mr. Newton, in his never enough to be admired book, has demonstrated several propositions, which are so many new truths before unknown to the world, and are further advances in mathematical knowledge; but, for the discovery of these, it was not the general *maxims, What is, is* or *The whole is bigger than a part,* or the like that helped him. . . . but by finding out intermediate *ideas* that showed the agreement or disagreement of the *ideas* as expressed in the propositions he demonstrated.[37]

---

these assessments have rather different objectives I would tend to support Axtell's rather than Cohen's. Cohen rather underplays the function of the review in the *Bibliothèque Universelle*. It must be remembered that Locke was in a sense trying to sell the *Principia* to a Cartesian-orientated public, who were, nevertheless, unlikely in general to be mathematically sophisticated. It is worth emphasizing that the non-mathematician, Locke, grasps immediately a crucial aspect of Newton's presentation which, notoriously, the mathematician Roger Cotes, in his Preface to the second edition of the *Principia*, completely missed, much to the annoyance of Newton. It is possible to doubt that Locke was the author of the review for there is no conclusive final evidence that he did write it. However, as Axtell argues, the comparison between Locke's manuscript notes and the published review, the presence of Locke in Holland, the known fact that he did write reviews for the journal, and the lack of any other candidate makes quite a strong case.

[35] It is worth underlining the fact that mathematics was for Locke not a discipline which had a unique method. It was exactly on a par with any other deductive argument which moved from idea to idea via necessary connection. It was precisely because of this that Locke believed that it was in theory possible to have deductive systems of physics in areas which were not mathematical. Once this is taken, then the otherwise puzzling remarks in *Essay,* IV, II, 9 ff. become clear

[36] *Essay,* IV, VII, 11. On the Ramist tradition and on Bacon see, for example Lisa Jardine, *Francis Bacon: Discovery and the Art of Discourse* (Cambridge 1974) esp. chapters 1, 2, and 3.

[37] *Essay,* IV, VII, 11.

It would thus appear that to read the *Principia* was not for Locke any sort of traumatic experience. Quite the contrary. It confirmed for him all his own methodological conclusions. The only way in which natural philosophy could be advanced was by the methods of observation and deduction, and, although there were definite limits to what could be learnt by the application of such techniques, Newton had shown that they were, nevertheless, capable of producing the most wonderful results. The *Principia* was for Locke the vindication of a general methodological approach to which he had subscribed for perhaps twenty years.

IV. *Locke and Newton: their personal acquaintance.*

There is no evidence to suggest that Locke met Newton prior to the former's return from Holland in 1689 after his absence since 1683. It is, however, just possible that they did meet before Locke's departure. Locke was elected Fellow of the Royal Society in 1668 and remained in London until November 1675, except for a month which he spent in France. Newton was elected a Fellow in January 1671/2, but he had been in London in 1669 and in February 1675. Whether on either of these occasions they did actually meet can only be a matter of conjecture. I have been able to uncover only one piece of documentary evidence which connects them prior to Locke's stay in Holland. In one of Locke's commonplace books for the years 1676-94 there occurs the following entry: "Aqua the weight of water to air is as 950 to one. Mr. Newton."[38] The entry is dated 1680. But it is unlikely that this information was conveyed personally to Locke from Newton. As it appears to have no published source, it is probable, that it was conveyed to Locke via a third party, and the most likely third party is Robert Boyle with whom Newton was then in correspondence, and with whom Locke was then collaborating.[39] By this stage Locke would already be familiar with Newton's work in optics which had been published in the Royal Society *Transactions* in 1672.

Whatever the truth about their earlier contact, Locke and Newton did not become friends until much later, for it was not until after Locke's return from Holland at the beginning of 1689 that they became well

[38] Bodleian Library, MS Locke C.42A f.244.
[39] Although Boyle is the most probable source he is not the only possible one. Isaac Barrow was another. Locke met Barrow in 1672 and Barrow gave Locke a copy of his *Lectiones Geometricae* (1670). The book is inscribed *"Ex Dono Authoris Viri cujus eruditiones pars minima est mathesis laudis doctrina."* On this see John Harrison and Peter Laslett, *The Library of John Locke*, 2nd ed. (Oxford, 1971), 44-73. It is totally unlikely that Barrow would have conveyed this information from Newton to Locke, but Barrow's acquaintance with Locke at this stage establishes a contact between Locke and Trinity College. For Barrow's influence on Newton's views on space and matter see E. W. Strong, "Barrow and Newton," *Journal of the History of Philosophy*, 8(1970), 155-72.

acquainted. It is traditionally assumed that Locke and Newton met in late 1689 or early 1690 at the salon of the Earl of Pembroke. Although there is no positive evidence for this it seems entirely plausible. Wherever it was, Locke and Newton had soon established a personal contact which was to become a friendship lasting until Locke's death. They must soon have recognized that they had much in common. Both were keenly interested in the natural sciences, though Locke's interests were wider and shallower than Newton's, both were deeply religious and believed that religion was capable of rational comprehension. Their family backgrounds were far from dissimilar. Both came from remote rural areas and both were from modest middle-class homes. Both remained life-long bachelors, both were disinclined to rush into print. More specifically, their intellectual outlooks were remarkably alike: both were Whig in politics; both were opposed to enthusiasm in the matter of religion; both, whilst strongly attracted to the philosophy of Descartes, were in fact set against what they took to be the fundamental flaws both in Cartesian theory and in Cartesian methodology; both were committed to the method in science which found expression in the work of the Royal Society.[40]

[40] Fully to document the claims made here in respect of the shared hostility to Cartesian methodology and the shared support of the method in science which found expression in the Royal Society would itself require a long paper. There are, however, some brief pertinent remarks which may be made. Both Locke and Newton rejected the Cartesian view that a theory in science can be accepted as established if it can be shown that the theory is compatible with all known empirical data. Descartes claimed in the *Principles of Philosophy* (Part IV Principle CCIV) that "I believe that I have done all that is required of me if the causes I have assigned are such that they correspond to all the phenomena manifested by nature." It was precisely this type of hypothetical explanation, which found expression in the work of many Cartesians, such as Rohault and Huygens, to which Newton was so strongly opposed. Newton's rejection of this "hypothetical" method not only found expression in the *Regulae,* the General Scholium of the *Principia,* and the 31st Query of the *Opticks,* but also in his manuscripts. The following two passages are, I believe, representative examples, both taken from drafts for the later *Queries:* 1. "Could all the phenomena of nature be (evidently) deduced from only three or four general suppositions there might be great reason to allow those suppositions to be true: but if for explaining every new Phenomenon you make a new Hypothesis if you suppose yᵗ yᵉ particles of Air are of such a figure size and frame, those of water of such another, those of vitriol of such another, those of Quicksilver of such another, those of flame of such another, those of Magnetick effluvia of such another. If you suppose that light consists in such a motion pression or force and that its various colours, are made by such & such variations of the motion & so of other things: your Philosophy will be nothing else than a systeme of Hypotheses. And what certainty can there be in a Philosophy wᶜ consists in as many Hypotheses as there are Phaenomena to be explained. To explain all nature is too difficult a task for any one man or even for any one age Tis much better to do a little with certainty & leave the rest for others that come after, than to explain all things by conjecture without making sure of anything And there is no other way of doing any thing with certainty than by drawing con

It is not too much of an exaggeration to say that a detailed account of the shared intellectual attitudes of Locke and Newton would go a long way to describing most of the major intellectual forces which shaped the eighteenth century.

University of Keele.

---

clusions from experiments & phaenomena untill you come at general Principles & then from those Principles giving an account of Nature. Whatever is certain in Philosophy is owing to this method & nothing can be done without it." (U.L.C. Add MS. 3970 f.479.)

2. ". . . if without deriving the properties of things from Phaenomena you feign Hypotheses & think by them to explain all nature you may make a plausible systeme of Philosophy for getting your self a name, but your systeme will be little better than a Romance." (U.L.C. Add MS. 3970 f.480.)

These quotations do not, of course, establish that Newton did in fact practice the method he preached. There is mounting evidence that often he did not. See, for example, R. S. Westfall, "Newton and the Fudge Factor," *Science*, 179 (1973); D. T. Whiteside, "Newton's Lunar Theory: From High Hope to Disenchantment," *Vistas in Astronomy*, 19 317-28. But I believe that at least we can say that Newton's "logic of justification," in contrast with his "logic of discovery," was entirely at one with principles argued by Locke and widely accepted amongst the early members of the Royal Society.

PART FOUR

THE SCIENCE OF MAN: BIOLOGY AND PHYSIOLOGY

Chapter XXIV

THE HISTORICAL ANTHROPOLOGY OF JOHN LOCKE

By William G. Batz

Political theory is not a discipline which treats of matters isolated from the many diverse realms of human experience, and political thought and action do not arise in a vacuum, but in a wide cultural context. A prudent political theorist, therefore, must take into account all the various historical, social, economic, and religious factors comprising the human situation, since Social Man, Economic Man, and Political Man are, ultimately and after all, one and the same fellow. Because political theory, moreover, is specifically concerned with decision-making in human collectivities, the theorist must be especially sensitive to the problematic issue of the nature, origins, and growth of human societies. Well-conceived historical and anthropological foundations are often one mark of a sophisticated political theory, and the great political philosophers have not failed to include general remarks on human society as elements in their treatments of human government in particular. A prime example of this principle is John Locke, whose *Two Treatises of Government* are also in large measure treatises of the nature and development of society in general. The sources of the historical and anthropological underpinnings in Lockean theory, furthermore, are not hidden or obscure, for it is known that the seventeenth-century theorist was well-read in histories of the early Americas and in descriptive accounts of primitive New World natives.[1] Locke undoubtedly wove into the fabric of his political theory a number of notions gleaned from this body of background reading.

In Lockean theory the "State of Nature" is described as the essential starting point of a developmental theory of "the True Original, Extent and End of Civil Government." No doubt Locke's pristine and aboriginal state is in part a logical construct, just as Hobbes's is. Whereas Hobbes, however, did not wish to defend the State of Nature as an historical fact, it does seem that Locke considered it not merely a logical fiction, but an historical reality as well. Addressing himself to this very question, "where are, or ever were, there any Men in such a State of Nature?"[2] his reply is twofold. First, heads of state vis-à-vis one another in international affairs are lacking in any contractual bonds, and so exist by definition in the natural state. Secondly, it seems possible that men may be "perfectly in a State of Nature" living and socializing "in the woods of America." Repeatedly in the *Two Treatises* Locke refers to the American wilderness as an unquestionable example of primitive social conditions. In one famous sentence he declares quite unequivocally: "thus in the beginning all the World was America."[3] In discussing "the Beginning of Political Societies," Locke specifically cites José d'Acosta, an early Spanish explorer in the

---

[1] A list of books acquired by Locke and included in his personal library may be found in John Locke, *Two Treatises of Government*, ed. Peter Laslett (Cambridge, 1960), Appendix B, 146–61.

[2] *Second Treatise*, par. 14.

[3] *Ibid.*, par. 49. America is also mentioned in the *First Treatise*, pars. 45, 144, 153; in *Second Treatise*, pars. 14, 36, 37, 41, 43, 45, 48, 65, 92, 102, 105, 108, 184.

Americas, to demonstrate with a Peruvian example his remarks about early human society.[4]

The reference to Acosta was not accidental. Locke was well-acquainted with the travelogue descriptions of the New World which were popular among the literate public of the mid-seventeenth century. Usually picaresque accounts of some individual's observations of the lands and natives of the New World, a number of these books were included in Locke's library and purchased and read prior to the writing of the *Two Treatises*. Acosta's book, *The Naturall and Morall Historie of the East and West Indies,* was published in an English translation in London in 1604. A large portion of the narrative concerns the social and political history of Mexico, or rather, the peoples living in Central America prior to and including the reign of Montezuma. Whether Acosta's account is completely accurate in an objective sense is probably irrelevant, since the Spaniard pretends to report only what the local inhabitants themselves have told him. Locke, furthermore, seems to accept Acosta's account as reasonably trustworthy.

Locke's library also included a French translation of the Spanish account of Rev. Cristobal d'Acuña, S.J., *Relation de la Rivière Des Amazons* (1682). Acuna's report is closely akin to Acosta's, except that the location is further south in the Brazilian jungles. Acuña records in similar fashion his impressions of the lands and peoples of the river basin. A parallel, though much earlier work, was also in Locke's possession, *Histoire d'un Voyage Fait en la Terre du Brésil* (1578) by Jean de Léry. Published over a hundred years before Acuña, this Frenchman's story focuses on his experiences among the tribal peoples of Portugese Brazil. Finally, among the South American travelogues, Locke also held a copy of one Englishman's work, *A New Survey of the West Indies* (1677) by Thomas Gage. The Gage book, however, only mentions earlier American tribes in passing, and concentrates on the Aztec civilization. In addition, Locke owned two travelogue accounts by a French Franciscan, Gabriel Sagard-Théodat, a missionary sent to New France to convert the North American Indians. *Le Grand Voyage du Pays des Hurons* (1632) and *Histoire du Canada et Voyages* (1636) relate the attributes of the country and the native tribes of the north, just as Acosta, Acuña, and Léry had done for the south.

To date, it seems, there has been no close examination of these Lockean source materials, no doubt because of the rarity, particularly in this country, of the original editions of these books.[5] Yet a perusal of these seventeenth-century publications and a comparison with the *Two Treatises* produces a series of interesting insights into Locke's mind and theory. It becomes readily apparent that the developmental aspect of Lockean political theory, as well as the attributes of his State of Nature, were the probable result not merely of logic and philosophical method (as with Hobbes), but may also have been suggested as historical realities by Locke's knowledge of pristine America. His reading in the history of American tribal peoples and the crude anthropological descriptions of French, English, and Spanish travellers in the New World, may have sup-

[4]*Second Treatise*, par. 102.
[5]The original editions of these works were available to me at the James Ford Bell Library of seventeenth- and eighteenth-century exploration literature, University of Minnesota, Minneapolis, Minn.

plied him with some motive and justification for postulating a primitive, natural state antecedent to property and civil government.

From his own words it is apparent that for Locke "all the World" was originally akin to America around 1600, which is to say, that the American wilderness was representative of the universal primal state. From his readings Locke could easily have made this general assumption. In traditional Judaeo-Christian thought, of course, the original state was the Garden of Eden—the universal human cradle. Every author whom Locke read repeatedly described the New World in Edenic terms. America emerges as an extant Paradise.[6] Acuña claims that the Amazon River is greater than the Euphrates, the sacred Mesopotamian river which purportedly formed one boundary of the original Garden. It flows through lands "full of large Gardens filled with flowers and fruit." "The places it waters are an Earthly Paradise."[7] Léry found the Amazon basin a land of unbelievable abundance "all year long and in every season," "toujours verdoyans," with flowers three feet in diameter.[8] This profusion of natural beauty was not confined to the tropics, however, for Sagard in New France found that plants and animals flourished in greater quantity and quality than anything in Europe.[9] Praising these "merveilles de Dieu," the copious supply of beautiful birds, flowers, and lakes filled with fish, Sagard again and again refers to Quebec as "nostre Jardin."[10]

Not only was the sheer physical setting of the American continent redolent of Eden. Its inhabitants too were reminiscent of the original peoples of the Book of Genesis. More specifically, the American natives impressed explorers by exhibiting that most striking pre-lapsarian trait: habitual and unashamed nudity. Sagard is amazed by the Hurons, "every man as nude as a child coming from his mother's womb. . . . For this they have neither shame nor scorn. . . . They never wear clothing."[11] Léry notes that the Amazons live all their lives naked as babes "without showing any sign of shame or scorn." In fact, says Léry, "nos pauvres Amériquains" are quite like Adam and Eve.[12] Acuña, who had already described the Amazon region as an Earthly Paradise, remarks of its native population:[13] "most of them go stark naked, Men as well as Women, and are no more ashamed of so appearing than if they were in the Primitive State of Innocency."

Through his reading, in short, Locke, like innumerable contemporaries, had probably absorbed this Edenic notion of the Americas and their indigents, enabling him to imagine the idyllic American state as an extant representation of the original condition of "all the World." If the Book of Genesis, however, provided little reliable political history, an anthropological history of America would fill the same need; and by virtue of its Edenic similarities, furthermore,

---

[6]For discussion of this notion of a New World Garden: Henry Nash Smith, *Virgin Land: American West as Symbol and Myth* (New York, 1950); R.W.B. Lewis, *The American Adam* (Chicago, 1955).

[7]Cristobal d' Acuña, S.J., *Relation de la Rivière Des Amazons* (Paris, 1682), 111–14.

[8]Jean de Léry, *Histoire d'un Voyage Fait en la Terre du Bresil* (LaRochelle, 1578), 40, 85–86.

[9]Gabriel Sagard-Théodat, *Histoire du Canada et Voyages* (Paris, 1636), 161.

[10]Gabriel Sagard-Théodat, *Le Grand Voyage du Pays des Hurons* (Paris, 1632), 210, 222, 242.

[11]Sagard, *Histoire*, 190, 193.   [12]Léry, 96, 115.   [13]Acuña, 214–15.

the American case could be presumed a universal prototype. So it is, then, that in sketching the hypothetical State of Nature in the *Two Treatises,* Locke presents as salient characteristics of the natural state items which, significantly enough, were also primary themes in the American anthropological reports with which he was familiar.

Unlike Hobbes, whose resolutive method broke society down into its simplest elements, i.e., atomized individuals, Locke considered man in essence to be at least semi-social. His anthropological background demanded this recognition. "Man," said Sagard in his comments on the Hurons, "is a social animal who cannot live without company."[14] The French missionary pointed out the ways in which the Great Lakes Indians naturally banded together in families and tribes under the leadership of their chiefs. The Hurons, said Sagard, "are a most prosperous and proud people. Bravery is inseparably attached and linked to their pride. . . . Their sons and daughters are like Nymphs, they are so well-conditioned, and like Does, they are so agile."[15] Sagard's Hurons offered an example of a people in a natural state, but also a people living properly in society.

Though social, of course, Lockean natural men acknowledge no authority.

Men living together according to reason, without a common Superior on Earth, with Authority to judge between them, is properly the State of Nature.[16]

This is precisely characteristic of the peoples described in the travelogues which Locke read. Acosta relates the existence of peoples in Central America several centuries prior to the civilization of the Aztecs. These "Chichimecas," as they were called, "lived onely [sic] by hunting."

They lived in the roughest partes of the mountains beastlike, without any policie, and they all went naked. . . . They had no superiors, nor did acknowledge or worship any gods. Neyther hadde they any manner of ceremonies or religion. There is yet to this day in New Spaine of this kinde of people, which live by their bowes and arrows, the which are very hurtfull.[17]

Léry's account of the Amazons, moreover, corroborated this view of the most primitive American peoples. Léry at one point described a particular jungle tribe, a very primitive society, "having neither among them any kings nor princes, and consequently . . . they are almost like grand lords, one as much as another."[18]

From the anthropological descriptions of the South American tribes, then Locke might have concluded that men in this State of Nature lived "without a common Superior." As mentioned concerning the Hurons, however, Locke was confronted among the northern Indians with the chieftain variety of tribal authority. Here seemingly were men in the State of Nature who also acknowledged political authority. More than tribal chiefs, in fact, existed among the Hurons. Sagard reported that all the tribal treasures were held by one elder who was akin to the "Treasurer of the Republic," dispersing goods for "the common welfare of all" on the orders of a Huron Council.[19] Fortunately for th

[14]Sagard, *Histoire,* 219.   [15]Sagard, *Le Grand Voyage,* 25 ▮
[16]*Second Treatise,* par. 19.
[17]José d'Acosta, *The Naturall and Morall Historie of the East and West Indie* (London, 1609), 497-98.   [18]Léry, 196
[19]Sagard, *Le Grand Voyage,* 261-62; *Histoire,* 234-35.

rest of Locke's theory, Huron property was communistically held. Yet here indeed was a regular structure of authority.

To resolve this problem Locke chose to distinguish between types of authority, and thus an analysis of paternal authority became appropriate. "Perhaps at first," says Locke, "some one good and excellent man" had a certain "deferment paid to his goodness" by being granted "a kind of natural authority."

I will not deny that, if we look back as far as history will direct us toward the original of commonwealths, we shall generally find them under the government and administration of one man.[20]

The answer of Locke is twofold. He would first insist that the authority of the Huron Chief is paternalistic, and secondly, that no individual property existed in this communistic tribe. On both counts the Hurons could not be said to have a civil government. By careful definition, therefore, Locke escapes the admission of civil authority among natural men, though the original statement— "Men living together . . . without a common Superior on Earth"—still seems too broad for the evidence.

Another anthropological ambiguity arises in Locke's distinction between the State of War and the State of Nature, and it parallels the logical difficulty that Professors MacPherson and Cox perceive in the same issue.[21] Locke, unlike Hobbes, insists that the State of Nature is peaceful. It is a "State of Peace, Good Will, Mutual Assistance, and Preservation," with men "living together according to reason."[22] Shortly thereafter, however, Locke expresses his fear that every contention in the natural state is apt to end in war. "One great reason of Men's putting themselves into Society and quitting the State of Nature" is "to avoid the State of War."[23] It seems that Locke has virtually agreed with Hobbes. Otherwise he must be distinguishing the states of nature and war, while simultaneously equating them in the long run.

This logical discrepancy may have originated from the confusion of Locke's anthropological background on the subject. Jean de Léry described the Amazon tribesmen as people who "live well together in peace," seeming to perceive innately "les loix divines et humaines." In random places Léry remarks on their amiability, hospitality, and helpfulness.[24] The Amazons seem genial and peace-loving. Yet both Acosta and Acuña emphasize precisely the opposite traits in primitive American peoples. Acosta calls the Chichimecas "barbarous and savage." "To fight with them were properly to hunt after savage beasts."[25] Acuña says frankly that the Amazons he observed "are in continual war, and are daily killing and making slaves of one another." Elsewhere he mentions their cannibalism as well.[26] Thus the anthropology of primitive American peoples available to Locke was strongly divided on the peacefulness or bellicosity of the State of Nature. Locke's logical ambiguity on the issue, as MacPherson, Cox, and others analyze it, is complemented by his conflicting anthropological knowledge. And as Locke is forced to conclude a

[20]*Second Treatise*, pars. 94, 105.
[21]C. B. MacPherson, *The Political Theory of Possessive Individualism* (New York, 1962), 238. Richard Cox, *Locke on War and Peace* (Oxford, 1960).
[22]*Second Treatise*, par. 19.
[23]*Ibid.*, par. 21.
[24]Léry, 272, 291–92.
[25]Acosta, 498.
[26]Acuña, 200.

potentially close affinity between the States of Nature and War (thus approximating Hobbes), so too, he suffered from an anthropological division on the subject, and the strong suggestion that the two states were nearly identical. It may be, however, that Locke had ulterior motives for maintaining the distinction between the State of Nature and the State of War. In order to justify property as a natural right antecedent to government, Locke needed to postulate first that natural men could recognize Natural Law, i.e., they could not have been the amoral agents of constant wars. Pre-contractual property logically implied pre-contractual rights, lawfulness, and peace. Yet it would be unfair to imply that Locke was playing a logical trick on his audience. Based on his readings he no doubt believed that men in the natural state did indeed recognize Natural Law, even though frequent wars marred its perfect implementation. The few men who foment war are described in the *Second Treatise* as "noxious," "degenerate," "having quit the Principles of Human Nature."[27] Locke's readings led him to believe that the majority of natural men were peaceful and law-abiding. The average "savage" in Sagard's books is described as a diligent, courageous provider and a devoted father. Léry's Amazon is a noble and friendly, warm fellow. Even the savages in Acuña's otherwise hostile account do at times seem somewhat humane. In all these societies, furthermore, adultery and incest are punished, honor is maintained. Though "inciviles et extravagantes," lacking "la lumière de la raison," the primitives hold onto "la pureté d'une nature espurée."[28]

From his readings in travelogues describing the Indians of North, Central, and South America, Locke seems, then, to have drawn some of the elements—and problems—of the concept of the State of Nature as hypothetically pictured in the *Two Treatises*. The American natives, living in society, lacking authority (except perhaps paternal), cognizant of Natural Law, though frequently falling into chaotic war—these are also the natural men who appear in the pages of Locke's work.

The final and perhaps most interesting parallel between seventeenth-century anthropological travelogues and the *Two Treatises*, however, appears in the pattern of development that Locke posits in discussing the emergence of peoples from the State of Nature to contractual, civil government. On this topic, needless to say, the issue of property is crucial, for the evolution of ownership is paramount in the entire Lockean explanation of the origin of government. A number of commentators[29] have pointed out three basic phases in Locke's developmental format.

There seems at first a period of society without individual, fixed property. The thrust of Locke's theoretical argument implies the likelihood that such peoples are nomadic, living perhaps by foraging and hunting. They hold to a purely subsistence economy and lack the institution of money. This is the first and purest period of the State of Nature, a "Golden Age" before "vain ambition . . . corrupted men's minds into a mistake of true power and honor."[30] The situation changed dramatically, however, when "ambition and luxury"

[27]*Second Treatise*, pars. 6, 8, 10.   [28]Sagard, *Histoire*, 19

[29]Richard Ashcraft, "Locke's State of Nature: Historical Fact or Moral Fiction?" *American Political Science Review*, 62 (1968), 910–11; also MacPherson, 210–1 Richard Aaron, *John Locke* (Oxford, 1955).

[30]*Second Treatise*, pars. 107, 162.

infected men. The most important event auguring the end of the first era was the invention of money which Locke traced to "the desire of having more than men needed."[31] As men began to enlarge their possessions, engage in trade, and use money as an exchange medium, there arose complicated transactions, disputes, and controversies. This is the second phase of the State of Nature.

Finally, of course, to protect property and settle conflicts, men leave the State of Nature altogether by contracting to establish civil government. Thus they have progressed from a nomadic state and a subsistence economy to a state of fixed property and an acquisitive economy, and then to civil government. Locke's developmental pattern is completed. This hypothetical model of political and economic evolution, moreover, may possibly have been suggested by a very similar developmental scheme encountered by Locke, once again, in his reading. Peter Laslett has stated that Locke was particularly interested in the book of José d'Acosta, calling it "one of the best works on the West Indies."[32] Indeed, Acosta is the one anthropological source directly cited in the *Second Treatise*, as mentioned earlier. It may be more than coincidental, then, that Acosta's history of the Aztec civilization corresponds quite closely with Locke's developmental hypothesis. Or rather, Locke's hypothesis seems an abstracted model closely related to Acosta's earlier history.

Unlike some explorers who simply wrote jealous descriptions of Aztec wealth, Acosta took a more detached, analytical approach to his subject. He was less impressed by the treasures of Montezuma, and more concerned with examining and describing the social and political structure of the kingdom. Aztec society, as he portrays it,[33] was rigidly hierarchic, far from the relative egalitarianism of the Lockean State of Nature. "Montezuma set Knighthood in its highest splendor, ordering military orders." The regime was strong and well-organized: "there was a good order and a settled policie for the revenues of the Crowne, for which there were officers divided throughout all the provinces." As for the young, says Acosta, the Aztecs "knew well that all the good hope of a common-weale consisted in the nurture and institution of youth" who attended regular school and led disciplined lives. By whatever standard, the Aztecs seemed to qualify as men in full possession of money, property, and civil government. Acosta continues by tracing the origins of this civilization.

The earliest peoples who migrated and lived in the region were the Chichimecas, mentioned already as possible prototypes of natural men. As recounted by Acosta, they lived without fixed property, money, or much common authority. Acosta believes that the Chichimecas alone occupied the region until the beginning of the eighth century. Around 720 A.D., he estimates, the land of the Chichimecas was invaded by tribes wandering from the north along the Pacific coast. These were the Navaltalcas, "a more civill and politike Nation." The Navaltalcas "did always entertain amitie together," and "seeking to increase and beautifie their common-weale,"[34] settled into communities to cultivate the land. Most of the Chichimecas were driven into the hills where they continued a nomadic existence. The Navaltalcas, on the other hand, divided the land into fixed portions, i.e., private property, though their government had no formal structure beyond sporadic, democratic assemblies. Eventually, notes Acosta in his hearsay history,

---

[31]*Ibid.*, par. 111.   [32]*Second Treatise*, par. 102, ftn.; in Laslett edit., 149.
[33]Acosta, 486–87, 489.   [34]*Ibid.*, 498, 502.

the barbarous Chichimecas, seeing what had passed, began to use some government, and to apparrell themselves. . . . They began to learn many things of them [the Navaltalcas] building small cottages . . . by means whereof they did in a manner quite abandon this brutish life.[35]

Notice at this point the parallel with Locke. Men acquire fixed property and leave the chaotic natural state in its pure form, though government is still minimal at best. The Navaltalcan society seems surprisingly similar to the second phase of the State of Nature as Locke was to later describe it in abstract, theoretical terms.

Eventually, of course, the Navaltalcan community was the victim of still another invasion, and the resultant mixed society united under the Aztec monarchy, i.e., civil government. As Acosta relates it, the monarchy was established through the consultation and agreement of "some excellent men," most likely the aristocrats.[36] His brevity and vagueness in reporting the specific details of the monarchy's origin, however, deprived Locke of definitive empirical evidence in support of his contract theory. Yet Acosta's account of Central American political history incorporated both the development of fixed property and, simultaneously, a series of conflicts and invasions making such property insecure. Civil government became the obvious recourse for order and stability. Locke, the admirer of Acosta, could easily have borrowed this evolutionary theme directly from the Spaniard, amending it only slightly to conform more explicitly to his contract theory. The developmental parallels seem even more plausible and compelling when it is noticed that Acosta himself prefaces his Aztec history with a summary of the three successive political stages in Central American history. Explorers, says Acosta,

have found three manner of governments at the Indes. The first and best, was a Monarchie, as that of the Inguas and of Montezuma, although for the most part they were tyrannous. The second was of Comminalties [i.e. Navaltalcan], where they were governed by the advise and authority of many. . . . The third kind of government [Chichimecan] is altogether barbarous, composed of Indians without Law, without King, and without any certaine place of abode, but go in troupes like savage beasts. As farre as I can conceive the first inhabitants of the Indes were of this kinde. . . . [Then] the other form of government was framed [Navaltalcan]. . . . [Then] grew the other form of government more mighty and potent, which did institute a Kingdom and a Monarchie.[37]

It is not impossible that Locke merely borrowed the order of Acosta's account, extracted the pattern from its Aztec embodiment, and so acquired the outline for his own developmental theory of political institutions.

Such strong parallels suggest that Locke was not working simply in an abstract, geometric, Hobbesian manner. Certainly the Two Treatises are in some measure the result of deductive reasoning, but, recognizing Locke's prior anthropological knowledge, it is also likely that they are the fruit of his collateral reading and vicarious social observation. Perhaps it is fitting, then, that Locke has given much to American political culture. From America, i seems, he took much as well.

University of Minnesota.

[35]Ibid., 502.　　　　　[36]Ibid., 502.　　　　　[37]Ibid., 471-72

Chapter XXV

VOLUNTARISM AND IMMANENCE: CONCEPTIONS OF NATURE IN EIGHTEENTH-CENTURY THOUGHT

By P. M. Heimann*

The traditional historiography of science has supposed that the metaphysical reorientation fundamental to the "scientific revolution" in the seventeenth century established the conceptual framework of eighteenth-century scientific thought.[1] This characterization of eighteenth-century ideas has been sustained by an interpretation of seventeenth-century thought that has placed emphasis on the modernity of the conceptual revolution associated with the establishment of the mechanical philosophy.[2] According to this interpretation, the mechanical philosophy conceived nature as a self-contained, law-governed system, in which God's relation to nature was viewed merely as a first efficient cause, and the appeal by natural philosophers to second causes (laws of nature) established knowledge of nature as independent of divine providence. Thus it is maintained that doctrines of providence declined in importance in the period, and the establishment of the mechanical philosophy is viewed in terms of the secularization of knowledge in the seventeenth century.[3] Newton and Boyle are regarded as having "prepared the ground for the deists of the Enlightenment"; for "deism, the religion of reason, steps full grown from the writings of the Christian virtuosi."[4]

This historiography is doubly misleading: in its account of doctrines of providence in the thought of Boyle and Newton, and of the consequent characterization of eighteenth-century intellectual history. Recent

* An early version of this paper was read as a lecture to The Society for the Humanities, Cornell University on 17 October, 1972. I am grateful to Professor Henry Guerlac for his kind invitation and for his comments on the paper. I am also grateful to Gerd Buchdahl, Ralph Grant, and J. E. McGuire for discussions on the themes of this paper.

[1] The following studies are representative: E. A. Burtt, *The Metaphysical Foundations of Modern Physical Science* (2nd ed., London, 1932); E. J. Dijksterhuis, *The Mechanization of the World-Picture* (Oxford, 1961). These studies and the works referred to in footnotes (2) to (4) below are cited here for their merits as important statements of the traditional historiography.

[2] M. Boas, "The establishment of the mechanical philosophy," *Osiris,* **10**(1952), 12-541.

[3] Richard S. Westfall, *Science and Religion in Seventeenth-Century England* (New Haven, 1958); Paul Hazard, *The European Mind 1680-1715* (London, 1953).

[4] Westfall, *op. cit.,* 219.

scholarship has questioned the traditional view that doctrines of providence declined in importance in late seventeenth-century natural philosophy. Stressing the influence of the voluntarist tradition of theology on Descartes, Boyle, and Newton, it has been argued that these men regarded God's will as the only causally efficacious agency in nature. To conceive nature as subject to laws did not obviate divine providence, for in regarding nature as a contingent artifact of divine omnipotence laws of nature were considered as being imposed on nature by God, having their source in the efficacy of the divine will. Laws and the abrogations of laws were both manifestations of divine providence.[5] The implications of this reconsideration of the theological dimension of seventeenth-century science are of considerable importance for an understanding of eighteenth-century thought. The assumption that Enlightenment skepticism was "already present in embryo among [the virtuosi]"[6] is clearly to be questioned. The current revaluation of seventeenth-century attitudes suggests that the transition from the natural theology of the virtuosi to the religion of reason of the eighteenth century involved a more complex shift in theological sensibility than has generally been supposed.

In this paper I am concerned to characterize the shift in theological sensibility associated with the emergence of new conceptions of nature in eighteenth-century British thought. The transition from the Newtonian view that the activity of the natural order was to be ascribed to the continued sustenance of passive matter by God's will to the theories of nature proposed in the late eighteenth century by Joseph Priestley and James Hutton which supposed—though in different ways—that activity was intrinsic to matter and immanent in the natural order, was associated with the rejection of Newton's voluntarist theory of nature which supposed that God's will "sustains the world in its minutest details." These eighteenth-century natural philosophers emphasized divine omniscience and rejected divine abrogation of the laws of nature as impugning divine foresight, rejecting the voluntarist conception of nature which stressed that God "gives order as well as deviation from order," a view that "diminishes the gap between the natural and the supernatural."[7] This was an important development in theological attitude towards the natural world, but these natural philosophers did not limit God's relation to nature as a first efficient cause, supposing a mechanical universe run by immutable natural laws established b

[5] Francis Oakley, "Christian Theology and the Newtonian Science: the ris of the concept of the laws of nature," *Church History*, 30(1961), 433-57; J. E McGuire, "Force, Active Principles and Newton's Invisible Realm," *Ambix*, 1 (1968), 187-208; *id.*, "Boyle's Conception of Nature," *JHI*, 33(1972), 523-42.
[6] Westfall, *op. cit.*, 219.
[7] R. Hooykaas, *The Principle of Uniformity in Geology, Biology and Theolog; Natural Law and Law and Divine Miracle* (Leiden, 1963), 170f. Hooykaas term this view of God's relation to nature the "Biblical" view.

God, which then maintained the operations of nature independently of divine energy, but supposed—though with different emphasis—that divine causality was manifested in the active powers[8] which were immanent in the fabric of nature. This shift in theological sensibility involved a change in attitude towards the causality of God and the relationship between God and nature.

I. The theological dimension of Newton's natural philosophy was familiar to eighteenth-century thinkers from his *Principia* and *Opticks* and also from the distinctively Newtonian cast of the writings of the Boyle lecturers, notably Samuel Clarke.[9] In the *Opticks* Newton emphasized that his conception of nature affirmed the voluntarist doctrine of divine omnipotence: everything in the world, he argued, is "subordinate to him, and subservient to his Will." As God's will was the only causally efficacious agency in nature, Newton declared that God "may vary the Laws of Nature, and make worlds of several sorts in several parts of the universe."[10] Newton distinguished between the role of active and passive principles in natural processes, maintaining that the laws of motion and the essential qualities of material substances—extension, impenetrability, inertia—were passive principles by which "there never could have been any motion in the world."[11] Newton concluded that the principles of the mechanical philosophy were limited in their comprehension of nature. As Hume later noted, "while Newton seemed to draw off the veil from some of the mysteries of nature, he showed at the same time the imperfections of the mechanical philosophy."[12] Newton argued that "some other principle [than the passive principles of matter and motion] was necessary for putting bodies into motion; and now they are in motion some other principle is necessary for conserving the motion." The passive laws of motion could neither originate nor sustain motion, and Newton concluded that a different category of causal agent, active principles, were responsible for "conserving and recruiting" activity and motion in nature, these active principles being "such as are the cause of gravity." In denying that the activity of nature was intrinsic to the natural order, Newton emphasized the role of active principles, which were defined in relation to divine omni-

---

[8] For an analysis of the significance of the concept of "power" in eighteenth-century British natural philosophy: P. M. Heimann and J. E. McGuire, "Newtonian Forces and Lockean Powers: Concepts of Matter in Eighteenth-Century Thought," *Historical Studies in the Physical Sciences*, 3(1971), 233-306; also Philip P. Wiener, "James Gregory: "On Power," *JHI*, 20(1959), 241-68.

[9] On the Newtonian cast of the Boyle Lectures: Henry Guerlac and M. C. Jacob, "Bentley, Newton and Providence," *JHI*, 30(1969), 307-18; M. C. Jacob, The Church and the Formulation of the Newtonian World View," *Journal of European Studies*, 1(1971), 128-48.

[10] Isaac Newton, *Opticks* (4th ed., rpt., London, 1952), 403f   [11] *Ibid.*, 397.

[12] David Hume, in his *History of England,* as quoted in Norman Kemp Smith, *The Philosophy of David Hume* (London, 1941), 58.

potence and conceived as the manifestations of God's causal agency in nature. Functioning as the cause of motion and gravity, active principles were regarded as "general Laws of Nature" rather than as divine abrogations of the laws of nature.[13] There was no conflict between Newton's stress on the lawlike function of active principles and their construal as manifestations of providence, for Newton argued that while all natural phenomena were constrained by God's will, nevertheless God also worked through second causes by divine concurrence with the order of nature that He had established. In terms of this voluntarist theology, the laws of nature as well as divine abrogations of law are expressions of divine providence. Newton bridged the dichotomy between natural laws and divine interventions, arguing that "miracles are so called not because they are the works of God but because they happen seldom and for that reason create wonder."[14] Newton did not publish this remark, but his ideas were echoed by Samuel Clarke in his famous correspondence with Leibniz.[15] Clarke declared that "*natural* and *supernatural* are nothing at all different with regard to God, but distinctions merely in our conceptions of things."[16] All of nature is subject to God's will, and whether we call an event a natural and lawlike phenomenon or an abrogation of law and a miracle lies "merely in the unusualness of God's doing it," for "with regard to God, no one possible thing is more miraculous than another."[17] In his *Discourse Concerning the Being and Attributes of God* (1705-06) Clarke stressed Newton's view that the activity of nature was dependent on an "Immaterial Power . . . *perpetually and actually* exerting itself every moment in every part of the world,"[18] for matter and motion were "arbitrary and dependent things."[19]

The import of Newton's concept of active principles is apparent in his theory of the aether developed in the 1717 edition of his *Opticks.*

---

[13] Newton, *Opticks*, 397-401; McGuire, "Force, Active Principles . . ." *op cit.*, 154-208.

[14] Newton MS quoted in Guerlac and Jacob, *op. cit.*, 309n.

[15] On Newton's role in the Leibniz-Clarke correspondence cf. A. Koyré and I. B. Cohen, "Newton and the Leibniz-Clarke Correspondence," *Arch. int. d'hist sci.*, 15(1962), 63-126; also F. E. L. Priestley, "The Clarke-Leibniz Controversy," *The Methodological Heritage of Newton*, ed. R. Butts and J. W. Davis (Oxford, 1970), 34-56.

[16] H. G. Alexander, ed. *The Leibniz-Clarke Correspondence* (Manchester 1956), 24.

[17] *Ibid.*, 114.

[18] Samuel Clarke, *Discourse Concerning the Being and Attributes of God*, 2 vols. (4th ed., London, 1716), II, 17. Clarke's Boyle Lectures were first published as: *A Demonstration of the Being and Attributes of God* (London 1705) and *A Discourse Concerning the Unchangeable Obligations of Natural Religion* (London, 1706).

[19] Clarke, *op. cit.*, I, 23.

The aether was employed as an explanation of gravity, and Newton was careful to imply that the aether functioned as an active principle, not as a passive or mechanical principle of matter and motion analogous to the Cartesian celestial vortices. In the General Scholium to the second edition of *Principia* in 1713, Newton had denied that gravity could be explained by "mechanical causes," and Newton implied that the aether, as a possible cause of gravity, was an active principle subordinate to God's will.[20] Newton's concept of the aether was echoed by Colin MacLaurin in his *Account of Sir Isaac Newton's Philosophical Discoveries* (1748). MacLaurin stressed that Newton was "particularly careful" to represent God as a "free agent . . . equally active and present everywhere,"[21] and in noting that gravity "seems to surpass mere mechanism" he pointed out that if gravity were "produced by a rare and elastic *aethereal medium*, as Sir *Isaac Newton* conjectured," then "the whole efficacy of this medium must be resolved into his power and will, who is the supreme cause." MacLaurin followed Newton in supposing that the aether was contingent on God's will; hence the supposition of an aether did not "derogate from the government and influence of the Deity" for God "is the source of all efficacy." MacLaurin thus affirmed Newton's voluntarism, viewing second causes as manifestations of the "power and will" of the Deity.[22]

However, by the 1740s natural philosophers were developing conceptions of nature in which the aether was considered as an active principle which was immanent in the fabric of nature, and which functioned as the source of the activity of nature. This transformation in thought involved a blurring of the distinctive categories of Newton's natural philosophy and a rejection of its theological overtones. Newton's natural philosophy was dualistic: a dualism of matter and force, attractive and repulsive forces, atoms and void space, and active and passive principles. By the middle of the eighteenth century conceptions of nature were being proposed in which there was a bridging of the dualism of these Newtonian categories. The emergence of a theory of nature in which activity was considered as immanent in the structure of nature led to a rejection of Newton's doctrine that all causal activity in nature was imposed by God's power and will.

The theory that nature was endowed with intrinsic active forces or powers had been proposed earlier in the century in opposition to the

[20] Isaac Newton, *Mathematical Principles of Natural Philosophy*, trans. and ed. A. Motte and F. Cajori (Berkeley, 1934), 546; *id., Opticks*, 349-54; Clarke, *op. cit.*, II, 16-19. On the background to Newton's aether: Henry Guerlac, "Newton's Optical Aether," *Notes and Records of the Royal Society of London*, 22(1967), 45-57.

[21] Colin MacLaurin, *An Account of Sir Isaac Newton's Philosophical Discoveries* (London, 1748), 381f.

[22] *Ibid.*, 387-89.

Newtonian world view, but these ideas had been rejected by Newton and Clarke. In his *Specimen Dynamicum* Leibniz had rejected the view that extension and motion were the defining characteristics of substance, arguing that force constituted the inmost nature of material substance,[23] and this rejection of the theory of the passivity of material entities had its counterpart in his hostility to Newton's voluntarism. As he later affirmed to Clarke. the Newtonians "acknowledge power, but not sufficient wisdom, in the principle or cause of all things." The inherent activity of matter did "not exclude God's providence, or his government of the world: on the contrary, it makes it perfect," for a "true providence of God requires a perfect foresight." Leibniz emphasized that the rejection of Newton's voluntarism did not restrict divine providence, denying that the world was a "machine," and affirming that "the creation wants to be continually influenc'd by its creator."[24] Nevertheless, Leibniz's opposition to a voluntarist conception of divine sustenance led to Clarke's vehement opposition to his natural philosophy. Clarke also dismissed the theory of a dynamic, inherently active universe proposed by John Toland in his *Letters to Serena* (1704). Asserting that the universe displayed constant activity, Toland claimed that "motion is essential to matter,"[25] but Clarke argued that matter could not be endowed with a self-existent principle of motion because "self-existence is necessary existence" and the existence of matter was contingent on God's will.[26]

From the early eighteenth century the concept of matter as an inherently active substance was developed explicitly in opposition to the Newtonian concept of nature. One of Newton's earliest English critics Robert Greene, maintained that "nature is active . . . [and] matter itself is so,"[27] and in rejecting the Newtonian theory of atoms argued that "Action or Force in general is the Essence or Substratum of Matter."[2] Greene did not suppose that the active forces constituting material substance were self-existent, arguing that if matter were self-existent it would have a "necessary, certain and unvaried principle of existing" however, natural phenomena were not unvaried but were diverse, an

---

[23] G. W. Leibniz, "Specimen Dynamicum," *Acta Eruditorum*, 14(1695), 14? 57. On Newton's reaction to this work, cf. J. E. McGuire, "Body and Void an Newton's *De Mundi Systemate*," *Arch. Hist. Exact Sci.*, 3(1966), 237.

[24] Alexander, *op. cit.*, 18f.

[25] John Toland, *Letters to Serena* (London, 1704), 158. On Toland's relation to Newton, cf. M. C. Jacob, "John Toland and the Newtonian Ideology *J. Warburg and Courtauld Institutes*, 32(1969), 307-31; also Rosalie L. Coli "Spinoza and the Early English Deists," *JHI*, 20(1959), 23-46.

[26] Clarke, *op. cit.*, 1, 49.

[27] Robert Greene, *The Principles of Natural Philosophy* (Cambridge, 1712 391. On Greene's concept of force, cf. Heimann and McGuire. *op. cit.* 254-6

[28] Robert Greene, *The Principles of the Philosophy of the Expansive an Contractive Forces* (Cambridge, 1727), 286.

"all Nature consists of an infinite number of actions different in their forces and contrary in their directions." Greene thus concluded that activity "cannot be self-existent," contending that the diversity of forces "must necessarily lead us to some Agent."[29] The immanent powers were not self-existent in nature but were dependent on divine agency for their activity.

The theory of activity as immanent in nature was a common assumption in the conceptions of nature developed in the 1740s, in which the aether was assimilated to Boerhaave's "active element" of fire[30] which was considered to be an active principle permeating the universe: "fire [was considered] as endowed with active Powers different from those of other Matter."[31] Electricity and fire were considered to be different modifications of the aether,[32] and the Newtonian notion that "motion comes immediately from the Divine Being" was rejected as "unphilosophical" in favor of supposing that activity was inherent in the aether, the aether being regarded as an active principle.[33] Newton's theory of the aether was transformed, so the aether was viewed as an active principle immanent in nature.

The implication of these developments in natural philosophy for Newton's doctrine of efficient causation as contingent on God's will is apparent in Hume's discussion of causation and the aether in his *Enquiry into the Human Understanding* (1748). Hume rejected the Newtonian doctrine of passive matter, the view—as he put it in his *Treatise of Human Nature* (1739)—that "the essence of matter . . . is endow'd with no efficacy," that because matter "is in itself entirely unactive, and depriv'd of any power" hence "the power . . . must lie in the DEITY." Hume thus opposed the notion that "the deity . . . is the prime mover of the universe, and who not only first created matter, and gave it its original impulse, but likewise by a continu'd exertion of omnipotence, supports its existence."[34] In his *Enquiry* Hume appealed to divine omniscience in rejecting the Newtonian doctrine that "nothing exists but by [God's]will," echoing Leibniz's arguments against Clarke in stating that the "purposes of providence" are manifested in the "perfect foresight"

[29] *Ibid.*, 108ff.

[30] Herman Boerhaave, *A New Method of Chemistry*, trans. P. Shaw (London, 741), 212. On the impact of Newton's theory of the aether and Boerhaave's concept of fire on eighteenth-century natural philosophy, cf. P. M. Heimann, 'Nature is a perpetual worker': Newton's aether and eighteenth-century natural hilosophy," *Ambix*, 20(1973), 1-25.

[31] John Rowning, *A Compendious System of Natural Philosophy* (London, 737-43), iii.

[32] I. B. Cohen ed., *Benjamin Franklin's Experiments* (Cambridge, Mass., 941), 210.

[33] C. Colden, *The Principles of Action in Matter* (London, 1751), 73.

[34] David Hume, *A Treatise of Human Nature* [1739-40], ed. L. A. Selby-igge (Oxford, 1888), 159.

by which the "fabric of the world" was contrived, for "it argues surely
more power in the Deity to delegate a certain degree of power . . . than
to produce every thing by his own immediate volition." This latter view
was in the realm of "fairy land."[35] Hume attributed the theory that all
agency in nature was derived from divine volition to Malebranche, and
ascribed the view that "matter has a real, though subordinate and derived [active] power" to the Newtonians. As an instance of the active
powers of matter which he claimed were supposed by Newton, Hume
appealed to Newton's "recourse to an etherial active fluid to explain
his [theory of] universal attraction," denying that Newton attributed
gravity to divine volition.[36] Hume maintained that the notion that
matter has a real power and energy can be made intelligible if this power
can be shown to be an instance of causal activity. Hence, subsuming
the phenomena of gravity under the action of an "etherial active fluid"
renders the power of gravity intelligible. Causal agency is thus seen as
only being intelligible in relation to physical explanation, in relation to
the laws of nature between material entities.[37]

In restricting the intelligibility of causal explanation to the formulation of laws of nature Hume rejected the notion of the efficient causality of God, of divine efficacy sustaining the natural world. Hume's
restriction of the causal principle to the formulation of physical explanations rendered the notion of divine sustenance unintelligible, and this
implication of Hume's arguments was resisted. The Scottish philosopher
Thomas Reid attempted a systematic refutation of Humean principles,
and in his Essays on the Active Powers of the Human Mind (1788) provided a full account of his theory of causality. Reid distinguished between causation in the sense of the formulation of laws of nature, which
was the concern of science (and which Hume accepted), and "efficient
causation," as in divine sustenance of the laws of nature, and sought to
justify the supposition of efficient causes. Reid pointed out that natural
philosophers were only concerned with the "cause of any phenomenon
of nature" in the sense of a "law of nature of which that phenomenon
is a necessary consequence." The laws of nature were merely "the rule
according to which the effects are produced," but science was not concerned with the postulation of the "efficient cause" of phenomena, the
supposition of a causal relation between an active agent and matter
However, it was meaningful to suppose an efficient cause of phenomena
"Upon the theatre of nature we see innumerable effects, which require
an agent endowed with active power; but the agent is behind the
scene. Whether it be the Supreme Cause alone, or a subordinate cause
or causes; and if subordinate causes be employed by the Almighty, wh

[35] David Hume, An Enquiry into the Human Understanding [1748], ed. L.
Selby-Bigge (2nd ed., Oxford, 1902), 71f.   [36] Ibid., 73
[37] Gerd Buchdahl, Metaphysics and the Philosophy of Science. The Classic
Origins: Descartes to Kant (Oxford, 1969), 325-87.

their nature, their number, and their different offices may be are things hid, for wise reasons without doubt, from the human eye."[38] Reid thus sought to justify efficient causation, the supposition that the activity of nature was a consequence of the causality of God, whether activity was imposed on nature by divine volition or was maintained by immanent active powers dependent on divine energy for their efficacy. In distinguishing between laws of nature and efficient causes Reid sought to anaesthetize the thrust of the Humean critique. Nevertheless in making this distinction his argument reflects Hume's critique of Newtonian voluntarism. In seeking to validate the notion of divine sustenance without stressing divine volition as the cause of phenomena, Reid's argument attests to the shift in theological sensibility consequent on the rejection of Newton's theory that active principles were imposed by divine volition on passive matter, and on the development of theories of natural philosophy which employed the concept of the aether as an active principle immanent in nature.

II. These intellectual developments are apparent in the writings of Joseph Priestley and James Hutton, two scientists active in the latter part of the eighteenth century whose importance can be seen not only in their notable contributions to chemistry and geology, respectively, but also in their attempts to construct systematic systems of natural philosophy.

Priestley rejected the Newtonian duality of active and passive principles because of the difficulty in explaining God's causal relation to nature entailed by supposing that God "has no property whatever in common with matter." This would imply that "the divine being is necessarily cut off from all communication with, and all action and influence upon, his own creation."[39] Priestley resolved the problem of the interaction between matter and the immaterial deity by positing a monistic theory of nature, denying the Newtonian dualism of matter and force by defining matter as "a substance possessed of the property of extension and of powers of attraction or repulsion,"[40] thus asserting the "immateriality of matter"[41] and denying that "there are . . . two substances as distinct from each other" as matter and spirit.[42] If matter was considered as defined by the properties of extension and inherent

---

[38] Thomas Reid, *Essays on the Active Powers of the Human Mind* [1788], ed. B. Brody (Cambridge, Mass., 1969), 46f.

[39] Joseph Priestley, *Disquisitions Relating to Matter and Spirit* (London, 1777; 2nd ed., 2 vols., Birmingham, 1782), in *The Theological and Miscellaneous Works of Joseph Priestley*, ed. J. T. Rutt, 25 vols. (London, 1817-31), III, 98 (2nd ed. quoted); hereafter Priestley, *Disquisitions*.

[40] Priestley, *Disquisitions* in *Works*, III, 219. For an analysis of Priestley's theory of matter, cf. Heimann and McGuire, *op. cit.*, 268-81.

[41] Joseph Priestley, *The History and Present State of Discoveries Relating to Vision, Light and Colours* (London, 1772), 392.

[42] Priestley, *Disquisitions* in *Works*, III, 223.

powers of attraction and repulsion, then the nature of matter was compatible with "that substance which . . . we have been used to call immaterial."[43] Priestley rejected the Newtonian concept of passive matter together with Newton's doctrine of the causal relation between God and nature, claiming that the Newtonian theory of matter supposed "something to be *independent of the divine power*" in postulating "two original independent principles."[44] Priestley argued that his monistic theory was thus consonant to the notion of God's "filling all in all."[45]

Priestley did not suppose that the powers which constituted matter were "self-existent in it"[46] but maintained that the activity of matter was sustained by divine agency, asserting that "the Deity not only attends to everything, but must be capable of either *producing* or *annihilating* anything."[47] Thus God's "power is the very life and soul of everything that exists . . . without him, we are, as well as can do, nothing,"[48] and without divine sustenance "substance ceases to exist, or is annihilated."[49] Priestley nevertheless rejected Newton's voluntarism, arguing that God acts by necessity not volition: God's causality "could not but have acted from all eternity."[50] He argued that the activity of nature was sustained by divine energy and that causal connections in nature were a necessary consequence of divine power, for God "was the same first cause from which all the powers of nature are derived"[51] and "all the *powers of nature* . . . can only be the effect of the Divine energy perpetually acting,"[52] concluding that causal connections in nature were "necessary" because there must be "some sufficient reason" for them.[53]

There are Leibnizian resonances in these statements, and Priestley like Leibniz, viewed nature as being "influenced" by God while rejecting the voluntarist doctrine of divine causality; as Leibniz expressed it

---

[43] *Ibid.*, 230.   [44] *Ibid.*, 241.   [45] *Ibid.*, 301.   [46] *Ibid.*, 224

[47] *Ibid.*, 297. With reference to this and other statements of Priestley's, cf. J. G. McEvoy and J. E. McGuire, "God and Nature: Priestley's Way of Rational Dissent," *Historical Studies in the Physical Sciences*, 6(1975), 332f, argue that Priestley's thought developed from voluntarist to rationalist theism after the publication of the first edition of his *Disquisitions* in 1777. This is possible though Priestley's writings are ambiguous; as they note, this statement of Priestley in the first edition of the *Disquisitions* is not an overt statement of a voluntarist position.

[48] Priestley, *Disquisitions*, in *Works*, III, 241.   [49] *Ibid.*, 22

[50] Joseph Priestley, *Letters to a Philosophical Unbeliever* (London, 1780 in *Works*, IV, 343; hereafter Priestley, *Philosophical Unbeliever*.

[51] Joseph Priestley, *A Free Discussion of the Doctrines of Materialism and Philosophical Necessity, in a Correspondence between Dr. Price and Dr. Priestley* (London, 1778), in *Works*, IV, 107.

[52] Joseph Priestley, *Institutes of Natural and Revealed Religion*, 2 vols., 2nd ed. (Birmingham, 1782), in *Works*, II, 15.

[53] Priestley, *Philosophical Unbeliever*, in *Works*, IV, 403.

God was "the efficient and exemplary cause" of all phenomena.[54] For Priestley the laws of nature and the active powers were the effect of divine energy permeating nature, and—given his monism and his theory of divine causality—the laws of nature and active powers constituting nature were regarded as being immanent in the fabric of nature, not imposed by divine volition. In conceiving the structure and activity of nature as arising necessarily from divine energy, Priestley's ideas have a slight affinity—which was seized on by Coleridge[55]—to Spinoza's conception of divine causality. Priestley, however, was concerned to disavow any suspicion of such a similarity. Incorrectly interpreting Spinoza as denying any conceptual distinction between God and the aggregate totality of all things,[56] Priestley repudiated the suggestion that his own conception of nature, which supposed "the Deity to *be* as well as to *do* everything," was "anything like the opinion of Spinoza," for Priestley claimed that he distinguished (as Spinoza did not) between "infinite power" and "inferior beings" and hence, between God and nature.[57] While there is quite possibly a substantive relation between Priestley's ideas and Leibniz's arguments, the influence of Spinoza is doubtful,[58] but whatever Priestley's links to these thinkers, it is apparent that his rejection of Newtonian dualism and voluntarism and his supposition of a monistic theory of nature and concept of active powers as immanent in nature is grounded on a doctrine of divine causality that considers nature as dependent for its existence on divine sustenance.

In his *Dissertations on Different Subjects in Natural Philosophy* (1792) and *Investigation of the Principles of Knowledge* (1794), Hutton firmly opposed the Newtonian doctrine that "bodies are composed of atoms which are absolutely inert . . . infinitely hard, and perfectly incompressible,"[59] arguing that this "received opinion of philosophers"[60] merely supposed as the defining principles of gross bodies "nothing but the bodies themselves under the pedantic designation of atoms."[61] Hutton claimed that "magnitude and figure [the defining characteristics of atoms] have no other existence than in the conceiving faculty of our mind,"[62] and that sensory experience—far from providing

---

[54] Alexander, *op. cit.*, 84.

[55] Thomas McFarland, *Coleridge and the Pantheist Tradition* (Oxford, 1969), 170, 175.

[56] H. A. Wolfson, *The Philosophy of Spinoza*, 2 vols. (Cambridge, Mass., 1934), I, 324f.   [57] Priestley, *Disquisitions*, in *Works*, III, 241.

[58] *Cf.* McEvoy and McGuire, *op. cit.*, 332, for a different view of Priestley's elation to Spinoza.

[59] James Hutton, *Dissertations on Different Subjects in Natural Philosophy* (Edinburgh, 1792), 669; hereafter Hutton, *Dissertations*.

[60] *Ibid.*, 292.   [61] *Ibid.*, 669.

[62] James Hutton, *An Investigation of the Principles of Knowledge, and of the Progress of Reason, from Sense to Science and Philosophy*, 3 vols. (Edinburgh, 1794), II, 393; hereafter Hutton, *Investigation*.

knowledge of passive, hard atoms—only gave us evidence of "resisting powers in bodies, by which their volume and figure are presented to us."[63] Thus "power, the cause of our sensation, is to be considered as a first cause."[64] Hutton considered that activity was an essential property of substances, asserting that "instead of considering matter as a thing inert, and only passive in its nature . . . we find it necessary to conceive power of action to exist in external things," and concluding that "matter [is] thus conceived as having power or efficacy."[65] Activity was immanent in matter, and in rejecting the Newtonian theory of passive matter he dismissed Newton's doctrine that the active powers of matter were maintained by God's will, the view that the activity of nature was to be ascribed "to God as the immediate cause."[66]

In discussing God's relation to nature, Hutton emphasized teleology and divine wisdom. In his opinion, "the proper purpose of philosophy is to see the general order that is established among the different species of events, by which the whole of nature, and the wisdom of the system, is to be perceived."[67] Final causes were "the proper object of our knowledge"[68] in pursuing the "science of physics," and only when final causes were discovered could "the law of nature [be] investigated." Laws of nature could be known only in relation to final causes, and the design of the universe was manifested in the lawlike structure of nature: "in every law of nature there is system or design . . . it is then that in the system of nature we perceive wisdom, in seeing the purpose of those laws of nature."[69] In comprehending final causes the natural philosopher understands divine wisdom.

Hutton thus supposed that matter was active, and in stressing divine omniscience he claimed that the laws of nature could not be abrogated by divine action; in his view "we must deny the possibility of anything happening preternaturally or contrary to the common course of things."[70] In rejecting divine intervention in natural phenomena Hutton echoed Leibniz's statement to Clarke that "when God works miracles, he does not do it in order to supply the wants of nature, but those of grace,"[71] arguing that although the abrogation of the natural order would impugn the wisdom and foresight of God, this did not exclude God's supernatural intervention in cases where, as Hutton put it, "truths . . . [were] not to be discovered by natural means."[72] Echoing Leibniz in stressing divine wisdom and foresight, Hutton affirmed that the "laws of nature . . . [were] the decrees of God" and demonstrated "the existence of a superintending Being, who has conceived every thing in wisdom."[73]

[63] Hutton, *Dissertations*, 290.   [64] Hutton, *Investigation*, II, 387

[65] *Ibid.*, 404. For an account of Hutton's theory of matter and natural philosophy, cf. Heimann and McGuire, *op. cit.*, 281-93..   [66] Hutton, *Investigation*, II, 415

[67] Hutton, *Dissertations*, 262.   [68] *Ibid.*, 624.   [69] *Ibid.*, 66

[70] Hutton, *Investigation*, II, 309.   [71] Alexander, *op. cit.*, 1

[72] Hutton, *Investigation*, II, 309n.   [73] *Ibid.*, II, 31

Hutton's theory of nature supposed a system of active powers whose self-sufficiency was not to be abrogated by divine intervention, but in regarding the active powers as immanent in nature he did not subsume God's agency under the laws of nature. Hutton pointed out that the term "nature" was figurative, corresponding to our structuring of experience, being a "creature of [our] fancy." The term "nature" applied to the "known part of the wise design, and powerful conduct of that infinite Being of whom we cannot form an adequate idea." Nature was "subordinate to God, who is the author of nature," and in formulating scientific explanations it was inappropriate to "ascribe this power of the universe to God, as the immediate cause." Because it was inappropriate for the natural philosopher to be "employing the term *God* in place of nature," the formulation of laws of "nature" could be regarded as "delegating the power of God, for the purposes that are perceived in natural things." Nevertheless, these statements were figurative, for God and divine power could not be regarded as being contained in or equivalent to "nature." Nature was "limited and changing" but God "is a Being which we cannot limit"; God is "infinite and unchangeable." Whereas "nature" is comprehended in terms of space and time it was absurd to suppose that "He who gave us the ideas of time and space can be limited by either of these," and Hutton dismissed the suggestion that "the author of nature was limited by natural things." God was transcendent over the order of nature, and "every existence is to be resolved . . . to that infinite Being and superintending mind."[74] The active powers immanent in the fabric of nature were thus grounded on divine agency.

The theories of the relationship between God and nature formulated by Priestley and Hutton attest to the shift in theological sensibility corresponding to the rejection of Newtonian principles in eighteenth-century British natural philosophy. In emphasizing divine omniscience rather than omnipotence, the foresight rather than the will of God, their ideas can be represented as a "religion of reason," but for these natural philosophers divine causality in nature was not to be subsumed under the concept of laws of nature.

University of Lancaster, England.

[74] *Ibid.*, II, 415-17.

Chapter XXVI

THEOLOGICAL VOLUNTARISM AND
BIOLOGICAL ANALOGIES
IN NEWTON'S PHYSICAL THOUGHT

By Henry Guerlac*

My title needs a word of explanation. We do not think first, if at all, of biology, anatomical knowledge, or vitalistic excursions when we hear the name of Sir Isaac Newton. Moreover, the word "biology" is of course an anachronism since it was coined long after Newton's time, but for simple convenience I shall use it. In any case, the scholarship of recent years—heavily indebted to the study of manuscript sources—has moved us well beyond the old image of Newton as the quintessential skeptical scientist, loath to "frame," that is to conjure up, hypotheses.

The articles of J. E. McGuire, focussing less on Newton's physics than on what he calls Newton's "natural Philosophy," a much-cited paper by David Kubrin, and the pioneer studies on Newton's alchemy by B. J. Dobbs, Karen Figala, and Richard Westfall have called our attention to less familiar traits of Newton's thought: the private and covert speculations to which there are cryptic allusions and tantalizing hints in his published writings.

Newton's greatest work, the *Principia* of 1687, that foundation of rational mechanics, offers hardly a hint of the speculative currents running deep beneath the cool, mathematical surface of that great book. There is but a single passage suggesting concern for living matter, and only a passing and ephemeral reference to divine guidance in nature until the appearance of the second edition of the *Principia* in 1713.[1]

But the *Opticks,* with which I shall be mainly concerned, is quite another matter. First published in 1704, long after his classic paper on light and color, and soon translated into Latin for Continental consumption, it was destined in the author's later years to appear in two later English editions, a second Latin translation, and two French

* Read at a conference on "Science, Myth, and Knowledge" of the Northeastern American Society for Eighteenth-Century Studies held at M.I.T. in October 198?

[1] The word "ephemeral" applies because Newton dropped this short passage from later editions. See I. Bernard Cohen, *Introduction to Newton's 'Principia'* (Cambridge, Mass., 1971), 154-156. Professor Cohen suggests that Newton eliminated it because it was out of place, or because it was singled out by Leibniz in his review of the *Principia* in the *Acta Eruditorum.* I think it just as likely that the addition in 1713 of the General Scholium, with its elaborate theological treatment, rendered the earlier passage superfluous.

editions. In this process it underwent successive modifications notably, but not exclusively, in the so-called Queries appended to the main
work. The Queries are deliberately set apart from the body of the text,
and are cast in the interrogative voice. They are frankly speculative,
but constitute nevertheless an avowal of Newton's underlying convictions or at least his serious conjectures. It is here, in the Queries, that
Newton "indulged bold and excentric thoughts," as Joseph Priestley
put it long after, revealing that "quick conception of distant analogies,
which is the great key to unlock the secrets of nature."[2] These are
sometimes stated clearly, more often they are cryptic and opaque
pronouncements. Such matters I shall touch upon later; but first, I
wish only to derive from the *Opticks* some notion of Newton's awareness and considerable knowledge of living nature.

Since the *Opticks* deals with light and color, we are not surprised
to find in it several passages relating to human vision. Here and there,
too, are references to color phenomena from the biological world: the
iridescence of a peacock's tail, color effects seen in the webs of
spiders, the changing colors of dying flowers or of autumn foliage.
Vision, of course, receives the closest attention. Newton wonders
how we see, suggesting early in the book (in Axiom VII, which means
he takes it as established) that images on the retina are "propagated
by Motion along the Fibres of the Optick Nerves into the Brain."[3]

In rough terms (by today's standards) Newton understood the
chief anatomical structures of the human eye and how they perform.
His knowledge was doubtless mainly derivative.[4] Ever since Kepler,
indeed earlier in a reference by the Swiss physician, Félix Platter
(1536-1614), scientists had recognized the crystalline humor (the lens)
as the chief focussing element of the eye, and the retina as the screen
on which the image appears, inverted as in the *camera obscura*.
Newton remarks that anatomists, after removing the tough outer coat,
what we call the *sclera*, have seen "the Pictures of Objects lively
painted" on the retina.[5] Like Descartes, whose *Dioptrique* (1637) was
a chief source for Newton's knowledge of physiological optics, he

[2] Joseph Priestley: *Experiments and Observations on Different Kinds of Air*
London, 1774), 249.
[3] *Opticks* (Dover Publications, New York, 1952) Ax. VII, 14-16. This paperback
is a photographic reprint of the edition published by G. Bell (London, 1931) based on
the probably fraudulent 4th edition of 1730. It is by no means a reliable text. I cite it
only because of its ready availability, hoping that a critical, annotated edition of the
Opticks may soon become available.
[4] Yet among Newton's manuscripts is a large drawing of a sheep's eye, accompanied by careful measurements which are surely by Newton. This was reproduced
by David Brewster in his *Memoirs of the Life, Writings, and Discoveries of Sir Isaac
Newton* (2 vols, London, 1855) I, 20-421.
[5] *Opticks*, 15. Newton refers to removing "that outward and most thick Coat
called the *Dura Mater*." This is clearly a mistake.

compares the functioning of the eye to this "vulgar experiment" of the *camera obscura*, made popular by the *Natural Magick* of G. B. Della Porta. He goes on, perhaps surprisingly, to describe the *optic chiasma*, where there is a 'decussation' or crossing over of the optic nerves, nerves from the right eye passing to the occipital lobe on the left side of the brain, and nerves from the left eye going to the right hemisphere. Newton suggests that this is probably a feature found only in higher animals with binocular vision.[6]

Newton's understandable concern for *color* vision took some interesting by-ways. He noted the apparent harmony and dissonance of different pairs of colors, as well as the persistence of color sensations. And he reports his discovery that the maximum sensitivity of the human eye is to the yellow-orange portion of the spectrum, a fact that psycho-physiologists and traffic experts have amply confirmed.

The Queries appended to the *Opticks*, phrased as questions, allowed Newton great freedom to raise possible solutions to problems and to suggest answers to be tested by later investigators. In one of the Queries of 1704 (others were added later), Newton, elaborating what he had announced in Axiom VII, suggests that the rays of light excite vibrations in the retina and that these "being propagated along the solid Fibres of the optick Nerves into the Brain, cause the Sense of seeing."[7] The very next Query, Query 13, asks whether the "several sorts of Rays make Vibrations of several bignesses, which according to their bignesses excite Sensations of several Colours, much after the manner that the Vibrations of the Air, according to their several bignesses excite Sensations of several Sounds?"[8] When later, for reasons I shall not explore here, Newton introduced into his *Opticks*, in 1717/18, the notion of a tenuous aether, he asks whether vision is performed, not (as he had suggested earlier) by vibrations in the solid substance of the nerve fibers but by the vibrations of this subtle medium passing along the nerves.[9] He takes matters a step further, and asks whether muscular contraction may not originate in "Vibrations of this Medium, excited in the Brain by the *power of the Will*, and propagated from thence through the solid, pellucid and uniform Capillamenta of the Nerves into the Muscles, for contracting and dilating them?"[10]

We may now inquire whether there was a deeper sense in which the world of living things helped shape Newton's philosophy of nature? Nature, which he described as "very conformable to herself,'

---

[6] *Opticks*, Query 15, 346-347. For Newton's theory of "semi-decussation," see Brewster, I, 226-229 and Appendix III. It was first set forth in MS. Add. 3975, fols 17-18. In the Portsmouth Papers of the University Library, Cambridge.
[7] *Opticks*, Query 12, p. 345.   [8] *Opticks*, Query 13, ibi
[9] *Opticks*, Query 23, p. 353. [10] *Opticks*, Query, 24, 353-354. The italics are min

is, despite her infinite variety, marked by an inner simplicity and fitness, clearly the result of Divine Wisdom. This applies not only to the order of the planetary scheme, but also, of course—as John Ray had shown in almost tiresome detail—to the world of living forms. So Newton, playing the natural theologian, argued, according to the rules of what was later called the argument from design and the text of the Book of Nature, that just as the wonderful uniformity of the solar system must be the result of choice, so must be too the often similar design in the bodies of higher animals—their bilateral symmetry, the homologous structures in vertebrates, and the artful contrivances of specialized organs. A somewhat surprising example of the latter in his list of the "artificial" parts of creatures is the swim bladder, the *vesica natandi*, an organ in bony fish that assists their vertical motion in water. First described by Guillaume Rondelet in the sixteenth century, mentioned by Henry More and also by John Ray in his *Wisdom of God manifested in the Works of Creation* (1691), the function of the swim bladder was first carefully analyzed by Giovanni Borelli in his posthumous *De motu animalium* (1680), where it is prefaced by an elegant account of Archimedes on floating bodies to make the functioning of this interesting structure clear. Newton had both books (John Ray's and Borelli's) in his library, so it is hard to say which was his source.[11]

Newton's was no static universe, and as we probe more deeply we note his interest in the *transformations* that are everywhere to be seen, above all in the world of living things. Such changes, he remarks, are "very conformable to the Course of Nature, which seems delighted with Transmutations." After giving examples of chemical and physical change, he writes:

Eggs grow from insensible Magnitudes, and change into Animals; Tadpoles into Frogs; and Worms into Flies,[12]

comments that suggest his awareness of the results obtained by Francesco Redi, Swammerdam, and Malpighi in their studies of animal generation and insect metamorphosis. The work of all these men was accessible to Newton from accounts in the Royal Society's *Philosophical Transactions* and from John Ray's *Wisdom of God*. But Newton continues:

All Birds, Beasts and Fishes, Insects, Trees, and other Vegetables, with their several Parts, grow out of Water and watry tinctures and Salts, and by Putrefaction return again into watry Substances.[13]

[11] John Harrison: *The Library of Isaac Newton* (Cambridge, 1978), No. 245, p. 106 and No. 1376, p. 224. Newton's copy of Ray's *Wisdom of God* was the second edition of 1692 "very much enlarged." A passing reference to the swim bladder occurs in Henry More's *Antidote against Atheisme* (1653), which Newton also had in his library.   [12] *Opticks*, Query 30, p. 375.   [13] *Ibid.*

There are surely echoes here of Van Helmont's willow tree experiment, and the similar attempts of Robert Boyle to prove that only water is required for the growth of plants. Earlier, in the *Principia*, Newton was even more specific, noting that

the seas are absolutely necessary to the constitution of our earth, that from them, the sun, by its heat, may exhale a sufficient quantity of vapors, which, being gathered together into clouds, may drop down in rain, for watering the earth and for the production and nourishment of vegetables . . . for all vegetables entirely derive their growths from fluids.[14]

Newton's preoccupation with transmutation found expression in a curious picture of a great cycle of change in which all aspects of nature take part. The key to his imagined transformation was Newton's belief, set forth even in the *Principia* of 1687, that the tails of comets consist of a very fine vapor which, continuously rarefied and dilated by the sun's heat, is scattered through the heavens where it is attracted towards the planets by their gravitational force, and mixed with their atmospheres. In this way the bulk of the earth is maintained or increased, and its fluids "if they are not supplied from without" in this manner "must be in a continual decrease, and quite fail at last."[15]

In mid-career, while immersed in his alchemical studies, Newton concluded that the processes of generation and growth, and the spectacle of so many diverse living forms, could not be explained (any more than the orderly motion of the planets) by purely mechanical agencies. From his tireless reading in the alchemical literature and his own alchemical experiments, he conceived of a process taking place on a level deeper than ordinary physical and chemical change, a process he called "vegetation." Despite its name, "vegetation" underlay changes in *all* three kingdoms of nature: the mineral as well as the animal or vegetable. Newton called its active agent the "vegetative spirit."[16] For a time he thought that an aether might play that role, but later he wrote that perhaps the aether merely served as the vehicle for "some more active spirit," and this he identified with the "body of light." He could never completely free himself from this alluring

[14] *Principia* (1687), 506. For the English, see *Sir Isaac Newton's Mathematical Principles of Natural Philosophy*. Trans. by Andrew Motte, ed. Florian Cajori (Berkeley, 1934), 529-30, to be cited as Motte-Cajori.

[15] *Principia* (1687), 506; Motte-Cajori, 530.

[16] "Of nature's obvious laws and processes in vegetation," Burndy MS 16, Smithsonian Institution, Washington, D.C. This manuscript was first described by B. J. T. Dobbs, who generously supplied me with a copy of her unpublished paper "Newton's Alchemy and His Theory of Matter." Ellen B. Wells, Rare Book Librarian, Smithsonian Institution Libraries, kindly sent me a xerox copy of this interesting manuscript.

notion, and there are traces of it in the early Queries in the *Opticks* of 1704. Nevertheless, although the "vegetative spirit" is never mentioned, this conception seems to have prepared his mind for his treatment of "active principles" as the cause of motion.

For a very special reason, the problem of the cause of motion deeply concerned Newton in his later years. Criticism of his doctrine of gravitational attraction, which Leibniz and the Cartesians described as an *occult quality*, was bad enough. But in 1704, the year that saw the publication of the *Opticks*, the radical deist, John Toland, brought out his *Letters to Serena*. In this slim book, Toland raised the ghostly demon that Newton, for many years, had hoped to exorcise.[17] This was the idea that matter, far from being absolutely inert, as Henry More and Newton too had insisted, was inherently active. Thus the gravitation of bodies resulted from an innate, or *essential*, quality of matter, the cause of motion. To make things worse, Toland appeared to link his doctrine with Newton, on whom he lavished fulsome praise. Yet all his professional life, at least, we can be sure, from the time of his famous exchanges with Richard Bentley, Newton was firm in his belief that to conceive of matter as having the capacity for motion as an essential, defining quality was a sure path to atheism since it implied a material universe totally self-sufficient, operating without the intercession of a Deity.[18]

Newton's disciple, Samuel Clarke, defended Newton from this imputation in his Boyle Lectures of 1705, specifically referring to Toland. And it was doubtless in reply to Toland that Newton added to the Latin edition of his *Opticks* in 1706 the flat statement that matter is inert and endowed only with a *vis inertiae*, a "passive principle" by which bodies remain at rest or in motion, but this "passive principle" cannot generate motion: "Some other Principle is necessary for putting Bodies into Motion" and for conserving this motion once it is produced.[19] Such "active principles" had for some time played a key role in Newton's imaginary universe. Since, he wrote in the *Opticks*, the "variety of Motion we find in the World is always decreasing,

---

[17] John Toland: *Letters to Serena* (London, 1704). See esp. Letter V. A modern facsimile, which I have not seen, was published in Stuttgart in 1964. For other aspects of Toland's life see Margaret C. Jacob, "Clandestine Culture in the Early Enlightenment," in Harry Woolf ed., *The Analytic Spirit* (Ithaca, N.Y., 1981), 122-45 and her *The Radical Enlightenment: Pantheists, Freemasons and Republicans* (London, 1981), *passim* and bibliography.

[18] See my *Newton et Epicure* (Paris, Palais de la Découverte, 1963), reprinted in my *Essays and Papers in the History of Modern Science* (Baltimore and London, 1977). The subject is treated from a different point of view by Ernan McMullin in his *Newton on Matter and Activity* (Notre Dame, Indiana, and London, 1978).

[19] For the Latin original see Newton's *Optice: sive de Reflexionibus, Refractionibus, Inflexionibus & Coloribus* (London, 1706, 340-41.

there is a necessity of conserving and recruiting it by active Principles," such as are the cause of gravity and cohesion; by which "Bodies acquire great Motions in falling;" and which are the cause of Fermentation, by which the "Heart and Blood of Animals are kept in perpetual Motion and Heat."[20] Indeed, he goes on, "we meet with very little Motion in the World, besides what is owing to these active Principles." An interesting modification appears in the Latin of 1706: "praeterquam quod vel ex his Principiis actuosis, *vel ex imperio Voluntatis*, manifesto oritur."[21] This we may give as it appears in the English version of Quaestio 23 where Newton wrote to be rendered into Latin: "besides what is visibly owing to these active principles and the power of the will." The "either . . . or" construction that we find in the Latin (vel . . . vel) is significantly not present. The reference to will (*voluntas*) is dropped from the second English edition of 1717 and the second Latin of 1719.

The subject of *active* and *passive* principles has been taken up with typical verve by my friend J. E. McGuire in several articles, notably (from my point of view) a paper of 1977 presented at a Clark Library Seminar at U.C.L.A.[22] He will not protest, I hope, if I use certain of his findings and expand on them somewhat.

The dualism between the *active principle,* responsible for motion and change, and the *passive principle* on which they act, goes back at least to Aristotle with his activating 'form' and passive 'matter.' Drawing upon the testimony of Seneca, Cicero, and Galen, Justus Lipsius describes the Stoics as building their scheme of nature on a similar duality. The Greek physicians, we know, divided the four qualities characterizing the 'humours' of the human body into two that are active (the hot and the cold) and two that are passive (the dry and the wet). Likewise the alchemists and some seventeenth-century chemists divided their five 'elements' into two classes: three active chemical principles ('spirit', oil, and salt) and two passive (water and earth). The doctrine is mentioned without enthusiasm in Robert Boyle's *Sceptical Chymist* (1661) and in Nicolas Lemery's immensely popular *Cours de Chymie,* a book that Newton knew well in the English translation of 1698. Among theologians and philosophers the doctrine was familiar to Henry More and Ralph Cudworth, the two Cambridge Platonists who influenced Newton, and to John Locke and John Ray as well.

---

[20] *Opticks,* Query 31, p. 399.

[21] *Optice* (1706), 343. My italics except for the word '*Voluntatis.*'

[22] J. E. McGuire, "Neoplatonism and Active Principles: Newton and the Corpus Hermeticum," in Robert S. Westman and J. E. McGuire, *Hermeticism and the Scientific Revolution* (Los Angeles, 1977), 95-133.

More and Cudworth, in what Mr. McGuire calls a "spiritualization of nature," sought to "restate the program of the mechanical philosophy." They both believed that God must operate on the physical universe through some inferior spiritual intelligences, beings that alone can produce motion and change in inert passive matter. More called his the *hylarchic spirit*—the matter-ruling spirit—while Cudworth speaks of *plastick natures* as the agents that execute the laws of nature. John Ray, in his *Wisdom of God*, gave wide circulation to Cudworth's doctrine and asserted that God, to effect the generation and growth of plants, indeed their whole "Oeconomy," invokes "the subordinate Ministry of some inferior Plastick Nature, as, in the Works of Providence, he doth of Angels."

Yet Ray points out that Robert Boyle in his *Christian Virtuoso* (1690) had no use for such entities mediating between God and the physical universe. For Boyle, God acts, as Newton believed to be the case, immediately and directly.

In the later editions Newton repeats what he believes these "active Principles" *do*, but he does not even hint at what they *are* or how these arise in the first place. They are not, he insists, *occult qualities*, but must be deemed "general Laws of Nature, by which the Things themselves are form'd; their Truth appearing to us by Phaenomena, though their Cause be not yet discover'd."[23] This, of course, is the familiar, quasi-positivistic stance Newton adopts in defending *the fact* of universal gravitation. Although he disclaims any knowledge of the cause of gravity, he can nevertheless describe in precise mathematical language *how* it operates.

There is little doubt Newton believed that God, directly or indirectly, was the cause of motion, as of everything else. There are certain passages that suggest that "active principles" are the agents or intermediaries of God's *will*, like More's hylarchical principles or Cudworth's "plastick natures." But this may have been a passing aberration.[24] It seems to be widely accepted that for Newton, God's action is direct. In a 1962 paper by Alexandre Koyré and I. Bernard Cohen, "Newton and the Leibniz-Clarke Correspondence," we read

[23] *Opticks*, p. 401.
[24] In the 1670s there are at least two instances. In his "Hypothesis explaining the Properties of Light" (1675) he wrote: "God, who gave animals self-motion beyond our understanding, is, without doubt, able to implant other principles of motion in bodies, which we may understand as little." Thomas Birch, *History of the Royal Society*, III, 255 and Newton, *Correspondence* I, 370. In the "De Aere et Aethere" which the Halls date between 1673 and 1675, we read that "God may have created a certain incorporeal nature which seeks to repel bodies and make them less packed together." Much later, Samuel Clarke, the voice of Newton in his exchange of letters with Leibniz, wrote: "In all void space, God is certainly present, and possibly many other substances which are not matter; being neither tangible, nor objects of our senses." H. G. Alexander, ed. *The Leibniz-Clarke Correspondence* (Manchester, 1956), 47.

". . . in the Newtonian metaphysics there was really no place for the 'hylarchical principle,' an entity mediating between God and the world. The Newtonian God did not need such a mediator: he acted himself."[25] There is a famous passage in the *Opticks* (Query 31) which first appeared in the Latin of 1706 where Newton, in suggesting that space is, or is like, God's sensorium, writes as if God's action is immediate and direct. "God, a powerful, ever-living Agent, who being in all places is more able by *his Will* to move bodies within his boundless uniform Sensorium, and thereby to form and reform the Parts of the Universe, than we *by our Will* to move the Parts of our own Bodies. . . . He is a uniform Being, void of . . . Members or Parts, and they [living forms and inert matter] are his Creatures subordinate to him, and *subservient to his will.* . . ."[26]

The theological roots of this stress on the divine Will are clear enough and of great age, though to trace them in detail would exceed my capacity.[27] But I need hardly remind you that in Christian theology, both Catholic and Protestant, God's perfection or his essence was understood to consist of three fundamental attributes: His *Wisdom,* His *Goodness,* and His *Power.*

Medieval theologians of the Latin West, for the most part, followed St. Thomas Aquinas who held what is called the *intellectualist* position in which the Wisdom and Goodness of God's essence are stressed at the expense of His Power. Later philosophers, notably Duns Scotus and William of Ockham, insisted that God's Will was subject to no such limitations. With the Reformation, this *voluntarist* position enjoyed great popularity among Protestant thinkers. In England and America the Calvinist Puritans especially exalted the Divine Will over God's other attributes.[28] Not all Protestant divines took this position, of course, and the voluntarism of Thomas Hobbes came under attack from the Cambridge Platonists, Henry More and Ralph Cudworth, who in other matters, as we know, exerted a strong influence on Newton. More, for example, wrote in his *Divine Dialogues* (1668) that rational goodness, rather than power, is the true basis of God's sovereignty.

Here again Newton parted company with these early influences upon him. In Newton's religious manuscripts housed in Jerusalem, and recently studied by Frank Manuel, we find a strongly expressed

---

[25] Alexandre Koyré and I. Bernard Cohen: "Newton and the Leibniz-Clark Correspondence," *Archives Internationales d'Histoire des Sciences,* **15** (1962), 58, note 57.

[26] *Opticks,* 403. The italics are mine.

[27] A useful introduction to voluntarism is Vernon J. Bourke's *Will in Western Thought: An Historico-Critical Survey* (New York, 1964).

[28] Perry Miller, *The New England Mind* (reissue, Cambridge, Mass., 1954), espec 101, 233-34. (First published in 1938.)

voluntarist view of the Divinity. In one manuscript Newton writes that God "required of us to be celebrated not so much for his essence as for his actions, the creating, preserving, and governing of all things according to his good will and pleasure." And again: "For the word God relates not to the metaphysical nature of God but to his *dominion*."[29] These and other passages anticipate the famous General Scholium with which Newton in 1713 concluded the second edition of his *Principia*. Here stress on Divine Will and God's dominion is a major theme. For those who have not read it recently, a few sentences can give the flavor of this extraordinary ending to Newton's masterpiece on rational mechanics: God "governs all things, not as the soul of the world, but as Lord over all; and on account of his dominion he is wont to be called Lord God *Pantokrator,* or *Universal Ruler;* for *God* is a relative word, and has a respect to servants." . . . "a being however perfect, without dominion, cannot be said to be Lord God . . . We know him only by his most wise and excellent contrivances of things . . . but we reverence and adore him as his servants; and a god without dominion, providence, and final causes, is nothing else than Fate and Nature. . . . All that diversity of natural things which we find suited to different times and places could arise from nothing but the ideas and *will* of a Being necessarily existing.[30]

As is well known, I trust, the most important use Newton makes of the concept of Divine Will in his science is when he calls upon God's direct action to explain that the solar system is touched up when it "wants a reformation." What has interested me most in this paper is that God's active will was understood by Newton through an analogy with human will and animal volition. This is why I devoted so much space to Newton's familiarity with biological matters; but clearly he does not know how the will, divine or animal, actually operates. This is explicit in Query 28 of the *Opticks* where he asks: "How do the Motions of the [living] Body follow from the Will?" Of course he can only guess, as he does in the puzzling last paragraph of the General Scholium. But he is fully aware of a power within himself which men call "will." Locke had already expressed similar views in the *Essay Concerning Human Understanding:*

Another idea we have of body, is the power of *communication of motion by impulse;* and of our souls, the power of *exciting motion by thought*. These ideas, the one of body, the other of our minds, every day's experience clearly furnishes us with.

And in words reminiscent of Newton's, he adds:

[29] Cited by Frank Manuel in his *The Religion of Isaac Newton* (Oxford, 1974), 1-22.
[30] Motte-Cajori (1934), 544-546. The italicized last word is my emphasis.

And if we consider the active power of moving . . . it is much clearer in spirit than body. . . . The mind every day affords us ideas of an active power of moving our bodies; and therefore it is worth our consideration, whether *active* power be not the proper attribute of spirits, and passive power of matter.[31]

Newton does not hesitate to include such a power, or "active principle" in his view of the universe. It is a non-mechanical agency, as he makes clear, that can only be understood by analogy with the world of living creatures. This is quite openly stated in manuscripts of the last of the Queries. In an English draft, written about 1705 for Samuel Clarke to render into Latin as Quaestio 23, Newton begins his list of active principles with "the power of life and will by which animals move their bodies with great and lasting force."[32] This, to be sure, is crossed out, and does not appear in print. In a still earlier English manuscript version, we catch a glimpse of how Newton's mind is working behind the scenes:

We find in ourselves a power of moving our bodies by our thought. Life and Will are active Principles by which we move our bodies, and thence arise other laws of motion unknown to us. And since the matter duly formed is attended by signs of life, and all things are with perfect art frames and wisdom, and nature does nothing in vain; if there be an universal life and all space be the sensorium of a thinking being, . . . [then] *the laws of motion arising from life or will* may be of universal extent.[33]

Newton's closest associates were quite aware of these ideas, that in all nature there operate forces that transcend the merely mechanical, but seem to resemble the mysterious volitional activity of men and animals, and derive from God. As Newton's disciple and translator, Samuel Clarke, expressing these ideas to Leibniz in their famous epistolary exchange, wrote in 1716

The means by which two bodies attract each other may be invisible and intangible, and of a different nature from mechanism; and yet, acting regularly and constantly, may well be called natural; being much less wonderful than animal motion, which yet is never called a miracle.[34]

Cornell University.

---

[31] *Essay Concerning Human Understanding*, Book II, Chap. 23, par. 28.
[32] University Library Cambridge, MS. Add. 3970, fols. 248-256.
[33] University Library Cambridge, MS. Add. 3970, fol. 619. My italics.
[34] *The Leibniz-Clarke Correspondence*, ed. Alexander, 53.

Chapter XXVII

VOLTAIRE VERSUS NEEDHAM: ATHEISM, MATERIALISM, AND THE GENERATION OF LIFE

By Shirley A. Roe

During the mid-eighteenth century, the relationship between biological theories and materialism became a source of increasing concern to a number of individuals, among them Voltaire. In the last fourteen years of his life, Voltaire (1694-1778) showed a keen interest in biological subjects, especially those having to do with the nature of generation. He supported the doctrine of preformation, the popular eighteenth-century view that all organisms had preexisted from the Creation; and he opposed several mid-century attempts, notably by Maupertuis, Needham, and Buffon, to challenge this theory. As in so many other areas of contemporary thought, Voltaire's critique served to crystallize many of the underlying concerns of Enlightenment biology.

Voltaire was not alone in using preformation to combat biological materialism. Charles Bonnet, Albrecht von Haller, and Lazzaro Spallanzani, preformation's major proponents in the 1760s and 1770s, were similarly concerned about the materialist and atheistic implications of epigenetic theories. The theory of preexistence of germs, or *emboîtement*, had first been proposed, in the late seventeenth century, within an explicit religious and mechanistic context.[1] The belief that the clockwork universe had been created by an intelligent and all-powerful God demanded that God's involvement in the creation of living creatures play a fundamental role in explanations of their generation. For there was always a danger in the mechanist world view that God as Creator might be a superfluous entity and that matter and motion might themselves be responsible for all of the phenomena of the universe, including the creation of life and the existence of the human soul. Preformation undercut these dangers by making both God and mechanical laws essential to the explanation of generation. On the theory of preexistence, all organisms had been formed at the Creation and encased within one another, but their development from miniature to full-fledged organisms occurred through mechanical means during each instance of reproduction.

In the 1740s, three epigenetic theories of generation arose to challenge the dominance of preformation. The first appeared in Maupertuis's *Dissertation physique à l'occasion du nègre blanc* in 1744, followed by the

---

[1] On eighteenth-century theories of generation, see Jacques Roger, *Les Sciences de la vie dans la pensée française du XVIIIe siècle: La génération des animaux de Descartes à l'Encyclopédie* (Paris, 1963, 1971); and Shirley A. Roe, *Matter, Life, and Generation: Eighteenth-Century Embryology and the Haller-Wolff Debate* (Cambridge, 1981), Chap. 1.

theories of Needham and Buffon, presented in 1748 and 1749.[2] Maupertuis argued that the embryo is formed through the agency of an attractive force acting on particles that issue from all parts of the body and that possess a kind of instinct for their eventual organization. Buffon's theory, similar in several respects to Maupertuis's, added to the idea that representative particles come from all parts of the body the concept of an "internal mold" that organizes the particles into a new organism. Finally, Needham argued in a more general manner for the existence of a vegetative force that operates at all levels of nature to produce generation.

In this paper, I examine Voltaire's biological views within the context of his opposition to atheism and materialism. As with many aspects of Voltaire's thought, his own opinions were expressed principally in his critiques of the views of others. He was adamantly opposed to the theories of Maupertuis, Buffon, and Needham, and all three suffered the sting of his witticisms and ridicule. Needham's work in particular raised Voltaire's ire, for Needham became a symbol of all that Voltaire opposed in the new biological theories of the mid-eighteenth century. A controversy ensued between the two of them, arising originally over the subject of miracles and lasting for over a decade. Yet although Needham figures frequently in Voltaire's writings in the 1760s and 1770s, few historians have fully investigated this episode in Voltaire's career.[3] My purpose, therefore, is threefold: to dispel some erroneous conceptions about Needham's work that have arisen in the Voltaire literature, to examine the events of the Needham-Voltaire clash, and to elucidate the motivations underlying each of their attitudes toward biological subjects.

Needham's Biological Views.—In 1745, John Turberville Needham (1713-81) published his first major work, *An Account of some New Microscopical Discoveries,* which contained observations made with the microscope on a number of organisms, among them tiny eels found in the grains of blighted wheat.[4] Needham found that the grains affected with

[2] Maupertuis's *Dissertation* was republished the following year as the first part of the *Vénus physique* (Leiden, 1745). John Turberville Needham, "A Summary of some late Observations upon the Generation, Composition, and Decomposition of Animal and Vegetable Substances," *Philosophical Transactions,* **45** (1748), 615-66; Georges Louis Leclerc, comte de Buffon, *Histoire Naturelle, générale et particulière,* II (Paris, 1749).

[3] On Voltaire's biological views, including his controversy with Needham, see Roger, *op. cit., Les Sciences,* 732-48; Jean A. Perkins, "Voltaire and the Natural Sciences," *Studies on Voltaire and the Eighteenth Century,* **37** (1965), 61-76; and Jacques Marx, "Voltaire et les sciences," *Episteme,* **9** (1975), 270-84.

[4] Chap. 8, 85-89. Needham's discovery of eels *(nematode larvae)* in blighted wheat was first briefly reported in "A Letter from Mr. Turbevil Needham, to the President; concerning certain chalky tubulous Concretions, called Malm: With some Microscopical Observations on the Farina of the Red Lily, and of Worms discovered in Smutty Corn," *Phil. Trans.,* **42** (1743), 634-41. On Needham's scientific and philosophical beliefs, see Roger, *Les Sciences,* 494-520; and Shirley A. Roe, "John Turberville Needham and the Generation of Living Organisms," *Isis,* **74** (1983), 159-84.

this malady contained whitish fibers that, to his surprise, exhibited signs of life when put into water. Furthermore, he reported that the same phenomenon had occurred two years later on grains from the same original lot. Needham did not propose any explanation for the origins of these unusual animals at this time, suggesting only that humid conditions in the ground or in grain storage might cause the onset of blight.

Needham also observed microscopic eels in paste made of flour and water. Some of these observations were made jointly with James Sherwood, who reported in a paper published in 1746 that he and Needham had discovered, partly by accident, that these eels contained offspring inside them, and thus reproduced viviparously.[5] Again, no explanation of their origin in flour was suggested, only that being viviparous, they could not arise from eggs deposited from the air.

Needham's first major statement of his views on the generation of living organisms was presented to the Royal Society in 1748 and published in the *Philosophical Transactions*. Two years later a greatly expanded French version of this paper appeared as *Nouvelles observations microscopiques*.[6] Here Needham proposed a theory of universal vegetation based on observations he had made, partly with Buffon, on microscopic bodies produced in organic infusions. Needham and Buffon had joined forces in the spring of 1748 to investigate Buffon's hypothesis that all microorganisms, spermatozoa included, are the product of random combinations of organic particles. Many of their infusions were made of seeds and grains, in which they observed, after a few days, a prodigious number of moving microscopic beings. Needham's most well-known infusion was made with mutton broth, which he sealed and heated to exclude contamination from the air and to kill any existing organisms in the broth. Even in this infusion, he reported, microorganisms could be observed after only a few days.[7]

Needham postulated that there exists a universal vegetative force responsible for the generation of living organisms from the lowest to the highest levels. Rejecting the theory of preexistent germs, Needham proposed instead an epigenetic account of generation. He claimed that vegetation operates through two component agents, an expansive force and a force of resistance that together govern the decomposition and composition of living organisms. When living material is infused or when it decomposes after death, it attains a state of exaltation, in which the expansive force acts to produce a succession of microorganisms. With

---

[5] James Sherwood, "A Letter from Mr. James Sherwood, Surgeon, to Martin Folkes, Esq.; President of the Royal Society, concerning the minute Eels in Paste being viviparous," *Phil. Trans.*, **44** (1746), 67-69.

[6] The *Nouvelles observations microscopiques, avec des découvertes intéressantes sur la composition & la décomposition des corps organisés* (Paris, 1750), contained also a French translation of Needham's *New Microscopical Discoveries*. This had been published separately as *Nouvelles découvertes faites avec le microscope* (Leiden, 1747).

[7] "A Summary," 634-39.

these same forces, Needham maintained, one could account for the formation of the embryo in higher organisms.

Needham now explained the origin of eels in blighted wheat on the basis of vegetation as well. A humid atmosphere, he argued, produced a vegetation of the contents of the grains into a state of exaltation, resulting in the formation of fibers that then exhibited characteristics of life. Needham suggested that one could account in a similar manner for the origins of paste eels from the vegetation of flour and water, even though these eels could later produce other eels viviparously. He did however admit that he was not completely satisfied with his account of their generation.[8]

Needham argued that his theory of universal vegetation was not a theory of equivocal generation, that is, of generation through chance events, but rather one that proposed a regular, lawlike process that always resulted in the proper organism. At higher levels, an offspring similar to the parent was produced. And in the microscopic world, he claimed, one always observed the same succession of microorganisms in infusions made of the same material. All generation, he concluded, occurs through laws that had been established at the Creation by God. Therefore, in no way could one interpret his theory as one based on equivocal, or chance, causes.

Needham was also concerned to defend his theory against the charge of materialism. If one was called a materialist in the eighteenth century, it generally meant two things: the denial of the separate, incorporeal, and eternal existence of the human soul; and second, the attribution of creative powers to matter. Furthermore, materialism also often included the idea that the universe had arisen by chance through material causation. All of these components added up to materialism's most disturbing aspect— a denial of the existence of God and any divine role in the creation and preservation of the world.

Needham continually argued that his theory had nothing in common with materialism, although, as we shall see, his biological views were used by materialists in ways he did not approve. Needham maintained that his theory of generation did not challenge the existence of the human soul, for he believed that animals possess a sensitive principle and humans an intellectual soul, neither of which arise through the process of vegetation. In his later works, Needham defined a new class of organisms, "vital beings," to denote microscopic organisms that multiply by dividing distinct from true sensitive animals that reproduce through normal means.[9] He also argued against the materialists that God played just as central a role in his theory as in the theory of preexistence. What difference

---

[8] *Ibid.,* 647-48, 659.

[9] Lazzaro Spallanzani, *Nouvelles recherches sur les découvertes microscopiques, et la génération des corps organisés,* trans. abbé Regley, with notes by John Turberville Needham (London & Paris, 1769), 150.

did it make, Needham asked, if God made all organisms at the beginning of the world or if, instead, he simply established the laws through which future generation would take place?

Needham's theory of generation met with little positive reaction among his preformationist contemporaries. Spallanzani published a refutation of his observations in 1765, followed by an even more thorough disproof in 1776.[10] Bonnet and Haller rejected in particular Needham's concept of a vegetative force, for neither could accept the idea that a force could be capable of forming life on its own.[11] And although they both accepted Needham's defense of his theory against equivocal generation and materialism, they were clearly worried about the implications of any epigenetic theory for the existence of God. This concern was reflected and amplified by Voltaire, whose opposition to Needham's work stemmed almost entirely from what he perceived as its materialist and atheistic overtones. But before I discuss the particulars of the Voltaire-Needham exchange, I turn to Voltaire's own scientific and religious beliefs.

Voltaire's Newtonian Deism.—From the 1730s Voltaire was a confirmed Newtonian. His *Lettres philosophiques (Letters Concerning the English Nation),* published first in 1733, contained his famous comparison of Cartesian Paris and Newtonian London, of a world that is full with one that is empty, moved by impulsion in Paris and by gravity in London. Only a year before these letters were published, Voltaire had written to Maupertuis, perhaps the earliest proponent of Newtonianism in France, "Here I am a Newtonian of your kind; . . . The more I glimpse of this philosophy, the more I admire it. One finds at each step that the whole universe is arranged by mathematical laws that are eternal and necessary."[12] During these years Voltaire also composed his best known scientific work, *Eléments de la philosophie de Newton,* published in its complete form in 1741.

The three principal conceptions that Voltaire adopted from the New-

---

[10] Spallanzani, *Saggio di osservazioni microscopiche concernenti il sistema della generazione dei signori di Needham e Buffon* in *Dissertazioni due* (Modena, 1765), and *Opuscoli di fisica animale e vegetabile* (Modena, 1776).

[11] Charles Bonnet, *Considérations sur les corps organisés* (Amsterdam, 1762) in *Oeuvres d'histoire naturelle et de philosophie,* 18 vols. (Neuchatel, 1779-83), VI, 299-300; Albrecht von Haller, *Elementa physiologiae corporis humani,* 8 vols. (Lausanne/Berne, 1757-66), VIII, pt. 1, 112.

[12] Voltaire, *Correspondence and Related Documents,* definitive edition by Theodore Besterman, vols. 85-135 of *Les Oeuvres complètes de Voltaire* (Geneva and Oxford, 1968-), D534, 3 November 1732. Hereafter Best. D. On Voltaire's Newtonianism and scientific beliefs, see Margaret Sherwood Libby, *The Attitude of Voltaire to Magic and the Sciences* (New York, 1935); Ira Wade, *Studies on Voltaire* (Princeton, 1947); Colm Kiernan, *The Enlightenment and Science in Eighteenth-Century France, Stud. Volt.,* **59a** (1973); and Martin S. Staum, "Newton and Voltaire: Constructive Sceptics," *Stud. Volt.,* 2 (1968), 29-56. See also note 3 above.

tonian world view were the uniformity and constancy of physical law, the passivity of matter, and the existence of an intelligent and free designer of the universe. Voltaire's deistic belief that the order and harmony of the universe testified to the existence of an intelligent cause, that a watch demanded a watchmaker, as he put it, pervaded his scientific writings until his death. He opposed Cartesian and Leibnizian conceptions of matter, arguing that matter is helpless on its own, and that motion and other active principles are given to it by God. Furthermore, he adopted Newtonian voluntarism in claiming that the world is a product of divine will rather than necessity. Finally, Voltaire ascribed to scientific skepticism, that is, he believed that human beings could understand the operations of the universe to only a limited extent: "We will know the first causes [of things] when we are gods," he wrote. "It is given to us to calculate, to weigh, to measure, to observe: this is natural philosophy; almost all the rest is chimera."[13]

Although during these early years Voltaire published no works devoted exclusively to biological topics, a section of his *Métaphysique de Newton,* written in 1740, clearly indicated the direction his future attitudes toward biology would take. Arguing against the Cartesian notion that at its basic level matter is uniform in nature, Voltaire asked how such matter could produce the diversity we observe in the world; specifically, how could living organisms, uniform within species yet so diverse from one another, be the result of matter and motion:

Now if no movement, no art has ever been able to produce fish instead of wheat in a field, nor medlars instead of a lamb in the womb of a sheep, nor roses at the top of an oak, nor sole in a beehive, etc.; if all species are invariably the same, should I not believe first, with some reason, that all species have been determined by the Master of the world; that there are as many different designs as there are different species, and that from matter and motion only eternal chaos could be born without these designs?

All experience confirms me in this belief. If I examine on the one hand a man or a silkworm, and on the other a bird or a fish, I see them all formed from the beginning of things; I see in them only a development.[14]

This is Voltaire's first indication of his acceptance of the theory of preformation. His belief in the preexistence of originally created germs coupled with his rejection of the formative powers of matter, became a central tenet of his biological views.

Voltaire's scientific interests in the 1730s and early 1740s were confined principally to physics. Although he published two papers in the

---

[13] Voltaire, *Oeuvres complètes,* ed. Louis Moland, 52 vols. (Paris, 1877-85), XVIII, 56. Hereafter M.

[14] M. XXII, 429. See also Roger, *Les Sciences,* 736. The *Métaphysique de Newton ou, parallèle des sentimens de Newton et de Leibniz* (Amsterdam, 1740) was incorporated into the 1741 edition of the *Eléments de la philosophie de Newton* (London [Paris]).

mid-1740s on the albino Negro and on geological subjects,[15] his preoccupation with topics in the life sciences really did not begin until 1764. Yet for the remaining fourteen years of his life, biological subjects, particularly the nature of generation, figured widely in his writings. His support for preformation, his opposition to, and ridicule of, the theories of generation proposed by Maupertuis, Buffon, and Needham, and his belief in the manifest design of the living world found expression in a variety of his publications.

Voltaire first indicated his familiarity with Maupertuis's views on generation in 1752, when he published a review of Maupertuis's *Oeuvres,* containing the *Vénus physique.*[16] Yet although he was critical of Maupertuis's theory, it was not until after the mid-1760s that Maupertuis's views on generation began to be ridiculed on a regular basis by Voltaire. In 1764 Voltaire published a review of Bonnet's *Considérations sur les corps organisés,* a strongly preformationist work that had appeared in 1762.[17] Voltaire's review endorsed preexistence and criticized Maupertuis's and Buffon's views on generation, although Voltaire had probably not yet read Buffon directly, relying rather on Bonnet's account of Buffon's theory.[18] In *Des singularités de la nature,* published in 1768, Voltaire reiterated his belief in preformation: ". . . It is today demonstrated to the eyes and to reason that there is neither vegetable nor animal that does not have a germ. One finds it in the egg of a chicken as in the acorn of an oak. A formative power presides at all these developments from one end of the universe to the other."[19]

After 1764, Voltaire became increasingly concerned over materialism and atheism, and the scientific, especially biological, grounds upon which these heretical positions might be based. Moreover, he began to see in preformation a defense against these dangerous biological positions. As he remarked in the article "Athée, Athéisme" of the *Dictionnaire philosophique* (1764), "there are fewer atheists today than ever, since philosophers have recognized that there is no vegetating being without a germ, no germ without design, etc., and that wheat does not come from corruption."[20] His subsequent attacks on Needham stemmed not so much

---

[15] "Relation touchant un maure blanc amené d'Afrique à Paris en 1744" (1744), M. XXIII, 189-91; "Dissertation sur les changements arrivés dans notre globe et sur les pétrifications qu'on prétend en être encore les témoignages" (1746), M. XXIII, 219-30.

[16] *Bibliothèque raisonnée* (juillet, août, septembre, 1752), M. XXIII, 535-43. Voltaire owned only a 1751 edition of the *Vénus physique.* See *Biblioteka Vol'tera: Katalog knig; Bibliothèque de Voltaire: Catalogue des livres* (Moscow & Leningrad, 1961), 604.

[17] *Gazette littéraire de l'Europe* (4 April 1764), M. XXV, 153-58.

[18] See Voltaire's marginal markings in his copy of Bonnet's *Considérations* in *Corpus des notes marginales de Voltaire* (Berlin, 1979), I, 393-94. Although Voltaire marked the preceding and succeeding chapters, he made no marks in Bonnet's chapter on Needham. On Voltaire's first reading of Buffon see note 38 below.

[19] M. XXVII, 161.

[20] M. XVII, 476.

from the particulars of Needham's work, which Voltaire never fully understood, as from what Needham's views symbolized for Voltaire. Voltaire's entire scientific world view was called into play in his defense of a preordained, ordered universe against what he saw as the chaos of materialism. And it was through Voltaire's critiques of Needham's work that this defense was most explicitly voiced.

The Clash.—Voltaire first learned of Needham's work from Maupertuis's *Lettres,* published in 1752. In Letter XVII, which was devoted to the subject of generation, Maupertuis referred to Needham's observations on calamary, a type of squid, then continuing,

But there are even greater marvels! In diluted flour one immediately finds eels large enough to be seen by simple sight: these eels are full of other small eels to which they give birth. One sees the grains of *blighted* wheat separate in water into filaments, each of which immediately becomes animated, and looks to the eye like a small fish; which when allowed to dry and to be without life for entire years, is always ready to be revived when one returns it to its element. Where does this leave us? Does not all of this plunge the mystery of generation back into an obscurity even more profound than that from which we had wanted to draw it? [21]

Maupertuis did not mention Needham's observations on infusions, nor did he amplify these remarks concerning Needham's work on the eels of flour paste and blighted wheat.

As I mentioned, Voltaire reviewed an edition of Maupertuis's works in 1752. Here Voltaire briefly criticized Maupertuis's *Vénus physique,* which he characterized as "*Vénus* trop peu *physique* et trop indécente," citing in particular Maupertuis's use of attraction and instinct in explaining the formation of the embryo. During 1752 and 1753 Voltaire also wrote several pamphlets in which he satirized Maupertuis and several aspects of his work. Prompted by Maupertuis's priority dispute with Koenig over the law of least action, Voltaire's pamphlets included a humorously written examination of Maupertuis's *Lettres* by an Inquisitor from Rome. "We will pass over several things that would fatigue the patience of the reader and the intelligence of M. the inquisitor;" Voltaire wrote, "but we believe that he would be very surprised to learn that the young student [Maupertuis] ... causes eels *pregnant* with other eels to be born from diluted flour, and fish from grains of wheat." In a "*séance mémorable,*" a parody of the Berlin Academy of Sciences, of which Maupertuis was president from 1746 to 1756, Voltaire had the "*galant*"

[21] Pierre Louis Moreau de Maupertuis, *Oeuvres* (Lyon, 1756), II, 281 (Letter XIV in this edition). Maupertuis cited Needham's *Nouvelles observations microscopiques* and Buffon's report of Needham's observations in his *Histoire naturelle,* II, chap. 9. For translation of Maupertuis's letter on generation, see Michael H. Hoffheimer, "Maupertuis and the Eighteenth-Century Critique of Preexistence," *Journal of the History of Biology* 15 (1982), 119-44.

president serve the ladies present "a superb dish composed of pâté of eels all one within the other and born suddenly from a mixture of diluted flour" as well as "great platters of fish that were formed immediately from grains of germinated wheat." [22]

In 1753, Voltaire was not particularly worried by Needham's observations. They simply served as further grist for the mill in his attack on Maupertuis, providing yet another belief of Maupertuis's to be ridiculed. Voltaire's real clash with Needham began in the mid-1760s and continued in one form or another until Voltaire's death in 1778. Within the Needham-Voltaire controversy we can discern three fairly distinct periods comprising, first, the debate over miracles of 1765; second, the rash of works dealing with science published by Voltaire in 1767 and 1768; and, finally, Voltaire's efforts to refute d'Holbach's *Système de la nature,* which appeared in 1770.

The Question of Miracles.—In 1765, while traveling as a schoolmaster, Needham spent several months in Geneva. There he encountered some anonymously published pamphlets on the subject of miracles, written by Voltaire in reply to Claparède's *Considérations sur les miracles,* which had appeared earlier in the year. Claparède's book was itself a reply to Rousseau's *Lettres écrites de la montagne* of 1764. The theme of all these works was whether or not miracles could occur and what role they had played and should play in the promotion of religious belief.

Voltaire, who was residing at Ferney (near Geneva), wrote the first of his letters on miracles in July 1765. By the end of the year these had grown to twenty.[23] Many themes are present in these pamphlets, including Voltaire's familiar attacks on church dogmas, here directed at the Calvinists, and on the massacres and martyrdoms of organized religion, as well as a critical assessment of Genevan politics. I concentrate here on those aspects of these pamphlets that shed light on Voltaire's attitude toward Needham.

After the first three of Voltaire's letters had appeared, Needham began to write his own replies in the form of three anonymous pamphlets.[24]

[22] M. XXIII, 568, 573. On the Voltaire-Maupertuis controversy, see "L'*Akakia* de Voltaire," ed. Charles Fleischauer, *Stud. Volt.,* **30** (1964), 7-145; and the Introduction to Voltaire, *Histoire du docteur Akakia et du natif de St-Malo,* ed. Jacques Tuffet (Paris, 1967).
[23] On the dating of these pamphlets, see the editorial comments in M. XXV, 357-58; and Georges Bengesco, *Voltaire: bibliographie de ses oeuvres* (Paris, 1882-90), II, 153-59.
[24] Needham's pamphlets were titled *Réponse d'un théologien au docte proposant des autres questions, Parodie de la troisième lettre du proposant addressée à un philosophe,* and *Projet de notes instructives, véridiques, théologiques, historiques & critiques sur certaines brochures polémiques du tem[p]s, adressées aux dignes éditeurs des doctes ouvrages du proposant.* Needham's *Réponse* and *Parodie* were written in August 1765, and the *Projet* probably in November 1765. Needham also published a second edition of the *Parodie* in February 1766. For a more detailed discussion of these pamphlets, see Renato G. Mazzolini and Shirley A. Roe, eds., *Science against the Unbelievers: The Correspondence of*

The first of these, intended to answer Voltaire's second letter, discussed the question of whether miracles are reasonable from a scientific point of view, an issue that had been raised in Rousseau's *Lettres écrites de la montagne*. Voltaire had argued that it seemed ridiculous that God would violate the laws of nature and the eternal plain of the universe only for a particular reason. Why, for example, would He have made the sun and moon stand still in the heavens for several hours so that Joshua could massacre the Amorites if the result would have been a major disturbance of the planetary system? The only conceivable reason, Voltaire remarked, was "so that on this small pile of mud called earth, the Popes might finally seize Rome, the benedictines might become too rich, Anne Dubourg might be hanged in Paris and Servetus burned alive in Geneva." [25] Needham, who was a Catholic priest, replied that miracles are only local exceptions, that God does not need to disturb the general system, and that miracles have served to establish morality among mankind. Miracles, Needham maintained, are "very intelligible and very believable for the loyal Christian who, knowing the voice of God, relies on his power, his wisdom, and his veracity." [26]

Although Voltaire devoted his fourth letter to answering Needham's first pamphlet, he did not yet know that Needham had been its author. He soon learned, however; and in his fifth letter, Voltaire began a series of personal attacks on Needham that were to run through the remaining fifteen letters he wrote. What piqued Voltaire's ire even more than Needham's specific arguments on miracles was that Needham had alluded directly to Voltaire, even mentioning his name, in his pamphlet.[27] Yet it was Needham's biological views that Voltaire found most worrisome. As he remarked in his fifth letter, "You had made a small reputation for yourself among atheists by having made eels from flour, and from that you have concluded that if flour produces eels, all animals, starting with

---

Charles Bonnet and John Turberville Needham, 1760-1780, Introduction, sect. 5, *Stud. Volt.* (forthcoming). See also Graham Gargett, *Voltaire and Protestantism, Stud. Volt.* **188** (1980), 226-28. Voltaire anonymously published annotated versions of Needham' pamphlets, along with his own twenty letters, as *Collection des lettres sur les miracles écrites à Genève et à Neufchâtel par Mr. le proposant Théro, Monsieur Covelle, Monsieur Néedham, Mr. Beaudinet & Mr. de Montmolin, &c.* (Neufchâtel, 1765 and 1767). Needham published an edition of his own pamphlets (with some additions), including extract from four of Voltaire's pamphlets, as *Questions sur les miracles, à Mr. Claparède, Professeur de Théologie à Genève, par un proposant: ou extrait de diverses lettres de M. de Voltaire, avec des réponses par M. Néedham* (London/Paris, 1769). Spelling modernized
[25] M. XXV, 373.
[26] *Réponse*, 14; *Questions sur les miracles*, 45.
[27] Neither of Needham's references to Voltaire (*Réponse*, 6, 9; *Questions sur les miracles*, 37, 39-40) stated *directly* that Voltaire was the proposant. The impropriety of Needham's allusions, however, was noted in November 1765 in the *Correspondance littéraire* (Paris, 1877-83), VI, 408.

man, could have been born in approximately the same manner." [28] In the *Avertissement* that Voltaire added to this pamphlet in his *Collection,* he made his concern over the implications of Needham's biological work even more explicit. Falsely characterizing Needham as an Irish Jesuit [29] who was disguised in secular clothing and who roamed the countryside spreading papist dogma, Voltaire remarked, "What was even more astonishing is that this disguised priest was the same one who, several years earlier, meddled with experiments on insects and who believed he had discovered with his microscope that the flour of blighted wheat, diluted in water, at once changed into small animals resembling eels. The fact was false, as an Italian savant has demonstrated. . . ." Voltaire here referred to Spallanzani's experimental refutation of Needham's work, which had just been published. But, Voltaire continued, Needham's claim "was false for another even more superior reason, namely, that the fact is impossible. If animals are born without germs, there would no longer be a cause of generation: a man could be born from a lump of earth just as well as an eel from a piece of paste. This ridiculous system would moreover obviously lead to atheism. Indeed it happened that several philosophers, believing in the experiment of Needham without having seen it, claimed that matter could organize itself; and the microscope of Needham came to be seen as the laboratory of atheists." [30]

Needham now became the butt of Voltaire's satire throughout the remaining pamphlets. Dubbing Needham "l'Anguillard," the eelmonger, calling him a "slanderous jesuit" and an Irish papist who made dangerous miracles, Voltaire charged that Needham even confused his own name with that of Jesus Christ: "If one says that Jesus Christ changed water into wine, immediately Needham thinks of his flour that he has changed into eels. . . ." [31] And in Voltaire's final pamphlet, Needham was subjected to a mock trial in Neufchâtel and sentenced to be stoned outside the city walls.

Many other themes emerge from the Needham-Voltaire exchange over miracles, but the most significant thing about this controversy with regard to Voltaire's biological views is that these letters provide us with the first evidence that Voltaire had identified Needham's work with theism. This was to be the underlying theme of all of Voltaire's sub-

---

[28] M. XXV, 394.

[29] Needham was in fact neither Irish nor a Jesuit. He was born in London, educated under the secular clergy at the English College at Douai, and ordained a Catholic priest in 1738. For Needham's biography, see the abbé Mann's eulogy in *Mémoires de l'Académie impériale et Royale des Sciences et Belles-Lettres de Bruxelles,* **4** (1783), xxxiii-xli. See also *Biographie nationale, publiée par l'Académie Royale des Sciences, des Lettres et des Beaux-Arts de Belgique,* XV, 520-28; and the *Dictionary of National Biography,* XIV, 57-59.

[30] M. XXV, 393-94.

[31] *Ibid.,* 395.

sequent attacks on Needham. Voltaire's erroneous description of Needham as an Irish Jesuit, when Needham was in fact English and a secular priest, was not a simple error on Voltaire's part; it was rather his way of heightening both his ridicule for organized Catholicism and his growing unease over the implications of Needham's views.

What had changed with regard to Voltaire's knowledge of Needham's work in the years between 1753 and 1765? It is clear from Voltaire's remarks on Needham's observations in the pamphlets on miracles that he had not yet read Needham's scientific works directly and was still relying on the comments on Needham's observations that Maupertuis had included in his *Lettres.*[32] These Voltaire slightly distorted, erroneously conflating Needham's observations on flour paste and on blighted wheat into observations on the flour of blighted wheat. What clearly had changed, however, was Voltaire's connection of certain kinds of biological views with atheism. As he succinctly expressed this during the miracles dispute, "he who writes that animals grow without germs, writes against God."[33] Pommeau, in his book on Voltaire's religion, has claimed that it was a visit that Damilaville paid to Voltaire that prompted Voltaire's worries over the rise of atheism and materialism.[34] Damilaville had apparently presented pro-atheism arguments to Voltaire, partly under the exhortation of Diderot,[35] and had explained Diderot's growing belief in biological materialism. Damilaville was in Geneva from July to September of 1765, overlapping Needham's visit and the publication of most of Voltaire's and Needham's pamphlets on miracles, so that it is likely that he and Voltaire discussed Needham's observations.[36] It was quite probably from these conversations that Voltaire began to connect Needham's work with atheism.

After the letters on miracles, Voltaire was to repeat the same line of argument against Needham in a number of subsequent works. If eels can form from flour, could not man originate from matter as well, and consequently, is there any need for a creative God? Voltaire did not fully understand Needham's observations, but he had no doubts about why he opposed them. Writing a congratulatory letter to Spallanzani after receiving his refutation of Needham's work, Voltaire stated, "You are most right to combat the alleged experiments of Mr. Needham. He wa

---

[32] In addition to Needham's pamphlets on miracles, Voltaire owned, but did not annotate, the volume of the *Philosophical Transactions* in which Needham's paper had appeared in 1748 and the *Nouvelles recherches* of 1769. See *Biblioteka Vol'tera,* 648-49, 689.

[33] M. XXV, 403 n.2.

[34] René Pomeau, *La Religion de Voltaire,* rev. ed. (Paris, 1969), 393-94.

[35] See Diderot's letter to Damilaville, sent to him at Ferney on 12 September 1765. Diderot, *Correspondance,* ed. Georges Roth, 16 vols. (Paris, 1955-70), V, 117-21.

[36] See Voltaire's letter to Damilaville of 13 November [1765], Besterman, D1297, where Needham's work on eels is mentioned.

attacked not long ago in Geneva on miracles. He could boast indeed of having made miracles if he had been able to produce eels without germs. One must be wary of all these dangerous experiments that contradict the laws of nature." [37]

Voltaire's Publications of 1767-1768. —After the miracles episode, two events rekindled Voltaire's attacks on Needham—his reading of Buffon's *Histoire naturelle* in 1767 and of an anonymous translation of Lucretius's *De rerum natura* in 1768. Both works brought once again to his attention some of the more dangerous tendencies of contemporary biological views. And in both, Needham's work played a key role. Although the first two volumes of Buffon's *Histoire naturelle* were published originally in 1749, evidence exists to suggest that Voltaire did not receive or read any volumes until 1767.[38] There are numerous marginal notes in Voltaire's copies of the first two volumes of the *Histoire naturelle,* which dealt with Buffon's theory of the earth and his views on generation. Although Buffon's ideas on the origins of mountains and fossils disturbed Voltaire as much as or more than his theory of generation, I do not concentrate on these here. Suffice it to say that Voltaire opposed a naturalistic explanation for the origins of both fossils and the earth's features, preferring to believe that God had created the earth as we see it and that fossils were the remains of travelers' meals.[39]

Many passages in volume two of Buffon's *Histoire naturelle* were marked simply "chimera" by Voltaire. To a mention of Needham's observations on the formation of spermatozoa in the seminal fluid of calamary, Voltaire responded, "Needham has seen, has imagined, has said only foolishness." And in the margin of a passage where Buffon discussed Needham's observations on eels in blighted wheat, Voltaire wrote, "Is it possible that you have been able to repeat after Maupertuis this enormous foolishness of the imbecile Needham!" Finally, annotating Buffon's summary chapter, Voltaire left no doubt about his preference for preformation over Buffon's theory of organic particles: "It seems ridiculous to suppose that organic particles that have not nourished the body then become bodies that have movement and thought; so that one of these particles is an alexander or a newton. Another particle is shit [or] urine [or] mucous. The ancient system is much more reasonable that admits all the descendents in the semen of a grandfather, as all the little elms in the fruit of an elm tree, and all the peaches in the stone of a peach tree. This

---

[37] Best. D13177, 17 February 1766. See also *Lazzaro Spallanzani: Epistolario,* ed. Benedetto Biagi (Florence, 1958-64), I, 57n.

[38] Voltaire's correspondence indicates that he first received some of the volumes of the *Histoire naturelle* in 1767. It is a second edition (1750-70) in which his annotations appear. See *Corpus,* 559-612, 655 n.413.

[39] See, for example, Voltaire's "Dissertation sur les changements arrivés dans notre globe" (cit. n.15 above). Theory of the earth was, during this period, another area of controversy involving atheism and materialism.

system frightens the imagination but the other one terrifies common sense." [40]

By mid-1768 Voltaire had also seen Lagrange's anonymous translation of Lucretius's *De rerum natura* in which Lagrange spoke positively about Needham's observations.[41] In a footnote to a passage on the formation of worms in rotting flesh, Lagrange reported that most people in his day believed that all organisms were preformed in eggs, even those that appeared to come from putrefaction. "But this principle of physics," Lagrange remarked, "as well as others one regards as equally certain, has been refuted by experience. Everyone knows that of M. Needham, who discovered with the aid of a microscope eels in flour diluted with water." [42] Lagrange also referred to a repetition by Heinrich Friedrich Delius of Needham's sealed infusion of heated mutton broth, which had resulted in microorganisms just as Needham's had.[43]

Lagrange was now added, although Voltaire never knew his name, to Maupertuis, Buffon, and Needham on Voltaire's list of dangerous biological thinkers. In a letter to d'Alembert, Voltaire commented on his "just sorrow at seeing that the translator of Lucretius adopts again the alleged creation of worms from blighted wheat and from the juice of mutton. It is very humorous that this chimera of an Irish jesuit named Needham could still seduce some physicists. Our nation is too ridiculous." [44] This is Voltaire's first mention of Needham's use of mutton broth in his experiments, which he apparently took from Lagrange's footnote. Still not having read Needham directly, Voltaire further misrepresented Needham's work, for Needham's observations on infusions of mutton broth were made with regard to the production of microorganisms, not eels. Lagrange did not make this distinction clear, and so neither did Voltaire. Almost all of Voltaire's subsequent references to Needham's work include the formation of eels in mutton broth as well as in flour paste.

[40] *Corpus,* 593, 604, 606. Voltaire's various comments on preexistence indicate an ambivalence over ovist versus animalculist preformation. Most of his statements support an ovist view; this is his most explicit endorsement of animalculism.

[41] This translation is first mentioned in Voltaire's correspondence in August 1768 (see Best. D15189). Very little is known about Lagrange (including his first name), who was tutor to d'Holbach's children and who apparently produced this translation at the request of d'Holbach and Diderot and with some editorial help from Diderot and Naigeon. See *Biographie universelle,* XXIII, 156-57; *Nouvelle biographie générale,* XXVIII, 847-48; and Alan Charles Kors, *D'Holbach's Coterie: An Enlightenment in Paris* (Princeton, 1976), 87.

[42] *Lucrèce, De la nature des choses,* traduction nouvelle, avec des notes par M. L* G** (Paris, 1768), I, 407. Voltaire owned and annotated this edition (*Biblioteka Vol'tera* 575).

[43] Lagrange cited a report of Delius's observations in *Commentarii de rebus in scientia naturali et medicina gestis,* 11 (1758), 531-32.

[44] Best. D15199, 2 September [1768].

Voltaire responded to Buffon and Lagrange in *La Défense de mon oncle* (1767), in *Des singularités de la nature* (1768), in *Les Colimaçons du Révérend père l'Escarbotier* (1768), and in *L'Homme aux quarante écus* (1768). In all of these, Needham, Buffon, and Maupertuis figured as the villains of the story. Completely confusing Needham's observations on the viviparous eels of flour paste with those on the eels of blighted wheat and microorganisms found in infusions of mutton broth, Voltaire erroneously referred to heated and sealed infusions of blighted wheat that yielded viviparous eels. In *La Défense de mon oncle* Voltaire repeated his equation of the formation of eels with the formation of man, resulting in no further use for God.[45] This was reiterated in *Des singularités de la nature*, where, after describing Needham's experiments, Voltaire remarked, "Immediately several philosophers did their best to cry marvel, and to say: There is no germ; everything is formed, everything is regenerated by a living force of nature. It is attraction, said one [Maupertuis]; it is organized matter, said another [Buffon]; these are living organic molecules that have found their molds. Good physicists were deceived by a jesuit." [46] Voltaire referred also to Lagrange's approval of Needham's observations and to Spallanzani's disproof, and concluded with a firm espousal of the theory of preexistence.

Les Colimaçons du Révérend père l'Escarbotier was written after Voltaire had learned of Spallanzani's experiments on decapitated snails, which were able to regenerate new heads.[47] This was one of the few areas of biology in which Voltaire actually made his own experiments, although he did not have as much success as Spallanzani. Opening with a comparison of Jesuits with snails in which Voltaire remarked that snails will endure longer than religious orders, since decapitated monks could accept no novices, Voltaire again turned to Needham's observations. Criticizing Buffon for forming a universe on the basis of a chimerical experiment, Voltaire praised Spallanzani's refutation. "No sooner was the father of organic molecules halfway through his creation," Voltaire wrote, "then *voilà* the mother and daughter eels disappear. M. Spallanzani, an excellent observer, showed to the eye the chimera of these so-called animals, born from corruption, as reason demonstrated them to the mind. Organic molecules flee with the eels into the nothingness from which they came: there they join the attraction with which an empty dream formed children in his *Vénus physique*. God resumes his rights; he says to all the architects

---

[45] M. XXVI, 408-9.

[46] M. XXVII, 159.

[47] See Spallanzani's *Prodromo di un opera da imprimersi sopra le riproduzioni animali* Modena, 1768). Voltaire owned and annotated a French translation titled *Programme u précis d'un ouvrage sur les réproductions animales* (Geneva, 1768). (See *Biblioteka 'ol'tera,* 804.) See also Voltaire's letters to Spallanzani of 20 May 1776 and 6 June 1776 Besterman D20133, 20158); and Spallanzani's reply of 31 May 1776 (Best. D20148 and :pistolario, II, 106-7).

of systems, as to the sea; *Procedes huc, et non ibis amplius* [Proceed this far, and go no further]." And so, Voltaire concluded, "It is given to man to see, to measure, to count, and to contemplate the works of God; but it is not given to him to make them." [48]

During 1767 and 1768, Voltaire's position on Needham solidified into an often repeated argument. Needham's observations provided grounds for atheism and materialism, Voltaire claimed; and, even though they were erroneous, they had seduced other good philosophers, notably Buffon, Maupertuis, and the translator of Lucretius, into falling into the trap of believing that matter can form life. All of this reinforced Voltaire's own leanings toward preformation into an inflexible and almost fanatic defense of preexistent germs against epigenesis. And all of Voltaire's discussions of Needham, as I have mentioned, were based on a thorough misunderstanding of Needham's observations gleaned from the descriptions Voltaire encountered in the works of Maupertuis, Buffon, and Lagrange.

The D'Holbach Episode. — After a brief respite of two years, Needham was once again brought to Voltaire's attention when in the infamous *Système de la nature,* published in 1770, the disguised author, d'Holbach, claimed an intellectual kinship with Needham. In an early chapter on the relationship between matter and motion, where d'Holbach attempted to prove that matter possesses active powers on its own, he gave two examples. The first was chemical combustion, where hidden powers of matter are frequently manifested in violent explosions. The second example involved the transition from nonlife to life: "by moistening flour with water and by enclosing this mixture," d'Holbach pointed out, "one will find after a little time, with the aid of a microscope, that it has produced organized beings that enjoy a life of which one believed flour and water incapable. It is thus that inanimate matter can pass into life, which is itself only an assemblage of movements." In a footnote, d'Holbach continued, "See the *observations microscopiques* of M. Needham, who fully confirms this opinion. For a man who reflects [on this], would the production of a man independently from the ordinary means be more marvelous than that of an insect from flour and water? Fermentation and putrefaction visibly produce living animals. The generation that one calls *Equivocal* is only thus for those who do not permit themselves to attentively observe nature." [49] It is interesting to note that even d'Holbach described Needham's observations not quite accurately in saying that one encloses the mixture of flour and water as in an infusion.

The *Système de la nature* began to circulate in early 1770; by July Voltaire had received a copy, and he was incensed. For the rest of th

---

[48] M. XXVII, 220-21. The Latin quotation is from the book of Job.
[49] [Paul-Henri Thiry d'Holbach], *Système de la nature, ou des loix du monde physique et du monde moral,* par M. Mirabaud (London [Amsterdam], 1770), I, 23 and n.5.

year his letters are full of complaints about the *Système,* not the least of which was its reliance on Needham. To one correspondent he described the *Système* as "a book that has made much noise among the ignorant, and that shocks all men of good sense. It is rather shameful to our nation that so many people have so quickly embraced such a ridiculous opinion. . . . But the height of impertinence is to have founded an entire system on a false experiment made by an Irish jesuit who has been mistaken for a philosopher." [50] Similar remarks can be found in several letters from these same months.[51]

The culmination of Voltaire's reaction to d'Holbach's materialism was his article "Dieu, Dieux," written during the summer of 1770 and published in the *Questions sur l'encyclopédie* in 1771. In the third and fourth sections of this article, parts of which had been separately published in 1770,[52] Voltaire objected to d'Holbach's views on matter and his attack on the existence of God. In a special subsection Voltaire devoted himself to the "story of the eels," which he described as the foundation of d'Holbach's system. Voltaire presented the now familiar argument that if flour could produce eels, men could originate this way also, and there would no longer be a need for God—an argument in which Voltaire had anticipated by five years the materialist view made explicit by d'Holbach. He proceeded through the same list of duped philosophers and pointed again to Spallanzani's refutation. The theme of Voltaire's defense against d'Holbach was an affirmation of the existence of God and of the incapacity of matter to produce life and intelligence. "The author claims that matter, blind and without choice, produces intelligent animals. To produce without intelligence beings that have intelligence! Is this conceivable? Is this system based on the least likelihood? Such a contradictory opinion would require proofs as astonishing as itself. The author gives none; he never proves anything, and he affirms everything he advances. What chaos! What confusion! But what temerity!" [53] Voltaire concluded that thinking, sensing beings could be created only by a power superior to mankind.

Voltaire continued to ridicule Needham in his works, notably in "Les Cabales" (1772), *Histoire de Jenni, ou l'Athée et le sage* (1775), and finally *Dialogues d'Evhèmere* (1777), published the year before Voltaire's death. The theme remained the same, and d'Holbach was simply added to the list of those misled into materialism by the experiments of the Irish Jesuit. In 1776 Voltaire received Spallanzani's *Opuscoli di fisica animale e vegetabile,* which contained even further experiments made in refutation of Needham. To Spallanzani Voltaire wrote gratefully, "You give the final

---

[50] Best. D16666, 26 September 1770.
[51] See, for instance, Best. D16602, 16673, 16693, 16736, 16786, 17066.
[52] *Dieu. Réponse de Mr. de Voltaire au Système de la nature* (Château de Ferney, '70).
[53] M. XVIII, 375.

blow, Monsieur, to the eels of the jesuit Needham. It is useless for them to wriggle, they are dead. . . . Animals born without germs could not live very long. It is your book that will live because it is founded on experiment and on reason." [54]

Voltaire's campaign against Needham was motivated more by his worries over atheism and materialism than by any real scientific opposition. As we have seen, Voltaire never understood Needham's observations, constantly confusing and misrepresenting them. Initially they were a means to ridicule Maupertuis during the Koenig affair. But after the miracles episode and the visit from Damilaville, Needham's work became the symbol for Voltaire of the dangerous trends he witnessed in biology. The work of Buffon, the discussion of Needham by Lagrange, and finally the explicit materialism of d'Holbach served only to add fuel to the fire. Voltaire's opposition, so often expressed in ridicule, crystallized around the scandalous Jesuit who had duped so many good philosophers by his alleged creation of life. Voltaire really never had to read Needham because what was most important for Voltaire was the use others had made of his observations.

Needham's Response. — How did Needham respond to Voltaire's invectives and ridicule? In the miracles pamphlets Needham confined himself to the discussion of miracles and religion, never defending himself against Voltaire's attacks on his scientific work. Only once did Needham even allude to the "misunderstood discoveries" of the "Anguillard." [55] In his next publication, a French edition of Spallanzani's critique of his microscopical observations to which Needham had added his own commentary in response, Needham mentioned Voltaire only once. Claiming in reference to the letters on miracles, that "this author omits nothing to entertain the public at my expense with ingenious jests," Needham said he would not respond. "M. M. de Voltaire and de Lignac [another critic] do not understand us or do not want to understand us," Needham concluded; "everything that they read of ours they explain in their own fashion and they criticize it according to their own ideas." [56]

Needham also published an anonymous essay comparing Voltaire and Rousseau, thinly disguised as Tévilaor and Suasoure, in an appendix to *Les Vrais quakers,* a book Needham edited and published in 1770. Voltaire, the vain poet, did not fare well against the gentle philosophe Rousseau, for "if the one had the fault of finding no friend worthy of his soul, the other never had a soul worthy of a friend; . . . . the one misled our minds under the dictates of his heart, so the other corrupted

[54] Best. D20133, 20 May 1776.
[55] *Projet,* 8-9; *Questions sur les miracles,* 105-06.
[56] *Nouvelles recherches,* 213.

our hearts under the dictates of the mind."[57] No references to Voltaire's biological views or to his attacks on Needham exist in this brief sketch. After the publication of d'Holbach's *Système de la nature,* Needham decided he had to respond publicly to the double challenge of d'Holbach's misuse of his ideas and Voltaire's critique of d'Holbach via Needham. In 1774 he added a long note to Blaise Monestier's *La Vraie philosophie* (of which Needham was the editor) in which Needham replied to the charge of materialism implicit in d'Holbach's reference to his observations. This note was republished in the *Journal ecclésiastique* in 1774, and in 1776 and 1781 as a separate work. The latter was titled *Idée sommaire, ou vue générale du système physique et métaphysique de Monsieur Needham, sur la génération des corps organisés,* contained as well a letter he had published in the *Journal encyclopédique* in 1771 against d'Holbach's *Système* and a brief remark on Voltaire's response to d'Holbach.

Needham explained in the opening of the *Idée sommaire* that he felt it necessary to give a précis of his views because "Certain modern authors, and especially the so-called philosopher Voltaire, seem to confuse the eels of blighted wheat with those of flour paste, which I have described in my new microscopical discoveries." Needham then proceeded to explain once again that his biological theory was not a materialist one and that he had never challenged the existence of the human soul. Admitting that his earlier statements on the origin of eels in flour paste might have led some people to conclude erroneously that he believed in equivocal generation, Needham nevertheless claimed that d'Holbach had misrepresented his views in the *Système de la nature:* ". . . It is vain to hope that a writer such as the author of the System of Nature do justice to others, and I am not surprised that to cover the absurdity of his hypothesis he confuses heaven and earth by mixing my experiments on the vital parts that detached themselves continually in my infusions of organized bodies, with those that I made before on the eels of flour." Describing the *Système de la nature* as a "sad and somber" book that had "come from the abyss of impiety," Needham observed that "the world recoils in horror at the blasphemies hurled there against its Creator."[58]

Nor was Needham happy with Voltaire's response to d'Holbach. Claiming that in all of Voltaire's works one found "the same false spirit,

---

[57] [Henri-Camille Colmont de Vaulgrenand], *Les Vrais quakers, ou les exhortations, harangues, & prédictions des vrais serviteurs du Seigneur Dieu: A un méchant frère, spécialement au sujet de ses maximes sur le luxe, & de ses persécutions contre un frère dans le malheur. Ouvrage à la suite du quel on a inseré un mémoire vraiment curieux sur son étonnante analogie avec ce qui précède* (London, 1770), 103. A second edition appeared in 1771.

[58] *Idée sommaire* (Brussels, 1781), 3, 13, 21. See also Jacques Marx, "Des anguilles la philosophie méchanique. Deux réfutations peu connues du 'Système de la nature' ", *Tijdschrift voor de studie van de Verlichting,* **1** (1973), 69-87.

[and] the same mania," Needham objected in particular to the misuse of his own ideas. "If he had wanted just once to come out from his house to interrogate the truth of things by the light of day, he would perhaps have been able to be satisfied that neither he nor the author of the System of Nature have any right to cite my experiments as favorable to materialism." Needham was displeased as well with "the deception in which he [Voltaire] persists since my quarrel with him in Geneva of making me pass for a Jesuit and an Irish man."[59]

There really was nothing more Needham could say to Voltaire. Before the explicit tie d'Holbach drew between his observations and materialism, Needham had simply let the matter lie. But after the publication of the *Système,* he felt compelled not only to proclaim again that he was not a materialist but to object to the specific misuse that Voltaire as well as d'Holbach had made of his scientific work. Needham was in an unenviable position. Seen as an ally by the materialists, attacked as a materialist himself by those who did not understand his biological views, and rejected by the preformationists who did understand his views but found them unacceptable, Needham was forced to defend his system on all fronts.

Conclusion.—Two years before he died, Needham wrote a letter to Bonnet in which he outlined the rationale behind his scientific work. When he had first come to Paris in 1746, Needham explained, he found that the new philosophy was too frivolous for his tastes. Having been taught from his earliest days, "to consider moral science as the first and the only truly useful one," Needham was concerned to see how shaky the underpinnings were for religion and morals. The two dominant hypotheses, preexistence of germs and innate ideas, both clearly served the purpose of convincing people of the presence of God and the immutability of morals; yet the only problem was that these hypotheses were both wrong. Consequently, Needham claimed, "false philosophers . . . had conceived the wild hope that in overthrowing them they would be able to sap the foundations of all religion, natural or revealed, and radically to destroy it." Both hypotheses served the same purpose, he reported that is, "to fix and to stop, if it was possible, research of the human mind that was too thorny and even dangerous on the first origins of things and on the source from which our intellectual operations derive." What was Needham to do? "Seeing [this] consequently," he told Bonnet, "from the beginning of my philosophical career and foreseeing that these different Cartesian resources and others in favor of religion could easily be made to fail us, at the same time as morality, without which society could not subsist, would perish if one did not take precautions to provide for a second retrenchment stronger than the first, I wanted to forestall

[59] *Idée sommaire,* 27.

the fatal consequences."[60] Needham's goal was to provide a biological account of generation that would offer an alternative to preexistent germs while still remaining a foundation for religion and morality. Likewise, he proposed alternative metaphysical and epistemological theories to substitute for the Cartesian conception of innate ideas. His purpose was never to offer new biological evidence for materialism but just the opposite: to ensure that when preexistent germs failed, materialism and atheism would not triumph.

Needham's disquietude over the immorality of contemporary society was expressed in a letter written from Paris to another correspondent in 1767: "Society decays apace in the great world, not only revealed religion, but even the law of nature has become an object of ridicule; materialism, and a metaphysical kind of atheism is substituted. . . man in his present situation has abandoned faith, reason, and morality without any fixed mechanical principle whatsoever to restrain him; what is left but Luxury, libertinism, caprice in the midst of gaity, and passion in their most serious moments variable as the wind?"[61] In a similar vein Needham remarked in another letter, "I know no philosophy going forward here, that I can either learn from books or conversation, but that which they call by that name, irreligion."[62] Struck by the decadence of Parisian society even more forcefully in the late 1760s then he had initially been in the 1740s, Needham sought to stem the tide of atheism and materialism and thereby to provide a new basis for morality and society.

Voltaire's concerns were in many ways quite similar: like Needham, Voltaire was seriously worried about the relationship of biological theories to atheism and materialism. And like Needham, his disquietude over irreligion was closely tied to a concern for morality. In 1768, Voltaire wrote a letter to the Marquis de Villevielle in which he made his worries over the implications of biology for atheism explicit. Remarking that he was glad his correspondent was not an atheist, Voltaire commented that atheists had never been able to answer the argument "that a watch proves a watchmaker." Mentioning the work of Needham who had "recently furnished arms to atheistic philosophy in pretending that animals can form themselves all alone," and "another fool called Maupertuis," Voltaire proclaimed "May God preserve us from such atheists." Finally, Voltaire concluded simply, "My dear Marquis, there is nothing good in atheism. This system is very bad in physics and in morals. An honest man can protest strongly against superstition and fanaticism; he can detest persecution, he renders a service to the human race if he spreads human

[60] Letter of 28 October (September) 1779; MS Bonnet, *35,* 100r-100v (Bibliothèque Publique et Universitaire, Geneva).
[61] Needham to Honoré-Auguste Sabatier de Cabre, 9 January 1767 (Brotherton Library, University of Leeds, Leeds).
[62] Needham to Emanuel Mendez Da Costa, 12 February 1767; Add. MS 28540, 101v British Library, London).

principles of toleration; but what service can he render if he spreads atheism?"[63] This was perhaps the fundamental theme of Voltaire's opposition to irreligion during these years—the threat to society its popularity would entail.

This concern was echoed two years later in another letter written in response to d'Holbach's *Système*. Pointing once again to Needham's "false experiment" as the foundation of d'Holbach's views, Voltaire revealed that he was extremely anxious that his own disapproval of d'Holbach's principles be made known to others. "Moreover," Voltaire continued, "I think that it is always very good to support the doctrine of the existence of a rewarding and vengeful God, society needs this opinion. I do not know if you recognize this verse, 'If god did not exist, it would be necessary to invent him.' "[64] This verse was in fact Voltaire's, written a year earlier in a poem intended as a reply to the infamous anonymous tract, *Traité des trois imposteurs* (1765).[65] Whatever Voltaire's own personal views were with regard to God, he felt that belief in God's existence was essential to preserve the social order, in addition to being demonstrated by the natural order. For Voltaire the proper society required a government based on an enlightened monarch and a moral code founded on justice, toleration, and a belief in God.[66]

Yet whatever the similarities between Voltaire's and Needham's opinions on science and religion, there were also wide differences between their world views—partly due to an age differential: Voltaire was 71 in 1765, the year their quarrel commenced, Needham was nearly twenty years younger. Voltaire's scientific and philosophical convictions had been forged in the 1720s and 1730s, and a belief in a divinely ordered Newtonian universe never left him. His was an essentially static view, of an unchanging world created by God in which all organisms already existed and even matter was seen as fundamentally passive. A confirmed deist Voltaire was frankly worried about the direction the *philosophe* movement had taken with the younger generation. Needham on the other hand did not share Voltaire's static Newtonian view but proposed rather a Leibnizian dynamic metaphysics in its stead.[67] Convinced that matter consists essentially of active agents rather than passive extension, Needham con

---

[63] Best. D15189, 26 August 1768. On the theme of God and social order, see als "Athée, Athéisme," M. XVII, 472-76; and "Dieu, Dieux," M. XVIII, 376-81.

[64] Best. D16736, 1 November 1770.

[65] "Epître à l'auteur du livre des trois imposteurs" (1769), M. X, 402-05.

[66] On this point see Theodore Besterman, "Voltaire, Absolute Monarchy, and th Enlightened Monarch," *Stud. Volt.,* **32** (1965), 7-21; Besterman, "Voltaire's god," *Stud Volt.,* **55** (1967), 23-41; H. T. Mason, *Pierre Bayle and Voltaire* (Oxford, 1963), 78-8! Pomeau, *La Religion,* 391-427; and Margaret C. Jacob, *The Radical Enlightenmen Pantheists, Freemasons and Republicans* (London, 1981), 101-06.

[67] On Needham's metaphysics and their Leibnizian ties, see Roe, "John Turbervil Needham." See footnote 4 above.

structed a picture of the physical and living worlds strikingly different from Voltaire's. For Needham, all operations in the universe were due to the action and reaction of expansive and resistive agents. The reproduction of an organism was not the development of an already existing miniature organism but rather the emergence of a new being through a truly developmental process. Yet all of these natural processes operated only through divinely ordained laws. God was as much a necessity in Needham's world as in Voltaire's—the source of the intelligent design and predetermined causes evident throughout the physical as well as the living universe.

Both Needham and Voltaire were responding to the same kinds of dangers they saw threatening religion and society. Both rejected atheism and materialism, and both attempted to provide a biological basis for religion and morality. Yet each perceived these dangers differently, and their solutions differed accordingly. That neither ever fully appreciated the other's position is not really very surprising. What little Voltaire knew of Needham's views was enough for him to seek no further; and his ridicule of Needham alienated Voltaire from even his preformationist allies. Yet their controversy offers us an insightful episode in the eighteenth-century's struggle to balance scientific, religious, and social concerns in an age of intellectual and political ferment.

Harvard University

Chapter XXVIII

BIOLOGY AND SOCIETY IN THE AGE OF ENLIGHTENMENT

BY FRANCESCA RIGOTTI

I. *Introduction.*—The movement of ideas which evolved and came to the fore in the eighteenth century under the generic definition of progress had many facets. A variety of concepts contributed to the formation of an image of progress: temporality, change, development, perfectibility, transformation. . . . These concepts were also applied to different fields of knowledge within both the study of human behavior and the study of the phenomena of the material world.

The new hypotheses which arose from the application of these concepts to the life sciences and the social sciences interacted and supplied conceptual models and working tools for both fields. Broadly speaking, in the eighteenth century the view of the history (progress) of mankind that developed portrayed the various ages linked in a chain of causes and effects such that the condition of mankind appeared as a continuous and logically directed whole. The corresponding picture of nature was composed of a continuous sequence of beings located in a hierarchy of a regular and consistent order. This correspondence was not, however, symmetrical, nor did the processes follow parallel lines; affinities did indeed exist, but there was also a sharp division between the "progressive" image in the field of social behavior and in the area of "natural" beings. A political-philosophical approach tended to dominate thinking about the phenomena of the human world, and here a dynamic model took precedence over a static one. Within the social world it became accepted, "new" phenomena may occur but not in the natural world. The ideas of the natural world remained static for a longer period, and the action of nature was thought only to reproduce and to develop a preordained order in which there was no place for either novelty or the unexpected.

Throughout the eighteenth century the prevailing idea in the field of the life sciences was still that which Arthur O. Lovejoy included in the "great chain of being."[1] Although eighteenth-century thinkers tended on the whole to understand the structure of the universe through this metaphor, they must nevertheless be credited with having introduced an idea of capital importance: instead of a *descending* order of beings from the most perfect to the least developed, the Enlightenment conceived an *ascending* order, that is, from the most primitive to the most perfect.

In elaborating this schema of perfectibility in their description of social and natural phenomena, the eighteenth-century naturalistic phi-

[1] A. O. Lovejoy, *The Great Chain of Being* (Cambridge, Mass., 1936), 64.

losophers took a decisive step forward. In fact their inversion of the classical model not only led to the theory of evolution in the biological sciences but also provided the basis for those political doctrines which place the attainment of man's happiness and his fulfillment in the future.

II. *The Leibnizian inheritance.*—For many eighteenth-century naturalists the universe of natural phenomena was a *full* one, based on the assumption of action by contact. Against the theories of Descartes, who had offered a plenistic schema of the universe with vortices and who had also later accepted its behavior as mechanical and based on purely physical predicates, many naturalists preferred Leibniz's paradigm, based on the principles of continuity, the plenum, preestablished harmony, and sufficient reason. These principles were clearly laid out in those works by Leibniz that had been read by the *philosophes* before the publication in 1765 of the *Nouveaux essais sur l'entendement humain*: the *Théodicée,* the *Correspondence with Clarke,* and the *Monadology.*[2] In the latter work, continuity, the plenum, and harmony in the universe were guaranteed by the principle of sufficient reason. Everything in nature is complete, and everything is connected with all possible order and harmony (the present is "gros de l'avenir, chargé du passé," each monad is in the present "pregnant with the future," which can be read in the past, "what is far off is expressed in what is near"). But since nothing occurs, according to Leibniz, without a sufficient reason to determine why a thing has occurred thus and not otherwise, the introduction of a Democritean discontinuity and void into the world would constitute a violation of Leibniz's principle of the need for a sufficient reason and would also accuse God of imperfect creation.[3]

The complete universe is that which contains the highest level of perfection. Even the divine choice among infinite possible worlds has to be inspired by the principle of sufficient reason, and the reason for the divine choice lies in the fitness and the degrees of perfection that these worlds contain, since each one has the right to claim existence in proportion to the perfection it contains. All possible perfection is provided by the principle of the greatest *variety* and *order* within the smallest compass.[4]

The main concern of Leibniz was therefore in conceptual terms to eliminate from the universe every possible source of disorder and imperfection. Thus, beings and the classes of beings are arranged as the ordinates of a single curve, closely joined together in strict observance of the law of continuity and the plenum. Since the law of continuity

---

[2] Y. Belaval, *L'Héritage leibnizien au siècle des lumières,* in *Leibniz, Aspects de l'homme et de l'oeuvre 1646-1716* (Paris, 1968), 253.

[3] G. W. Leibniz, *Correspondence with Clarke,* in *Leibniz' Philosophical Writings,* ed. M. Morris (London, 1934), 209.

[4] *The Monadology,* in *Philosophical Papers and Letters* (Chicago, 1956), II, 1053.

requires that, when the essential determinations of one being resemble those of another, all the properties of the first must draw close to those of the other; and all the order of natural beings must form a single chain, in which the different classes are so closely joined to one another that the senses and the imagination cannot distinguish the exact point at which one begins or ends. All the species alongisde or inside the border regions must be equivocal and endowed with characteristics that can be equally attributed to the neighboring species.[5]

The law of continuity holds a central place in the methodological interests of Leibniz.[6] The schema of the structure of the universe derived from it is seemingly of a static type, in which the aspiration of potential beings to existence is fulfilled in the perfection of the present world and where the only dynamic process permitted is the development of an order preordained *ab initio* by God.

Leibniz's belief in preformation, so far as the reproduction of living beings is concerned, seems to contribute to the static nature of this structure. Preformation is the doctrine which held that animal seed is encapsulated in the loins of the first progenitor,[7] as in a Russian doll enclosing a series of similar dolls. The notion of preformation, or evolution of the preformed, that is, the development of what is enveloped, the unwinding of what is wound up, in fact ensures that once the divine act of creation has taken place, nothing new will be added to the created nature. This is opposed to the epigenesist doctrine, which held that the living being grows from the germ to the acquisition and subsequent formation of new parts.

The reproductive mechanism must therefore, for Leibniz, admit the preformation of the seeds in the bodies that are born, contained in those from which they have been born, right back to the first seeds. Thus, excluding miracles and chaos and in order to maintain the principles of harmony and the plenum, it must be concluded that God preformed things so that new organizations should be only an automatic consequence of a previous organic constitution.[8]

A hypothesis that explains nature's becoming as a successive unfolding of a predetermined order, and not as an autonomous generation of an order through the iteration and temporal continuity of the processes, is bound to a static model of nature in which individuals and species are granted development but not a sudden transformation from the embryonic to the adult condition, according to the preestablished schema.

The perfection of the present world and preformist hypotheses might

[5] Letter to Varignon of 2nd February 1702, *ibid,* II, 886.

[6] G. Tonelli, "The Law of Continuity in the Eighteenth Century," *Studies on Voltaire and the Eighteenth Century* (1963), 1621.

[7] G. W. Leibniz, *The Principles of Nature and of Grace, Based on Reason,* in *Philosophical Papers,* II, 1037.

[8] *Essais de théodicée,* in *Philosophischen Schriften,* ed. Gerhardt (Berlin, 1885), VI.

seem to be a sufficient foundation on which to base an indestructibly
static view of nature; but there is, at least to my knowledge, one point
where the Leibnizian philosophy seems to waver and to be open to other
hypotheses.

Between the spring and summer of 1715, a year before his death,
Leibniz began to correspond with Louis Bourguet (1678-1742), a philosopher, man of letters, and naturalist of Geneva, on the question of
the perfection of nature. In his meditation on nature, Bourguet had come
to wonder whether it was possible to think of succession without conceiving an initial point from which all the successive states derive. Perplexed by the problem, he asked Leibniz for clarification. The reply
arrived after some months and was slightly ambiguous.

Since in nature there is no term which is fundamental for all the
others, no seat of God so to speak, there is no reason why it should be
necessary to conceive an initial principal instant. Even if a difference
between the instants and the terms does exist, Leibniz continued, a primal
instant does not necessarily exist, in that one term in the universe does
not have priority in nature over the other terms, whereas a preceding
instant always has priority over the following instant, not only in time
but also in nature. If it is true that the primary notion of a unit-class is
resolvable in the notion of units, which can be considered as a primary,
it does not follow that the notion of different instants must be resolved
in a primal instant. Nevertheless, even if we may not affirm the existence
of a primal instant, we cannot deny it either. Leibniz formulated two
hypotheses: either nature is already perfect, or it grows continually in
perfection.

The first case is shown by rectangle A (fig. 1) which represents the
hypothesis of equal perfection, in which it is more probable that there is
no beginning:

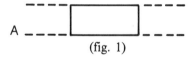
(fig. 1)

The second case (that nature always grows in perfection, supposing
that it is not possible for it to be endowed contemporaneously with all
perfection) is further divided by Leibniz in two ways, with the ordinates
of hyperbola B or with those of triangle C (fig. 2).

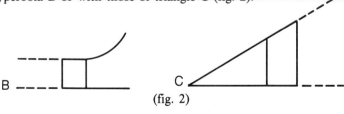
(fig. 2)

According to the hypothesis of hyperbola B, the world would have no beginning, and the instants would be growing in perfection from eternity. But in the hypothesis of triangle C, there would have been a beginning. Mere reason, Leibniz went on to say, does not enable us to make a definite choice. The only conclusion he felt able to draw was that, though according to the hypothesis of growth the state of the world at any given instant could never be absolutely perfect, yet the existing succession would be the most perfect of all possible successions because God always chooses the best possible.[9]

Leibniz retained divine choice in any case as the best possible; but, while not making too apodictic a declaration, he did not reject the idea of nature's growth in perfection, leaving room in his construction (which for this reason we have regarded as *apparently static*) for the idea of perfection in time and therefore of change for the better.

The theoretical foundation inherited from Leibniz by the French biologists thus consisted of something more than a "panpsychism" according to which living nature is the sum and substance of infinite individual beings (the original monads) endowed with autonomous activity and sensitivity. It also provided a structured scale of perfectibility ascending from the embryo, which left room for transformist interpretations.

III. *The continuum theorist: Bourguet, Plouquet, Kästner, Boscovich.*—Leibniz's reply caused Bourguet some perplexity at the time, but the following year he decided to make a definite statement on the triangle hypothesis,[10] even though he never fully realized the importance of Leibniz's intuitions.

Louis Bourguet, who conceived and contributed to the *Bibliothèque italique,* for which he was best known, was the author of several works on geology written over the 1720s and '30s.[11] In these works his technical analysis and classification of fossils and crystals followed a logical schema based on the scale of beings. Apparently unaware of the illustrious tradition that had preceded him on this subject, Bourguet claimed to be the first to set up the hypothesis of the scale of beings, although he admitted having been influenced by Leibniz.[12] His aim was to show the gradation of beings, even in the mineral kingdom, from the most simple to the

[9] Letter from Bourguet to Leibniz of 15th April 1715, in L. Isely, "Leibniz et Bourguet. Correspondance scientifique et philosophique (1707-1716),"*Bulletin de la Société neuchâtelaise des sciences naturelles* (1903-04), 202-05, and letter from Leibniz to Bourguet of 5th August, 1715, in G. W. Leibniz, *Philosophischen Schriften,* III, 282-83.

[10] Letter from Bourguet to Leibniz of 16th March, 1716 in L. Isely, *op. cit.,* 207.

[11] L. Bourguet, *Lettres philosophiques sur la formation des sels et des cristaux et sur la génération et le méchanisme des plantes et des animaux à l'occasion de la pierre belemnite et de la pierre lenticulaire* (Amsterdam, 1729); *Mémoire sur la théorie de la terre* (Amsterdam, 1729); with P. Cartier, *Traité des pétrifications* (Paris, 1742).

[12] "Lettre de M. L. B. P. à Monsieur Antoine Vallisnieri premier professeur de la médecine théoretique à Padoue, sur la gradation et l'échelle des fossiles," *Bibliothèque italique,* II (1728), 102-03.

most complex, from the least to the most perfect. In his writings Bourguet tried to avoid theological discussion, excluding God from his scale as being too far above limited beings to be considered on the same level.

Despite the benefits of his correspondence with Leibniz (they wrote to each other from June 1709 to July 1716), Bourguet was still too conditioned by the creationist way of thinking to accept a single direction in the movement of nature. Saying that nature ascends by degrees towards more perfect creations is only one way of interpreting gradation, which may just as easily be depicted going in the other direction, as a scale that descends from the most perfect beings to the coarsest of natures.

Other authors were, however, much more critical of the possibility of applying the continuity principle to the study of the natural world. During the middle of the century these writers were concerned with the law of continuity in mathematics and physics in relation to the problem of hard bodies. Bourguet's doubt as to whether it might be possible to compose a gradation including immaterial beings more perfect than man and beings whose soul is tied to a body appears many years later in the writings of Plouquet (1716-1790). But whereas Bourguet's answer was affirmative, Plouquet's was entirely negative. On the very basis of the *lex continui,* it is illogical to formulate a continuous sequence with non-homogeneous elements like spirit and matter. For the same reason it is not possible to fit God into the same continuous scale (although Bourguet had already thought of leaving God out), since the Deity is *infinite,* and everything that exists apart from God is by definition *finite.* In this case also the lack of homogeneity mars the continuity of the gradation. If unlike is compared with unlike, we cannot free ourselves of contradiction. But difficulties also arise from the comparison of like with like and are not easily overcome, for if it is possible for the species to be plotted as the ordinates of a single curve, as Leibniz maintained, there must never be an intermediary discrete species between two others. But the very nature of the continuum forbids absolute proximity.[13] The error lies in the fact that the gradation of being takes on the category of the discrete, which is confused with that of the continuous. Plouquet's conclusion in the name of the defense of the law of continuity is categorical. This law cannot be transferred from the physical world to the behavior of the species for the two above-mentioned reasons: 1) It is impossible to construct a perfect system with dissimilar beings, to say nothing of irregular and "eccentric" beings, in it. 2) It is equally impossible to imagine an absolute similarity between two species. Both these conditions would be in contradiction to the law of continuity.[14]

---

[13] G. Plouquet, *Dissertatio historico-cosmologica de lege continuitatis sive gradationibus leibnitiana* (Tübingen, 1761), 64. Analogous questions are discussed also in *De Corporum organisatorum generatione disquisitio philosophice . . .* (Berlin, 1749).

[14] G. Plouquet, *Dissertatio historico-cosmologica,* 65.

Towards the middle of the eighteenth century A. G. Kästner (1719-1800) expressed a similar perplexity in his *De Lege continui in natura*.[15] When applied to changes in nature, "lex continui" means that anything that changes must go through all the changes necessary to reach the ultimate; in reality, Kästner observed, not only is it impossible to set up a chain without interruptions (since the distance between the most perfect created being and its creator is greater than that existing between the most perfect and the lowest of creatures, and since, above all, the gap between creature and creator is unbridgeable); but it is contrary to Leibniz's view that nature makes no leaps (*natura non facit saltus*). These rigorous defenders of the law of continuity in mathematics and physics then maintained its inapplicability to the scale of nature and especially made use of it in the analysis of generation and of the development of the embryo into the adult individual.

IV. *Charles Bonnet.*—Bonnet and Robinet, however, declared themselves faithful disciples of Leibniz and champions of a law of continuity strictly applied to both the physical and the living world. They were eccentric characters, half naturalists, half philosophers; but their contributions to the reversal of the model of nature going from *descending* to *ascending* and to the conception of the perfectibility of nature, individuals, and society, were of lasting influence.

Charles Bonnet (1770-1793), a Genevan, biologist and strong supporter of the performist thesis, tells in his memoires how he came into contact with Leibniz's thinking. In the winter of 1748 he first read Leibniz's *Théodicée*, and from that moment he referred to the event as one of the most important in his intellectual life.[16] His enthusiastic statements should not be taken too literally, since a few lines later, Bonnet himself candidly confesses that he had not understood either the monadology or the doctrine of preordained harmony. His Leibnizian inspiration can therefore be reduced to the doctrine of the preexistence of germs and souls in particular, as well as to the hypothesis of the chain of being and the principle of continuity.

The enchanting prospect opened up by Leibniz's philosophy was rather one of nature proceeding by degrees from one creation to another, without gaps on its way. Bonnet's universe is systematic: everything contained in it is arranged, related, linked, chained together. Every single thing is the immediate effect of something that has preceded it and in turn determines the existence of what follows.[17] Nature does not proceed by leaps and bounds; everything that exists has a sufficient reason, which for Bonnet was identified with the proximate and immediate cause. The

[15] Leipzig, 1750.

[16] Ch. Bonnet, *Mémoirs autobiographiques*, ed. R. Savioz (Paris, 1948), 100.

[17] *Contemplation de la nature*, in *Oeuvres d'histoire naturelle et de philosophie* (Neuchâtel, 1779-1783), VII, 36.

present state of a body is the result or product of its antecedent's state, for as there is a gradation in the growth of beings, so there is between one being and another. Bonnet wholly accepted the concept of the universal chain (from which its creator is excluded) that unites all beings, joins all worlds, and embraces all spheres from the lowest to the highest degree of bodily or spiritual perfection. Just as Tremblay's (1700-1784) polyp had come to fill the apparent void between the animal and the plant world, so sooner or later, Bonnet concluded, some other being would be discovered that bridges the gap that nature seems to have left in passing from plants to minerals. Our knowledge, Bonnet stated, is only just beginning to scratch the surface of the realm of nature, for nature has infinite creations about whose existence we know nothing and whose exact nomenclature we do not even possess. Here Bonnet formed a hypothesis: the intermediary between plants and minerals might be fossils, even though there is still a vast gulf between the most regular and plant-like fossil and the least organized plant, for fossils do not grow, feed or reproduce. However this might be, the void between plants and minerals would one day be filled, corroborating the wonderful gradation existing between all beings.[18]

On this subject Bonnet engaged in controversy with Maupertuis (1698-1759). In his *Essai de cosmologie* (1751) Maupertuis had in fact hypothesized that a natural catastrophe, such as a collision with a comet, could have destroyed a part of the species. Thus Maupertuis offered an explanation for the disappearance of certain natural species for whose previous existence there was clear evidence. As far as Bonnet was concerned, however, it was only a question of ignorance when anyone believed there were breaks in the great chain of being. When natural history, still in its infancy, reached maturity and when we had the exact nomenclature for all the species contained in our globe, then and only then would we be able to state whether the scale of beings is really interrupted. It is true that Bonnet admitted that the state of the present natural world might be different from the original one. But instead of imagining, as Maupertuis did, some catastrophic, destructive intervention, or even, as the latter seems to have intuited, a real and natural filiation of living beings, Bonnet simply attributed the differentiation of beings and their increase in number with respect to their original state to climate or diet, or to hybridization.

This differentiation of the species due to external climatic or environmental factors did not, however, alter the performist beliefs of Bonnet. Whether he was speaking in terms of evolution or preformation, preexistence of germs or preordination, his thinking remained developmentalist. He held that everything had been formed *ab initio*, nothing is generated. What we improperly call generation is only the beginning of a devel-

---

[18] *Considérations sur les corps organisés*, in *Oeuvres d'histoire naturelle*, V, 87-88; 191-6.

opment which will make visible and palpable what is invisible and impalpable. This is the only certitude deducible from the occurrence of two different orders of causation, *emboîtement* or *panspermia* (original dissemination of germs in all the parts of nature), and to neither of these two ideas did Bonnet adhere, although he tended towards the first.[19]

Bonnet's schema seems to deny all sudden evolution, all creative spontaneity, every break or interruption in continuity. Thus in the realm of immobilism the only change he permitted was a quite particular "perfectibility," in which progress, conservation, and gradation were included.

The premise set out in the *Palingénésie* rests on the belief in the limitless perfectibility of animals, together with the character of divine goodness that cannot but desire the growth of happiness of its creatures. Since this growth is inseparable from bodily and spiritual perfection, we may infer, Bonnet concluded, that each animal species is ordained to attain a perfection whose organic principles were foreseen at the beginning but whose development (which could rise to the knowledge of God) is ordained according to the future state of the globe. In perfecting its own limbs, its own senses, its own intellectual faculties, every animal species will achieve a step forward in quality which will enable it to go up one step in the scale of nature, allowing the species immediately below it, which in the meantime will have undergone an analogous process, to occupy the step previously filled by the first species. As the scale and the linearity remain intact, this metaphoric movement will allow a process of perfecting in time which is real even if imperceptible, so that the very gradation of beings will be maintained in the future but according to other degrees of proportion, determined by the grade of perfectibility reached by each species.[20]

Amusement over the idea of monkey-like Newtons and Leibnizes and ideas such as Robinet's fish-men have often sidetracked us from grasping how great was the affinity between this chain of beings, quivering with life and pointing towards a future perfection, and contemporary philosophies of history focussing on the triumph of mankind in constant progress towards betterment. If the evolution-epigenesist movement (Maupertuis-Buffon-Diderot) gave history that dynamic and genetic sense that was to find full development in the nineteenth century, the foundation of that striving towards perfection, or at least the image of a better future than the present, is to be found in the naturalistic movement founded on continuity.

V. *Robinet or "la nature qui apprend à faire l'homme".*—Similar opinions were expressed by another naturalist-philosopher of the second half of the eighteenth century, J. B. Robinet (1735-1820), whose writings

[19] *La Palingénésie philosophique, ou idées sur l'état passé et sur l'état futur des êtres vivans etc.* (Genève, 1769), I, t.I, 204-05.
[20] *Op. cit.*, 198-99 and 203-04.

Bonnet knew, although he did not share his opinions. For Robinet the hierarchic order of the scale of nature had its counterpart in the hierarchic order of society. The harmony of the latter had to correspond to the harmony of the former. Robinet was very concerned with a possible disturbance of the social order which might affect the equilibrium of good and evil which regulated the efficient working of society, and he tried to face the problem by tackling it from a metaphysical point of view. He seemed in fact even more obsessed by the problem of evil than Bonnet was,[21] and he tried to justify and offset its presence in the world by establishing the existence of an exactly equivalent proportion of good. The harmony of nature is the perfect equilibrium of good and evil. Its variety equals the sum of the combinations of these two essences, which are opposite yet always united. The quantity of evil is equal to the quantity of good. Pure, absolute evil cannot exist because it would be an imperfection in the total good, which cannot be infinite, at least in the finite field.[22] In nature there exists a precise gradation of the species, but despite the subordination which places, the lowest below the highest, the equilibrium of good and evil present in each species guarantees its perfect equality.

Comparing these pages of *De la Nature* with those in the same volume concerned with the study of society, we find a perfect parallelism between natural species and social ranks. When writing of nature, however, Robinet was descriptive, whereas when dealing with society, he became prescriptive. If every social state possessed pleasure and pain in like measure, a preferable condition would not exist. The inequality of ranks, Robinet explained, did not consist in an excess of good in the highest ranks nor in a great amount of evil in the lowest but rather in the fact that the lowest classes are such because they are less "fortunate" as well as less "unfortunate" than the higher ones. Following the graduated arrangement of the ranks, it could easily be noted that growth occurred according to a proportionate increase of good and some evils (the shift from singular to plural here is significant). Because of the acquisition of both in equal amounts, it might be concluded that no condition existed which could really be defined as better or worse than another, whatever the distance between the two might be. In concrete terms it was important for the happiness of society that its humble components remained in the condition in which they were born. If they had a less ignoble soul and if society contrived to increase their sensitivity and their education, they would realize the degradation in which they lived and would no longer enjoy the simple pleasures with which they were content; they would refuse heavy work, the only thing they enjoyed. The same thing would

---

[21] See J. Marx, "Charles Bonnet contre les lumières (1738-1850)," *Studies on Voltaire and the Eighteenth Century* (1976), 145.
[22] J. B. Robinet, *De la Nature,* I, 97, 182.

happen to the negro slaves, strong and stupid as Robinet assumed they were. Anyone awakening their sensitivity, their knowledge, and their good sense would be doing them a great disservice, for their condition would soon become unbearable for them. They would no longer carry out humble tasks and hard work, and they would stop at nothing to harm their masters. Anyone thinking of bettering the French peasant or the American Negro would be upsetting the equilibrium of the individual and disturbing the harmony of the State, preventing the happiness of both. But who indeed, concluded Robinet, could possibly be so crazy as to wish to exchange the healthy life of the strong peasant, content in his vulgar pleasures, for the dramatic existence of the lord whose excess of sensual pleasures prevented him from enjoying even the sweetness of love?[23]

The *scala naturae* set up by Robinet, which reflects the hierarchical organization of society, had the normal requisites of classical Greek thinking, which had been reaffirmed by Leibniz. Robinet acknowledged that it had been Leibniz who first discussed the importance of the principle of continuity,[24] as well as the description of nature as an infinite scale bounded at one end by nothing and at the other by infinite existence.

Comparing the construction of Robinet with that conceived in the same period by Bonnet, it may be noted that the hypothesis of a unity of design which directs the general plan of creation is very similar in both. Although Bonnet's acceptance of it was cautious, Robinet embraced it more enthusiastically. For Bonnet the various productions of nature are only different sections of the same general design, which embraces all the parts of earthly creation, or rather different points of a single section which, with its infinitely varied circumvolutions, traces the shapes, proportions, and the linking of all terrestial beings.[25] The unity of the design is revealed first when the design itself is traced and then at the moment of deciphering, which can only be completely carried out by the same hand that traced it. For Robinet the unity is even stronger, since it appears not only at the moment of the composition and description of the design but also, and particularly, in the behavior of nature. Nature is a unique activity which comprises past, present, and future phenomena and ensures in its permanence the duration of things. Creation is an original but permanent impulse which makes the universe and the immense chain of different beings which compose it live and move eternally. Everything operates according to this single creative act, and everything would cease if this act were to end. For Robinet the whole stands, exists,

[23] *Op. cit.,* 114 ff.
[24] J. B. Robinet, *Considérations philosophiques de la gradation naturelle des formes de l'être, ou les essais de la nature qui apprend à faire l'homme* (Paris, 1768), 7. See also *De la Nature,* IV, 8-9.
[25] Ch. Bonnet, *Contemplation de la nature,* VIII, 214-15.

and acts only by virtue of the mutual connection of its parts; and it is inconceivable that one phenomenon be detached from the whole or one truth be affirmed independently of it.[26]

A closer study of this unitary design leads us, however, to understand the difference between Bonnet's and Robinet's standpoints. On one point in particular the divergence is "abysmal."[27] Bonnet in fact, after questioning the validity of the methodical classifications based on the hypothesis of a real and absolute separation of the different orders which make up the scale of beings, puts forward in his turn a classification by classes. This aroused Robinet's profound indignation. It mattered very little if Bonnet's taxonomy was based on a new criterion (the "organization" of beings). Even if one single essential quality, in Bonnet's case organization, or any other quality belonging to a certain number of beings were assumed to the exclusion of the others, this would be sufficient for the isolated class, defined on the basis of any qualitative criterion, to break the chain and violate the law of continuity.

Robinet's objection was far from superficial. To be able to uphold the division into classes and at the same time maintain the principle of continuity, links would have to be set up between non-homogeneous categories, such as organized and nonorganized, animate and inanimate. But the intermediary beings linking the two ought to be part of the two contraries which mutually exclude each other, and this is impossible. The principle was stated several times in De la Nature, in which Bonnet was the antagonist.

The process of nature's becoming, in Robinet's schema, could be seen as a dialectic process which places importance on the element of continuity and unity over oppositions. Each of the moments forming the process must be connected to the others, must indeed involve the others to be able to permit, in their unwinding (in the literal sense of unravelling something previously wound up), a continuous and unitary process which affirms the principle of the organic whole at every moment.

The cornerstones of Robinet's doctrine, from that aforementioned single act of nature to the concept of the prototype, all aim at assuring the process of becoming that is connected to the substantial unity and identity of nature.

The prototype, a concept which Robinet introduced and discussed in the Considérations philosophiques, is essentially a primitive design on the basis of which all beings are conceived, formed, and graduated to infinity.[28] Moreover, the prototype is a principle of force that manifests

---

[26] J. B. Robinet, De la Nature, I, 24; Considérations philosophiques, 2. See also J. Marx, op.cit., I, 355-56.

[27] As Paolo Rossi rightly points out in I Segni del tempo. Storia della terra e storia delle nazioni da Hooke a Vico (Milano, 1979), 123.

[28] J. B. Robinet, Considérations philosophiques, 6.

itself as a tendency to change which is continuously and necessarily exerted. The unitary nature of this principle and the presence of this "quality," which is common to all beings, enabled Robinet to present his strict affirmation of the fundamental law of continuity.

Nature works on the original prototype, which is altered, modified, and enriched as it is realized in matter. Every variation of the prototype gives rise to a new being; and nature itself, in its progress, grows perfect, so to speak, in the elaboration of its most perfect creation, man, so that every variation of the prototype seems to be a study carried out by nature in order to learn how to create man. Man will thus be composed from the prototype plus, not all of the qualities of the other beings but the result—compatible in one essence—of all the combinations that the prototype has undergone in passing through all the degrees of the universal progression of being.

And what else can we learn from fossils, asked Robinet, if not that they are the first attempts of nature to express the human form? Nature has sowed the human form everywhere along the scale of beings to announce in an intelligible way in which direction the first metamorphoses of being are moving.

Robinet was faithful to the principle of the presence of a single quality possessed to a greater or lesser degree in all things. As a guarantee of the law of continuity, he considered fossils and in general minerals as endowed with an organization and a level of life, even if minimal; thus, they may possess the same property as animals and plants. In so doing, Robinet was merely drawing extreme consequences from principles which were almost universally accepted. Proceeding by analogy on the basis of that philosophical apriorism which was characteristic of all his research, Robinet conjectured that minerals, whose life is undeniable, reproduce themselves through a fusion of male and female seed and thus undergo a process of growth from being soft to becoming gradually harder.

His opinion on caudate men or sirens was even more implausible. They were supposed to represent the beings that link inferior animals to men in the same way that the "fibrous stones" form the transition between minerals and plants. Not content with basing this hypothesis on his a priori method founded on a strict *esprit de système,* Robinet supported his reasoning with dozens of accounts of fishermen and sailors who had witnessed amazing catches of mermen and mermaids;[29] he also resorted to the authority of writers such as Pliny, La Mothe le Vayer, Athanasius Kircher, and Benoît de Maillet.

These eccentricities, however, cannot relegate Robinet to the band of dreamers or failures. We are not concerned, in our study of eighteenth century naturalists, with yet another application of an evolutionistic criterion such as natural selection, which considers the legacy of Leibniz'

[29] *Op.cit.,* 112, and *passim.*

lex continui as the blind alley in which the reproduction of a species incapable of adapting to its environment comes to an end. It is pointless to look for a true transformism arranged in chronological series in the biological writers of the second half of the eighteenth century. But it would be wrong to deny their positive contribution or fail to acknowledge the step forward from the simple to the complex by seeing their representation of the world as fixed and unchangeable.[30]

In Robinet as in Bonnet, the static concept of the chain of being became dynamic.[31] Nature moves forward slowly and gradually, Robinet explained, in a fashion analogous to art (which proceeds from the most primitive representations to our masterpieces) or to the series of natural numbers (which starts from a unit and increases by addition). It is evident, especially in the example of numbers, that there is no hypothesis of autogeneration. But it is likewise evident that in Robinet the principle of perfectibility plays the central role, according to which living forms are created through a progressive process of development which goes from the simple to the complex. Everything begins its existence in its simplest and smallest form and grows larger by means of a uniform gradation until it reaches the point of perfection.

VI. *De Beaurieu, Delille, Delisle de Sales.* —The theme of the chain of being and of its unity of plan was continually taken up in the second half of the eighteenth century by writers who were more like Robinet in adopting literary-political-philosophical claims than like Bonnet in his experimentalistic attitude,[32] but who were nevertheless inspired by both and achieved a notable success with their works, which were intended for a wide reading public.

Gaspard-Guillard de Beaurieu (1728-1795) was the author of *L'Elève de la nature* (1766), a book written for young people, which tells the story of a young boy's acquisition of sense and reasoning, when, after having lived for fifteen years in a cave where he never saw the light of day nor spoke or heard people speak, he began to be aware of the world on a desert island. De Beaurieu also wrote a lengthy *Cours d'histoire naturelle ou tableau de la nature,* published in seven volumes in 1770. Whereas the first work reveals the writer's admiration for Locke and Rousseau (*L'Elève de la nature* was often attributed to the latter), the *Tableau de la nature* displays his acceptance of Bonnet's finalism. De Beaurieu, in fact, adopted the schema of the scale of beings and represented it as a pyramid whose base is formed by the minerals, the center by plants, and the top by animals. Within this pyramid the level of

---

[30] They are all thesis of François Jacob presented in *La Logique du vivant: une histoire de l'hérédité* (Paris, 1970).

[31] See L. G. Crocker, *Diderot and Eighteenth-Century French Transformism,* in *Forerunners of Darwin: 1745-1859,* eds. B. Glass, O. Temkin, and W. L. Strauss, Jr. (Baltimore, 1959), 135.

[32] See J. Marx, *op.cit.,* I, 357-58.

organization and the *esprit de vie* gradually increase from the base to the top, while the quantity of *materia bruta* decreases. The universe is composed of two elements, living matter and dead matter. From the different combinations of these two elements all possible beings are born. The unity of design and of action intended by the divine order and wisdom is revealed in the general resemblance of creatures, just as their infinite variety of forms testifies to the omnipotence of divine performance. The harmony of the universe, reflecting the eternal order which is divine, produces the immense chain of the whole universe which is perpetually in motion and whose links are never jumbled or crossed.

If a debt to Robinet can be discerned in de Beaurieu's insistence on the harmony of the universe, his influence is even more evident in his positioning of man in the scale of beings. The human body can be graduated in its internal economy like the model that nature followed in the formation of all the other animals, so that anything said of its mechanism, its senses, and its other parts is a necessary introduction to the history of the other animals.[33]

Another bio-philosopher and author, writing under the pseudonym of Delisle de Sales, was as well-known during his lifetime as he was presumptuous: Jean Baptiste Claude Isoard (1743?-1816) was the author of the *Histoire philosophique du monde primitif* in seven volumes (1780), and the author of the *De la Philosophie de la nature* (1766), which became the object of scandal and was burnt but which was nevertheless reprinted right up to the beginning of the nineteenth century. In this study he recognized that nature proceeds by imperceptible changes and gradations, moving from the simple to the complex; he postulated the need for the existence of an intermediary organization between the one realm and the next. He maintained no doubts about the immense lengths of time which must have passed between the first developments of organized nature in marine life and the birth of vegetation on the land after emerging from the sea, and between the development of plant life on earth and the birth of man.

Like Bonnet, Delisle de Sales denied that the scale of beings could cover, in his hierarchy, the entire range of existence up to divinity, since between a created intelligence and infinite intelligence there exists not only an interval of space too vast to be filled with a series of gradations but a real qualitative gap which demonstrates the disparity of the two. God is "chained" to the world, Delisle explained, only in the sense that he holds the chain in his hands, but the divinity cannot properly be submitted to the eternal laws of nature.[34] Unlike Bonnet, he did deny the permanently dynamic character of the scale of beings. The vital thrust

---

[33] G. G. de Beaurieu, *Cours d'histoire naturelle ou tableau de la nature* (Paris, 1770), I, 45-46.

[34] J. B. Delisle de Sales, *De la Philosophie de la nature* (Amsterdam, 1770), I, 7.

of nature, which brought about the development and the perfectioning of the world, will sooner or later come to an end when the internal energy is exhausted, and the universe will move in downward gradation towards its end. The process through which the organization of nature has passed from the simple to the complex will one day be repeated in reverse, and with imperceptible gradations the scale will descend again from the most complex to the simplest being endowed with the most elementary structure.

In the portrayal of Jacques Delille (1738-1813), however, nature's activity is much more reassuring. The most famous of his poetic works, *Les trois Règnes de la nature* (1803), proclaimed in verse the continuity and the gradation of the *scala naturae,* the quality of the "fibrous stones" which represent the link between the mineral realm and the plant world, and the triumph of the polyp. The poetry of this French Alexander Pope displayed before his readers' eyes the fluid unwinding of the great chain of being in its reassuring continuity.

VII. *The encounter with Newtonianism.*—In order to meet the requirements of gradation and continuity, the chain of being had to operate within a full universe characterized by action through contact, of Cartesian-Leibnizian derivation. The mathematicians and philosophers of continuity (Plouquet, Kästner, Boscovich) upheld this concept of action by contact, and Bonnet, Robinet, Delille, and Delisle de Sales modelled their *scalae naturae* on this assumption. But an opposing movement of thinking was being elaborated at the same time during the eighteenth century, namely, the Newtonian model of the void universe and action at a distance. What were the consequences of the introduction of these principles on the questions concerning us here?

One example may be taken from the application of Newtonianism to biology made by Maupertuis. Reason and experience, stated Maupertuis, prove that, as opposed to the opinion that the whole of matter forms a continuum without interruptions between the parts, there is, on the contrary, a void in nature, and that the bodies are scattered in space without any need for reciprocal contact.[35] The same force of gravitation-attraction which controls the behavior of bodies in space governs the formation of organic bodies. However, as the force of attraction is transformed, in Maupertuis's terminology, into *affinity,* it loses the characteristics of the simple mechanical phenomenon of the Newtonian model and gains "Leibnizian" qualities. A uniform, blind attraction spread over the parts of matter would not explain how these parts are arranged to form the most rudimentary organized bodies. If they all possess the same tendency and the same force to join them together, why then do some go to form the eye and others the ear? Why is there this wonderful arrangement? Why

---

[35] P. L. M. de Maupertuis, *Système de la nature* in *Oeuvres* (Hildesheim, 1965), II, 174-75.

do they not join haphazardly? If an explanation is to be attempted, even if founded entirely on analogy, some principle of intelligence must be applied, something similar to what we call desire, aversion, memory. Thus, for Maupertuis, in order to explain the formation of organized bodies, psychic properties must be added to the physical properties of matter; and he takes from Leibniz the consciousness and the will of the simple substances that make up the world. By endowing the "living particles"—which in Maupertuis's system represent the elementary units that make up living beings—with a kind of memory, the regularity of the unfolding of organic processes and even the existence of that otherwise inexplicable phenomenon, the heredity of character, can be explained.[36]

The arrangement of the parts is not made, according to this model, by an external order but by an internal one within the parts themselves. Each of them "knows" (so to speak) how and where it must join the others because it preserves a kind of memory of its previous situation. A process is generated from the old one, which may preserve some characteristic of the previous one but which is new and different.

The role played by Maupertuis's "particles" in the world of living beings is similar to that of Buffon's "organic molecules," although for Buffon the power of Newtonian mechanics over the ambit of the organization of the living beings is even more explicit.[37] In formulating a theory of generation, Buffon took as a model the Newtonian idea of a system of matter in motion in a void. The living organic molecules which animate all organized bodies and which are used to nourish and generate all beings are controlled in their movements by forces that, having the capacity to permeate them thoroughly, are comparable to the force of attraction. The molecules are indestructible and always active; they are continually joining to form organized bodies,[38] controlled in their distribution and behavior by that principle of force which Buffon called *moule intérieur*. In Buffon's case also we may notice how his rejection of the plenistic assumption led him to make formulations of a dynamic nature which can also be found in his account of the formation of an inhabitable world.

The theories of generation by epigenesis gave fundamental impetus to the development of a dynamic and transformist doctrine in eighteenth-century biological science. Moreover, epigenism helped to modify theological-philosophical thinking by enriching it with the notion of creation extended in time, while the doctrine of preexistence implied the single and simultaneous creation of all beings.

It was Diderot who seemed especially to have given the concept of nature the qualities of dynamism and individuality, of self-generating and

---

[36] *Op.cit.*, 146-47, 179.
[37] G. Canguilhem, *La Connaissance de la vie* (Paris, 1952).
[38] G. L. L. de Buffon, *Les Époques de la nature*, ed. J. Roger (Paris, 1962).

temporal process, subsuming concepts of both the Leibnizian and the Newtonian world systems in his thinking. His idea of nature can in fact be defined as unifying, continuistic, and also dynamic. Nature performed a *single act,* in virtue of which it continuously recreates ("nature is still at work") and the results of which can be seen in the continuity of the great chain.[39] But in his chain of being the links have become degrees; the process of temporalization has been fully completed.

VIII. *Biology and society.*—In a period when biological questions were treated within philosophy, it was easy to move from theories about the natural world to ideas of the social world and vice versa. For instance, it was natural for Robinet to move from the analysis of the hierarchy of natural beings to that of the human races. Voltaire was fully aware of this tendency and was, much like Johnson and Blumenbach, one of the harshest critics of the theory of the perfect continuity of the scale of nature. Voltaire believed that the series of forms was interrupted and realized that the concept of the unbroken chain of being seemed designed to impress and please public imagination. "Good people" like to recognize in this hierarchy "the pope and cardinals, followed by the archbishops and bishops, after whom are the vicars, curates and priests, the deacons and subdeacons, then come the monks and the capuchins bring up the rear."[40] It must indeed be asked whether this emphasis on the definition of the world as an entity under the aegis of an overall providential harmony, where a rigidly continuistic interpretation of phenomena excludes the least overlap, was not in fact deliberately aimed at directing the behavior of a society which was in conflict—a society which was in conflict but which saw itself as immovable in its vertical cross-section, or within which at most a sideways movement might be possible along an axis, so that the distances between classes might be strictly retained, while the classes themselves improved their position without any of them taking an inferior role or advancing at the expense of another. In this sense the metaphor of the chain of being as applied to society is slightly altered to show a reality without conflicts or problems—certainly not a true image, particularly at that time, when society was preparing for a revolution.

We may thus ask whether this metaphorical portrayal was not intended to describe the world as it is but rather to suggest how it should be. The prescriptive aim seems to appear insistently whenever natural or scientific models are applied to the sphere of social behavior. This purely descriptive value when limited to the biological sphere changes into a specifically normative one when grafted onto the social sphere. Description is formalized in norm. If nature does not change, neither does society change, nor *must* it. The maintenance of equilibrium and social harmony

[39] D. Diderot, *De l'Interprétation de la nature* (Paris, 1753), 31-33.
[40] Voltaire, *A Philosophical Dictionary* (London, s.d.), I, 255.

is attainable only when nature's example is followed. God, providence, or nature has already arranged for all beings the best condition for their existence, in which perfectibility is also possible. Living beings settle in the lines of the natural plot, where they find equilibrium and the possibility of fulfillment. The social beings must do likewise.

Georg-August-Universität, Göttingen.

Chapter XXIX

HYSTERIA AND MECHANICAL MAN*

By John P. Wright

For different ends the busy head is fill'd
With different spirits from the blood distill'd.[1]

The study of hysteria and related diseases has played a central role in the development of a major twentieth-century conception of man and the nature of the human mind. It was research into these diseases by Charcot, Freud, and others which led to the belief that even "normal" people are affected by ideas and instincts which are somehow cut off from consciousness, and over which they have very little control. In hysteria these unconscious processes cause local loss of sensation, pains, paralysis, and gross motor disturbances. Freud claimed that these symptoms are substitutes for "wishes and desires which . . . have been prevented from obtaining discharge in psychical activity that is admissible to consciousness."[2] These wishes and desires, which represent universal innate sexual tendencies, are kept from consciousness by a process called "repression." Freud thought that neuroses develop out of an inevitable conflict between ego and sexuality" which is somehow solved by normal people, but not by those who suffer from the illness in question.[3] Thus we are led to the view of man (and the human mind) as a bipolar creature whose ego is opposed by wishes and desires which are constantly seeking for fulfillment.

Interest in hysteria and its explanation has not been confined to the late nineteenth and early twentieth centuries. Thomas Sydenham writes about hysteria in 1682 because hysteria, next to fever, is the most common disease, especially among women: ". . . If we except those who lead a hard and hardy life," there is rarely one who is wholly free from it]."[4] He also found the disease remarkable because of the multiformity of shapes which it puts on. It is a Proteus or chameleon and "whatever part of the body it attacks, it will create the proper symptom of that

*An earlier version of this paper was read at the XVth International Congress the History of Science in Edinburgh, August 1977. Research was supported by the Canada Council Killam Program. I am indebted to Renée Isenberg Wright for her criticisms of earlier versions of this paper, especially of my earlier views Freud.

[1] Sir Richard Blackmore, *The Nature of Man: A Poem* (London, 1711).

[2] Sigmund Freud, *Three Essays on the Theory of Sexuality*, trans. & ed. James Strachey (New York, 1962), 55.

[3] *A General Introduction to Psychoanalysis*, trans. Joan Riviere (New York, 1966), 359.

[4] *Epistle to Dr. Cole, The Works of Thomas Sydenham*, trans. R. D. Latham (London: Sydenham Society, 1852), II, 85, cf. 56.

234   JOHN P. WRIGHT

part."[5] Observations about the multiform symptoms of this disease go
back to ancient times. Sydenham cites a letter from Democritus to
Hippocrates in which it is said that the womb (the seat of the disorder
for the ancients) is the cause of "six hundred miseries, and innumerable
calamities."[6] Hippocrates himself describes how the womb wanders
around the body causing disorders in the various organs it encounters.[7]

If interest in this curious disease goes back a long way in the history
of western medicine, then so does its close connection with a theoretical
interest in the nature of man. In his *Timaeus* Plato gives us an account
of hysteria which is directly related to the physical description of the
disease that we find in the Hippocratic writings. Plato describes the
womb as an animal which becomes disobedient to reason and courses
through the body causing disease. It is,

desirous of procreating children and when remaining unfruitful long beyond
its proper time, gets discontented and angry, and wandering in every direction through the body, closes up the passages of the breath, and by obstruct-
ing respiration drives [the woman] to extremity, causing all variety of disease.

This account is closely connected with Plato's general notion of the
soul as consisting of three parts (appetite, spirit, and reason), each o
which has its own motions.[9] Inactivity of one part, causes that part t
become the strongest and results in imbalance and ill health. Plato'
theory of hysteria fits in well with his account in the *Republic* (439d
of a war in the soul between reason and desire. Freud recognized that i
associating hysteria with sexuality he was "going back to the ver
beginnings of medicine and reviving a thought of Plato's."[10] For in Plat
one finds something very like the Freudian conflict of ego and sexuality
though the teleological description of sexuality in the Platonic account
as bound up with desire of procreation, is foreign to the Freudian notio
of sexuality. Freud insists that the sexual instinct exists quite apar
from any procreative function.[11] However both accounts regard the eg
as being opposed to a lower bodily soul which has its own desire
and goals.

In the course of Sydenham's century, the seventeenth, the seat c
hysteria shifted from the womb to the brain and nervous system. At th
beginning of the century one still finds some of the elements of th
wandering womb theory contained in Eduuard Jorden's *A Briefe Di.*

[5] *Ibid.*, 85.
[6] T. Sydenham, *Dissertatio Epistolaris ad Gulielmum Cole, M.D.* . . . (Londo
1682), 117. Latham is not faithful to Sydenham's Latin original here.
[7] *Oeuvres Complètes d'Hippocrates*, trad. E. Littré (Amsterdam, 1967
VIII, 33.
[8] *Timaeus, Dialogues of Plato*, trans. B. Jowett (Oxford, 1964), III, sect. 91
[9] *Ibid.*, 89e.
[10] S. Freud, *An Autobiographical Study*, trans. James Strachey (Londc
1935), 42.   [11] *General Introduction*, 312

course of a Disease called Suffocation of the Mother (1603).[12] Jorden speaks of the womb as "being grievously anoyed [sic] with the malignity of those vapours" which (according to the Galenic theory) arise from putrified menses and female seminal fluid which have not been properly excreted from the body.[13] The womb rises upwards in the body in order to escape these noxious odors. It is significant that one finds this animism in Jorden who is looking for the best established medical theories in order to attack those who are prosecuting the sufferers of this disease as witches. The theory of the rising womb is still found in 1651 in the writings of William Harvey who, like Jorden, attributes hysteria to sexual abstinence.[14] However in 1618 the French physician Charles Lepois centered the disease in the head and more particularly in the seat of common sense (*sensorium commune*).[15] Lepois attacks the womb theory by noting that almost all the symptoms occur in men as well as women. By the time the celebrated English "neurocartographer" Thomas Willis writes about hysteria in 1667 the womb theory is clearly on the decline. He cites both Lepois and Dr. Highmore as having shown that that theory is untenable. Willis considers the disease as primarily convulsive, due to the explosions of the "animal spirits" in the brain.[16] Between 1700 and 1765 no book-length English language study of hysteria and related disorders (I have discovered eight) regards the disease as centered in the womb.

[12] Unless otherwise indicated works referred to are published in London.

[13] *Op. cit.,* 5.

[14] See Ilza Veith, *Hysteria: The History of a Disease* (Chicago, 1965), 130-31. While it contains an extremely useful general account of the history of hysteria, Veith's book does not appear to me to give an entirely accurate picture of 17th and 18th-century views on the disease. The views of Sydenham seem to be closer to those of Willis than Veith acknowledges. See H. Isler, *Thomas Willis* (New York, 1968), esp. 139-40. Veith comments that, in opposition to Willis, Sydenham held that hysteria was due to "an imbalance of the mind-body relationship." But the real issue between Willis and Sydenham concerned the question of the extent to which visceral organs were involved in hysteria. Willis was generally regarded as holding that the disorder originated in the spleen: see, e.g., Sir Richard Blackmore's *A Treatise on the Spleen and Vapours* (1725), 237. It also is important to carefully weigh Veith's contention (147) that Baglivi—an Italian iatromechanist, much influenced by Sydenham—introduced "the concept of psychosomatic medicine." *In a certain sense* most 17th-century iatromechanists were willing to allow for the influence of the mind on the body; the difficulty is to discover that exact sense.

[15] C. Piso, *Selectorum Observationum . . .* (Pont-à-Mousson, 1618), quoted in G. Abricossoff, *L'Hystérie aux XVIIe et XVIIIe siècles* (Paris: Thèse, 1897), 5-26. This work on hysteria by a former student of Charcot was never published. In contrast to Veith, Abricossoff gives high grades to authors who ascribe hysteria to a malfunction in the central nervous system. Curiously, she does not discuss the question of the ideogenic character of hysterical symptoms.

[16] Willis, *Pathologiae cerebri et nervosi generis specimen* (Oxford, 1667), 48. Hereafter I will refer to the English translation, *An Essay of the Pathology of the Brain . . . ,* trans. S. Pordage (London, 1681), 77-78.

236JOHNP.WRIGHT

Corresponding to this shift in the location of the disease there is a shift in the analysis of its essential nature. Hysteria is completely divorced from any connection with frustrated sexual desires. At best sexual appetite receives brief mention as one of the purely physical perturbations which can act upon an already overly sensitive nervous system.[17] For most physicians of the period 1667–1765 the essence of the disease lies in this heightened nervous sensitivity which causes the nervous system to react violently to stimuli of various kinds. It is this sensitivity, rather than an unsatisfied sexual appetite, which was used to account for the predominance of the disease among women.[18]

At the same time it must be said that the nature of this disease as a *mental* disorder was clearly recognized, and is apparent in the description of the disease given by Sydenham, a description frequently repeated in eighteenth-century accounts of hysteria. Sydenham followed a Baconian methodology which led him to the presentation of what he called a "history of the disease," a careful listing of the symptoms of the disease which was preliminary to its reduction to a "definite and certain species."[19] After a careful listing of the complex and varied physiological symptoms of hysteria, Sydenham notes that, in this disease, "the mind sickens [even] more than the body."[20] He goes on to describe the severe emotional disorders of his patients. The worst passions of the human mind arise without any reason: despair, melancholy forebodings, fear, anger, and jealousy. Their feelings toward others change suddenly, without any reason, from immoderate love to immoderate hatred. Sydenham gives a vivid description of the guilt felt by his patients: ". . . they are racked in both mind and body as if life were a purgatory wherein they expiated and paid the penalty of crimes committed in a previous state." He goes so far as to cite the passions themselves as the chief occasioning cause of the disease, that which leads to the onset of physical, as well as mental, symptoms.[21]

But while Sydenham shows this clear recognition of the mental character of the disease, he resolves both the mental and physical symptoms into a disorder of (what he takes to be) the microstructure of the nervous system. In giving "the efficient, internal, and immediate causes" of hysteria Sydenham describes what he calls "a disorder (ataxy)

[17] *Ibid.*, 79. Willis speaks of the disordered spirits becoming "entangled with all the perturbations both of the concupiscable and irrascible appetite." Sir Richard Blackmore (see below p. 244) may have the same thing in mind when he speaks of the latent causes of the diseases being "assisted and promoted by the ferment of puberty" (*op cit.*, 110).

[18] *Ibid.*, 82. Also Sydenham, *Epistle to Dr. Cole*, sect. 80.

[19] *Medical Observations Concerning the History and Cure of Acute Diseases*, Preface third ed., in *Works* . . .I, 13.

[20] *Epistle to Dr. Cole*, sect. 75.   [21] *Ibid.*, sect. 78

of the animal spirits,"[22] a purely physical disorder due to the weakened state of the nervous fluids themselves which makes it possible for them to fly off in disarray at the slightest stimulus. Emotional dysfunctions, no less than purely physical ones, are caused by the improper disposition of the nervous fluids. To use terms later made famous by Sydenham's associate John Locke, the mental symptoms form part of the nominal essence of the disease, but not part of the real essence.[23] The real essence consists in the peculiar structure of the nervous fluids which were supposed to form the basis of muscular movement as well as the passions of the mind.

Sydenham does not give a psychic analysis of the causes of the emotional symptoms of hysteria. In spite of his vivid description of the guilt experienced by his hysterical patients, he never seems to have thought it relevant to ask the reason for that guilt. His theory stands in sharp contrast to the psychoanalytic one, where the reasons for the guilt of hysterical persons become all important. According to Freud's account the persons who suffer from this disease expiate and pay the penalty for the perverse infantile sexual desires which lie hidden in the unconscious part of their minds.[24] These desires are the reason that these people feel ashamed, for the desires constitute a threat to the ego. Sydenham, on the other hand, thinks that the emotional states of his hysterical patients arise without any reason. Hence he turns to a discussion of their mechanical causes. For Sydenham the symptoms of hysteria have mechanical causes, but not reasons.

The role of mind in Sydenham's theory of hysteria is completely different from its role in the theories of Freud and Plato. For Sydenham, the mind plays an entirely passive role in the genesis of the disease. While Freud frequently claims that psychoanalysis showed the powerlessness that human beings have over their destinies, the fact of the matter is that both his and the Platonic theory represent the mind, taken as a whole, as remarkably active. The desires of the unconscious part of the mind are essentially active forces involved in the production of the symptoms of hysteria. However, in Sydenham's account, all activity lies in the nervous system and purely physiological forces are responsible for the production of the mental symptoms of the disease. Sydenham's account of mental disease is fully in accord with the theory of the nature of the human being and the nature of the human mind that was gaining ascendency in his own day.

The rejection of the Platonic division of the soul is central to the theory of man which became predominant during the period of the rise of modern science. Descartes, one of the major proponents of the

[22] *Ibid.*, sect. 79.
[23] John Locke, *Essay Concerning Human Understanding*, ed. J. W. Yolton (London, 1964), II, 43 (3, 6, 2). (First ed. 1690.)
[24] *General Introduction*, 318.

theory, argued that "there is only one soul in us, and that soul does not have in itself any diversity of parts."[25] The perceptions of will, desire, appetite, are reserved for the soul itself: there is no bodily soul in us with desires of its own. Strictly speaking there are no 'carnal' desires. The act of will is said to be the chief, or perhaps the only, operation of the soul itself.[26] All appetites such as sexuality *belong* to the soul, though Descartes thought that their *cause* was a certain physiological process.[27] The will can only act indirectly on the appetites by making changes in the physiological processes of the body.[28] These processes must be understood to be purely physical, describable purely in terms of the categories of matter and motion. Anything that the soul suffers, that is passively received, is the result of purely physical motions. Thus all the actions which lie outside of the soul itself must be describable in purely physical terms. The Cartesian unconscious is purely physical.

Descartes is best remembered for his strict division of man into a mind and a body which are entirely distinct one from the other. He bases this distinction on the claim that one can have a complete conception of oneself as a thinking thing quite apart from one's conception of matter, and one can have a complete conception of matter and material processes quite apart from any mental categories.[29] At the same time Descartes always insists as much upon the substantial union of the mind and body as he does upon their division. In his *Discourse on Method* he writes that the mind depends so strongly upon the body that, if it is possible to make men wiser and more intelligent than they now are, it is in medicine that the means must be sought.[30] The medicine which Descartes proposed was not that practiced in his own day, but one which was founded upon the basic notions of his mechanical physics. He sees this medical progress as leading to the prevention of *mental* as well as purely physical diseases. While Descartes does not believe that thought as such is produced by the nervous system, he does believe that disorders of the faculty of thought in mental illness are caused, not by the mind itself, but by faults in the mechanical organs of the body.[31]

Descartes is a major proponent of the mechanical theory of man. On the one hand the human body is held to be a machine or engine which responds in a reflex and frequently adaptive way to its environment. On the other hand man is said to have an active mind

---

[25] Descartes, *Les Passions de L'Ame,* (Paris, 1649), *Oeuvres et Lettres,* ed. André Bridoux (Paris, ed. Pléiade, 1953), art. 47. All references to works by Descartes will be to this edition. I am responsible for the translations.

[26] Art. 13.   [27] Art. 47.   [28] Art. 41

[29] *Méditations,* 6, 323-24 (first published 1641).

[30] *Le Discours de la Méthode* (Paris, 1637), 6e partie, 168-69.

[31] *Réponses aux 4e Objections,* 447.

which, through knowledge of the laws of the operation of this machine, can correct and improve both the condition of the machine itself, and that of the passive part of the mind which depends upon it. Hence the mind stands in two kinds of relation to the mechanical body. The mind relates to the body actively like the pilot of a boat who guides it through knowledge of its various parts. Robert Boyle, who employs this image, claims that the mind is capable, "especially if instructed in the physician's art," of going beyond the spontaneous adaptive processes of the machine itself, and making changes to preserve it, and correct any faults in its operation.[32] In the second place, as Descartes himself says, "I am not only lodged in my body like a pilot in his vessel, but, besides that, I am very tightly conjoined to it, and so confused and mixed that I compose with it a single whole."[33] This union of the mind and the body into a substantial whole relates to the mind's passive receptive nature wherein it is dependent upon the laws of the mechanical operation of the body.

Descartes regards most 'psychological' processes as being dependent upon physiological structures and motions in the brain and nervous system. Among the psychological functions which he attempts to model in a purely mechanical way are sensation, memory and imagination, appetite and passions, and the automatic behaviour which results from stimuli from these various sources.[34] These functions can all arise from purely physical processes. But even when these activities arise in the mind itself, as does the activity of imagination involved in geometrical reasoning, they depend upon the physical structures in the brain.[35] And judgment concerning the veracity of our senses, freely suspended during the process of doubt to which Descartes subjects himself in the first of his *Meditations,* is itself dependent upon the memory by which we join our present with our past experiences.[36] Such a memory is, according to Descartes' theory, dependent upon the traces left in the brain by these

[32] *A Free Inquiry into the Vulgarly Received Notion of Nature, The Works of Robert Boyle* (London, 1772), V, 236.

[33] *Méditations* 6,326. The words "besides that" are missing from the most commonly used English translation by E. Haldane & G. R. T. Ross, *The Philosophical Works of Descartes* (Cambridge, England, 1931), I, 192. These words are conveyed by the French "outre cela." The original Latin word "ille" *may* be ambiguous, but for Descartes' use of the French to resolve any ambiguity in the Latin see his introduction to the French translation in Adam & Tannery, *Oeuvres de Descartes,* IX, 2-3.

[34] *Traité de l'homme,* 873, published posthumously in 1664. In his more mature works Descartes still attributed most of what his contemporaries called sensation and human action entirely to the body: ". . . pour ce qui est du sentiment et du marcher, je les rapporte aussi, pour la plus grande partie, au corps, et je n'attribue rien à l'âme de ce qui les concerne que cela seule qui est une pensée" (*Réponses aux 5ᵉ Objections,* 478; cf. *Réponses aux 4ᵉ Objections,* 448).

[35] *Méditations* 6, 319; also *Règles pour la direction de l'esprit,* #12, 78.

[36] *Méditations* 6, 333-34.

earlier experiences.[37] Thus failure in judgment itself, can, on Descartes'
view, be attributed to faults in the physical organs of memory.[38]

The extensive dependence of the mind upon the body is apparent
in Descartes' theory of the passions. He defines the passions as certain
perceptions which are "caused, supported and fortified by a certain
movement of the [animal] spirits."[39] In so doing he is assigning the passions to that physiological entity which, according to the Galenic theory
accepted by most of the physicians of his day, was responsible for
sensation and movement. In the Cartesian theory these spirits are
purely physical: they consist of the finest and most agitated particles
of the blood, which enter into the cavities of the brain after being rarified
by the heat of the heart.[40] From the brain the animal spirits are directed
into the nerves (conceived of as hollow tubes) which lead to some
muscle or other. Muscular movement is caused by the elongation and
shortening of opposing sets of muscles due to the increased flow of the
animals spirits from the brain toward one of them.[41] Thus the passions,
by way of the animal spirits, have a direct relation to certain muscular
movements. The direction and flow of the animal spirits from the brain
into muscles depends upon the microstructure of these animal spirits
themselves, as well as certain other conditions.[42] This microstructure of
the animal spirits, which is also the direct cause of the passions, is itself
dependent upon two factors: in the first place, upon certain changes
wrought in the body by the impressions of external objects upon the
senses;[43] and in the second place, upon the dispositions of the organs
involved in the manufacture of the animal spirits, i.e., upon the disposition of the heart, the liver, the stomach, and the spleen.[44]

The objects of the senses constitute what Descartes calls the "most
ordinary and principle cause of the passions."[45] The object-stimuli
agitate the animal spirits in an entirely automatic way causing a certain
desire in the soul and certain disposition in the body to perform a certain
action.[46] The animal spirits of a healthy person are so constituted that,
when stimulated by objects of the senses, they tend to form desires and
actions which are adaptive in character. On Descartes' view the mechanism of our nature teaches us adaptive responses which we are to make
in the light of certain environmental stimuli. Thus certain objects natu-

[37] *Traité de l'homme*, 852-53; Letter to Hysperaspistes, Aug. 1641, 1131;
Letter to Arnauld, July 1648, 1307.

[38] Cf. Michel Foucault, *Histoire de la Folie à l'âge classique*, 2nd ed. (Paris,
1972), 56-59. Foucault argues that madness, for Descartes, lies entirely outside
the realm of the *cogito*. But he seems to miss the fact that in the fully reconstituted
Cartesian metaphysics, judgment concerning the accuracy of the senses, and hence
concerning that which is useful for our ordinary lives, is equally dependent upon
conditions outside the *cogito* itself.

[39] *Les Passions de l'Ame*, Arts. 27, 29.
[40] Art. 10; also *Traité de l'Homme*, 812 ff.   [41] *Ibid.*, Art. 11.
[42] Art. 14; also *Traité de l'Homme*, 867 ff.   [43] *Ibid.*, Art. 13.   [44] Art. 15.
[45] Art. 51.   [46] Art. 52. See also Art. 36.

rally cause fear, the desire to flee, and the muscular responses which serve to that end.

But while our nature forms these original *prima facie* adaptive reactions, it does not always do so. Passions can become linked to other stimuli than their original ones through a process of conditioning.[47] Thus we might become fearful and desire to flee in the face of an entirely harmless object. I shall return to this point. For present purposes it is important to realize that, for Descartes, *faults* in the bodily organs themselves can cause useless or positively harmful desires to arise in the soul. What is remarkable is that Descartes attributes such "perverse" desires to human nature itself.[48] He gives the example of the person suffering from dropsy who desires to drink even though drinking will cause him positive harm.[49] Descartes compares the dropsical man to a clock which fails to indicate the correct time merely because of a change in its hidden mechanical parts. But, in contrast to the clock, Descartes considers the man's nature to be positively deceitful in such a case since, having both a mind and a body, he *desires* what will harm his body. In attributing such a failure to the man's nature itself, Descartes is implicitly attacking a traditional notion which regards nature as a beneficial force, independent of the mechanism of the body, and always tending toward the good of the organism.[50]

Thus the difference between adaptive and reasonable responses to the environmental stimuli, and useless or positively harmful ones, reduces to a mere variation in the physical condition of the body mechanism. A qualitative difference of response reduces to a mere structural difference in the nervous system. Similarly inappropriate passions will differ from appropriate ones due to variations in the material conditions on which the passions depend.

Sydenham's attribution of hysteria to a disorder of the animal spirits appears as a logical extension of the mechanical theory of the passions. Hysteria is characterized by distinctive muscular contractions (the hysterical fits) and certain disorders of the passions. In the Cartesian theory normal adaptive muscular movements and normal passions are determined by physical changes in the animal spirits. Thus it seems logical to conclude, as Sydenham does, that "the disturbance and inconsistency of both the mind and the body" in hysteria is caused by a physical difference in the initial basic structure of the animal spirits.[51] Sydenham stresses in particular the close connection between thought and the animal spirits:

---

[47] Art. 50.

[48] *Méditations* 6, 333; "La nature de l'homme . . . ne peut qu'elle ne soit quelquefois fautive et trompeuse."   [49] *Ibid.,* 6, 329-30.

[50] See also Robert Boyle's *Free Inquiry . . . , op. cit.,* 237. Boyle is explicitly discussing a common interpretation of the dictum of Hippocrates "Natura est morborum medicatrix."

[51] Sydenham, *Epistle to Dr. Cole,* Sect. 90.

. . . The strength and constancy of the mind, so long as it lies in this our bodily crust of clay, depends most especially upon the strength and constancy of the spirits that lodge along with it. [1]

It is, therefore, the lack of strength and inconsistency of the spirits which accounts for the unreasonable or inappropriate passions which arise in the mind of hysterical patients. At the same time Sydenham recognizes that the disorder of the animal spirits is merely "cognizable to the eye of reason."[52] For the microphysical imbalance of these fluids can only be inferred. Nevertheless Sydenham seems certain enough of the standard theory of the rarefaction of these spirits out of the blood that his cure of the disease lies in the restoration of the blood, "the fount and source of the spirits," with iron salts.[53] (Sydenham also recommends horseback riding, but only because he thinks that this exercise helps in a purely physical way in ridding the blood of waste products.)[54]

It is the weakened state of the animal spirits which is used to explain the fact that hysterical symptoms arise from external stimuli of various kinds. Sydenham considers emotional upsets to constitute the chief "remote or external causes" of hysteria,[55] and Willis claimed that the symptoms of the disease often arise from "sudden fear, great sadness, or anger and other violent passions."[56] But there is no reason to think that either Sydenham or Willis conceive that the passions bring about any bodily change except through the motions of the animal spirits with which they are correlated. The same reduction would seem to apply here as in the case of the passions when they are considered as symptoms of the disease. The fundamental reason why passions which are stimulated in normal ways have disastrous effects on hysterical patients is that their nervous fluids are in a weakened state. One can, thinks Sydenham, as easily cure the disease by recommending that a person become indifferent to their passions as cure a toothache "by a resolution forbidding one's jaws to give pain."[57]

One contemporary of Sydenham and Willis who seems to have a clear idea of the operation of external stimuli in the production of hysterical symptoms is Robert Boyle. In *Some Considerations Touching the Usefulnesse of Experimental Naturall Philosophy* (second ed., 1664), Boyle reports that it commonly happens that one hysterical woman, when she observes another undergoing a fit, will soon be "infected with the like strange discomposure."[58] Elsewhere, in *A Free Inquiry into the Vulgarly Received Notion of Nature*, he claims that there are certain odors which will bring about fainting fits in hysterical people.[59] These fits are so severe that the pulse is barely detectable. He also reports the case of a woman who fell into such a fainting fit merely at the sound

[52] Sect. 80.   [53] Sects. 94, 96.   [54] Sect. 116.   [55] Sect. 78
[56] Willis, *An Essay of the Pathology of the Brain*, 78-79.
[57] Sydenham, *Epistle to Dr. Cole*, Sect. 90.
[58] Boyle, *Op. cit.* (Oxford, 1664), 248.   [59] *Op. cit.*, 235

of a bell.[60] But in each of these cases Boyle thinks that there is nothing going on besides a purely physical process. To help his reader understand this Boyle reminds him that the human body is an engine, the parts of which are so connected together, that great changes can be wrought by a "very weak and inconsiderable impression of adventitious matter."[61] This bit of adventitious matter is nothing else but the sensual stimulus which brings on such severe symptoms in hysterical patients. But what is crucial in these cases is not the stimulus itself; for the same bit of matter can affect a normal person without the same consequences. For Boyle the pathological reaction depends upon the "peculiar contrivance" of the body which he likens to a loaded and cocked musket.[62] Because of this peculiar contrivance the effects of very small disturbances can produce very great and abnormal alterations in the whole machine. The lady who suffered fainting fits when she heard a bell did so because of the "texture of her body in reference to physical sounds."[63] The proof that the agencies operating are no more than physical lies in the fact that she was cured by merely physical remedies. And in the *Free Inquiry* . . . , where Boyle explicitly claims that the active elements in the human body are the fluids, he attributes the sensitivity of hysterical patients to certain odors to "the spirits and the *genus nervosum*."[64] Clearly it was the attempt to say something about the cause of the "peculiar disposition" of these spirits which set the problem of hysteria for physicians like Sydenham and Willis.

Boyle thought that if the full meaning of the mechanist hypothesis was grasped there would be no difficulty in admitting that the very ideas of imagination could bring about severe somatic disorders. He claims to have found a number of cases in the books of physicians to show "that imagination is able to so alter the imagining person's body, as to work such a disposition in the spirits, blood, and humours of it" to produce a disease which a person has very much feared.[65] Boyle considered the ideas of imagination, no less than those of sense, to be merely physical entities which can bring about extreme changes in the body machine.

The role of imagination in the production of hysteria is taken seriously in an eighteenth-century account of hysteria which closely follows that of Sydenham, Sir Richard Blackmore's *A Treatise on the Spleen and Vapours* (1725). In the course of an argument against those who think that hysteria and related diseases should not be taken seriously, because they arise merely from delusive imagination, Blackmore allows that ideas can in fact be the source of the symptoms of hysteria.[66] However he argues that this does not provide any real comfort to the sufferers of hysteria since the painful effect is not less real than if it arose from any

---

[60] *Some Considerations* . . . , 248. [61] *Ibid.*, 246.
[62] *Ibid.* [63] *Ibid.*, 248. [64] *Free Inquiry* . . . , 235.
[65] *Some Considerations* . . . , 244.
[66] Blackmore, *op. cit.*, 99.

other source. In order to help his reader understand how ideas can bring about real bodily change Blackmore reminds him how dreadful objects presented to the mind in dreams can, by putting the spirits into a hurry and confusion, "cause great inquietude and grievous pains."[67] But clearly Blackmore considers the effects of images in the case of hysteria to be far more extreme than usual because of a difference in basic structure of the nervous system. Like Sydenham he thinks that the source of the disease lies in "the weak and too delicate texture of the nervous system and the volatile dissipable temperament of the spirits."[68] This is the fundamental reason that, in hysterical people, ideas can have the severe effects that they do.

It should be recognized that the role of imagination in the production of passions and somatic effects of normal people was well accepted by the mechanistic philosophers. Boyle notes that the passions of the mind "are often excited by the bare, if attentive, thoughts of absent things."[69] He claims that the memory of a "loathsome potion" excites such horror in him that he feels a slight convulsion in his stomach whenever he has the thought of it. But the clearest account of the role of past experience in the production of the passions of normal people was given by Descartes.

In the writings of Descartes we find a clear account of the unconscious effect of early childhood experiences on later adult life.[70] In the *Passions of the Soul* Descartes explains the strange aversions which people have to a certain odor, or to the presence of an animal, by the fact that the odor, may have caused a severe headache when they were still in the cradle, or the animal may have frightened them without their "retaining any memory of it afterwards." He gives the example of a cat jumping into the baby's cradle and the resulting adult aversion to cats.[71] Elsewhere, in a letter, Descartes recounts the fact that for a number of years he had had an attraction for cross-eyed women without knowing the reason why. Eventually, he claims, he remembered that when he was a young child he had loved a girl who had this defect. (In a curious anticipation of a psychoanalytic cure, Descartes notes that, when he finally made this reflection, he was no longer affected!) But Descartes attributes these effects totally to the body, and a certain "disposition of the parts of the brain." Such adult behaviour and feelings have their source in the associational links forged in the brain of the child when a certain sensual stimulus is experienced together with a certain passion. Descartes' explanation of his attraction for cross-eyed women lies in the fact that "the impression which was made in (his) brain by the sense of sight," when he looked into the wandering eyes of his child-

[67] *Ibid.*   [68] *Ibid.*, 101.
[69] *Some Considerations . . .* , 243.
[70] See the important book by Geneviève Lewis, *Le Problème de l'Inconscien et le Cartésianisme* (Paris, 1950), esp. 51.
[71] Descartes, *op. cit.*, 136.

hood sweetheart, "joined itself to such an extent with that which evoked the passion of love," that a resembling visual stimulus (wandering eyes), made much later, evoked the same effect.[72] Descartes conceived of latent unconscious ideas[73] as the tendency of certain parts of the brain to bend in a certain way when stimulated by appropriate impressions. The unconscious ideas of Cartesian philosophy are purely physical dispositions.

Does this mechanical account of the unconscious effect of early childhood experiences bring us any closer to twentieth-century ideas of hysteria? One's answer to this question depends upon one's understanding of the twentieth-century idea of the unconscious. It is certainly true that writers around the turn of the century thought that hysterical attacks were at least partly due to unconscious ideational complexes which were connected with various traumatic experiences, often in the patient's childhood. From this point of view it seems that we can see the roots of their analysis in the suggestions of Descartes and his successors: for it would be easy to fit Descartes' conception of unconscious processes with the account of genesis of hysterical symptoms by ideas in Blackmore and Boyle. On the other hand, right at the beginning of the early psychoanalytic work on hysteria, Breuer insists on the distinction between ideas as immediate objects of experience and "cortical excitations" as their merely hypothetical correlates.[74] This suggests that there might be an incompatibility between the psychoanalytic view and the fundamental principle of the Cartesian unconscious; namely, the unconscious ideas must correspond to some brain structures. Moreover, from the time of this early work, Freud insists, along with Breuer, on the existence of a resistance on the part of the hysterical person's ego that accounts for the fact that ideas which are so full of affect are cut off from consciousness. This resistance is described in purely psychological language as an *intentional* repression of the traumatic ideas from the person's consciousness.[75] Though this process of intentional repression is itself not conscious, it is difficult to see how it can ever be described in purely physiological terms. As the idea of innate perverse sexual desires tends to replace (or at least dominate over) that of traumatic experiences in Freud's theory of hysteria, the intentional processes of the ego become

---

[72] *Letter to Chanut,* 6 June 1647, 1277.

[73] Descartes' use of "idea" in *Passions,* Art. 136, appears to be at odds with his stipulation about the use of this word in his definition in *Réponses aux 2ᵉ Objections,* 390. But that Descartes has an established use of the notion of a corporeal idea has been shown by Norman Kemp Smith, *New Studies in the Philosophy of Descartes* (London, 1952), Chap. VI "The Embodied Self." See also S. Hall's discussion in his translation of Descartes' *Treatise of Man* (Cambridge, 1972), 87, n. 136; also notes 137, 140.

[74] J. Breuer & S. Freud, *Studies on Hysteria, The Complete Psychological Works of Sigmund Freud,* ed. & trans. James Strachey (London, 1957) **II,** 5.

[75] *Ibid.,* 10.

more important.[76] For it is these processes that come to determine the difference between people who become abnormal and those who become normal. Such a description differs markedly from that which ascribes such difference to a difference in the structures of nervous fluids.

The structures and functions to which seventeenth-century philosophers and physicians attributed mental functions were almost entirely hypothetical. According to the epistemology of Descartes the presence of a hypothetical cause is not an irredeemable fault: he thought that, for purposes of practical arts such as medicine, a good deal was accomplished by assigning physical causes which could conceivably produce effects like those that are in fact perceived, even if they are not the actual causes which do produce those effects.[77] In assigning mechanical causes for psychological functions he was satisfied with what we today would call a *model*. Descartes thought that such a procedure was justified because the real causes of such phenomena were too small to be perceived by the senses.[78] It is however a good deal more surprising to find Sydenham, a physician whose methodological works ring with warnings about avoiding physiological hypotheses, turning to the animal spirit theory in order to explain the disorders connected with hysteria. One explanation of this lies in the fact that Sydenham was willing to rely not only on "the testimony of our senses," but also on "anatomical investigations of long standing."[79] The animal spirit theory of nervous and muscular action was so well established that, despite various experiments which put it into serious doubt, it was still the prevailing view of nervous and muscular action in the mid-eighteenth century. But perhaps the real explanation of its resilience to experimental refutation lay in the need, felt by the leading thinkers of this time, to assign psychological functions to physiological processes. In any case one finds a number of leading 'empiricist' writers employing and even arguing for the animal spirit theory right into the eighteenth century.[80]

The methodological attitude of a seventeenth-century physician like Sydenham stands in marked contrast to that adopted more than 20 years later by Freud who, after spending a number of years doing empirical research which attempted to link psychological function with neurological structure, turned to a purely psychological analysis of diseases like hysteria. It seems that it was at least partly his empiricism which led Freud to label unconscious processes *mental* rather than physical. He claims that, while the physical characteristics of such processes "are totally inaccessible to us," there are solid empirical reasons

---

[76] *General Introduction*, 353ff. Despite Freud's denials it seems clear that the importance of trauma has waned considerably from his earlier studies.

[77] *Les Principes de la Philosophie* (1644), IVe partie, 204, 667.

[78] *Ibid.*, #203, 266.

[79] *Medical Observations . . . , op. cit.* (n. 19 above), Sect. 20.

[80] For example, Bernard de Mandeville, *Treatise on the Hypochondriack and Hysterical Passions*, 2nd. ed. (London, 1730), 215.

for applying to them the same "categories which we employ to describe conscious mental acts such as ideas, purposes, resolutions, and so on."[81] He argues that premature identification of unconscious processes with physical ones would cause people to abandon empirical psychological research without having anything better to rely upon.

However there are good reasons to think that Freud goes beyond this methodological empiricism to challenge the basic "Enlightenment" conception of man and the nature of the human mind. Freud goes so far as to speak of the "insoluble difficulties of psychophysical parallelism."[82] This implies that his application of psychological categories to the unconscious might be ultimate. We have also seen that Freud following Plato, considers the human being to be composed of an ego and a lower bodily soul from which it is distinguished. If Freud means to use the concept of "unconscious mental processes" in any ontological sense, to represent what really exists in the world, then the conscious ego would be opposed by a bodily will and bodily desires. We have seen that this involves the rejection of the conception of man and the human mind promulgated by Descartes, and a very different view of the nature of the forces which have to be mastered by the conscious ego.

University of Western Ontario, Dept. of History of Medicine
    and Science

[81] "The Unconscious," *The Complete Psychological Works of Sigmund Freud,* XIV, 168.
    [82] *Ibid.*

Chapter XXX

FROM *HOMME MACHINE* TO *HOMME SENSIBLE:*

CHANGING EIGHTEENTH-CENTURY MODELS OF MAN'S IMAGE

BY SERGIO MORAVIA

"Sixty years ago, when I was young," wrote the Bolognese doctor and mathematician Domenico Guglielmini in 1707, "nothing else was spoken of in the field of medicine but innate heat, radical humidity, primary qualities." A short time later everything changed: "the physiologists proclaimed the necessity for closer contact with the physicists, while repudiating the Aristotelian doctrines and introducing into the medical field the systems of Descartes and Gassendi, systems which have been distorted to a point at which we can no longer tell upon what physiological foundations a doctor bases his personal theories or establishes his therapy." Not to mention the invasion of the field of life sciences by mathematics, added Guglielmini, which increased the confusion.[1]

Testimonies such as Guglielmini's could be multiplied without the slightest difficulty. In the second half of the seventeenth century the situation in the medical sciences was, to say the least, difficult and frustrating. In this field, too, new methodological concepts and the new mechanistic world image developed by the scientific revolution had produced extremely good results. And yet even some of the protagonists of that revolution had soon realized the difficulty of using, in the science of living nature, and especially in medicine, solely mechanical presuppositions and mathematical procedures employed with success in other branches of knowledge. At a certain moment Descartes himself had begun to express, in numerous texts and in certain letters, his own awareness of this difficulty. It was certainly great pity, he wrote to Princess Elizabeth, not to have clarified in the *Passions de l'Âme* the "principes de physique" which accompany the various passions. But this would have required an explanation in physical key "de toutes les parties du corps humain," which had seemed to him, and still did, "une chose si difficile que je ne l'oserois encore entreprendre."[2] On close examination it was not possible to describe a human being in terms of a "machine."[3] For this reason, after having

---

[1] D. Guglielmini, *Symposium medicum, sive Quaestio convivalis de usu mathematum in arte medica*, in *Opera omnia mathematica, hydraulica, medica physica* (Geneva, 1719), II, 518-19.

[2] Descartes, *Correspondance*, ed. Ch. Adam-G. Milhaud (Paris, 1960), VII, 5

[3] M. Gueroult, *Descartes selon l'ordre des raisons* (Paris, 1953), II, 178ff., 24

long cherished the dream of deducing medicine and the science of man from physics, Descartes recognized the failure of this design in a letter to Chanut: "Il y a un fort grand intervalle entre la notion générale du Ciel et de la Terre, que j'ai tâché de donner dans mes *Principes,* et la connaissance particulière de la Nature de l'Homme."[4]

However, many scholars, more trusting (or less cautious) than Descartes, had continued to pursue an ideal which, though certainly attractive, was at the same time in many ways risky. At the beginning of the eighteenth century, medical mechanists (or iatromechanists) were not only unwilling to recognize the theoretical and practical difficulties, but seemed decided on celebrating their great triumphs. "Since doctors," wrote Giorgio Baglivi in 1696, "have begun to examine the structure and action (*effectus*) of the animate body on the basis of geometrical and mechanical principles, as well as of physical, mechanical, and chemical experiments, they have not only discovered innumerable phenomena unknown to preceding centuries, but have also realized that as far as its natural actions are concerned the human body is nothing more than a complex system of mechanical and chemical movements that obey mathematical laws."[5]

Baglivi, and with him Borelli and Bellini, Pitcairne and Cole, Lamy and Chirac were, of course, worthy and even excellent scholars. Moreover, it should be stressed that they made important contributions to the knowledge of the human body precisely because their doctrines were iatromechanical. Their comparison of the human body with a machine led them to examine with particular care all the *quantitative* aspects of the living organism. The sympathy with which many historians of medicine have spoken of the revolution caused by mechanism is therefore not unjustified. But these historians did not adequately analyze the epistemological and philosophical implications of iatromechanical doctrines, and therefore did not fully understand the sense and direction of the criticism made in the eighteenth century of such doctrines. Certain texts, even of very recent scholars, seem to suggest that iatromechanical theory represents the train of thought which has most decidedly turned its back on philosophy in order to take at last the "true" road of science. "It would seem clear from the history of biology," Giuseppe Montalenti has written, "that the greatest progress, both in theoretical knowledge and in the domain of phenomena usable for practical purposes, has been made because of the application of the mechanistic method. The life principle, on the contrary, has very rarely acted as a stimulus, but rather almost always as an inhibiting factor, both to research and to progress."[6]

---

[4] Descartes, *Correspondance,* VII, 82-83.

[5] G. Baglivi, *De Praxi medica,* in *Opera omnia medico-practica et anatomica* (Venice, 1727), 78.

[6] G. Montalenti, *Storia della biologia e della medicina,* in N. Abbagnano, ed.,

In point of fact, even a summary examination of iatromechanical texts reveals how greatly "philosophy"—not always of the highest quality—inspired and conditioned them, both from a methodological and an interpretive point of view.[7] First and most obviously, iatromechanism tends to reduce organic matter to mere *res extensa,* to postulate the identity of biological phenomena (in a broad sense) with physical and mechanical phenomena, and to explain life and the living organism as if their phenomenology and their laws would be *a priori* of a determinate type. Secondly, the explanatory techniques which, for the most part, characterize the work of the followers of iatromechanism are those of hypothesis and analogy. It has been rightly observed that iatromechanist thought implies in some way a vicious circle based on a *petitio principii:* the iatromechanists claim to *arrive* at the demonstration of the mechanical nature of certain phenomena, whereas they actually *began* by surreptitiously attributing to those phenomena the specific characteristics which would favor the planned demonstration. Thirdly, on a more detailed level, iatromechanism prefers the structural to a functional analysis of the organism, reduces physiology to anatomy, and either ignores the dynamics of the organic forces or tends to reduce them within kinematic schemes of a physical and mechanical nature. Finally, the fundamental inspiring principle of the iatromechanical plan consists of an extremely precise interpretation of the life force and of the living being: life is movement and the living being—even the human being—is a machine. There is "philosophy" enough in these doctrines for anyone. It is, however, only by reading at first hand certain key texts of the iatromechanical school that one can perceive the radical nature of a doctrine that had so great an influence on European culture in the late seventeenth and early eighteenth centuries. To this end we could analyze some of the works of Giovanni Alfonso Borelli or consider the impassioned philomechanistic peroration contained in the *De usu ratiocinii mechanici in medicina* of Hermann Boerhaave, who was in fact a more prudent and better balanced scholar than other exponents of the school.[8] But we prefer to take up once again the previously quoted

---

Storia della scienze (Torino, 1962), III, t. I., 610; S. Moravia, "Filosofia 'sciences de la vie' nel secolo XVIII," *Giornale critico della filosofia Italiana,* 4. (1966), 64-109.

[7] G. Canguilhem, "Aspects du vitalisme," *La Connaissance de la vie,* 2nd ed (Paris, 1965), 83-100; R. Collin, "Mécanisme et animisme en biologie," *Revue de Métaphysique et de Morale,* 35(1935), 385-418.

[8] L. Premuda, "La filosofia anatomica di Boerhaave," *Minerva medica,* 5 (1966), 3229-35; *idem,* "La reazione metodologica di H. Boerhaave alla scienza cartesiana," *Atti della V^a Biennale della Marca e dello Studio Firmano* (Fermo 1963), 437-47; H. Lindeboom, *Hermann Boerhaave, The Man and his Work* (London, 1968), and the chapters devoted to Boerhaave by L. S. King, in *The Medical World of the Eighteenth Century* (Chicago, 1958).

Baglivi: "Whoever examines the bodily organism with attention will certainly not fail to discern pincers in the jaws and teeth; a container in the stomach; watermains in the veins, the arteries and the other ducts; a piston in the heart; sieves or filters in the bowels; in the lungs, bellows; in the muscles, the force of the lever; in the corner of the eye, a pulley, and so on. So let the chemists continue to explain natural phenomena in complex terms such as fusion, sublimation, precipitation, etc., thus founding a separate philosophy. It remains unquestionable that all these phenomena must be seen in the forces of the wedge, of equilibrium, of the lever, of the spring, and of all the other principles of mechanics. In short, the natural functions of the living body can be explained in no other way so clearly and easily as by means of the experimental and mathematical principles with which nature herself speaks."[9]

The text, as we see, is most peremptory. Many historians of medicine have failed, however, to take account of the kinds and extent of the reactions provoked by this sort of declaration. Even during the seventeenth century, scholars of various tendencies did in fact express manifold reservations about iatromechanical doctrines. These reservations were well-taken, since a great many observations and experimental discoveries seemed to sanction an image of the living organism quite different from that proposed by the followers of iatromechanism. In the second half of the seventeenth century, while Leeuwenhoek was discovering the existence of spermatozoa and Malpighi the complex properties of cellular tissue, Swammerdam was demonstrating the disquieting capacity of the muscles to respond to nervous stimulus even after the severing of every connection with the spinal cord.[10] After studying them and other phenomena, an English scientist Francis Glisson did not hesitate to attribute to the organism a real force (*vis insita in materia*) which he called "irritability." In 1672, his great physiological treatise *De naturae substantia energetica* indicated by its very title a new philosophic and scientific orientation, considerably different from that which inspired the iatromechanical school.[11] In 1680, reflecting on the new studies of the structure and functioning of the *machine animale*, Claude

[9] Baglivi, *op. cit.,* 78.

[10] Bibliography on these biological and physiological researches is increasingly conspicuous. E. Bastholm, *The History of Muscle Physiology* (Copenhagen, 1950); G. Canguilhem, *La formation du concept de réflexe aux XVIIe et XVIIIe siècles* (Paris, 1955); J. Roger, *Les sciences de la vie dans la pensée française du XVIIIe siècle* (Paris, 1963); K. E. Rothschuh, *Physiologie* (Freiburg-München, 1968); Th. S. Hall, *Ideas of Life and Matter* (Chicago-London, 1969), 2 vols.

[11] Ch. Daremberg, *Histoire des doctrines médicales* (Paris, 1870); M. Verworn, *Irritability* (New Haven, 1913); G. Canguilhem, and O. Temkin, "The Classical Roots of Glisson's Doctrine of Irritation," *Bulletin of the History of Medicine,* 38(1964), 297-328.

Perrault, a scholar well aware of the problems and scientific debates of his time, declared that it was time to challenge "les sentimens de la nouvelle secte . . . où l'on croid [sic] que par le moyen de la Méchanique on peut connoître et expliquer tout ce qui appartient aux animaux."[12]

In the face of this body of doubts and data (here only summarily touched upon), theoretical questions of a more general significance immediately came to mind. Could one really believe that life is nothing but the movement of solid and liquid parts; that organic matter is identical with inert matter; that the living being is really devoid of principles and forces that are in some way active; in short, that the organism is really a *machine,* functioning according to processes and laws of an exclusively physical and mechanical nature? As time passed, and the *secte* of iatromechanists obstinately continued to defend their theses, a growing number of scholars tended to give negative answers to these questions. Among other things (perhaps this has not been sufficiently emphasized), the doctrines of Leibniz and even more so of Newton encouraged scholars to reconsider the existence of forces in some way immanent in matter and acting perhaps (we may recall Leibnizian biology) according to their own teleological principles.[13] Despite all this, even at the end of the seventeenth and the beginning of the eighteenth century the elaboration of a new interpretive model of bioanthropological phenomena appears to have met with insuperable difficulties. The *facts* are there (or at least a reasonable number of facts), but the *theory* is missing. And for want of the theory (that is to say, of a theory which corresponds to the epistemological principles worked out by the scientific "revolution" of the seventeenth century, some scholars of the day did not hesitate, when they needed to operate in a new way in a certain field of study, to have recourse even to the oldest and most thoroughly discredited doctrines.

In this context, perhaps no scientist-philosopher seems more typical than Georg-Ernst Stahl (1660-1734). Stahl does not at all wish to deny the "mechanicalness" of the functioning of the living organism At the same time, however, he appears to be convinced that an *exclusively* mechanical interpretation cannot explain either the specific nature of certain functions or the origin and the action of the forces clearly at work in every living being. It is therefore necessary, in his opinion, for the scientist to learn to formulate questions far more complex than those elaborated by the *mécanistes.* To begin with the

[12] Cl. Perrault, *De la mécanique des animaux,* in *Oeuvres diverses de physique et de mécanique* (Paris, 1721), 330-31.

[13] Lecture by J. Steudel, *Leibniz und die Medizin* (Bonn, 1960), and Th. S Hall, "On Biological Analogs of Newton Paradigms," *Philosophy of Science, 3* (1968), 6-27; P. M. Heimann and J. E. MacGuire, "Newtonian Forces and Lockean Powers: Concepts of Matter in Eighteenth Century Thought," *Historical Studies of Physical Sciences* (1971), 233-306.

problem of life itself: "Before anything else," we read in his most famous work, the *Theoria medica vera,* "we must know the exact meaning of what is vulgarly called life. What does it formally consist of? What is its function, both from the material and subjective point of view, and from the final and objective point of view? What use has it, what need is there for it in the body? What does it offer? And how useful or even necessary is it?"[14]

On the basis of such relevant questions Stahl tried to analyze the particular characteristics of the living organism. Certain of his studies, such as those which treat of the difference between mechanism and organism,[15] appear promising, at least on the programmatic level. But the answers which he gave to those questions (doubtless valid) are generally rather disappointing. Stahl is still far from seeking answers in the data offered by experimental investigation. In his research he does not employ the new biological and physiological contributions that would have supported some of their theses. As a ground for the "specificity" of the living phenomenon, he relies on a soul whose task is to govern the various functions of the organism, from which, however, it remains distinct. The heavy, scholastic structure of Stahl's doctrine, with its frequent references to unreliable texts and data, certainly does not render his work stimulating or show it to be abreast of the time and its problems.[16]

But the history of scientific knowledge does not proceed from "positive truth" to "positive truth" along a road completely separated from contemporary philosophy. Despite its considerable limitation, the fact is that, during the late seventeenth and the early decades of the eighteenth century, the work of Stahl constitutes one of the most remarkable points of reference of the anti-mechanistic reaction in the medical field. It could be said that the Stahlian theses occurred at the

[14] G. E. Stahl, *Theoria medica vera* (Halle, 1708), 254. In the nineteenth century the works of Stahl were translated into French by Ch. Blondin. G. E. Stahl, *Oeuvres Médico-philosophiques et pratiques* (Montpellier-Strasbourg, 1859-63), 6 vols.

[15] Stahl, *Disquisito de mechanismi et organismi diversitate* (Halle, 1706).

[16] On Stahl, see the work by A. Lemoine, *Le vitalisme et l'animisme de Stahl* (Paris, 1864); J. E. Chancerel, *Recherches sur la pensée biologique de Stahl* (Paris, 1934); H. Metzger, *Les doctrines chimiques en France du début du XVIIᵉ à la fin du XVIIIᵉ siècle* (Paris, 1923; new ed. Paris, 1969); idem, *Newton, Stahl, Boerhaave et la doctrine chimique* (Paris, 1930). More useful in our context are the following articles: L. J. Rather, "G. E. Stahl's Psychological Physiology," *Bulletin of the History of Medicine,* 35(1961), 37-49; L. S. King, 'Stahl and Hoffmann: a Study in Eighteenth Century Animism," *Journal of the History of Medicine,* 19(1964), 118-30. On the fortune of Stahl in the eighteenth century: P. Naville, *D'Holbach et la philosophie scientifique au XVIIIᵉ siècle* (Paris, 1943; new ed. Paris, 1967); E. Callot, *La philosophie de la vie au XVIIIᵉ siècle* (Paris, 1965).

right moment, for they gave expression to needs that could no longer be ignored. For this reason, many scholars did not hesitate to accept a doctrine that was explicitly animistic and metaphysical. To physiologists who intended to transform radically a certain image of the living organism and of the science relating to it, it did not seem impossible to separate, in Stahlian thought, its old-fashioned and unacceptable aspects from the theses which could be considered valid or at least usable in an anti-mechanistic perspective. They had only to shift certain accents and to manipulate freely certain principles or doctrines. The Stahlian texts would, perhaps, be distorted; but the *science de la vie* would certainly benefit.[17]

To cite just one example (but the most important one): whoever takes up the texts of the Medical School of Montpellier cannot fail to notice that the operation described above was exactly the one carried out by certain exponents of that ancient and renowned Faculty of Medicine.[18] In the opinion of Boissier de Sauvages, Bordeu, and Barthez, Stahl had understood the need to admit the irreducible vitality of organic bodies, to seek the source of this vitality, and to analyze the most salient aspects and manifestations (beginning with its sensitivity, so greatly ignored by the iatromechanists) of the "interiority" of the living organism. To be sure, the sympathy that these *médecins-philosophes* demonstrated for the theoretician of animism essentially stops there. The scientists of Montpellier were in general fervent devotees of Hippocratic experimentalism and among contemporary philosophers they preferred Bacon and Locke. If they rejected iatromechanism, it was because it presented hypotheses and generalizations that were not confirmed by empirical evidence. If they had recourse (with explicit theoretical reservations) to animist doctrines, it was because, if nothing

[17] For a richer analysis of anti-mechanistic animism between the seventeenth and eighteenth centuries: Th. S. Hall, *Ideas of Life and Matter*, and R. K. French, *Robert Whytt, The Soul, and Medicine* (London, 1969); R. K. French "Sauvages, Whytt and the Motion of the Heart: Aspects of Eighteenth Century Animism," *Clio Medica*, 7(1972), 35-54 L. S. King, "Basic Concepts of Eighteenth Century Animism," *American Journal of Psychiatry*, 124(1967), 797-802 Valuable remarks on the connection between Mechanism, Animism, and Vitalism, as well as on other themes discussed in the present article, can be found in Joseph Schiller, "Queries, Answers, and Unsolved Problems in Eighteenth Century Biology," *History of Science*, XII(1974), 184-99.

[18] On the vitalism of the Montpellier medical school: F. Bérard, *La doctrin médicale de Montpellier* (Montpellier, 1819); Ch. Daremberg, *op. cit.*, II, Ch. 32 L. Dulieu, "Le mouvement scientifique montpelliérain au XVIIIe siècle," *Revu d'histoire des sciences*, 11(1958), 227-49; J. Roger, *op. cit.*, 615ff. S. Moravia "Philosophie et médecine en France à la fin du XVIIIe siècle," in Th. Bestermar ed., *Studies on Voltaire and the XVIII Century* (Banbury, 1972), 89, 1089-115 G. Gusdorf, *Dieu, la nature et l'homme au siècle des Lumières* (Paris, 1972) 471-76.

else, they admitted the existence in living reality of dynamic and organic phenomena inexplicable by the physical and mechanical theories then prevalent. Not unlike scholars from other schools of thought, they tended to recover, to a certain extent, those forces and powers that a too rigid and unilateral *philosophie mécanique* had banished from nature.

It is not by chance that some of them quoted Newton and cited his discoveries concerning universal attraction.[19] How can one admit that organic nature is completely devoid of an energy of its own, if even physical nature seems to be filled with immanent *vis*? The moderns—Boissier de Sauvages wrote—had banished the faculties of the living organism from the School of Medicine, but they were wrong to have done so. He warned against any diffidence that might lead one to deny the existence of certain forces simply because they were unknown. Otherwise, those "moderns" should "also abolish the names of elasticity [and] of gravity, the essence of which we do not know." The essential point, Boissier de Sauvages significantly emphasized, is not to reify, as Stahl had done, these unknown forces and faculties, but instead to consider them (such is the remarkable thesis of the *savant* of Montpellier) as the *x* and *y* so successfully used in mathematics.[20]

But this combination of the critical use of Stahl's doctrines together with the rejection of his more outmoded ideas can most clearly be seen within the School of Montpellier in the work of Théophile Bordeu (1722-76), future friend of Diderot, remembered today (though unjustly) only as being one of the protagonists of the *Rêve de d'Alembert*. It is in fact with Bordeu that a genuinely new concept of the science of man begins to take shape. In the opinion of Bordeu, Stahl's animism is clearly to be rejected, for the same reasons for which this scientist and *philosophe*, admirer of Hippocrates and Locke, rejects every kind of metaphysical reification of abstract beings and principles.[21]

The principal enemy, however, remained for him, iatromechanism in its various aspects and trends. In the battle against this enemy, Stahlian doctrines had, in the opinion of Bordeu, undeniably made an important contribution—beginning with the assertion of the autonomy of vital phenomena vis-à-vis mechanical phenomena.[22] But it would be necessary to proceed with more adequate instruments than those used by Stahl. After all, the professor from Halle had done nothing

[19] E.g., L. La Caze, *Idée de l'homme physique et moral* (Paris, 1755). P. J. Barthez, *Nouveaux élémens de la Science de l'Homme* (Paris, 1778).

[20] Boissier de Sauvages, *Nosologia methodica* (Venice, 1764), 32.

[21] Th. Bordeu, *Recherches anatomiques sur la fonction des glandes et sur ur action*, in *Oeuvres complètes* (Paris, 1828), I, 204-06. Even more forceful his critique of Stahlian animism in his *Recherches sur les crises, ed. cit.*, I, 224.

[22] Bordeu, *Recherches su l'histoire de la médecine, ed. cit.*, II, 666-67, 671; *nalyse médicinale du sang, ed. cit.*, II, 1025.

more than *add* to a mechanistic conception of living reality an integrative animistic doctrine. On the contrary, Bordeu intends to confute such a conception through a radical recasting of the notion of matter that lies at its base. He intends above all to elaborate a pattern of organic matter that will explain the nature and the different aspects of life in reliable and verifiable terms. Bordeu is not really a speculator, as was Stahl and to some extent Descartes himself. He is a doctor, a scholar of anatomy and physiology. He devoted long years of research to the observation and experimental analysis of living beings. He studied the mucous membranes, noting their rich and complex organic properties. He examined the dynamics of the secretory processes, revealing their various characteristics. He analyzed (in an essay of particular importance) the action of the glands, demonstrating by experiments the groundlessness of the iatromechanical doctrines in this field. He worked for a long time on the origins and development of pathological disorders in the organism.[23] During the course of this research, Bordeu was able to ascertain on an experimental level the impossibility of interpreting particular organic phenomena as a result of movements or pressures of physical and mechanical kind. And he also ascertained the existence in the living organism of functions which clearly presuppose (at least for those scientists who do not admit the presence of the soul) the action of forces which are innate in living matter itself.

Beginning with the above mentioned Glisson, various other scholars had admitted the presence of some *vis insita* in living organisms. In the same period in which Bordeu was carrying out his research, Albrecht von Haller had distinguished in a vigorously experimental way force inherent in muscular fiber which he, like Glisson, had called irritability; and he had also demonstrated, once again by means of detailed experimental research, that in nerve fibers there exists another important property—sensitivity.[24] In comparison with Haller, Bordeu

---

[23] Bordeu, *Recherches sur les tissus muqueux ou l'organisation cellulaire; Recherches anatomiques sur la fonction des glandes; Recherches sur les crises; Recherches sur les maladies chroniques.* All these studies are in the *Oeuvres complètes. ed. cit.*

[24] A. von Haller, *De partibus corporis humani sensibilibus et irritabilibus* (Göttingen, 1752-53). However, this work became widely known mainly in the French version, translated by Simon-André Tissot, a Swiss scientist who was close friend of Haller. A. von Haller, *Dissertation sur les parties irritables sensibles des animaux* (Lausanne, 1755). Haller was the author of many scientific works, and particularly of two important physiological treatises: *Primæ lineae Physiologiae* (Göttingen, 1751) and *Elementa Physiologiae* (Lausanne 1757-66), 8 vols. In 1936, O. Temkin published the anonymous English translation of the first study on sensibility and irritability: A. von Haller, *A Dissertation on the Sensible and Irritable Parts of Animals* (London, 1755; Baltimore 1936).

was certainly a less rigorous scientist. But we must recognize that his vitalism inspired him with several physiological conceptions that are in some ways more modern than Haller's. Haller seems to have been more interested in a static and abstract analysis of the properties of organic fibers considered separately from the study of the actual dynamic and concrete functioning of the living organism (he defined physiology as "animate anatomy"). In fact, irritability appeared to him, not only as a force completely separate from and independent of the other organic properties, but also as one which acted in a blind and mechanical manner. On the other hand, sensitivity was first of all reduced (in quite a restrictive way) to mere perception of pain, and secondly was attributed to the nerve fibers: but only in the sense that the nerves carry certain impulses to the soul, which remains the only center able to perceive ("feel") sensations.[25]

Bordeu, on the contrary, sketches a quite different image of the living organism and of the science of such an organism. He regards Haller's punctilious distinction between sensitivity and irritability as too abstract in that these two properties seem to be, in the concrete phenomenology of the living being, closely connected (perhaps, Bordeu wrongly opines, they even constitute and express a *single* force). In the opinion of Bordeu, the point to be emphasized, as Stahl had guessed, is that organic beings seem to possess a peculiar capacity of self-control, to act in accordance with particular aims or ends, and to participate harmoniously, by means of ceaseless reciprocal interaction, in that complex dynamism (not at all "mécanique") which constitutes the life of the living being. For Bordeu, at this point, it would be a great mistake to attribute the responsibility for all this to a metaphysical substance. With all due respect for proven facts, it had to be admitted that the organism possesses something that we may call a "force"—being careful to emphasize that it is *sui generis,* "intelligent," or at least capable of executing functions that no blind "mechanical" motor could. This force Bordeu called "sensitivity," a property which he considered to be diffused by the nerves, not only to some parts of the organism, but throughout the whole organism: "Chaque partie organique du corps

[25] We still lack an exhaustive and satisfactory study on Hallerian physiology in its connections with eighteenth-century science and philosophy. See nevertheless the comprehensive introduction by L. S. King to the anastatic re-edition of the English translation (1786) of the *Primae lineae Physiologiae* (London, New York, 1966); also G. Rudolph "*Hallers Lehre von der Irritabilität un Sensibilität* in K. E. Rothschuh, ed., *Von Boerhaave bis Berger* (Stuttgart, 1964); *idem,* "De partibus sensibilibus," *Sudhoffs Archiv für Geschichte der Medizin und Naturwissenschaften,* 49(1965), 423-30. Of some use are the pages devoted to Haller by Bastholm, Hall, Rothschuh, and Roger in their works cited above. Among the monographs on Haller: S. O'Irsay, *Albrecht von Haller* (Leipzig, 1930); M. Hochdoerfer, *The Conflict between the Religious and Scientific Views of Haller* (Lincoln, Nebr., 1932); G. Tonelli, *Poesia e pensiero in Albrecht von Haller* (Turin, 1965).

vivant a des nerfs qui ont une sensibilité, une espèce ou un degré particulier de sentiment. . . ."[26]

This is an important turning point. For the iatromechanists, life was movement; for Bordeu, life is sensitivity. For the iatromechanists, man was a mechanical apparatus; for Bordeu, man is an organism. When considered as an interpretive model, the latter opinion appears far closer to the real, concrete facts before the eyes of all *observateurs:* "l'organisme moderne laisse bien loin derrière lui les copistes et les commentateurs des Hacquet, Baglivi et autres de cette espèce, qui ont tant parlé de ressorts, d'élasticité, de battements, de fibrilles. Ces physiciens légers furent aussi éloignés des vrais principes de l'observation, qui conduisent dans les détours des fonctions de l'économie animale, que des enfants qui jouent avec des morceaux de cartes, pour bâtir des petits châteaux, sont éloignés des belles règles d'architecture. . . ."[27]

Nor must we believe that Bordeu considers his duty as a physiologist to end with having shown "sensitivity" to be the rational source of all organic functions and processes. On the contrary, he seems particularly concerned to examine the specific action of sensitive properties in the psychophysical being of man. Here, too, he starts with a concrete analysis of the way this being functions. Such an analysis seems to him to show, among other things, that the various organs of the body have behavior patterns or characteristics that are for the most part independent and autonomous, even though these organs seem to interact closely with one another, and that some organic functions are substantially independent of the action or control of the brain.

Up to this point we have been given the facts. But how can they be arranged and interpreted at a theoretical level? Here we observe another instance of the bold utilization of metaphysical speculation by the part of a branch of learning that considered itself (and for the most part was) *scientific*—and this speculation was, in this case, among the most obsolete and compromised that the seventeenth century could offer: that of van Helmont (1577-1644).

Alchemist, medical man, and philosopher, van Helmont had reacted against the first mechanistic interpretations of living nature, elaborating a complex system which attributed to every part or to every living organ an energetic spiritual principle (the famous *archaeus*), which could simultaneously make that part or organ act in a relatively autonomous way and also introduce it harmoniously into the vital process of the entire being to which the said organ belonged.[28] Despite the high opin-

[26] Bordeu, *Recherches sur les pouls,* in *Oeuvres complètes,* I. 420.
[27] Bordeu, *Recherches sur l'histoire de la médecine,* II, 670.
[28] J. B. van Helmont, *Hortus medicinae, id est initia Physicae inaudita. Progressus medicinae novus* (Amsterdam, 1648). On van Helmont: W. Pagel, *Th*

ion (certainly greatly exaggerated) that Bordeu expressed for van Helmont,[29] he was very careful not to accept the whole of his fanciful
doctrine without a grain of salt. And yet it seems to suggest to him,
despite all its unacceptable aspects, an explanatory model for efficiently interpreting the observed phenomena. Man, writes Bordeu,
is not a unitary-monarchic being. That is to say, he is not a being
who is unitarily and uniformly subject to the action of the soul, of the
consciousness, or of the brain. He is, on the contrary, an articulate
complex, and, so to speak, "decentralized" being. He constitutes, in
short, a "federation of organs"—to use a term that can be traced back
to van Helmont. Bordeu expressed all this in an image which, from
Maupertuis to Diderot, was to fascinate the entire mainstream of Enlightenment culture: "Nous comparons le corps vivant, pour bien sentir
l'action particulière de chaque partie, à un essaim d'abeilles qui se
ramassent en pelotons, et qui se suspendent à un arbre en manière de
grappe; on n'a pas trouvé mauvais qu'un célèbre ancien ait dit d'un des
viscères du bas ventre, qu'il étoit *animal in animali*. . . . Ainsi, pour
suivre la comparaison de la grappe d'abeilles, elle est un *tout* collé à
une branche d'arbre, par l'action de bien des abeilles qui doivent agir
ensemble pour se bien tenir; toutes concourrent [sic] à former un corps
assez solide, et chacune cependant a son action à part. L'application est aisée; les organes du corps sont liés les uns aux autres; ils
ont chacun leur district et leur action; les rapports de ces actions,
l'harmonie qui en résulte, font la santé. Si cette harmonie se dérange,
soit qu'une partie se relâche, soit qu'une autre l'emporte sur celle qui
lui sert d'antagoniste, si les actions sont renversées, si elles ne suivent
pas l'ordre naturel. ces changemens constitueront des maladies plus ou
moins graves."[30]

    It is easy to regard this image ironically, as those historians of
science who attach importance only to the discoveries of "positive" facts
have done—even if, after all, it is difficult to understand why the
mechanistic metaphors of the "man-machine" or of the "man-water
pump" should be *a priori* more valid than the vitalistic one used by
Bordeu. The essential point, however, is not so much to discuss the
value in itself of one metaphor over another as to perceive what is
expressed in the concepts that lie behind them. Behind the revival
(extremely partial and prudent, as has already been mentioned) of the
old-fashioned animistic mythology of van Helmont, there lay embedded
in Bordeu's work several theses of the greatest importance. The great
maître of Montpellier understood, in the first place, the fact that every

Religious and Philosophical Aspects of Van Helmont's Science of Medicine
Baltimore, 1944).
    [29] Bordeu, *Recherches sur l'histoire de la médecine*, II, 670 ff.
    [30] Bordeu, *Recherches anatomiques sur la position des glandes*, I, 187.

reflection on life must start with the principle of the irreducible vitality of the organs. Next, Bordeu hastened to translate this doctrine into terms that were as empirical and experimental as possible. Far from deriving from the action of some *archaeus* or other metaphysical being, the animation of living organs is connected with the existence within these organs of concrete and visible nerve filaments. And this is not all. While developing the study of these filaments (see, above all, the essay on glandular functions), Bordeu realized that they are not connected only at the brain center. They are also grouped in many special *ganglions,* which are situated in all the peripheral organs of the body and operate according to laws that had yet to be discovered.

It is at this point that, together with a certain idea of the living organism, Bordeu and his friends and followers seem to change their minds about the task of the science of living beings. Until that moment scientists and physiologists had devoted themselves to distinguishing the *general* functions and laws of the organism, on the tacit assumption (of mechanistic origin) that all its parts are perfectly identical, not only as regards their nature, but also their behavior. Now, however, there grew up the conviction that these different parts or organs can behave in different ways, or at least may possess different aspects and implica- tions that should not be ignored in favor of the principle of functiona' uniformity—a principle which is certainly not lacking. In short, there arises and develops what could be called a "regional" medicine or phys iology. As Herbert Dieckmann has observed, Bordeu made an im portant theoretical contribution to this physiology in that he emphasize the relative autonomy of the various organs and the fact that each o: them is connected to the brain (the controlling organ) but executes whole series of independent functions with its nerve *ganglions*—fron reactions to determined external stimuli to the accomplishment of cer tain internal physiological *operations* to which the conscious brai center seems completely alien.[31] Do the sexual organs, the digestiv organs, or the glands act under the exclusive control of the brain Certainly not. Each of these organic "compartemens" has the capacit to operate in a largely independent manner, in accordance with a phe nomenology which is extremely complex and in no way to be deduce *a priori* from the known laws of mechanical physics.

Greatly struck by these facts, aware of the existence of many livin, beings in which even serious cerebral lesions had not in any way intel rupted the accomplishment of organic functions, Bordeu meant t express all this by distinguishing within every living individual tw fundamental dimensions of the phenomenon of life. The first dimensio

---

[31] H. Dieckmann, "Théophile Bordeu und Diderot's Rêve de l'Alembert *Romanische Forschungen,* **52**(1938), 55-122. This essay is the only useful artic' on this *médecin-philosophe* of Montpellier, but see Roger, *op. cit.,* 618-30.

is that constituted by the life of the organism considered in its psychophysical totality and unity. The second is that constituted by the (relatively independent) life of the parts which make up such an organism.
Thus, in the opinion of Bordeu, there exists a "general" sensitivity,
nervous tension, and blood circulation, which are directly controlled by
the brain; and at the same time there exists a "particular" sensitivity,
nervous tension, and circulation, autonomously controlled by the
peripheral organs.[32] "Le corps vivant," Bordeu emphasizes elsewhere,
"est un assemblage de plusieurs organes qui vivent chacun à leur
manière, qui sentent plus ou moins, et qui se meuvent, agissent ou se
reposent dans des temps marqués; car suivant Hippocrate, toutes les
parties des animaux sont animées."[33] Although expressed in a rather
careless manner, such considerations can in no way be ignored. It is
upon principles of this type ("decentralization" of sensitivity, admission
of more than one nervous system, etc.) that Bordeu and other scholars
developed the study of the involuntary and unconscious motion-impulses,
of the peripheral nervous system, and of the functions of the organic
instincts.[34]

In concluding this essay, I wish to offer some considerations of a
more general nature. What Bordeu has derived from a happy combination of his own Hippocratic experimentalism and the doctrines of Stahl
and van Helmont is a highly important conception of life and of the
living organism. Life is a reality which to a great extent cannot be
compared to anything else; for this reason it requires from a cognitive
point of view that autonomous place and status which modern physiology has finally conceded it. As for the living individual, it is no longer
(not even metaphorically) a *machine,* but an *être sensible.* It is an
organic being made up of flesh, nerves, and muscles; possessing dynamic
forces and impulses; and characterized by processes that have nothing
to do with the working of a machine. This image of the living being,
opportunely elaborated (by Cabanis especially) would soon be contrasted, not only to the iatromechanical model of the man-machine, but
also to Condillac's model of the man-statue. Unlike the machine and
the statue, the living organism does not lead a life which is exclusively
determined by the external environment and its modifications. Made up
of sentiment and dynamic centers, Bordeu's man possesses an internal
vitality and activity as well. His organs carry out determined functions,
produce determined sensations, and interact among one another independently from external stimuli. Whereas the sensationalist school
stressed (in ways sometimes exaggerated or not adequately justified) the

[32] Bordeu, *Recherches sur la position des glandes,* I, 187.
[33] Bordeu, *Recherches sur les maladies chroniques,* II, 829.
[34] Bastholm, *The History of Muscle Physiology.* These studies should be developed and enlarged, keeping in mind the important psychological and philosophical implications of certain bio-physiological researches.

importance of the external *milieu,* Bordeu and the Vitalists centered attention on the organic *intérieur* of man—a motion which some late eighteenth-century *philosophes* would find very stimulating.[35]

There were some scholars who saw in the vitalism of the School of Monpellier an inclination towards materialism. They were certainly not wrong. It does not escape the observer's attention that if the living subject assumes a dynamic autonomy all its own in relation to the environment, this happens because of the great powers of material and bodily organization. The concept of organization is thus raised from the position (see Condillac) of mere intermediary between *milieu* and *âme* to that of active protagonist of a complex vital phenomenology. The materialistic inclinations inherent in a certain type of physiological vitalism were distinguished above all from the way in which Bordeu (and even more so his Parisian heirs) seemed to shape the structure and functioning of the so-called "superior" activities of the human being. Until then, these activities had been attributed to the soul or to an intellectual and conscious center, often considered (more or less tacitly) to be of a slightly *sui generis* nature. And how could it be otherwise, at least within the iatromechanical doctrine, since the body as such was considered a mere aggregate of inert and insensible mechanical *ressorts?* Bordeu tends, on the contrary, to modify the traditional status of the problem. Not only does the soul appear to be cut off from any actual psychic process; but the "monarchic" supremacy of the conscious intellectual center is replaced (as we know) by a "federation" of many bodily centers. These centers are, in turn, endowed with highly developed sensitive faculties and, because they are connected by the nerves to the brain (which remains the source, but no longer isolated and autonomous, of ideas), can actively participate in the psychoaffective life of man. In short, the functions of the *physique* (to use terms employed by the vitalists of Montpellier and Paris) are intrinsically and jointly interwoven with the functions of the *moral.*[36]

It is a pity that Bordeu did not develop these themes systematically, but instead limited himself to a few indications of the influence that, through the voice of the instincts and of unconscious sensitivity, the body exercises over the *esprit.* But following his lead, other scholars, from Diderot to Cabanis, would subject traditional psychology to a radical criticism, emphasizing with the greatest energy the abstractness of any

[35] We think first of Diderot, not only for his well-known *Réfutation* of the "environmental" doctrines of Helvétius and for his passionate defense of the concreteness of the body, but also for the thesis contained in that important text *Élémens de Physiologie,* where Diderot's debt to the neovitalism of the Montpellier medical school is explicitly recognized by Diderot. See on this subject the introduction by Jean Mayer to his critical edition of the *Élémens* (Paris, 1964) also his *Diderot, homme de science* (Paris, 1959).

[36] Bordeu, *Recherches sur les maladies chroniques,* II, 799-802, 952.

study of the "superior" activities separated from the study of bodily activities and functions. The purpose of this group of scientists was to find, exactly as Bordeu had once suggested,[37] an organic and dynamic psychophysiology of man. Or perhaps theirs was another, more general aim, that of refuting once and for all the mechanistic image of the living being, by showing how far from inert, how autonomously active and vital, is the bodily substance of this being. The materialistic inspiration, or at least the materialistic implications of this twofold plan, should be quite evident. And it is an instructive paradox to see how the animistic fantasies of Stahl and van Helmont ended by propitiating (if through various intermediaries) a materialistic science of man. It is this science of man which coincides with an organic analysis of the relationships between *moral* and *physique,* that Cabanis (a reader full of sympathy for the animist and vitalist *savants,* from van Helmont and Stahl to Barthez and Bordeu) will feel disposed one day to call *anthropologie.*[38]

University of Florence.

[37] "La connaissance de l'homme physique et moral nous paroît être le but auquel doivent tendre tous les efforts et toutes les études d'un médecin-philosophe." *Ibid.,* II, 828.

[38] P. Cabanis, *Rapports du physique et du moral de l'homme,* in *Oeuvres philosophiques,* ed. Lehec-Cazeneuve (Paris, 1956), I, 126. On that page Cabanis seems aware that the word was already used in Germany by E. Platner in his *Neue Anthropologie in pragmatischer Hinsicht* (Koenigsberg, 1798), but seems to ignore the work by A. Chavannes, *Anthropologie, ou Science de l'Homme* (Lausanne, 1788). On the concept of "science de l'homme": S. Moravia, *La scienza dell'uomo nel Settecento* (Bari, 1970). On the Cabanisian psycho-physiology: *idem, Il pensiero degli idéologues. Scienze e filosofia in Francia, 1785-1815* (Florence, 1974), Pt. I, Ch. V.

PART FIVE

LARGER ISSUES

Chapter XXXI

MILLENARIANISM AND SCIENCE IN THE
LATE SEVENTEENTH CENTURY*

By Margaret C. Jacob

When historians have dealt with seventeenth-century English millenarianism they have invariably focused on the political ideologies and religious aspirations of the radical sectaries.[1] Very recent scholarship, however, has brought to light the millenarian beliefs and speculations of such disparate social conservatives as Richard Baxter, Isaac Newton, and Thomas Hobbes.[2] My own research into the intellectual interests of late seventeenth-century churchmen has convinced me that millenarianism was more widespread than has generally been assumed and that, more particularly, millenarian beliefs were commonly held in the late seventeenth century by latitudinarian churchmen. Many of these same Anglican churchmen or their friends and protégés also shared a marked interest in the new science, especially in the Newtonian natural philosophy. In exploring the nature of Anglican millenarianism I wish to relate it to the latitudinarian acceptance of the new science and its concomitant natural philosophy. What strikes us as so curious—that in many instances the same churchmen who championed the new science should also have been millenarians—will, I hope, appear less so when we are able to integrate the thought of these churchmen with their social and political interests. For those interests rendered science and millenarianism compatible.

Both millenarianism and science played vital roles in the social ideology constructed by churchmen to secure the church's interests. Consequently we should not be surprised to find churchmen of Newtonian persuasion convinced that the ordered and mathematically regulated universe explicated in the *Principia* would, at an appointed time, physically disintegrate, destroyed by an act of God foretold by Scriptural prophecies. That the author of the *Principia* himself espoused markedly millenarian views, particularly in his private conversations and writings,[3] should appear less curious or idiosyncratic when we

*This paper was delivered first as a lecture to a scheduled session of the annual meeting of the American Historical Association, in San Francisco, Dec. 1973. I am grateful to Professors J. G. A. Pocock and Richard Schlatter for their comments on that occasion.

[1] E.g., Christopher Hill, *Antichrist in Seventeenth Century England* (London, 1971); Norman Cohn, *The Pursuit of the Millennium* (London, 1970), 252, *et seq.,* and appendix.

[2] J. G. A. Pocock, "Time, History and Eschatology in the Thought of Thomas Hobbes," in J. H. Elliott and H. G. Koenigsberger, eds., *The Diversity of History* (London, 1970); William Lamont, "Richard Baxter, the Apocalypse and the Mad Major," *Past and Present,* **55** (1972), 68–90; L. Trengove, "Newton's Theological Views," *Annals of Science,* **22** (Dec. 1966), 277–94; Frank Manuel, *Isaac Newton Historian* (Cambridge, 1963), 146–47. I disagree with Manuel's conclusions. The conclusions of that book are modified in F. Manuel's *The Religion of Isaac Newton* (Oxford, 1974).

[3] D. Kubrin, "Newton and the Cyclical Cosmos: Providence and the Mechanical Philosophy," JHI, **28** (1967), 325–46; H. W. Turnbull, ed., *The Correspondence of Sir*

realize that the church circle with which he associated, both socially and intellectually,[4] displayed a deep and abiding interest in the millenarian prophecies.

In the light of recent controversies[5] about who in the seventeenth century should rightly deserve the title "millenarian" I should be explicit about the definition of that term. Seventeenth-century religious convictions and their organized proponents display the delightful characteristic of defying the historian's attempt at categorization. This is nowhere truer than in the ranks of the millenarians, however tepid or enthusiastic their fervor. Millenarianism simply means a belief in an approaching millennium or earthly paradise, an event foretold in the Scriptural prophecies, and in turn capable of being predicted either by specially enlightened saints or by cautious and exacting scholarship. This new state of human existence would be instituted by divine intervention. The dates of its arrival, the method chosen by God for its enactment, the beneficiaries in the "new heaven and the new earth," the joy or fear induced by the contemplation of this fundamental alteration in the human condition—on these important aspects of millenarianism we readily admit enormous differences among seventeenth-century believers. Certainly the millenarian speculations and beliefs of later century churchmen differed quite purposefully from those held by mid-century radicals. For the churchmen discussed in this paper millenarianism was only occasionally a fitting subject for church sermons; it lent itself too easily to misinterpretation and hence to encouraging the growth of enthusiastical religious movements. Furthermore, the millenarian vision of churchmen placed the church, and not simply the saints, as triumphant in the "new heaven and the new earth." In the millenarian paradise, and consequently in the historical process that would lead to its creation, the church and the more powerful and prominent members of its laity would lead the nation and finally the world along the stable and peaceful course preordained and guided by providence.

Certain stages were inevitably part of this providential plan as churchmen interpreted it: the Protestant Reformation with the English church as its vanguard would convert both the old and the new worlds to its teachings; the Antichrist Rome, and more immediately its main political defender, the French king, would suffer defeat and finally destruction at the hands of Protestant forces. Indispensable to the fulfillment of the providential plan was political stability and prosperity in England, as well as the maintenance of the church's political and moral power in a society that churchmen believed to be dangerously corrupted by rapacious self-interest, and infested by intellectual and political radicals, the so-called atheists, freethinkers, Hobbists, and Epi-

Isaac Newton (Cambridge, 1961), III, 245; Newton MSS from Jewish National and University Library, Cambridge University Library, microfilm 664, f. 2–3; B.L. MSS. ADD. 4478b, ff 142–150; Royal Society, Gregory MS, f. 87.

[4] H. Guerlac and M. C. Jacob, "Bentley, Newton and Providence: the Boyle Lectures Once More," *JHI*, 30 (Nov. 1969), 307–17; T. Birch, ed., *The Works of . . . John Tillotson* (London, 1752), I, XIV.

[5] Bernard Capp, "*Godly Rule* and English Millenarianism," *Past and Present*, 52 (1971), 117; William Lamont, *loc. cit.*; Bernard Capp, "The Millennium and Eschatology in England," *Past and Present*, 57 (1972), 156–62.

cureans.[6] To secure the church's political and social position, particularly as its power further declined in consequence of the Revolution Settlement of 1688–89, the latitudinarian faction that ascended to high ecclesiastical offices in the 1690's preached with renewed fervor their unique social ideology.

In this latitudinarian ideology providence guaranteed social and political stability in the world politic just as it ordered and harmonized, through laws discernible by scientific inquiry, the world natural. On this analogy between the world politic and the world natural, which we find consistently used in the sermons of Isaac Barrow, John Tillotson, and the Newtonians, Bentley, Clarke, Harris, Derham, and Whiston, the latitudinarians hung their vision of the ordered society.[7] In such a society prosperity came to the industrious and God-fearing, self-interest worked for the interests of the public weal, and the church alone stood guard over the moral temper of a nation called by God to fulfill the Protestant Reformation and thereby to usher in the millenarian paradise. Millenarianism made urgent the church's social mission and gave historical purpose to its social teachings. The earthly paradise would come into being only after men established a stable, prosperous, and Protestant polity, guided by providence. The natural philosophy and scientific discoveries of men like Boyle and Newton seemed to provide incontrovertible proof for the efficacy of providence and for the harmony and reason inherent in the natural order. In retrospect, latitudinarian social philosophy may appear to have been a somewhat unsuccessful attempt to joust with Mammon; at the time it was intended as a weapon in the historical struggle with Antichrist.

In many instances the genealogy of latitudinarian millenarianism leads back to Cambridge, to Henry More, John Worthington, and others, as well as to the writings of Joseph Mede and the Elizabethan mathematician, John Napier. Thomas Burnet, master of Charterhouse in the late 1680's and firm opponent of James II's policies, almost certainly imbibed his millenarianism from the Cambridge Platonists. As Wilfrid Lockwood and I have argued elsewhere, Burnet's *Sacred Theory,* if read in its original Latin text, is a millenarian document.[8] Among those churchmen who shared or supported Burnet's theories I would include Drue Cressener, Simon Patrick, Bishop of Chichester, and his brother, John—all Cambridge men. Newton's affiliation with Cambridge is, of course, well known.

Millenarian beliefs also prevailed among the church's ecclesiastical

---

[6]M. C. Jacob, "John Toland and the Newtonian Ideology," *The Journal of the Warburg and Courtauld Institutes,* 32 (1969), 307–31; J. R. Jacob, "The Ideological Origins of Robert Boyle's Natural Philosophy," *Journal of European Studies,* 2 (1972), 1–21.

[7]Isaac Barrow, *The Theological Works,* ed. A. Napier (Cambridge, 1859), V, 203–07, 231–32; John Tillotson, *The Works of . . .* ed. T. Birch (London, 1752), 554–55; William Derham, *Physico-Theology: or, A Demonstration of the Being and Attributes of God, from his Works of Creation* (London, 1714); William Whiston, *The Accomplishment of Scripture Prophecies* (London, 1708); Samuel Clarke, *A Discourse concerning the Unalterable Obligation of Natural Religion* in R. Watson, ed., *A Collection of Theological Tracts* (1st ed., London, 1785), IV, 177–78; Richard Bentley, *The Works . . .* ed. A. Dyce (London, 1838), III, 174–75.

[8]M. C. Jacob and W. A. Lockwood, "Political Millenarianism and Burnet's *Sacred Theory.*" *Science Studies,* 2 (1972), 265–79.

leadership. In 1689 Archbishop Sancroft listened closely and seriously to the predictions of that most avid Anglican millenarian, William Lloyd, Bishop of St. Asaph.[9] Edward Fowler, Bishop of Gloucester, John Tillotson, Archbishop from 1691 until his death in 1695, and Thomas Tenison, his successor in that office, all express apocalyptic sentiments in their sermons.[10] In the early eighteenth century Fowler was so gripped by millenarian fervor that his name appears on a manuscript list of followers drawn up by the millenarian and enthusiastic French prophets.[11] As late as 1710 Pierre Allix, a refugée and recipient of latitudinarian patronage, whose name also appears on the prophets' list, was busily at work still trying to unravel the cryptic utterances of Scripture about the final days of the world.[12]

Anglican millenarianism surfaces most dramatically in the late 1680's, and again during the reign of Anne. In 1685 the revocation of the Edict of Nantes and the advent of a Catholic monarch alarmed English Protestants of whatever persuasion. But James II's policies primarily endangered the church's interests. In turn the Revolution of 1688–89 and its Settlement provoked a crisis of conscience within the church, and out of that experience the latitudinarian faction emerged most amenable to the new political order.[13] After 1688–89 it provided the church with its ecclesiastical and intellectual leadership.

In 1688 when the threat to the church was most critical John Evelyn, a prominent member of the latitudinarian camp, close friend to Robert Boyle and Thomas Tenison, and also himself a proponent of the new mechanical philosophy, penned a treatise for the Countess of Clarendon, entitled "Concerning the Millennium." Written before Williams' invasion, this manuscript, now deposited amid Evelyn's papers at Christ Church, reveals Evelyn's profound millenarianism. In it he is at pains to make clear that his version of the new heaven and the new earth is "not as the Millenaries of old, or Fifth Monarchists of Late, have fancied for a Thousand years only before the final consumation; but [as I have said] after it . . . when our Blessed Savior shall reign with his Saints forever, I do not say, on this earth at all; but in that Renewed Heaven and Earth to come."[14] Church millenaries like Evelyn and

[9] E. de Beer, ed., *The Diary of John Evelyn* (London, 1955), IV, 636; cf. Lambeth Palace Library, MS 930, f. 42, and MS 1029, f. 109.

[10] Edward Fowler, *A Sermon Preached in the Chapel of Guildhall . . . 1704 . . . being the day of Public Thanksgiving . . .* (London, 1704), esp. 16; John Tillotson, *op. cit.,* II, 575–76, III, 170–72, 247–48; Thomas Tenison, *A Sermon against Self-Love . . .* (London, 1689), 14, and *A Friendly Debate . . .* (London, 1688), 18; also the Boyle lectures of John Williams, *The Possibility, Expedience and Necessity of Divine Revelation* (London, 1696), in S. Letsome and J. Nicholl, eds., *A Defense of Natural and Revealed Religion* (London, 1739), I, 246; and Kidder's lectures in Letsome and Nicholl, I, 95–96.

[11] Fatio de Duillier MSS, Bibliothèque Publique et Universitaire de Genève, MS Français 603.

[12] P. Allix, *Two Treatises* (London, 1707) and his MSS in the Cambridge University Library; also Lambeth Palace Library, MS 953, Lloyd to Allix, 1697. I am grateful to Hillel Schwartz for pointing out Allix's involvement, whatever it may have been, with the prophets.

[13] G. V. Bennett, "King William III and the Episcopate," *Essays in Modern English Church History,* eds. G. V. Bennett and J. Walsh (London, 1966), 104–31.

[14] Christ Church, Evelyn MS. 35, f. 2.

Burnet always insisted on the destruction of this earth by Christ and the establishment of an earthly, but new kingdom. The social message here is obvious: the radicals could never establish a millenarian kingdom in this world according to their principles in anticipation of the second coming. Their millennium contradicts Scripture; yet Scripture quite clearly predicts the advent of the millennial paradise. Evelyn tells the Countess:

For this Earth in which dwell nothing but wickedness (as St. Peter tells us) shall be burnt up, purged and made another thing; the glorious state of which you will find described, through the whole Sixtieth Chapter of Isaiah. . . . And upon this Hope, the Apostle persuades them to Repentance and Conversion; That thereby they might partake of that Refreshment when Christ (whom the Heavens must receive in the meane time) shall be sent, as god had spoken by the mouths of his holy prophets since ye world began.[15]

Evelyn believes that only the saints, those who have repented their sinful ways and undergone conversion, will be spared during that final destruction in order that they may rule triumphantly in the new heaven and new earth. In the best landowning tradition "they shall build houses, and inhabit them" and enjoy "those earthly possessions of plenty and prosperity in the Land of Promise." In Evelyn's version of the saintly inheritance no amelioration of existing economic inequities is ever hinted at, much less imagined. The saints' progress toward spiritual and material fulfillment in the new heaven and the new earth proceeds gradually, and one essential step will be the freeing of God's people from the tyrant Herod, the subsequent "revival of a purer Church," and the destruction of Antichrist. It is difficult to doubt that by naming Herod, Evelyn was referring to James II and to his hope for a restitution of the Protestant religion. Evelyn, of course, sought its recovery by any means except revolution. On November 2, 1688 he anxiously wrote to Pepys about the possibility of James II's promoting Stillingfleet and Tillotson to bishoprics, presumably to stave off "the impendent Revolution,"[16] and in another letter Evelyn assured Sancroft that he had no use for invaders "be they Dutch or Irish."[17]

Despite his fear of Revolution, Evelyn accepted the new order once the church's political influence had been secured. Evelyn's well-developed sense of self-interest conspired with his millenarianism to render him a supporter of the Revolution Settlement. As trustee of the Boyle lectureship he became, until his death in 1706, one of the most important guardians of church thinking and a promoter of natural religion based on Newtonian principles. Among the motivations for Evelyn's actions, whether political or intellectual, we must include his fervent belief in the approaching apocalypse. His extensive notations made in his private Bible reveal Evelyn's scheme for the fulfillment of the prophecies:

The 7th Viale poured on Antichrist was the preaching of Luther, etc., and continues to this day: by all the reformed; figured by the Earthquake . . . and that by the Harvest is figured, ye Reformation of ye last century. The Vintage is now to come: from anno 1689 or thereabout and to last till the full destruction of ye Roman Babylon.[18]

[15] *Ibid.,* f. 3.
[16] Christ Church, Evelyn MS. 39, f. 105.
[17] *Ibid.,* f. 104, 10 October, 1688.
[18] Christ Church, Evelyn MS 46, notes after Revelation XXII.

For Evelyn the world would not end in 1689; like Cressener, Lloyd, and possibly Burnet, he assumed rather that in 1689 or thereabouts the tide would turn against Babylon. From the late seventeenth century onwards, the Reformed church would assume the ascendancy in Europe and the task of its leaders would be to convert the recalcitrant to the Protestant way and thereby insure their reign in the millennial paradise. After many misgivings and uncertainties Evelyn and his fellow churchmen came to see the Revolution as a step along the prophetic path revealed in Scripture. By 1692 Tillotson recorded in his private Commonplace book: "I look at the King and Queen as two angels in human shape sent down to us to pluck a whole nation out of Sodom that we may not be destroyed." [19] A year earlier Thomas Burnet rejoiced to John Patrick, brother of Simon, about English victories in Ireland, worried about the military campaign on the Continent but concluded optimistically: "ye Resurrection of ye Witnesses goes on very well in Savoy and Dauphine, and that another argument to hope all will end well." [20] In 1694 Drue Cressener was still pursuing his study of Scripture and he assured Simon Patrick that only in the reign of Justinian had the Roman Church ever been completely in control of state affairs. [21]

In conjunction with the millenarianism of the low-church faction went its dedication to the new science, and in particular after 1689, to the Newtonian natural philosophy. As trustees of the Boyle lectureship, Evelyn and Tenison appointed the Newtonians as lecturers, and the lectures of Bentley, Clarke, Whiston, and Derham constituted the first public expositions of Newton's achievements. They embraced and preached Newton's system of the world, in all probability with his approval, as the new and essential foundation upon which, by analogy, rested justification for their vision of the "world politick." How then did the millenarian beliefs of churchmen such as John Evelyn, Simon Patrick, Thomas Burnet, Thomas Tenison, and William Whiston blend with their advocacy of the new science and with their acceptance of the mechanical philosophy as developed by Boyle, Wilkins, and others and applied to the workings of the universe by Sir Isaac Newton?

Millenarianism gave human application to scientific theories, in particular to the new mechanical philosophy. The church's vision of the historical process by which the Scripture prophecies would be fulfilled demanded the creation of a stable political and social environment. In direct contradiction to the challenge to that order posed by the radical millenarians, the latitudinarian church sought the attainment of its paradise through the acceptance of a broad and tolerant Protestantism that rewarded private endeavor and at the same time maintained the church's vested interests. Because churchmen believed the political and moral order to be inextricably guided by the natural order they accepted the new mechanical philosophy because it argued for the operation of God in that order. In Newton's universe matter is passive, all motion originates with and is controlled by the deity; universal gravitation operates in nature through a series of active principles, in effect through the agency of divine will. The order and stability imposed by God in the natural

[19] Quoted in D. D. Brown, "An edition of Selected Sermons of John Tillotson (1630–1694) from MS. Rawlinson E. 125 in the Bodleian Library ..." (M. A. Thesis, University of London, 1956), lxi.
[20] Bodleian Library, Tanner MS, XXVI, f. 44.
[21] Bodleian Library, Tanner MS, XXV, f. 216.

world provided churchmen with what they believed was a new and invincible argument for the operation of providence in human affairs.

Providential action in the historical process, as they understood it, would culminate in the creation of an earthly paradise. The millenarian dreams of the latitudinarians facilitated their acceptance of the new science because it articulated an ordered, providentially guided pattern, pervasive in the natural world. That pattern corresponded to, and more importantly, reinforced the order and stability so desperately desired by churchmen for their world. Indeed, the entire historical plan hung on that order, and with its accomplishment a beleaguered church would reign triumphant amid the plenty and prosperity promised to the saints in their earthly millennial paradise.

Baruch College, C.U.N.Y.

Chapter XXXII

PHYSICS AND METAPHYSICS IN NEWTON, LEIBNIZ, AND CLARKE

By Margula R. Perl

Just what are the philosophical differences between Newton and Leibniz? Where do they differ as to the scope of natural philosophy, i.e. physics, the requirements for a physical theory, the role of metaphysics and of God, methodological principles, and the relation between physics and metaphysics? The classical source for the answers to this question is the Leibniz-Clarke correspondence. It is argued, and recently with vehemence, that Clarke was not only Newton's spokesman, but that evidence exists to show that Newton provided notes for some of the replies and that further, he dictated others.[1] This evidence seems well-founded. Yet it seems important to examine other relevant texts of both Newton and Leibniz, as well as of Clarke, for the following reasons.

The Leibniz-Clarke correspondence was initiated in 1715. Leibniz, always fond of polemics as well as of royal correspondents, conveyed his fears about natural religion in England to Princess Caroline. Samuel Clarke was chosen to defend England. This ultimately involved the defense of some inferences from Newton's natural philosophy which were then current. This took place almost three decades after Newton had completed most of his scientific work. From 1696 on, Newton was engaged first as Warden and then as Master of the Mint. Several other historical factors may be relevant here as well. The exchange of letters between Leibniz and Clarke followed a bitter, futile controversy over priority in the invention of the calculus. The year 1712 marked the appearance of the *Commercium Epistolicum,* issued by the Royal Society. This report on the priority question, in the formulation of which Newton presumably participated, was of course unfavorable to Leibniz. This engendered further bitterness. The details are here irrelevant; neither Newton nor Leibniz behaved particularly well, since each knew that the other had achieved his results indepen-

---

[1] Cf. A. R. Hall and M. B. Hall, "Clarke and Newton" *Isis,* 52 (Dec. 1961), 583–5. Here they cite a note in Newton's handwriting, apparently for Clarke's use, on miracles, occult qualities, and other topics in the correspondence; but the Halls note that no passage of Clarke's precisely refutes Newton's jottings, although there are parallels in the Fifth Reply. Cf. also A. Koyré and I. Bernard Cohen, "The Case of the Missing Tanquam," *Arch. Int. Hist. Sci.* XVI (Jan.–June, 1962), 63ff., where it is argued that in the Leibniz-Clarke correspondence there is a serious opposition of two philosophers, and the issue is not one of wounded vanities. They list many published objections of Leibniz, from 1710 on, to Newton's statements on gravity, miracles, etc., and argue that Newton helped Clarke in drafting replies to Leibniz, and that Clarke is a reliable spokesman.

dently.[2] But a far more important consequence of this personal feud was that neither one regarded as successful the solutions of specific scientific problems offered by the other, as had previously been the case.[3] (It may be noted that most of Leibniz's objections to Newton in the Correspondence are directed to the Queries in the *Optics* rather than to the systematic part of the *Optics* or to the *Principia*.) The community of scientists gave way to two camps of feuding metaphysicians. Thus Newton writes of Leibniz in 1715: "As for Philosophy, he colludes in the significations of words, calling those things miracles which create no wonder; and those things occult qualities, where causes are occult, though the qualities themselves be manifest; and those things the souls of men which do not animate their bodies. His *Harmonia Praestabilita* is miraculous, and contradicts the daily experience of all mankind . . . . He prefers hypotheses to arguments of induction drawn from experiments . . . and instead of proposing questions to be examined by experiments before they are admitted into Philosophy, he proposes hypotheses to be admitted and believed, before they are examined . . . ."[4] (Descartes' three elements are distinguished from each other by their subtlety, i.e. fineness and degree of moveability. There are particles of the first element, the second, and the third, which are present in the sun and stars and are luminous, those in the skies which are transparent, and those of the earth and planets which are opaque, respectively. The most subtle account for the plenum. Cf. *Principia Philosophiae* III, 52.) The choice of Clarke, the theologian, rather than Cotes or even Pemberton, the more competent scientists in the Newtonian ranks, is almost symbolic of this feud.

Samuel Clarke, C. D. Broad states, had first-rate mathematical and philosophical ability.[5] This seems rather doubtful for the following reasons. First, let us consider Clarke's edition of the Cartesian Rohault's textbook of physics. This appeared in 1697, after the publication of Newton's *Principia*, with footnotes by Clarke which have been said to provide refutations of the Cartesian physics which comprise the book. Let us grant the apologists for Clarke the need for a complete textbook of natural philosophy which includes chapters on "Snow Hail and Hoar-Frost and Honey-Dew extraordinary Rain and Manna," and Part IV entitled "Of the Animated or Living Body." It is not yet

[2]Not only differences in the symbolism of each, but also differences in the specific kinds of problems dealt with by each attest to this.

[3]Cf. Leibniz' letters to Huygens, 1692 1694, selections from which appear in Loemker's *Leibniz' Philosophic Papers and Letters* (Chicago, 1956), II, 678–88. Cf. also Leibniz' letter to Hartsoeker in which he writes that on the question of the original color of light he prefers Newton's theory to Mariotte's since Newton made a large number of experiments. (Letter of 12 December, 1706), *Gerhardt* III, 488.

[4]Newton's *Opera Omnia*, ed. Horsley Linden, 1779 1785, IV, 598. Cf. E. W. Strong "Newtonian Explications of Natural Philosophy," *JHI*, (Jan. 1957), 49 83.

[5]CF. C. D. Broad, "Leibniz' Last Controversy with the Newtonians," *Theoria*, XII (1946), 143 68.

clear how Clarke was able fully to understand Newton and still accept
even the style of Rohault's text. Even the lack of one equation in Cartesian physics may be noted, as well as the inconsistencies, not to mention the method. As for the notes which Clarke provides, which have
been cited in his defense, it many be illuminating to cite a few examples, as well as to consider flagrant omissions. To Rohault's explanation of the rectilinear reflection of two bodies in perpendicular
impact that "there being no reason why it should incline one way
rather than another,"[6] Clarke makes no comment. He neither comments on Rohault's discussion of substantial forms,[7] nor objects to
Rohault's argument against the chemists who restrict themselves to
the observable and do not deal with the ether.[8] Clarke's objections
to the Cartesian three elements are that they are fictitious and dependent upon a Plenum, but especially that it is absurd that everything is
composed of three elements "without any Interposition afterwards
either of God himself, or any other intelligent Cause."[9] Where Clarke
cites Newton as an opposing authority, he quotes from the Queries to
the *Optics,* which are replete with conjectures and speculations, and
can hardly be considered sufficient as a serious basis for refuting Cartesian physics. Newton's own refutations of Descartes in the *Principia*
are much more impressive.

In a letter from Clarke to Benjamin Hoadly, a number of curious
remarks cast further suspicion on Clarke as a fair representative of
Newtonian science. We may quickly pass over Clarke's statement
that mathematics is a real science "founded in the necessary nature of
things,"[10] since it is well known that Newton refused to commit himself on the ultimate nature of things, as well as on what is "necessary."
Perhaps Clarke is merely misconstruing Newton's remark that geometry is founded in mechanical practice. But of greater interest is
Clarke's argument against Leibniz's assertion of the proportionality of
force to the square of the velocity for a body in motion (the principle
of *vis viva*). Clarke argues as follows: Every effect is proportional to
its cause, i.e. the action of the cause or the power exerted at the time
when the effect is produced. To suppose the effect is proportional to
the square or the cube of its cause is to suppose the effect arises partly
from the cause, partly from nothing.[11] The sheer ineptness of the
argument is apparent. Clarke goes on to claim that force is proportional to two causes taken together, the quantity of matter and the
velocity, and that in free fall, the cause of the quantity of space described is both the force and time of action, the force varying as the
velocity.[12]

[6]Jacques Rohault, *Rohault's System of Natural Philosophy*, ill. with Dr. Samuel
Clarke's Notes, tr. John Clarke, 3rd ed. (London, 1735), 81.
    [7]*Ibid.*, 103.   [8]*Ibid.*, 110.   [9]*Ibid.*, 114–17.
    [10]A Letter from the Rev. Dr. Samuel Clarke to Mr. Benjamin Hoadly F. R. S.,
Works of Samuel Clarke (London, 1738), IV, 737–40.   [11]*Ibid.*   [12]*Ibid*

In dealing with the Correspondence, we shall cite a number of Clarke's claims, and compare these with Newton's treatment of the same topic. The point is that Clarke characteristically asserts categorically what Newton has said conjecturally or hypothetically. In referring to the perfectly solid parts of all matter, Clarke writes, ". . . all Bodies, fluid and solid are equally compounded of such sort of Particles entirely solid and perfectly hard."[13] Yet Newton's commitment to atomism is undeniably only to a mathematical atomism in which the particles of the *Principia* are limits. Newton explicitly writes that by particles he means "evanescent divisible quantities,"[14] and where he speaks of corpuscles in the *Principia* he means theoretical mass points. Even when he discusses the undivided particles "as far as we can see," Newton allows that it is an experimental question whether these are *divisible* or not. According to Newton, the separability of parts of bodies is observable. Thus, Newton, far from accepting metaphysically necessary, indivisible atoms, rather inclined toward a crude, empirical atomism. This much seems clear as far as the *Principia* of 1686 is concerned.

What then of the corpuscular metaphysic attributed to Newton in a good deal of the literature? The problem does not arise in a view like Hélène Metzger's that "atom" is the subject of the verb "attract" just as "ether" is the subject of "undulate." For clearly here "atom" means mass point which is clearly a theoretical entity of the sort that Newton calls "mathematical." The problem arises with those who attribute to Newton an underlying, pervasive metaphysic in an effort to show that Newtonian science is replete with metaphysical commitments. Newton does talk of ether corpuscles, of possible color corpuscles, of corpuscles of varying sizes and shapes. In these cases, what a corpuscle is for Newton in some specific context depends on the particular aspect of phenomena with which he is concerned. Where Newton later writes of "particles" (in the *Opticks*), he is still not referring to absolutely dense atoms. For these, whether he calls them particles or corpuscles, can swell and shrink, can be divided into smaller parts, are of variable density, and above all, constantly bear some relation to experiment.

What is often seized on by various writers is Newton's talk of hard particles in the last Query to the *Opticks,* which incidentally, apparently conflicts with his remark in the *Principia* that there are no absolutely hard particles. In the latter case, I suspect that by "hard" he means perfectly elastic, whereas in the *Opticks* he is dealing with a problem in which such a construal would be inappropriate. For he is

[13]Dr. Clarke's Fourth Reply in *The Leibniz-Clarke Correspondence*, ed. H. G. Alexander (Manchester, England, 1956), 45.
[14]*Mathematical Principles of Natural Philosophy*, tr. Motte, ed. F. Cajori, (Berkeley, 1934), 38; (hereafter *Principia)* in a scholium in which Newton discusses limits.

here in the *Opticks* concerned with the experimental phenomena of congealing and precipitation. His evidence is experimental, as is his inference, although the extrapolation is a poor one.[15]

As for the belief in the existence of a vacuum, there is no clear answer to be found within Newton's texts. There are rare and denser spaces. But the fact that Newton sought mechanical explanations of gravitation, and worked at ether theories indicates that the question of the existence of a vacuum was not a fundamental one. Leibniz's objections, if aimed at Newton, then become irrelevant, for they are not based on Newton's lack of evidence, but rather on Leibniz's principle of the identity of indiscernibles, which hardly applies to Newton's corpuscles, although the objection may well apply to Clarke's remarks.[16]

Clarke claims that the mathematical principles of philosophy "prove matter, or body, to be the smallest and most inconsiderable part of the universe,"[17] and are thus repugnant to atheism. For, he argues, "so far as metaphysical consequences follow demonstratively from mathematical principles, so far the mathematical principles may be called metaphysical principles."[18] For Newton, not only do mathematical principles have no connection at all with metaphysical principles, but from mathematical principles no physical principles follow. This is obviously intended to defend Newton against charges of materialism, but certainly the *Principia* is silent on this speculation, and in principle irrelevant to questions of the quantitative constitution of the universe. Clarke is then open to Leibniz's objection that mathematics is concerned with arithmetic and geometry, while metaphysics has more general concerns, and metaphysical principles are properly to be opposed to materialism, but not to mathematics. Leibniz can then use the principle of sufficient reason in his arguments against Clarke, which he could not do had Clarke not confused mathematical demonstration with metaphysical argument. Clarke's attempt to withdraw later by writing that mathematical reasonings are applied to physical and metaphysical subjects is of no avail; also, he does not clarify his position.

The distinction between the mathematical and the physical is both basic and pervasive in Newton. He is extremely cautious with regard to the degree of commitment involved in assent to those propositions which are in his system said to be mathematical. These are hypothetical formulations; as such they are not descriptive of the world, and require specification, restriction, and interpretation before they can be used to refer to phenomena. In brief, most of Newton's mathematical principles, on his view, have systematic import, but are not to be taken straightforwardly as empirically true.

[15]*Opticks* (New York, 1952), Queries (pp. 30 ff.).
[16]Leibniz-Clarke Correspondence, 65, 36–7.
[17]*Ibid.*, 12.   [18]*Ibid.*, 20.

Equally strange are Clarke's views on action. He writes: "...every action is the giving of a new force to the thing acted upon. . . .all mere mechanical communications of motion are not properly action, but mere passiveness, both in the bodies that impel and that are impelled. Action, is the beginning of a motion where there was none before, from a principle of life or activity."[19] These differ considerably from the views of Newton, which are that an action is essentially a dynamical event, one which is mathematically analyzed into components referred to as action and reaction, but there is no *one* cause. Newton generally speaks of action not only in the case of attraction, but also in mechanical situations.[20]

Clarke's misunderstanding of Newton is equally noteworthy with respect to the question of gravitation. Clarke writes: "Gravity . . . is an original, connate and immutable affection of all matter."[21] Now it is true that Newton *wrote* all sorts of speculations in the Queries to the *Opticks*. But he *worked out* a number of basic principles applicable to the question of gravitation. He developed a mathematical physics of central forces and applied it to the explanation of astronomical motions. He also proved that the force of terrestrial gravitation and the central forces in the sun and planets are subsumed under the same universal force of gravitation. We shall confine most of our discussion to what is found in the *Principia*, in the introduction to which Newton characterizes his program as follows: ". . . by the propositions mathematically demonstrated in the former Books, in the third I derive from the celestial phenomena the forces of gravity with which mere bodies tend to the sun . . . from these forces, by other propositions which are also mathematical, I deduce the motions of the planets. . . ."[22] Gravity is an instance of a measurable central force used in making calculations and inferences. Central forces are characterized by Newton as being "mathematical," meaning thereby that one avoids all "questions about the nature or quality of this force."[23] The geometrical representation of force is accomplished in the *Principia*, and force can thus be dealt with as a mathematical concept. The application of the Third Law (of action and reaction) to theorems on central forces makes all actions reciprocal. When these theorems are applied to particular bodies, the mathematical forces become specific, e.g., they become gravitational forces.

The existence of a force of gravity, as asserted by Newton, means that the laws governing gravitation, when suitably specified, provide

[19]*Ibid.*, 110.
[20]On this, see my "Newton's Justification of the Laws," *JHI* XXVII, No. 4, Oct.-Dec. 1966), 585-92.   [21]Rohault, *op. cit.*, 66.
[22]*Principia*, p. xviii (Preface); also Section XI, p. 164, and the Scholium on p. 192. Cf. E. W. Strong, "Newton's 'Mathematical Way,' " *JHI*, XII (Jan. 1951), 90-110.
[23]*Principia*, 550 (System of the World).

true descriptions of planetary and terrestrial motions. Gravity is "learned" from "experiments and astronomical observations." Descartes (in his *Principia Philosophiae*, IV, 20) attempted to explain gravitation; Galileo thought it not worthwhile. Newton attempted mechanical explanations in his avowedly speculative writings; but even there he added that the laws of attraction must be known prior to any effort at explanation or accounting of the causes of gravitation. The *Principia* speaks of gravity "acting according to the laws we have explained,"[24] and mentions no "Law of Gravitation." "Hypotheses non fingo" is consistent with Newton's treatment of gravitation in the *Principia*. Initially Leibniz wrote approvingly to Huygens, "Planets move as if there were only one motion of trajection . . . combined with gravity, as he (Newton) has observed."[25] The use of "as if" here is equivalent to one sense of Newton's "mathematical way," i.e. the manner of action, the causes, the qualities of attracting forces are irrelevant. Also, Leibniz wrote to Conti that he approved of Newton's physico-mathematical work and of his method. And elsewhere Leibniz again writes of Newton: "That remarkable man is one of the few who have advanced the frontiers of the sciences."[26] Writing partly in a Newtonian and partly in a Keplerian vein, Leibniz said: "Leaving out of consideration the physical basis of gravity, and remaining within mathematical concepts, I consider gravity as an attraction caused by certain radii . . . going out from an attracting center."[27] Why then did he attack Newton by referring to Newtonian attraction as either an occult quality or a miracle? Why did he write, "the attraction of bodies is a miraculous thing"? And why did he write to Huygens that he didn't understand Newton's concept of weight? Or later yet, that attraction is a long banned chimera, a poor sophism?[28]

Leibniz's objections to action at a distance are not central. Newton generally disavowed *physical* action at a distance. Leibniz himself in a scholium to his *Essay de Dynamique* writes: ". . . on peut concevoir le mouvement comme dans le vide, afin qu'il n'y ait point de résistance du milieu, et on peut s'imaginer que les surfaces des plans et des globes sont parfaitement unies, afin qu'il n'y ait point de frottement et ainsi du reste."[29] This is equivalent to affirmation of action at a distance even though it is prefaced by an 'as if.' But this 'as if,' is much like Newton's 'as ifs' when he engages in activity he calls 'mathematical.' At any rate, the view that a body can act on another so that there is simultaneous motion of all the parts presupposes action at a distance. This is so even when the action is rigorously mechanical, i.e., a push

[24] *Ibid.*, 546.   [25] Loemker, *op. cit.*, 68
[26] *The Correspondence of Sir Isaac Newton*, ed. Turnbull (Cambridge, 1961) Vol. III (1688-1694), 4.   [27] Loemker, *op. cit.*, 67
[28] Letter to Bourget, *Leibniz' Philosophische Schriften*, ed. Gerhardt, III, 593; also Letter to Huygens (Oct. 1690), Turnbull, *op. cit.*, III, 80.
[29] Pierre Costabel, *Leibniz et la dynamique: Les Textes de 1692*, (Paris 1960), 9

that meets all the Cartesian requirements of contact. Here it may be noted that Leibniz also speaks of a vacuum which is of course, necessary for a theoretical particle dynamics. Clarke argues that gravity implies the existence of a vacuum; Newton made no such claim and could not. For it could not be a mathematical posit; and in his search for a physical explanation, mechanical explanation would be a major desideratum, and vacuua are thereby excluded.

Leibniz's real objections to gravitation are more fundamental in character. His claim "that all matter is heavy . . . is certainly not proved by experiments,"[30] is certainly true, but the way he formulated this claim merely reveals that the relational character of gravity was not understood. But he was not alone in this. Even Newton speaks of bodies being endowed with a principle of mutual gravitation, although the 'mutual' does indicate the relational aspect. A purely relational account of the behavior of substances would never satisfy Leibniz. Nor would he admit gravity as ultimate in any descriptive or explanatory scheme since attraction is not admitted as part of the nature of bodies. Gravitation is not an inherent force, and force is the essential attribute of substance for Leibniz. It is here that we find one ultimate difference between Newton and Leibniz which is genuine. For Newton speaks of the force *on* a body, language which requires the consideration of the relation between two bodies and precludes speaking strictly of forces in isolation. Newton's alternate way of putting this point is in his stating that forces are measured by their effects, i.e. accelerations. Leibniz speaks of the force *of* or *in* a substance, which requires no other substance for the phrase to have reference. Force, being an essential attribute of monads, is an ultimate existent for Leibniz. His view of the ideality of relations precludes forces having the relational character which a particle mechanics requires. Further, Leibniz disallows the action of substances upon each other since the monads are not causally connected at all. But surely Leibniz is not thereby denying the validity of classical particle mechanics. He is merely claiming that as it stands it is not ultimately descriptive of the real, i.e. substances. These arguments against Newton are then quite beside the point. For mechanics applies to phenomena for both Newton and Leibniz, and in a sense would define the range of *phenomena bene fundata* for Leibniz. The problem for Leibniz here is the relation between the physical and metaphysical domain, which his concept of force is intended to bridge. For he writes that it is force, as the cause of motion, which really exists.[31] Further, nature based its laws on that which is most real, and force is viewed as being most real in nature, more real than either mass or motion. Yet observable properties of nature are at best *phenomena bene fundata*. What is the relation between the force of sub-

[30]Letter to Bourget, *loc. cit.*   [31]Costabel, *op. cit.*, 42.

stance, and natural forces? In order to answer this question we must consider a whole host of general questions concerning science and metaphysics and nature.

Leibniz writes: "It is not sufficient to say: God has made such a law of Nature, therefore the thing is natural. It is necessary that the law should be capable of being fulfilled by the nature of created things."[32] Here is implied a distinction between the laws to which things conform and their nature. We may ask whether Leibniz can maintain such a distinction. At one point he characterizes nature as inherent law, which would eliminate any distinction between "how things are" and "the laws according to which they behave." Yet Leibniz's reference to his dynamics as containing "an appraisal of the laws of nature and of motion that is true and in harmony with things"[33] would require the distinction. It would furthermore follow that there are criteria of adequacy in addition to applicability or truth, for laws of nature, since there is an implied distinction, related to the aforementioned one, between truth and being "in harmony with things."

Pure mathematics as such contains, for Leibniz, only the concepts of number, figure, and motion; a law of nature is but mathematics applied to the world. Mechanical laws are the applications of geometry to motion.[34] The reality of phenomena consists in their subjection to the "rules of mathematical thinking."[35] Yet, truth concerning phenomena has only moral certainty: phenomena need only meet requirements of constancy and coherence. For mathematics does not follow the order of nature. Maintaining the distinction between the order of knowing and the order of existence, Leibniz abandoned his earlier claims that because geometry is a science, space is a substance.[36] Only in practical disciplines are the order of nature and the order of knowing the same since the nature of the objects considered originates in thought and production. Thus Newton's statement that geometry is founded in mechanical practice would imply that geometry is a practical discipline in this sense. For Leibniz, mathematical time, extension, and motion are merely ideal, because they are unanalyzable into their primary constituents; extension is not primitive, but resolvable. The mathematical ideal of uniform motion is never found in nature. The laws according to which things behave must be formulated in terms of the simple concepts, the unanalyzables which do not merely relate, but refer, to real things. The laws of mechanics do not, as such, conform to the order of existence. They must be brought into harmony with things, for the adequate understanding of the operations of a body requires the consideration of the arrangement of the parts—the unanalyzable, non-mathematical, ultimate simples. Mathematics, even

[32]Loemker, *op. cit.*, 803 and *Correspondence* p. 94.
[33]Loemker, *op. cit.*, 814 (This was written in 1698.)
[34]*Ibid.*, 291.   [35]*Ibid.*, 950.   [36]*Ibid.*, 126

when applied, can provide only magnitude, figure, and situation. For predications involving existence, duration, action and passion, or force of action one must have recourse to metaphysics. In brief, we may say that Leibniz does not accept Newton's extension of the term "mathematical" to include various theoretical concepts of physics.

Leibniz objects to those who "use only incomplete and abstract concepts which thought supports but which nature does not know in their bare form."[37] Such is the consideration of what is treated only mathematically, e.g. when derivative forces are dealt with. While mathematicians engaged in mathematical activity need be concerned only with consistency, and need have no concern for metaphysical questions, the situation is different when the question of the application of mathematics arises. Perhaps for this reason Leibniz is concerned to show that algebra assumes the infinitesimal and the principles of continuity, for then mathematics is shown to be in some sense founded in reason. The importance of this for Leibniz lies in the fact that mere sensibilia attain the status of well ordered phenomena when they are consistent with each other and with "rational principles," which apparently for Leibniz means mathematics.[38] Here Leibniz's concern may be interestingly contrasted with Newton's requirement that his calculus be compatible only with the *method* of synthesis of the ancient geometers. It is true that in writings other than the *Principia* Newton wants further grounding for his formulations of the calculus. But constructibility suffices for the *Principia*. Thus, satisfied with his geometrical representation of limits, Newton is content with the mathematical model of a limit as the meaning of "particle."[39] Leibniz, on the other hand, does not consider extension to be an adequate concept since it is not conceived in itself and thought is completed only in the concept of force.[40] The criterion invoked here is not that of systematic completeness, or suitable application of a method. Thought is properly completed when the ultimate ontological order is reached. While admitting the difficulty of arriving at concepts of ultimate simplicity, or unity, and at times allowing of their non-necessity, Leibniz more consistently requires them. For the metaphysical demand of true unities from which multiplicities derive their reality is ultimate. Because of the activity in things, these simples must be active; full intelligibility is found in the concept of force. Hence the monads are units of force. Leibniz insists that it would not be conformable to reason if we were to deny that an active creative force resides in things.

For Leibniz nature is only superficially a mechanism of bodies; we view it as such only if we employ derivative principles. Activity cannot derive from the essentially inactive. The origin of the natural mech-

---

[37]*Ibid.*, 861.   [38]*Ibid.*, 631.
[39]*Principia*, Book I, Section I, pp. 29–39, especially pp. 38–39.
[40]Loemker, *op. cit.*, 861.

anism is then not a material principle and mathematical reasons alone, but a higher metaphysical source. The mathematical concept of motion is only ideal. Real motion involves, in addition to a body and change, a reason for and determinant of change. This consideration of real motion as change may be contrasted with Newton's conception of motion as a state. This is clear from the Law of Inertia. As such, motion requires no explanation; only change of motion, i.e. acceleration does. This means that phenomena are considered in such a way that only changes of motion will require analysis and explanation using the axioms and theorems of the system. To ask for the reasons of motion in Newtonian mechanics would hardly make sense. Yet there are further considerations which reveal a more complicated situation than the foregoing simple contrast would indicate.

Newton distinguishes mathematical from physical motion— or "absolute" and "relative" motion—just as he distinguishes absolute from relative time and space. The grounds for the distinction between the latter two is primarily methodological, i.e. any description in which there is commitment only to the satisfaction of certain mathematical relations is to be distinguished from those in which various empirical factors have to be taken into account, e.g. observables or measurement procedures. Thus, one must distinguish mathematical propositions about motion from physical propositions which assert how the motions actually take place. For example, the former may involve analyses into several motions when in fact there is but one; one motion cannot be physically analyzed into two. Mathematical motions are also such a attractions of bodies toward an immovable center "though very probably there is no such thing existent in nature."[40a] The import of these distinctions is that absolute time, space, and motion serve as concepts which can be used independently of any actual state of affairs

In Leibniz we find the term "absolute space," which he defines as the "locus of all loci."[41] This is distinguished from the space which is the order of co-existents. The former is much like Newton's absolute space; the latter involves quality (relative space). The distinction is that between *locus* and *situs*, and bears a certain resemblance to one sense of Newton's mathematical-physical distinction. But Leibniz does not use the distinction in connection with the problem of motion. The lines are drawn differently, and one might say that for him the only apparent connection between them is that both mathematics and motion are subject to the principle of continuity. We thus have the infinitesimal calculus subject to the principle on the one hand, and rest considered as motion having a velocity less than any assignable value on the other. From the above, it seems clearly absurd to write, as is often done, that Newton and Leibniz are straightforwardly opposed on the question of space and time, Newton holding an absolute, Leibniz a relative view

[40a] *Principia*, p. 164.   [41] *Ibid.*, 108

Leibniz explicitly grants the applicability of mathematical concepts such as "the concept of time as well as of space or merely mathematical extension, purely passive masses, motion in the mathematical sense, etc.,"[42] explains their manageability (due to their being definable "merely by theory"), and then cautions us that such concepts do not correspond to entities in nature. In the *Nouveaux Essais* we find Leibniz writing that time determination requires something uniform in nature "as space likewise could not be determined if there were no fixed or immoveable body," which is very much like Newton's Hypothesis I in the Third Book of the *Principia* (of an immovable center for the solar system to which to refer motion).[43] Much of the debate in the Leibniz —Clarke correspondence on the question of space, time and motion loses a good deal of significance if we consider Newton's use of the distinction between the absolute and relative, and Leibniz's understanding of this distinction as *used* for purposes of theoretical mechanics, as opposed to Newton's pronouncements in the General Scholium and Clarke's elaborations thereof. At any rate, the discussion, even in the correspondence, does not quite fit the categories of scholastic ontology as subsequent attempts to so construe them insist upon.

The difference between Newton and Leibniz appears most clearly when we consider their views of phenomenal motion. Phenomena for Newton are generally ordered measurable appearances. In the *System of the World*, for example, his list of phenomena includes instantiations of Kepler's laws for various planets, which as generalizations can be merely descriptive, so that the requirement of lawfulness seems foremost here. Subsumability to laws is also Leibniz's criterion for all *phenomena bene fundata*, but Leibniz does not regard phenomenal motion as real as the metaphysical cause of all change, namely, the living force (*vis viva*) within each monad or substance. Observable bodies as such are but quasi-substances, and are not so much the subjects of change as they are products of change. The subjects of change

[42]Philip P. Wiener, ed. *Leibniz Selections* (New York, 1951), 180. Cf. also L. Couturat, ed. *Opuscules et Fragments Inédits de Leibniz*, (590), where Leibniz writes: "Motus in rigore Mathematico nihil aliud est, quam mutatio situs corporum inter se, neque adeo absolutum quiddam est, sed in relatione consistit." Mathematically motion is relational and not absolute.

[43]Wiener, *op. cit.*, 180. We may note another Leibniz text in this connection: "Donc pour trouver ces unités réelles, je suis contraint de recourir à un point réel et animé pour ainsi dire, ou à un Atome de substance qui doit envelopper quelque chose de forme ou d'actif, pour faire un Estre complet." Gerhardt writes that Leibniz later changed this to: "or la multitude ne pouvant avoir sa réalité que des unités véritables qui viennent d'ailleurs et sont tout autre chose que les points dont il est constant que le continu ne scauroit estre composé; donc pour trouver ces unités réelles, je suis contraint de recourir à un atome formel puis qu'un estre matériel ne scauroit estre en même temps matériel et parfoitement indivisble ou doué d'une véritable unité." Gerhardt, *op. cit.*, IV, 471. The *Nouveaux Essais* quotation is from Langley's translation, *New Essays Concerning the Human Understanding* (Lasalle, 1916), 156.

for Leibniz are monads, the real substances, but monads can only change in degree of internal activity or perception. Yet another problem arises here. Leibniz explicitly says that in nature there can only be simple substances and the aggregates resulting from them. In actual bodies there is a multitude of monads, although in any sensible aggregate there may be more than any given number. Here is a clear claim that sensible gross bodies are literally composed of monads in much the same way that wooden logs are composed of cellulose molecules. But Leibniz also says that bodies are real, as composites with definite parts, and are "specified in a fixed way according to the divisions which nature introduces through the varieties of motion."[44] Bodies are the results of fixed primary constituents, real unities, although these bodies are not as permanent as their components. Bodies result from monads and matter is but a phenomenon grounded in their activity. The incompatibility between these two accounts of the relation between material bodies and monads appears in two important logical questions: If bodies are composites of monads, then how can their extension arise from their unextended components, and how can diverse monads form the continuum? But, it may also be asked, what explanatory value monads under their dynamical aspect can have if they are entities as real as the bodies which they compose?[45]

If Leibniz's conceptual analysis of contingent things into monads is physical though infinitely incompletable, then there is still an atomism on the level of imagination, which Leibniz opposes. If then monads are the results of logical analysis, and bodies are logical constructions of monads, the following problem arises: Primary force obtrudes into the world as *vis viva*, the cause of all observed change. But if all we need consider for physics is mv^2, according to Leibniz, why do we need metaphysically primary "living forces" at all? At least part of our answer is found in the *Discourse on Metaphysics* of 1686. Here Leibni

[44]Letter to De Volder, Loemker, *op. cit.*, 873.

[45]It is indeed tempting to speculate on the degree of neoplatonic influence on Leibniz's thought. For while Leibniz offers a variety of arguments for his monadistic ontology, there yet remains the question of what sort of model underlies it. For while it is true that the infinitesimal calculus supplies a structural model, this does not explain some of the vitalistic peculiarities of the monad system. Certain features of Plotinus's thought seem to illuminate some of these. The first obvious analogy to appear is that between Plotinus's One and Leibniz's monad. Besides the unity and simplicity common to each, there is the activity, the internality of each. Fundamentally Plotinus's activity of contemplation and Leibniz's monadic act of perception do not differ greatly. For Plotinus's hierarchical universe is arranged according to different degrees of contemplation, much as Leibniz's monads are ranked according to degrees of perception. The neoplatonic panzooism also bears similarity to the monad as souls. The neoplatonic emphasis on unity as the essential principle of being also fundamental in Leibniz. The distinction in Leibniz between primitive force as the law of the series, and the derivative force as the actual present instance is similar to Plotinus's distinction between nature and the logos. The continuity of the system of monads is also like the continuity of beings in the Plotinian universe.

writes that primary qualities like size and shape are relative to perception, though somewhat less so than secondary qualities, and include
something imaginary which precludes their concepts being fully distinct; hence they cannot constitute any substance: "And if there is no
other principle of identity in body than those we have just mentioned,
no body can ever subsist longer than a moment."[46] Metaphysics is
necessary in order that we may have some referent in view of the infinitesimal character of physical states, which are states "at an instant."
One almost suspects that because of his mathematical knowledge of
continua (especially that a continuous line is not composed of
points),[46a] Leibniz abandoned his youthful atomism of atoms of mass
or minimum extension. Yet, in a sense, Leibniz has not conceptually
abandoned this youthful atomism in assuming that phenomena are
fundamentally monadic. There is another kind of atomism also assumed by both Hume and Kant. Although Hume's is an atomistic sensationalism, and Kant speaks of the "rhapsody of sensations," the
underlying assumption of atomic elements in one form or another is
common to all. Kant's solution to the problem of how one may talk
about the world lies in his transcendental idealism; Leibniz's attack is
straightforwardly metaphysical: we must ultimately refer to monads,
which provides us with constant reference, although the monad is itself in part a formal "spiritual" atom.

Leibniz is consistent in his demand that the conceptual scheme of
monads is not to be used in particular natural explanations, or in establishing general principles; but these general principles, mechanical in
nature, are to be applied to particular phenomena of motion or physical
or chemical changes, which are *given* not merely as phenomena, but as
functions of substances. The language of monads is part of the language
used in describing that to which scientific theory applies, and is not part
of that theoretical language. Monads are not theoretical constructs,
but ontological posits. At the same time they have a peculiar role in
providing significance for the physical concept of force.

The laws of mechanics, says Leibniz, account for the laws of nature,
which we learn from experience. The former require the concept of
living force, which is metaphysical. Atoms of substance, the real
unities, i.e. monads, are the sources of action. Body is not a true unity,
and thus not fully real but a mere *ens rationis* of phenomenal being.
Real substances are characterized by the possession of primitive force,
inherent activity. This primitive force is characterized by the law of
the series, while the derivative force of bodies distinguishes some particular term in the series. Motion follows from derivative force, but
derivative force is a mere vanishing modification within each body

[46]Loemker, *op. cit.*, 475.
[46a] "New System of Nature and the Communication of Substances" in *Leibniz Selections*, ed. Wiener, 107.

which itself requires something permanent. To assume only derivative forces in bodies is to take the incomplete for the complete. For derivative forces explain diversities in phenomena, but are not ultimately explanatory in any sense of explanation which provides completeness and maximal coherence. The primitive forces which are then required are also characterized by Leibniz as primary entelechies, as inherent powers of acting, as primary motive forces of substances. Leibniz gives a dynamical argument for the existence of primitive forces. In impact, conservation of momentum is insufficient to account for the action, and conservation of *vis viva* (mv^2) must also be considered. This *vis viva* is the constant quantity in the universe, and thus the permanent, the real, the force of substances.

The varieties of Leibnizian arguments and characterization of force are almost by sheer quantity sufficient to reveal the manifold implications of the difference between speaking of a force on a body and the force of a substance. The difference is not only that Newton speaks of the origin of impressed force in percussion, pressure, or centripetal force, and that he defines force in terms of change in momentum, while Leibniz defines force (*vis viva*) as mv^2 which gives us a quantity proportional to kinetic energy,[47] for this is relatively insignificant. The important difference is that for Leibniz the correlate of *vis viva* is the monad, while for Newton the correlate of the mathematical concept of say a central force is a measurable laboratory weight. The fact that Leibniz writes ". . . la force ne se doit pas estimer par la composition de la vitesse et de la grandeur, mais l'effet futur,"[48] indicates that Leibniz grasps something of the dispositional character of force, very similar to Newton's talk of an action as a disposition of two bodies. Yet, Leibniz must also have a corresponding entity, a substance which exists beneath the dispositions.

In the context of Leibniz' views on force we find an interesting example of basic misunderstanding in Leibniz' Fourth Paper. He there argues that one cannot speak of dynamically identical states. His argument is:

To say that God can cause the whole universe to move forward in a right line or in any other line, without making otherwise any alteration in it; is another chimerical supposition. For, two states indiscernible from each other, are the same state; and consequently 'tis a change without any change.[49]

But surely this is to miss the point, which is not that inertial motion is not change, and thus there can be no question of identity of indis-

[47]In this connection it may be relevant to cite Brian Ellis' argument that Newton' concept of force derives from a primitive concept of a push or a kick. But Newton careful to add, in speaking of force, that the Second Law holds regardless of how the force is impressed. "Newton's Concept of Motive force," *J.H.I.*, XXIII, 2 (April 1962 273–78.

[48]Costabel, *op. cit.*, 42.   [49]Leibniz-Clarke Correspondence, 3

cernibles, or of discernibles either for that matter. Clarke's retort that two different places are not identical misses the mark, for the question of dynamical identity is independent of place.[50] What is involved here is the matter of the equivalence of inertial frames. And it is strange that Clarke does not refer to Newton's Fifth Corollary to the Laws: "The motions of bodies included in a given space are the same among themselves whether that space is at rest or moves uniformly forwards in a right line without any circular motion."[51]

While Leibniz does talk of resistance to change (*antitypia*), he does not seem to clearly grasp that inertia involves resistance to acceleration, and he persists in talk of motion *vs.* rest. Nor does he seem to grasp that change in dynamics is change of velocity and not of position. And I think that this is because motion for Leibniz is merely phenomenal, as distinguished from the real metaphysical *vis viva* which is its cause.[52] That he considered a conserved quantity such a mv^2 rather than ma may stem initially from his critique of Descartes. But it may rather be that the use of a conserved quantity is thus compatible with a permanence of substance as a metaphysical requirement, for Leibniz seems to find great significance in his refutation of conservation of momentum for the universe in general.

There are further differences between Newton and Leibniz. Thus where Newton's talk of causality is of instrumental causes, Leibniz's quest is for intelligible reasons. Newton retains a skepticism with regard to "real causes," which culminates in *"hypothesis non fingo,"* and contents himself with equations which can be applied to phenomena upon suitable interpretation. Leibniz speaks in a different language: "When the particular disposition of one substance provides a reason for change occurring in an intelligible manner, in such a way that we can conclude that the other substances have been adapted to it in this point from the beginning according to the order of the divine decree that substance should be thought then of as *acting* upon the others in this sense."[53] It is odd to find Popper attacking Newton for "essentialism" on the ground that Newton would have stopped asking questions if he had found a mechanical explanation for gravitation[54] (which is probably not true, since there is enough evidence in the Newtonian corpus that Newton would have looked for more general principles covering both dynamical laws and optical acoustic, magnetic, etc. laws). In the *Principia* Newton writes that he suspects that all de-

---

[50]*Ibid.*, 48.

[51]*Principia*, 20. In other discussions Leibniz does consider this corollary. But further, he wants to maintain the equivalence in cases of circular motion as well, which reveals that metaphysical "neatness" is his prime consideration.

[52]More clearly, we may say that phenomenal motion is for Leibniz at most a matter of kinematics, in which velocity-acceleration distinctions would hardly enter.   [53]Loemker, *op. cit.*, 749.

[54]*Cf.* Karl R. Popper, *Conjectures and Refutations* (London, 1963), 106–9.

pends on certain forces by which particles are compelled or repelled.[55] It is odd to laud Leibniz for having asked "why can bodies push one another," when the sort of answer Leibniz accepts as an account of mechanism is hardly of the kind to spur scientific investigation. Besides which, Leibniz has his own list of what needs no explaining, e.g. the fluidity of matter. He writes, "It is unnecessary to investigate the cause of fluidity, for matter is itself fluid except insofar as there are motions within it which are disturbed by the separation of certain parts,"[56] etc. His reasons are somewhat crude. An account of mechanism or mechanical laws for Leibniz can only be metaphysical, in terms of final causes. Of course, there is an innocuous sense of "final cause" in Leibniz, that of some minimax principle, e.g. the law of least action would be such for him, least-path equations, etc. But there is also a less innocent sense in which Leibniz speaks of laws of nature as originating "in the wisdom of their author or in the principle of greatest perfection."[57] And further, he adds, "the principles of mechanics themselves cannot be explained geometrically, since they depend on more sublime principles which show the wisdom of the Author in the order and perfection of his work." Now the odd thing about all this is that Leibniz does accept the requirement of mechanical explanation (in the Cartesian sense) for science since it was he who grasped, earlier than others, the concept of functionality. For action at a distance should rather have appealed to Leibniz, and perhaps the real objection to action at a distance is that there may be a violation of continuity.

The issue of religion which instigated the Leibniz-Clarke correspondence does reveal some differences between Newton and Leibniz. But again, these are not connected with Newtonian science, nor would either Newton or Leibniz admit religious considerations into scientific explanation. The points of dissent arise from several remarks of Newton, all of which are well known and, on my view, equally insignificant. Space as God's sensorium is a piece of Newtonian philosophical naiveté. And the need for God's interventions in the universe, which Newton suggests in various speculations, is on the whole supported by him by factual considerations.[58] These do not appear to be for Newton matters of philosophical argument. Leibniz's arguments here involve such distinctions as those between nature and grace, God's power and wisdom, and metaphysical and moral necessity, and are on the whole philosophical arguments. There are other theological questions in the correspondence which are of greater interest.

On questions of theology, Clarke is a fairly reliable Newtonian. For his views on questions of divine providence accord with Newton's

[55]*Principia*, xviii.
[56]Loemker, *op. cit.*, 671.　　　　　　　　　　　　　　　　　　　　　　　　[57]*Ibid.*, 779
[58]Cf. E. W. Strong, "Newton and God," *JHI*, XIII (April 1952), 147-67.

voluntaristic view of God, as opposed to the intellectualistic view of
Leibniz. Clarke writes that a sufficient reason may often be "the mere
will of God." But it is important to note that his examples are of the
sort that one would list under boundary conditions, and not such as
would occur in any scientific explanation. For both Newton and Clarke
would grant that the world is a function of divine providence, that
God's will is efficacious, and neither would find anything problematic
therein. At the same time, neither considered the kinds of theological
questions in which logical issues arise, as did Leibniz.

Leibniz and Clarke disagree on the distinction between the natural
and the supernatural. For Clarke, the difference is one of the kind of
explanation offered, and to him not every unexplained event is therefore miraculous. Leibniz's rationalism requires that every event
classed as natural be not only explicable but its description deducible
from an account of the nature of things. Anything else would be
miraculous. Newton writes quite consistently that the world as such is
explicable only by God. By this he does not mean that God completes
incomplete scientific explanations nor that any account of the world
follows from the nature of God. For from an early age Newton maintained that natural philosophy and religion are to be distinct, and he
disallowed the intrusion of the arguments of one into the domain of
the other. Yet he did claim that from appearances we can infer divine
teleology. But this is discourse different from that of mathematical
philosophy.

The problem is however rather subtler. For Leibniz's view requires
that we have an adequate, complete science, which he clearly knew
that he did not have. Newton can come out much better in this sort of
argument since he explicitly writes that we don't know what the real
substance of anything is. Leibniz confronts here part of a more general
problem, that of reconciling the contingency of empirical science with
the necessity of metaphysics. This is presumably done by having science fulfill certain methodological and metaphysical principles, such as
the principles of continuity and sufficient reason. However, the merely
moral certainty of science—together with the fact that Leibniz does
allow, for example, conjectures and hypotheses in science—does not
give him a sufficient basis for defining the extent of natural explanation, in order to make room for the supernatural.

We may note that both Newton and Leibniz agree on teleology in
nature as evidence for God. And it is further of interest to note their
similar use of language in different contexts. Newton, in discussing a
possible explanatory use of aether, writes "and after condensation
wrought into various forms, at first by the immediate hand of the
Creator, and ever since by the power of nature, who, by virtue of the
command, increase and multiply, became a complete imitator. . . ."[59]

[59]Cf. the Queries to the *Opticks.*

And Leibniz, arguing for his view of nature writes, ". . . there is a certain efficacy residing in things, a form or force such as we usually designate by the name of nature, from which the series of phenomena follows according to the prescription of the first command."[60] Although Leibniz puts conditions on the first command and Newton does not, they are still in agreement.

There are two interesting differences between the accounts given by the two on the relation between God and the world which in a way sum up their divergence. For Leibniz, the origin of mechanism is said to be not in a material principle and mathematical reasons alone, but in a higher metaphysical source. On the other hand, Newton does not call the world a mechanism, nor is his God metaphysical.

It is of interest to compare Newton and Leibniz when each uses the same key terms, and each is in a relatively critical mood. It may be noticed that the sources for this are not the usual texts. In defense of his attribution of space to God's sensorium, Newton notes the "unavoidable narrowness of language."[61] Thus, when speaking of infinite space as the qualities or properties of eternal Substance this is not to be taken in the sense of vulgar metaphysics, but rather as "Consequents of the Existence of a Being which is really necessarily and substantially Omnipresent and Eternal."[62] By "infinite" is meant not a substance or quality, but a mode of existence. "Immense" and "eternal" are answers to *ubi* and *quando*. It seems sufficiently clear from this that Newton is not merely restating Henry More.

The Leibnizian text is from a *Réfutation Inédite de Spinoza par Leibniz*. Leibniz writes (in the French translation of the Latin text):

Quant 'a moi, je penserais que tout est en Dieu, non pas comme la partie dans le tout, ni comme un accident dans le sujet, mais comme le lieu dans ce qu'il remplit, lieu spirituel ou subsistant et non mesuré ou partagé, car Dieu est immense; il est partout, le monde lui est présent, et c'est ainsi que toutes choses sont en lui, car il est où elles sont et ne sont pas; il demeure quand elles s'en vont, et il a déjà été là où elles arrivent.[63]

The connection between God and place is an ancient, traditional, if not philosophical one. And it seems that Newton and Leibniz were familiar with the religious sources and unselfconsciously employed the metaphor which was intended to express omnipresence.

It appears then sufficiently clear that what is at issue between Newton and Leibniz is not disagreement on fundamentals of scientific method. Nor is the disagreement on the question of space and time to

---

[60]Loemker, *op. cit.*, 813.   [61]*Ibid.*, 811

[62]Cf. Koyre and Cohen, *op. cit.*, 96–97. The source is from drafts of Des Maizeau *Recueil de diverses pièces . . . par Messrs Leibniz, Clarke, Newton, & autres auteurs célèbres* (Amsterdam, 1720), and letters related thereto.

[63]A. Foucher de Careil, *Réfutation Inédite de Spinoza par Leibniz* (Paris, 1854), 38–39.

be glibly phrased as one of opposition between absolute and relative space, time and motion. For Newton's distinctions are methodological and Leibniz's arguments in the Correspondence are ontological. Where Leibniz addresses himself to the sort of questions that concern Newton, his distinctions, though not developed or applied extensively are much more similar to Newton's than is evident if one confines oneself to the text of the Correspondence. Leibniz's ontology of substances is too often neglected in speaking of his relativistic view of space and time. And in view of Newton's deliberate lack of ontological commitment, it is indeed odd to speak of metaphysical disagreement here.

But surely, it may be objected, there is profound disagreement between the two.[64] And we may then consider this objection in the following way. What more or other than a scientific account of the world is involved in a metaphysical account of the world? In the case of Leibnizian metaphysics the answer might roughly be that if we accept a distinction between how things appear and how they really are, a metaphysical account of the latter enables us to account for those features of experience which are not accessible to the restricted methods of science. Among these are moral experiences, religious experiences, teleology, and so on. It may of course be added that the requirements for substance could never in principle be met by any observed entity, and experimental methods cannot disclose harmony.

For Newton, such a metaphysical account of the world is superfluous. What is not properly accounted for in natural philosophy is readily accounted for by God, and any metaphysical account is in his view, replete with fictions. We have here a theistic, anti-metaphysical view in a fairly pure, medieval form. Newton's theological writings provide further evidence for this.

No, we can't view the two thinkers as engaged in a contest, for they were doing different things. If we want to award points, Leibniz's philosophical sophistication can be matched by Newton's experimental sophistication. Newton's mechanics needs no commendation here. *Vis viva*, while foreshadowing the modern energy concepts, was not significantly developed by Leibniz. Concepts which do not occur in developed theories are not in themselves of great significance.

Temple University (1967–68).

[64]In connection with such claims it is very illuminating to take a concrete point of comparison, the criticisms each makes of Descartes. Leibniz's criticism of Descartes in the *Animadversiones* is well known; it is essentially aimed at Cartesian epistemology and metaphysics, and is directed to the first two Books of the *Principia Philosophiae*. Leibniz does attack the Cartesian Dynamics as well. In his *De Gravitatione et aequipondro Fluidorium* Newton also gives detailed criticisms' of Descartes' *Principia*, but his attention is directed to Book II, from Principle 4 to Book III, Principle 140. Where Leibniz talks of substance, Newton talks of body; Leibniz is concerned with God and the will, Newton deals with questions of astronomy and meteorology.

Chapter XXXIII

SAMUEL CLARKE, NEWTONIANISM, AND THE FACTIONS OF POST-REVOLUTIONARY ENGLAND

By Larry Stewart

The High-Church alarm of "Church in Danger" which rang throughout Anne's reign was no mere electoral gambit. It represented a real fear that the Church was being destroyed by insidious forces from within, embodied by the activities of the Newtonian theologians, Whiston and Clarke. While this concern manifested itself most often in the politics of Convocation and from time to time in Parliament, there remained the more fundamental issue of the roots of those differences of which the warfare between High Church and Low was only a symptom. Well hidden at the time of the prosecutions of Whiston and Clarke was the question of the influence of Newtonian natural philosophy in the unorthodox scriptural interpretations of the two deviant divines. While the debate on the Trinity aroused a swarm of pamphlets alternately repelled and attracted by Clarke's *Scripture-Doctrine*, the metaphysical assumptions of the Newtonian natural philosophy were also called into question.[1] Some went so far as to suggest that the Newtonian metaphysics, of which Clarke was the leading exponent, was the foundation of an unorthodox view of the Trinity. This connection, as we shall see, was made by Newtonian and anti-Newtonian alike, although more often in private correspondence than in print.

The emergence of a popular Newtonianism in the early eighteenth century meant that natural philosophy was injected with political and social ideology: the Newtonians were increasingly identified with the rise of a Whig oligarchy and with the difficult adjustments which followed the Revolution of 1687-89. It was thus not merely a political

---

[1] Thomas Herne, *An Account of all the Considerable Books and Pamphlets that have been wrote on either Side In the Controversy Concerning the Trinity, Since the Year 1712, In which is also contained, An Account of the Pamphlets Writ this last Year on each Side by the Dissenters, To the End of the Year, 1719* (London, 1720). J. Hay Colligan mistakenly identifies the author as Thomas Hearne the Oxford antiquarian; in fact, the author Thomas Herne was a controversialist who, as a follower of Samuel Clarke and Benjamin Hoadly, represented the Latitudinarian arm of the Church. Under the pseudonym "Phileleutherus Cantabrigiensis," he wrote pamphlets in both the Arian and Bangorian controversies. *Dictionary of National Biography*, IX, 701. Cf. J. Hay Colligan, *The Arian Movement in England* (Manchester, 1913), 52 n. 1.

or intellectual revolution; for Newton and many of his enthusiastic followers, it was both.

In the first decade of the eighteenth century the public face of Newtonian science was formed. The years 1704 through 1706 were especially important: they included the first appearance of Newton's *Opticks* and Harris's *Lexicon Technicum*, the early work of Ditton, Cheyne, and Mead, followed by Samuel Clarke's Latin translation of the *Optice*, in 1706, with the new queries added by Newton. But it was also a time when the scent of deism was still strong, perhaps a result of the debates of the world-makers like Thomas Burnet.[2] In 1704, Samuel Clarke in his Boyle Lectures took it upon himself to deliver a blast against the deniers of revelation. A particular target was John Toland who had asserted in his *Letters to Serena* (1704) that motion was essential to matter. Toland had the temerity to quote from Newton's explanation of *vis inertiae* (Definition III of the *Principia*) in defense of his own assertion that matter is inherently active: "one Motion is always succeeded by another Motion, and never by absolute Rest, no more than in any Parcel of Matter the ceasing of one Figure is the ceasing of all, which is impossible."[3] Toland translated the final portion of Definition III in a manner which emphasized the relative nature of motion and rest:

The Vulgar attribute Resistance to quiescent, and Impulse to movent Bodys; but Motion and Rest, as commonly conceived, are only respectively distinguish'd from one another, nor are those things always in true Repose, which are vulgarly consider'd as quiescent.[4]

But Toland was not really looking to Newton for support. He described the passivity of matter as a notion of sects in philosophy as well as of the vulgar. For Toland, the idea of "defining Matter only by extension, of making it naturally inactive, and of thinking it divided into real Parts every way independent of one another" necessarily resulted in the "erroneous consequence"[5] of a void space. Thus his *conatus of motion* was the basis of an anti-Newtonian system.

It was necessary that Toland be answered. Humphry Ditton re-

---

[2] M.C. Jacob, *The Newtonians and the English Revolution, 1689-1720* (Ithaca, 1976), Ch. III; Jacob and W.A. Lockwood, "Political Millenarianism and Burnet's Sacred Theory," *Science Studies* (1972), 265-79.

[3] John Toland, *Letters to Serena* (London, 1704; reprint ed. Stuttgart-Bad Cannstatt, 1964), 231.

[4] *Ibid.*, 201-02. This differs from the Motte-Cajori version in one important, if subtle, way—in the translation of *vulgus/vulgo*. Motte-Cajori indicate this as "usually" or "commonly," which may be close to Toland's sense. The word *vulgus* has an eristic quality which did not escape Newton's critics. See below on Roger North. Cf. Florian Cajori, *Sir Isaac Newton's Mathematical Principles of Natural Philosophy* (Berkeley, 1971), 2.   [5] Toland, *Letters to Serena*, 172-73.

plied with sarcasm in the Preface to his *General Laws of Matter and Motion*. William Wotton, chaplain to the family of Heneage Finch, and who evidently had some role in the selection of the Boyle lectures, quarreled with Toland's citing Newton's law of gravitation and yet refusing to admit a void space: "The truth is, a Man that can comprehend the Grounds upon which Mr *Newton* builds that noble Discovery, will hardly ever afterwards talk with Gravity against a *Void*."[6]

While Wotton wrote his censure of the deist, Samuel Clarke delivered his Boyle lectures. Clarke, to whom Wotton was indebted in the *Letter to Eusebia*, had Toland specifically in mind in 1704 when he ascribed to atheists the idea of motion as essential.[7] Both Wotton and Clarke were determined to establish the reality of empty space and to this end they both cited Newton's argument (in Corollaries III and IV to Proposition VI of Book III of *Principia*) that variations in the specific gravities of bodies resulted from the fact that all spaces are not equally full and hence a vacuum must be granted. In his Boyle lectures of 1704, Clarke argued:

If bare Matter be the Necessarily-existing Being, (for that there can be but One such, shall be proved hereafter;) then in that Necessary Existence there is either included the Power of Gravitation, or not: If not, then in a World *merely Material*, and in which no Intelligent Being presides, there never could have been any Motion; because Motion, as has been already shown, and is now granted in the Question, is not Necessary of *itself*: But if the Power of Gravitation *be* included in the Necessary Existence of Matter; then, it following necessarily that there must be a Vacuum, (as the incomparable Sir Isaac Newton has abundantly demonstrated that there must, if gravitation be an Universal Quality or Affection of Matter;) it follows likewise, that matter is not a Necessary Being: For if a Vacuum actually be, then it is plainly more than possible for matter not to Be.[8]

Thus, as Newton argued, from the principle of a vacuum it not only followed that specific gravity was proportional to the spaces between the particles of a body, but also that the inertial force of a body was proportional to its mass.[9] Hence, the significance of Clarke's critique of Toland's distortion of Definition III: neither matter nor motion was "a Necessary Being."

[6] [Will Wotton], *A Letter to Eusebia: Occasioned by Mr. Toland's Letters to Serena* (London, 1704), 66.

[7] *Ibid.*, 71; Samuel Clarke, *A Demonstration of the Being and Attributes of God* (London, 1705), 45-59.

[8] Wotton, *Letter to Eusebia*, 66-67; Clarke, *A Demonstration of the Being and Attributes of God*. 2nd ed. (London, 1706), 40, quoted here as the argument is more precise than in the 1705 edition.

[9] *Principia*, Book I, Definition III. Cajori, ed., *Newton's Mathematical Principles*, 2.

The Newtonian Idea of the Trinity

In his Boyle lectures on the Being and Attributes of God, Clarke dismissed infinite materiality by demonstrating that it was possible for matter not to be, i.e., for a vacuum to exist. Thus, with due regard to God's spiritual nature, it was evident that matter could not be a necessary Being.[10] From this Clarke launched into the *a priori* argument based on the necessity of a universal self-existent Being whose attributes must be eternity, infinity, and unity.[11] This theological view obviously bears a close resemblance to the Newtonian view of absolute space, a doctrine founded upon immateriality, which in turn may have led the way to Clarke's metaphysical view of the Trinity. However, it is quite evident that as early as 1704, Clarke was aware of the potential conflict between the Athanasian Doctrine of the three persons of the Trinity and the view of God determined by the *a priori* argument. To be sure, there was only a hint of this in 1704: "The Self-Existent Being, must of Necessity be but One." To think otherwise, Clarke argued, was to imply a contradiction as . . . "Necessity Absolute in itself, is Simple and Uniform, without any possible Difference or Variety. . . ."[12]

Clarke's initial intention was to undermine the materialism of Toland and others that both God and matter could be considered self-existent principles. Clarke followed the same aim in his dispute with Henry Dodwell by denying the divisibility of consciousness or soul.[13] About the time of his Boyle lectures, in 1704 and 1705, when he was also preparing the translation of the *Opticks*, Clarke first came to entertain serious doubts as to the authenticity of the Athanasian Doctrine.[14] What had initially been an argument against materiality was transformed, *a priori*, into the foundation of the necessity of Divine unity. Much was to rest on the essence of that unity, to be sure, but in the first printed version of Clarke's lectures there is a discussion of unity which includes, in the margin, a brief reference to the Trinity. By 1711, in the third edition of the lectures the year before he published his *Scripture-Doctrine*, Clarke made the reference quite explicit:

That the *Unity* of God, is an *Unity of Nature*, or essence: For of *This* it is that we must be understood, if we would argue Intelligibly, when we speak

[10] Clarke, *A Demonstration of the Being and Attributes of God* (London, 1705), 49-50.

[11] James P. Ferguson, *The Philosophy of Dr. Samuel Clarke and Its Critics* (New York, 1974), 23-26.

[12] Clarke, *A Demonstration of the Being and Attributes of God* (London, 1705), 93-94.   [13] *Ibid.*, 96.

[14] William Whiston, *Historical Memoirs of the Life of Dr. Samuel Clarke* (London, 1730), 10-13.

of Necessity or Self-Existence. As to the *Diversity of Persons* in the ever-blessed *Trinity*; that is, whether notwithstanding the Unity of the Divine Nature, there may not coexist with the First Supreme Cause, such Excellent Emanations from it, as may themselves be really Eternal, Infinite, and Perfect, by a complete Communication of Divine Attributes in an incomprehensible Manner; always excepting Self-Origination, Self-Existence, or absolute Independency: Of this, I say; as there is nothing in bare Reason, by which it can be demonstrated that there is actually any such thing; so neither is there any Argument, by which it can be proved impossible or unreasonable to be supposed; and therefore when declared and made known to us by clear Revelation, it ought to be believed.[15]

As late as 1711, Clarke was still able to declare the desirability of belief in the doctrine of the Trinity, although it is important to note that the question of its metaphysical viability had been raised as a result of the necessity of unity in a self-existent being. But his final statement implies a question which could only be answered through the study of Scripture. Thus, there appeared in 1712 Clarke's famous analysis of the texts of the New Testament which concerned the doctrine of the Trinity. What he found confirmed his suspicions.

While his analysis was scriptural, his concerns remained primarily metaphysical. Clarke asserted that while the New Testament did not expressly indicate whether the Son was created of the Necessity of nature or by the power of the will of God, the terms of Scripture— "Son" and "Beget"—implied an act of will. If this were so, then the eternal, absolute, attributes of God were not those of the Son whose attributes must therefore be relative, the result of divine authority over man.[16] Clarke had, he thought, established a difference between the absolute and the relative in the Trinity—a difference which was fundamental to the Newtonian philosophy. Whether his theological views derived from his metaphysical principles was to be the occasion of much debate. The aspersions of Arianism which were so quickly cast in his direction, while obviously a matter of Church politics, involved a considerable interest in the philosophical assumptions upon which Clarke had initiated his investigations. Thus, the attack upon Clarke took the form of a detailed examination of his metaphysics, while political battles raged in a time uncertain of the succession and High-Church Tories seemed bent on self-destruction.

The shift in the axis of the political world which followed the death of Queen Anne gave the Low Church some hope that religious persecutions might be curtailed. Certainly, it seems the decline of the High-Church party ensured Clarke's work an influence which it might otherwise have had only in freethinking circles. On Christmas Day,

[15] Clarke, *A Discourse Concerning the Being and Attributes of God, The Obligations of Natural Religion, and the Truth and Certainty of the Christian Revelation*. Third edition, corrected (London, 1711), 51.

[16] Clarke, *The Scripture Doctrine of the Trinity* (London, 1712), 280, 290.

1714, John Jackson, the Rector of Rossington, wrote to Samuel
Clarke to indicate that he had been so convinced by the *Scripture-
Doctrine* that he had ceased to read the Athanasian Creed during
service.[17] This was not a sudden decision. Jackson and Clarke had
been in correspondence at least since the time of Clarke's difficulties
with Convocation. Since Jackson was not yet willing to risk the wrath
of the High Church, he published anonymously in 1714 a portion of
his correspondence with Clarke. Here Jackson defended Clarke from
the charges of heresy and tried to draw a line between the supposed
Arianism of Whiston's Primitive Christianity (which seemed to
suggest that the Son was created) and Clarke's view of the unity of
God. Clarke replied that he regarded the idea of three persons in the
same individual substance to be a "self-evident . . . Contradiction."
Clarke then perhaps gave away why he had made his opinions on the
matter public in the form of an examination of Scripture rather than as
a philosophical disquisition. He was well aware of the criticism that
had been voiced against natural reason "because the Great popular
Objection against Men that think seriously and carefully about these
things, is, that they are apt to adhere to their own *Reason* more than
to the *Scripture*: which is a most unjust Suggestion."[18]

Metaphysics and Newtonianism

Until the prosecution of Clarke was halted by the bishops in the
summer of 1714, most of the criticism directed at him had been within
the context of the politics of the Church, or at the very least, of what
we might call the politics of the reason vs. revelation debate. One
notable exception, from the pen of a young student at the Dissenting
Academy at Tewkesbury, Joseph Butler, took the form of a series of
letters that he wrote to Clarke between November 1713 and February
1714. These letters were later published by Clarke with his replies but
without identifying Butler as the "Gentleman in Glostershire." Butler
had pressed Clarke on the necessity of unity in the self-existent being
which allowed no division of natures. It became clear from Clarke's
answers that his view was based entirely upon the assumptions of the
necessity of the existence of space and time which Newton had demonstrated as the only solution. For Newton, it was absolute
mathematical space, and not relative space, which was real. Clarke
seems to have introduced a subtle difference into this view although
this may well be one of expression only. He described space and time
as "very *abstruse*" which were "*Affections which belong, and in the
order of our Thoughts are antecedently necessary, to the Existence of*

---

[17] B.M. Add. MSS, 4370, f. 27. Jackson to Clarke. Christmas Day, 1714.
[18] [John Jackson] *Three Letters to Dr. Clarke, From A Clergyman of the Church
of England; Concerning his Scripture-Doctrine of the Trinity* (London, 1714), 31.
Clarke to Jackson, Oct. 23, 1714.

all Things." [19] For Clarke, since space was necessarily existent, space was a property of the self-existent substance. However, space was not substance. All substances, other than the self-existent, were in space; "but the Self-existent Substance is not *IN Space*, nor *penetrated by it*, but is itself (if I may so to speak) the *Substratum of Space.*" [20]

It is of great significance that Space, for both Clarke and Newton, was a property, not self-existent in its own right but an effect of self-existence. This was not the same as the essence of self-existence which we cannot distinctly know.[21] That this discussion had taken place within a few months of the appearance, at the end of June 1713, of the second edition of the *Principia* with its new "General Scholium" is important. In his fifth reply to Butler, when he sought once again to make it clear that space and duration were not of themselves substances, Clarke cited the scholium to Definition VIII where Newton distinguished between absolute and relative. Moreover, when discussing the substance upon which the existence of space and duration depend, Clarke cited directly from the General Scholium: "*Deus* non est *Aeternitas* vel *Infinitas*, sed aeternus & infinitus. . . ." For Clarke and his followers, this Newtonian view of God was the foundation upon which rested so much of their theology. Clarke's reply to Butler, in the spring of 1714, represents the first time that Clarke had been prepared to make the relation between his scriptural views and the Newtonian metaphysics explicit:

> How universally have men for many Ages believed, that *Eternity* is not *Duration* at all, and *Infinity* no *Amplitude*? Something of the like kind has happened in the matter of *Transubstantiation*, and (I think) in the Scholastick Notion of the *Trinity*, etc.[22]

While Joseph Butler questioned the metaphysical basis of Clarke's Boyle lectures, Clarke received a far more sympathetic hearing from John Jackson.

After having read Clarke's *Scripture-Doctrine*, Jackson initiated a

---

[19] Clarke, *A Discourse Concerning the Being and Attributes of God . . . Fifth edition, Corrected. There are added in this Edition, Several Letters to Dr. Clarke from a Gentleman in Gloucestershire, relating to the first Volume; with the Drs Answers* (London, 1715), 14. Clarke to Butler, Nov. 23, 1713. See also, John H. Gay, "Matter and Freedom in the Thought of Samuel Clarke," *JHI*, **24** (1963), 96-97; and Ferguson, *Philosophy of Dr. Samuel Clarke,* 32-34.

[20] Clarke, *Discourse* (1719), 21. Clarke to Butler, Dec. 10, 1713.

[21] Clarke, *A Discourse Concerning the Unchangeable Obligations of Natural Religion, and the Truth and Certainty of the Christian Revelation. Being Eight Sermons Preach'd at the Cathedral Church of St. Paul in the Year 1705, at the Lecture Founded by the Honourable Robert Boyle, Esq.* Third edition, corrected (London, 1711), 4, note.

[22] Clarke, *Discourse* (1719), 33. Clarke to Butler, April 8, 1713/14.

correspondence only part of which was published in 1714 after Clarke's difficulties with Convocation. While Jackson's anonymous *Three Letters* were significant discussions of the problem of the Athanasian Creed, they represent only a minor part of a lengthy correspondence and cooperation in the face of his and Clarke's theological and indeed, political, enemies. In a sense, the failure of scholars to find much of the Clarke-Jackson correspondence in print may represent the myopia of those who see the history of seventeenth-century science simply in terms of such great works as the *Principia*. This is all the more puzzling as the Jackson-Clarke letters overlap the well-known queries of Joseph Butler to Clarke and the far more famous correspondence of Clarke with Leibniz. These three sets of letters should not be too readily separated, for together they demonstrate a growing realization on the part of Clarke's readers, and perhaps to some extent an increasing willingness on the part of Clarke, to admit that his theology rested largely on Newtonian metaphysics. This relationship of Clarke to Newton became widely recognized and accepted. Clarke's defenders found in Newton a foundation for their scriptural views while his detractors, whose innate tendency to the High-Church ground was well-known, simply saw in this the confirmation of all their suspicions about the new philosophy.

It was in his letters to Jackson that Clarke indicated the source of his metaphysics: as it pertained to the *real* existence of absolutes this had been the Scholium to Definition VIII of Newton's *Principia*.[23] Thus, the General Scholium of the second edition (1713) was not a necessity for the formation of a Newtonian metaphysic. It is not without interest that Clarke's admission came shortly after the initiation of the famous exchange with Leibniz on the perfection of God. Apparently Jackson had already recognized the significance of the *Principia*. On January 30, 1715 (just after Clarke's second reply to Leibniz) he wrote to Clarke; Jackson's letter is remarkable not only for the timely expression of his loyalty to "our good and Gracious K. George" but also because he informed Clarke:

About a Year ago I Consulted the Scholium to *Sir Isaac Newton's Princip: Mathemat:* Concerning the true Notion of God, and found it Exactly agreeable to your *scripture Doctrine*; I found also that the most learned Knight did ascribe a *Corpus* to the supreme God; which manner of speaking had Extreamly puzzled Dr Edwards and his Friends; but I suppose he means by *Corpus* there the *Substance* of God, . . .[24]

---

[23] Cambridge University Library, Add. MSS, 7113, f.21. Clarke to Jackson, Last day of year 1715.

[24] B.M. Add. MSS, 4370, fols. 37-38. Jackson to Clarke, Jan. 30, 1715/16. The reference is to John Edwards who regarded the General Scholium as the joint effort of Newton and Clarke. See Ferguson, *The Philosophy of Dr. Samuel Clarke*, 42.

This is clearly a reference to the General Scholium of the second edition. But, as Clarke undoubtedly realized, the General Scholium only made explicit what had been there in the first *Principia*. As I. B. Cohen has pointed out, the General Scholium merely follows what had already been laid down in Newton's discussion of relative and absolute terms in the Scholium following the Definitions in Book 1.[25] Clarke had made that distinction clear to Jackson. Newton's God was infinitely more than an Old Testament creator.[26] With Jackson the relationship between Scripture and natural philosophy had come full circle. Whereas Clarke's initial suspicions regarding the Trinity seem, in part, to have been aroused by his Newtonian metaphysics, Jackson now had found in Newton's General Scholium a proof of Clarke's scriptural program to eliminate the Athanasian Creed.

The High Ground

The connection which Clarke and Jackson had made between Newtonian metaphysics and the meaning of the Trinity suggested that the Newtonian philosophy could not hope to escape the attention of those who pursued heretics. This, of course, is precisely what happened. The most significant part of the debate came after the publication of Clarke's *Scripture-Doctrine* in 1712. The division of opinion concerning the theological work of Samuel Clarke and his followers seemed to follow lines of political and religious divergence. Similarly, the response to Newtonian natural philosophy and its role in the formation of heterodox theology depended to a considerable extent upon political, religious, and probably even metaphysical sentiments or attitudes rather than precise formulations of cause and effect. We cannot say that all High-Church theologians were hostile to Newtonian science. Nor can we categorically determine that all Latitudinarians were predisposed to support the new philosophy. One might expect the most orthodox members of the Church to fear that Newtonian natural philosophy might pose a threat to Anglican doctrine. To a considerable extent this fear was a vestige of the late seventeenth century when the Royal Society came under scrutiny because of aspersions that mechanical philosophy led to atheism. The hunt for deists in the early eighteenth century kept such views alive, and natural philosophy seemed to be fair game. When Whiston and Clarke began to expound on the Trinity during the Tory ascendency in the latter part of Anne's reign, it was inevitable that Newtonianism should be suspected as the root of heresy.

Such suspicion probably had the greatest effect among those who

---

[25] I. Bernard Cohen, "Isaac Newton's *Principia*, the Scriptures, and Divine Providence," in *Philosophy, Science and Method. Essays in Honor of Ernest Nagel*, eds. Sidney Morgenbesser, Patrick Suppes, Morton White (New York, 1969), 524-26.
[26] Cf. Frank Manuel, *The Religion of Isaac Newton* (Oxford, 1974), 75-76.

regarded the Low Church, and especially the Whig Junto, with a particular animosity which was conspicuously evident among the Non-Jurors, those clergymen and laymen who, after the Revolution of 1688, balked at taking the oaths to the new dynasty of the House of Orange. On the whole, those who consistently refused to have any part of the government and the Church of which William was the head did so on the grounds that support would have constituted a violation of the Tory principle of divine right and hereditary succession. As a result, they were forced to give up their positions within both the Church and the structure of government. For the most part, they were also High Churchmen with a very conservative attitude toward changes in the liturgy of the prayerbook. Like their High-Church brethren, they refused to make any accommodation with those Whigs who supported a policy of religious moderation and an end to the political constraints upon non-conformists. However, unlike the rest of the High Church, they preferred to take a stand on principle against the validity of the Revolution. As a result, many of the Non-Jurors held not very secret sympathies for the Pretender biding his time in France.[27] Foremost among these was the Non-Juring Bishop, George Hickes.

By the time Samuel Clarke and William Whiston began those investigations which led them to the verge of heresy, George Hickes was the sole surviving Non-Juring bishop. His influence was so pervasive in the tiny Non-Juring community that it became known as the "Communion of Dr. Hickes."[28] It was a community continually under siege, always suspected of harboring Jacobites preparing for the return of the Stuarts. Such accusations came not only from the Whigs but also from those who were generally sympathetic to the scriptural investigations of the Latitudinarian clergy.[29] There was some foundation for these impressions, which tended to connect the Non-Jurors with the political sympathies of some of the High-Church Tories. When Hickes decided to continue the succession of the Non-Juring bishops by the consecration of Jeremy Collier, Samuel Hawes, and Nathaniel Spinkes, the ceremony apparently took place at St. Andrew's, Holborn in 1713, the very church to which Sacheverell was presented.[30] Indeed, in the aftermath of the Jacobite rebellion of 1715 Hickes's papers which charged the Church with "heresy, schism, perjury, and treason" were seized by the nervous authorities.[31] So

[27] H. Broxap, "Jacobites and Non-Jurors," *The Social and Political Ideas of Some English Thinkers of the Augustan Age, A.D. 1650-1750*. J.F.C. Hearnshaw, ed. (London, 1928), 101-02.   [28] *Ibid.*, 101.

[29] John Disney, *Memoirs of the Life and Writings of Arthur Ashley Sykes, D.D.* (London, 1785), 35. Disney, much influenced by the work of Clarke, left the Church and declared his Unitarianism. See C. Robbins, *Eighteenth-Century Commonwealthman, passim*.

[30] Broxap, "Jacobites and Non-Jurors," 103; and, *D.N.B.*, IX, 803.

[31] Disney, *Memoirs of Sykes*, 35-36.

concerned was the government over the influence of Hickes that his death in 1715 did not prevent the authorities from continuing to search out sedition amongst his followers. When *The Constitution of the Catholick Church* was published posthumously, in 1716, the printer's premises were searched upon information that it was a treasonable pamphlet. The reply by Benjamin Hoadly, *Preservative Against the Principles and Practices of the Nonjurors*, represented the immediate origins of the Bangorian Controversy.[32]

Hickes's attitudes towards the major theological issues of the day indicate his sympathy with the High Church. He held a particular dislike of Whiston; in 1712 he went through the notes of the deceased Dr. John Grabe and published a commentary upon Whiston's view of the Trinity.[33] Hickes was also a prolific letter writer so that his attitudes are best revealed through a private correspondence which he continued over a number of years with one of the most prominent of the lay Non-Jurors, Roger North.

Most well-known to historians of literature for his masterly *Lives of the Norths*, Roger had been a prosperous lawyer under the Stuarts and solicitor to the Queen at the time of the Revolution. Thereafter he had nothing to do with the new dynasty, and by 1695 retired to his country estate at Rougham. Through the papers of the captured Jacobite spy Christopher Layer, North was implicated in attempts to supply support to the Pretender. Although the evidence provided by Layer's imagination may be suspect, there is no doubt that North was sympathetic to the Stuarts. In 1696 he married the daughter of Sir Robert Gayer who had managed to escape to the Continent after having been implicated in the plot of 1695.[34] But North's long standing membership in a community defined by its objection to the Revolution, and his subsequent attack upon Newtonianism, make him representative of the orthodox attitude toward the new philosophy founded upon the *Principia* in 1687.

Despite his retirement, North was active in the pursuit of what he considered to be doubtful political opinion. In the intoxicating Tory days of the spring of 1710, a week before Sacheverell made his triumphal entrance into Oxford, Bishop Hickes urged North to under-

[32] William Bradford Gardner, "George Hickes and the Origin of the Bangorian Controversy," *Studies in Philology*, **39** (1942), 66-67.

[33] J.G. Barnish, "Orthodoxy and Heterodoxy: The Trinitarian Dispute in the Church of England, 1710-1730" (B.D. thesis, Oxford, 1966), Chap. II, 48; also, Bodleian, Ballard MS, 12, f. 196. Hickes to Charlett, Feb. 21. 1711/12.

[34] Paul S. Fritz, *The English Ministers and Jacobitism between the Rebellions of 1715 and 1745* (Toronto, 1975), 71, 80, Appendix 2, 143; G.V. Bennett, "Jacobitism and the Rise of Walpole," in *Historical Perspectives: Studies in English Thought and Society*, ed. Neil McKendrick (London, 1974), 88-89; Roger North, *The Lives of the Right Hon. Francis North, Baron Guilford; The Hon. Sir Dudley North; and the Hon. and Rev. Dr. John North*, ed. Augustus Jessop. 3 vols. (London, 1890), 3, Supplementary, 300-01.

take an answer to White Kennett's Whig history, *A Complete History of England*. The result was the *Examen* which was finished in 1713 along with a ''scornful'' pamphlet on John Locke.[35] More important, North was also the author of an acrimonious manuscript attack on the theology of Samuel Clarke. North probably had some contact with Clarke about some ''phisiological matters'' [*sic*] prior to the publication in 1712 of *The Scripture Doctrine of the Trinity*. However, the occasion of the ''Answer to Dr Clarke'' was the solicitation by Clarke of North's views on the subject.[36] A copy was passed to Hickes for his comments. North obliged his Bishop by accusing Clarke of attempting ''to set up reason against Revelation.'' This was the predictable High-Church position; the attitude that all revelation was at stake was characteristic of the High-Church mentality. One hears echoes of Erasmus Warren's fears in the 1690s when he wrote against Thomas Burnet. In North, a man displaced by the Revolution, a Non-Juror by choice whose father-in-law was a hunted Jacobite, there prevails a sense of an impending battle, that it must be all or nothing:

... I shall In ye Mean time take ye freedom to Remark that Things will Not lye tho Men may and ye latter Even in so doing discover their falsity, by ye nature of those things they medle with, as for Instance, the declared Enimys of all Revealed Religion, doe not or very seldome apply their force against Religion itself directly, or say there is no Revelation of any, but they fall foul upon the Misterys of our faith and Endeavour to demolish them; supposing If they can once prevail to have misterys laid aside, or wch is as bad, or wors, Interpreted into worldly Resemblances, & so Reduced to Nothing, that then all Revealed Religion must Tumble; for ye Argument is Thro-stitch, and Must conclude, all or None. . . .[37]

North was absolutely determined to defend the revelation of the Trinity against Clarke's *Scripture-Doctrine* which he considered to be in complicity with atheism.[38] A copy of this ''Answer'' was sent to Hickes for his comments, as the work of North fitted readily into the campaign which Hickes had been conducting against the Latitudinarian clergy. The acknowledgment by Hickes, which is to be found among North's manuscripts, is one of the most instructive documents relating to the High-Church perception of Newton's science. The reply is dated May 23, 1713, notably just *before* the appearance of the

[35] P.T. Millard, ''The Chronology of Roger North's Main Works,'' *Review of English Studies*, n.s., **24** (1973), 287-89.

[36] B.M. Add. MSS, 32551, f. 1ʳ. Works of Roger North, XXIV. This ''Answer'' was the second version and can be dated from internal evidence after the death of Hickes in 1715 but probably before 1719. The first version, Add. MSS, 32550 is dated Feb. 20 [?], 1712/13.

[37] B.M. Add. MSS, 32550, f. 12. Works of Roger North, XXIII. Rougham, Feb. 20 [?], 1712/13.   [38] B.M. Add. MSS, 32550, fols. 12, 22-23.

second edition of the *Principia* with its General Scholium.[39] Hickes was not one to hide his feelings on a matter of such fundamental importance:

. . . Methinks ye telling him wee can have No Idea of ye devine Essence, should be an humbling consideration to him, & make him Reflect, that IF wee had bin capable of conceiving the HOW of a Trinity and unity of 3 persons In one essence, God would Not only have Revealed the thing but have made us clearly understand ye how of it, and so have made it ye object of our understanding as well as ye Matter of our belief. . . . You seem to have a Mind to animadvert [?] on their New philosophy and I hope you will have health, & leisure to doe it. *It is their Newtonian philosophy wch hath Made Not onely so many Arians but Theists, and that Not onely among ye laity but I fear among our devines.* I desire to keep yr Letter a litle Longer, wch If you would Consent to have it Made publick, I would consent to prepare it with a few Inconsiderable alterations for the press, I hope something he will say to it privately or publiquely will make it Needful to be published, for it is great pity it should be confined to private hands.[40]

For Hickes, as well as for many in the High Church, Newtonianism produced a questionable theology. What resulted was a multivolume attack on Newton.

It is a singular misfortune that many of North's works have never been published. Even his celebrated *Lives of the Norths* appeared posthumously. The large bulk of his manuscripts, the compilations and revisions of a serious scholar after his retirement at Rougham in 1695, remain unpublished. From the point of view of the historian of science, as perhaps also for the political historian, this is easily explained. The manuscripts represent both a philosophical and a political failure: North was a Cartesian and a Tory with a framework of the world which was rapidly to expire amongst the intelligentsia. And it is the progressive, not the regressive, which has captured the attention of the historian of science. But as his Tory *Examen* represents a valuable view of the late Stuart period, his critique of Newtonian natural philosophy establishes how thoroughly North believed that Newtonianism and heterodoxy were woven together.

North's interest in natural philosophy dates from his early days as an undergraduate of Jesus College, Cambridge, where he read Descartes, presumably the *Principles*, three times until he understood him. From then on he was captured by the "vortices, vapours, and striata" from whose whirl he was never to escape. One of his early

---

[39] The second edition of the *Principia* did not appear until between June 18 and July 1, 1713. I. Bernard Cohen, *Introduction to Newton's Principia* (Cambridge, Mass., 1971), 246-47.

[40] B.M. Add. MSS, 32551, f. 34. George Hickes to North. May 23, 1713. My italics.

sources was Father Ignace Pardies, an eminent Cartesian and one of the first critics of Newton's optical experiments. Nevertheless, North did have some esteem for Newton's theory of colors although he did not regard the issue as finally settled.[41] While North was predisposed to criticize Newton, his view was a unique one. North had nothing but admiration for Newton's mathematical achievements which he regarded as masterly, but, as he wrote to his nephew at Peterhouse in 1706, Newton's reputation would only have been enhanced had he "let dabbling in physics alone." This may now amuse us and for North's nineteenth-century editor it caused some consternation, leading him to suggest that what North really meant was dabbling in religious matters. We are to believe in a slip of the pen, but as we shall see, North wrote precisely what he believed. It is true, nevertheless, that theological consequences were never far from North's mind. In the same letter he refers to Whiston as the "Apolcalyptic Geometer."[42] For North, as well as for many of a High-Church persuasion, heterodox theology and the new philosophy were intimately related. Long before Leibniz, Roger North complained of the occult in Newton's philosophy.

One might be inclined to think that the encouragement of Bishop Hickes led Roger North to demonstrate what he considered to be the flaws in the Newtonian system. It is more likely, however, that Hickes's letter of 1713 merely prodded North to complete intentions he held from the 1690s. North's manuscripts, although evidently revised for publication from time to time, remained essentially his own jottings on philosophical matters which he considered of the utmost importance.[43] North was at his acerbic best when he reached the foundation of the Newtonian system, in the distinction between "absolutes and relatives." This was, as we are aware, of some significance in the debate which had surrounded the metaphysics of Samuel

[41] North, *Lives of the Norths,* III, 15, 21, 25-26, 63-66; Louis Trenchard More, *Isaac Newton* (New York, 1962), 86-88, 104. North's brother, Dr. John North, was Master of Trinity College from 1677 to 1683 during Newton's residence at Cambridge.

[42] North, *Lives of the Norths,* III, 254-55. Roger North to Philip Foley, December 22, 1706. Cf. Augustus Jessop, 255, n. 1 & 2. Jessop would also have us believe that the disparagement of Whiston refers to his publication of Newton's *Arithmetica Universalis* in 1707. There is some merit in this. North may simply mean Whiston's *Astronomical Lectures* published as *Praelectiones astronomicae. Cantabrigiae in scholis publicis habitae* (1707). However, in view of the religious connotation, it is at least possible that the lectures to which North refers are Whiston's Boyle Lectures on "The Accomplishment of Scripture Prophecies" which he was to deliver in 1707.

[43] Millard, "Chronology of Roger North's Main Works," 289-90; Millard, "An Edition of Roger North's *Life of Dr. John North* With a Critical Introduction" (D. Phil. thesis, Oxford, 1969), 55. My thanks to Dr. Millard for allowing me to examine a copy of his thesis.

Clarke. North, then, had some interest in examining the philosophical aspects of this issue:

I doe not know any subject matter Relating to a true Judgment of Natural things more obnoxious to most pertinacious prejudice then this of absolutes & Relativs; therefore I intend to bend all my artistry against them. It is a notion of ye vulgar, that place is a most stated sure thing, as Is their church steeple, and If all ye world sunk into Nothing, yet here and there would be the same. . . . These I say are the opinions of the vulgar, but however Great philosofers, and chiefly Sr Is. N. think fitt to maintain them, I conceiv it is from ye same force of prejudice In them all, but it is so deep Rooted In humaine nature that philosofy is too weak and If tainted with popularity Not willing to remove it. . . .

But then let there be space, that must be Infinite, I deny there is any here or there in it, but onely Relatively, that is Respecting somewhat or other . . . for suppose but one body In space infinite, it is all one where it is, Nothing can be affirmed of it differently from situation, but still it is In vacuo Infinito, and thats all. Sr Is. N. will affirm otherwise, that there is absolute space, and so will ye Rabble, but neither give a reason, but that None can imagine . . . So for Motion, If a body be solitary In vacuo Infinito (I comply with ye Notion) can any one say, that such body moves, or rests. . . .[44]

Throughout his manuscripts, North returned time and again to Newton's Scholium to Definition VIII. In view of his theological preoccupation with Clarke this is not surprising. There is no doubt that the distinction between absolute and relative terms was at the root of Clarke's metaphysics. This distinction North regarded as vulgar, an idea which Newton had argued into reality; along with attractions, qualities, and tendencies, it "perverts the knowledg of things, into a logick of words."[45] Newton and Clarke had proposed the necessary reality of absolutes from the necessity of their conceptions. But to North, the necessity of the absolutes of space and time, or at least to argue that space and time coincided with a Deity, was to encroach upon the power of the Deity "and so come neer to Hobbisme."[46] These notions of absolutes and relatives, of gravity, attractions, inertia, and void space, North intended to replace with a Cartesian aether the vortex of which rotated swiftest at the centre and slower away from it, which he was willing, like the Newtonians, to argue from the observed effects.[47] If the universe operated by way of a material aether the motion of which was originally imparted to it by God, then there was no need to distinguish between the creations of matter, space, and time. Space and time had likewise been created

---

[44] B.M. Add. MSS, 32545, fols, 220-21.

[45] Millard, "Life of Dr. John North," 149, 124, 130-32, 144-46. Also, Add. MSS. 32548, f. 61r; Add. MSS, 32546, fols. 174-75. "Works of Roger North," XIX.

[46] Millard, "Life of Dr. John North," 146; B.M. Add. MSS, 32546, f. 174.

[47] M.M. Add. MSS, 32548, fols. 66ff.

and were not necessary in themselves. Thus was banished the distinction between absolutes and relatives. Space could be created and destroyed by an infinite power. Either, argued North, space and time were limited or God's power was limited and the latter was heresy.[48]

North's intentions in his attack upon the Newtonian system were quite clear. He had set out to show the falsity of the metaphysical system upon which the heresy of Samuel Clarke was constructed. In one of his later manuscripts, which appears to date from about 1722, North denied there were degrees in existence between absolutes and relatives, "between something and nothing." To have admitted such an hypothesis would have been to admit a limitation to God's power, which was impossible. All this rested fundamentally upon the necessity of revelation. North's entire purpose had been to defend Christian revelation and belief in miracles:

. . . wch shew [Almighty power] indubitably, and also what may be his will with respect to us, how to be worshiped, . . . by repentance in Christ, and How farr wee may pretend to know his Essence wch can be no otherwise then hath bin Revealed to us in the Ineffable Trinnity: with other scriptural articles of the Christian Religion. All wch have bin so well deduced from the knowne Miracles Recorded for demonstration beyond contradiction. . . .[49]

North's position was that of the High-Church hostility to Newtonianism, a philosophy which was seen as a threat to revealed religion. The Doctrine of the Trinity became a crucial issue. Only by accepting the revelations, North argued, could those whom he suspected were "sceptical Atheists" be "cured of their perversity."[50] In this category were undoubtedly the Newtonians whose metaphysical distinctions had led them to anti-Trinitarian heresy.

Faction in Philosophy

The Newtonian natural philosophy became, explicitly, part of the political debate in post-Revolutionary England. Whether or not Newtonian concepts of universal gravitation, attraction, or of absolutes and relatives were acceptable seemed to turn partly upon the religious or theological attitudes which formed part of the system of co-ordinates distinguishing city from country, Low Church from High, and Whig from Tory. To some it followed that Newtonianism might be viewed as a sect or even a party in philosophy. This was certainly the opinion of Ephraim Chambers.[51] But his argument on behalf of

[48] B.M. Add. MSS. 32548, No. 5, f. 144r; and, Add. MSS. 32546, f. 174r.

[49] B.M. Add. MSS. 32548, f. 149r; also, fols. 140r, 146r.   [50] Ibid., f. 149r.

[51] Ephraim Chambers, F.R.S., *Cyclopaedia: Or, an Universal Dictionary of Arts and Science; Containing An Explication of the Terms, and an Account of the Things Signified Thereby, In the Several Arts, Both Liberal and the Several Sciences, Human and Divine: The Figures Kinds, Properties, Productions, Preparations, and*

specific scientific propositions might be characterized as justification after the fact of the victory of Newtonianism in England, a particularly Whiggish notion of progress in philosophy in which one view of the natural world was replaced by another which could explain the phenomena more accurately—a sense not unlike the *ex post facto* justification of the Revolution on the part of some Whigs. But this approach was largely, if not exclusively, based on a subjective judgment. The reply of those who might be described as holding Tory sensibilities was not entirely to defend the old paradigm, whether Cartesian or Leibnizian, but was rather to deny the validity of sects in philosophy or, in political terms, to refuse to accept the legitimate existence of faction. Thus, the elusive distinction between a Whig and a Tory in the early eighteenth century may have had more subtle roots in the defense of party on the one hand, by Walpole for example, and on the other, the attack on political division as merely factions of self-interested men, an opinion expressed often enough by Bolingbroke.[52] In many respects, the Tory attack on party as factionalism which clearly existed by the 1690s is only superficially an attack on the Whigs. This kind of criticism reflects a far more fundamental distrust of political difference and self-interest expressed in Swift's satire on Lilliputian low-heels and high-heels.[53]

A similar judgment can be found in the criticism directed against Newtonianism as well as against all faction in philosophy. Like Samuel Clarke's theological conjectures, Roger North's attitudes toward natural philosophy and his view of political and religious matters were also "thro-stitched." This is revealed in the many volumes of his crabbed writings which have survived. For North the Newtonian philosophy represented far more than another attempt to explain the forces of the natural world: it was, above all, representative of a world in which the forces of British society were dramatically shifting, when the discussions of philosophers were not confined to the cloisters or to the colleges but were extended, literally, to a more common run of men like the coffee-house virtuosi and the traders of the metropolis.

For the Newtonians, their philosophy was a clear alternative to the systems of Descartes and Leibniz. This is reflected not only in the debates with Leibniz but also in Ephraim Chambers' view of the

Uses of Things Natural and Artificial: The Rise, Progress, and State of Things Ecclesiastical, Civil, Military and Commercial. . . ., The Fourth edition (London 1741), s.v. "Newtonian Philosophy," "Sect."

[52] Isaac Kramnick, *Bolingbroke and his Circle: the Politics of Nostalgia in the Age of Walpole* (Cambridge, Mass., 1968), 158-63.

[53] Phillip Harth, "The Problem of Political Allegory in *Gulliver's Travels*," *Modern Philology*, 73, Supplement (May, 1976), 46-47. For a general discussion of the issue, see Pat Rogers, "Swift and Bolingbroke on Faction," *Journal of British Studies*, 9 (May, 1970), 71-101.

various sects in philosophy. Roger North, however, seems to have regarded much of the attack on Descartes as the result of the introduction of faction, "whereby if one party is in ye right, another is all wrong." Hence, words like attraction and inertia were part of a polemic.[54] The existence of such factions was deplored at great length by North. From his country-Tory, High-Church perspective, he saw the result to be detrimental to the investigation of nature much as he had been disgusted by the growth of political faction in the seventeenth century which he felt had destroyed the political basis of the Stuart monarchy.[55] As North saw things, the Newtonians were to blame for the growth of sects in philosophy. Newton and his followers had deliberately set themselves up against Descartes and Leibniz, but the invective was contagious and North was certainly not immune. So far as he was concerned, the battle between the sects could not end in truth; any follower of Descartes, whatever the merits of that particular philosopher, was "Gone for a Cartesian, and made appear as wretched & Ignorant a sectator as ye other was a vain Inconsiderate philosofer."[56]

North, nevertheless, desired to examine the Newtonian philosophy dispassionately. He was willing to admit the achievement of Newton in mathematics, but beyond that the problem lay in Newton's physical system of gravity and attractions. North's criticism of Newton, while ostensibly philosophical, went much farther. His objections to Newton, and especially to his followers whom he described as "all our second, third, & fourth hand philosophers," were a reflection of his social attitudes as well. In his mind, sects in philosophy, faction, and rabble were merely differing shades of disorder and republicanism.[57] This association between republicanism and the new philosophy, and to some extent deism, may partially explain his attitude toward Newton and his disciples.[58] While he recognized that Descartes could be legitimately criticized, especially on the types of matter in the universe, North regarded much of the complaint against Descartes to be the work of "proletarian scriblasters" led as "a parcel of Nose ledd Ignoramuses" by a new authority: the new standard in natural philosophy was Newton's *Principia*.[59] Thus, North's objections rested simultaneously at two levels, a philosophical as well as a social criticism. Success and the kind of

[54] B.M. Add. MSS, 32548, No. 2, f. 63.

[55] Roger North, *Examen: Or, An Enquiry into the Credit and Veracity of A Pretended Complete History* (London, 1740), 303, 319-35.

[56] B.M. Add. MSS, 32548, No. 2, f. 63r.

[57] B.M. Add. MSS, 32548, No. 2, f. 42; and, North, *Lives of the Norths*, 2, 320.

[58] For a discussion of this phenomenon, see J.G.A. Pocock, *The Machiavellian Moment: Florentine Political Thought and the Atlantic Republican Tradition* (Princeton, 1975), 476-77.

[59] B.M. Add. MSS, 32548, No. 2, f. 39.   [60] North, *Lives of the Norths*, 2, 320-21.

popularization we have seen were sins of equal magnitude when based upon a mistaken philosophy.

Although ostensibly the opinion of Dr. John North, we can take as Roger's sentiment the description of the populace of a nation as a "Brute beast indeed."[60] The rabble meant only disorder. Disorder is what Roger North thought had become of natural philosophy, and Newton was largely to blame. The attempt to establish the properties of the forces of nature by way of experiment or demonstration was, in North's opinion, a "pompous Pretence." He thought that experiment could never reveal the elementary differences between the particles of compound bodies.[61] It would be unfortunate if we dismissed this argument out of hand as the complaint of a disappointed Cartesian. What, I think, North was expressing in his manuscripts was a feeling that there was a relationship between experimentalism, the rage for scientific demonstration in which so many of the Newtonians were engaged, and a world that was enamored of what the eighteenth century regarded as sensibles, those recognizable effects of nature. One must understand that for North this was a view of the world which he instinctively distrusted. It was, after all, in the coffee houses of the late seventeenth and early eighteenth centuries, places which he thought were seedbeds of sedition and atheism, where scientific demonstration became the vogue.[62] All of this smacked of the rabble.

One of the greatest objections North had against Newton was the use of a vocabulary which lent itself to the accusation of being occult. It was Newton who had overturned the motto of the Royal Society, *nullis in verba,* by reintroducing into natural philosophy words like "attraction" which few could understand.[63] In North's opinion, many of the difficulties of Newtonian natural philosophy were the result of abstract words used substantively. "Motion" was a word which described a phenomenon but "attraction" was a descriptive word which had come to signify a cause. North's perception of the problem of the Newtonian vocabulary was certainly not distorted—Leibniz simultaneously took Clarke to task on the same point, and as we know attraction had become the doctrine of most of the Newtonian commentators. William Derham, in the notes to his Boyle lectures of 1711, continually mentioned "the Newtonian Attraction."[64] However, despite the popularity of such ideas, or perhaps because of it, in the philosophical digression of his life of Dr. John North, Roger also

[61] B.M. Add. MSS, 32548, No. 2, fols. 54-55.
[62] For his comments on coffee-houses, see the *Examen,* 320-21, 370, 597.
[63] B.M. Add. MSS, 32548, No. 2, fols. 41-42.
[64] W. Derham, *Physico-Theology: Or, A Demonstration of the Being and Attributes of God, from His Works of Creation,* 2nd ed. (London, 1714), 31 n. 1; 40 n. 1; 52 n. 5.

expressed doubts about the nature of attractions which he found much less satisfactory than the Cartesian notion of an aether:

If any one sees a vessell in the Thames thrown up by a still tide towards London, would he not say it is conveyed by the stream rather than attracted by that monstrous Citty. And the like of the planets, swifter or slower as the state of the fluid in their severall places require.[65]

It was when the Newtonians began to talk about gravitation and attraction as synonymous that North wondered whether this was merely a device to "catch the common people by their familiarity of acquaintance."[66] It was, in North's opinion, the great reliance upon similar effects described in like terms which confound understanding.

North had a long list of Newtonian terms like attraction, gravitation, ray, and *vis inertia* which he thought merely distorted natural philosophy. His opinion is founded not so much in the failure of the precision of the Newtonian language but seems to lie upon a concern with philosophy as a matter of common understanding and popular discourse. When North described *vis inertia* as a "meer vulgar Idea," he clearly associated the popularization of natural philosophy with his feelings about the rabble.[67] It was, in terms like gravitation, which North regarded as a popular notion, that he perceived Newton's philosophy to stand or fall.[68] Gravity was defined as force, and this necessarily coincided with the concept of action at a distance, between bodies across a vacuum, the void to which the virtuosi had become addicted since the *Principia* and the *Opticks*. This was only to re-admit into philosophy "ye peripatetick Inanity of words," to reintroduce occult qualities under the influence of which natural philosophers followed "as harmless sheep, one after another in a track."[69] To individuals like Roger North it may have seemed that the seventeenth-century warnings against mechanical philosophy had come to fruition in the Newtonian philosophy. To the High Church, who looked at Clarke and Whiston with disgust, it was the Newtonian philosophy which should be held responsible. The theological lines were clearly drawn. North did not think the results so harmless.

University of Saskatchewan.

---

[65] Millard, "Life of Dr. John North," 95. Also, B.M. Add. MSS, 32548, No. 2, fols. 51-52.
[66] B.M. Add. MSS, 32548, No. 2, f. 52r. [67] B.M. Add. MSS, 32548, No. 2, f. 53r.
[68] B.M. Add. MSS, 32548, No. 2, f. 43r, and f. 65.
[69] B.M. Add. MSS, 32548, No. 2, f. 45r; Add. MSS, 32545, f. 210, "Works of Roger North," XVIII.